Taking a GapYear

Susan Griffith

Distributed in the USA by
The Globe Pequot Press, Guilford, Connecticut

Published by Vacation Work, 9 Park End Street, Oxford
www.vacationwork.co.uk

First published 1999
Second edition 2001
Third edition 2003

TAKING A GAP YEAR
by Susan Griffith

Cover Design by Miller Craig & Cocking Design Partnership

Text design and typesetting by Brendan Cole

Illustrations by John Taylor

Publicity: Roger Musker

Printed and bound in Italy by Legoprint SpA, Trento

Taking a
GapYear

Contents

PART I – PREPARATIONS

PART II – GAP YEAR PLACEMENTS

PART III – COUNTRY BY COUNTRY

Europe

Worldwide

PART IV – APPENDICES

Acknowledgments

This third edition of *Taking a Gap Year* would not have been possible without the help of many gap year students, year out organisations and an army of travel informants who have generously shared their information and stories with me by letter, email, telephone and in a few cases down the pub.

Lucy Bale, Roger Blake, Willem Boshoff, Rosie Bywaters, Ben Clark, Peter Colledge, Amelia Cook, Clare Cooper, Keri Craig, Carisa Fey, Anna Fooks, Cathleen Graham, Claire Grew, Karl Harrison, Sebastiane Haye, Annabel Iglehart, Sam James & Sophie Ellison, Niall Johnson, Victoria Jossel, Peta Miller, Graham Milner, Rosna Mortuza, Ronan O'Kelly, Hannah Peck, Elizabeth Petchey, Juliette Radford, Ben Spencer and Katherine Wratten.

Preface

Young people approaching the end of school or university are uniquely privileged to be able to contemplate taking a year off before going on to the next phase of their lives. It is an opportunity that is unlikely to be repeated. Although it is still a minority of school leavers who take a year off, the figure is steadily rising by about ten percent per year, reflecting the democratisation of the gap year. While working in order to save money for university may be the primary motivation for some in this post-grant era, many more are attracted by the prospect of novelty and excitement in choosing from the fantastic range of options available.

Gap years have acquired so much status and respectability over the past decade or so that the Department for Education & Skills and UCAS officially endorse them and royal princes opt for them. Perhaps Prince Charles has more justification than the rest of us to think, as he does, that no one wants to have his or her life mapped out along predictable lines. This accounts for his enthusiastic attitude towards first Prince William and now Prince Harry deciding to take a year out after finishing school. The range of choices open to young people these days is astonishing; if your parents express envy of your gap year, give them a copy of the sister volume *Taking a Career Break* for Christmas.

Organising a year off would be daunting for people of any age, but more so for 17 or 18 year olds. Most gap years comprise a medley of activities which complement one another, work and play, earning and spending, challenge and self-indulgence, worthiness and fun. Fortunately the rising popularity of taking a year out has prompted a dramatic increase in the number of programmes and schemes targeted at young people. The path to exciting and memorable gap year experiences whether in Manchester, Massachusetts or Mongolia may be smoother than you think.

Within the generalised increase in take-up of the gap year option, other trends can be noted. Interest in Latin America has escalated strongly (possibly because it is in the opposite direction to the troubled Middle East) and many providers have initiated interesting projects in Mexico, Costa Rica, Peru etc. Gap year programmes connected with sport are also on the rise, whether it is snowboard training in Canada or football coaching in Ghana. Interestingly, a number of the main gap year providers have introduced shorter (and therefore cheaper) trips into their programmes, so that it is possible to participate in a month-long adventure for less than £1,000.

This book aims to canvas the possibilities comprehensively, and covers a wealth of both mainstream and obscure options. While browsing through its pages you will find detailed studies of the solid integrated programmes offered by gap year specialist organisations in all the continents of the world. You may also stumble across never dreamed-of possibilities like a film-making course in New York, organic gardening in New Zealand, turtle-monitoring in Madagascar, work experience with a record company in London, teaching in Paraguay, a homestay in Korea, helping at an orphanage in Russia. The amazing thing is that the vast majority of these opportunities are open to everyone.

Enterprising and energetic students from all backgrounds and schools are beginning to realise that the opportunity to take a year out is open to them, whether to join a project in some exotic part of the world, to earn some money and gain maturity before proceeding to university, to improve their CVs through work experience or learning a language, or simply to see the world.

Susan Griffith
Cambridge
July 2003

PART I

Preparation

Introduction

Planning & Preparation

Travel

Introduction

Deciding whether to take a year off and then how to spend it may not be as momentous as some other life decisions like getting married, having babies, choosing or changing careers, but it is as individual. No book or even trusted adviser can make the decision for you. All that outsiders can do is set out the possibilities and see if any of them takes your fancy enough to pursue. Do as much research as possible, let the ideas swill around in your head and see what floats up.

DECIDING TO TAKE A GAP YEAR

For many young people approaching the end of school, the decision about gap years is a difficult and complex one. The first question to ask yourself is does the idea have a strong appeal? If you close your eyes and imagine yourself in the student union bar at university and then transport yourself in your imagination to a Costa Rican rainforest or a Tanzanian village school or an Italian language class, which gives you more of a buzz? Think of the bad bits. Think of yourself sitting in a college library with an essay crisis and then think of yourself swatting mosquitoes and doing some manual job in tropical heat. If the idea of striking off to some remote corner of the world, far away from family and (most likely) friends, gives you the heebie-jeebies, then maybe a gap year is not for you. What you want to avoid is spending a year hanging around waiting for something to show up (though in some cases this also might be beneficial in sorting yourself out).

There is no doubt that it is easier to stay on the funicular which leads directly from the sixth form to higher education. After all, the majority of school leavers still do it. Yet the number of people deferring is much higher than it used to be and an increasing number of students from a variety of social backgrounds are at least giving the idea some serious thought. Of course not every school leaver who defers is bound for exotic travels and exciting overseas projects. With the demise of the grant, many students are taking a year off before higher education to work and save to support themselves.

In many circles, taking a gap year is still considered something that only the rich and privileged do; but the explosion in the number of specialist organisations helping students to set up gap years is the result of a democratisation of the concept. Of course there are still plenty of people from public schools and privileged backgrounds who take gap years (take Prince William for example and now Prince Harry plans to do likewise) but anybody who is determined and enthusiastic enough can do it. Figures from the long-established gap year provider GAP Activity Projects from 2003/4 indicate that more than two thirds were from state schools (71% from the state sector, 29% from independent schools).

Widening Access

During its election campaign, the Labour Party proposed to deposit cash in an account for every baby born in the UK and to implement a formula whereby any money saved by parents and deposited in that account would be matched. The money will become available on the child's 18th birthday (see page 38). The policy is intended to encourage a habit of saving in the large swathe of the population who don't have bank accounts, nest eggs or pensions. When pressed to identify concrete uses to which the money could be put, a structured gap year was mentioned by several MPs, illustrating how far up the agenda the idea of taking a constructive year out between school and university has moved. Speaking on a Radio 4 programme, one MP said that the benefits derived by so many middle class school leavers from taking a gap year abroad could be extended to a broader cross section of the population. It would be disingenuous to claim that taking a gap year is open to all since clearly anything that costs in the neighbourhood of £2,000 or more is not open to all. However in this case the government is putting its money where its mouth is.

Pros and Cons

Employers have been shown to value gap years. Some company application forms are beginning to include a question about the gap year and possibly to pay more attention to that than to your hobbies. Nearly three-quarters of employers surveyed by the Royal Mail thought that a gap year made young people more self-confident and over half claimed that they would be more likely to offer a job to a graduate who had taken a gap year. In the gap year literature from CESA, a language course booking service, the Recruitment Manager of Ernst & Young is quoted:

> *Travel or a year out will not in itself be a positive factor. However if the candidate can demonstrate that they have learnt and developed as a result of the experience this would be seen as a strength.*

According to UCAS statistics, a record 25,310 students deferred entry in 2002/2003, a massive increase of 10% over two years (i.e. the lifetime of this book). This means that approximately one in 15 university applicants defers their place for a year, a significantly higher percentage than a decade ago. The culture is changing slowly; education is no longer seen as a linear progression without interruption. Yet universities, parents and friends often go on assuming that there is no real alternative and it is all too easy to stay on the loop, especially if none of your friends or contemporaries is planning to take time out. But it is worth stepping back at some point (preferably early on, but not necessarily) and considering alternatives. Fifteen months is a miraculous period of time in which to pursue dreams and create memories. There will of course be opportunities later in life to take a break from routine – after university, between jobs, after having a child, sabbatical leave, after retirement, etc. But the combination of freedom from responsibility and leisure time is much harder to manage later on.

The standard objections raised by the doubting Thomases of the academic and parental world go as follows:

O You'll be a year behind your friends

O You'll lose the impetus to study (though you may lose that over the four months between A-levels and university anyway)

O You'll be seduced by travel and find it difficult to settle back into a comparatively boring routine on your return

O You'll be seduced by the things that money can buy if you spend your year out earning enough money to save and spend and then will find it difficult to contemplate reverting to the poverty of studenthood

O You'll be seduced full stop and abandon everything for love

Your parents will be relieved to learn that the vast majority of gap year students do not lose their way. Some are changed enormously but very few bring grief to their families by cashing in their return ticket to settle in Koh Samui or Goa. The experience of working hard at a local job in order to fund a gap year experience is usually enough to persuade even those who are lukewarm about the benefits of higher education to stay on as a student for a few more years.

Whereas six months of slogging at a local chain store or pizza restaurant usually works wonders as aversion therapy, six months of working in a developing culture can alter your view of what you want to do with your life. For example **Stephanie Lee** spent time with *Gap Activity Projects* teaching in Vietnam which led (by chance) to a close involvement with Burmese refugees. On her return Stephanie decided to give up her place at art college in favour of attending the School of Oriental and African Studies at the University

changing worlds

A year out with changing worlds, change your life forever.

For details of our voluntary and paid placements,
telephone: 01883 340960 or
visit: www.changingworlds.co.uk

Australia

Canada

Chile

India

Nepal

New Zealand

Romania

Changing Worlds: 11 Doctors Lane Chaldon Surrey CR3 5AE UK   Tanzania of London where she decided to study Thai and Burmese languages with a view to making a future career in development.

Parents worry that a gap year will alter future plans. But of course there are thousands of school leavers with precious few plans to alter and travel might be a catalyst for moving in one direction or another. This was the case with **Carisa Fey** from Germany who headed off to England when she was 18 and scraped a living in various jobs before travelling to Mexico and South America for an extended period. She eventually returned to Stuttgart and found to her surprise that she enjoyed working in a 'real' job:

When I started out I didn't have much of an idea what I wanted to do afterwards. But pretty soon in my travels the idea of studying became more and more attractive. Especially since one can realise one's own abilities and preferences a lot better while on the road. When I was 18 I was absolutely sure I'd never want to work in an office. But now I love my office and my computer. If I studied now it would not be music or history (dreams of the 18 year old) but business or economics (which I always thought extremely boring). Some of my friends' kids say, you see, no need to study or make a proper training. Look at Carisa, she just travelled around the world and came home to land a great job. But I learned things you can't learn in any university, how you get out of any situation yourself, to stand up for yourself, to get along with all kinds of people. And I didn't just sit at the beach. I was working very very hard. And in every job I did, I learned all I could and gave my best. No matter if I waited tables, worked in a factory, did gardening or whatever. You can learn something everywhere. Even if it is just that you are a bloody lucky person because you hate doing nightshifts at the frozen chips factory; for some people that is their life, but you can get out.

If major doubts remain about what the next step in your life should be, there is nothing better than taking a year out to do something completely different, to give yourself time and space to decide, away from all the pressures of home and school. Students repeatedly say that travelling and/or working abroad really help to focus their minds on what they want to do with their lives.

In **Rachel Thomas's** case, the pros easily outweighed the cons, and she enthusiastically accepted a place teaching in China through GAP Activity Projects:

I never had any doubts about a gap year as it was something I had planned to do for as long as I can remember. It took longer to convince my parents, but once they recognised my commitment, they supported me wholeheartedly. The gap year provides the ultimate opportunity for independence and to prove yourself. I knew I would be experiencing new places and cultures which appealed to my sense of adventure. I had worked very hard for my A-levels while also working as a part-time waitress and so I was exhausted. I had been under a lot of stress and I wanted a break before returning to studies. I knew I needed to relax and take the chance to step back to assess my future choices. More practically, if I failed to get the grades I needed to do medicine, I also had the option to retake once I returned. I was somewhat worried about homesickness and missing friends, family and boyfriend, and there was the expense to consider, but in the end I didn't need to deliberate very long.

Jake Lee found that he had lots of motives for wanting to take a gap year:
My parents are pretty liberal and wanted me to see the world. But I had my own reasons. I wanted to break through the middle class bubble that we're all living in back here. I wanted to see how the rest of the world lived. I wanted to do something for myself, gloriously independent of interfering teachers, parents and friends. Most importantly I wanted to grow up.

DECIDING HOW TO SPEND YOUR GAP YEAR

After deciding to take a year out, it is necessary to decide how to divide it up. The options are open-ended but usually involve a combination of working locally to save money, travelling and possibly signing up with an organisation for an expedition or placement overseas. Deciding whether you want to join a project overseas or just travel is crucial.

One advantage of joining a scheme is that it makes you stay put for an extended period instead of drifting from place to place in what can end up giving a superficial view of the countries visited. The great travel writer Dervla Murphy expressed her views on this subject in an essay in *The Traveller's Handbook* published by WEXAS (£14.99):

The past decade or so has seen the emergence of another, hybrid category: young-sters who spend a year or more wandering around the world in a holidaymaking spirit, occasionally taking temporary jobs. Some gain enormously from this experience but many seem to cover too much ground too quickly, sampling everywhere and becoming familiar with nowhere. They have been from Alaska to Adelaide, Berlin to Bali, Calcutta to Cuzco, Lhasa to London. They tend to wander in couples or small packs, swapping yarns about the benefits - or otherwise - of staying here, doing that, buying this. They make a considerable impact where they happen to perch for a week or so, often bringing with them standards (sometimes too low) and expectations (sometimes too high) which unsettle their local contemporaries.

Of course one rejoices that the young are free to roam as never before, yet such rapid 'round-the-worlding' is, for many, more confusing than enlightening. It would be good if this fashion soon changed, if the young became more discriminating, allowing themselves time to travel seriously in a limited area that they had chosen because of its particular appeal to them, as individuals.

The chapters that make up this book survey the range of possibilities and provide lots of concrete information to help you decide whether to earn a salary in a high-tech industry in Britain or join an expedition to Patagonia (or both). Details are provided on voluntary work in residential situations in the UK and abroad, work experience, courses and homestays, seasonal jobs like working in ski resorts, au pairing, English teaching, travelling around Europe: all are covered.

In some sixth forms a certain amount of one-upmanship prevails about who can do the most adventurous and exotic trip (though most end up going to Thailand or India where there are whole colonies of gap year students). Paraguay and Outer Mongolia are great if you have a particular interest in those regions but if you would be happier working on an American summer camp or a Scottish sailing school or attending a language school in Barcelona, so be it. It is possibly a mistake to think of the Himalayan gap year as vastly superior to the one spent closer to home. Trekking in Northern Thailand does not

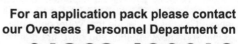

necessarily trump working in a Swiss ski resort or volunteering to teach gypsy children in Spain. Do not fall into the trap of making plans to impress. Find the route that suits you.

Using a Gap Year Agency

The ambition of many gap year students is to explore Europe. But if you have set your sights on more distant places, you (and your parents) may not feel happy about wandering around without any structure. Although some 18 year olds fresh from school have the confidence and maturity to set off without anything set up (perhaps with a working holiday visa for Australia or a return ticket to Lima) most will prefer to enlist the help of a mediating organisation or agency to set up a placement and provide a back-up service if things go wrong.

Broadly speaking, you must decide whether to throw in your lot with a sending organisation or arrange something independently. Many of the advantages of going on an organised scheme are self-evident but it is worth canvassing a few here:

1. Makes the choice available less overwhelming since placement agencies have a finite number of destinations and opportunities.
2. Saves you the time of contacting many organisations abroad and the anxiety of liaising with them assuming they do express interest. Pre-departure orientation will be provided. Even just a briefing booklet can be helpful and reassuring. Agencies are usually in a position to give reliable advice on necessary health precautions, insurance and flights.
3. Back-up is available if you have an accident, become ill or the placement is unacceptable in some way.
4. Reassurance for anxious parents. The agency often provides a conduit of communication between gap year student and family.
5. Placement is normally in groups or pairs, so moral support is always available from gap year or volunteer partners.

The majority of students coming home from a gap year are grateful for the help and back-up given to them by their agency, claiming that they considered the fee they paid well spent. On the other hand, some find that their agency's local rep is not easy to contact and therefore not of much use. Others who end up not needing to make use of the support network begrudge the fee. The fee paid to a sending agency can be viewed as an insurance policy which many students and their parents are more than happy to pay.

Of course there are also drawbacks to signing up with an organisation, principally the expense. Orientations and back-up in the field cost money, with some commercial organisations charging more than charitable ones. Up to a point these schemes are inflexible. Naturally you will be expected to commit yourself to a certain length of stay, possibly even 11 or 12 months. A lot can change in that time: you can fall in love, become lonely and homesick, decide that your contribution is pointless.

Only you know whether you have the stamina and initiative to create a constructive gap year without the shelter of an umbrella in the form of a placement organisation. Bear in mind that locally-run NGOs may profess to need your help but may have little experience of dealing with the kinds of problem faced by homesick 18 year olds. Without contact with a like-minded person, you can feel lonely and isolated. On the other hand, some gap year students do arrange their own job/placement, with or without contacts, and find the experience immensely gratifying. Arranging something independently shows great initiative (always something worth boasting about on future CVs) and of course saves the money which would otherwise go to a middle man. This is something which **Rachel Sedley** wishes she had done instead of signing up with a gap organisation to teach in Kathmandu:

It's frustrating to see in retrospect how easy it would have been just to come here and present myself to a school. I have met several people from various schools and orphanages far more needy that the one where I'm working who would love English volunteers. Back in England of course I had no idea, so I paid up without questioning. The training course was held in a beautiful stately home with delicious meals and friendly staff, but in retrospect was probably superfluous and extremely expensive.

The old proverb, 'It is easy to be wise after the event' may be apt here.

Schemes and pre-arranged projects are not for everyone. **Eleanor Padfield** decided to avoid them because she wanted to make her way on her own in the Spanish-speaking world (Salamanca, Bolivia, Chile) away from all her gap year contemporaries. **Emma Hoare** did lots of research on a gap year but couldn't find an approach that suited her at first:

> *For years I had always been saying 'yes, I really want to travel…maybe after A-levels, maybe after my degree, maybe when I retire' and all my friends would go 'yeah, me too, definitely' and all my family, teachers, elders and betters would smile and nod in that way they do when a young person starts talking vaguely about the Big Things, that there is really no fear of them actually doing.*
>
> *On results day I found that I had managed to get four A grades. At some point in all the celebrations I decided that, no, I didn't want to go straight to university. I wanted to go backpacking, see the world, have a spiritual epiphany, etc. To say this did not please my mother, teachers, etc. is an understatement. When I started talking about cancelling my place at York University and reapplying the next year, every adult I knew (except my Dad) was 100% against it. They did have a small point, I suppose. I didn't have any plans, though I had about £1,000, not even enough for a ticket to New Zealand as it turned out.*
>
> *So I had about four days before I had to accept or decline my place at York. By the end of the third day, I had been pretty much convinced that it would be a stupid thing to go gallivanting around the world. I went into my local careers advisory centre and was sat down with a pile of leaflets dealing with gap years. Every single one of these dealt with either a structured voluntary course abroad or how to arrange work experience. 'On the road' it wasn't. Then – portentous roll of thunder, sudden bright light – one of the receptionists gave me a book that had just come in, 'Work Your Way Around the World'. No exaggeration, I promise you. I sat there and read it until they closed the centre. Then I went straight to Waterstones and bought a copy. Then I went home and wrote to York University declining my place. Three months later I was off to New Zealand… As you can probably surmise from the gushing tone of this letter, I had an amazing time. I crewed on a yacht, helped with haymaking, went to a sheep-shearers' reunion, did a 12,000ft skydive, saw sperm whales, etc… And now I'm off to start my degree (at Oxford!). I can assure you the transformation is nothing short of miraculous.*

Overcoming Anxiety

Often the hardest step is committing yourself to a decision, i.e. fixing a departure date and destination. Once you have booked a place on a scheme or bought a ticket and explained to your friends and family that you are off to see the world, the rest seems to fall into place. Inevitably first-time travellers suffer pre-departure anxieties as they contemplate leaving behind the comfortable routines of home. But these are usually much worse in anticipation than in retrospect.

Prepare yourself for a horrid 48 hours after saying good-bye at the airport (tip: don't look back after going through Passport Control). **Jake Lee** who went to Sri Lanka in his gap year puts it rather brutally:

Let me just state for the record. It doesn't matter who you are, but if you are travel-

ling alone to a faraway place for a relatively long time, you will cack yourself on the plane. The excitement you previously had turns to fear, and you are desperate for the plane to turn around. I don't think there is anything you can do about this. Just ride it out. As a Buddhist monk at my school always said, 'There is never anything to worry about - Nothing.' This is true.

Sources of Information

If you happen to come from a school with no tradition of sending students on gap years, you will have to do your own research. Access to the internet makes this task much easier and at the same time more complicated since there is so much information scattered through cyberspace. One obvious starting point is www.gapyear.com set up in 1998 by Tom Griffiths. Members can access monthly e-newsletters, use the messageboards, find travel mates and access the database of opportunities. This is of course a commercial venture.

The non-profit trade association, the Year Out Group, aims to promote and advise on structured years out. Their website (www.yearoutgroup.org) has links to its 28 member organisations and contains guidelines and questions to ask when comparing year out providers; more information about the Year Out Group can be found in the introduction to the chapter 'Specialist Gap Year Programmes'.

As further illustration of how the whole field of taking a year out has proliferated in recent years, the mainstream student travel agencies and travel insurance companies have programmes, hotlines and brochures dedicated to the gap year (see later chapters). Springboard is a web-based advisory service for young people aged 16-18 which has some information on gap year choices (www.springboard.co.uk/gap.cfm). Its links are patchy because of the commercial nature of the site. Anyone who is in the early stages of thinking about a gap year and wants to discuss the educational and career implications with someone might approach Connexions, the Government's new information, advice and guidance service for 13-19 year olds whose brief is to encourage young people not to abandon their schooling prematurely.

The Jobs Abroad Bulletin is a useful one-man and one-woman site (www.payaway.co.uk) which dispenses with pretty graphics to deliver actual job vacancy details each month. E-mail subscriptions to what is billed as an 'on-line magazine for working abroad and taking a gap year' are free.

An independent gap year consultancy *Gap Enterprise* offers private client consultations and training for planning a gap year. The director John Vessey can save students and their parents the time and effort of researching the vast range of possibilities and will try to match specific requirements to a tried and tested programme; contact details may be found in the 'Directory of Specialist Gap Year Programmes'.

THE REWARDS

Any number of publications and careers documents list the advantages of taking a gap year which are mostly to do with gaining self-confidence and independence. All of one's education is a movement in this direction. The first time primary school age children are taken camping for a few nights, they are learning to depend on themselves rather than on their parents to keep track of their socks and their pocket money. A gap year abroad moves the individual in the same direction probably at a faster rate than if they had continued straight to university (without passing Goa).

While some of the rewards of taking a gap year may be unpredictable, others are more obvious: the interesting characters and lifestyles you are sure to meet, the appetite to see more of the world that it will engender, the wealth of anecdotes you will collect with which you can regale your grandchildren and photos with which you can bore your friends, learning how to do your own cooking and laundry, a feeling of achievement, an increased self-reliance and maturity, learning to budget, a better perspective on your own country and your own habits, a good sun tan... the list could continue. **Stephen Psallidas** summed up his views on travelling:

> *Meeting people from all over the world gives you a more tolerant attitude to other nationalities, races, etc. More importantly you learn to tolerate yourself, to learn more about your strengths and weaknesses. While we're on the clichés, you definitely 'find yourself, man'.*

A host of gap travellers have mentioned how much they value their collection of memories and photos. When looking back on your year off, you are not going to remember that it was the year you gained self-confidence or learned how to live within a budget; you will remember being invited to a Buddhist initiation ceremony, learning a few words of Spanish from a Mexican fisherman, your encounter with what might have been a redback spider at a Queensland barbecue or how you nearly missed your plane in Nairobi.

In 2003, **Sebastien Haye** joined a project for street children in Calcutta through *Cosmic Volunteers.* Although English is not his first language he describes his impressions after just a few weeks, which are typical of many gap year students' initial experience of life in a developing country:

> *People are really poor, children are far from a good hygiene and most of them are under lack of nutrition. However, I saw a lot of smiles, dignity and hospitality, even in the poorest houses, that I have never seen before. All these experiences are permanent 'life lessons' for me and all this courage and hope growing from the dirtiest and saddest place you can imagine force my biggest admiration. Even though the air is highly polluted, I feel good in this place and all the people I meet are really nice with me, always wanting to learn about my famly, see my photos and give me food or tea. As a first report, I can tell you that I am actually living the most humbling and interesting experience of my life.*

Long-term Benefits
Gap years can change you and change the direction of your life forever. After enjoying her gap year carrying out conservation work in the coral reefs of Tanzania through Frontier (see entry in the 'Directory of Specialist Gap Year Programmes') **Emily Jimsor** changed her university course:

> *To me the most important part of the experience has been the effect it has had on my career. I became really involved in the conservation side of things while I was in Tanzania, particularly looking at the effects of pollution on coral reefs. I learnt so much from the field staff out there and their enthusiasm really inspired me. When I came home I contacted my university (Portsmouth) and told them I really wanted to study marine biology. The tutors were very understanding and I was able to swap courses. My entire life has changed, all thanks to that one article I read in the local paper about three years ago.*

Sometimes travels abroad have a similar impact. After working his way around the world in many low-paid and exploitative jobs, **Ken Smith** decided to specialise in studying employment law. Several gap year students have become so involved with their destination community that they carry on raising funds and sometimes recruiting volunteers to carry on the work. After his gap year in Kenya **Rob Breare** set up a charity called Harambee Schools Kenya that continues to support the education of village children in the Central Highlands. The repercussions of **Rachel Battilana's** gap year in Africa were quite different. When choosing a fourth year structural engineering project, she was attracted to one which involved re-designing a tent for refugees. She claims that she managed to be accepted onto the project by referring to her gap year in Uganda (and her many family camping holidays) and her tent went on to win an award at the 2001 Science, Engineering and Technology Student of the Year awards.

Nearer home, you might come back from a work experience placement or language course on the Continent feeling a part of Europe rather than just English, Scottish or Welsh. Such experiences will enhance your CV if you ever want to pursue a job with a European dimension. Volunteering in the UK can provide a useful taster of an alternative career especially if you have decided that the world of commerce is not for you and you are considering the caring professions or development field.

A gap year is often a defining moment in the life of an almost-adult. Mostly the rewards are highly personal. Successful gap years abroad allow you to learn how to relinquish your own customs, desires and expectations. Exposure to a completely different way of viewing and managing time is something that might teach you to resist stress and competition in our own culture. A young participant who went on an expedition to Kenya with the *Borders Exploration Group* felt he had had a revelation about different attitudes to life:

> *Most people feel that we are so much better off; we are in money, but in what else? They have lots of fun and laughter, even though their lives are so hard. It's a lesson to all of us.*

Learning to find joy and pleasure in simple things like running water or the sunset over the desert is a lesson worth learning. Exposure to new people and cultures teaches you that you can (generally) rely on instinct about whether a stranger is trustworthy or not.

Prolonged exposure to people with different value systems is bound to change your perspective and teach you how subjective one's values and view of society are. Just before taking his final exams at Cambridge, **Matthew Applewhite** reflected on the impact the six months of his gap year spent working at an outback school for Aboriginal people had had on his subsequent development and attitudes. His students in the Northern Territory had drawn pictures, written poems, made friends but hadn't been made to do any exams. He realised that whatever the class of degree he ends up with doesn't matter nearly as much as his certainty that he has acquired an education in the broadest sense; he has made friends, read books, pursued new ideas, indulged his passion for the theatre and generally had a very worthwhile three years at university.

Meeting the challenge of doing something completely different from the norm can have a positive effect on your personal development too. Like millions of others, **Edward Brown** is from a 'sheltered and safe' middle class background. After graduating, he was determined not to slide into an office job and spotted an advert for CSV (see 'Directory of Voluntary Placements in the UK'). No one is turned away by CSV and soon Edward had taken up his placement in London working with young offenders:

> *London filled me with fear. I thought I would be surrounded by hardened criminals. But I soon realised that the young people I work with are just like everyone else and not at all as I imagined. My role has had a really positive effect. It hasn't been easy and things have been very slow to change and very unpredictable. I'm much more streetwise now. I used to be very shy and now I feel like I am being myself more and more. I wanted to experience some real life. I'm much more tuned into things and am able to communicate to people on loads of different levels. Being a volunteer is a life-changing experience. It helps you to discover who you are and what your strengths and weaknesses are. It has helped to shape my future.*

Annabel Iglehart waited until after university to plan an ambitious gap year so that she would be in a better position to make the most of the opportunities. After a three-month intensive Spanish course in Salamanca with *Mester* and three months at home in Edinburgh fundraising, she travelled to Quito in March 2003 under the auspices of *Challenges Worldwide* to join a project promoting environmental awareness among children.

> **Apart from finding the whole experience 'fun and invaluable,' Annabel Iglehart also found it easy to identify the long-term benefits:**
> *My placement here has been an incredibly valuable experience for me. I have been involved in a variety of tasks that have highlighted my skills to me, whilst living in a completely different culture. Taking part in the placement has helped me decide on a career direction and has increased my confidence. I have had to overcome difficulties that don't exist in Western countries and have had to come up with productive and creative solutions to problems.*

THE RISKS

Of course things can go desperately wrong. Several young women and men who have been on gap year projects have had fatal accidents such as the three young women on a year out in Malawi in 2001 who were killed in a jeep accident. A much less remote possibility is losing your passport or having your backpack stolen. You may get sick or lonely or fed up. You may make a fool of yourself by allowing yourself to be tricked by a con-man who sells you some fake gems or rips you off in a currency transaction. You may feel desperately homesick for a situation in which you do not have to behave like an adult when you have only had an adolescent's experiences.

While some identify the initial decision to go abroad as the hardest part, others find the inevitable troughs, such as finding yourself alone in a cheap hotel room on your birthday, running out of money faster than anticipated, getting travellers' diarrhoea, more difficult to cope with. But if travelling requires a much greater investment of energy than staying at home, it will reward the effort many times over.

Friends and family are seldom reluctant to offer advice, and normally the perceived risks are far greater than the actual ones. When **Cathleen Graham** from Canada announced that she was bound for rural South Africa with the charity SCORE (see Africa chapter), many came forward to express grave concerns for her safety as a young woman:

> *People's reactions to my choice of destination were determined by what they saw portrayed about South Africa in the media. Of course, people who knew me best knew this was an opportunity that suited me. You really need to develop a strong filter about listening to people's opinions before you go: are they sound and balanced, or more reflecting the person's own fears and anxieties if they were the one going?*

Barry Robinson from Reading had to put up with a similar catalogue of dire warnings when he went off to teach English in Moscow:

> *Moscow is one of those places which suffers due to misconceptions ranging from the ill-informed to the downright ludicrous. Prior to my initial visit to Moscow, I was warned about (believe it or not!) bears meandering through the streets at night, the omnipresent Russian Mafia, sub-zero Siberian gales of 50 below zero, lengthy food queues, and the Russian predilection for all things beetroot. So, in order to prevent lunacy begetting lunacy, I would like to start by dispelling such ill-founded fancies before they fester into facts: I have never been mauled by carnivorous beasties. In fact the only Grizzlies I've encountered were behind bars at the Moscow Zoo. I have never had any encounters with the Russian Mafia. Believe me, they are concerned with frying bigger fish than you and I. There are no lengthy food queues anymore, except lunchtime at Macdonalds, which is still obscenely popular with Muscovites. Russian cuisine is rich, diverse and plentiful. The supermarket shelves are always replete with everything from Russian Pelemini (a kind of meat ravioli in soup) to tubes of Pringles.*

Some might find this cultural globalisation a little disappointing. Some gap year travellers undergo a process of disillusionment, which is not a bad thing in itself, since no one wants to live in a world of illusions. You harbour a desire to see some famous monument and find it surrounded by touts or chintzy boutiques. The reality of seeing the Taj Mahal or walking down the Gorge of Samaria in Crete or meeting an Amazonian Indian may be less romantic than you had imagined. (See Alain de Botton's elegant *The Art of Travel* for an in-depth study of the conflict between dreams of travel and the reality.)

Of the thousands of placements which gap year students accept, a few are bound to be disappointing. **Victoria Greaves** describes how what she found on arrival at a farm in France (where she had been taken on as a volunteer assistant during her gap year) failed to match her expectations:

Before setting off I made particular efforts to check the reliability of the organisation with the local tourist information office, etc. However when I arrived, the situation was not as I had been led to believe. On arrival I discovered that I was the only person there apart from Monsieur, although he had led me to believe that he lived with his wife and son, and that there would be other volunteers on site. After a 20-hour journey I was put to work immediately mucking out the horses. Monsieur refused to let me phone home. I spent the next day cleaning the buildings and stables which had obviously not been done for some weeks. There was no suitable vegetarian food available although he had promised to make arrangements. At one point I actually found him in my dormitory reading my personal letters and diary. My visit was an extremely traumatic experience which ended after three days, with me being dismissed at 30 minutes notice and my employer dumping me in the nearby town with no travel arrangements and nowhere to stay. It was a totally unsuitable environment for an 18 year old volunteer, especially a female on her own.

In rare cases, students can be traumatised by what they experience in a gap year. According to the Senior Tutor of a Cambridge college who regularly meets students before and after their gap year, most come back much more changed than the students who have not deferred for a year. Some benefit enormously, but not all. He recalls one in particular who had been sent to work in a Romanian orphanage with young children with AIDS. She came back so traumatised that she suffered from nightmares for a long time afterwards. But usually the changes are not so dire. A tutor at St. Anne's College Oxford wrote in the college magazine how offended students are if she fails to recognise them, even though there can be a two year gap between interview and arrival: 'The problem is that they can have changed in appearance completely, from scrubbed and tidy interview candidate to world-weary international traveller, sans hair but plus several ear or facial rings.'

REASSURANCE FOR PARENTS

The departure of a child from the family home is traumatic enough when they're merely going to university, but is made much more frightening if he or she is travelling to the ends of the earth on a year out adventure. When you were 18, you probably hadn't even heard of, let alone considered visiting, some of the destinations that gap travellers now visit, from Vientiane to Antananarivo, Port Douglas to Sulawesi. The relative cheapness of long-distance flights, the range of gap year providers offering remote destinations and the raised expectations of the new generation account for these heightened travel ambitions. How you as a parent react will have a lot to do with what you did when you were 18. The parents who motorcycled through Afghanistan to India or hitch-hiked round Greece with no money will be more sympathetic than the ones who carried straight through from school to university or a job.

The parental imagination is bound to dwell on the possible disasters. Feelings of helplessness when a child is far away fuel these anxieties. But a calm assessment of the risks will result in a startling realisation, that staying at home is just as risky. Clubbing in a city centre or driving on a British road poses risks, too, though parents don't tend to focus on those. According to an article in *The Times* headed 'Gap year away safer than rock festival at home,' research published in the *Journal of the Royal Society of Medicine* showed that taking part in a structured expedition brought with it less risk of death or injury than attending a music festival in Britain or going to a Scout camp.

As the numbers of young people taking gap years abroad increase, it is inevitable that more accidents will occur. The raised profile of young people travelling abroad on their gap year means that these accidents tend to be widely reported. So if a young man slips down a waterfall in Costa Rica or a British girl is killed by a freak accident with a high voltage cable in Ecuador or a bus carrying overlanding travellers is held up by armed bandits in the Andes, the world hears about it. By the same token some reported tragedies take place in Britain, as in the case of a young woman working at a Plymouth supermarket in her gap year who was murdered by the store manager. But mostly, if an 18 year old dies of a drug overdose or is killed on his bicycle in his hometown, this is not reported nationally.

It is arguable that children nowadays are overprotected and should be given more not less freedom so that from an early age they learn to be street-wise and how to navigate dangers outside the home. Some say that adventures are now too easy. Young people are lulled into a false sense of security by the number of people doing likewise. A trek round Annapurna can be arranged in an instant, but that does not mean that a blizzard won't reduce visibility to nil inside 20 minutes.

Still, a parent will want to take every possible precaution on his or her child's behalf, knowing that all 18 year olds believe themselves immortal. They should check with the Foreign Office on world trouble spots (www.www.fco.gov.uk/travel; 020-7008 0232/3). They should make sure that their child hasn't skimped on insurance and if necessary top it up to a policy that will fly them home in an emergency, cover dangerous sports, legal problems, search and rescue, etc. If you have resisted going on e-mail, now is the time to relent, because your child is almost guaranteed to spend time in internet cafés and will be able to let you know that all is well at more frequent intervals than they could if they have to rely on phones. Try not to be too prescriptive about how often your son or daughter contacts you because if they are out of contact for some reason, you will worry unnecessarily. A few causes of tragedy are avoidable, such as in the case of an A-level girl who died of heat stroke and dehydration on an expedition in Borneo. Urging your child to take sensible precautions like dressing modestly in countries where it is expected, not flaunting valuables, not falling prey to smooth-tongued con men, and so on may have some beneficial effect. Those who can't rein in their anxiety might investigate enrolling their progeny on a gap year preparation course, at least one of which run by a former member of the SAS (see entries for *Objective Team* and *The Knowledge Gap*).

But really the hard truth is that it is time to let go. Try to give your child lots of credit for their initiative, enterprise and courage and remind yourself daily that they are now grown-up.

The Beaten Track

Two years ago a report was published by an academic lambasting the negative impact that backpackers have on places where they congregate (Sinai, Kathmandu, Goa, Kho Pha-Ngan, Machu Picchu, etc). The organisation for responsible tourism Tourism Concern (www.tourismconcern.org.uk) is also worried by the number of young people who travel to places they are not really interested in just to meet up with other travellers, to eat, drink and socialise in exactly the way they would at home but without as many inhibitions. There is even a novel about it. For a satirical account of the wrong way to go about being a gap year traveller, read William Sutcliffe's novel *Are You Experienced?* based on his own gap year experiences. In this extract, the anti-hero Dave is being lectured by an old-India hand:

Hippies coming for spiritual enlightenment have been replaced by morons on a pov-erty-tourism adventure holiday. Going to India is no longer an act of rebellion but an act of conformity for ambitious middle-class kids who believe that a trip to the third world shows the kind of initiative which companies are looking for. You come here and cling to each other as if you're on some kind of extended management-bonding exercise in Epping Forest... It's a modern circumcision ritual, a badge of suffering you have to wear to be welcomed into the tribe of Britain's future elite. Your kind of travel is all about low horizons dressed up as open-mindedness. You have no inter-est in India and no sensitivity for the problems this country is trying to face up to. You treat Indians with a mixture of contempt and suspicion reminiscent of the Victorian colonials. Your presence here in my opinion is offensive and you should all go home to Surrey.

Hard-hitting stuff but worth pondering.

Choosing a culturally sensitive organisation with which to work can prevent this kind of situation from arising, as **Rosie Bywaters** found when she joined an *SPW* health and sanitation project in India:

For the first time, SPW India has partnered Indian volunteers with western volun-teers. This makes the projects more easily sustainable and ensures that we are sensitive to the community's needs. I have found it tremendously helpful and enlight-ening to be working with our six counterpart volunteers. Not only is their knowledge of Tamil a geat asset, but they guide and support us in all sorts of way, even with the difficult task of crossing the street without getting run over by a bus, autorickshaw or stray cow. My counterpart is called Sasikala. She is the same age as me (21) and has a degree in Nutrition and Dietetics. She calls me her right hand but I feel that it is she who is my right hand, teaching me about her culture and introducing me to a whole new way of being. India is a very special place, impossible to describe, impossible to forget. I cried so much when I had to leave and say goodbye to some amazing friends, but it just makes me all the more sure that I want to go back as soon as I can.

Coming Home

Coming home and experiencing reverse culture shock is a problem for some. Settling back will take time especially if you have not been able to set aside some money for 'The Return'. It can be a wretched feeling after some glorious adventures to find yourself with nothing to start over on. Life at home may seem dull and routine at first, while the outlook of your friends and family can strike you as narrow and limited. If you have been round the world between school and further study, you may find it difficult to bridge the gulf between you and your stay-at-home peers who may feel a little threatened or belittled by your experiences.

Peta Miller came back to the same grey airport she'd left six months before to go to Ghana with a classic case of reverse culture shock:

I had thought it would be relatively easy to slot back into my life seeing friends, socialising and in the end looking for my first proper job. But my soul was true to Ghana. I scrutinised those around me and found the way they behaved rude, selfish and pretentious. They looked sallow, pale and unhealthy as they shuttled back and forth between home and the office, compressed into tube compartments, breathing black air. Nobody smiled or communicated. Train tickets, bars of chocolate, cinema tickets could all be purchased without uttering a word. Even my own friends seemed changed into frivolous consumers intent on image and appearance. There was no colour, no sincerity and no content. People seemed to be wasting the working week doing jobs that made rich men richer so that at the weekends they could go on fren-

TourismConcern

Exploring the World

Being sensitive to these ideas means getting more out of your travels – and giving more back to the people you meet and the places you visit.

● *Learn about the country you're visiting*
Start enjoying your travels before you leave by tapping into as many sources of information as you can.

● *The cost of your holiday*
Think about where your money goes - be fair and realistic about how cheaply you travel. Try and put money into local people's hands; drink local beer or fruit juice rather than imported brands and stay in locally owned accommodation.

Haggle with humour and not aggressively. Pay what something is worth to you and remember how wealthy you are compared to local people.

● *Culture*
Open your mind to new cultures and traditions - it will transform your experience.

Think carefully about what's appropriate in terms of your clothes and the way you behave. You'll earn respect and be more readily welcomed by local people.

Respect local laws and attitudes towards drugs and alcohol that vary in different countries and communities. Think about the impact you could have. *"The effect on the local community of travellers taking drugs when visiting the hilltribes of Thailand can be devastating. People become trapped into selling drugs to travellers and become addicted themselves, especially young people who want to be like the travellers."* Jaranya Daengnoy, REST

● *How big is your footprint? – minimise your environmental impact*
Think about what happens to your rubbish - take biodegradable products and a water filter bottle. Be sensitive to limited resources like water, fuel and electricity.

Help preserve local wildlife and habitats by respecting rules and regulations, such as sticking to footpaths, not standing on coral and not buying products made from endangered plants or animals.

● *Guidebooks*
Use your guidebook as a starting point, not the only source of information. Talk to local people, then discover your own adventure!

● *Photography*
Don't treat people as part of the landscape, they may not want their picture taken. Put yourself in their shoes, ask first and respect their wishes.

The ideas expressed in this code were developed by and for independent travellers. They show what individuals can do to play their part towards Tourism Concern's goal of more ethical and fairly traded tourism. For more information see Tourism Concern's website: www.tourismconcern.org.uk   Telephone: +44 (0)20 7753 3330

This TourismConcern initiative is supported by

zied shopping trips. From such a perspective the world seemed to have gone mad. Five months later I'm better acclimatised. But the fact remains that Ghanaians smile and laugh more than we do because their pleasures are simpler, more easily and more often fulfilled.

Another returned traveller who has struggled with western consumerism is **Chris Miksovsky** from Colorado who made the mistake of letting his eyes wander round a supermarket:

Memories of the trip already come racing back at the oddest of times. A few days after returning to the US, I went to a large grocery store with my mother. It was overwhelming. Rows and rows of colours and logos all screaming to get your attention. I wandered over to the popcorn display and stood dumbfounded by the variety: buttered, lite, generic, Redenbacker, Paul Newman's au naturel, from single serving sachet through economy family popcorn-orgy size. I counted over 25 unique offerings... of popcorn.

But it passes. The restlessness passes, the reverse culture shock wears off soon enough and you will begin to feel reintegrated. Gap year experiences are great conversation openers when you're meeting new people at university. **Simon Rowland** found that of the 16 other first years in his hall of residence at York University, the four who had taken a gap year gravitated to one another and ended up sharing a unit. As has been noted, it provides an easy topic of conversation for future interviews so in official contexts you should be prepared to put as positive a spin on it as possible.

UNIVERSITY APPLICATION

Applying to university is a stressful and complicated business on which your school should offer detailed advice. The worst aspect of it is the uncertainty of outcome. Conditional offers are the bugbear of prospective students because it means it is difficult to make definite plans until you know your A-level results. Of course the specialist placement organisations are used to coping with the problem and can offer support throughout.

Many school leavers feel forced to make up their minds about university courses too early. More mature students make better decisions about what they want to study and are statistically less likely to drop out.

Taking a lead from Tony Higgins, Chief Executive of UCAS who has given his endorsement to the Year Out Group, organisations involved in gap year travel always urge students to sort out their university applications before taking off. It is also important to ascertain what line the department or college you're applying to takes on gap years. Brian Heap's book *Degree Course Offers* (£24.99 for 2004 edition) includes a sentence or two about the attitude taken by individual institutions to gap years. The vast majority are more than tolerant of them, provided you can demonstrate that you will do something constructive with your year out. Perfecting the art of sleeping until 11am and watching morning television may turn out to be good preparation for university, but not according to admissions tutors.

Even the most inventive interviewee or CV-writer will find it hard to dress up days spent packing videos in a Sydney warehouse or selling ice cream in a New Jersey resort followed by nights of partying. But a lot depends on presentation: any evidence of initiative and organisational abilities will help. If you travel alone you can boast of your independence; if you travel with friends you can claim to have learned about co-operation and team work.

Timing

Wherever possible, students should begin preparations for a gap year well in advance. There are so many plans to make and problems to sort out that the best way to avoid panics and disappointments is not to leave things to the last minute. On the other hand, not all applications are dealt with swiftly. In the November of his last year of high school in Victoria, Canada, **Graham Milner** got excited about a gap year scheme to assist at boarding schools in England, which his school recommended:

> *The application deadline was the first week of December, and we just got letters to say we were accepted the first week of June. They seemed to put a lot of weight on the interview rather than the written application. Anyway, be prepared to wait.*

At last report Graham was investigating cheap flights to London to take up his placement at a school in Hertfordshire in September 2003.

University application forms have to be submitted to the Universities and Colleges Admissions Service, UCAS, by December 15th of your A-level year at the latest (earlier for Oxbridge and some courses). This leaves seven months until exams finish, which may seem plenty of time to decide how to spend your gap year until you realise that some of the schemes are already filling up or that you'll have to raise several thousand pounds in order to join your preferred programme. Similarly, many *Year in Industry* jobs require early application to ensure the chosen company and placement have places left.

Whatever decision is made about your gap year, it is important to keep the university informed. They are unlikely to look favourably on someone asking for deferred entry at the last minute, nor are they likely to permit it.

Pre A-Level Application

The pros and cons of taking a gap year need to be weighed up for a period of time to ensure that the idea has substance and is not just a passing whim. Students need to crystallise their reasons for taking a gap year before speaking to university admissions tutors. It may be beneficial to stress the fact that time spent in the 'real world' will encourage a more mature outlook. Tutors are fully aware of the fact that many students who defer for a year go on to do comparatively better at university. According to a survey carried out on behalf of the Year Out Group, nine out of ten university vice-chancellors agreed that a 'structured year out benefits the personal development of the typical undergraduate'.

However, there is evidence of hostility to deferring entry to certain courses such as maths and possibly music. Equally, students pursuing a particularly long course such as veterinary studies and architecture may choose not to delay embarking upon the long haul of the course. The date for entering the working world is already far in the future; to delay this by yet another year is not always an appealing idea.

The received wisdom on the subject of gap years and medical studies is that a year out will be tolerated only if it is spent in some way related to medicine. **Tom Watkins** who hoped to be accepted for medicine disagrees strongly with the claim that medical schools are suspicious of gap years. His impression is that they do not want to accept people straight out of school and would really prefer older students who will have more chance of sticking the course. His plan was to apply after getting his A-level results in August and then to work as a care worker with damaged children (via an agency like the British Nursing Association) until university interviews in the winter (between December and February). After that he was looking into going to Accra, Ghana with *Projects Abroad* to work in a hospital where he hoped to be involved in the setting up of an immunisation programme.

Students need to impress upon the university that they really want to have a place on that particular course and that come hell or high water they will return to take it. Universities have been made uneasy in the past by too many students provisionally accepting courses and then changing their minds. Having a coherent plan and focusing on the potential benefits will make the university realise that you are serious about spending the year in a responsible manner. Questions about gap years often form a large part of an interview and can potentially be impressive.

Once it has been decided that a gap year is the best plan, this needs to be indicated on the UCAS forms in section 3j. To offer a deferred-entry place is then at the university's discretion and they will send their conditions to UCAS, who in turn send this to the student. Provided the student fulfils the requirements, their place is assured for the September following the gap year. If there are any queries about the university application process, UCAS can be contacted on 01242 222444 while information on retakes is available on the UCAS enquiries line 01242 227788.

Post A-Level Application

In the words of Robert Burns, 'the best-laid schemes of mice and men gang aft agley'. Come results day, some students find that they have not done as well as anticipated and have not met the requirements of their preferred university. Several options are now possible:

1.   Contact your first choice university to see if they will take you for the following year.
2.   Proceed to early entry in Clearing. Courses with vacancies are published in the *Independent* and on the UCAS website www.ucas.com. Speed of reaction and decisiveness are essential at this stage because lots of people are competing for remaining places. You must communicate directly with the institutions which is easier said than done since the phone lines are often jammed in the days following results day. The BBC operates a Student Essentials Helpline in August which includes advice on what to do (including how to break bad news to your parents); check on their website for the number.
3.   Plan to retake and reapply to your preferred university.
4.   Carry on with your gap year plans and apply again the following year with the same exam results.

If the first choice university will not offer a place, you need to ask yourself some hard questions. Was the original choice of course suitable anyway? Would it be better to apply for something else? If the first course was vocational, it could be worthwhile having a serious chat with the Careers Service to reassess the situation, particularly if the grades were a long way below the offer. Reapplying post A-level for the following year is straightforward; universities will either make an unconditional offer or reject your application.

> **Some people choose to have a gap year and some have one thrust upon them. Nicky Stead fell into the latter category when she discovered in August that she had not quite met her offer from Bristol University, though they did offer her a place the following year:**
>
> *Unfortunately I hadn't been swayed while at school by reports of fantastic gap years and had decided to go straight to university from school. Then on results day, my results (AAC) weren't good enough for Bristol, who had offered me ABB, though they said they'd give me a place for the following year. I could have gone to Edinburgh straightaway but I was very keen on Bristol and suddenly realised if I played my cards right I could use a year out to my advantage. I was stuck at the end of August with a year in front of me to fill. I had no money, and I was disappointed that so many gap year opportunities were closed to me because I hadn't spent the last year raising money for travelling, etc. and also because many months notice were required for a lot of projects. GAP Activity Projects had only about ten placements left anywhere and I didn't like the sound of them. Everyone else had applied to GAP the previous October.*
>
> *So I had to get a job and decided that to make the best of things I should get a job relevant to my preferred career and which would look good on my CV as well as raise money for travelling. I got a job inputting mortgage applications for my local building society for six months, which I loved. I felt grown up which was*

> *great. My appraisal was good and they encouraged me to stay. But I felt it would be a waste of the year not to see some of the world. That was when an old teacher handed me a leaflet about conservation projects in Australia through i-to-i. Going to Australia was the best thing I ever did. Now I would encourage anyone to take a year out. I go to Bristol on October 1st, much more confident than a year ago, with an improved CV and many great friends and memories behind me.*

Retakes

Another reason you may end up having to take an unplanned gap year is if you decide to retake one or more exams in the winter or spring. Not many schools will allow students to stay on for an extra year to resit nor is it really advisable. It would be more beneficial to have different tuition to provide a fresh approach to the subject. Even the keenest student will be reluctant to dredge up and study from the same tired old notes all over again.

Tutorial colleges or crammers cater specifically for students needing to retake. Students will resit just the subjects in which they need to boost their grades, thus making them part-time students and leaving lots of time for other pursuits like working and earning, gaining extra skills or doing voluntary work. The downside is that they are extremely expensive. Private colleges charge up to £3,500 for each subject and anxious parents have been known to invest £14,000 on improving their son or daughter's overall grades. Students need to be really sure that they are serious about resitting and are prepared to put in the hard work to make it worthwhile spending such large amounts of money.

If you can't find a suitable tutorial college close to home, you may have to consider travelling elsewhere to cram for your resits. Students need to be mature and self-disciplined to avoid the temptations that arise when one leaves home for the first time. Further information about tutorial colleges can be found from CIFE (Council for Independent Further Education); their website www.thecapability.uk.com/cife has links to their 32 member tutorial colleges around the country and offers more detailed information about retake courses.

The timetable below may serve as a useful guide to where you should be in your application and arrangement of gap year activities. Ideally, students should be around for Results Day in case results are not as expected so that decisions can be made by the students. Alternative arrangements may need to be made, although if the entry is deferred there is plenty of time to do this.

TIMETABLE FOR UNIVERSITY APPLICATION

Plan A

Lower Sixth	*Autumn/Spring*	Begin to think about university courses and the possibility of taking a Gap Year
	Spring/Summer	Visit university Open Days. Speak to Admissions tutors about taking Gap Years. Students should try to visit as many universities as possible to get a feel for the place.
Upper Sixth	*Sept-Dec*	Fill in UCAS forms and clearly mark preference for deferred entry. Hand in no later than 15th December (or 15th October for Medicine and Oxbridge applications)
	Oct-Apr	Make plans for Gap Year (apply to placement scheme/s, volunteer organisations, consider travel options, etc.). Earn as much money as possible to fund your Gap Year
	Jan-March	Receive conditional offers from universities
	Around April	Submit final decision for first and second choice university courses
	May/June	Sit Exams
	August	Results Day i) Sufficient grades; accept the place and enjoy the Gap Year ii) Insufficient grades; implement Plan B

Plan B

Upper Sixth	*Late August*	Phone universities to see if they will still offer a place. Be prepared to stay on the phone for a week If yes, take the place offered and proceed with original Gap Year plans If no, reapply the next year for alternative courses and proceed with original plans Find a tutorial college and proceed as below.
Gap Year	*Sept-May*	Study at tutorial college and spend spare time working, doing voluntary work, taking a skills course, etc.
	Sept-Dec	Reapply to universities via UCAS (presumably no deferred entry this time)
	Jan-March	Receive offers
	May/June	Resit examinations
	June-Sept	Free time for travelling, work, etc.
	August	Results Day (again)
First Year	*Sept-Oct*	Freshers' Week at university

Planning & Preparation

Every successful gap year combines periodic flights of fancy with methodical planning; any homework you do ahead of time will benefit you later, if only because it will give you more confidence. Your first task in the planning stages, is to consider some of the programmes and organisations described in this book and to obtain details from the addresses and websites given. If an organisation offers a project that appeals, the next step is to find out whether you are eligible. The hardest part is not usually being accepted to join but raising enough money to fund it.

FUNDRAISING

For many gap year students, a shortage of money is the main obstacle. As we have seen, many of the most attractive gap year schemes are expensive (£3,000+) so fundraising becomes a major issue for those sixth formers who have decided to take a gap year. Others who simply want to travel will also have to save a substantial sum that should include a contingency fund as well as the minimum for airfares and living expenses.

Once you have resolved to meet a particular target, it is surprising how single-mindedly you can pursue it. Most sending agencies provide extensive advice and support on fundraising, and a lot of useful tips and tricks can be found on the web. Try for example the Jubilee Sailing Trust site www.jst.org.uk, while www.gapyear.com carries plenty of information and links to real life examples. See also the section in a later chapter on Expeditions.

If you have signed up for an organised placement, you will probably have been sent a timetable for paying the placement fee in instalments. Estimate how long it will take you to reach your target and stick to the deadline come what may. It might help to break the saving down into smaller amounts, so that you aim to save £X per week. Dedicated savers consider a 70-hour week at a local job quite tolerable (which will have the additional advantage of leaving you too tired to conduct an expensive social life). Bear in mind that saving over a long period, especially from a job which doesn't pay well, can be depressing since you will have to deny yourself all those expensive little treats. **Georgina Hartley** from Cambridge worked as many hours as she could at her local Marks & Spencer, lived frugally and had saved about £3,000 well before the deadline for her GAP placement in New Zealand. **Kitty Hill** is just one of the many gap year students who spent six months working 60-hour weeks and the valuable thing she learned from that experience was that 'it is a million times nicer to be in a job you enjoy than a job you hate but pays a bit better'.

Letter Writing

Some year out organisations provide a template of a letter seeking sponsorship and a list of suggested trusts to try. It helps to include a photo and make the letter succinct. Although time-consuming, hand-written letters are thought to attract more attention than slick computer-generated ones. The more obvious care you have taken, the better your chances of success so, for example, you should try to find out the name and job title of the person to whom your request will be referred, and enclose a letter of endorsement from your head teacher.

Zoe Nisbet from Madras College in St. Andrew's published a fundraising diary on www.kayem.co.uk/zoe/projecttrust, recording all the ways she used to reach her target of £3,350 to go to Malawi with the Project Trust. Perusing such a detailed breakdown could be instructive, since it makes clear how much dogged effort is needed. In Zoe's case she baked cakes and sold them in the staff room every week. But a few of her many letters to charities and trusts met with a positive response and a donation of £800 in February meant that she exceeded her target months before she was due to depart.

In writing a report about her very successful post-university gap year in Ghana in 2003, Clare Cooper describes the trepidation she felt at the prospect of undertaking to raise the necessary funds to join an AfricaTrust Networks team:

I accepted the offer (against the better judgement of some friends and family) and, armed with positivity, I began the mammoth task of raising £2,500. Already working as a care assistant to cover rent and living costs, I took on two extra jobs in a bar and cinema to begin saving. I wrote literally hundreds of letters to local shops, businesses, schools, charities and churches explaining what I was doing and appealing for sponsorship. To raise awareness of my fundraising, the local newspaper ran a story on me explaining that I would be working with orphans in West Africa and any help with my fundraising would be much appreciated. I followed up this article by visiting local businesses in person asking them if they had received my letter and if not could I leave them another one. I found that using the local paper and visiting people in person really effective.

Still a fair distance from my financial target I had exactly six weeks left to raise the money or I couldn't go. As I worked in a cinema in a thriving local arts centre I decided to organise a fundraising art exhibition. After a couple of weeks of manic organisation and with the invaluable help of friends, family and local artists we held an exhibition of local arts, craft and textiles. The day was a real success, with lots of visitors and many of the artists selling work. With less than a month to go, I was closer to my financial target, but still not there, and running out of time and ideas. With the priceless help and support from the managers, staff and locals in the bar I worked in we organised an African-themed fundraising day. We had a BBQ, bring-and-buy stall, face painting, children's games, art and craft and traditional story telling followed by an evening of music from a number of local bands, a raffle with great prizes provided by local shops, restaurants and businesses and a fantastic African fire sculpture and fireworks display. As well as raising the rest of the money, the night was a great way of saying thank you and good-bye to all my friends and people who had been fundamental to my fundraising.

Target organisations, companies, schools and clubs with which you or your family have links, or which might have some connection with your project. The skill of fundraising is itself impressive when it appears on a CV. Local businesses are usually inundated with requests for donations and raffle prizes and are unlikely to give cash but some might donate some useful items of equipment. Keep track of all the individuals and businesses which have contributed and be sure to send them a thank you note mentioning your fundraising target and progress and then another letter describing the success of your gap year venture.

If you want to go down the route of applying to trusts and charitable bodies, consult a library copy of the *Directory of Grant Making Trusts* compiled and published in three volumes by the Charities Aid Foundation. Also check the National Charities Database on www.charitiesdirect.com or search www.caritasdata.co.uk. In fact not many are willing to support individuals and so you may meet mostly with rejections, especially at this time when the financial markets are at a low ebb and investments are giving low returns. (One enterprising fundraiser got his friends and family to sponsor him for every rejection.) If you are going through a registered charity, always include the number in your letter of request since this may be needed by their accountant.

One potential source of benefactors cannot be found in the library or on the internet but in your parents' address book. Kitty Hill hit upon a more painless way to raise money than her 60 hour-a-week job:

For sponsorship I wrote to everyone on my parents' Christmas card list asking them to sponsor me for a day of my trip, at about £30 a day. Then I promised to send them a postcard on that day. I raised about £2,500 with this method.

Fundraising Ideas

The ingenuity which sixth-formers have demonstrated in organising money-making events, etc. is impressive. If you happen to recall ideas that worked for Comic Relief, think of ways of adapting these. For example one fundraiser got everybody he knew to sponsor him to stay up a tree for a week. You may choose to shave your head, jump out of an aeroplane, organise a fancy dress pub crawl or a thousand other ways to raise money. Try to organise events that will be fun as well as expensive for your well-wishers. For example if you organise a fund-raising quiz in your local pub, give away a few prizes like glitter nail polish. If you have been sponsored to do a bungy jump or swim a mile, hand out sweets when you go round to collect the pledges. If you are seeking sponsorship from businesses, think of ways in which they might benefit, e.g. promise to wear the company T-shirt in a publicity photo on the top of Kilimanjaro or down the Amazon. Other ideas include holding a sweepstake on a big sporting event, hosting a garden fete with stalls and raffles, charging admission to a ceilidh or a salsa evening. One gap year student who went to Mexico organised a huge fashion show which cost £5,000 to put on but raised a massive £11,000.

Publicise your plans and your need of funds wherever you can. Local papers and radio stations will usually carry details of your planned expedition, which may prompt a few local readers/listeners to support you. Ask family and friends to give cash instead of birthday and

Christmas presents. Consider possibilities for organising a fundraising event like a concert or a barn dance, a quiz night, wine tasting or an auction of promises. (If your mum was ever on the PTA ask her for advice but don't expect her to run your campaign for you.)

Sources of Funding

From September 2003, the Chancellor of the Exchequer is proposing to deposit £250 in a Child Trust Fund for every baby born in the form of a voucher, colloquially called the baby bond. A further £50 will be added at ages 5, 11 and 16 (or £100 for the less well off). This money can be accessed at age 18 (approx £1,500) and can be used for higher education, driving lessons or, of course, a gap year project, course or trip. Parents and grandparents are given an incentive to add to this fund by tax breaks.

A small percentage of schemes operate as scholarships and bring with them their own funding, e.g. the *Youth for Understanding* Japan exchange. *European Voluntary Service* (see entry in the 'Directory of Specialist Gap Year Programmes') provides full funding in some cases for a 6-12 month stint as a volunteer on socially beneficial projects in Europe and beyond.

Some schools (not exclusively fee-paying schools) have odd bursaries and travel scholarships which the careers teachers will be able to tell you about. Various scholarships and grants are available to those who fulfil the necessary requirements. To take just a couple of examples: the Caley Gap Scholarship of up to £1,000 is offered by the Royal Caledonian Schools Trust (80a High St, Bushey, Herts. WD23 3DE; rcst@caleybushey.demon.co.uk) to the children of Scottish servicemen and women or people with a Scottish parent living on a low income in Greater London. Applicants must submit a proposal for a worthwhile project abroad. The Peter Kirk Memorial Scholarship (c/o Secretary, 17 St. Paul's Rise, Addingham, Ilkley, Yorks LS29 0QD (mail@kirkfund.org.uk; www.kirkfund.org.uk) funds 10-12 young people aged 18-26 to investigate and write about some aspect of modern Europe. Awards of up to £1,000 are made to those carrying out research over two or three months. The deadline for applications is the middle of February.

The Winston Churchill Memorial Trust (15 Queen's Gate Terrace, London SW7 5PR; www.wcmt.org.uk) awards about 100 four to eight week travelling fellowships to UK citizens of any age or background who wish to undertake a specific project or study related to their personal interests, job or community. The deadline for applications falls in October. Past winners are listed on the website with their age and topic of study; most are older than school leavers but a handful are 18-21. One winner looked at youth circus in Colombia, Australia and Germany; another project took as its theme inspiring young British athletes in Australia and the US.

The Millennium Commission with funding from the National Lottery has been dispensing Youth Millennium Awards through the British Council. Young people aged 18-25 who want to carry out an international project that can be shown to benefit their community can apply (at least 16 weeks in advance) for funding; ring the British Council on 020-7389 4046 for details (www.britishcouncil.org/education/yec/mill.htm).

Archaeology Abroad (www.britarch.ac.uk/archabroad; with an entry in the 'Directory of Voluntary Placements Abroad') makes Fieldwork Awards of £100-£200 and scholarships to selected candidates joining an archaeological excavation who must be subscribers to *Archaeology Abroad* (see first-hand account in the chapter on Greece).

The Young People's Trust for the Environment and Nature Conservation or YPTENC (8 Leapale Road, Guildford, GU1 4JX; awards@yptenc.org.uk) has the task of allocating funding from the Millennium Commission to young people who can design and then implement an environmental education project normally in their home towns. Check www.livingforthefuture.org.uk/faqframe.cfm to see the scope of the projects the Trust is keen to support.

INSURANCE

Any student heading beyond Europe should have travel insurance. Within Europe private insurance is not absolutely essential because European nationals are eligible for reciprocal emergency health care in the EEA. From June 2004 a Europe-wide health card is to be launched which will replace the antiquated old E111 form. In the first phase of introduction it will cover health care for short stays and in the second phase, it will take the place of the current E128 and E119 which cover longer stays for students and job-seekers. The ultimate ambition is to introduce an electronic 'smart-card' but that is some way off.

At present this reciprocal cover is extended only to emergency treatment, though this may change in the coming years. Therefore at present it may still be wise to purchase private travel insurance, not least because you may have to cope with theft. Most students shop around to find the cheapest policy, e.g. with Endsleigh Insurance which specialises in the student market. But if you are going anywhere risky, give some thought to what the policy covers, for example look closely at whether the policy will repatriate you or fly out a parent in an emergency. Check the exclusions carefully and the amount of excess you'll have to pay if you claim.

In situations where you might be two days from civilisation, it is imperative that you (or your sending agency) have water-tight insurance. During **Tom Watkins'** expedition with *BSES* to Lesotho, one of the members of the expedition had a fit. He was picked up by helicopter in less than half an hour (and was subsequently fine). At that point Tom was very glad that his expedition organisers had the best insurance policy that money could buy, even though earlier he had felt disappointed that he had not been allowed to go rock-climbing for reasons of insurance.

Most insurance companies offer a standard rate that covers medical emergencies and a premium rate that covers personal baggage, cancellation, etc. Always read the fine print. Sometimes activities like bungy-jumping (now quite commonplace in parts of the world) are excluded for being too risky. Some travel policies list as one of their exclusions: 'any claims which arise while the Insured is engaged in any manual employment'. If you are not planning to visit North America, the premiums will be much less expensive. Most insurance companies operate 24-hour helplines in the UK which can be dialled from anywhere in the world.

Companies to consider are listed here with an estimate of their premiums for 12 months of worldwide cover (including the USA). Expect to pay roughly £20-£25 per month for basic cover and £35-£40 for more extensive cover.

Boots Insurance Services, Travel Cover Centre, PO Box 1940, Kings Orchard, 1 Queen St, Bristol BS99 2TT (0845 840 2020; www.bootsinsurance.com). Dedicated Gap Year travel cover which costs £295 for one year. Available to anyone up to 64!

Club Direct, Dominican House, St John's St, Chichester, W Sussex (0800 083 2455; www.clubdirect.com). Work abroad is included provided it does not involve using heavy machinery. £179 for basic year-long cover (renewable); £249 including baggage cover.

Columbus Direct, 17 Devonshire Square, London EC2M 4SQ (020-7375 0011; 08450 761030). Globetrotter policy (basic medical cover only) costs £188 for one year. More extensive cover is offered for £312 and £364.

Coverworks, 47a Barony Road, Nantwich, Cheshire CW5 7PB (01270 625431; www.coverworks.com). Policy specially designed for working travellers.

Downunder Worldwide Travel Insurance. 3 Spring St, Paddington, London W2 3RA (0800 393908; www.duinsure.com). Backpacker policy covers working holidays (excluding ladders and heavy machinery). £185 or £235 with baggage cover.

Endsleigh Insurance, Endsleigh House, Cheltenham, Glos GL50 3NR. Offices in most university towns. Twelve months of cover in Europe costs from £215, worldwide £338 (£299 and £485 respectively for a higher level of cover).

Europ-Assistance Ltd, Sussex House, Perrymount Road, Haywards Heath, W Sussex RH16 1DN (01444 442365; www.europ-assistance.co.uk). World's largest assistance organisation with a network of doctors, air ambulances, agents and vehicle rescue services in 208 countries offering emergency assistance abroad 24 hours a day. The Voyager Travel policy covering periods from 6 to 18 months costs £265 for 12 months in Europe and £545 worldwide.

gosure.com, www.gosure.com offer a worldwide backpacker policy (which doesn't cover lost baggage) for just over £200 to cover 18 months including up to 3 months in North America.

Insure and Go, 0870 901 3674; www.insureandgo.com. £240 worldwide; £187 for Australia/New Zealand only. Allows people who take out its plan to cancel if they do not get the A-level grades required for university.

insureyourgap.com – Specialist policy promoted by gapyear.com.

MRL Insurance, 0870 876 7677; www.mrlinsurance.co.uk. Backpacker's Long Stay Travel Insurance targets gap year students and working holiday makers. £199.

Options, 0870 848 0870; www.optionsinsurance.co.uk. £250

Preferential Direct Worldtrekker Policy, 01702 423280; www.worldtrekker.com. For people 18-35. £175 or £264.

Primary Direct, 0870 444 3434; www.primaryinsurance.co.uk. £229. Possible to extend cover on-the-road.

STA Travel, Priory House, 6 Wrights Lane, London W8 6TA (0870 160 6070; www.statravel.co.uk). £180 basic backpacker cover; £275 standard, £379 premier.

Travel Insurance Agency, 775B High Road, North Finchley, London N12 8JY (020-8446 5414/5).

Travel Insurance Club. 01702 423398/0800 316 5520. £189. www.travelinsuranceclub.co .uk. Backpacker policy includes working holidays. £175.

HEALTH & SAFETY

No matter what country you are heading for, you should obtain the Department of Health leaflet T6 *Health Advice for Travellers*. This leaflet should be available from any post office or you can request a free copy on the Health Literature Line 0800 555777.

If you are a national of the European Economic Area and will be working in another EEA country, you will be covered by the European Community Social Security Regulations. Advice and the leaflet SA29 *Your Social Security Insurance, Benefits and Health Care Rights in the European Community and in Iceland, Liechtenstein and Norway* may be obtained free of charge from the Inland Revenue National Insurance Contributions Office, International Services, Benton Park View, Newcastle-upon-Tyne NE98 1ZZ (08459 154811, local rate call; www.inlandrevenue.gov.uk/nic).

If you are planning to include developing countries on your itinerary, you will want to take the necessary health precautions, though this won't be cheap unless you happen to have a well informed GP who doesn't charge much for non-essential injections. Competition among private travel clinics may bring prices down, though this benefits the 'consumer' only in London. At many clinics you will pay between £20 and £40 per vaccine, and more for hepatitis A and B. An added difficulty is that GPs cannot be expected to keep abreast of all the complexities of obscure tropical diseases and malaria prophylaxis for different areas, etc. Many are downright ignorant, though internet access to expert sites has alleviated this problem to some extent.

You can trust the advice of Nomad Travel Clinics which specialise in longhaul travel. For the Hospital for Tropical Diseases in Bloomsbury, ring 020-7388 9600 for appointments or 09061 337733 for automated information costing 50p per minute. Consultations are offered at their clinic near Oxford Circus for £15 but if you have your jabs there, the fee is waived. The respected travel agent Trailfinders operates a Travel Clinic at 194 Kensington High St (020-7983 3999).

Some countries have introduced HIV antibody testing for long-stay foreigners and the certificate may be required to obtain a work or residence visa. If you are going to be spending a lot of time in countries where blood screening is not reliable you should consider carrying a sterile medical kit. These are sold by MASTA (Medical Advisory Service for Travellers Abroad) at the London School of Hygiene and Tropical Medicine, Keppel St, London WC1E 7HT. MASTA (www.masta.org) maintains an up-to-date database on travellers' diseases and their prevention. You can ring their interactive Travellers' Health

Line on 0906 822 4100 with your destinations (up to six countries) and they will send you a basic health brief by return, for the price of the telephone call (60p per minute).

Mercifully the SARS disease seems to have been brought under control, but these crises that seem to come out of nowhere (not to mention the Bali bombing) are bound to give your parents nightmares (and maybe you too).

For advice on protecting your sexual health, Marie Stopes International (0845 300 8090; www.mariestopes.org.uk) is helpful. The government's free booklet 'Drugs Abroad' has sound advice. The National Drugs Helpline (0800 776600 or +44 151 706 7324 from abroad) can give information on drugs laws abroad.

For routine travellers' complaints, it is worth looking at a general guide to travel medicine such as *Bugs, Bites and Bowels* by Dr. Jane Wilson Howarth (Cadogan, 2002, £9.99), *Traveller's Health: How to Stay Healthy Abroad* by Richard Dawood or Ted Lankester's *The Traveller's Good Health Guide* (2002, £7.99). These books emphasise the necessity of avoiding tap water and recommend ways to purify your drinking water by filtering, boiling or chemical additives (i.e. iodine is more reliable than chlorine). MASTA and Nomad market various water purifiers; one of the best is the 'Travel Well Trekker'. Tap water throughout Western Europe is safe to drink.

Increasingly, people are seeking advice via the internet; check for example www.fitfort ravel.scot.nhs.uk; www.tripprep.com; www.tmb.ie and www.travelhealth.co.uk. The private internet-based medical service www.e-med.co.uk has a large travel section with a detailed immunisation schedule. A pre-travel consultation costs £40. The Highway to Health website has a straightforward-to-use database of medical personnel including pharmacies around the world and listings of emergency numbers (www.highwaytohealth.com/public/ doctor_search/by_location.cfm).

Americans seeking general travel health advice should ring the Center for Disease Control & Prevention Hotline in Atlanta on 404-332-4559; www.cdc.gov/travel/destinat.htm.

Malaria is continuing to make a serious comeback in many parts of the world, due to the resistance of certain strains of mosquito to the pesticides and preventative medications which have been so extensively relied upon in the past. You must be particularly careful if travelling to a place where there is falciparum malaria which is potentially fatal. Out of 2,000+ British travellers who return home to the UK with malaria each year, up to 20 will die. All travellers are urged to protect themselves against mosquito bites. Wearing fine silk clothes discourages bites. The Nomad Travel Store in London (40 Bernard St, Russell Square; 02907833 4114; www.nomadtravel.co.uk) can offer expert advice; their Travel Health Line is 09068 633414 (60p a minute). Oasis Nets (High St, Stoke Ferry, Norfolk PE33 9SP; 01366 500466) market mosquito repellents and nets and will send a free fact sheet about malaria in your destination country. Catch 22 in Lancashire is also recommended for a full range of products (01257 473118; www.catch22products.co.uk).

There are two principal types of drug which can be obtained over the counter: Chloroquine-based and Proguanil (brand name Paludrine). Many areas of the world are reporting resistance to one of the drugs, and a new drug Malarone is recommended for some circumstances, though at present it is very expensive and Larium might be a worthwhile alternative if you don't suffer side effects. These drugs plus Mefloquine are available only on prescription and should be tried out before travelling to test for side effects. Unfortunately these prophylactic medications are not foolproof, and even those who have scrupulously swallowed their pills before and after their trip as well as during it have been known to contract the disease. It is therefore also essential to take mechanical precautions against mosquitoes. If possible, screen the windows and sleep under an insecticide-impregnated mosquito net. Marcus Scrace bought some netting intended for prams which occupied virtually no space in his luggage. If these are unavailable, cover your limbs at nightfall with light-coloured garments, apply insect repellent with the active ingredient DEET and sleep with a fan on.

The International Association for Medical Assistance to Travellers (IAMAT) continues to collate news and information about health risks abroad. This organisation co-ordinates doctors and clinics around the world who maintain high medical standards at reasonable cost e.g. US$60 per consultation for IAMAT members. They will send you a directory listing IAMAT centres throughout the world as well as detailed leaflets about malaria and other tropical diseases and country-by-country climate and hygiene charts. There is no set fee for joining the association, but donations are welcome; at the very least you should cover their postage and printing costs. Further information is available on their website www.iamat.org including their world malaria chart and immunisation recommendations country-by-country.

Consider taking a first aid course before leaving. The St. John Ambulance (020-7324 4000) offers a range of Lifesaver and Lifesaver Plus courses. The standard one-day course costs £35-£50 (depending on region). Two new short courses specialise in preparing young people for potential danger and unpredictable situations abroad; see entries for *Objective Team* and *The Knowledge Gap* ('Directory of Gap Preparation Courses'). A company called Adventure Lifesigns (01483 459139; www.adventurelifesigns.co.uk) offers first aid training for overseas explorers and mountaineers. In July 2003 the Royal Geographical Society (020-7591 3030) offered an evening session on planning a gap year, for parents and students, and it might be worth finding out if this will be repeated.

RED TAPE

Passports

A ten-year UK passport costs £28 for 32 pages and £38 for 48 pages, and should be processed by the Passport Agency within ten days, though it is safer to allow more time. Queuing in person at one of the six passport offices (in Liverpool, London, Newport, Peterborough, Glasgow and Belfast) will speed things up in an emergency but will incur a surcharge of £12; addresses are listed on passport application forms (available from main post offices). Ring the Passport Agency on 08705 210410 (www.passports.gov.uk).

Travel Visas

Outside the Schengen Area of Europe in which border controls have been largely abolished, you can't continue in one direction for very long before you are impeded by border guards demanding to see your papers. EU nationals who confine their travels to Europe have little to worry about. Everyone else should do their homework. Always check with the Consulate, the internet or a clued-up travel agent who will have access to current visa regulations.

Up-to-date visa information is available on many websites such as that of the visa agency Thames Consular Services in London (www.thamesconsular.com) which allows you to search visa requirements and costs for individual countries. Addresses for some foreign Consulates and High Commissions in London are listed in Appendix II. Getting visas is a headache anywhere and often an expensive headache, but is usually easier in your home country. The health consultancy MASTA operates a Visa and Passport line charged at £1 a minute (0897 501 1000) providing accurate and comprehensive visa information for all destinations.

If you are short of time or live a long way from the Embassies in London, there are private visa agencies such as the VisaService, 2 Northdown St, London N1 9BG (www.visaservice.co.uk) which will obtain the relevant visa for a handling fee starting at £25 plus VAT per visa. They have a premium visa info line on 09068 34 36 38 though quite a lot of information is available on embassy websites. Alternatives include Benmar Visa Service (020-7379 6418; www.visaservice.uk.com) and Thames Consular (www.thames consular.com).

If you intend to cross a great many borders, especially on an overland trip through Africa, ensure that you have all the relevant documentation and that your passport contains as many blank pages as frontiers which you intend to cross. Travellers have been turned back purely because the border guard refused to use a page with another stamp on it.

Work Visas

The free reciprocity of labour within the European Union means that the red tape has been simplified (though not done away with completely). The standard situation among all EU countries (plus Norway and Iceland which belong to the European Economic Area or EEA) is that nationals of any EU state have the right to look for work in another member state for up to three months. At the end of that period they should apply to the police or the local authority for a residence permit, showing their passport and job contract. (See section 'Working in Europe' in the chapter *Work Experience* for information about the new member states of the European Union.)

Outside Europe, obtaining permission to work is next to impossible for short periods during a gap year unless you are participating in an organised exchange programme where the red tape is taken care of by your sponsoring organisation. If you come up against bureaucratic obstacles, try to work around it as **Jaime Burnell** did in her gap year:

> *I wanted to find work in South Africa but work permits were too difficult and expensive. Instead, I exchanged au pair work for room and board and enjoyed two months in Durban.*

Student and Youth Hostel Cards

With an International Student Identity Card (ISIC) it is often possible to obtain reduced fares on trains, planes and buses, £1 off each night's stay at a youth hostel in the UK, discounted admission to museums and theatres, and other perks. The ISIC is available to all students in full-time education. There is no age limit though some flight carriers do not apply discounts for students over 31. To obtain a card (which is valid for 15 months from September) you will need to complete the ISIC application form, provide a passport photo, proof of full-time student status (NUS card or official letter) and the fee of £7. Take these to any students' union, local student travel office or send to ISIC Mail Order, PO Box 36, Glossop, Derbyshire SK13 8HT (enquiries@nussl.co.uk). When issued with an ISIC, students also receive a handbook containing travel tips, details of national and international discounts and how to get in touch with the ISIC helpline, a special service for travelling students who need advice in an emergency.

Membership in the Youth Hostels Association costs £13.50 or £6.75 for the under 18s; contact the YHA at Trevelyan House, Dimple Road, Matlock, Derbyshire DE4 3YH (0870 770 8868; www.yha.org.uk). Seasonal demand abroad can be high, so it is always preferable to book in advance if you know your itinerary. You can pre-book beds over the internet on www.iyhf.org or through individual hostels and national offices listed in the *Hostelling International Guides*: Volume I covers Europe and the Mediterranean, Volume II covers the rest of the world. They can be ordered by ringing Customer Services on the above number or online for £8.50 each including postage.

A growing number of privately-owned hostels is providing lively competition for the International Youth Hostels Federation; check the websites www.hostels.com, www.hostelworld.com or www.hostels.net for a selection worldwide. VIP Backpacker Resorts of Australia (www.backpackers.com.au) have hundreds of hostels in Australia, New Zealand and worldwide.

Three hundred hostels are listed in the pocket-sized annually revised *Independent Hostel Guide* from the Backpackers Press, Speedwell House, Upperwood, Matlock Bath, Derbyshire DE4 3PE (☎/fax 01629 580427; june@backpackerspress.com), at a cost of £4.95 (plus £1 postage); most are in the UK. Independent hostels are a good source of temporary work, often providing a few hours a day of work in return for bed and board.

For many travellers, hostels are the key to an excellent holiday. Not only do they provide an affordable place to sleep (typically £10 in the first world, much less in developing countries), they provide access to a valuable range of information about what to see, how to get there and who to go with. Additional services are often provided such as bicycle hire or canoeing and trekking trips.

Travel Warnings

The Foreign & Commonwealth Office has a Travel Advice Unit which can advise on how risky travel to certain war zones, etc. might be. It can be contacted on 020-7008 0232/3; www.fco.gov.uk/travel. If you have access to BBC Ceefax look at pages 470 and following. Two years ago the FCO launched a 'Know Before You Go' campaign to raise awareness among backpackers and independent travellers of potential risks and dangers and how to guard against them, principally by having a good insurance policy. According to FCO research younger travellers are twice as likely as the average to get into some kind of trouble abroad.

General advice on minimising the risks of independent travel is contained in the book *World Wise – Your Passport to Safer Travel* published by Thomas Cook in association with the Suzy Lamplugh Trust and the Foreign Office (www.suzylamplugh.org/worldwise; £6.99 plus £2 postage). Arguably its advice is over-cautious, advising travellers never to hitch-hike, ride a motorbike or accept an invitation to a private house. Travellers will have to decide for themselves when to follow this advice and when to ignore it.

Taxation

Students who find holiday jobs often have more tax deducted by their employers than they are liable for. If you earn less than the annual tax-free personal allowance (£4,615 in 2003), you should pay no tax at all. It is a time-consuming and bothersome business to claim back what you've overpaid at the end of the tax year (April 6th). It is better to obtain the relevant form P38(S) from the Inland Revenue before starting work which proves that you are a student doing a vacation job; note that it does not apply to longer-term work even if you are a student.

In theory EU students working in the EU for less than six months are not liable for tax, so students should always show their employers documents to prove their status. In many countries your employer will expect you to clarify your tax position with the local tax office at the beginning of your work period. This can be to your advantage for example in Denmark or Australia where, unless you obtain a tax card, you will be put on a very high emergency rate of tax.

MONEY

The average budget of a travelling student is £25 a day though many survive on half that. Whatever the size of your travelling fund, you should give some thought to how and in what form to carry your money. Travellers' cheques are safer than cash, though they cost an extra 1% and banks able to encash them are not always near to hand. The most universally recognised brands are American Express and Visa (Thomas Cook now sells American Express products). It is advisable also to keep a small amount of cash. Sterling is fine for most countries but US dollars or euros are preferred in much of the world such as Latin America, Eastern Europe and Israel. The easiest way to look up the exchange rate of any world currency is to check on the internet (e.g. www.xe.net/ucc) or to look at the Monday edition of the *Financial Times*. A Currency Conversion Chart is included in Appendix I.

Hole-in-the-wall machines can be found in major cities around the world and generally incur a fairly low transaction charge. Ask your bank for a list of cash machines in the countries you intend to visit. Otherwise you can check the ATM locator on www.mastercard.com (where you'll learn where the facility is in Antarctica) or http://visaatm.infonow.net.

Theft takes many forms, from the highly trained gangs of gypsy children who artfully pick pockets in European railway stations to violent attacks on the streets of American cities. Risks can be reduced by carrying your wealth in several places including a comfortable money belt worn inside your clothing, steering clear of seedy or crowded areas and moderating your intake of alcohol. If you are robbed, you must obtain a police report (often for a fee) to stand any chance of recouping part of your loss from your insurer (assuming the loss of cash is covered in your policy) or from your travellers' cheque company. Always keep a separate record of the cheque numbers you are carrying, so you will know instantly the numbers of the ones that have been taken.

Haggling is a topic of endless fascination among world travellers. Try to avoid boasting about how hard a bargain you are able to drive. Remember that in some countries, the rickshaw driver or temple guide could feed his family that day with the 20p you saved. But spreading largesse randomly is not advisable either. It is not uncommon for children to skip school in order to frequent tourist haunts where they stand a chance of being given a few coins.

Transferring Money

Assuming your account at home remains in credit and you have access to a compatible ATM, it shouldn't be necessary to have money wired to you urgently. If you run out of money abroad, whether through mismanagement, loss or theft and cannot use an ATM, you can contact your bank back home by telephone, fax or on-line, and ask them to wire money to you. This will be easier if you have set up a telephone or internet bank account before leaving home since they will then have the correct security checks in place to authorise a transfer without having to receive something from you in writing with your signature. You can request that the necessary sum be transferred from your bank to a named bank in the town you are in – something you have to arrange with your own bank, so you know where to pick the money up.

Western Union offers an international money transfer service whereby cash deposited at one branch (by, say, your mum) can be withdrawn by you from any other branch or agency, which your benefactor need not specify. Western Union agents – there are 90,000 of them in 200 countries – come in all shapes and sizes, e.g. travel agencies, stationers, chemists. Unfortunately it is not well represented outside the developed world. The person sending money to you simply turns up at a Western Union counter, pays in the desired sum plus the fee, which is £14 for up to £100 transferred, £21 for £100-200, £37 for £500 and so on. For an extra £7 your benefactor can do this over the phone with a credit card. In the UK, ring 0800-833833 for further details, a list of outlets and a complete rate schedule. The website www.westernunion.com allows you to search for the nearest outlet.

Thomas Cook, American Express and the UK Post Office offer a similar service called Moneygram. Cash deposited at one of their foreign exchange counters is available within ten minutes at the named destination or can be collected up to 45 days later at one of 37,000 co-operating agents in 150 countries. The fee is £12 for sending £100, £18 for up to £200, £23 for up to £300, £44 for between £750 and £1,000 and so on. Ring 0800 018 0104 for details.

WHAT TO TAKE

Packing for travelling as a backpacker will always entail compromises because you will be limited in the amount of clothes and equipment you can take with you. When you're buying a backpack/rucksack in a shop try to place a significant weight in it so you can feel how comfortable it might be to carry on your back, otherwise you'll be misled by lifting something usually filled with foam.

Another important consideration is what you take for sleeping. A tropical quilt might be preferable to a sleeping bag for travel in hot climates. Either you can spread out the quilt as a bed to sleep on or it can be folded to create a lightweight sleeping bag. The other advantage is that it is much lighter to carry and takes up less room in your luggage. Alternatively, it can be wrapped around your shoulders for warmth in an air-conditioned space or on a chilly evening in the mountains. After washing, the quilt dries in 20 minutes. However, it will not provide enough warmth if you're planning to travel at high altitudes. A down vest might be a solution for travelling at altitude and can also double up as a comfortable pillow.

While aiming to travel as lightly as possible, you should consider the advantage of taking certain extra pieces of equipment like comfortable walking boots or a tent if you will have the chance to travel independently. One travelling tip is to carry dental floss, useful not only for your teeth but as strong twine for mending backpacks, hanging up laundry, etc.

In the tropics you must carry water, in order to prevent dehydration. Belts with zips worn under a shirt are very handy for carrying money unobtrusively. A bandana is also advisable in the tropics to mop up sweat or to put round your face in windy desert conditions. Some even have backgammon and chess sets printed on them to provide portable entertainment.

When packing it's best to roll clothes to save space and put the heaviest objects at the bottom of the pack. One bizarre piece of advice passed on by a backpacker is to take a spare set of clothes to your local butcher and ask to have them vaccum-packed, to keep an emergency set of clothes dry and clean. Always carry liquids (like shampoo or iodine for purifying water) inside a plastic bag in case they leak.

If you have plumped for a placement scheme which is sending you to one place for a long period of time like a village school or kibbutz, you might allow yourself the odd (lightweight) luxury, such as a favourite cassette, short-wave radio or jar of marmite.

HANDY TRAVEL TIPS FOR BACKPACKERS

- Keep a record of vital travel documents like passport number, driving licence, travellers' cheque serial numbers, insurance policy, tickets, emergency number for cancelling credit cards, etc. Make two copies: stow one away in your luggage and give the other to a friend or relation at home.
- Make sure your passport will remain valid for at least three months beyond the expected duration of your trip; some countries require six months worth of validity.
- Carry valuable items (like passport, essential medicines and of course money) on your person rather than relegating them to a piece of luggage which might be lost or stolen.
- Only take items you are prepared to lose.
- When deciding on clothes to take, start at your feet and work your way up the body; then try to shed up to half. If you find that you really need some missing item of clothing, you can always buy it en route
- Take waterproof and dustproof luggage.
- Remember to ask permission before taking photographs of individuals or groups. In some cultures it can be insulting.
- Take advantage of the loos in expensive hotels and fast food chains.
- Use the libraries of the British Council which can be found in most capital cities. The luxuries on offer include British newspapers and air-conditioning.
- Take a list of consular addresses in the countries you intend to visit in case of emergency

---

Good maps and guides always enhance one's enjoyment of a trip. Most people you will meet on the road will probably be carrying a *Rough Guide* or a *Travel Survival Kit* from Lonely Planet. These are both excellent series, though try not to become enslaved by their advice and preferences. Rough Guides has brought out a new title which could be of interest to gap year students *First Time Around the World*. Even though so much advance information is available over the internet (for example www.travelleronline.co.uk allows you to link to selected extracts of Rough Guides and London Planet publications), nothing can compete with a proper guide book to pore over and take away with you. If you are going to be based in a major city, buy a map ahead of time. If you are in London, visit the famous travel book shop Stanfords (12-14 Long Acre, Covent Garden, WC2E 9LP; 020-7836 1321/fax 020-7836 0189) and Daunt Books for Travellers (83 Marylebone High Street, W1M 4DE; 020-7224 2295) which stocks fiction and travel writing alongside guide books and maps. The Map Shop (15 High St, Upton-on-Severn, Worcestershire WR8 0HJ; 01684 593146/e-mail: Themapshop@btinternet.com) does an extensive mail order business and will send you the relevant catalogue for the part of the world you are intending to visit.

Preparation is half the fun but choose like-minded company before discussing your intended anti-malarial regimen and your water sterilising equipment since you don't want to turn into a pub bore.

What to leave behind

Make sure you leave a record of all important documents with your parents plus at least four signed passport photos which are needed for university loan applications and by some university admissions departments. Whereas forms can be e-mailed, faxed or posted to you abroad for your attention, it is difficult to arrange for photos to be sent and impossible if you are on a placement teaching at a village school in Tanzania or Nepal.

Depending on your destination, don't take your trendy clothes and trainers. For tropical countries, leave behind anything that isn't made of cotton or silk.

STAYING IN TOUCH

The revolution in communication technology means that you are never far from home. Internet cafés can be found in almost every corner of the world where, for a small fee, you can access your e-mail or check relevant information on the web. Internet cafés can easily be located on arrival in virtually any place in the world simply by asking around. Angus Kennedy's *The Rough Guide to the Internet* contains practical advice and, for constantly updated listings, check the revealingly named www.cybercaptive.com. The technically minded might wish to take a digital camera in order to be able to send photos home electronically. Many gap year travellers also set up their own websites so that they can share their travelogue.

Fixing yourself up with a roving e-mail account before leaving home is now virtually compulsory. This allows you to keep in touch with and receive messages from home and also with friends met on the road. The most heavily subscribed service for travellers is hotmail (www.hotmail.com) though its popularity occasionally places strains on the system. Alternatives include BT's btopenworld.com and http://mail.yahoo.com. Spending time in travel chatrooms like Lonely Planet's thorntree or www.gapyear.com might turn up gems of little-known travel wisdom or put you on your way to connecting up with a like-minded companion.

People on a peripatetic year out are increasingly using e-mail not just to keep in touch with home but to meet people on-line, to keep in touch with people they've met travelling, to find out information about a place and to publish their own adventures. The danger for people who rely too heavily on the new technology is that they spend so much time tracking down and inhabiting cybercafés that they end up not having the encounters and adventures they might have otherwise. Just as the young mobile phone generation is finding it harder to cut ties with home knowing that a parent or a school friend is only a few digits away wherever they are, so too travellers who spend an inordinate amount of time online risk failing to look round the destination country in depth. They are so busy communicating with their fellow travellers that they miss out on meeting locals in the old-fashioned, strike-up-a-conversation, getting-in-and-out-of-scrapes way. They will also be deprived of another old-fashioned treat: arriving at a poste restante address and experiencing the pleasure (sweeter because deferred) of reading their mail.

A plethora of companies sell pre-paid phone cards intended to simplify international phone calls as well as make them cheaper. After registering, you credit your card account with an amount of your choice (normally starting at £10 or £20). Then you are given an access code which can be used internationally. Conditions vary but with a BT International Prepaid Card, there is no minimum charge on any single call and you can check to see how much credit you have left at any point. You can buy the BT card at branches of Travelex, for example at the currency exchange desks at airports.

Lonely Planet, the Australian travel publisher, has an easy-to-use communications card called eKno which combines low cost calls, voice mail, email and internet and travel information. For information ring 0800 376 2366 or log on www.ekno.lonelyplanet.com.

Try to ascertain that your card will work in your destination country. Nineteen-year-old **Eloise Weddell** was anxious at first about staying with a Mexican family in order to improve her Spanish and naturally wanted to keep in touch with home. The card she bought locally allowed her to make very cheap calls within Cuernavaca but it cost her £7 for a 3-minute call to England. **Lucy Jackson** fared even worse on her first homesick night in a Quito hotel; her phone card didn't work at all, so she paid $17 on the hotel phone for one minute's reassurances from her father.

The cost of taking a mobile phone abroad differs wildly between brands and tariffs but can be as much as £1.80 per minute to receive a call. Whether or not to take your mobile phone will have to be considered in light of the views of Joseph Tame who went travelling when he was 18 some years ago:

Is a mobile phone necessary when travelling abroad? Well, despite owning four of them, I'd have to say No. The first thing to remember is that Pay-as-you-talk doesn't work abroad. Also, if you're going to America you'll need a Tri-Band handset, and when in Japan you'll need a new one altogether, all a bit complicated. Usually I think the best thing to do is only get one if you stay in one country for a long time - and buy it when you get there. What I would recommend is having a voice mailbox whereby people can call a number and leave a message for you. You can then call your mail-box once a week and listen to your friends telling you how jealous they are.

The radio might offer a more conventional way of keeping in touch. Access to the World Service can be a comfort. You will need a good short-wave radio with several bands powerful enough to pick up the BBC. 'Dedicated' short-wave receivers which are about the size of a paperback start at £65. If you are travelling via the Middle East or Hong Kong, think about buying one duty-free. Alternative English language broadcasting organisations are Voice of America, Radio Canada International and Swiss Radio International.

A British Consul can:
- Issue an emergency passport
- Contact relatives and friends to ask them for help with money or tickets
- Tell you how to transfer money
- Cash a sterling cheque worth up to £100 if supported by a valid banker's card
- As a last resort give you a loan to return to the UK
- Put you in touch with local lawyers, interpreters or doctors
- Arrange for next of kin to be told of an accident or death
- Visit you in case of arrest or imprisonment and arrange for a message to be sent to relatives or friends
- Give guidance on organisations who can help trace missing persons
- Speak to the local authorities for you

But a British Consul cannot:
- Intervene in court cases
- Get you out of prison
- Give legal advice or start court proceedings for you
- Obtain better treatment in hospital or prison than is given to local nationals
- Investigate a crime
- Pay your hotel, legal, medical, or any other bills
- Pay your travel costs, except in rare circumstances
- Perform work normally done by travel agents, airlines, banks or motoring organisations
- Find you somewhere to live or a job or work permit
- Formally help you if you are a dual national in the country of your second nationality
- A Foreign & Commonwealth Office leaflet 'Backpacking and Independent Travellers' is widely distributed at British airports, etc.

Travel

It would be a pretty sad gap year that didn't include at least some travel. Placement schemes abound which can set you down in near or far destinations and give you a chance to get to know a foreign city or region while working, volunteering or studying there. But of course many people taking a year out will simply decide to spend part of it on holiday, usually near the end after they have had a chance to earn and save some money. If you have a friend who wants to go with you, many happy sessions can be spent in the pub planning the itinerary. If your friends are all disappearing in different directions, do not give up on the idea of going on a trip.

Many gap travellers have found that even if they start off alone, they soon meet like-minded travellers in hostels, trains, cyber-cafés and so on. Some even bump into someone from their school by chance as happened to Ben Hartley when he was changing buses in outback Australia. People who pluck up the courage to travel on their own often find that it is easier for them to have contact with local people.

One solution to the problem of having no available travel companions is to join a group of like-minded people on an overland expedition. There are distinct advantages to having your travel arrangements organised for you en route. Travelling with an overland company saves time and stress usually expended on things like the bureaucratic snags of border crossings and provides help with food, accommodation, activities and excursions. Taking advantage of such insider knowledge removes all the hassle of solitary independent travel. For example Oasis Overland (www.oasisoverland.co.uk) specialises in adventure travel for young travellers with truck-based overland expeditions in South America, Africa and the Middle East lasting 19 days to 29 weeks. Some trips attract more mature travellers while others (such as their 'Egypt Encompassed' trip) tend to emphasise partying. So it is worth making enquiries before booking.

Most overland companies cater for the backpacking market and keep prices down by providing basic accommodation, often camping, and expecting participants to share the cooking duties. Overland trips include optional adventurous excursions, such as mountain trekking, white water rafting or adrenaline sports. An average trip would cost between £100 and £150 a week plus £40-£50 a week for the food kitty. The longer the trip the lower the weekly cost, for example Oasis Overland trips start at £65 per week plus £30 a week local payment (for food and camping fees) on 29-week trips and go up to around £135 a week for shorter South American trips (see *Directory of Expeditions*).

Overland Tour Operators

Here is a selected list of overland operators whose websites provide detailed information about their trips. The average age on most of these would be 20-30 with a higher ratio of women to men. For more companies, see the directory of tour operators maintained by Overland Expedition Resources (www.go-overland.com). Specialist companies which operate only in one region (e.g. Africa) are mentioned in the relevant chapter.

Dragoman, Camp Green, Kenton Road, Debenham, Suffolk IP14 6LA (01728 861133; www.dragoman.co.uk). Incorporates Encounter (www.encounter.co.uk).

Exodus, 9 Weir Road, London SW12 0LT (www.exodus.co.uk). Africa, Asia and the Americas.

Explore Worldwide Ltd, 1 Frederick St, Aldershot, Hants. GU11 1LQ (01252 760200; www.exploreworldwide.co.uk). Europe's largest adventure tour operator with trips in Europe, Africa, Asia and the Americas.

First 48, PO Box 48, Pudsey, W. Yorks LS28 5GY (0700 423 8368; www.first48.com).

Guerba Expeditions, Wessex House, 40 Station Road, Westbury, Wilts. BA13 3JN (01373 826611; www.guerba.co.uk). Originally an Africa specialist, now runs trips to other continents.

Imaginative Traveller, 1 Betts Avenue, Martlesham Heath, Suffolk IP5 7RH (0800 316 2717; www.imaginative-traveller.com) runs small group adventures around the globe.

Kumuka Expeditions, 40 Earl's Court Road, London W8 6EJ (020-7937 8855; www.kumuka.co.uk).

Oasis Overland, The Marsh, Henstridge, Somerset BA8 0TF (01963 363400; info@oasis overland.co.uk). Africa, Middle East, Egypt and Latin America.

Travelbag Adventures, 15 Turk St, Alton, Hants. GU34 1AG (01420 541007; www.travelbag-adventures.com).

Cost is usually the crucial factor for gap students wondering where to go or how to get there. Those who go through a sending agency will either have their travel arranged for them or be offered plenty of guidance. But for those students who want to organise their own trip, here are some travel tips to get started.

AIR TRAVEL

Scheduled airfares as laid down by IATA, the airlines' cartel, are best avoided. They are primarily designed for airline accountants and businessmen on expense accounts. You should be looking at no frills airlines, discounted student tickets, cheap charters and tickets from unpopular carriers (e.g. Garuda instead of Qantas). Air travel within individual countries and continents is not always subject to this choice, though some special deals are available.

High street travel agents and mainstream internet travel agents can offer exceptional deals. But the very lowest fares are still found by doing some careful shopping around on the telephone and internet. Even if you choose not to book online and want the reassurance of dealing with a human being, the web can still be a great source of information about prices and options.

For longhaul flights, especially to Asia, Australasia and more recently Latin America, discounted tickets are available in plenty and there should never be any need to pay the official full fare. The major student travel agency *STA Travel* is one of the best starting places. STA Travel are specialists in student and youth travel offering low cost flights, accommodation, insurance, car hire, round-the-world tickets, overland travel, adventure tours, ski, and gap year travel. STA Travel have almost 70 branches in the UK and over 450 worldwide staffed by experienced travellers. A reverse chargeable helpdesk provides help before, after and during your trip. STA Travel is interested in courting gap year students and publish a year out brochure which includes information about organising a gap year; a free copy may be obtained by ringing 020-7361 6166 or can be picked up in any branch. STA Travel attend lots of gap year fairs at schools around the country in co-operation with a selection of leading gap year placement organisations. For bookings and enquiries call STA Travel on 0870 160 6070 or log on at www.statravel.co.uk to find fares, check availability, enter competitions, find your nearest branch or book online. It is now possible to book onto a TEFL course or voluntary programme with i-to-i at any STA Travel branch and on to selected other gap year programmes mentioned on the STA Travel website.

The price of round-the-world tickets has been coming down over the past few years. Check the specialist site www.roundtheworldflights.com (0870 442 4842) or its sister site www.globalvillageflights.com (0870 422 4848). RTW fares start at about £860 plus tax; the cheapest fares involve one or more gaps which you must cover overland. Most are valid for up to a year. An example of a good fare (available through STA Travel) is £924 plus £120 tax which uses Virgin Atlantic, Singapore Airlines and Air New Zealand. This fare can be applied to a large number of routes, though the most popular would be London – Bangkok – surface to Singapore – Perth – surface to Sydney – Christchurch – surface to Auckland – Fiji – LA – surface to New York – London.

Other reliable agencies specialising in longhaul travel including for student and budget travellers are:

Trailfinders Ltd, 194 Kensington High St, London W8 7RG (020-7938 3939 longhaul; 020-7937 5400 transatlantic; 020-7937 1234 Europe). Also travel centres in Birmingham, Manchester, Newcastle, Bristol, Cambridge, Glasgow, Dublin, Belfast, Sydney, Brisbane and Cairns Australia.

Marco Polo Travel 24A Park St, Bristol BS1 5JA (0117-929 4123). Discounted airfares worldwide.

Student Flights UK, c/o Flight Centre, Level 3, Broadway House, 112-134 The Broadway, Wimbledon SW19 1RL (08708 988 8989 or 08708 900092; www.studentflights.co.uk). Cheap student flights and extra services (e.g. working holiday packages).

North South Travel, Moulsham Mill Centre, Parkway, Chelmsford, Essex CM2 7PX (01245 608291). Discount travel agency that donates all its profits to projects in the developing world.

Quest Travel – 0870 444 5552; www.questtravel.com.

Bridge the World – 0870 444 1716; www.bridgetheworld.com.

All of these offer a wide choice of fares including RTW. When purchasing a discounted fare, you should be aware of whether or not the ticket is refundable, whether the date can be changed and if so at what cost, whether taxes are included, and so on. **Roger Blake** was pleased with the round-the-world ticket he bought from STA for £940 that took in Johannesburg, Australia and South America. But once he embarked he wanted to stay in Africa longer than he had anticipated and wanted to alter the onward flight dates:

> *That is the biggest problem of having an air ticket. I had planned for six months in Africa but I've already spent five months in only three countries. I have been into the British Airways office here in Kampala to try my verbal skills but have been told*

the 12-month period of validity is non-negotiable. How stupid I was to presume I would get a refund when it states clearly on the back of the ticket that they may be able to offer refunds/credit. A lesson for me and a warning to future world travellers, to check before they buy whether or not the ticket is refundable/extendable.

Ben Spenser came to a similar conclusion when his travel plans changed and he regretted not having studied the fine print of his ticket which indicated that he could change the date but not the route. Having booked a return flight London-Hong Kong and Moscow-London on Lufthansa (for £500 with STA), his plans changed and he decided to extend his stay. When making enquiries in Moscow, the airline claimed that changes could only be done by the travel agent and the travel agent claimed that they could only be made by the airline. So he bought an exceedingly cheap ticket from St. Petersburg to Tallinn & Helsinki and then a new one-way flight Helsinki-London on SAS for £100 (via email with STA in Helsinki). Again, he did not use this ticket because he was hospitalised in Moscow and his insurance company (Columbus) arranged for his return flight (accompanied by a nurse).

Discount agents advertise in London weeklies like *TNT* and *Time Out,* as well as in the travel pages of newspapers like the *Independent.* Phone a few outfits and pick the best price. Those with access to the internet should start by checking relevant websites, for example www.cheapflights.co.uk which has links to other useful sources of travel information. Alternatives are www.travelocity.com and www.lastminute.com.

If you are spending time in North America through *BUNAC* or *Camp America,* you will have had to book your return ticket before leaving the UK. But if you are in the US without a ticket and need to find a cheap transatlantic or onward flight, the best bet by far is available to people who are flexible about departure dates and destinations and are prepared to travel on a standby basis. The passenger chooses a block of possible dates (up to a five-day 'window') and preferred destinations. One company that tries to match these requirements with empty airline seats at knock-down prices is Air-Tech at 588 Broadway, Suite 1007, New York, NY 10012 (212-219-7000; www.airtech.com). The transatlantic fares being advertised at the time of writing were $165 one way from the east coast, $233 from the west coast and $199 from Chicago, all excluding tax, a registration fee of $29 and a FedEx delivery charge of $18+. Discounted fares of $250 return between the US and Mexico or the Caribbean are also available.

EUROPE

Airfares

From the UK to Europe it is often cheaper to fly on one of the new no-frills ticketless airlines shuttling between Stansted or Luton and many European destinations than it is by rail or bus. The explosion of competition on European routes has seen some amazingly low fares, though recent buy-outs in the industry may mean a loss of competition, i.e. Easyjet bought Go so that it could have Stansted as well as Luton as a base and Ryanair has acquired Buzz. Richard Branson's Virgin Express, whose hub is Brussels, has stopped flying to the UK. On the other hand several new no-frills airlines have joined the fray including BMI's no-frills offshoot bmibaby and MyTravelLite. These airlines do not take bookings via travel agents so it is necessary to contact them directly, preferably booking over the internet since that invariably saves money, usually £5 per ticket. When comparing prices always factor the tax in which routinely adds £20-£30 to fares and often represents more than 100% of the fare cost:

Easyjet – 0870 6000000; www.easyjet.com. Flies from Luton, Stansted, Gatwick and other UK airports to Nice, Barcelona, Amsterdam, Madrid, Malaga, Palma de Mallorca, Alicante, Athens, Geneva, Zurich, Munich, Lyon, Paris, Rome, Naples and Venice.

Ryanair – 0871 246 0000; www.ryanair.com. To Irish airports and dozens of European cities. Amazing bargains on internet such as return fares from £10.

BMIbaby – www.bmibaby.com. Based at East Midlands Airport. Quoted fares include tax.

MyTravelLite – 08701 564564; www.mytravellite.com. Part of My Travel Group (formerly tour operator Airtours). Connects Birmingham with Geneva, Malaga, Murcia, Alicante, Amsterdam, Knock and others

Eclipse Direct, part of First Choice Holidays, offer some cheap fares on long stay flights which depart from the UK for European resorts in the winter and return before the holiday season begins. For example a two-month return from Cardiff to Tenerife or from Birmingham to Malta should cost well under £100. Details from 08705 329326. Other holiday companies out of peak season try to fill up seats on charter flights, by advertising or (increasingly) over the internet.

Europe's largest and best-connected scheduled coach tour operator is Eurolines serving 500 destinations in 25 countries from Killarney on the west coast of Ireland to Bucharest. Prices start at £36 return for London-Amsterdam. You can write to Eurolines (UK) head office for schedules and prices at 4 Cardiff Road, Luton, Beds LU1 1PP or call 08705 143219 for reservations or check fares and times on www.eurolines.com. Passengers under the age of 26 are eligible for a 10% discount.

For smaller independent coach operators, check advertisements in London magazines like *TNT*. For example Kingscourt Express (125 Balham High Road, London SW12 9AJ; 020-8673 7500; www.kce.cz) runs daily between London and Prague or Brno; fares start at £64 return.

An unusual way of locating cheap flights is available from Adventurair (PO Box 757, Maidenhead, SL6 7XD; 01293 405777; www.rideguide.com) who produce *The Ride Guide* as a book or CD which gives details of companies operating cargo planes, aircraft deliveries and private planes. Any of these may have seats available for bargain prices. The book costs £15.99 in the UK ($19.99) plus £1.50 postage.

Rail

On the whole the railways of Europe are expensive, even with under-26 discounts available through Rail Europe. One of the classic gap year experiences is to Inter-Rail around Europe. It may sound a little tame compared to round-the-world flights or Himalayan treks, but it can provide an amazing taste of the delights of Europe which you can explore in more detail on future trips. For the Inter-Rail pass, you must choose how many zones you intend to cover and bear in mind that seat reservations will cost extra; current prices for the under-26s are £195 for a month's travel in two zones, £225 for three and £265 for four. Anyone intending to do some concentrated travelling by train should contact a specialist operator like Rail Europe (0990 848848) or Rail Choice (www.railchoice.co.uk) who sell a large range of European and international rail passes.

Other youth and student discounts can be very useful; for example the *Wochenendticket* (weekend ticket) in Germany is valid for the whole country on Saturdays and Sundays but only on regional trains. It costs €20 for up to five people which means that you can get from Salzburg to Denmark for about £2.50 each.

The Thomas Cook *Overseas Timetable* is the bible for overland travellers outside Europe; within Europe, consult the *Continental Timetable*.

Coach

Europe's largest and best-connected scheduled coach tour operator is Eurolines serving 500 destinations in 25 countries from Killarney on the west coast of Ireland to Bucharest. Prices start at £33 return for London-Amsterdam. You can write to Eurolines (UK) head office for schedules and prices at 4 Cardiff Road, Luton, Beds LU1 1PP or call 08705 143219 for reservations or check fares and times on www.eurolines.com. Passengers under the age of 26 are eligible for a 10% discount.

For smaller independent coach operators, check advertisements in London magazines like *TNT*. For example Kingscourt Express (125 Balham High Road, London SW12 9AJ; 020-8673 7500/ www.kce.cz) runs daily between London and Prague or Brno; fares start at £64 return.

One of the most interesting revolutions in youth travel has been the explosion of backpackers' bus services which are hop-on hop-off coach services following prescribed routes. These can be found in New Zealand, Australia, Ireland, Scotland, England and the continent including the first backpacker bus in Russia, the Beetroot Bus. For example 15 days of travel within two months on Busabout (258 Vauxhall Bridge Road, London SW1V 1BS; 020-7950 1661/www.busabout.com) costs £319 for those under 26.

Shared Lifts

The European land mass is one of the most expensive areas of the world to traverse. If your mum is unhappy about the idea of hitching, reassure her that in Europe a network of lift-sharing agencies makes hitching respectable. The practice is especially widespread in Germany where there are Citynetz offices in Berlin, Düsseldorf, Freiburg, Hamburg, Munich, etc. For a varying fee (usually £10-£20 plus a share of the petrol) they will try to find a driver going to your chosen destination. They are certainly worth trying if, say, you are signed up for a four-week language course and know some weeks in advance when you want to move on or head home.

Here are some details of European agencies:

France: Allostop Provoya, 8 rue Rochambeau, 75009 Paris (1-53 20 42 42/fax 01-53 20 42 44). Prices are set according to distance of journey, e.g. €6 for less than 200km, €8 for 200-300km, €10 for 300-500km and so on. The website http://astop.gnafour.net helps people arrange lifts within France.

Belgium: Taxistop/Eurostop, 28 rue Fossé-aux-Loups, 1000 Brussels (02-223 23 31/fax 02-223 22 32; www.taxistop.be). Taxistop Flanders, Onderbergen 51, 9000 Gent (09-223 23 10/fax 09-224 31 44). The admin fee charged to passengers by Taxistop is €0.8 per 100km (minimum €6.2, maximum €20). In addition passengers pay drivers €2.5 per 100km.

Netherlands: International Lift Centre, NZ Voorburgwal 256, 1012 RS Amsterdam (020-622 43 42). The joining fee is €10 plus a small sum per kilometre has to be paid to the driver.

Germany: Citynetz-Mitzfahrzentrale – www.citynetz-mitfahrzentrale.de. Website gives addresses and phone numbers of offices around Germany, for example Saarstr. 22, D-50677 Köln (0221-19444). Prices work out at approximately 3 or 4 cents per kilometre.

Spain: Iberstop Mitzfahrcentrale, 85 C/ Elvira, 18010 Granada (958-29 29 20). Offices also in Almeria, Barcelona, Lloret de Mar, Malaga, Oviedo, Salamanca, San Sebastian, Santiago de Compostela, Seville and Valladolid.

Elsewhere try to locate Eurolift in Portugal (01-888 5002 in Lisbon), Auto Tip in Prague (02-204383) and Mitfahrzentrale in Vienna (022-408 2210).

NORTH AMERICA

Incredibly, the price of flying across the Atlantic has been steadily decreasing over the past decade. Off-peak student returns to New York start at less than £200. Competition is fiercest and therefore prices lowest on the main routes between London and New York, Miami and Los Angeles. In many cases, summer fares will be twice as high as winter ones. One-way fares are also available to eastern seaboard cities like Washington for £100-£150. When comparing fares, always take the taxes into consideration since they now represent about £45-£50.

Outside summer and the Christmas period you should have no problems getting a seat; at peak times, a reliable alternative is to buy a discounted ticket on one of the less fashionable carriers which fly to New York, such as Air India or El Al. A one-year return London-New York on Kuwait Air might start at £250 plus taxes.

The USA and Canada share the longest common frontier in the world, which gives some idea of the potential problems and expense of getting around. You will want to consider Drive-aways (see *United States* chapter) and also bus and air travel which are both cheaper than in Europe. The Greyhound bus pass (Ameripass) is alive and well, and represents a bargain for people who want to cover a lot of ground. Greyhound no longer has an office in the UK but their Discovery Passes can be bought through STA Travel, BUNAC, Bridge the World Travel and a few others. In 2003, Greyhound (www.greyhound.com) were offering 7, 10, 15, 21, 30, 45 and 60 day passes to students for $177, $222, $265, $310, $344, $389 and $486; passes for non-students cost 10%-15% more. Once you are in the US timetable and fare information is available 24 hours a day on the toll-free number 1-800-231-2222. Greyhound also offer a Canada Pass which costs C$218 for 7 days, C$360 for 21 days up to $491 for 60 days.

Other forms of transport in the USA are probably more expensive but may have their own attractions, such as the trips run by *Green Tortoise* (494 Broadway, San Francisco, California 94133; 800-867-8647/ www.greentortoise.com) which uses vehicles converted to sleep about 35 people and which make interesting detours and stopovers. There may even be an option to swap your labour for a free ride.

For accommodation in North America (mainly Canada), get hold of the list of hostels from *Backpackers Hostels Canada* (Longhouse Village, RR 13, Thunder Bay, Ontario P7B 5E4; www.backpackers.ca). The list can be downloaded from the net for free or sent by post in exchange for $5 or four IRCs.

LATIN AMERICA

A fully-bonded agency which specialises in travel to and around this area of the world is Journey Latin America (12-13 Heathfield Terrace, Chiswick, London W4 4JE; 020-8747 3108; www.journeylatinamerica.co.uk) who consistently offer the lowest fares and the most expertise. Another advantage is that they deal exclusively with Latin America and hence are the best source of up-to-date travel information. One of the best deals at the time of writing was on Delta who were offering a six-month return to Lima for £478 plus £45 tax.

Heavy taxes are levied on international flights within South America: the cheapest way to fly from one capital to another (assuming you have plenty of time) is to take a domestic flight (within, say, Brazil), cross the border by land and then buy another domestic ticket (within, say, Peru). The alternatives include the remnants of a British-built railway system and the ubiquitous bus, both of which are extremely cheap and interesting. A rough estimate of the price of bus travel in South America is US$1.50 for every hour of travel.

For information on travel in Latin America join *South America Explorers* who maintain clubhouses in Lima, Cusco and Quito. The US office is at 126 Indian Creek Rd, Ithaca, NY 14850 (607-277-0488; www.samexplo.org) and membership costs $40.

AFRICA

Flights to Cairo are advertised from £150 single, £200 return, while the special offers to Nairobi start from £280 single, £395 return. A specialist agency for Southern Africa is Melhart Travel in East London (020-8953 4222; info@melharttravel.com). A 12-month return to Johannesburg on Virgin in the low season was costing about £550 before tax at the time of writing. Another agency to try is the Africa Travel Centre (21 Leigh St, London WC1H 9QX; 020-7387 1211).

As noted above, the overland routes are fraught with difficulties, and so joining a trip with an established overland tour company is a good idea.

ASIA

Most gap year travellers take advantage of the competitive discount flight market from London to Asian destinations. For example the cheapest quoted return price London to Delhi is about £300. The cheapest carrier to Bangkok is Tarom, the Romanian airline, which has a one-year return for £330. The price of flights to Japan has dropped significantly in the past few years, especially if you are willing to fly on the Russian carrier Aeroflot.

Once you're installed in Asia, travel is highly affordable. The railways of the Indian sub-continent are a fascinating social phenomenon that cost next to nothing. Throughout Asia, airfares are not expensive, particularly around the discount triangle of Bangkok, Hong Kong and Singapore. The notable exception to the generalisation about cheap public transport in Asia is Japan, where the possibility of hitching marginally compensates for the high cost of living and travelling.

AUSTRALASIA

The Australian Tourist Commission's *Traveller's Guide* contains quite a bit of hard information and useful telephone numbers as well as all the advertising; request a copy by ringing 0906 863 3235. An excellent free guide for backpackers is the *Australia & New Zealand Independent Travel Guide* from TNT (14-15 Child's Place, London SW5 9RX; 020-7373 3377); send an A5 s.a.e. with a 70p stamp.

Per mile, the flight to the Antipodes is cheaper than most. The cheapest fares become available when airline promotions are advertised. For example in early 2003, Malaysian Air was selling return flights to Sydney through Austravel (0870 166 2100) for less than £500 before tax, though at most times fares will start at around £600.

Your transport problems are by no means over when you land in Perth or Sydney. The distances in Australia may be much greater than you are accustomed to and so you will have to give some thought to how you intend to get around, though Richard Branson's Virgin Blue (www.virginblue.com.au) has made a big difference. It has expanded its network enormously over the last couple of years and (as with no-frills flights in the UK) special promotions are advertised over the internet. There are also other discounts for booking at the last minute, and for travelling at unsocial hours or standby.

If you plan a major tour of the country you might consider purchasing a Greyhound Pioneer coach pass along a pre-set route (☎ 13 20 30; www.greyhound.com.au). Sample prices are A$290 for the nearly 3,000km trip between Sydney and Cairns and the all-Australia pass costing $2,333; people with YHA or other cards should be entitled to a 10%-15% discount. If you just want to get from one coast to another as quickly as possible and qualify for the very cheapest deals, you will pay around A$370 one way on the coach or train (excluding berth and meals). A multiplicity of private operators has sprung up to serve the backpacking market such as Oz Experience and Wayward Bus.

Unfortunately the flight from Australia to New Zealand is not particularly cheap unless bought in conjunction with a long-haul flight. The standard return fare of A$750-A$800 can be nearly halved by canny shopping; check out www.travel.com.au or investigate the no-frills New Zealand airline Freedom Air (www.freedomair.co.nz).

PART II

Gap Year Placement Organisations

Specialist Gap Year Programmes

Expeditions

Work Experience

Volunteering

A Year Off for North Americans

Paid Seasonal Jobs

Au Pairing

Courses

Specialist Gap Year Programmes

Specialist gap year placement organisations can arrange the logistics and save you (and your parents) a great deal of anxiety. They find voluntary and occasionally paid placements, provide orientation and sometimes group travel and, crucially, provide back-up, usually in the form of an in-country representative who can sort out problems. Mediating agencies come in all shapes and sizes. Some are bastions of the establishment with longstanding programmes in a range of countries and links forged over many years with certain schools. Others are more entrepreneurial and are always seeking new projects in developing countries to which they can send paying volunteers.

A plethora of organisations both charitable and commercial offer a wide range of packaged possibilities, from work experience placements in French businesses to teaching in Himalayan schools. This section provides a general description of the programmes run by the major gap year placement agencies. Younger school leavers should be aware that 18 is often quoted as a minimum age, which might exclude them. Further details of programmes mentioned here are (if available) included in the country-by-country chapters, with stories of people who have done placements.

All participants must fund-raise substantial sums which are paid to the mediating agency. In recent years the expectation that parents will finance the year off has declined and most organisations provide much detailed advice on how to obtain sponsorship and raise money. Fees and services differ enormously, so research is essential, preferably well in advance. Generally speaking the high profile organisations that invest a lot in publicity are considerably more expensive than the more obscure small charities active in just one country. Before committing yourself and your backers to a large financial outlay, you must be sure that your choice of organisation is sound. Researching all the possibilities is time-consuming and sometimes confusing since it can be difficult to compare programmes simply on the basis of their publicity.

In May 2000 the Year Out Group was launched by 23 founding member organisations. The launch took place in the presence of two MPs including Margaret Hodge, then Minister for Employment and Equal Opportunities, proof that the gap year has moved onto the political agenda. The founding members plus the seven organisations that have joined since all have entries in this chapter and their entries indicate their membership.

Year Out Group members are working towards models of good practice and seeking to maintain high standards of quality (while at the same time being in competition with one another). The role of the non-profit Year Out Group is to promote and advise on structured years out. Their website contains guidelines and questions to ask when comparing providers, most of which are common sense, e.g. find out whether it is a charity or a profit-making company, look at safety procedures and in-placement support, ask for a breakdown of costs, and so on. The Year Out Group may be contacted at Queensfield, 28 Kings Road, Easterton, Wilts. SN10 4PX (07980 395789; info@yearoutgroup.org/ www.yearoutgroup.org). Note that it cannot intervene in any dispute between member companies and disgruntled clients.

Everybody will tell you that you have to set the wheels in motion about a year before you're ready to go. But in fact lots of people start their gap year with nothing fixed up. It turns out that all those organisations whose literature contains dire warnings of the consequences of procrastination often have last minute vacancies due to cancellations, so it is worth ringing around whenever you decide you want to go for it. In many cases they need you more than you need them.

This chapter sets out the programmes of about 60 leading organisations which are equipped to organise all or part of your gap year for you. The majority is based in the UK though some American organisations welcome all nationalities onto their programmes. For agencies and organisations that target North American school leavers, see the chapter *A Year Off for North Americans*. The organisations listed below specifically target gap year students. Many other organisations listed in the other directories in the chapters on Volunteering, Work Experience, Au Pairing, Courses and also in the country chapters welcome gap year students with open arms but do not specialise in catering for them.

Directory of Specialist Gap Year Programmes

ACADEMIC ASSOCIATES INTERNATIONAL
Academic Year in the USA & Europe, 46 High Street, Ewell Village, Surrey KT17 1RW. ☎ 020-8786 7711. Fax: 020-8786 7755. E-mail: enquiry@aaiuk.org. Website: www.aaiuk.org.
Founding member of the Year Out Group. Promotes cultural exchange, international study and volunteer opportunities for year out students.
Programme description: Academic year or shorter stays can be arranged in USA and Europe. Participants live with families, study languages and join in extracurricular activities including winter and summer sports, music, drama and community opportunities.
Destinations: USA, France, Germany, Italy and Spain.

Prerequisites: Ages 16-21.
Duration and time of placements: 3, 4, 5 or 9 months starting August/ September/ October or January/February.
Cost: Programme fees from £3,280. Students must also have fully comprehensive insurance which will cost a further £395. Fee includes meals and accommodation with host family and in-country student support.

ADVENTURE ALTERNATIVE
31 Myrtledene Road, Belfast BT8 6GQ. ☎/fax: 02890 701476. Also Dun-leckney Manor, Bagenalstown, Co. Carlow, Ireland; +353 503 21932. E-mail: office@adventurealternative.com. Website: www.adventurealternative.com.
Three-month programmes for gap year students (among others) in Kenya and Nepal.
Programme description: Combine 8 weeks of teaching/community work, group activities (e.g. climbing, trekking, rafting, safaris) and independent travel. In Kenya participants teach and work in HIV-education in rural schools. In Nepal, participants help to build a village school. Medical electives also available for medical students and doctors.
Destinations: rural Kenya and Himalayan Nepal.
Number of placements per year: 32 for Kenya, 60 for Nepal.
Prerequisites: Minimum age 17; average age 22. Hard-working committed enthusiastic gap year students who are not fazed by the hardships of living in a developing country. All nationalities.
Duration and time of placements: 3 months.
Costs: £1,700 plus £300-£600 in-country expenses plus £650-£700 for flights, insurance and other necessities. Total from £2,635
Contact: Gavin Bate, Director; or Chris Little, Expedition Co-ordinator.

AFRICA AND ASIA VENTURE
10 Market Place, Devizes, Wiltshire SN10 1HT. ☎ 01380 729009. Fax: 01380 720060. E-mail: av@aventure.co.uk. Website: www.aventure.co.uk.
Founding member of the Year Out Group. Africa and Asia Venture is an organisation which enables students to gain work experience (unpaid) with youth in Africa, Northern India, Nepal and Mexico.
Programme description: Students are placed in selected rural secondary and primary schools for approximately three months, teaching a variety of subjects and helping with extracurricular activities, especially sports. This is followed by two weeks of backpacking before going on safari to areas of interest and outstanding beauty in the chosen country. Also opportunities to join community and conservation projects.
Destinations: Kenya, Tanzania, Botswana, Uganda, Malawi, India, Nepal and Mexico.
Number of placements per year: 430-460.
Prerequisites: A-level students going on to Further Education or undergraduates considering taking time out can apply. Students must be aged 18 when they join the scheme and enjoy working with young people.
Duration and time of placements: 4/5 months, with departures to Africa in September, January and late April, to Nepal in October or January, and to India in September or April.
Selection procedures and orientation: On application students are invited to an interview to assess suitability. Applications should be submitted as early as possible since places are on a first-come-first-served basis for interview.
Cost: The basic cost is approximately £2,500 which covers living allowance, food, accommodation, safari, health and personal effects insurance and an orientation course. Fee does not include airfares, entry visas and extra spending money.

AFRICAN CONSERVATION EXPERIENCE
PO Box 9706, Solihull, West Midlands B91 3FF. ☎ 0870 241 5816. E-mail: info@ConservationAfrica.net. Website: www.ConservationAfrica.net.

AFRICA & ASIA VENTURE

An Experience for Life

Projects, challenges and adventure
in your 'year out' in Kenya, Uganda,
Tanzania, Malawi, Botswana,
India, Nepal and Mexico

www.aventure.co.uk
for news and opportunities

Member of the Year Out Group.
Programme description: Conservation work placements for young people on game reserves in Southern Africa. Tasks may include darting rhino for relocation or elephant for fitting tracking collars. Game capture, tagging, assisting with veterinary work, game counts and monitoring may be part of the work programme. Alien plant control and the re-introduction of indigenous plants are often involved.
Destinations: Southern Africa including South Africa, Botswana and Zimbabwe.
Prerequisites: Must have reasonable physical fitness and be able to cope mentally. Most important qualification is enthusiasm for conservation. Programme may be of special interest to students of environmental, zoological and biological sciences, veterinary science and animal care.
Duration and time of placements: 4-12 weeks throughout the year.
Selection procedures & orientation: Candidates are matched to a suitable project on the information provided on their application form but do have final say on their placement. Optional Open Days are held at various locations in the UK.
Cost: Varies depending on reserve and time of year. Students can expect an average total cost of about £2,600 for 4 weeks up to £3,600 for 12 weeks, which includes international flights (from London), transfers, accommodation and all meals. Support and advice given on fund-raising.
Contact: Lisa Hewston, Volunteer Administrator.

AFRICATRUST NETWORKS
Africatrust Chambers, PO Box 551, Portsmouth, Hants. PO5 1ZN. ☎ 02392 838098. E-mail: info@africatrust.gi. Website: www.africatrust.gi.
Programme description: Ghanaian NGO that works with disadvantaged young people in Africa. Residential placements for pre-university and post-university students, to teach young children, help with disabled, homeless, blind and orphaned children, etc.
Destinations: Ghana (Cape Coast and Kumasi), Mali (Bamako) and from January 2005 Morocco.
Prerequisites: Volunteers must be 18-25, in good health and have an EU passport. A-level French is needed for Mali.
Duration and time of placements: 3 and 6 months.
Selection procedures and orientation: Application form available on website. References will be taken up and interviews scheduled in London. Briefing information on health, fundraising and projects are sent. There is a compulsory pre-departure briefing in London for volunteers and their families plus 2-week in-country induction course.
Cost: 3-month programme will be at least £2,200 and 6 months will cost £3,400. Volunteers are also expected to raise donations, typically £500/£750 which the volunteers as a team distribute themselves in-country. Costs include all travel, food, accommodation, induction courses, mid-visit holiday tour programme and management supervision/review programme.
Contact: David Denison (UK Director) or Dr. K. Kwansah-Filson DVM (Ghana Director).

AFS INTERCULTURAL PROGRAMMES UK
Leeming House, Vicar Lane, Leeds LS2 7JF. ☎ 0113-242 6136. Fax: 0113-243 0631. E-mail: info-unitedkingdom@afs.org. Website: www.afsuk.org.
According to its mission statement, AFS is an international, voluntary, non-governmental, non-profit organisation that provides intercultural learning opportunities to help people develop the knowledge, skills and understanding needed to create a more just and peaceful world. AFS currently has 54 member countries.
Programme description: On the International Volunteer Programme, participants spend 6 months in another country, living with a family and volunteering on a local community project. On the Schools Programme, participants spend an academic year in another country, attending a local school and living with a local family. 3-month placements on the Schools Programme can be requested.

Destinations: Brazil, Costa Rica, Ecuador, France, Ghana, Guatemala, Honduras, Hong Kong, Indonesia, Italy, Mexico, Panama, Peru, South Africa, Thailand, USA and Venezuela.

Number of placements per year: AFS tries to place anyone eligible who applies.

Prerequisites: Applicants for the International Volunteer Programme are normally aged 18-29 at the time of departure. Older applicants are welcomed. No particular qualifications or skills are needed but experience of voluntary work or skills in a particular area would enhance the suitability of the applicant. Applicants for the Schools Programme must be aged 15-18 at the time of departure.

Duration and time of placements: 6 months for volunteers, departing January/February and July/August. One academic year for the Schools Programme with departures throughout the UK summer. 3-month placements from September are available on request.

Selection procedures and orientation: Initial application form must be accompanied by a £10 fee. Selection is conducted at a group event, after which a full application will have to be completed. It is preferred that applications are sent at least six months before the intended departure to give time to raise contribution costs and for the organisation to find a suitable placement. Selection for the Schools Programme is a group activity for applicants and parents. A pre-departure orientation is held for all programmes.

Costs: For the International Volunteer Programme, each participant is requested to raise £3,300. Advice and support for fundraising are given. For the Schools Programme, participants are requested to contribute £3,950 for a year-long programme and £2,950 for a 3-month programme. The money raised covers travel, medical insurance, orientation materials and events, language tuition and emergency support. The host family provides food and accommodation. Some financial assistance may be available for the Schools Programme.

THE ARMY
HQ Recruiting Group, ATRA, Bldg 165, Trenchard Lines, Upavon, Wiltshire SN9 6BE. ☎ 08457 300111. Website: www.armyofficer.co.uk.

The British Army offers gap year students the opportunity to spend a year in the Army. The Gap Year Commission (formerly called the Short Service Limited Commission), offers the opportunity for students taking a year out to be placed in an Army regiment. There is no obligation after the year has been completed for the student to have any further links with the Army. However those who do wish to use their Gap Year Pass to enter after university may do so. Financial sponsorship is available through university.

Programme description: A 4-week course is undertaken at Sandhurst before joining the regiment. At first students serve under supervision of an experienced officer, but soon are given their own responsibilities. The most promising students are invited to become officers.

Destinations: Virtually anywhere around the world. Previous participants have travelled to the Rockies of Canada, Norway, Hong Kong and Guatemala.

Number of placements per year: Around 90.

Prerequisites: Applicants must have a confirmed place at a UK university with all A-level examinations completed before entry to Sandhurst. Applicants must have been resident in the UK for 5 years and be a British or Commonwealth citizen.

Duration and time of placements: The minimum service is 4 months; maximum is 18 months. Six weeks' notice must be given to terminate commission.

Selection procedures and orientation: Students must be recommended by their Head Teacher, have reached the age of 18 and be less than 20 on the day of commissioning, be accepted by the Corps or Regiment of their choice and have passed an Army Medical Board and Regular Commissions Board. The most successful candidates are those of high academic ability with a history of leadership at school, such as sports captain or prefect. A taste for active outdoor pursuits and a sense of adventure is of paramount importance. Sandhurst courses are in September so applications must be made early in the upper sixth and certainly by the end of January.

Payment: Gap Year Commission officers are paid at a special rate of £13,907 per year rising to £15,221 after 9 months. Additional allowances, e.g. for clothes, may also be paid.

ART HISTORY ABROAD
26 De Laune St, London SE17 3UU. ☎ 020-7277 4514. Fax: 020-7740 6126. E-mail: info@arthistoryabroad.com. Website: www.arthistoryabroad.com.
Founding member of the Year Out Group.

Programme description: Unique programme designed for the Year Out that looks to broaden participants' sense of self as well as cultural and intellectual horizons. Programme includes art, history, Italian sociology, architecture, politics, philosophy, economics, music, poetry, theology, literature and classics. 6 weeks of travel throughout Italy including Venice, Verona, Florence, Siena, Naples and Rome plus at least 6 other cities. All tuition is on-site and in groups of no more than 8.

Number of placements per year: 24 per course.

Duration and time of placement: 6-week course offered 3 times a year (Autumn, Spring and Early Summer) and 2-week course offered in July/August.

Cost: £5,100 for the Autumn, Spring and Early Summer courses and £2,100 for the shorter Summer course.

Accommodation: Shared rooms in hotels in the centre of each city visited.

AU PAIR IN AMERICA
37 Queen's Gate, London SW7 5HR. ☎ 020-7581 7300. Fax: 020-7581 7355. E-mail: info@aupairamerica.co.uk. Website: www.aupairamerica.co.uk
Parent organisation (American Institute for Foreign Study) founded in 1967 and the au pair programme authorised in 1986.

Programme description: Au Pair in America operates the largest and longest established legal childcare programme to the United States. Au pairs are placed with a screened American family for 12 months. Other programmes that run alongside are the EduCare in America (for students who work shorter hours to allow more time for studies and receive less pocket money) and Au Pair Extraordinaire (for qualified and experienced childcarers).

Number of placements per year: 4,000+.

Duration and time of placements: 12 months. Au pairs provide 45 hours of childcare per week.

Prerequisites: All nationalities are eligible provided there is an established interviewer network in their country. Ages 18-26. Must have recent practical childcare experience, hold a full driving licence and be available for 12 months.

Selection procedures and orientation: Applicants must submit a complete application and attend a personal interview with an appointed Au Pair in America interviewer. Contact

Au Pair in America for a full colour brochure.

Cost: $75 non-refundable placement fee; $400 Good Faith Deposit and $100 contribution to medical and personal liability insurance to be paid on receipt of confirmation of placement. Au pairs receive $139 (approximately £80) per week.

Benefits: 4-day orientation programme held near New York, legal J-1 visa, $500 study tuition allowance, medical insurance, 2 weeks paid holidays, optional 13th month travel, year-long support from US community counsellor and placement in an established au pair 'cluster group'.

BASE CAMP GROUP
Howick, Balls Cross, Petworth, West Sussex GU28 9JY. ☎ 01403 820899. Fax: 01403 820063. E-mail: contact@basecampgroup.com. Website: www.basecampgroup.com.

Programme description: Gap Snowsports Programme in the Alps and Rockies. (See entry in 'Directory of Sports Courses').

BRITISH COUNCIL ASSISTANTS PROGRAMME
10 Spring Gardens, London SW1A 2BN. ☎ 020-7389 4596. E-mail: education.enquiries @britishcouncil.org. Website: www.britishcouncil.org/education.

Also in Scotland: The Tun (3rd Floor), 4 Jackson's Entry, Holyrood Road, Edinburgh EH8 5EG; 0131-524 5700.

Northern Ireland: Norwich Union House, 7 Fountain St, Belfast BT1 5EG; 028-9024 8220.

Wales: 28 Park Place, Cardiff CF10 3QE; 029 2039 7346.

The British Council's Education and Training Group manages various programmes for students and young people such as IAESTE and the Leonardo Programme (see chapter on *Work Experience*). General enquiries to the British Council Information Centre (Bridgewater House, 58 Whitworth St, Manchester M1 6BB; 0161-957 7755).

Programme description: *English Language Assistants Programme* for modern language students and recent graduates. Applicants should normally be aged 20-30 with at least two years of university level education in the language of the destination country.

Destinations: Country-by-country details are available from the British Council (020-7389 4596; assistants@britishcouncil.org/ www.languageassistant.co.uk). Most posts are in France, Germany, Austria, Belgium, Switzerland and Latin America.

Duration and time of placements: One academic year, i.e. September or October to May or June, depending on country.

Selection procedures & orientation: Application forms are available from October; the deadline is 1st December of the year prior to placement.

Cost: None, except for China; allowance paid. Accommodation rarely provided.

THE BRITISH INSTITUTE OF FLORENCE
Palazzo Strozzino, Piazza Strozzi 2, 50123, Florence, Italy. ☎ 055-26 77 82 00. Fax: 055-26 77 82 22. E-mail: info@britishinstitute.it. Website: www.britishinstitute.it.

Modern centre of cultural exchange which runs short and long term courses in Italian language and art history, and also Italian culture, life drawing, opera, landscape watercolours, Tuscan cooking and (new since 2003) fresco painting.

Programme description: Various events such as lectures, concerts and films are arranged on a weekly basis for students and local people at the Institute's library and cultural centre.

Duration and time of placements: Courses last from 2 days to a year and start year round. Summer courses are also available near the Tuscan coast.

Cost: Tuition fees vary according to length and intensity of the course chosen. For example a 4-week Italian Language course costs from €430 (£296) approximately, and a 3-day History of Art course costs €230 (£158). Accommodation can be arranged in local homes, *pensione* and hotels starting at €22 (£15) a day.

BSES EXPEDITIONS
Royal Geographical Society, 1 Kensington Gore, London SW7 2AR. ☎ 020-7591 3141. Fax: 020-7591 3140. E-mail: bses@rgs.org. Website: www.bses.org.uk.

Founding member of the Year Out Group. BSES Expeditions organises expeditions worldwide for people 16-20. See entry in 'Directory of Expeditions'.

BUNAC
16 Bowling Green Lane, London EC1R 0QH. ☎ 020-7251 3472. Fax: 020-7251 0215. E-mail: enquiries@bunac.org.uk. Website: www.bunac.org.

Founding member of the Year Out Group. BUNAC is a non-profit national student club offering work and travel programmes worldwide. It acts as an aide before and after arrival in the country of travel and acts as a 'security blanket' if situations go wrong whilst the student is abroad.

Programme description: Various work programmes in North America and elsewhere. A large number of students and non-students are placed on summer camps. Also arrange internships in America for students and non-students of any nationality on the Overseas Practical Training programme (OPT USA). BUNAC makes it possible for candidates to obtain the necessary visas and publishes its own job directories which help members to fix up short-term jobs before or after arrival.

Destinations: USA, Canada, New Zealand, Australia, South Africa, Ghana and Costa Rica.

Prerequisites: For Work Canada and Work America students must have documentary evidence that they are returning to a university degree or HND course, or already be a full-time student. Work Australia and New Zealand is open to anyone who is eligible for the working holiday visa (see country chapters).

Duration and time of placements: 9 weeks on summer camps in the US. Participants on the Work America programme must return to a full-time course in the UK in September/ October. Other programmes in other countries can last up to a year.

Selection procedures and orientation: Students need to join BUNAC, either through the local club at university or at the time of applying. Applicants must also provide proof of student status, the fee and (if relevant) a job offer. In some cases, an attendance certificate from a BUNAC presentation (held at university campuses) is compulsory.

Cost: £4 BUNAC membership fee, plus programme fee from £62 for employment on summer camps to £1,700 for Work New Zealand. First-time Work America participants must purchase BUNAC's travel package (average of £650 includes flight and airport taxes, airport collection and the first night's accommodation). Reductions are available to those applying early. Students cover living costs by working. Compulsory insurance for the summer costs about £120.

CACTUS WORLDWIDE LTD.
4 Clarence House, 30-31 North St, Brighton BN1 1EB. ☎ 0845 130 4775. Fax: 01273 775868. E-mail: enquiry@cactusenglish.com. Website: www.cactusenglish.com.
Provider of language courses worldwide. In Latin America in conjunction with voluntary placements (see *Directory of Language Courses*). Also acts as a language and teaching consultancy.

Destinations: Guatemala, Costa Rica, Peru, Ecuador, Bolivia and Argentina. Language courses in Germany, France, Spain, Italy, Greece, Russia and many others.

Duration and time of placements: Combination language and volunteer programme in Latin America lasts 8 or 12 weeks: 4-week language course followed by volunteering.

Costs: from £739 for 8 weeks in Guatemala to £1,939 for 12 weeks in Costa Rica. Language course costs clearly searchable on Cactus website.

CALEDONIA LANGUAGES ABROAD
The Clockhouse, Bonnington Mill, 72 Newhaven Road, Edinburgh EH6 5QG. ☎ 0131-621 7721/2. Fax: 0131-621 7723. E-mail: info@caledonialanguages.co.uk. Website: www.caledonialanguages.co.uk.
Established in 1994. As well as offering independent advice on language courses in Europe, Latin America and Russia, Caledonia can arrange for clients to participate in volunteer community projects. Activities include learning the language of the country, visiting places of local interest, working on projects alongside local people and living in their homes.

Destinations: Caledonia's partner language schools are all over Europe and in Peru, Mexico, Ecuador, Cuba, Costa Rica, Brazil, Mexico, Bolivia and Argentina. (see entry in

'Directory of Language Courses').

Duration of courses: 3 weeks to 6 months.

Selection procedures and orientation: Briefing meetings are held during the pre-placement language courses and regular discussion with the language school. Depending on the location, site visits can be organised before the placement. In-country back-up support is given.

Cost: Volunteers must pay for the pre-placement language course in the overseas country plus accommodation and travel. In Costa Rica 3 weeks Spanish course plus 3 weeks voluntary service plus accommodation would cost from £1,150. In Peru, 3 weeks intensive Spanish course followed by 3 weeks voluntary work and accommodation throughout would cost from £1,120.

CAMP COUNSELORS USA (CCUSA)

Green Dragon House, 64-70 High St, Croydon CR0 9XN. ☎ 020-8688 9051. Fax: 020-8681 8168. E-mail: info@ccusa.co.uk. Website: www.ccusaweusa.co.uk. Northern office: 27 Woodside Gardens, Musselburgh, Scotland EH21 7LJ (0131-665 5843; 101355.257@compuserve.com). US headquarters of CCUSA are at 2330 Marinship Way, Suite 250, Sausalito, CA 94965, USA (www.campcounsel ors.com).

Programme description: Camp counsellor placement in the US plus Work Experience in the US, Australia, New Zealand and Brazil. Placements on summer camps in Russia and Croatia.

Prerequisites: Ages 18-30 for most programmes.

Duration and time of placements: 9 weeks for camp counsellors, 3-4 months working in the US (between late May and October), 3 or 6 months in Brazil and up to 12 months in Australia and New Zealand.

Cost: Camp Counselors USA fee from £245, Work Experience USA £635 or £735

including flights and insurance; Work Experience Downunder £375. First year counsellors aged 18 earn $400 in pocket money.

CAMPS INTERNATIONAL LIMITED
PO Box 67, Stroud, Glos. GL5 1ZR. ☎ 01453 767901. Fax: 01453 767967. E-mail: info@campsinternational.com. Website: www.campsinternational.com.
Run gap year safari camps and expeditions in Kenya and Tanzania, based in local communities where participants undertake a range of wildlife and community projects.
Destinations: Kenya and Tanzania including national parks and possibility to climb Mount Kenya, Mount Kilimanjaro or to do a scuba diving course.
Duration and time of placements: 2 weeks to 3 months.
Selection procedures and orientation: Must be motivated.
Costs: Sample price of £900 for 28-day Gap adventure which includes 20 days of voluntary work assisting rangers, teaching or building costs, excluding flights and insurance. 3-month programme costs £2,100-£2,700.
Contact: Stuart Rees Jones.

CESA LANGUAGES ABROAD
CESA House, Pennance Road, Lanner, Cornwall TR16 5TQ. ☎ 01209 211800. Fax: 01209 211830. E-mail: info@cesalanguages.com. Website: www.cesalanguages.com.
Founding member of the Year Out Group. Major provider of language courses in France, Guadeloupe, Spain, Ecuador, Costa Rica, Mexico, Germany, Austria, Italy, Portugal, Greece, Russia, Mexico, Morocco and Japan. See entry in 'Directory of Courses'.

CHALLENGE EDUCATIONAL SERVICES
101 Lorna Road, Hove, East Sussex BN3 3EL. ☎ 01273 220261. Fax: 01273 220376. E-mail: info@challengeuk.com. Website: www.challengeuk.com.
Programme description: Challenge Educational Services is a specialist provider of total immersion language courses and Gap Year opportunities in France, Spain, Germany and the USA. Challenge offers tailor-made courses for all ages and abilities. Opportunities in the USA include an Academic Exchange programme with students living in the US for 5 or 10 months and studying at an American High School.
Destinations: Currently France and the USA.
Prerequisites: Students must be educated to A-level standard (any subject) to apply for a French University programme.
Duration and time of placements: From one week at any time of year to a full Academic Year.
Selection procedures and orientation: Students are required for interview for the Academic Year in the USA programme. There are also pre-departure meetings and an orientation on arrival into the US.
Cost: The Academic Year in the USA costs approximately £3,495 including visa, flights and accommodation. Students could expect to pay approximately £7,000 for an Academic Year in a French University with student residence accommodation (£10,790 for the Sorbonne in Paris).
Contact: Gill Lowe, Overseas Programme Manager.

CHANGING WORLDS
11 Doctors Lane, Caterham, Surrey CR3 5AE. ☎ 01883 340960. Fax: 01883 330783. E-mail: welcome@changingworlds.co.uk. Website: www.changingworlds.co.uk.
Member of the Year Out Group. Aims to provide full cultural immersion through challenging and worthwhile work placements with a safety net if required.
Programme description: A range of gap year placements ranging from voluntary teaching placements in developing countries to paid placements in prestigious hotels.

Destinations: Australia, Canada, Chile, India, Nepal, New Zealand, Romania and Tanzania.
Number of placements per year: 200.
Prerequisites: A-levels or equivalent plus initiative, determination, adaptability and social skills.
Duration and time of placements: from 3 to 6 months. Minimum placement time for Canada is 6 months. Placements begin throughout the year.
Selection procedures and orientation: Interview days held in Surrey every 6-8 weeks. All participants attend a pre-departure briefing; for those going to a developing country, this is a 2-day residential course. Participants are met on arrival in-country and attend orientation with the local representative before proceeding to placement. Local representatives act as support during placement.
Cost: From £1,895 for 6 months in Banff, Canada. Prices include return flights but exclude insurance (approximately £200 for 6 months).
Contact: David Gill, Director.

CIEE (Council on International Educational Exchange)
52 Poland Street, London W1F 7AB. ☎ 020-7478 2020. Fax: 020-7734 7322. E-mail: infouk@councilexchanges.org.uk. Website: www.ciee.org.uk.
Member of the Year Out Group. CIEE offers work, teaching and study abroad programmes for UK students, graduates and young professionals. Programmes include Work & Travel USA, Internship USA, Professional Career Training in the USA, Work & Travel Australia, Work & Travel New Zealand, Internship Canada, Teach in China and Teach in Thailand. CIEE also arrange Language Study Abroad programmes in 23 destinations across Europe and Latin America.
Number of placements per year: 8,000 worldwide of whom 1,500 come from the UK.

CORAL CAY CONSERVATION
The Tower, 13ᵗʰ Floor, 125 High Street, Colliers Wood, London SW19 2JG. ☎ 0870 750 0668. Fax: 0870 750 0667. E-mail: info@coralcay.org. Website: www.coralcay.org
Founding member of the Year Out Group. Hundreds of volunteers join CCC projects each year to assist in conserving fragile tropical marine and terrestrial environments.
Programme description: The aim of CCC expeditions is to help gather data for the protection and sustainable use of tropical resources and to provide alternative livelihood opportunities for local communities.
CCC also offers intern opportunities at their London Head Office (see *Directory of Work Experience*).
Destinations: Malaysia, Mexico, Cuba, the Philippines, Honduras and Fiji.
Number of placements per year: hundreds. Sites vary in the number of volunteers they

can accommodate.

Prerequisites: No previous experience is required. Volunteers come from a diverse range of ages, nationalities and backgrounds but want to do something positive for the environment, learn new skills, meet new people and explore new environments. Volunteers are provided with scientific and scuba diving tuition.

Duration and time of placements: Expeditions depart monthly throughout the year. Minimum stay 2 weeks (no maximum stay).

Selection procedures and orientation: A free information pack is available on request. Full training is provided on location.

Cost: A fortnight's Marine Skills Training costs £700 and surveying starts at £300 per week. Dive trainees pay £400 for PADI Advanced Open Water certification. Terrestrial training is a one-week course at £350, followed by surveying at £200 per week. A sample 6-week marine project would cost £1,800 (£2,200 for dive trainee) and a 6-week Terrestrial project would cost £1,150. Prices exclude flights and insurance.

Cross-Cultural Solutions
AN INTERNATIONAL VOLUNTEER PROGRAMME

Want to see the world?

Volunteer abroad and see a country through the eyes of its people. Programmes run from 2-12 weeks, longer programmes can be arranged. Participate in meaningful community development by contacting us today.

info@crossculturalsolutions.org • US: 800 380 4777 • UK: 0845 458 2781

www.crossculturalsolutions.org

CROSS-CULTURAL SOLUTIONS
US Head Office: 800-380-4777. UK Information Office: 0845 458 2781. E-mail: info@crossculturalsolutions.org. Website: www.crossculturalsolutions.org. See website for US and UK postal addresses.
A non-profit international volunteer organisation founded in 1995.

Programme description: Opportunity for participants to work side-by-side with local people, on locally designed and driven projects. Volunteer programmes are designed to facilitate hands-on service and cultural exchange with the aim of fostering cultural understanding.

Destinations: Central America, South America, Africa, Asia and Eastern Europe.

Number of placements per year: 1,000+.

Prerequisites: No language or specialist skills are necessary. All nationalities welcome.

Duration and time of placements: 2-12 weeks. Longer programmes may be arranged. Monthly start dates run throughout the year.

Cost: Programme fees start at $1,985 (approximately £1,200) and cover the costs of services like staffing and volunteer placement, and in-country expenses like lodging, meals and ground transport as well as travel, medical and emergency evacuation insurance. International airfares not included.

CSV
Community Service Volunteers, 237 Pentonville Road, London N1 9NJ. ☎ 0800 374991/020-7278 6601. E-mail: volunteer@csv.org.uk. Website: www.csv.org.uk.

Founding member of the Year Out Group. CSV is the largest voluntary placement organisation in the UK. It guarantees a voluntary placement to anyone aged over 16 who commits him or herself to a minimum of 4 months full-time volunteering in a huge range of social care projects. Foreign volunteers over 18 also welcome; placement fee for non-residents is £512. See entry in 'Directory of Voluntary Placements in the UK'.

THE DANEFORD TRUST
45-47 Blythe Street, London E2 6LN. ☎ 020-7729 1928. Fax: 020-7729 1928. E-mail: dfdtrust@aol.com.

Small educational trust which aims to encourage education and work exchanges between young people from inner-city London and young people from Africa, Asia and the Caribbean.

Programme description: Limited number of assistant teacher, youth worker and general worker placements in selected locations worldwide.

Destinations: Bangladesh, Botswana, Namibia, South Africa, Zimbabwe, St Vincent, St Lucia and Jamaica.

Number of placements per year: 15-20.

Prerequisites: Must be from London, Asia, Africa or the Caribbean.

Duration and time of placement: Minimum 3 months, maximum 1 year. Standard length is 6-9 months.

Selection procedures and orientation: There are monthly briefings and a residential seminar prior to departure. Monitoring is limited whilst the volunteer is overseas.

Cost: All costs are raised by the volunteer and Trust in partnership. No one who is committed gets left behind.

Contact: Anthony Stevens, Trust Co-ordinator.

ECO AFRICA EXPERIENCE
Guardian House, Borough Road, Godalming, Surrey GU7 2AE. ☎ 01483 860560. Fax: 01483 860391. E-mail: info@EcoAfricaExperience.com. Website: www.EcoAfricaExperience.com.

Programme description: Unique conservation opportunity for volunteers to work on some of Southern Africa's premier private game reserves or leading Marine ocean research projects. Participants get involved in conservation projects covering anti-poaching patrols, monitoring and counting of wildlife, darting and animal capture, bush rehabilitation and the day-to-day maintenance of the reserve. Working with Africa's big five (lion, leopard, elephant, rhino, buffalo) as well as marine life such as dolphins, whales, sharks and seals. Participants will be taught bush skills and learn about the wildlife and the environment by participating in most of the reserve's day-to-day activities. Exposure to the local community's outreach programmes will bring volunteers closer to the many diverse cultures of Southern Africa.

Number of placements per year: 100-150.

Prerequisites: No particular skills needed but should be passionate about conservation. All nationalities accepted.

Duration and time of placements: 4, 8 or 12 weeks. Summer holiday or gap year.

Selection procedures and orientation: Applications accepted year round. Interviews are informal and can be done by telephone. Occasional open days are arranged to meet potential volunteers. Full medical and personal checklist is supplied during preparation.

Costs: £2,500 for a 4-week placement; £3,500 for a 12-week placement, inclusive of international flights, meals, accommodation (furnished and comfortable, shared between two) and placement activities. Accommodation is fully furnished and extremely comfortable.

Contact: William Moolman, Marketing Manager.

ECOLOGIA TRUST
The Park, Forres, Moray, Scotland IV36 3TZ. ☎ 01309 690995. Fax: 01309 691009. E-mail: gap@ecologia.org.uk. Website: www.ecologia.org.uk.
Programme description: Volunteer programme specifically for gap year students at the Kitezh Children's Community for orphans in western Russia. Russian language is not essential although students of Russian will quickly become fluent. (See entry in 'Directory of Voluntary Placements Abroad' and further details in chapter on Russia.)

EF GAP YEAR
EF House, 36-38 St Aubyn's, Hove, Sussex BN3 2PD. ☎ 08707 200735. Website: www.ef.com/master.gy.
International language schools.
Programme description: 3-4 week TEFL training course in London or Brighton (including accommodation), followed by placement in international language school to spend 12 weeks learning the language and then posting to an EF language school for 6 month teaching job.
Destinations: Language course offered in Barcelona, Quito, Shanghai, Nice and St.

Petersburg; teaching post in Quito, China (various), Indonesia, Casablanca or Moscow.
Prerequisites: participants must do 4-week EF TEFL training course.
Duration and time of placements: 4 weeks in UK, 12 weeks in first destination, 6 months in next destination (of choice).
Costs: From £5,400 for two phases in Quito to £6,800 for two phases in Russia.

EIL: EXPERIMENT IN INTERNATIONAL LIVING
287 Worcester Road, Malvern, Worcs. WR14 1AB. ☎ 0800 018 4015. Fax: 01684 562212. E-mail: info@eiluk.org. Website: www.eiluk.org.
Focuses on educational and cultural travel and offers a variety of opportunities for young people in their gap year or long vacations. Partner offices in 30 countries.
Programme description: Various programmes include European Voluntary Service (EVS) described below, Farmstays and Work & Travel programmes in the USA, internships in Ghana and Spain, volunteer programmes in Argentina, Chile, Ecuador, Ghana, Guatemala, Ireland, Kenya, Mexico, Nepal, Nigeria, South Africa and Thailand. Also homestays worldwide.
Destinations: USA, Europe, Ghana, Kenya, Ecuador and Mexico.
Number of placements per year: Thousands.
Duration and time of placements: Varies from 2-weeks volunteer stay in Latin America to 12 months at EVS host institution on the Continent.
Cost: Costs vary depending upon the type of stay chosen.

EN FAMILLE OVERSEAS
4 St Helena Road, Colchester CO3 3BA. ☎ 01206 546741. Fax: 01206 546740. E-mail: marylou_toms@btinternet.com. Website: www.enfamilleoverseas.co.uk.
En Famille Overseas has been in business for over 50 years, arranging homestays with families in Europe.
Programme description: Homestays can be arranged for teenagers, gap year students, families, etc. Paying guests are treated as one of the family and become fully immersed in family life, experiencing how other cultures live and work. Alternatively students can attend a small local school, allowing more independence.
Destinations: France, Germany, Italy and Spain.
Number of placements per year: Around 600.
Prerequisites: A very basic knowledge of the language of the country is preferable together with an ability to adapt and a sense of humour.
Duration and time of placement: From 1 week to 1 year, all year round.
Selection procedures and orientation: An application form must be filled in with as much information as possible so a suitable family can be chosen. Once an acceptance has been received from the host family, a provisional booking can be made.
Cost: A language course with a homestay in Tours would cost £470 for 15 hours tuition and full board. Private one-to-one tuition with a qualified teacher costs £600 for 2 weeks with full board. A £35 enrolment fee must also be paid.
Contact: Mary-Lou Toms.

ENGLISH SPEAKING UNION
Dartmouth House, 37 Charles Street, London W1J 5ED. ☎ 020-7529 1550. Fax: 020-7495 6108. E-mail: mary_dawson@esu.org. Website: www.esu.org.
The ESU was founded in 1918 and has played an important role in fostering links between different nationalities. It stresses the importance of the English language as a means of shared communication between different races and cultures.
Programme description: The ESU's Secondary School Exchange makes it possible for students to spend 6 months or a full academic year in one of about 50 participating independent schools in the US and Canada. There are also plenty of opportunities to travel in the school holidays and at the end of the academic year.
Destinations: USA and Canada.

Number of placements per year: Approximately 30.
Prerequisites: A-levels or equivalent, an outgoing personality and past participation in extra-curricular activities.
Duration and time of placement: 6 months from January or 9 months from September.
Selection procedures and orientation: Students are selected for interview on the basis of a submitted application form. Prior to departure there is a lot of contact with the ESU and former scholars. A compulsory pre-departure briefing is held. Students are expected to make their own travel arrangements although an ESU representative or member of the school will meet them at the destination.
Cost: Board and tuition are free as part of the scholarship. Travel and other expenses (insurance, visa and spending money) of £2,500 must be met by scholar and his or her family.
Contact: Mary Dawson, Education Officer.

EUROPEAN VOLUNTARY SERVICE (EVS)
Connect Youth International, The British Council, 10 Spring Gardens, London SW1A 2BN. ☎ 020 7389-4030. Fax: 020-7389 4033. Website: www.britishcouncil.org/education.connectyouth/programmes/eyp/evs.htm.
Programme description: EVS programme offers thousands of young people aged 18-25 the opportunity to take up fully funded placements lasting 6 but preferably 12 months in Europe or beyond. Participants work as full-time volunteers on a social project, e.g. working with children with special needs.
Destinations: Member countries of the EU, central and Eastern Europe, the Mediterranean region and Latin America.
Number of placements per year: Around 2,500 places.
Prerequisites: Applicants must be aged 18-25 and be legally resident in one of the EU member states, Norway or Iceland. No specific qualifications are needed. Language training may form part of the voluntary service.
Duration and time of placements: Standard term of voluntary service is 6 or 12 months. Short-term projects between 3 weeks and 6 months are open to disadvantaged young people who for some reason cannot undertake the standard placement.
Selection procedures and orientation: Applicants may apply directly to EVS at Connect Youth International as above, or they may apply through a partner organisation like AFS, EIL (see entries in this Directory), VSO and many others.
Cost: No cost to volunteers; programme is funded by the EU.

EUROYOUTH
301 Westborough Road, Westcliff-on-Sea, Southend-on-Sea, Essex SS0 9PT. ☎ 01702 341434. Fax: 01702 330104.
Since 1961, Euroyouth has been organising holiday and paying guest placements for young people wishing to spend a period of time abroad.
Programmes offered: Euroyouth offers the chance for students (either those taking a Gap Year, undergraduates or post-graduates) to live with a host family, either as a paying guest or as a holiday guest. The former allows the student to live in a home and adapt to family life. Holiday guests receive free accommodation and food in return for making conversation in English with some members of the family. There is also time for the student to practise the foreign language or even receive language tuition.
Destinations: France, Germany, Italy and Spain. Enquire about other countries.
Number of placements per year: Over 200.
Prerequisites: Applicants tend to be between 17 and 25, although older people can be catered for.
Duration and time of placements: Usually 2-3 weeks, although some guests may be invited to stay for longer. School holiday periods tend to be the most sought-after time for placements.
Selection procedures and orientation: Application form must be submitted along with

a medical certificate, and a recommendation from a Headteacher, in the case of school pupils.
Cost: Registration fees of £80 and £100 for the paying guest and holiday guest respectively plus varying fees payable to families.
Contact: Mrs. R. Hancock.

FLYING FISH
25 Union Road, Cowes, Isle of Wight PO31 7TW. ☎ 0871 250 2500. Fax: 01983 281821. E-mail: mail@flyingfishonline.com. Website: www.flyingfishonli ne.com.
Member of the Year Out Group. Flying Fish trains watersports staff and arranges employment for sailors, divers, surfers and windsurfers. Founded in 1993 it can help young people to fix up a year of travel, training and adventure, or to start a career in watersports.
Programme description: A gap year with Flying Fish starts with a course leading to qualification as a surf, sail or windsurf instructor, yacht skipper, Divemaster or dive instructor (see entry in 'Directory of Sports Courses'). After qualifying you can choose a period of work experience or go into a paid job in many locations worldwide, with advice from a Flying Fish careers adviser.
Destinations: Training courses are run at Poole in the UK, at Sydney and the Whitsunday Islands in Australia and at Vassiliki in Greece. Jobs are worldwide with main employers located in Australia, the South Pacific, the Caribbean and the Mediterranean.
Number of placements per year: 500.
Duration and time of placements: 3-12 months with start dates year round.
Selection procedures & orientation: Applicants submit an application before training and will be asked to attend job interviews.
Cost: Fees range from £800 to £8,000 but most gap year students choose a programme costing about £3,500. Accommodation and airfares are provided, with normal wages during employment.

FRIENDS OF ISRAEL EDUCATIONAL FOUNDATION
Bridge Programme, PO Box 7545, London NW2 2QZ. ☎ 020-7435 6803. Fax: 020-7794 0291. E-mail: info@foi-asg.org. Website: www.foi-asg.org.
British foundation established to promote an understanding of Israel and to forge working links between the UK and Israel. Bridge scheme has been in operation since 1961.
Programme description: Provides gap year scholarships which help candidates to take part in kibbutz work, community action and teaching. Programme includes a stint on a kibbutz, two months community service on a northern Israeli moshav, contact with a whole range of religious and secular communities and free time to travel in Jordan and Egypt.
Destinations: Israel, both Jewish and Arab communities.
Number of placements per year: 12.
Prerequisites: Minimum age 18; most candidates are 18/19. Must be willing to work hard and adapt to sometimes demanding circumstances. Medical certificate of fitness needed. No requirement to speak Hebrew or Arabic.
Duration and time of placements: 6 months between January and July.
Selection procedures & orientation: Shortlist drawn up on basis of written application which will include a minimum 400 word essay setting out reasons for wanting to spend time in Israel. Deadline for applications is July 1st. Informal interviews in London in July.
Cost: Scholarship covers all expenses including insurance but not spending money (approximately £600). Accommodation provided in self-catering flat, hostel or as homestay. Optional extra to join an archaeological dig.
Contact: John Levy, Director.

FRONTIER
50-52 Rivington St, London EC2A 3QP. ☎ 020-7613 2422. E-mail: info@front ierconservation.org. Website: www.frontierconservation.org.
Founding member of the Year Out Group. Frontier has been involved with conservation expeditions since 1989. It aims to work with local people in order to find out as much as possible about the areas so that relevant and necessary conservation work can be pursued.

Programme description: Frontier offers the opportunity to work in coral reefs, savannas, forests and mangrove areas as part of conservation programmes in far-off destinations. Programmes are established in response to problems; surveys of damaged areas are carried out so that possible solutions can be identified. For example, dynamite fishing in Tanzania was damaging the web of delicate marine life. Frontier volunteers carried out more than 6,000 dives, resulting in the establishment of a Marine Park where the marine life is protected.

Destinations: Tanzania, Madagascar, Vietnam, the Andaman Islands and Nicaragua.

Number of placements per year: 250+.

Prerequisites: Minimum age 17. No specific qualifications required as training is provided in the field leading to a BTEC Level 3 in Tropical Habitat Conservation.

Duration and time of placements: 4, 8, 10 or 20 weeks.

Selection procedures and orientation: Informal information sessions are held on Saturdays and Wednesdays (check website for dates) where interested parties can find out more from past volunteers. After an application has been submitted and a telephone briefing, applicants will hear within a week whether they have been accepted. Prior to the expedition, a briefing weekend is held in the UK.

Cost: Depending on location and duration, international volunteers raise from £1,400 for 4 weeks, £1,800 for 8 weeks, £2,200 for 10 weeks and £3,400 for 20 weeks, which covers all individual costs, including a UK weekend briefing, scientific and dive training, travel, visas, insurance, food and accommodation but excludes flights. The organisation helps with fund-raising ideas but the onus is on the individual.

GAP ACTIVITY PROJECTS (GAP) LTD
44 Queen's Road, Reading, RG1 4BB. ☎ 0118 959 4914. Fax: 0118 957 6634. E-mail: Volunteer@gap.org.uk. Website: www.gap.org.uk.
Founding member of the Year Out Group. GAP Activity Projects is an educational charity more than 30 years experience of sending 18/19 year old volunteers to work overseas during their year out. GAP is committed to the principle of service to others and intercultural exchange.

Programme description: Voluntary work placements are organised in various fields, including teaching English as a foreign language, assisting with sport, drama and general activities in schools, care work with the disadvantaged and people with disabilities, outdoor education, environmental and hospital work.

Destinations: 32 countries worldwide.

Number of placements per year: 2,000+.

Prerequisites: Applicants must be 18 or 19 in their year between school/college and higher education, employment or training.

Duration and time of placements: From 4-12 months (average 6 months).

Selection procedures and orientation: The GAP brochure is published annually in July/August for placements starting from September the following year. After an application is received, a face-to-face interview will be held, after which the applicant will hear if he or she has been offered a place. There is a briefing which the applicant must attend, preferably with a parent or guardian. Any necessary courses (e.g. TEFL) must be attended before leaving for the destination country or sometimes on arrival.

Cost: Applicants pay a fee, currently £750. All places are subsidised by GAP's own fundraising by over 20%. Additional costs are airfares, insurance and medical costs, but accommodation and food in the destination country are provided. In most cases pocket money will also be paid.

GAP CHALLENGE – see World Challenge below

GAP ENTERPRISE
East Manor Barn, Fringford, Oxfordshire OX27 8DG. ☎ 01869 278346. E-mail: johnvessey@gapenterprise.co.uk. Website: www.gapenterprise.co.uk.
Gap year consultancy.
Programme description: Gap Enterprise can assist in the planning and support of a structured year out, whether taken as an academic course, skills training, work experience, paid employment, expedition, volunteer placement or travel.
Destinations: Worldwide. Library of information and computerised database of projects and activities around the world.
Other services: Seminars held on relevant topics such as risk assessment, health and safety, insurance, red tape, cultural orientation and fundraising.
Cost: From £250 for a consultation consisting of detailed confidential questionnaire, three-hour interview, comprehensive 50-page written report (including client-specific contacts list) and follow-up. A review with recommendations on university application is included.
Contact: John Vessey, Director.

GAP SPORTS ABROAD (GSA)
39 Guinions Road, High Wycombe, Bucks. HGP13 7NT. ☎/fax: 01494 769090.
E-mail: info@gapsportsabroad.co.uk. Website: www.gapsportsabroad.co.uk.
Programme description: Provides sports coaching placements in football, basketball, tennis and boxing in Ghana. Other placements relate to teaching, art and design, media, sports psychology, physiotherapy and medicine. Participants are based at a football academy with the support team and other volunteers.
Destinations: Ghana.
Number of placements per year: 50-100.
Prerequisites: Minimum age 18. Relevant experience of qualifications needed for some projects; others require only a willingness to learn.
Duration and time of placements: 3-4 months on average though possible to stay up to 12 months. Also 5-week specials and 2-week sports tours.
Selection procedures and orientation: Applications should be submitted at least 6 weeks before departure. Interviews not required.
Costs: £495-£1,755.
Contact: James Burton, Director.

GAPWORK.COM
☎ 0113-274 0252. E-mail: info@gapwork.com. Website: www.gapwork.com.
Programme description: gapwork is a publisher and provider of gap year and working holiday information. The website provides a range of information on taking a gap year including listings of accommodation providers, employment opportunities and gap year organisations. Gapwork also publish gap year guidebooks and produce a free e-mail newsletter.
Destinations: Europe (including Ibiza and the UK), Australia, New Zealand, Canada and the USA.
Cost: Gap packs (Australia/New Zealand, Canada, Europe, and the USA) cost £12.99 each but can sometimes be bought for £9.99 using a promotions code.
Contact: Rachel Morgan-Trimmer.

GAPYEAR.COM
E-mail: info@gapyear.com. Website: www.gapyear.com.
Largest gap year community in the UK dedicated to helping people plan and prepare for a gap year. This web-based company also produces *gapyear magazine* and other

publications including a monthly e-newsletter and membership. Users of the website can create profiles, find travel mates, access a database with thousands of opportunities, and use the message boards. Gapyear.com also runs gapyearshop.com (specialist gap year travel kit site) and insureyourgap.com (specialist gap year insurance).

GLOBAL VISION INTERNATIONAL (GVI)
Nomansland, Wheathampstead, St. Albans, Herts. AL4 8EJ. ☎ 01582 831300. Fax: 01582 834002. E-mail: info@gvi.co.uk. Website: www.gvi.co.uk.
Programme description: 25 overseas expeditions and conservation projects in Africa, Latin America, Asia and Australasia. See relevant chapters for details.
Destinations: South Africa, Swaziland, Madagascar, Ecuador, Brazil, Mexico, Panama, Guatemala, Nepal, China, Indonesia, Thailand and New Zealand.
Number of placements per year: 500-600.
Prerequisites: None. Minimum age 18. All nationalities welcome.
Duration and time of placements: 2 weeks to one year.
Selection procedures and orientation: Some projects require a telephone interview; others require only a completed application form.
Cost: from £595 to £2,995.
Contact: James Scipioni, Volunteer Co-ordinator.

GREENFORCE
11-15 Betterton Street, Covent Garden, London WC2H 9BP. ☎ 020-7470 8888. Fax: 020-7470 8889. E-mail: info@greenforce.org. Website: www.greenforce.org.
Member of the Year Out Group. Greenforce invites people from all backgrounds to 'Work on the Wild Side' on one of their five wildlife research projects around the world.
Projects work to protect endangered species and habitats on behalf of a host country authority. Establishing new protection zones and managing wildlife resources are the main objectives of these long-term conservation projects.
Programme description: Volunteers work as Fieldwork Assistants, carrying out tasks such as tracking animal movements and studying coral reef species over a 10-week project phase. All training is provided including diver training and rope access (Amazon project). Greenforce offers a traineeship to one member of each volunteer team; the selected trainee stays on camp for a further expedition as a staff assistant at no further cost. The position is aimed at those seeking to develop a career in conservation.
Destinations: Peruvian Amazon, Zambia, Malaysian Borneo, Fiji and the Bahamas.
Number of placements per year: 320 per year. 4 volunteers per member of staff.
Prerequisites: No previous experience is necessary; no qualifications required. Applicants must be over the age of 18.

Duration and time of placements: 10 weeks, commencing January, April, July and October. Limited number of 4-week placements in summer months.
Selection procedures and orientation: Applicants may attend one of the regular, informal open evenings. A briefing pack is provided, giving information about fund-raising and relevant medical advice, etc. Volunteers can attend a training weekend 6 weeks prior to joining the project (cost included in contribution). The first week of the expedition is spent undertaking further training and familiarisation with the project and host country.
Cost: From £2,550 ($4,220) for 10 weeks in Peru and Zambia; £2,750 ($4,500) for the others. Summer expeditions cost £1,500 (Amazon and Africa), £1,600 for Borneo. These fees cover all training and instruction, food, accommodation, visas and medical insurance but not flights. Diving equipment and training are provided at no extra cost.

ICYE: INTER-CULTURAL YOUTH EXCHANGE
Latin American House, Kingsgate Place, London NW6 4TA. ☎/fax: 020-7681 0983. E-mail: info@icye.co.uk. Website: www.icye.co.uk.
Non profit-making international exchange organisation that arranges for people aged 18-30 to spend 6 or 12 months in many countries worldwide (see 'Directory of Voluntary Placements Abroad').

IDP EDUCATION AUSTRALIA (UK) LTD
Suite 210, Business Design Centre, 52 Upper Street, Islington, London N1 0QH. ☎ 020-7288 6828. Fax: 020-7288 6829. E-mail: info@london.idp.com. Website: www.idp.com/uk.
Programme description: Gap Australia StudyExperience (GAS) programme being developed in conjunction with Australian colleges of further education. To combine study, work and travel. Studies can be on-campus or off-campus, across a range of subjects (e.g. Aboriginal art, equestrian studies, music production) as well as more standard training courses, e.g. in bar management or IT to assist in getting holiday jobs afterwards. Work experience placements possible.
Destinations: Throughout Australia.
Duration and time of placements: 3 weeks - 3 months.
Selection procedures and orientation: IDP UK can assist with the preparation and departure, provide information on the full range of courses available, assist with enrolment, visas, accommodation, etc. and host pre-departure briefings.
Contact: Dee Roach, Director.

THE INTERNATIONAL ACADEMY plc
St Hilary Court, Copthorne Way, Culverhouse Cross, Cardiff CF5 6ES. ☎ 02920 672500. Fax: 02920 672510. E-mail: info@international-academy.com. Website: www.international-academy.com.
Member of the Year Out Group. Instructor training in skiing, snowboarding, whitewater rafting and diving to help people on a gap year, career break or others become qualified as instructors. See 'Directory of Sports Courses'.

INTERNATIONAL EXCHANGE CENTER (IEC)
35 Ivor Place, London NW1 6EA. ☎ 020-7724 4493. Fax: 020-7224 8234. E-mail: isec@btconnect.com. Website: www.isecworld.co.uk.
Programme description: Cultural exchanges with large range of countries in Europe and worldwide, including au pairing, volunteering, paid work, volunteering, etc.
Destinations: Denmark, Finland, France, Germany, Italy, Netherlands, Norway, Sweden, Russia and states of the former Soviet Union, Australia, New Zealand, USA, South Africa, Brazil and Latin America.
Number of placements per year: 200+.
Prerequisites: Majority of programmes open to all over 18. Some have language requirements (au pairing on the continent), some dependent on degree/qualifications (e.g.

some teaching programmes).
Duration and time of placements: mostly 6-12 months though some shorter and longer.
Selection procedures and orientation: Informal telephone interviews often sufficient.
Cost: Varies by programme, $100-$1,200.
Contact: Outbound Department.

INTERNATIONAL EXCHANGE PROGRAM UK LTD (IEPUK)
The Old Rectory, Belton, Rutland LE15 9LE. ☎ 01572 717381. Fax: 01572 717343. E-mail: GY@iepuk.com. Website: www.iepuk.com.
Equine staff agency (formerly called Stablemate) with partners in Australia and the USA.
Programme description: International Exchange Program offers work placements in agriculture, equine studies, horticulture, landscaping and winemaking. IEP also acts as a recruitment agency making permanent and relief placements in the equestrian and agricultural industry.
Destinations: Australia, New Zealand, USA, South Africa, Europe and UK.
Number of placements per year: 300/400.
Prerequisites: Equestrian staff require suitable background. One year of practical experience usually needed though many placements offer additional training. Placements as general farm assistants may not require experience.
Duration and time of placements: Usually one year, but variable.
Selection procedures and orientation: Interviews and orientation are required for work overseas.
Cost: IEP fee is about £1,800 including airfares.

i-to-i
Woodside House, 261 Low Lane, Horsforth, Leeds LS18 5NY. Tel: 0870 333 2332. Fax: 0113 205 4619. E-mail: info@i-to-i.com. Website: www.i-to-i.com.
Founding member of the Year Out Group with Investor in People status and Open and Distance Learning Quality Council accreditation for TEFL. i-to-i is a teacher training and volunteer travel organisation.
Programme description: 450 projects in 23 countries involving teaching, conservation, caring, building, media etc. Voluntary English teaching and community development projects (including TEFL certificate) in Bolivia, Brazil, Cambodia, China, Costa Rica, Croatia, Dominican Republic, Ecuador, El Salvador, Ghana, Guatemala, Honduras, India, Kenya, Mongolia, Nepal, Peru, South Africa, Sri Lanka, Thailand, Vietnam,; conservation projects in Australia, Bolivia, Brazil, Costa Rica, Croatia, Ecuador, Guatemala, Honduras, India, Ireland, Kenya, Peru, South Africa and Sri Lanka. Plus building, health, museums, archaeology, media, marketing and tourism projects available. i-to-i also organise 40-hour weekend TEFL training courses across the UK and an online version for those with little time or who live in remote areas.
Number of placements per year: 6,000.
Prerequisites: Fluency in English and some placements (e.g. media) require a CV).
Duration and time of placements: From 1 week to a full year out, available all year round. TEFL courses or volunteer travel placements can be booked at any branch of STA Travel and Student Flights/Flight Centre.
Selection procedures and orientation: All i-Venture placements include full pre-departure travel advice and work briefing, full project inventories and information packs, comprehensive insurance, pre-arranged accommodation, in-country co-ordinator to help deal with emergencies, language lessons and orientation in-country. All teaching/community development placements include free i-to-i Online TEFL course , CD-ROM and teaching worksheets, TEFL Toolkit of teaching activities for any classroom, and back-up from trained TEFL teachers in the UK.
Cost: £750-£1,750 (excluding airfares). £195 for TEFL course only. Free taster TEFL course on-line at www.onlinetefl.com.

JET PROGRAMME
c/o JET Desk, Japanese Embassy, 101-104 Piccadilly, London W1J 7JT. ☎ 020-7465 6668/6670. E-mail: jet@embjapan.org.uk. Website: www.embjapan.org.uk/eng/education.jet.html.
Programme description: Government-run Japan Exchange & Teaching Programme (JET) allows graduates to spend one or more years teaching in Japan.
Destinations: Throughout Japan.
Number of placements per year: 1,000+
Prerequisites: Must have a BA and be under 40.
Duration and time of placements: One-year contracts begin in late July.
Selection procedures and orientation: The application deadline is early December. Orientations given in London and Tokyo.
Cost: None. Return airfares provided to those who complete contract. Salary of 3,760,000 yen paid (currently about £19,000+).

JOHN HALL PRE-UNIVERSITY COURSE
12 Gainsborough Road, Ipswich, Suffolk IP4 2UR. ☎ 01473 251223. Fax: 01473 288009. E-mail: info@johnhallpre-university.com. Website: www.johnhallpre-university.com.
Annual pre-university course on European civilisation specially designed for gap year students, held in London and Venice between January and March. Emphasis is on the visual arts and music. Cost for 1 week in London and 6 weeks in Venice is £5,800 with optional extra periods in Florence and Rome. See 'Directory of Art Courses'.

KIBBUTZ REPRESENTATIVES
1A Accommodation Road, London NW11 8ED. ☎ 020-8458 9235. Fax: 020-8455 7930. E-mail: enquiries@kibbutz.org.uk. Website: www.kibbutz.org.il.

Programme description: KR represents the Israeli kibbutz movement in the UK and recruits volunteers for kibbutzim on their behalf. The newest programme is 'The Israel Experience' which over three months combines a political and cultural introduction to the country, language instruction (Hebrew or English) and volunteering.
Prerequisities: Must be aged 18-35.
Duration and time of placements: Minimum stay is 8 weeks, with departures year round.
Selection procedures and orientation: Candidates attend an informal interview in London or Manchester, and provide a signed declaration of medical fitness. Processing takes from 3-5 weeks (summer is the busiest time).
Cost: Package costs from £400 including flights plus compulsory insurance from £75.

KWA MADWALA

PO Box 192, Hectorspruit 1330, South Africa. ☎ 13-792 4526. Fax: 13-792 4219. E-mail: gazebog@mweb.co.za. Website: www.kwamadwala.co.za. UK representatives are Rob & Libby Aarvold, Thaningtong, Chichester Road, Dorking, Surrey RH4 1CR (01306 884924; kmgapyear@hotmail.com). Private game reserve in South Africa which offers a 3-month gap year experience. Kwa Madwala is located on the south side of the Kruger National Park between Swaziland and Mozambique.
Programme description: Game conservation course that covers tracking, spoor identification, conservation control, snake and snakebite identification, survival skills, game counting, etc.
Duration and time of placements: 6 starting dates throughout the year, the 1st and 15th of January, May and September.
Costs: 90-day programme costs 50,000 Rand (£3,900) all-inclusive. Shorter stay of 25 days available for 20,000 Rand (£1,560).

LANGUAGE COURSES ABROAD LTD

67 Ashby Road, Loughborough, Leicestershire LE11 3AA. ☎ 01509 211612. Fax: 01509 260037. E-mail: info@languagesabroad.co.uk. Website: www.langua gesabroad.co.uk.
Parent company, Spanish Study Holidays Ltd., is a member of FIYTO (Federation of International Youth Travel Organisations), ALTO (Association of Language Travel Organisations) and GWEA (Global Work Experience Association).
Programme description: In-country language courses in Spanish, French, German, Italian, Portuguese and Russian (see entry in 'Directory of Language Courses' often in conjunction with work experience placements, available in Spain, Latin America, France, Germany and Italy (see entry in 'Directory of Work Experience').
Contact: Mike Cummins, Director.

MADVENTURER

Adamson House, 65 Westgate Road, Newcastle-upon-Tyne NE1 1SG. ☎ 0845 121 1996. Fax: 0191-280 2860. E-mail: team@madventurer.com. Website: www.madventurer.com.
Madventurer enables young people to gain experience through work and travel in the developing world. Non-profit-making organisation with network of volunteer societies at UK universities.
Programme description: Expeditions that give students the opportunity to undertake a range of voluntary work (building, teaching, sports instruction, healthcare) and adventurous travel. 3-month placements include 2 months of volunteering for a grassroots community or environmental project followed by a one-month group adventure (trekking, rafting, touring). Placements can sometimes be arranged to complement area of academic study.
Destinations: Peru, Bolivia, Chile, Ghana, Tanzania, Togo, Uganda and Kenya.

Prerequisites: Minimum age 17.
Duration and time of placements: From 3 weeks at Easter to 3-month placements with various departure dates throughout the year. Some volunteers extend their stay for up to 6 months. Also 8-week group projects operate in the summer holidays in which 15-20 volunteers live and work in a village for 4-5 weeks followed by adventure travel.
Selection procedures and orientation: Volunteers are assigned a mentor to lend support throughout placement. Pre-departure information session held in the UK.
Cost: £1,585 (Africa), £1,870 (Latin America) for summer trip (not including flights).
Contact: John Lawler.

MONDOCHALLENGE
Galliford Building, Gayton Rd, Milton Malsor, Northampton NN7 3AB. ☎ 01604 858225. Fax: 01604 859323. E-mail: info@mondochallenge.org. Website: www.mondochallenge.org.
Programme description: Volunteers of all ages including some of their gap year (pre and post university) are sent to villages in Nepal, India, Sri Lanka, Tanzania, Kenya, Gambia and Chile, mainly to teach. Some business development programmes. Fee for 3 months is £800. (See entry in 'Directory of Voluntary Placements Abroad'.)

NONSTOPSKI
1A Bickersteth Road, London SW17 9SE. ☎/fax: 020-8772 7852. E-mail: info@nonstopski.com. Website: www.nonstopski.com.
Programme description: Ski and Snowboard Instructor Courses in Fernie, British Columbia, Canada (see entry in 'Directory of Sports Courses').

OPERATION WALLACEA
Hope House, Old Bolingbroke, Nr Spilsby, Lincolnshire PE23 4EX. ☎

01790 763194. Fax: 01790 763825. E-mail: info@opwall.com. Website: www.opwall.com.
Programme description: Scientific research projects on Indonesian island of Sulawesi and Honduras. Volunteer students, divers and naturalists assist with surveys of marine and rainforest habitats.
Destinations: Southeast Sulawesi and Northern Honduras.
Prerequisites: Minimum age 16. Enthusiasm needed.
Duration and time of placements: 2, 4, 6 or 8 weeks between the beginning of June and the end of September.
Selection procedures and orientation: Telephone interview. No deadlines. Dive training can be given.
Cost: £875 for 2 weeks, £1,700 for 4 weeks, £2,300 for 6 weeks and £2,700 for 8 weeks, exclusive of flights and accommodation.
Contact: Alexis Bain.

Outreach International

GAP Year and Voluntary Projects in **Cambodia, Mexico** and **Ecuador**
Volunteers are needed to work on the following projects for three to nine months:

* Orphanages and Street Children
* Rehabilitation centres for land mine and polio victims
* Disabled children centres
* Special needs school

* Teaching English and sport in Pacific coast villages
* Art and craft. Dance
* Conservation work in the Amazon
* Work with whales, dolphins and giant sea turtles

Do you have an interest in immersing yourself in a fascinating foreign culture whilst working on an important, locally initiated, grass roots project?

Gap@Outreachinternational.co.uk www.Outreachinternational.co.uk Tel/Fax James Chapman on: 01458 274957

OUTREACH INTERNATIONAL
Bartletts Farm, Hayes Road, Compton Dundon, Somerset TA11 6PF.
☎/fax: 01458 274957. E-mail: gap@outreachinternational.co.uk. Website: www.outreachinternational.co.uk.
Member of the Year Out Group. Outreach International is a small gap year specialist with carefully selected projects with enough variety to ensure that the interests and skills of individual volunteers can be put to good use.
Programme description: Volunteers participate in local initiatives allowing them to live in communities and work alongside local people. Cambodian placements include working with young land mine and polio victims and children who have become victims of human trafficking. Volunteers teach English, computer skills and art skills. Mexican projects are on the Pacific coast in traditional villages. The projects are with orphans, disabled children, teaching in local schools or working with giant sea turtles. In Ecuador, volunteers work in an orphanage and also carry out conservation work in the Amazon rainforest.
Destinations: Mexico, Cambodia and Ecuador.
Prerequisites: Ideal for confident young people with a desire to travel, learn a language and offer their help to a damaged society.
Duration and time of placements: 3+ months.
Selection procedures and orientation: Applicants will be invited to interview within 3 weeks of applying.
Cost: £3,100 for 3 months includes air tickets, full insurance, language course, in-country support, food, accommodation and all project costs. Additional months are approximately £400 per month.
Contact: James Chapman, UK Director.

PEAK LEADERS
Mansfield, Strathmiglo, Fife KY14 7QE, Scotland. ☎ 01337 860079. Fax: 01337 868176. E-mail: info@peakleaders.com. Website: www.peakleaders.com.
Gap year ski and snowboard instructor courses in the Canadian Rockies and Argentina, and Jungle Expedition Leader gap year programme with diving and sailing in Sumatra, Indonesia (see *Directory of Sports Courses*).

THE PROJECT TRUST
Hebridean Centre, Ballyhough, Isle of Coll, Argyll PA78 6TE. ☎ 01879 230444. Fax: 01879 230357. London office: 12 East Passage, London EC1A 7LP. ☎ 020-7796 1170. Fax: 020-7796 1172. E-mail: info@projecttrust.org.uk. Website: www.projecttrust.org.uk.
Founding member of the Year Out Group.
Programme description: Voluntary placements specifically for gap year students throughout the developing world. Volunteers can choose to take part in care work, community development and wildlife projects, educational projects or outdoor activity projects, or they can act as English language assistants at schools.
Destinations: Africa (Uganda, Lesotho, Botswana, South Africa, Malawi, Namibia, Mozambique, Niger, Mauritania and Morocco), South and Central America (Honduras, Cuba, Chile, Bolivia, Peru, Guyana and the Dominican Republic), Asia and the Middle East (Thailand, China, Egypt, Jordan, Sri Lanka, Japan, Malaysia, Vietnam, South Korea and Pakistan).
Number of placements per year: Around 200 (80% from state schools).
Prerequisites: Applicants should be between 17 and 19 and be aiming for university.
Duration and time of placements: 12 months from August. Limited number of 9-month placements for those needing to attend a university interview in the autumn.
Selection procedures and orientation: In the period between August and March, candidates attend a 4-day course on the Hebridean Isle of Coll where their skills and interests are assessed. About 80% of those who take the selection course are offered a place within a week of leaving Coll. Training courses are held, also on the Isle of Coll, during July and August to teach skills such as river crossing, navigation, menu planning, leadership and emergency procedures, and to provide country-specific briefings. Once in the destination country there is always at least one local representative on hand to help volunteers settle in. There is also a 24-hour medical telephone number in case of emergencies.
Cost: Volunteers are required to raise £3,850 which includes the costs of selection, training, supervising, debriefing, airfares, medical insurance, board and lodging and a living allowance.

QUEST OVERSEAS
32 Clapham Mansions, Nightingale Lane, London SW4 9AQ. ☎ 020-8673 3313. Fax: 020-8637 7623. E-mail: emailus@questoverseas.com. Website: www.questoverseas.com.
Founding member of the Year Out Group. Quest Overseas specialises in combining worthwhile voluntary work projects with challenging expeditions to Africa and South America for small teams of gap year students. Throughout the summer Quest Overseas run separate projects and expeditions lasting 6 weeks. Quest Overseas students raise tens of thousands of pounds each year for UK registered charities (see chapter on Latin America).
Programme description: The South America programme is split into 3 phases: Phase I – 3-week intensive Spanish language course in Quito, Ecuador or Sucre, Bolivia; Phase II – 4-week voluntary work projects, either conservation work in the cloudforests or rainforests of Ecuador, or looking after children in the suburb district of Villa Maria, Lima, Peru or working in Ambue Ari animal rehabilitation project in Bolivia. Phase III – 6-week Andean expedition covering over 1,000km of Peru, Chile and Bolivia including Amazon

jungle and Machu Picchu.

Destinations: Ecuador, Peru, Chile and Bolivia. The Africa programme is split into 2 phases: Phase I – 6-week voluntary work project, either conservation work in Swaziland or a community development project in Tanzania. Phase II – 6-week expedition through Swaziland, Mozambique, South Africa, Botswana and Zambia.

Number of placements per year: 16 students in each team and 12 expeditions per year.

Prerequisites: All students involved are gap students aged 18-19.

Duration and time of placements: 13-week programmes depart throughout January-April, with summer expeditions departing July. Flights can be open returns so stays can be extended.

Selection procedures and orientation: Selection is by interview. Preparation and Expedition Skills weekends are organised 3-4 months prior to departure.

Cost: £2,790-£3,985 (South America) and £3,470 (Africa), excluding costs of return flights (approximately £570), individual insurance (about £150) and personal pocket money for souvenirs and luxuries.

RALEIGH INTERNATIONAL

Raleigh House, 27 Parsons Green Lane, London SW6 4HZ. ☎ 020-7371 8585. Fax: 020-7371 5116. E-mail: info@raleigh.org.uk. Website: www.raleighinternational.org.

Founding member of the Year Out Group. Leading youth development charity which offers young people the chance to take part in challenging environmental, community and adventure projects as part of 3-month expeditions overseas.

Programme description: Volunteers aged 17-25 from a wide range of backgrounds and nationalities take part in 10-week expeditions in one of 5-6 expedition countries. Every volunteer completes one community, adventure and environmental project, such as trekking in Mongolia's Gobi Desert, helping to build clinics/schools in Namibia, or completing environmental research in Costa Rica's rainforest.

Destinations: Costa Rica, Nicaragua, Chile, Ghana, Namibia and Sabah-Borneo.

Prerequisites: Applicants must be aged between 17 and 25 and able to understand English, to swim and to be enthusiastic, committed and motivated.

Duration and time of placements: 10 weeks with the opportunity to travel independently after the expedition for up to three months at no extra cost.

Selection procedures and orientation: Self-selection process starting with an Introduction Day. Briefing day prior to departure and a training weekend two months beforehand. Once in the country, 5 days are spent as orientation.

Cost: Fundraising target of £3,500 covers all costs towards the expedition, including return flight, with the exception of personal kit.

Contact: James Phipps, Venturer Recruitment & Support Team.

ROTARY INTERNATIONAL IN GREAT BRITAIN AND IRELAND (RIBI)
Kinwarton Road, Alcester, Warwickshire B49 6PB. ☎ 01789 765411. Fax: 01789 765570. E-mail: paulaw@ribi.org. Website: www.youthribi.org.
Programme description: One-year international exchanges to promote international understanding and peace through exposure to different cultures. Exchange students stay with families in host country and attend a place of academic or vocational learning.
Number of placements per year: Over 9,000 worldwide (see chapter *A Year Off for North Americans*) but around 20 on Gap Year from UK at present.
Prerequisites: Minimum age 16; average age 18. All nationalities. Students are expected to get involved in the activities of their host Rotary Club.
Duration and time of placements: 10-12 months.
Costs: Students pay for costs of travel and insurance plus approximately £200 for orientation and sundries. They receive pocket money of £60 per month.
Selection procedures and orientation: Deadline for applications is the end of February. Interviews held in candidate's home with parents. Students should be from the top 10% of their school year in overall achievement. Weekend residential orientation in March and local orientation of half a day prior to leaving. Students receive orientation within one month of arriving in their host country.
Contact: Andrew Page (andrew@cavideo.co.uk), RIBI Youth Exchange

SKI LE GAP
220 Wheeler St, Mont Tremblant, Quebec J8E 1V3, Canada. ☎ +001-819-429-6599. E-mail: info@skilegap.com. Website: www.skilegap.com.
Programme description: Ski and Snowboard instructor's programme in Quebec, Canada, designed for gap year students from Britain. See entry in 'Directory of Sports Courses' and further details in chapter on Canada.

THE SMALLPEICE TRUST
Holly House, 74 Upper Holly Walk, Leamington Spa, Warwickshire CV32 4JL. ☎ 01926 333200. Fax: 01926 333202. E-mail: gen@smallpeicetrust.org.uk. Website: www.smallpeicetrust.org.uk.
Associate member of the Year Out Group. Runs the Smallpeice Engineering Gap Year (SEGY) for gap year students (see entry in 'Directory of Work Experience').

SPW – STUDENTS PARTNERSHIP WORLDWIDE
17 Dean's Yard, London SW1P 3PB. ☎ 020-7222 0138. Fax: 020-7233 0008. E-mail: spwuk@gn.apc.org. Website: www.spw.org.
Member of the Year Out Group. Groups of European volunteers aged 18-28 are recruited to work in partnership with counterpart groups from Africa and Asia. In pairs or groups

they live and work in rural communities for 4-9 months. Their input builds awareness and begins to change attitudes and behaviour to important health, social and environmental issues amongst young people and communities. All volunteers take part in training which covers health, hygiene, sanitation, nutrition and the environment, with a particular emphasis on HIV transmission.

Programme description: SPW runs health education and environment programmes. These programmes tackle youth problems from different perspectives. All placements are in rural villages.

Destinations: India, Nepal, South Africa, Tanzania, Uganda and Zambia.

Number of placements per year: 250 places for European volunteers.

Prerequisites: A-level or equivalent qualifications. Volunteers need to be physically and mentally healthy, hard working, open-minded, enthusiastic and have good communication skills.

Duration and time of placements: 4-9 months with starting dates throughout the year.

Selection procedures and orientation: Applicants should request an application form from the London office. Every applicant is required to attend an Information and Selection day in London. This also gives them the opportunity to meet staff and ex-volunteers. Following selection, volunteers are accepted on a first come first served basis, so early application is recommended.

Cost: £2,900-£3,300 all-inclusive of open return flight, accommodation, basic living allowance, insurance, in-country visa, UK briefings and general administrative support, and extensive overseas training and support. SPW is a non-profit making charity, so volunteer fees cover costs only.

STUDENT ACTION INDIA
c/o HomeNet, Office 20, 30-38 Dock Street, Leeds LS10 1JF. ☎ 07071-225866. Fax: 0870 135 3906. E-mail:info@studentactionindia.org.uk. Website: www.studentactionindia.org.uk.

Programme description: Arrange voluntary attachments to various Indian non-governmental organisations for 2 months in summer or 5 months from September. See entry in 'Directory of Voluntary Placements Abroad'.

TEACHING ABROAD
Gerrard House, Rustington, West Sussex BN16 1AW. ☎ 01903 859911. Fax: 01903 785779. E-mail: info@teaching-abroad.co.uk. Website: www.teaching-abroad.co.uk.

Founding member of the Year Out Group. Company arranges voluntary TEFL posts in a range of countries. Sister organisation Projects Abroad (see 'Directory of Work Experience') makes placements in medicine, media and other fields in selected destinations.

Destinations: Bolivia, Chile, China, Ghana, India, Mexico, Mongolia, Nepal, Peru, Romania, Russia, South Africa, Sri Lanka, Thailand, Togo and Ukraine.Destinations and programmes can be combined; their 'Grand Gap' combines three or four destinations.

Number of placements per year: 2,500.

Prerequisites: Minimum age 17+. University entrance qualifications needed. Optional UK briefing and TEFL weekend courses before departure.

Duration and time of placements: Very flexible, with departures year round. Placements last 1-12 months.

Selection procedures and orientation: Paid staff in all destinations arrange and vet placements, accommodation and work supervisors. They meet volunteers on arrival and provide a final briefing before the placements.

Cost: Placements are self-funded and the fee charged includes insurance, food, accommodation and overseas support. Three-month placements cost between £895 and £1,795, depending on placement, excluding travel costs.

THE LEAP OVERSEAS LTD
Windy Hollow, Sheepdrove, Lambourn, Berks. RG17 7XA. ☎ 0870 240 4187. Fax: 01488 71311. E-mail: info@theleap.co.uk. Website: www.theleap.co.uk.
New company providing British students (and employees taking career sabbaticals) with work placements in a number of African countries plus Nepal.
Programme description: Overseas voluntary work placements focused on eco-tourism with an emphasis on conservation and community issues.
Destinations: Kenya, Tanzania, Malawi, Botswana, Namibia, South Africa, Zambia and Nepal.
Number of placements per year: 45.
Prerequisites: Ages 18-60. Must be committed, enthusiastic and motivated to work in a team and get stuck in.
Duration and time of placements: 3-month placements departing September, December, March and June or to suit the hosts' seasonal requirements.
Selection procedures and orientation: Face-to-face interviews preferred or attendance at 2-day Familiarisation and Selection course for suitability and training/briefing.
Other services: Flights can be arranged through ATOL partner agency Safari Drive Ltd.
Costs: £1,950-£2,100 excluding travel and visas.
Contact: Guy Whitehead, Director.

TRAVELLERS
7 Mulberry Close, Ferring, West Sussex BN12 5HY. ☎ 01903 502595. Fax: 01903 500364. E-mail: info@travellersworldwide.com. Website: www.travellers worldwide.com.
Founder member of the Year Out Group.
Programme description: Teaching conversational English (and other subjects), conservation, language courses, structured work experience and cultural courses (photography, tango, etc.).
Destinations: Argentina, Brazil, Brunei, China, Cuba, Ghana, India, Kenya, Malaysia, Nepal, Russia, South Africa, Sri Lanka, Ukraine and Vietnam.
Number of placements per year: 1,000+.
Prerequisites: No formal qualifications required.
Duration and time of placements: From a month to a year with flexible start dates all year round.
Cost: Sample charges for 3 months in Sri Lanka are £1,345 and Ukraine £895. Prices include food and accommodation but do not include international travel, visas or insurance. (Travellers can arrange the latter but many volunteers prefer the flexibility of organising their own.)
Contact: Philip Perkes, Director.

TREKFORCE EXPEDITIONS
34 Buckingham Palace Road, London SW1W 0RE. ☎ 020-7828 2275. Fax: 020-7828 2276. E-mail: info@trekforce.org.uk. Website: www.trekforce.org.uk.
Founding member of the Year Out Group. Established since 1989.

Programme description: Expedition programme specially designed for gap year students concentrating on vital conservation, community and scientific projects. Destinations include Central America (Belize and Guatemala), South America (Guyana and Brazil) and East Malaysia (Sarawak and Sabah). Expeditions last for two months or up to five months for those who opt for expedition work, language learning (Spanish or Portuguese) and teaching in rural communities such as the Maya and the Kelabit, or Amerindian villages.

Prerequisites: Minimum age 18. Must be enthusiastic, and generally fit and healthy.

Duration and time of placements: 2, 3, 4 or 5 months all year round.

Selection procedures & orientation: Interested participants attend an informal introductory day or visit the Trekforce office for an interview. Briefing day and in-country training is provided for expedition members.

Cost: £2,570 for 8 weeks, £3,200 for 12 weeks, £3,600 for 17 weeks extended programme in Sarawak; £3,800 for 20-week extended programme in Belize or Guyana (excluding flights).

Contact: Sarah Bruce.

VAE TEACHERS KENYA
Bell Lane Cottage, Pudleston, Nr. Leominster, Herefordshire HR6 0RE. ☎ 01568 750329. Fax: 01568 750636. E-mail: vaekenya@hotmail.com. Website: www.vaekenya.co.uk. Kenya address: PO Box 246, Gilgil, Kenya.
VAE runs two associated charities: Harambee Schools Kenya providing educational infrastructure and materials (www.hsk.org.uk) and Langalanga Scholarship Fund providing secondary education to bright children who would not otherwise be able to afford it (www.llsf.org.uk).

Programme description: School leavers or graduates to teach in extremely poor rural schools based around the town of Gilgil in Kenya. Volunteers are placed only in schools with a shortage of teachers and resources, and must assume major responsibility as they become integrated and live as part of an African community. VAE is also involved with the local town street children.

Duration and time of placements: Preferred departure time January for 6 months.

Cost: About £3,000, including flight, insurance, salary, accommodation, etc.

Contact: Simon C. D. Harris, VAE Director.

VENTURE CO WORLDWIDE
The Ironyard, 64-66 The Market Place, Warwick CV34 4SD. ☎ 01926 411122. Fax: 01926 411133. E-mail: mail@ventureco-worldwide.com. Website: www.ventureco-worldwide.com.
Member of the Year Out Group. Hold an ATOL license.

Programme description: Gap Year and Career Gap specialist with programmes that combine language schools, local aid projects and expeditions.

Destinations: *Inca Venture:* Ecuador, Peru, Chile and Bolivia. *Patagonia Venture:* Peru, Bolivia, Chile, Argentina and Tierra del Fuego. *Maya Venture:* Guatemala, Belize, Honduras, Mexico, Nicaragua, Costa Rica and Cuba. *Himalaya Venture:* India and Nepal. *L'Afrique Venture:* Morocco, Mali, Niger, Nigeria, Cameroon and Gabon. *Indochina Venture* (career gap only): Cambodia, Vietnam, Laos and China. Live Venture reports and dossiers available from website.

Number of placements per year: 175.

Prerequisites: Gap Year 17½-19; Career Gap minimum age 20. Must have motivation, enthusiasm and desire to be part of a Venture team.

Duration and time of placements: Programmes are 4 months long with departures year round.

Selection procedures & orientation: Selection is by interview. Preparation weekends held in UK, and expeditions skills training in-country.
Cost: Approximately £4,500 including flights and insurance.
Contacts: Mark Davison and David Gordon, Directors.
See also chapters on Latin America and Asia.

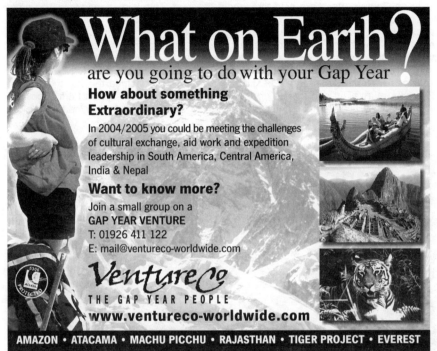

WORLD CHALLENGE EXPEDITIONS
**Black Arrow House, 2 Chandos Road, London NW10 6NF. ☎ 020-8728 7200.
E-mail: welcome@world-challenge.co.uk. Website: www.world-challenge.co.uk.**
Founding member of the Year Out Group. World Challenge Expeditions run four flexible skills development programmes for schools and individuals: Gap Challenge (described here), Team Challenge and First Challenge (see 'Directory of Expeditions') and Leadership Challenge (see 'Directory of Courses'). Each of the programmes works to raise motivation through developing skills in leadership, team building, decision making and problem solving. World Challenge Expeditions started in 1987.
Programme description: Gap Challenge offers a variety of paid and voluntary work placements for 3 or 6 months in 13 countries. Voluntary placements in developing countries and paid work arranged in Canada and New Zealand. Teaching placements in secondary or primary schools in Belize, Nepal, Malaysia, Tanzania, Peru, Mexico, Costa Rica and Ecuador. Conservation placements in Belize, Ecuador, Costa Rica, Malaysia, Peru, Mexico and South Africa. Care work in South Africa, Malaysia, Belize, Ecuador and Peru. Medical work in Peru, Ecuador and Mexico. Youth recreation or paid agricultural work in Australia and New Zealand.
Destinations: India, Nepal, Malaysia, Tanzania, South Africa, Ecuador, Peru, Belize, Costa Rica, Mexico, Canada, Australia and New Zealand.
Number of placements per year: Approximately 450.
Prerequisites: Programmes open to people aged 18-25 taking a year out between school

and university or after university. Applicants under 18 must submit consent form signed by parent or guardian.

Duration and time of placements: From 3 and 6 months to a maximum of 9 months. Departures are in September, January, March/April and June/July.

Selection procedures & orientation: All applicants are required to attend a two-day Selection Course; these are held throughout the year. This is a chance to get to meet the applicants and check that they and their choice of destination and placement are compatible. Once selected there is an obligatory Skills Training course before departure where they can meet past Gap Challengers and receive training and briefings from qualified staff.

Cost: Fees range from £1,588 for a placement in Canada to £2,887 for a placement trekking, river rafting and jungle trekking in Nepal. Prices include the training course, 12-month return flight and transfer to the destination, in-country support from appointed representatives and 24-hour emergency back-up and support from World Challenge Expeditions in London.

Contact: World Challenge Expeditions on 020-8728 7274.

WORLDWIDE VOLUNTEERING FOR YOUNG PEOPLE

7 North Street Workshops, Stoke sub Hamdon, Somerset TA14 6QR. ☎ 01935 825588. Fax: 01935 825775. E-mail: worldvol@worldvol.co.uk. Website: www.www.org.uk.

Worldwide Volunteering aims to make information about worldwide volunteering programmes in the UK and worldwide more accessible to young people.

Programme description: Maintains a database of volunteer opportunities around the world geared particularly to 16-35 year olds. The software matches volunteers' requirements with those of 950 organisations offering a potential total of 300,000

placements.
Destinations: All over the world.
Prerequisites: These vary from organisation to organisation and will be specified in the database. Anyone can use the database.
Selection procedures and orientation: Once volunteers have found information on the database, they can then get in contact with the organisations that interest them using the email and weblinks provided. The database provides a wealth of information about organisations.
Cost: The *Worldwide Volunteering Database* is available for individuals on-line and for subscribers on-line or by CD-ROM (stand-alone or network) at an annual subscription fee which includes free data update after six months. Some subscribing schools and careers centres, libraries and volunteer bureaux will allow enquirers to access the information free of charge. A list of these subscribers is found on the WWW website. Note that the print version *Worldwide Volunteering for Young People* (2001) is distributed by How To Books, Plymbridge House, Estover Road, Plymouth PL6 7PZ for £15.95.
Contact: Roger Potter.

YEAR IN INDUSTRY
The University of Southampton, Southampton SO17 1BJ. ☎ 02380 597061. E-mail: enquiries@yini.org.uk. Website: www.yini.org.uk.
Founding member of the Year Out Group. Major provider of gap year industrial placements throughout the UK. See entry in 'Directory of Work Experience'.

YEAR OUT DRAMA COMPANY
Stratford-upon-Avon College, Alcester Road, Stratford-upon-Avon, Warks. CV37 9QR. ☎ 01789 266245. Fax: 01789 267524. E-mail: yearoutdrama@strat-avon.ac.uk.
Founding member of the Year Out Group. One-year course covers acting, directing, performance, voice work, movement and design. See entry in 'Directory of Courses'.

YOUTH FOR UNDERSTANDING
15 Hawthorn Road, Erskine, Renfrewshire PA8 7BT. ☎/fax: 0141-812 5561. E-mail: yfu@holliday123.freeserve.co.uk.
Programme description: Scholarship exchange programme funded by government of Japan which grew out of international educational exchanges set up in the US in the 1950s.
Destinations: Japan.
Number of placements per year: 10-20.
Prerequisites: 16-18 year olds placed in secondary schools abroad. Must have interest in Japan and be prepared to learn the basics of the language.
Duration and time of placements: 10 months departing in March. Shorter stays may be possible.
Selection procedures and orientation: Application deadline is end of August. Two interviews are held in Glasgow or London, one with Programme Co-ordinator, the other in front of a panel including representatives from the Japanese Embassy. Orientation weekends held before departure, during programme and prior to arriving home.
Cost: The Programme is funded but candidates have to pay for a school trip taken during the year in Japan (£500-£800) plus pocket money (£100-£150 per month). Airfares from Heathrow are covered by the programme and internal travel in Japan. Homestay accommodation provided free of charge.
Contact: Lorraine Holliday, Programme Co-ordinator.

Also see directories at the end of the chapters on Volunteering, Work Experience, Au Pairing and Courses for other organisations that welcome gap year students (among others).

Expeditions

Adolescence is a good time to discover tales of adventure from the literature of exploration whether it is the casual descriptions of suffering by mountaineers or sailors, classics by Robert Byron or Freya Stark, or more recent classics by Bruce Chatwin, Redmond O'Hanlon or Dervla Murphy. Books can be very influential at a time when life is circumscribed by family and school. Reading a book like the explorer Robin Hanbury-Tenison's *Worlds Apart* can easily inspire a longing to visit the wild and woolly corners of the world instead of joining the annual family holiday to a self-catering cottage in Yorkshire or Tuscany.

It might seem an impossible dream for a 16 or 17 year old with no money and no travel experience beyond a youth hostelling weekend in the Peak District. But a number of organisations cater specifically for gap year students looking for adventures in remote places. These are open to anyone who is mentally and physically fit and who is prepared to raise the fees (typically £2,500-£3,500). Although the fund-raising target is fairly high, so are the rewards, according to **Hannah Peck** who joined a *BSES* expedition to arctic Svalbard in 2002:

> *My reasons for taking a gap year were to travel to a remote environment away from city life to try to regain some direction and inspiration. Now near the end, I feel that*

my confidence has grown incredibly while I've been here, both socially and physically. In particular I can mix more easily with 'blokes' as having been at an all-girls school I have not had much chance to live and work with them. This should make moving on to university a much smoother and more enjoyable experience. I have gained more understanding of my physical strengths and limits and have been pleasantly surprised to see how well I cope under harsh conditions and pleased to see that I can easily keep up with boys. So now I know that being a girl should be of no real consequence for future expeditions. Living here on Svalbard has allowed me to experience the importance of preservation of the wilderness through everyday watching the natural goings on, the weather, wildlife and sea ice, as well as experiencing the silence. I have learnt to be entertained easily and now know the things I rely so much on at home to entertain me are really not that great.

Many bemoan a decline in youth culture, arguing that life at the beginning of the 21st century is too materialistic, too soft and that young people are emerging into adulthood afraid to take risks, not to mention unfit and overweight. There is no equivalent in our culture to the coming-of-age tests and initiation rites to which so many other cultures expose their young people, whether giving them a painful tattoo or sending them into the wilderness to fend alone for a given period. In fact this was going on in Britain as recently as 1933, if Roald Dahl's autobiography *Boy* (Puffin, 2001) is to be believed, where he describes the summer after finishing school:

That summer, for the first time in my life, I did not accompany the family to Norway. I somehow felt the need for a special kind of last fling before I became a businessman. So while still at school during my last term, I signed up to spend August with something called the Public Schools' Exploring Society. The leader of this outfit was a man who had gone with Captain Scott on his last expedition to the South Pole, and he was taking a party of senior schoolboys to explore the interior of Newfoundland during the summer holidays. It sounded like fun.

Our ship sailed from Liverpool at the beginning of August and took six days to reach St. John's. There were about 30 boys of my own age on the expedition as well as four experienced adult leaders. But Newfoundland, as I soon found out, was not much of a country. For three weeks we trudged all over that desolate land with enormous loads on our backs. We carried tents and groundsheets and sleeping bags and saucepans and food and axes and everything else one needs in the interior of an unmapped, uninhabitable and inhospitable country. My own load, I know, weighed exactly 114 pounds, and someone else always had to help me hoist the rucksack on to my back. We lived on pemmican and lentils and the 12 of us who went separately on what was called the Long March from the north to the south of the island and back again suffered a good deal from lack of food. I can remember very clearly how we experimented with eating boiled lichen and reindeer moss to supplement our diet. But it was a genuine adventure and I returned home hard and fit and ready for anything.

Significantly this anecdote comes right at the end of *Boy* before he proceeds to the second part of his autobiography called *Going Solo*.

If you feel the need for a similar last fling or would like to show your friends and family what stern stuff you are made of, then a gap year is the perfect time to think about going on an expedition.

After participating on one of the trails through unspoiled places organised by the Wilderness Trust, 18 year old Willem Boshoff reflected:
For me personally, the one single thing which held the most meaning for me, was certainly the fact that my own existence was once more placed in perspective. The wilderness simply indicated once again just how relative and insignificant

academic and other values which we consider so important really are. For a change, one is forced to consider again one's place in the whole creation - and that place is surprisingly small!

Helpful Organisations

The *Royal Geographical Society* (1 Kensington Gore, London SW7 2AR) encourages and assists many British expeditions. The Expedition Advisory Centre at the RGS distributes a booklet *Joining an Expedition* (2001, £7.50) which includes about 60 organisations that regularly arrange expeditions. The EAC also hosts a weekend 'Explore' seminar every November on 'Planning a Small Expedition', which covers fundraising and budgeting for expeditions as well as issues of safety and logistics. If you want personal advice on mounting an expedition, you can make an appointment to visit the EAC (020-7591 3030; eac@rgs.org). The Society's historic map room is open to the public daily from 11am to 5pm. The Expedition Advisory Centre has generously put online most of the grant-giving organisations listed in its publication *Fund-raising and Budgeting for Expeditions*. Although many grants are ring-fenced (e.g. must live within eight miles of Exmouth Town Hall) it is certainly worth checking and applying as widely as possible.

The *Young Explorers' Trust* offers to help groups of students organise their own expedition during their gap year. The organisation was established as a charity over 25 years ago to provide for young people participating in exploration, discovery and outdoor activities. YET does not offer pre-arranged expeditions but offers an expert panel of advisors and assessors for expedition plans. It also organises occasional weekend Expedition Planning Courses open to everyone for a residential fee of £70. YET also publishes two Codes of Practice for youth expeditions: 'Safe and Responsible Expeditions' and 'Environmental Responsibility for Expeditions'. Some grant aid may be made available to YET-approved expeditions.

Raleigh International (www.raleighinternational.org) is the longest established and most experienced expedition organisation, having run more than 200 three-month expeditions overseas. Their aim is to enable people to reach their full potential through challenging community, environmental and adventure projects as part of an overseas expedition. Trekking through the Andes Mountains in Chile, building schools/clinics in Namibia or collecting scientific data in Costa Rica are examples of projects undertaken in Raleigh International's expedition countries. Applicants attend an introduction day and are asked to fundraise £3,500 (see entry in 'Directory of Specialist Gap Year Programmes' and mentions in the chapters on Africa, Asia and Latin America).

School-leavers who have attended schools with a tradition of sending students on expeditions will be at an advantage in tracking down suitable opportunities in their gap year. An expedition forms part of the requirements to gain a Duke of Edinburgh Award. Most take place in the UK (usually the Lake District or Wales) but some go abroad e.g. on canoeing expeditions to Canada. The Duke of Edinburgh's Award Scheme supports personal and social development of young people aged 14-25 and has links with the main youth expedition organisers like *Adventureworks*. Most people become involved through their local school or youth club though it is possible to enlist through an Open Award Centre. Details are available on the DoE website (www.theaward.org) which includes a selection of 'Expedition Memories' including one by **Elisabeth Atkins**:

My favourite section throughout the Award was the Expedition, which gave me the opportunity to explore some exciting and beautiful places in the UK. The pinnacle was my Gold Award Exploration in Adelboden, Switzerland, where we explored the mountains and studied the course of the river from its source in the mountains to the town. Some of the Expeditions were gruelling at times, negotiating our way through mud and rain, but I have fond memories, even of the tough parts! The Award was a wonderful way to try new activities, to learn new skills, to meet interesting people and to gain a great sense of achievement.
The British Schools Exploring Society (see entry for BSES Expeditions below) organ-

ises an impressive range of expeditions. In most cases, they achieve a reasonable balance of participants, about half girls, half boys, about half from private schools and half from state, and a good distribution of regional origins (with a traditional concentration from Devon and some from Scotland and Wales). Expedition members undergo a training weekend outside Sheffield in April so that they can meet the others going on the expedition and can be assessed for fitness. At the weekend there are presentations by the project leaders about the various environmental projects on the expedition and a chance to learn how to use all the new equipment.

Another organisation that aims to prepare young people aged 16-18 for adulthood through a structured leadership programme is Fulcrum Challenge (Unit 7, Luccombe Business Centre, Milton Abbas, Dorset DT11 OBD; 01258 881399; office@fulcrum-challenge.org). Challenges organised for carefully selected candidates include an intensive team-building weekend, an environmental weekend, introduction to financial management, a two-week overseas visit to a developing country and a post-placement conference focusing on business and careers. School leavers must have the endorsement of their headteachers in order to be considered for one of the six challenges held each year. The cost of the programme is about £1,400, though there are some assisted places.

Sailing Adventures

Several youth-oriented organisations and charities take young people on character-building sailing expeditions, some on traditional tall ships. Fees vary enormously. The Association of Sea Training Organisations (ASTO) is the umbrella group for sail training organisations in the UK and their website is a useful link to sail training schemes (www.asto.org.uk). ASTO is based at the Royal Yachting Association, RYA House, Ensign Way, Hamble, Southampton SO31 4YA (0845 345 0400) and is affiliated to the newly set up international organisation Sail Training International (5 Mumby Road, Gosport, Hants. PO12 1AA; 023-9258 6367; office@sailtraininginternational.org). See entries for *Sail Training Association, Ocean Youth Trust* and *JST Youth Leadership @ Sea Scheme*.

Commercial crew agencies match willing sailors with sailing expeditions looking for

crew. For example Global Crew Network (145 Bracklyn Court, London N1 7EJ; 07773 361959; info@globalcrewnetwork.com/ www.globalcrewnetwork.com) specialises in crew recruitment for tall ships, traditional boats and luxury yachts worldwide; discounts on membership available for students. The Tall Ships People (Moorside, South Zeal Village, Okehampton, Devon EX20 2JX; ☎/fax 01837 840919; jacci@thetallshipspeople.freese rve.co.uk; www.tallshipspeople.com) co-ordinate crew placement for vessels taking part in the *Cutty Sark* Tall Ships Race. The 2004 race will visit the ports of Antwerp, Aalborg, Stavanger and Cuxhaven between July 21st and August 18th. Trainees are aged 15-25 and of mixed nationalities; some are using the trip as the residential element of the Duke of

Edinburgh Gold Award. The price begins at around £250. General sailing adventures are also available (from £150) for those who do not wish to race but to learn to sail, including navigation and standing watch.

Those who want to do some sail training during their gap year but who are short of funds should ask the training organisation whether any financial assistance is available. The Norfolk Boat (Harrisons Farmhouse, East Tuddenham, Dereham, Norfolk NR20 3NF; 01603 881121; info@norfolkboat.org.uk) offers financial assistance to East Anglian residents aged 12-24 or disabled people of any age who can't afford but would like to experience the challenge and fun of deep sea sailing with various accredited sailing organisations.

Fundraising

Expeditions tend to be among the most expensive among gap year placements, and some of the targets fixed by the major organisations are truly daunting. See the section on Fundraising in the chapter 'Planning and Preparation' for ideas on how to earn, save and persuade others to give you the necessary funds.

Those with a specialised project might discover that targeted funds are available from trusts and charities. However many, like the Mount Everest Foundation (www.mef.org.uk/mefguide.htm), are earmarked for high level expeditions undertaking first ascents, new routes and scientific research on mountains, which are beyond the capabilities of someone in a gap year.

Relevant companies are sometimes willing to give equipment in lieu of a cheque, though most manufacturers of hiking and camping equipment are inundated with requests. Successful supplicants often present imaginative ways in which they plan to publicise their benefactors' products.

Sponsored Expeditions for Charity

A large and growing number of charities in the UK now offer adventurous group travel to individuals who are prepared to undertake some serious fundraising on their behalf. So popular and so energetically marketed has this kind of trip become that it even warrants its own heading 'Travel for Charity' in the travel advertisements of the *Independent* broadsheet. Household names like Oxfam, the Youth Hostels Association and the Children's Society organise sponsored trips, as do many more obscure good causes. Specialist agent Charity Challenge allows you to select your trip and which charity you would like to support. They have an extensive brochure available (7th Floor, Northway House, 1379 High Road, London N20 9LP; 020-8557 0000; www.charitychallenge.com). Participants are asked to raise £2,300 (say) for the charity and in return receive a 'free' trip. You are in a far stronger position to ask people for donations if you can say you are supporting the Children's Society/British Heart Fund/Whale Conservation Society or whatever, than if you say you are trying to raise money for a holiday to Morocco/Patagonia/Borneo. These trips are usually of short duration and more attractive to older people looking for an interesting way to take a gap than to school-leavers.

DIRECTORY OF EXPEDITIONS

ADVENTUREWORKS
The Foundry Studios, 45 Mowbray St, Sheffield S3 8EN. ☎ 0114 276 3322 or 0845 345 8850. Fax: 0114 276 3344. E-mail: info@adventureworks.co.uk. Website: www.adventureworks.co.uk.
Youth arm of mountaineering expedition organiser Jagged Globe (www.jagged-globe.co.uk) at the same address. Company is keen to enable young people of all backgrounds to become involved in remote and wilderness travel.
Programme description: Organises climbing, trekking and other expeditions for schools and youth groups. Gap year expedition to Kilimanjaro for individuals organised in 2003.
Destinations: Primarily Peak District but also 9-day summer expedition based in the Benasque region of the Pyrénées. Jagged Globe has destinations worldwide including Antarctica.
Prerequisites: Caters primarily for groups including Duke of Edinburgh Gold Award expeditions. Fitness and enthusiasm required.
Selection procedures and orientation: Pre-expedition planning and training weekends in the Peak District. Courses in winter climbing offered in Wales and the Lake District. Distribute fundraising and sponsorship pack.
Cost: 7-day expeditionary trips in the UK cost from £200. Trip to Pyrénées costs £750 including flights to Barcelona, 2 days of acclimatisation, planning and preparation before undertaking 4-day expedition. Sample price of 24-day climb of Aconcagua in the Andes is £ 3,000.

BORDERS EXPLORATION GROUP
c/o Alan McGhee, 3 Burnfoot, Hawick TD9 8ED. ☎ 01450 376996. E-mail: Bordexpgp@Beeb.net. Website: www.borders-exploration-group.org.uk.
Borders Exploration Group is a non-profit making organisation which organises international expeditions every other year, primarily for young people resident in the Scottish borders.
Programme description: Expeditions are organised and led by teams of volunteer leaders. Every expedition consists of 4 phases: Community, Adventure, Environmental and Social.
Destinations: Previous expeditions have been to Lesotho, Ecuador, Kenya, Mongolia, India and (in 2003) Peru. In the years when no large international expedition takes place the group organises a smaller European expedition, most recently to Romania.
Number of placements per expedition: About 35 on international, 12 on European.
Prerequisites: Must live in Scottish Borders catchment area. Minimum age 16. Humour, stamina, initiative, communication and application are needed.
Selection procedures and orientation: Participants are selected during an outdoor adventure day. Training starts almost a year before the expedition departs and is run over 6 training weekends. Basic first aid and camping skills are taught.
Cost: Participants will be expected to raise their own funds (minimum £1,600 in 2003) through a wide range of fundraising initiatives.
Contact: Allan McGee or Alan Young.

BRATHAY EXPLORATION GROUP TRUST LTD
Brathay Hall, Ambleside, Cumbria LA22 0HP. ☎/fax: 01539 433942. E-mail: admin@brathayexploration.org.uk. Website: www.brathayexploration.org.uk.
Established 1947.
Programme description: Runs expeditions and expeditionary courses for young people. Emphasis on conservation of the environment.
Destinations: Worldwide, varying from year to year. 2003 expeditions to Tanzania, South Africa, Malaysia, Mongolia, New Zealand, Western USA, Morocco, Norway, the Alps and

some in the UK. 2004 expeditions to Belize, Bolivia, India, Northwest Canada, Corsica, the European Alps, Norway, the Shetland Islands, the Scottish Highlands and the Lake District.
Number of placements per year: 250.
Prerequisites: Ages 15-24. No qualifications needed. People with disabilities welcome to apply.
Duration and time of placements: 1-5 weeks between spring and autumn.
Selection procedures & orientation: Briefings and pre-departure training sessions on survival skills, first aid and scientific research.
Cost: Up to £2,000 for month-long overseas expeditions (excluding airfares); less for trips in UK, e.g. £415 for 15 day adventure on Mull.
Contact: Ron Barrow, Administrator.

BSES EXPEDITIONS
Royal Geographical Society, 1 Kensington Gore, London SW7 2AR. ☎ 020-7591 3141. Fax: 020-7591 3140. E-mail: bses@rgs.org. Website: www.bses.org.uk.
The British Schools Exploring Society is a UK charity which was founded by a member of Scott's Antarctic Expedition. It has provided the opportunity for young people to take part in exploratory expeditions in remote regions since 1932.
Programme description: The expeditions aim to combine living in gruelling and testing conditions with valuable scientific and environmental research. Past expeditions have included climbing a 22,000ft peak in India, investigating the rare spiral aloe plant in Lesotho, scientific field-work through the arctic winter in Eastern Greenland, sea kayaking in Alaska and a year-long expedition in the Arctic. In 2004 there will be a 6-week expedition to South Africa and 4/5-week expeditions to Arctic Svalbard, Tanzania and Iceland.
Destinations: Worldwide, for example Greenland, Scandinavia (including Svalbard, formerly Spitsbergen), Arctic Russia, Alaska, Antarctica, Kenya, Morocco, Sinai, Namibia, Lesotho, Nepal and India. Destinations change from year to year.
Number of placements per year: 180-220.
Prerequisites: Must be aged between 16 and 20 and in a good state of fitness both mental and physical. Candidates are chosen according to their suitability to a particular expedition.
Duration and time of placement: Expedition lengths vary from 4 weeks to 4 months and take place during the summer holidays and throughout the Gap Year.
Selection procedures and orientation: Places are allocated on a first come first served basis on completion of a successful interview. Short-listed applicants will be called for interview in London or a regional office. On accepting the offer of a place, Young Explorers take part in a briefing weekend held prior to their expedition, either in the North of England or at the RGS. Following the expedition an annual gathering is held for a presentation about the experience.
Cost: £2,500-£3,500. BSES Expeditions offer lots of help and guidance on fundraising. No one showing appropriate commitment and effort in raising the contribution will be denied a place.

CORAL CAY CONSERVATION
The Tower, 13ᵗʰ Floor, 125 High Street, Colliers Wood, London SW19 2JG. ☎ 0870 750 0668. Fax: 0870 750 0667. E-mail: info@coralcay.org. Website: www.coralcay.org
Recruits paying volunteers to assist with tropical forest and coral reef conservation expeditions in Honduras, Mexico, Cuba, Philippines, Malaysia and Fiji. Details in 'Directory of Specialist Gap Year Programmes'.

DORSET EXPEDITIONARY SOCIETY
Chickerell Road, Weymouth, Dorset DT4 9SY. ☎/fax: 01305 775599. E-mail: dorsetexp@wdi.co.uk. Website: www.dorsetexp.co.uk.

The Dorset Expeditionary Society encourages and organises adventurous opportunities for young people from throughout the UK. All leaders are volunteers. Expeditions can qualify for two elements of the Duke of Edinburgh Gold Award.

Programme description: Adventure holidays are organised where young people go trekking, mountain climbing, kayaking, white water rafting, mountain biking and on safari, and see other world cultures.

Destinations: Europe, North and South America, Africa, India and Asia, always to wilderness areas off the tourist track.

Prerequisites: Participants must be fit and healthy. Minimum age 15 for some expeditions, 16/18 for others.

Duration and time of placements: 3-5 weeks, usually in the summer holidays.

Selection procedures and orientation: Selection weekend to choose suitable candidates. Training courses for aspiring leaders are organised to gain nationally-recognised qualifications such as Basic Expedition Leaders Award, Mountain First Aid Certificate, Cave Leadership and Mountain Leadership Award.

Cost: £50 for the selection weekend plus expedition costs (roughly £400-£2,000). Guidance on fundraising is given.

Contact: Keith Eagleton, Secretary.

THE EXPEDITION COMPANY LTD
PO Box 17, Wiveliscombe, Taunton, Somerset TA4 2YL. ☎ 01984 624780. Fax: 01984 629045. E-mail: info@expedition.co.uk. Website: www.expedition.co.uk.

Programme description: Expedition consultants. Source and lead a variety of adventure and development training opportunities overseas to match clients' expectations.

Destinations: Worldwide, e.g. Tanzania, Morocco, Kenya, Nicaragua, Costa Rica, Corsica, Gozo (Malta) and North Wales.

Number of placements per expedition: 20-25 in pre-arranged groups from one school, university or company.

Prerequisites: Minimum age for short-haul destinations is 14, for longhaul 16 and for gap years 18-19. Must have certificate of fitness from doctor.

Duration and time of placements: 1-6 months.

Selection procedures and orientation: Rolling training programme starting every 3 months. Expeditions tend to have a 2-year life cycle to allow time for fundraising.

Cost: £1,500-£2,500. Price includes 7 days (in total) of training in Devon, but excludes airfares.

Contact: Matt Cambridge, Director.

FRONTIER
50-52 Rivington St, London EC2A 3QP. ☎ 020-7613 2422. E-mail: info@frontierconservation.org. Website: www.frontierconservation.org.

See 'Directory of Specialist Gap Year Programmes' for details of Frontier's conservation projects in Tanzania, Madagascar, Vietnam, the Andaman Islands and Nicaragua.

GLOBAL VISION INTERNATIONAL (GVI)
Nomansland, Wheathampstead, St. Albans, Herts. AL4 8EJ. ☎ 01582 831300. Fax: 01582 834002. E-mail: info@gvi.co.uk. Website: www.gvi.co.uk.

Programme description: Since 1998, GVI has been providing overseas expeditions in Africa, Latin America, Asia and Australasia. See relevant chapters for details.

Destinations: South Africa, Swaziland, Madagascar, Ecuador, Brazil, Mexico, Panama, Guatemala, Nepal, China, Indonesia, Thailand and New Zealand.

Number of placements per year: 500-600.

Prerequisites: None. Minimum age 18. All nationalities welcome.

Duration and time of placements: 2 weeks to one year.

Selection procedures and orientation: Some projects require a telephone interview; others require only a completed application form.

Cost: from £595 to £2,995.
Contact: James Scipioni, Volunteer Co-ordinator.

JST YOUTH LEADERSHIP @ SEA SCHEME
Jubilee Sailing Trust, Hazel Road, Woolston, Southampton SO19 7GB. ☎ 023-8044 9108. Fax: 023-8044 9145. E-mail: info@jst.org.uk. Website: www.jst.org.uk.
Courses offered: Leadership course on a sea voyage to develop communication, leadership and team skills.
Prerequisites: Ages 16-25.
Selection procedures and orientation: By written application; mark form with 'Youth Leadership @ Sea' and enclose short personal statement.
Cost: The JST Youth Leadership @ Sea Scheme offers young people aged 16-25 up to £300 towards the cost of any voyage (prices start from £495).

Fancy an Adventure with a Difference?

Why not take on the ultimate adventure onboard a spectacular square-rig sailing ship?

The Jubilee Sailing Trust (JST), provide adventure sailing holidays onboard The LORD NELSON and TENACIOUS, the only specially designed tall ships in the world that enable people of mixed abilities to crew a tall ship together on equal terms.

The ships sail to a range of destinations including popular UK and European ports, the Caribbean and the Canary Islands. For the ultimate sailing experience, the 4 weeks transatlantic voyage will give you a real taste of the challenge and adventure that crewing a tall ship provides.

Climb the mast, furl the sails and take the helm – all things that YOU will do as part of the active voyage crew. The JST runs a Leadership @ Sea scheme, which is a fantastic opportunity and a great way to spend a gap year for all 16-25 year olds. Onboard, you will get to develop your leadership, communication and seamanship skills by facing unique challenges and working outside of your usual environment. The JST Leadership @ Sea Scheme also qualifies you for the gold residential part of the Duke of Edinburgh's Award, is great fun and will look brilliant on your CV.

For more info visit www.jst.org.uk, email: leadership@jst.org.uk or tel: 02380 449108

OASIS OVERLAND
The Marsh, Henstridge, Somerset BA8 0TF. ☎ 01963 363400. Fax: 01963 363200. E-mail: info@oasisoverland.co.uk. Website: www.oasisoverland.co.uk.
Overland expedition company founded in 1997.
Destinations: South America, Africa, Middle East and Egypt.
Number of placements per expedition: Purpose-built trucks carry up to 24.
Duration: Large choice (see website) between 10 days and 29 weeks.
Cost: From £65 a week plus £30 kitty on longest trips, rising to £135 plus £60 kitty in South America. Sample expedition 105 days Quito to Rio costs £1,890 plus US$1,250 kitty paid locally.
Contact: Chris Wrede, Director.

OCEAN YOUTH TRUST SOUTH
Spur House, 1, The Spur, Alverstoke, Gosport, Hampshire PO12 2NA. ☎ 0870 241 2252. Fax: 0870 909 0230. E-mail: oytsouth@aol.com. Website: www.oyt.org.uk.
Adventure sail training organisation originally formed as Ocean Youth Club over 40 years ago, now operating as 6 separate regions altogether running more than 250 voyages from 40 UK ports every year and giving 3,000 young people the chance to sail. Links from above website to OYT North-east, North-west, Scotland, Northern Ireland and East. Each regional group sails one vessel with berths for 12 crew.
Programme description: Short sailing voyages on ocean-going yacht from ports around the coast of the UK.
Destinations: Website posts crew vacancies on forthcoming voyages.
Pre-requisites: Ages 12-25 years. Must be able to swim 50 metres. No sailing experience required.
Duration and time of placements: 2-7 days between March and November.
Selection procedures & orientation: By written application.
Cost: Vary according to duration and date, from £210 to £450 for a 6-day voyage. Mates' fees are less if sailing as sea staff. Grants are sometimes available to help with voyage fees.

OUTWARD BOUND GLOBAL
☎ 0870 513 4227. E-mail: globalexpeditions@outwardbound-uk.org. Website: www.outwardbound-uk.org/global.
Long-established organisation whose mission is to widen access for young people to experience adventure in the outdoors. Has centres in 30 countries.
Programme description: Recently introduced international expeditions for individuals and groups.
Destinations: in 2003 to Mount Kinabalu, Sabah (Malaysia), Tatras Mountains (Slovakia), Outeniqua Mountains (South Africa) and Carpathian Mountains (Romania). Planning expedition to Arctic Finland in 2004.
Prerequisites: age ranges vary, e.g. 16-20, 16-18 or 18-25.
Duration and time of placements: 2-4 weeks.
Cost: sample prices £2,200 for 22 days in Sabah for participants aged 16-18. £950 for 15 days in Slovakia.
Contact: Kevin or Dom.

RALEIGH INTERNATIONAL
Raleigh House, 27 Parsons Green Lane, London SW6 4HZ. ☎ 020-7371 8585. Fax: 020-7371 5116. E-mail: info@raleigh.org.uk. Website: www.raleighinterna tional.org.

Well-established youth development charity which sends groups of young people aged 17-25 on expeditions around the world where they take part in adventure, community and environmental projects. See further listings in the 'Directory of Specialist Gap Year Programmes', and in chapters on Africa, Asia and Latin America; the latter includes a first-hand account of a volunteer's experiences in Chile.

SAIL TRAINING ASSOCIATION
2A The Hard, Portsmouth, Hants. PO1 3PT. ☎ 023-9283 2055. Fax: 023-9281 5769. E-mail: TallShips@sta.org.uk. Website: www.sta.org.uk.
Youth charity which runs adventure sail training voyages year round on 60 metre square rigged ships *Prince William* and *Stavros S Niarchos*.
Programme description: Voyages lasting up to two weeks accept young people as crew members. These take place in the waters around the UK and Northern Europe in the summer and around the Canaries and Azores between November and May.
Prerequisites: Minimum age 16 with an upper age limit of 24 on most trips, though a few scheduled expeditions are intended for people 16-19.
Selection procedures & orientation: No previous sailing experience needed. Must demonstrate ability to work well with others.
Cost: About £65 per day (plus flights for voyages in the Canaries/Azores). Cash grants may be available.

SEASCAPE RESEARCH & EDUCATION
Mr. Pleasant, Bequia, St. Vincent, West Indies. ☎/fax: 784-528-6965. E-mail: earthship@acrossthesea.net. Website: www.acrossthesea.net.
Programme description: Multidisciplinary projects, sailing and scuba programmes aboard 200ft tall ship. Earthship programme offers marine science studies, management of coastal resources, etc. and accreditation in scuba (up to PADI Divemaster) and Ship's Crew (Bridge Watch Certification). People interested in Geography can study Geographic Information Systems (GIS).
Destinations: Caribbean Sea.
Number of placements per year: 30-60 staying for different periods. Participants come from all over the world.
Prerequisites: Must be highly motivated and possess patience, commitment, an ability to work in a team and tolerance of people from many backgrounds.
Duration and time of placements: 12-week Experience Programme, 1-month Internship, 15-week and 30-week Student Crew Programmes. Ship sails September to April with summer programmes pending.
Selection procedures and orientation: Telephone interviews before acceptance.
Cost: 2-weeks $1,250, 1 month $2,200, 15 weeks $4,200, 30 weeks $7,500. Reductions on 30-week programme possible for qualifying individuals. Scuba training costs extra ($200 a week) if staying less than 15 weeks.
Contact: Kurt Cordice, Programme Director/Co-ordinator.

TANGENT EXPEDITIONS
3 Millbeck, New Hutton, Kendal, Cumbria LA8 0BD. ☎ 01539 737757. Fax: 01539 737756. E-mail: paul@ tangent-expeditions.co.uk. Website: www.tangent-expeditions.co.uk.
Programme description: Mountaineering, climbing and ski-touring expeditions organised since 1989. Chance to make first ascents of previously unclimbed but easy grade alpine peaks in the Arctic.
Destinations: Greenland and Spitsbergen.
Prerequisites: Minimum age 18. Must have prior winter walking experience and attend a pre-expedition training weekend.
Duration and time of placements: Variable though most are 22 days.
Cost: £2,750-£5,000.

Contact: Paul Walker, Director.

TREKFORCE EXPEDITIONS
34 Buckingham Palace Road, London SW1W 0RE. ☎ 020-7828 2275. Fax: 020-7828 2276. E-mail: info@trekforce.org.uk. Website: www.trekforce.org.uk.
Expedition Programmes that suit gap year students (and others) in the rainforests of Central and South America and East Malaysia, concentrating on conservation and scientific expeditions. Extended programmes of up to five months offer a combination of conservation project work, learning languages (Spanish or Portuguese) and teaching in rural communities.

VENTURE CO WORLDWIDE
The Ironyard, 64-66 The Market Place, Warwick CV34 4SD. ☎ 01926 411122. Fax: 01926 411133. E-mail: mail@ventureco-worldwide.com. Website: www.ventureco-worldwide.com.
Programme description: Gap Year and Career Gap specialist whose 4-month programmes in Latin America, India/Nepal, West Africa and Indochina incorporate an 8 or 9 week expedition through the Andes, Himalayas, Sahara Desert and China highlands including the Everest Base Camp Trek. Trek route planning and day-to-day organisation is done by team members, and leadership roles are shared out (see entry in 'Directory of Specialist Gap Year Programmes').

WILDERNESS TRUST
The General's Orchard, The Ridge, Little Baddow, Essex CM3 4SX. ☎/fax 01245 221565. E-mail: info@wilderness-trust.org. Website: www.wilderness-trust.org.
Organisation dedicated to the preservation of wilderness and wild areas. Objectives are to educate about the value of wilderness, campaign for preservation of areas around the globe and to give direct experience of wild areas through sensitively guided trails and conservation volunteering (see *Directory of Voluntary Placements Abroad*).
Programme description: Annual trails to remote areas of South Africa, Norway and Scotland, in partnership with wilderness guides who emphasise the philosophical, spiritual and ecological elements of the wild. Trails have minimum impact on the environment, i.e. all equipment is carried in and out in backpacks and participants sleep under the stars.
Destinations: Norway (Arctic Circle), South Africa, Scotland, Canada.
Number of placements per expedition: up to 8.
Prerequisites: Must be at least 16.
Duration and time of placements: 5-15 days.
Cost: £325-£500 depending on length excluding travel to starting point.
Contact: Jo Roberts, Director.

WIND, SAND & STARS
6 Tyndale Terrace, London N1 2AT. ☎ 020-7359 7551. Fax: 020-7359 4936. E-mail: office@windsandstars.co.uk. Website: www.windsandstars.co.uk.
In operation for 13 years.
Programme description: Annual summer student expedition to the desert and mountains of the Sinai, travelling and working with local Bedouin families on community based projects. Opportunities for expedition Leaders, Assistant Leaders and Medical Officers.
Prerequisites: Ages 16-23.
Duration and time of placements: 4 weeks in the summer.
Selection procedures & orientation: Pre-departure training day.
Cost: Approximately £2,000 though special price for 2003: £1,300 plus return flight.
Contact: Amelia Stewart, Operations Executive.

WORLD CHALLENGE EXPEDITIONS
Black Arrow House, 2 Chandos Road, London NW10 6NF. ☎ 020-8728 7222.

E-mail: welcome@world-challenge.co.uk. Website: www.world-challenge.co.uk.
Parent company of Gap Challenge (see 'Directory of Specialist Gap Year Programmes').
Programme description: Two types of expedition: Team Challenge and First Challenge.
In a Team Challenge expedition, students plan and lead their own 4 or 6-week expedition,
e.g. trekking through the jungles of Borneo and hiking in the Andes. First Challenge offers
an introduction to an expedition from 8-14 days attempting to climb North Africa's highest
mountain in Morocco or crossing the Corinth Canal to the Peloponnese in Greece.
Destinations: Variety of countries worldwide.
Prerequisites: Team Challenge is the core programme of World Challenge Expeditions.
Each expedition lasts one month but is preceded by 15-20 months of careful planning and
preparation.
Duration: 4 weeks between June and September.

XCL LIMITED
**Reaseheath, Nantwich, Cheshire CW5 6DF. ☎/fax: 01270 625825. Fax: 01270
627014. E-mail: enquiries@xcl.info.**
Programme description: Bi-annual expedition to changing destination involves 2 weeks
of working alongside indigenous people followed by a week-long adventurous phase.
Destinations: Past expeditions have been run to Guyana, Uganda, India and Borneo.
Number of placements per expedition: 50.
Prerequisites: 'Ordinary people doing extraordinary things'.
Duration and time of placements: 2-3 weeks.
Selection procedures and orientation: Registration form and 2 residential training
weekends in the UK which include country and culture orientation, team working, health
and safety, project briefings and preparation.
Cost: £2,150 in total.
Contact: Naomi Starling.

YORKSHIRE SCHOOLS EXPLORING SOCIETY
**1A Garnett Street, Otley, West Yorkshire, LS21 1AL. ☎/fax: 01943 468049. E-
mail: admin@yses.freeserve.co.uk. Website: www.leeds.ac.uk/sports_science/yses.**
Programme description: Expeditions are organised to wilderness areas most recently to
Tibet and the American West. Young leaders are needed to assist with the expeditions.
Number of placements per year: Around 70/80.
Prerequisites: Students on the expeditions must be in full-time education in Yorkshire
(excluding Gap Year students). Leaders can come from anywhere and need not be in
full-time education.
Duration and time of placements: 4-5 weeks.
Selection procedures and orientation: Selection weekend held in the Yorkshire
Dales where applicants undertake rigorous mental and physical tasks. Good training is
given prior to departure, plus help with fundraising. Leaders are required to send a CV.
Experience is regarded as just as important as written qualifications. They may also have
to attend the selection weekend.
Cost: £1,500-£3,500.
Contact: Humaira Khan, Society Administrator.

YOUNG EXPLORERS' TRUST
**c/o YET Secretary, Stretton Cottage, Wellow Road, Ollerton, Newark, Notts.
NG22 9AX. ☎/fax: 01623 861027. E-mail: ted@theyet.org. Website:
www.theyet.org.**
The Young Explorers' Trust is the Association of Youth Exploration Societies which advises
and assists groups of students who wish to organise their own expedition during their gap
year. They organise short courses on how to plan for an expedition.

Work Experience

Any school leaver lucky enough to have some idea of what career he or she is aiming for can try to build into their gap year a component of working in a related field. Work experience considered in its broadest terms applies to any experience of the world of work. A steady stint in even a boring job will enhance your CV and it might also have the salutary effect of reinforcing your desire to get more education so that you won't be consigned forever to the kind of jobs normally available to 18 year olds.

Although all UK schools are obliged to organise five or ten-day work placements for students in Year 10, a longer period spent working in a particular area gives a much clearer idea of what a job is about and whether it is of interest for your potential future. Even if a work placement is irrelevant to your future plans, it will at least provide a useful introduction to how companies or organisations function.

Work placements are looked upon favourably by university admissions officers; experience of the 'real world' often helps students to develop a more mature outlook on life which enables them to do relatively better at university than their peers who come straight from school. Similarly, employers view students with work experience as more desirable. There is less risk for an employer in choosing someone who has already had some exposure to a particular career, and also less expense in training.

Employers, especially in companies with an international profile, look for employees who have demonstrated that they are open-minded and can adapt to different cultures. One way to impress these employers is with a CV that shows that you have successfully completed a period of work experience abroad. This is particularly impressive if the student uses or learns a foreign language as part of this experience. However, experience in the USA or Australia also tends to be popular and is also viewed favourably by companies.

Nowadays, the demand for many careers often outweighs supply, and exam qualifications no longer seem to be enough to get a job. Work experience can be used as a means of getting a foot in the door with particular companies and occupations. If you are interested in gaining work experience in a competitive field like media, publishing, broadcasting, museology, veterinary science, wildlife conservation, etc. you may find it very difficult to obtain paid work. If you're serious about enhancing your CV or simply getting a taste of what it will be really like, you should be prepared to work on a voluntary basis, which is now standard practice in many professions (for example conservation).

If you foresee yourself working in business, engineering, banking, accountancy or industry after graduation, you may be able to arrange a relevant work experience placement in your year between school and university. Not only are you likely to be able to earn and save money but with luck they will like you enough to offer you future vacation jobs or even a permanent career. **Nicky Stead** from West Yorkshire found herself in the unwelcome position of being forced to take a gap year when her A-level results were worse than expected. Undaunted, she decided to work locally before embarking on some world travels (see Australia chapter):

I had to get a job and decided that to make the best of things I should get a job that was relevant to my preferred career and would look good on my CV as well as raise money for travelling. I got a job inputting mortgage applications for Skipton Building Society for six months, which I really enjoyed. I made so many friends and I loved the business environment. I felt grown up, and it was great. My appraisal was good and they encouraged me to stay.

FINDING A PLACEMENT

Several companies which take students for work placements for a substantial period are listed at the end of this chapter. It is worth visiting the local careers centre for the names of local companies who take on students. Students can also write directly to companies enclosing a CV to ask if they offer work placements, though the ratio of favourable replies is likely to be discouraging. The direct approach is more personal and likely to please potential employers, especially if there is a particular aspect of the company which students can say has attracted them.

Much can be achieved by confidently and persistently asking for the chance to help out in your chosen workplace unpaid. **Laura Hitchcock** (from the US) managed to fix up two three-month positions in the field of her career interest by agreeing to pay her own expenses if they would take her on and help her find accommodation in local homes. Her jobs were in the publicity departments of the Ironbridge Gorge Museums (Coach Road, Coalbrookdale, Shropshire TF8 7DQ; education@ironbridge.org.uk) and then in a theatre-arts centre in East Anglia (The Quay at Sudbury, Quay Lane, Sudbury, Suffolk CO10 6AN). Laura discovered that if you were willing to help yourself people could be extremely helpful and encouraging.

However, there are often benefits to working for companies with specific Gap Year programmes. They tend to make their programmes interesting and varied to impress students. Work placement trainees are often regarded as a good investment as they may choose to take a job with the company after their degree, provided they are treated well. For example, the Accenture Horizons School Sponsorship Scheme is a gap year programme which lasts eight months from September and combines training with paid work experience. Accenture (formerly Andersen Consulting) pays £18,500 (pro rata, so equivalent to about £12,400 for the eight months) plus a travel bursary of £1,600 on completion of a satisfactory period of work, which leaves plenty of time and money for travelling before university in the autumn. Because of the high rewards, acceptance is very competitive as one contributor to the gapyear.com messageboard describes:

I applied for Accenture's 2002/03 gap year scheme and got through the first interview (which was friendly, though they definitely wanted to make sure I had done my research about the company). I was invited back for a further assessment afternoon where there were seven of us. We were split into two groups for a discussion on the most influential people of the 20th century – basically Accenture wanted to see how we worked with other people. I also had another interview which was pretty similar to the first. Although I felt that both these assessments went quite well, I didn't get offered a position. I think I probably just lacked a little bit of confidence compared to some of the others, although it was hard to tell exactly what Accenture was looking for. Basically, this is a tough scheme to get on, but the rewards are good. However, don't be disappointed if, like me, you are rejected! The actual selection process is good experience for job interviews and applications later in life, and on the plus side, I am now going to be spending more of my gap year abroad!

With the global downturn in business, companies that are household names like Marconi no longer accept gap year students claiming that 'the current market no longer supports student recruitment'. Yet many schemes are flourishingm including the ones run by *IBM* and *PriceWaterhouse Coopers* (see entries). The high profile gap year schemes are so competitive that many students seeking work experience will entertain more modest ambitions. Agency temping experience in different kinds of office can be a useful stepping stone not only to well-paid holiday work in the future but also to acquiring a broad acquaintance with the working world.

For more leads on work experience placements, check the website of the National Council for Work Experience, an organisation with charitable status which aims to promote work experience for students and thereby help the economy. The searchable list of opportunities is available on the national universities careers website www.prospects.ac.uk. The majority of work experience placements are designed for university students and many university careers services have excellent databases of prospective hiring companies.

The Windsor Fellowship offers sponsorship to high-achieving school-leavers from African, African-Caribbean and Asian communities in the UK who want to pursue careers in science, engineering and maths. The professional development programme funded by the Fellowship includes a work placement and its website (www.windsorfellowship.org) includes lots of information and advice on work experience.

Individual universities cater mainly to a local population but can be worth searching; try for example the University of Keele Careers website (www.keele.ac.uk/depts/aa/careers/wkexperience/workexp.htm) and the University of Stirling (www.careers.stir.ac.uk). Shorter placements may be found in the Vacation Trainee sections of the annually revised *Directory of Summer Jobs in Britain* from Vacation Work Publications (£9.99). These shorter placements are suitable for students who wish to spend their year out fitting in more than just work experience.

Robin Campbell graduated from Framlingham College and fixed up a work experience placement for the summer by applying to engineering companies listed on a leaflet put out by the Institution of Civil Engineers. He landed a job with Sir Robert McAlpine working on a building project in London's Docklands (which turned out to be in sharp contrast to his later gap year experiences, teaching in Sri Lanka through the Project Trust):

Well, here I am, one month since leaving school and I am sitting in my room, in a three storey house, half a mile from the Millennium Dome, working in the London Docklands - not bad! I'm here working on the Excel project for Sir Robert McAlpine for vocational employment during the summer. The Excel (or London International Exhibition Centre) is a huge building, looking similar to Stansted Airport's Terminal, with the largest roof in Europe, which means a lot of walking. It takes up all of the north side of the Royal Victoria Dock, which is located next to the Millennium Dome...Sir Robert McAlpine are a very high-up construction company, having built in part the Millennium Dome, the good bit of the Millennium Bridge...we could go on! Anyway they are a firm which seems to have a good atmosphere and treats its employees well. More importantly they are very keen to attract the 'next generation' of engineers, which translates to a very attractive set of sponsorship opportunities and graduate placements. That means money, experience and CV building stuff!... The sense of independence is only just beginning to sink in, I think the thing that hit it all home was driving to the supermarket on the first day, having to set out shopping for the coming week!

Year in Industry

The *Year in Industry* scheme is by far the most important provider of gap year industrial placements in the country. More than 600 students are placed in companies where they gain experience of real, hands-on work. This figure represents an increase of more than 50% on two years ago. Students should be interested in following a career in industry and must have met the requirements for a confirmed place at university. Most participants are intending to study engineering, science or business though other disciplines are acceptable. The placements generally last for 11 months, from August/September to mid-July, with a minimum salary of £8,000-£11,000. The work experience is reinforced by a compulsory series of structured short courses at a nearby college or university. The student is required to submit a project for presentation at the end of the year.

Some companies choose to sponsor a student through university or offer vacation work. One success story of the Year In Industry programme is **Alexander Taylor** who developed a new touch-screen monitor in record time at his work placement company, Densitron Computers Ltd. He was given full responsibility for developing a 15-inch flat screen monitor and was able to see the project through from start to finish:

I'd heard so many tales of students wasting their gap year that I was hesitant about making the break. However, I couldn't have been further from the truth. I have gained a valuable insight into engineering which can't be gained from any text book.

WORK EXPERIENCE ABROAD

According to a representative from the Global Work Experience Association, 'Work Experience is the fastest growing sector in the world of youth travel today.' Established in October 2003, the GWEA has about 100 member organisations actively engaged in arranging international work experience placements. The organisations include language schools providing work experience, youth exchange agencies, training organisations and student travel agencies. GWEA's stated aim is to 'promote work experience programmes for young people throughout the world in order to strengthen cultural and economic ties among nations'. Its website www.gwea.org includes clear links to its members and is a good starting place for anyone interested in fixing up work experience (most of which is unpaid) in Europe. Most mediating organisations charge a substantial fee for their services, normally between €750 and €1,500, which may not include living expenses.

Predictably it is easier for students a little further along in their education than their gap year to find a suitable placement. For example the agencies running the internship programme for the USA are looking for university students and recent graduates. Trainee exchange programmes like those run by *CIMO* in Finland and the *Swiss Federal Aliens Office* in Switzerland are also open to those who have completed part of their degree course (see country chapters).

Students and recent graduates in business, management science, marketing, accounting, finance, computer applications or economics may be interested in an organisation run by a global student network based in 87 countries. *AIESEC* – a French acronym for the International Association for Students of Economics and Management – has its UK headquarters at 29-31 Cowper St, 2nd Floor, London EC2A 4AP (www.workabroad.org.uk). It can organise placements in any of its member countries, aimed at giving participants an insight into living and working in another culture.

The *British Council* (10 Spring Gardens, London SW1A 2BN; www.britishcouncil.org/ education) has information about official work schemes and exchanges, many of them aimed at students. *IAESTE* is the abbreviation for the International Association for the Exchange of Students for Technical Experience (iaeste@britishcouncil.org; www.iaeste.org.uk). It provides international course-related vacation training for thousands of university-level students in 80 member countries. Placements are available in engineering, science, agriculture, architecture and related fields. Undergraduates at UK universities should apply directly to *IAESTE UK* in the autumn term for placements commencing the following summer. The registration form is available on the website www.iaeste.org.uk. Students at universities in other countries should contact their own national IAESTE office through the website www.iaeste.org.

Some training and exchange organisations like *Interspeak* can place school leavers in the European workplace, usually for a substantial fee. Interspeak (01829 250641/ www.interspeak.co.uk) can arrange short and longer term traineeships (internships or *stages*) in France, Spain and Germany in the fields of marketing, international trade, computing, tourism, etc. Successful candidates live with host families. Their booking fee starts at £300 for 4-24 week placements; accommodation and board are normally charged at about £150 per week. **Andy Green** was placed by Interspeak in an office in Limoges in France:

The work I did in Limoges was purely work experience. I was unpaid which was fair enough as I was costing them time in explaining things, etc. Much of my time was spent accompanying the company reps on the road. I also did some very basic office work. The company took the view that I was not there to fill a job, but merely to observe. I learnt a lot, but it did cost me. You certainly have to be able to speak reasonable French before you go, and have some money. It cost about £1,000 for two months' accommodation with a family and the agency fee. If you can afford it, anyone can do it.

Interspeak also offer 'mini-stages' which last just one or two weeks. These appeal mostly to 17-19 year olds who pay an all-inclusive price from £550 (excluding travel).

Often there is a large area of overlap between work experience and volunteering, as **Cathleen Graham** found when she became a volunteer with the SCORE Programme (Sports Coaches Outreach) in South Africa, while pursuing development studies at university in Canada:

An opportunity to gain some work experience overseas was a stepping stone toward my longer-term goals. Living and working locally in another culture, language and country for a year would develop some skills relevant to work areas I was interested in: intercultural communication, development project work, sports development. In terms of disadvantages, some people don't see this kind of opportunity as taking steps toward your future, but rather as sidelining it and I sometimes had to deal with people's judgements. I also had to look ahead to when I came back home and try ahead of time, for my peace of mind anyhow, to define the next steps for me and how I would build on this experience. That was kind of critical, financially anyhow, because you are unlikely to earn much in your year away and you will probably spend some savings.

WORKING IN EUROPE

Legislation has existed for many years guaranteeing the rights of all nationals of the European Union to travel, reside, study and work in any member country. In addition, a number of special exchanges and youth programmes exist to help young Europeans to move easily across borders for short and longer periods. Various schemes have been established by the European Commission to provide financial aid to young people (normally aged 18-25) who wish to study, gain work experience or undertake a joint project with other young people in the EU. Many of these projects cannot be applied for directly by the student, but must be supported by their school, college or university. The best source of information is the Education and Training Group at the *British Council.*

From May 2004 the EU will consist of the original 15 member states (Austria, Belgium, Denmark, Finland, France, Germany, Greece, Ireland, Italy, Luxembourg, the Netherlands, Portugal, Spain, Sweden and the United Kingdom) plus Hungary, Poland, the Czech Republic, Slovakia, Slovenia, Estonia, Latvia, Lithuania, Malta and Cyprus. However nationals of these new member states will not necessarily be allowed to work in other member states straightaway. For example Italy, France and Germany (but not the UK) are imposing transitional controls so that it will be up to seven years from accession before full mobility of labour is allowed. Even once the legislation is in place, there are no guarantees that the red tape will disappear for exchange students and seasonal workers who wish to stay in a member state for a period longer than three months.

European Employment Service & Exchanges

Every EU country possesses a network of employment offices similar to British Jobcentres. A Europe-wide employment service called *EURES* (EURopean Employment Service) operates as a network of more than 400 EuroAdvisers who can access a database of jobs within Europe. These vacancies are usually for six months or longer, and for skilled, semi-skilled and managerial jobs. Language skills are almost always a requirement. Ask at your local Jobcentre how to contact your nearest EuroAdviser. In the UK most of the expertise is concentrated in the headquarters of the national Employment Service. Details on the EURES service can be obtained from the Overseas Placing Unit (Level 4, Skills House, 3-7 Holy Green, Off the Moor, Sheffield S1 4AQ; 0114 259 6051), or from the EURES website: http://europa.eu.int/eures/index.jsp.

Euroguidance Centres covering European careers have been set up in all EU member states to provide information on training, education and employment in Europe, mostly to help careers services and their clients. Careers Europe, Onward House, Baptist Place, Bradford BD1 2PS (01274 829600/fax 01274 829610; europe@careersb.co.uk/www.careerseurope.co.uk) produce the Eurofacts and Globalfacts series of International Careers Information, and Exodus, the Careers Europe database of international careers information, all of which can be consulted at local Connexions careers offices. Another source of information on European programmes is Eurodesk (Community Learning Scotland, Rosebery House, 9 Haymarket Terrace, Edinburgh EH12 5EZ; 0131-313 2488) which has an on-line database (www.eurodesk.org.uk).

The aim of the EU's *Leonardo da Vinci* programme is to improve the quality of vocational training systems and their capacity for innovation. The mobility measure offers opportunities for students and recent graduates to undertake work placements of between 3 and 12 months (for students) or between 2 and 12 months (recent graduates) in one of 30 European countries. It must be noted that applications for Leonardo funding must be submitted by organisations, not individuals.

The Europass is a passport-like document used to record skills gained during a period of work-based training in another European country. As above, only organisations can apply for European documents. Details will be available from university Placement Offices or International Relations Offices, or directly from the Leonardo and Europass Unit at the British Council (leonardo@britishcouncil.org/ www.leonardo.org.uk and europass@ britishcouncil.org/ www.europass-uk.co.uk) and from specific agencies that deliver the programme.

The specialist gap year programme offered to future engineers by the *Smallpeice Trust* includes a three-month study period in the UK followed by a four-week language course and a three-month period of work experience in Europe. By the end participants should be able to take an active part in an engineering project.

All these European schemes are reciprocal with many European students coming to Britain. A number of agencies assist European students to arrange internships in Britain where they can improve their English, for example:

Eagle UK, Eagle House, 177 Stourbridge Rd, Halesowen, W Midlands B63 3UD (0121-585 6177; www.eagle-uk.demon.co.uk. Business placements for 1-12 months combined with family stay.

EWEP (European Work Experience Programme), Unit 1, Red Lion Court, Alexandra Rd, Hounslow, Middlesex TW3 1JS (020-8572 2993; www.ewep.com). Charges an admin fee of £265.

LAF Ltd. 101-91 Western Road, Brighton, E Sussex BN1 2NW (01273 746 932; www.aplacement4.com).

Trident Transnational, The Smokehouse, Smokehouse Yard, 44-46 St John St, London EC1M 4DF (020-7014 1420; www.trident-transnational.org).

work-uk, 5 Cwrt-yr-Onnen, Llanbadarn, Aberystwyth SY23 3TD (☎/fax 01970 625247; enquiries@work-uk.demon.co.uk). Candidates must pay £119 per week for service including room and board.

Directory of Work Experience in the UK

ACCENTURE HORIZONS SCHOOL SPONSORSHIP SCHEME
60 Queen Victoria St, London EC4N 4TW. ☎ 0500 100189 (Recruiting helpline). E-mail: ukgraduates@accenture.com. Website: www.accenture.com/ukgraduates.
Programme description: Provides students looking to take a gap year with a combination of training, work experience and the opportunity to travel before going to university. The job involves working alongside high profile clients to deliver Management and IT consultancy solutions. Upon successful completion of the placement, an opportunity is given to do further paid summer vacation work while at university and potentially an offer of a permanent position on graduation.
Destinations: London base, however the work will require travel to client sites across the UK.
Prerequisites: Must be an A-level student currently in the upper sixth year. A strong record of academic achievement is important with good grades in Maths and English at GCSE level and a minimum of 300 UCAS points or 4 B's at Scottish Highers predicted. Candidates should be confident, enthusiastic and mature with excellent communication and team working skills.
Duration and time of placements: 8-month internships from September to April.
Selection procedures & orientation: All applications should be made on-line at www.accenture.com/ukgraduates. Interviews will be held from the September of the candidate's final year at school. Refer to website for closing date.
Remuneration: Candidates are paid the pro rata equivalent of £18,500 per year, with a possible travel bursary of £1,600 awarded at the end of the scheme. Depending on performance, financial sponsorship through university (up to £1,500 per year) and the chance to come back and work during summer holidays is extended.

ALSTOM POWER TECHNOLOGY CENTRE
Cambridge Road, Whetstone, Leicester LE8 6LH. ☎ 0116 284 5601. Fax: 0116 284 5461. Website: www.techcentreuk.power.alstom.com.
The Whetstone site has been involved in gas turbines since the 1940s. Specialising in engineering design, research and development, the company aims to develop the technologies of the future.
Programme description: Vacation trainees work on specialised engineering projects and fulfil a variety of other duties.
Number of placements: About 4.
Prerequisites: Students must be studying for a degree in Engineering or related technical subjects at university.
Duration and time of placements: 10-12 weeks over the summer period, with occasional vacancies during Christmas and Easter.
Remuneration: Pay is commensurate with the candidate's age and qualifications.
Contact: Miss H. Watkins, Human Resources Officer.

THE ARMY
HQ Recruiting Group, ATRA, Bldg 165, Trenchard Lines, Upavon, Wiltshire SN9 6BE. ☎ 08457 300111. Website: www.armyofficer.co.uk.
The British Army offers gap year students the opportunity to spend a year in the Army. The Gap Year Commission offers the opportunity for students taking a year out to be placed in an army regiment. There is no obligation after the year has been completed for the student to have any links with the Army. For more information see entry in the 'Directory of Specialist Gap Year Programmes'.

BBC WORK EXPERIENCE PLACEMENTS
www.bbc.co.uk/workexperience.
Programme description: Chance for people to see what the working life of the BBC is like for a few days or up to 4 weeks.
Number of placements: 150+ placement areas from which to choose.
Prerequisites: See descriptions online for specific criteria.
Remuneration: none.
Selection procedures and orientation: Deadlines vary according to Directorate (e.g. Production, Resources, Broadcast). Up to 3 months needed to process applications.

BLACK & VEATCH CONSULTING LTD
Grosvenor House, 69 London Road, Redhill, Surrey RH1 1LQ. ☎ 01737 774155. Fax: 01737 772767. Website: www.bbv-ltd.com.
Civil engineering consultancy specialising in water supply, public health and environmental and power engineering. Much of their work involves bringing treated drinking water and sewage treatment to the developing world.
Programme description: Traineeships and summer positions available.
Number of placements per year: 2 pre-university plus 2-3 undergraduates for summer placements.
Prerequisites: Applicants should have Mathematics and Science A-levels and be applying to read Civil Engineering, Mathematics, Physics or Applied Science at university.
Duration and time of placements: Up to 12 months or 10 weeks for summer.
Selection procedures and orientation: Applications should be sent to Celia Morris, Training Manager by Easter.
Remuneration: Trainees receive around £9,000 p.a.

CADOGAN TIETZ CONSULTING ENGINEERS LTD
14 Clerkenwell Close, Clerkenwell, London EC1R 0PQ. ☎ 020-7490 5050. Fax: 020-7490 2160. E-mail: tietz.london@dial.pipex.com.
Independent civil and structural engineering consultancy.

Programme description: Trainees gain first-hand experience of structural and civil engineering. Also accept gap year students looking for Building Services experience.
Prerequisites: Students must be from university or college and studying Civil Engineering or related disciplines.
Selection procedures and orientation: Applicants from abroad will be considered. Applications should be sent by April.
Remuneration: Salary will be discussed at interview.
Contact: Andrew J Jolly, Managing Director.

CIVIL SERVICE CAREERS
Units 2-4, Lescren Way, Avonmouth, Bristol BS11 8DG. ☎ 0117-982 1171. Website: www.careers.civil-service.gov.uk.
More than 170 departments and executive agencies, employing nearly half a million people make the Civil Service one of the largest employers in the UK. A number of Government Departments and Agencies offer vacation opportunities for students; details are available from Careers Services or Civil Service Careers. (Note that the above telephone number is for despatch of copies only; please do not call it for further information on vacation work.) Very few opportunities listed in the booklet 'Work Experience in the Civil Service' are open to post-secondary school students; one of them is in the newly formed Department for Constitutional Affairs (formerly the Lord Chancellor's Department), Selbourne House, 54-60 Victoria St, London SW1E 6QW; Denise.Cook@lcd.gsi.gov.uk. Another possibility is in the Department for Environment, Food and Rural Affairs (Room 518, 10 Whitehall Place, London SW1A 2HH). Students are advised to apply early as most opportunities have deadlines for applications early in the year and by the end of March at the latest.

CORAL CAY CONSERVATION
The Tower, 13ᵗʰ Floor, 125 High Street, Colliers Wood, London SW19 2JG. ☎ 0870 750 0668. Fax: 0870 750 0667. E-mail: info@coralcay.org. Website: www.coralcay.org
Founding member of the Year Out Group that sends hundreds of volunteers to assist in conserving fragile tropical marine and terrestrial environments in Malaysia, Mexico, Cuba, the Philippines, Honduras and Fiji (see 'Directory of Specialist Gap Year Programmes').
Programme description: Opportunities for interns to work at London head office in the Science, Expedition Management and Marketing departments.

CORUS PLACEMENT SCHEME
Ashorne Hill Management College, Leamington Spa, Warks. CV33 9PE. ☎ 01926 488025. Fax: 01926 488024. E-mail: recruitment.web@corusgroup.com. Website: www.corusgroupcareers.com.
Number of placements: 12-month hands-on industrial placements for students of all disciplines and some summer vacation placements. Fields include engineering, metallurgical technology, Commercial, Human Resources, etc.
Prerequisites: Suitable mainly for undergraduates.
Selection procedures and orientation: Application should be made on-line.
Remuneration: About £200 per week, depending on age. If successful, possibility of receiving sponsorship for following academic year.

DATA CONNECTION LTD
100 Church Street, Enfield, Middlesex EN2 6BQ. ☎ 020-8366 1177. E-mail: recruit@dataconnection.com. Website: www.dataconnection.com.
Data Connection is one of the few UK companies working at the forefront of communications and networking technology. They develop leading edge software and hardware solutions for major IT and telecommunications companies such as BT, Microsoft and Cisco, as well as Internet service providers and technology start-ups.
Programme description: Vacation work is offered to exceptional students with an interest

in the development of complex software. The company provides challenging programming assignments, while offering help and support. Head office in Enfield, North London, and other offices in Edinburgh, Chester, San Francisco and Washington DC.
Prerequisites: Applicants will have all A grades at A-level.
Duration and time of placements: Minimum of 8 weeks over the summer. Early application is advised as vacancies are limited.
Remuneration: A salary of £1,100 per month for pre-university students increasing to £1,300 a month for university vacation students. Also subsidised accommodation in the company house. Many vacation students go on to join Data Connection as full-time employees, and some receive sponsorship whilst at university.

DAVY GROUP OF COMPANIES
59-63 Bermondsey St, London SE1 3XF. ☎ 020-7407 9670. E-mail: cdt@davy.co.uk. Website: www.davy.co.uk.
Programme description: Work experience placements with both on- and off-job training for those looking to enter the wine bar industry. Training and development courses include Basic Food Hygiene, Introduction to Wine and First Aid.
Number of placements per year: 8.
Prerequisites: Minimum age 18. Should have basic understanding of hospitality, sound spoken English and documented evidence confirming the right to work legally in the UK. Should also possess a strong sense of team spirit and a commitment to providing excellent customer service.
Duration and time of placements: 6-12 months. Some accommodation available.
Selection procedures & orientation: Written applications or e-mails quoting reference Gap.2003-06-03.
Remuneration: Paid work experience.
Contact: Recruitment Administration Officer.

EUROMONEY INSTITUTIONAL INVESTOR PLC
Nestor House, Playhouse Yard, London EC4 5EX. ☎ 020-7779 8888. Fax: 020-7779 8842. E-mail: people@euromoneyplc.com. Website: www.euromoneyplc.com.
International publications and events company.
Programme description: No formal scheme but offers work to undergraduates and gap year students with excellent grades. Positions available as researchers, in telesales, administration and data inputting.
Prerequisites: Students of any subject are considered but economics, law and languages are particularly useful.
Remuneration: Varies according to vacancy. No accommodation provided.
Contact: Kerry Velazquez; applications by e-mail only.

FORD MOTOR COMPANY
Room 1/419, Central Office, Eagle Way, Warley, Brentwood, Essex CM13 3BN. Website: www.ford.co.uk/recruitment.
Programme description: Vacation placements for undergraduates: engineering, finance, marketing, service, purchasing, etc. Also offer 12-15 month Business/Industrial Placements suitable for post-university year out.
Number of placements: 100.
Prerequisites: Any degree course acceptable except engineering department seeks engineering students. Application must be made online.
Duration and time of placements: 12 weeks in the summer.
Remuneration: £1,200 per month.

GLOBE EDUCATION
Shakespeare's Globe, Globe Education, 21 New Globe Walk, London SE1 9DT.

☎ 020-7902. Fax: 020-7902 1401. E-mail: education@shakespeares-globe.org. Website: www.shakespeares-globe.org.

Programme description: One year paid gap year student internship to assist with the running of the theatre's workshop and lecture programme for groups (which caters for 45,000 students annually). Shorter unpaid administrative work experience placements in various departments: exhibition, appeals/fundraising and communications. Students will be able to work on special projects and events and act as stewards during the summer.

Number of placements: 1 paid internship, 30 shorter ones.

Duration and time of placements: 12 months from September 1st for internship. 1-2 weeks work experience (or longer if gap year placement) or minimum 3 months unpaid internship.

Remuneration: Student internship stipend is from £6,500 with 25 days holiday, free access to the majority of Globe Education events and some free theatre tickets. No wage paid for short work experience placements and travel expenses are not covered.

Contact: Crispin Hunt, Lively Action Programme (for paid internship) and Alexandra Massey, Courses Administrator/Internships (for unpaid placements).

HALCROW GROUP LTD

16 Abercromby Place, Edinburgh EH3 6LB. ☎ 0131-272 3300. Fax: 0131-272 3302. E-mail: Beardl@halcrow.com. Website: www.halcrow.com/recruit/student_opps.asp.

Programme description: Short paid placements in large multi-disciplinary engineering and development planning company according to current workload. Tasks include surveys, data entry, analysis and research.

Destinations: Scotland.

Number of placements per year: 2-3.

Prerequisites: Minimum age 18, though university graduates preferred. Must be numerate and computer-literate with good command of spoken and written English. Ideally, candidates will have qualification in town planning, traffic engineering, economics, geography, environmental science or urban design.

Duration and time of placements: Variable.

Contact: Liz Beard, Associate Development Planner.

IBM UK

PO Box 41, North Harbour, Portsmouth PO6 3AU. ☎ 023 92 564104 (Student Recruitment Hotline) or 023 92 283777. E-mail: student_pgrs@uk.ibm.com. Website: www-5.ibm.com/employment/uk.

Programme description: Pre-University Employment scheme for able students in one of many locations around the UK and in various departments such as Finance Operations or Business Controls.

Prerequisites: Good personal, business and technical skills. Predicted A-level results of AAB (with minimum C in GCSE English). Deadline for applications end of January.

Duration and time of placements: 9-12 months starting in August/September.

Other services: Residential induction course at beginning of year.

Contact: Katherine Weeks, Student Recruitment Officer.

INDEPENDENT TELEVISION

Programme description: A limited number of work experience placements are sometimes available with the regional ITV companies. Vacancies are rarely known in advance and demand constantly outstrips supply.

Prerequisites: Applicants must be students on a recognised course of study at a college or university; their course must lead to the possibility of employment within the television industry (ideally, work experience would be a compulsory part of the course); and the student must be resident in the transmission area of the company offering the attachment, or in some cases, attending a course in that region. However, opportunities occasionally exist for students following computing, librarianship, finance, legal, administrative or management courses.

Duration and time of placements: Placements vary in length from half a day to several weeks or months, depending upon the work available and the candidate's requirements.

Remuneration: Students do not normally receive payment, although possibility that expenses will be paid. Students from sandwich courses who are on long-term attachments may be regarded as short-term employees and paid accordingly.

Selection procedures and orientation: Applications should be sent to the Personnel Department of the applicant's local ITV company. General information on working in media can be obtained from the National Training Organisation for Broadcast, Film, Video and Multi-media on 020-7520 5757 (fax 020-7520 5758; info@skillset.org; www.skillset.org) which has charitable status. Skills for Media (Prospect House, 80-110 New Oxford St, London WC1A 1HB) with a telephone helpline 08080 300900 (www.skillsformedia.com) offers one-to-one advisory sessions and career guidance for interested individuals.

LISHMAN, SIDWELL, CAMPBELL AND PRICE
Administrative Office, Eva Left House, 1 South Crescent, Ripon, Yorkshire HG4 1SN. ☎ 01765 608956. Fax: 01765 690296. E-mail: admin@lscp.com.
One of Yorkshire's largest independent Chartered Certified Accountants with 16 offices from Sheffield to Middlesbrough.

Programme description: The company offers vacation and other traineeships to students including those in their gap year.

Number of placements per year: 6.

Prerequisites: None; should be seriously contemplating accountancy as a career.

Duration and time of placements: Mostly summer but some throughout the year.

Selection procedures and orientation: Written applications.

Remuneration: Wage is £5-£6 per hour, according to age, experience and qualifications.

Contact: John D. Emptage, Personnel Training Manager.

MERIDIAN RECORDS
PO Box 317, Eltham, London SE9 4SF. ☎ 020-8857 3213. E-mail: mail@meridian-records.co.uk. Website: www.meridian-records.co.uk.
Meridian Records is a small record company specialising in the recording and production of classical records.

Programme description: Candidates are required to help with a wide variety of tasks including the preparation of art work, accounting, recording, editing and the maintenance of machines, buildings and grounds.

Number of placements per year: 1 or 2.

Prerequisites: Candidates need to demonstrate motivation and a keen interest in music. They should have a general interest in all aspects of running a record company. An ability to read music is an advantage but is not essential. It is also the policy of Meridian Records to employ only non-smokers.

Duration and time of placements: Varying number of weeks during the three main vacations.

Remuneration: The traineeships are unpaid although accommodation may be free on the premises.

NATIONAL CENTRE FOR YOUNG PEOPLE WITH EPILEPSY (NCYPE)
St. Piers Lane, Lingfield, Surrey RH7 6PW. ☎ 01342 832243. Fax: 01342 834639. E-mail: aboyce@ncype.org.uk. Website: www.ncype.org.uk.
Programme description: To support student development by contribution to student's education and social and developmental curriculum, as part of a co-ordinated team.

Number of placements: Up to 5.

Prerequisites: Minimum age 19; suitable for pre-university. Must be legally entitled to work in the UK, obtain enhanced police disclosure and have desire to work with young

students.
Duration and time of placements: 1 year minimum (September-July).
Remuneration: £12,629 (award pending).
Other services: Single hostel accommodation arranged.
Contact: Adrienne Boyce, Assistant Personnel Officer.

OXFAM
Volunteering Team, 274 Banbury Road, Oxford OX2 7DZ. ☎ 0845 3000 311/ 01865 313 3252. Website: www.oxfam.org.uk/involved/placements/index.htm.
Programme description: Volunteer Opportunities Scheme in charity/volunteer sector. Successful candidates can make a contribution to Oxfam's work in one of several divisions. Opportunities for specific training if relevant to assigned task, e.g. Influencing People and Time and Staff Management.
Destinations: UK only; most positions are at Oxford headquarters.
Prerequisites: Most candidates are post-university. Some positions can be filled only by people with the right qualifications and experience. Should have basic office and IT skills.
Duration and time of placements: 3-5 days per week for 3-12 months.
Remuneration: Work is unpaid. Lunch and travel expenses paid.

PRICEWATERHOUSECOOPERS
Southwark Towers, 32 London Bridge Street, London SE1 9SY. ☎ 0808 100 1500 (Student Information Line). Fax: 020-7804 8835. E-mail: zoe.gordon@uk.pwc.com. Website: www.pwc.com/uk/careers.
World's largest professional services organisation.
Programme description: Gap year students join one of 3 areas: Assurance and Business Advisory Services, Tax & Legal Services and Actuarial. Gap year students undertake real work with clients and develop skills for the future. Structured induction training programme given at beginning of placement. Vacancies in various offices in the UK.
Number of placements: 30 per year on the PwC Gap Year programme.
Prerequisites: Skills needed are teamwork, communication, motivation, flexibility, career focus and commercial awareness. Students should have 300 UCAS points (excluding General Studies). Students who require a work permit are not accepted. Applications via website, preferably before end of January when most vacancies are filled.
Duration and time of placements: 6 months, September to March.
Other services: Students have to find their own accommodation, though PwC puts other programme participants in touch with each other. Many gap year students return to work for PwC in university vacations.
Contact: Zoe Gordon (Gap Year Manager) or Louise Heatherson (Gap Year Co-ordinator).

QED EDUCATIONAL CONSULTANTS
90 Gloucester Place, London W1U 6HS. ☎ 020-7935 4909. Fax: 020-7486 9922. E-mail: info@qed-education.com. Website: www.qed-education.com.
Specialists in recruitment and training for independent schools.
Placements offered: Games or general assistant, mainly at preparatory schools in the UK.
Number of placements per year: 5-10.
Prerequisites: Must enjoy being in the company of young children. Generally competent games players but other skills and interests such as music and ICT are very useful. Must be willing to contribute to the life of a boarding school which entails weekend duties, usually on a rota basis.
Duration and time of placements: 1-3 terms.
Selection procedures and orientation: Students can apply at any time of year by sending an application letter with a CV.
Remuneration: From £100 per week and receive free board and lodging.

Contact: Angela Forsyth, Managing Director.

ROLLS-ROYCE PLC
PO Box 31, Derby DE24 8BJ. ☎ 01332 244306. E-mail: careers@rolls-royce.com. Website: www.rolls-royce.com/careers.
Programme description: Placements available for 3-12 months at Rolls-Royce's for students in at least their second year of study. Opportunities are available in engineering, finance, purchasing, human resources and logistics.
Duration and time of placements: 10 weeks to 12 months, usually starting around early summer.

ROYAL OPERA HOUSE EDUCATION
Covent Garden, London WC2E 9DD. ☎ 020-7212 9410. Fax: 020-7212 9441. E-mail: education@roh.org.uk. Website: www.royaloperahouse.org.
Placements offered: Work placements/internships offered across the organisation but predominantly in technical and production areas, e.g. archives, education, music library and publications.
Prerequisites: Minimum age 18. Students should have an interest in ballet or opera (though not necessarily performers).
Duration of courses: At mutually agreed start date and period of time.
Other services: 5-day 'Behind-the-Scenes' course in April (see entry in 'Directory of Courses').
Contact: Joanne Allen, Education Secretary/Work Placement Co-ordinator.

SIR ROBERT MCALPINE
Eaton Court, Maylands Avenue, Hemel Hempstead, Herts. HP2 7TR. Website: www.sir-robert-mcalpine.com.
One of UK's leading construction companies. Work experience opportunities available to gap year students as well as sponsorship for higher education and industrial placements.

STEP
11-13 Goldsmith Street, Nottingham NG1 5JS. ☎ 0115 941 5900. Fax: 0115 950 8321. E-mail: enquiries@step.org.uk. Website: www.secureyoursuccess.co.uk.
Government-supported initiative to match second and penultimate year undergraduates with small and medium sized businesses and community organisations for work experience.
Programme description: Summer work experience placements and year-long industrial placements for students as part of their degree.
Number of placements: 1,500.
Prerequisites: Must be studying full-time at a UK university. No age restrictions.
Duration and time of placements: 8 weeks over summer; part-time term-time up to 15 hours per week, 12 months otherwise.
Selection procedures and orientation: Application can be made online. Deadline for summer placements is 13th June.
Remuneration: Summer students receive £170 per week. Average 12-month placement pays £12,000. Travelling expenses are paid at the employer's discretion.

TRIDENT TRANSNATIONAL
The Smokehouse, Smokehouse Yard, 44-46 St John St, London EC1M 4DF. ☎ 020-7014 1420. Fax: 020-7430 9275. E-mail: info.transnational@trid.demon.co.uk. Website: www.trident-transnational.org.
International division of the Trident Trust, an educational charity and organiser of work experience programmes for overseas nationals in the UK.
Programme description: Work experience and working holiday schemes for young people aged 18-35 from the EEA. They send applicants' CVs round relevant companies

in the UK. Work placements are accredited with a certificate issued by the University of Cambridge Local Examinations Syndicate.

Duration and time of placements: 6 weeks to 12 months starting year round.

Selection procedures and orientation: Application should be made at least two months in advance. It is occasionally possible to find placements for non-European students who must obtain a TWES permit (Training & Work Experience Scheme) for the UK.

Fees: £235 (work experience); £195 (working holidays).

Contact: Paula Devries (paula@trid.demon.co.uk).

J. D. WETHERSPOON PLC
PO Box 616, Watford WD24 1YN. ☎ 01923 477777. Recruitment hotline: 0870 243 8243 for application forms. Fax: 01923 219810. Website: www.jdwetherspoon.co.uk.

Programme description: One-year placements for students. Trainees are trained to a level where they will be able to run a managed public house.

Number of placements: 30+.

Prerequisites: Minimum age 18. No experience necessary however candidates need to demonstrate motivation, confidence, drive, team leadership, attention to detail, customer focus and business skills.

Duration and time of placements: Minimum 48 weeks.

Selection procedures and orientation: Short-listed candidates are invited to recruitment forum, full day of interviews, pub tour, presentation and numeracy test. Full training given on acceptance.

Remuneration: From £13,000 outside London; £17,000, with London weighting.

YEAR IN INDUSTRY
The University of Southampton, Southampton SO17 1BJ. ☎ 02380 597061. E-mail: enquiries@yini.org.uk. Website: www.yini.org.uk.

Major provider of gap year industrial placements throughout the UK.

Programme description: Students are placed in companies where they gain experience of industry and may be given a lot of independence to develop new ideas. Participants are required to submit a project for presentation at the end of the year.

Number of placements per year: 600+.

Prerequisites: Students should be interested in following a career in industry and must have a confirmed place at university. Most participants are intending to study engineering, science or business though other disciplines are acceptable.

Duration and time of placements: Placements generally last for 11 months, from August/September to mid-July.

Selection procedures and orientation: Participants are required to attend formal courses in related field during the work placement.

Remuneration: Minimum recommended salary is £8,000-£11,000.

Directory of Work Experience Abroad

AFRICAN CONSERVATION EXPERIENCE
PO Box 9706, Solihull, West Midlands B91 3FF. ☎ 0870 241 5816. E-mail: info@ConservationAfrica.net. Website: www.ConservationAfrica.net.

Programme description: Conservation work placements for young people on game reserves in Southern Africa. See 'Directory of Specialist Gap Year Programmes' and 'Africa' chapter.

AGRIVENTURE

International Agricultural Exchange Association (IAEA), Long Clawson, Melton Mowbray, Leicestershire LE14 4NR. ☎ **01664 822335. Fax: 01664 823820. E-mail: post@agriventure.com. Website: www.agriventure.com.**

Programme description: International agricultural exchanges for young agriculturalists.

Destinations: Placements for UK and European participants in the USA, Canada, Australia, New Zealand and Japan.

Prerequisites: Must be aged 18 to 30 with good practical farming experience.

Duration and time of placements: Placements in the USA and Canada begin in February, March and April and last for seven or nine months. Placements for Australia and New Zealand begin in April, May, July, August and September and last for six to nine months. Placements in Japan begin in April and last four to twelve months. There are also several round-the-world itineraries which depart in the autumn to the southern hemisphere for six to seven months followed by another six to seven months in the northern hemisphere.

Selection procedures & orientation: Pre-departure information meeting.

Cost: Participants pay between £2,000 and £4,100 which includes airline tickets, visas, insurance, orientation seminar and board and lodging throughout with a host family. Trainees are then paid a realistic wage.

AMILI

Selva Alegre 1031 y La Isla, Ecuador. ☎ **+593 2-222 6947. Fax: +593-2-250 0669. E-mail: info@amili.org/amili@amili.com. Website: www.amili.com.**

Programme description: Internship programme in Ecuador. Unpaid internships in many fields such as media, tourism, computing, marine biology, event management, engineering and many others.

Destinations: Throughout Ecuador including Highlands, coastal areas, Amazonia and the Galapagos Islands.

Prerequisites: Good knowledge of Spanish is required. Must be able to adapt to different culture.

Duration of placements: Minimum 2 months, up to 6 months (since foreigners require no visa for stays of less than 6 months). Available any time of year.

Cost: $200 placement fee includes transfer from airport to host family. Language lessons cost $6 an hour (20 hours a week).

Accommodation: Accommodation with host families costs $12 per day including full board.

Contact: Patricia Fernández (Internship Consultant), Patricio Fernández (General Co-ordinator).

ARCH SCOTLAND

Olney Bank, The Ross, Comrie, Perthshire PH26 2JU. ☎ **01764 670653. E-mail: libby@grampus.co.uk. Website: www.grampus.co.uk.**

Independent Scottish training company, formerly called Grampus Heritage & Training Ltd.

Programme description: Authorised to make placements through European Commission schemes. 4-week placements through the Leonardo da Vinci Programme in the fields of culture and heritage management, and possibly also art, archaeology, forestry and countryside management.

Sample of Leonardo placements include reconstructing using traditional materials a house in a Nature Park in Germany and working on a community arts project in Gdansk.

Number of placements: About 20 per session.

Destinations: Germany, Poland, etc.

Duration and time of placements: 4 weeks in spring (after Easter) and autumn.

Remuneration: Programme covers all travel, accommodation, subsistence and insurance costs.

Contact: Libby Urquhart.

BLUE DOG ADVENTURES
Amwell Farm House, Nomansland, Wheathampstead, St. Albans, Herts. AL4 8EJ. ☎ 01582 831302. Fax: 01582 834002. E-mail: info@bluedogadventures.com. Website: www.bluedogadventures.com

Programme description: Adventure internships and equestrian experiences (see entry in *Directory of Sports Courses* for other trips.)

Destinations: Equestrian experience internships at ranch in southwestern Montana learning to break in colts. Also volunteer position at stables in Romania and with the Working Horse Organisation of Romania, an organisation dedicated to equine welfare and equestrian tourism.

Duration of courses: 1 month, possibly up to 3 months.

Prerequisites: Equestrian experience internships require a minimum level of expertise, ranging from beginner through advanced.

Cost: 1-month volunteering programme in Romania while receiving navigational training in the mountains of Transylvania costs £80 for accommodation and food. 1 month at DJ Bar Ranch in Montana costs £775.

Contact: Jenna Troy, Adventure Co-ordinator.

CDS INTERNATIONAL INC
871 United Nations Plaza, 15th floor, New York, NY 10017-1814, USA. ☎ (212) 497-3500. Fax: (212) 497-3535. E-mail: info@cdsintl.org. Website: www.cdsintl.org.

CDS International offers practical training placements in the US in a variety of fields including business, engineering and technology; and also overseas practical training internships for American students or recent graduates.

Programme description: CDS arranges various work experience, internships and work-study programmes for Americans in Germany and a number of other countries. For incoming participants to the US, CDS sponsors visa authorisation, arranges internships and provides programme during US stay.

Destinations: Germany, Turkey, Argentina, Ecuador, Switzerland, and incoming programme to the US.

Number of placements per year: 2,000+.

Prerequisites: The opportunities for internships are limited to young professionals, aged 18-35. Language proficiency required for most programmes (not Turkey), as well as relevant experience and a strong desire to gain international experience.

Duration and time of placements: Internships generally last 3-18 months, although 24-month placements may be available.

Selection procedures and orientation: Qualified applicants are interviewed by telephone. Pre-departure orientation materials are sent and support is provided throughout the programme.

Cost: Programme fee normally $500. Some internships are paid.

C.E.I. (CENTRE d'ECHANGES INTERNATIONAUX)
Club des 4 Vents, 1 rue Gozlin, 75006 Paris, France. ☎ 1-43 29 17 24. Fax: 1-43 29 06 21. E-mail: France@cei4vents.com. Website: www.cei4vents.com.

Programme description: Professional training, academic year abroad and homestays. Work experience in Brittany region.

Prerequisites: Minimum age 17.

Duration and time of placements: 2-4 weeks (or more) year round.

Cost: €750 for 2 weeks; €1,000 for 3 weeks, €1,250 for 4 weeks including full board accommodation with local family and ongoing back-up.

Other services: C.E.I. offers large range of French courses for young people aged 14-18 and linguistic holidays on the Mediterranean for 17-20 year olds. Also has residential language courses in Paris at Paris Langues (www.parislangues.com).

Contact: José Luis Ponti, Incoming Programmes Manager.

CIEE
52 Poland Street, London W1F 7AB. ☎ 020-7478 2020. Fax: 020-7734 7322. E-mail: infouk@councilexchanges.org.uk. Website: www.ciee.org.uk.
Founded in 1947 in the US, CIEE is a non-profit, non-governmental organisation offering work abroad programmes designed to improve cultural understanding and the skills necessary for living and working in a culturally diverse world.
Programme description: CIEE offers work, teaching and language study abroad programmes. They include Work & Travel USA, Internship USA and Professional Career Training USA, Work & Trravel Australia, Work & Travel New Zealand, Internship Canada, Teach in China and Teach in Thailand.
Destinations: USA, Canada, Thailand, Australia, New Zealand, Canada, Europe and Latin America.
Prerequisites: Different eligibility requirements for each programme. To work in the USA participants must either be a student, graduate or young professional. To work in Australasia, they must be over 18. To teach in Asia they must be a degree-holder.
Duration and time of placements: Anything from a few weeks up to 18 months. The Work & Travel USA summer programme is open between June and October. Internship USA and Professional Career Training USA can last up to 18 months and runs all year round. Students bound for Australia, New Zealand and Canada can go out for 12 months at any time of year. Five or ten month contracts for Teaching in China start in August or February and for Thailand they begin in May or October.
Selection procedures and orientation: The application deadlines are the end of June for Work and Travel USA; mid-November or early May for Teach in China; and mid-February and mid-July for Thailand. Participants receive orientation in London followed by 7 days of residential training in Shanghai or Bangkok, covering the essentials of TEFL and an introduction to Asia, its culture and language. Students participating in Work and Travel USA receive a pre-departure orientation. CIEE offers advice and support both in the UK and abroad and provides assistance with obtaining visas, insurance and placements.
Cost: Teachers in China and Thailand are paid a local wage which allows for a comfortable lifestyle. Work and Travel USA fee starts from £335 which includes first night's accommodation, employment directory and all support services. Other programme fees are listed in application materials, available on request or on the web.

DON QUIJOTE
2-4 Stoneleigh Park Road, Epsom, Surrey KT19 0QT. ☎ 020-8786 8081. Fax: 020-8786 8086. E-mail: info@donquijote.co.uk. Website: www.donquijote.co.uk.
Language school agency specialising in the Spanish language as taught in Spain and Latin America.
Programme description: Language course followed by internship programme in Barcelona and Madrid. 6 weeks intensive language course followed by 2 weeks professional orientation and 12-week internship.
Accommodation: Homestay, residence and flats.
Follow-up: Further courses can be arranged, particularly to specialise in business Spanish and including an internship placement programme in Madrid and Barcelona. Private tuition is available at all schools.
Cost: €920 for 120 Spanish classes over 6 weeks, €188 orientation and €1,750 internship.

EARTHCORPS
6310 NE 74th St, Suite 201E, Seattle, WA 98115. ☎ 206-322-9296 ext 224. Fax: 206-322-9312. E-mail: mark@earthcorps.org. Website: www.earthcorps.org.
Programme description: 6-month skill-based environmental restoration experience in Seattle. Trail construction, environmental education and invasive plant removal.
Number of placements per year: 20-25 (2 per country).
Prerequisites: All nationalities, so cross-cultural communication skills needed. Ages

18-24. People preferred who have experience of working in the field of environmental restoration.

Duration and time of placements: June-November (or April-August for second year applicants).

Selection procedures and orientation: Competitive selection. Applications due by middle of November.

Remuneration: $240 monthly stipend given to international participants (many of whom are from developing countries). Homestays arranged.

Contact: Mark Howard, International Co-ordinator.

EURO-ACADEMY LTD
67-71 Lewisham High St, London SE13 5JX. ☎ 020-8297 0505. Fax: 020-8297 0984. E-mail: enquiries@euroacademy.co.uk. Website: www.euroacademy.co.uk.
Language school agency in business for 30 years (see 'Directory of Language Courses') with Internship Department.

Programme description: Work experience in France (Paris, Lille, Reims, Strasbourg, Dijon, Lyon, Limoges, Bordeaux, Montpelier, Marseille, Cannes, Aix-en-Provence or Dinan), Germany (Munich, Berlin, Frankfurt), Italy and Spain. Placements are in the fields of agriculture, industry, sales, marketing, etc.

Duration and time of placements: 4, 8 or 12 weeks, plus shorter placements of 2, 3 or 4 weeks available in Brittany (Dinan). Weekly start dates, usually Monday.

Prerequisites: Candidates should have intermediate knowledge of the language and be able to submit CV in target language. Minimum age 18.

Selection procedures and orientation: Minimum 8 weeks notice needed.

Cost: Placement fee for France is £240 for 4 weeks, £300 for 8 and £360 for 12 plus accommodation, for example with host family from £22 per night. Brittany programme has different price structure: £545 for 2 weeks including half-board accommodation with host family, £725 for 3 weeks and £885 for 4 weeks. German Work Experience programme includes 4-week intermediate German course and host family accommodation: £950 for 4 weeks plus £125 per week bed and breakfast.

EUROLINGUA
61 Bollin Drive, Altrincham WA14 5QW. ☎/fax: 0161-972 0225. Website: www.eurolingua.com/Work_Experience.htm.
French-based international language training group offers work experience placements in UK for European students and in Europe for British students.

Programme description: Unpaid work experience in the hospitality industry for university students studying tourism whatever their nationality or those who are currently employed in a hotel.

Destinations: Germany, Italy, UK (for foreigners), etc.

Prerequisites: Normally candidates follow an in-country language course beforehand.

Cost: A one-month preparatory course in Italian followed by a two-month internship is €1,300.

EUROPEAN COMMISSION
Bureau des Stages, 200 Rue de la Loi, 1049 Brussels, Belgium. ☎ 02-299 23 39. Fax: 02-299 23 40. E-mail: eac-stages@cec.eu.int; http://europa.eu.int/comm/ stages or www.cec.org.uk/work/stage.htm.
The scheme is open only to graduates and is administered by the Training Office at the European Commission's General Secretariat in Brussels.

Programme description: Twice a year the Commission organises in-service training periods to give trainees a general idea of the objectives and problems of European integration and provide them with practical knowledge of the workings of Commission departments. Part of the period may be used to prepare a post-graduate thesis or academic paper.

Destinations: Most are in Luxembourg or Brussels.
Number of placements per year: 628.
Prerequisites: Applicants must have a thorough knowledge of one other EU official language in addition to their mother tongue. The age limit is 30. Applicants must also have completed their degree.
Duration and time of placements: 5 months. Training periods begin on 1st March and 1st October every year.
Selection procedures and orientation: Application forms must be submitted online. Deadlines are August 31st and March 1st. If applicants pass the first selection procedure, it is often helpful to attend informal interviews in Brussels.
Remuneration: All candidates are considered eligible for a grant. Most trainees are paid a grant and their travel expenses. The monthly allowance currently paid to the majority of trainees is about €700.

EURO-PRACTICE CORP S.L.
C/ Cibeles 4, Local 2, 18004 Granada, Spain. ☎ +34 958-535 866. Fax: +34 958 536 391. E-mail: spain@euro-practice.com. Website: www.euro-practice.com. Also offices in Germany (Kyffhäuserstr. 17, 50674 Cologne; germany@euro-practice.com) and France (13 rue Eugène Léris, 81100 Castres; france@euro-practice.com).
Programme description: International work placement organisation based in France, Germany and Spain. Clients can choose to fix up their own work placement from list of 30 selected companies supplied for a fee of €58 or they can have a placement made on their behalf for a fee of €751. Possible fields are marketing/communication, international trade, IT, office administration, translation and tourism.
Prerequisites: Must have competence in the language. Applications should be submitted 12 weeks in advance.
Duration and time of placements: Minimum 8 weeks up to 6 months.
Remuneration: Negotiable with employer.
Other services: Homestay accommodation arrangement fee of €75.
Contact: Jean-Louis Yague, Director.

EXPERIMENT PARIS
89 rue de Turbigo, 75003 Paris, France. ☎ 1-44 54 58 03. Fax: 1-44 54 58 01. E-mail: incoming@experiment.france.org. Website: www.experiment.france.org.
Programme description: Internship Programme in Montpellier region of France. Placements in hotels/restaurants or businesses, e.g. advertising, computing, import/export, etc.
Duration of courses: 3-6 months; 2 months in summer. Maximum 3 months for non-EU candidates.
Prerequisites: Ages 18-30. Must be able to function at an intermediate level of French. Internship placement fee is €580.
Remuneration: Hotel/restaurant staff receive monthly stipend of €150. Other businesses pay €230.
Other services: 20 hours of French classes may be arranged prior to internship. Accommodation can be arranged on request; host family providing half-board costs €220 per week; self-catering in student residence costs €150.
Contact: Anne Blassiau, Incoming Programs Manager.

FOREIGN & COMMONWEALTH OFFICE
Recruitment Section Room, 2/98, Old Admiralty Building, London, SW1A 2PA. ☎ 020-7008 0762. E-mail: recruitment.public@fco.gov.uk. Website: www.fco.gov.uk.
Overseas Undergraduate Attachment Scheme.
Programme description: Offers British university students in their penultimate year

Looking for a meaningful and productive year out?

Why not work as an 'animateur' with

French Encounters

the specialists in high level educational and language field trips for schools

Do you want to:
earn while you learn?
confront exciting challenges and broaden your horizons daily?
develop a variety of essential life and vocational skills?
improve your general communication and presentation skills?
learn to be a guide, courier and entertainer?
perfect your French language skills in France?
use your initiative?
live and work in a château in Normandy?
acquire some practical first aid skills?
work with a great variety of people and as part of a dynamic team?

and, of course, have fun in the process?

What previous animateurs have said of their experience:

"I still remember my time at FE with fondness" 1996
"A great time - I learned so much and had such fun" 1998
"It was really hard work, but worth every minute;
It was better than anything I've done since" 1999
"An indication of how much we enjoyed it . . . . we're returning
to the château to get married!" 1999
"The first time I took a group out I was terrified - by the end of the season,
I could cope with anything" 2000
"It's a fast way to grow up and get paid too" 2002
"What a good time we had . . . . we wish we could do it again" 2002

Season lasts from mid-February to mid-June

Interested ?

contact French Encounters
63 Fordhouse Road Bromsgrove Worcs B60 2LU
Tel: 01527 873645 Tel/Fax: 01527 832794
email: admin@frenchencounters.com
www.frenchencounters.com

unpaid summer work experience placements in consulates worldwide. The work is normally in the commercial or information sections of the embassy or high commission.
Destinations: Worldwide.
Number of placements per year: About 40.
Prerequisites: Competitive application procedure.
Duration and time of placements: 2-8 weeks in the summer.
Cost: Participants receive free travel and accommodation but must cover day-to-day living costs.
Other services: FCO also runs Work Experience Scheme for 16 and 17 year olds considering a career in the Diplomatic Service. They spend 2 weeks in October observing and doing straightforward jobs in an FCO department.

FRENCH ENCOUNTERS
63 Fordhouse Road, Bromsgrove, Worcestershire B60 2LU. ☎ 01527 873645. Fax: 01527 832794. E-mail: admin@frenchencounters.com. Website: www.frenc hencounters.com.
Company runs field study trips for 10-13 year olds based in two chateaux in Normandy with British staff who act as guides/couriers/teachers/entertainers/organisers.
Programme description: *Animateurs/animatrices* to work with groups of young people in France. Compulsory 2-week pre-service training includes English Speaking Board's 'Professional Presentation Skills' training and assessment, continuous on-the-job training and French Red Cross *(Croix Rouge)* First Aid Certificate Course.
Prerequisites: A-level French preferred. Minimum age 18. Must be committed enough to work long hours (on-call 24 hours a day) and tackle challenging tasks.
Duration and time of placements: 4 months from beginning or middle of February to mid-June. Applications should be submitted before the end of August for September interviews.
Remuneration: All expenses are paid including reasonable interview expenses, insurance, return travel to France, cost of all training and exam fees and board and lodging. In addition pocket money is paid (£80 in 2003) calculated to be below the taxable threshold. Weekend allowance also paid. Rooms are shared and not en suite. Chateaux are relatively isolated so accommodation normally provides TV and video.
Other services: Experience gives gap year students an opportunity to develop a range of management and business skills and knowledge of the service and tourism industries.
Contact: Patsy Musto, Owner/Director.

GALA SPANISH IN SPAIN
Woodcote House, 8 Leigh Lane, Farnham, Surrey GU9 8HP. ☎/fax: 01252 715319.
Gala offers an information, advisory and placement service for students of Spanish.
Programmes description: Hotel work experience in Lérida (Catalonia) in association with Hotels Association of Lérida.
Prerequisites: Should have at least intermediate level of Spanish (pre-placement language course can be arranged if needed). No experience needed for menial jobs, but some needed for better jobs such as receptionist and waiter. Must be over 18 and an EU national.
Duration and time of placements: 1-3 months during summer. Possibility of placements at other times of the year on request.
Remuneration: €360-€540 per month for 40 hour weeks (with 2 days off, not necessarily consecutive).
Selection procedures: Applications should be submitted by end of February. Later applications (before May 15th) will be surcharged €80.
Cost: Enrolment fee is €65; programme fee is €358.
Contact: Anne Thomas, Proprietor.

GLS SPRACHZENTRUM BERLIN
Kolonnenstr. 26, 10829 Berlin, Germany. ☎ 30-78 00 89/0. Fax: 30-787 41 92. E-mail: germancourses@gls-berlin.com. Website: www.german-courses.com.
Programme description: Minimum 4-week language course followed by an internship lasting 4, 8 or 12 weeks in a company in or near Berlin. Traineeships available in range of fields such as marketing, government and banking. One recent example was at Heinrich-Boell-Stiftung, the foundation of the German Green Party.
Prerequisites: Must be able to express yourself in German and understand everyday conversations. Must also show initiative. Minimum age 18/19.
Cost: Placement fee is €450.
Other services: GLS is a leading centre in Berlin for teaching German as a foreign language and is a founding member of GWEA (Global Work Experience Association).
Contact: Dorothee Robrecht, Director PR & Marketing.

INSTITUTE FOR EXPERIENTIAL LEARNING
Suite 201, 1776 Massachusetts Ave NW, Washington, DC 20036. ☎ 202-833-8581/800-435-0770. Fax: 202-833-8581. E-mail: info@ielnet.org. Website: www.ielnet.org.
Programme description: Academic internships in Washington DC.
Number of placements: 200.
Prerequisites: Must be in at least second year of university or college; normally in age range 19-30. Good academic record, good recommendations from professors, ability to write and speak English effectively and strong work ethic needed.
Duration and time of placements: 10 weeks in summer, 15 weeks in spring or autumn.
Selection procedures & orientation: Interviews for internships done by telephone. Successful students attend a 2-day orientation on IEL and on Washington DC following by on-the-job training with the organisation with which they are interning.
Remuneration: Accommodation arranged in furnished apartments shared by up to 4 students.
Contact: Lauren Day, Programme Co-ordinator for Student Recruitment, Admissions and Marketing.

INSTITUT LE ROSEY
Château du Rosey, 1180 Rolle, Switzerland. E-mail: rosey@rosey.ch. Website: www.rosey.ch.
Programme description: School laboratory assistant to help in setting up and clearing away apparatus for practicals and demonstrations, keeping labs in order, cleaning equipment, filing, etc.
Number of placements: 1.
Prerequisites: Ages 19-25. Post A-level, preferably with science background. Knowledge of French (or willingness to learn) an advantage.
Duration and time of placements: September to June with holidays during school vacations.
Remuneration: SFr800 per month plus free accommodation, meals, health insurance and laundry.
Other services: Single study bedroom accommodation with en suite is provided with job. No-frills flights to Geneva also provided free. May be a chance to attend in-house French course. Winter campus allows plenty of opportunities for skiing.
Selection procedures and orientation: Applications are considered in May.
Contact: M. R. Gray, Deputy Director.

INTERNATIONAL EXCHANGE PROGRAM UK LTD (IEPUK)
The Old Rectory, Belton-in-Rutland, Oakham, Rutland LE15 9LE. ☎ 01572 717381. Fax: 01572 717343. E-mail: GY@iepuk.com. Website: www.iepuk.com.

Equine staff agency with partners in Australia (PO Box 1206, Windsor, NSW 2756; 02-4576 4444; info@stablemate.net.au) and the USA (Communicating for Agriculture, 112 East Lincoln Avenue, Fergus Falls, MN 56537; 218-739-3241).
Programme description: Agricultural, equine, horticultural, landscaping and winemaking work placements. Also acts as a recruitment agency making permanent and relief placements in the equestrian and agricultural industry.
Destinations: Australia, New Zealand, USA, South Africa, Europe and many posts in UK.
Number of placements per year: 300/400.
Prerequisites: Equestrian staff require suitable background. One year of practical experience usually needed though many placements offer additional training. Placements as general farm assistants may not require experience.
Duration and time of placements: Usually one year, but variable.
Selection procedures and orientation: Interviews and orientation are required for work overseas.
Cost: IEP fee is about £1,800 including airfares.

INTERSPEAK
Placements and Homestays, Stretton Lower Hall, Stretton, Cheshire SY14 7HS.
☎ **01829 250641. Fax: 01829 250596. E-mail: enquiries@interspeak.co.uk. Website: www.interspeak.co.uk.**
Since 1981, Interspeak has placed students in homestays and internships.
Programme description: Short and longer term traineeships (unpaid internships/ *stages*) in Europe in the fields of marketing, international trade, computing, tourism, etc. Candidates live with host families.
Destinations: France (Paris, Lille, St. Malo, Limoges), Spain (Madrid) or Germany (Munich, Regensburg). Workplace placements for Europeans in England (London Manchester, Chester).
Number of placements per year: 300-400.
Prerequisites: Students must be at least 17. Some knowledge of the language required.
Duration and time of placement: 1-24 weeks. Applicants can specify their preferred date of departure.
Selection procedures and orientation: A CV in both English and the destination country's language must be sent, as well as a letter of motivation. This should specify why an Interspeak internship is being requested, what type of placement is preferred, what the student hopes to do during the internship and what relevant course work and experience qualifies them for this placement.
Cost: Agency fee starts at £300 for longer-term placements.
Contact: Irene and David Ratcliffe, Owners.

LANGUAGE COURSES ABROAD LTD
67 Ashby Road, Loughborough, Leicestershire LE11 3AA. ☎ 01509 211612. Fax: 01509 260037. E-mail: info@languagesabroad.co.uk. Website: www.langua gesabroad.co.uk.
Spanish Study Holidays Ltd, the parent company, is a member of GWEA (Global Work Experience Association).
Programme description: Work experience placements in range of countries. Any type of work experience can be provided as long as the student has relevant qualifications. A few work placements available in company's own schools.
Destinations: Spain, Latin America, France, Germany and Italy.
Number of placements per year: 100.
Prerequisites: Work placements require at least an intermediate level of the language. Most work placements are preceded by a 4-week in-country language course (see entry in 'Directory of Language Courses').
Duration and time of placements: 4 weeks minimum, normally 8-16 weeks.

Selection procedures and orientation: Applications should be sent at least 8 and preferably 12 weeks in advance. Personal monitor is appointed to oversee work placement.

Costs: Work placements not normally paid, except those in the hotel and catering industry for which students normally receive free board and lodging and sometimes also payment at national minimum wage levels. Fees included on company website.

Contact: Mike Cummins, Director.

M.B. LANGUAGE ASBL

41 rue Henri Bergé, 1030 Brussels, Belgium. ☎ 2-242 27 66. Fax: 2-242 25 36. E-mail: macbaron@chello.be.

Promotes linguistic and cultural exchanges within Europe.

Programme description: Organises work experience abroad for European students aged 16-18.

Destinations: Mainly in Brussels, also Hamburg.

Number of placements per year: 100-200.

Prerequisites: Language skills (French or German), organisation, enthusiasm and self-motivation are needed. Students ought to have studied French or German at school.

Duration and time of placements: 2 weeks or longer if requested throughout the year.

Selection procedures and orientation: A CV is required, but interviews are not essential.

Cost: Work experience fees are €450 for 2 weeks between October and May and €475 in July and August.

Contact: Xavier Mouffe, Manager.

MOSCOW INSTITUTE FOR ADVANCED STUDY

Lebyazhii Pereulok 8, Building 1, Moscow 119019, Russia. US office: 156 W 56th St, 7th Floor, New York, NY 10019. ☎ 212-245-0461. Fax: 212-489-4829. E-mail: info@mifas.org. Website: www.studyabroad.com/moscow.

Number of placements: Large number of placements in prestigious organisations like the Gorbachev Foundation and in major companies like American Express.

Prerequisites: For advanced language students or students fluent in Russian. Most internships are filled by students from the US.

Duration and time of placements: Most internships last at least one semester (autumn, spring or summer) and are offered on a part-time basis, 10-15 hours per week.

Accommodation: homestay or in double occupancy room in a dormitory.

S & S HUMAN RESOURCES DEVELOPMENT

PO Box TN 1501, Teshie-Nungua Estates, Accra, Ghana. ☎ +233-27-740 5512/ 743 2191; +233-21-7011154. Fax: 022-401336. E-mail: hrdev@ighmail.com. Website: www.hrdevghana.com.

Limited liability company that arranges paid and unpaid internships in Ghana.

Programme description: Practical training and summer work programmes in businesses and institutions in Ghana. Teaching programme at primary, secondary and tertiary levels.

Destinations: Accra, Kumasi, Cape Coast, Tema, Ho and Takoradi.

Prerequisites: Open to high school students, college students and professionals.

Duration and time of placements: Minimum of 6 weeks starting year round.

Remuneration: Allowance paid by employers rather than full salary. Unpaid positions for volunteers.

Other services: Optional cultural, educational and recreational tours in Ghana and West Africa. Room and board can be arranged on request.

Contact: Senyo T. Dake, Chief Executive.

IL SILLABO

Via Alberti 31, 52027 San Giovanni Valdarno (AR), Italy. ☎ 055-912 3238.

Fax: 055-942439. E-mail: info@sillabo.it. Website: www.sillabo.it.
Courses offered: Unpaid internships available to all who achieve an adequate level of Italian after minimum of 4-week intensive course. Most placements are in restaurants and hotels though some also available in travel agencies, farms (e.g. olive picking) and social work.
Duration of courses: 4-24 weeks (following on from language course of same duration).
Cost: fee is €155.
Accommodation: Provided free by employer with meals.
Other services: Many other courses offered in addition to language, e.g. art, cookery, archaeology, etc.
Contact: Anna Paola Bosi, Director.

The Smallpeice Engineering Gap Year is a programme aimed at students with deferred entry to university on an engineering-related degree course. It uniquely combines:

- 11 weeks academic study in engineering, management, IT
- 4 weeks language study in Europe
- 13 weeks work placement in Europe

If you are forward thinking, independent, intent on engineering as a career and ready for a really worthwhile gap year, contact:

The Smallpeice Trust
Holly House, 74 Upper Holly Walk, Leamington Spa, CV32 4JL
Tel: 01926 333200 Fax: 01926 333202
Email: gen@smallpeicetrust.org.uk www.smallpeicetrust.org.uk

THE SMALLPEICE TRUST
Holly House, 74 Upper Holly Walk, Leamington Spa, Warwickshire CV32 4JL.
☎ **01926 333200. Fax: 01926 333202. E-mail: gen@smallpeicetrust.org.uk.**
Website: www.smallpeicetrust.org.uk.
The Smallpeice Engineering Gap Year starts in September each year. It gives students a firm grounding in management and engineering skills, and encompasses a European language and work experience prior to pursuing their chosen engineering discipline in higher education.
Programme description: The programme is divided into four parts: academic, language course, work experience and awards ceremony. The academic part teaches basic engineering skills, supervisory management and computer-aided design. The language course at a European language school lasts 4 weeks and is generally to conversation level unless a qualification is already obtained, in which case a technical level may be achieved. The work experience lasts for 3 months in one of nine European countries and students are expected to become actively involved in engineering projects. Students meet up for a final awards ceremony in May.
Destinations: Work experience is in one of nine European countries.
Number of placements per year: 30 each year.
Prerequisites: Students must be 18 at the start of the course and have a deferred entry place for an engineering-related degree course at a university.
Duration and time of placement: Around seven months in total, beginning in the last week of September.
Selection procedure: Applications are invited from October onwards for the following year and interviews are held at the Smallpeice Trust. It is advisable to reserve a place early based on expected grades. Before the course starts, an induction day is held for students and parents. One week is spent team-building immediately prior to the academic study part of the course. Support is provided by a Smallpeice Trust mentor.
Cost: The fee per student is £4,950 for the complete course which includes

accommodation, subsistence, all tuition and return travel in Europe.
Contact: Derek Wiggins.

SPANNOCCHIA FOUNDATION

Tenuta di Spannocchia, 53012 Chiusdino, Siena (SI), Italy. ☎ 0577-75211. Fax: 0577-752224. E-mail: internships@spannocchia.org. Website: www.spannocchia.com.

Programme description: Internships Programme on 1,200-acre community organic farm and education centre in the hills of Tuscany. Three-quarters of time spent working alongside Italian farm staff in the vineyards, olive groves, forestry operations, etc. The rest of the time is devoted to structured courses, particularly in Italian language.

Number of placements: 8 per session, 24 per year.

Prerequisites: All nationalities though hoping to broaden range (most at present are Americans). Experience working with animals, gardening and/or manual labour is beneficial but not required. Working knowledge of Italian helpful, though interns mainly speak English on-site.

Duration and time of placements: 3 months starting March, June or September.

Cost: Interns are responsible for their airfare to Italy plus insurance and spending money. Financial aid available to people who can't afford programme.

Other services: Free accommodation and meals in exchange for working on the farm.

Contact: Madeline Yale, Internship Programme Director.

TEACHING & PROJECTS ABROAD

Gerrard House, Rustington, West Sussex BN16 1AW. ☎ 01903 859911. Fax: 01903 785779. E-mail: info@teaching-abroad.co.uk. Website: www.teaching-abroad.co.uk.

Teaching & Projects Abroad places fee-paying volunteers in English teaching posts in many countries (see 'Directory of Specialist Gap Year Programmes') and also arranges unpaid work experience.

Programme description: Voluntary work experience opportunities in selected destinations for business, conservation and other fields including archaeology, care, medical, media/journalism and supervised dissertations for degree courses.

Destinations: Include Bolivia, Chile, China, Ghana, India, Mexico, Mongolia, Nepal, Peru, Romania, South Africa, Sri Lanka, Thailand, Togo and Ukraine. Destinations and programmes can be combined.

Number of placements: 2,500 in total of which 60% are project placements and 40% teaching.

Prerequisites: Minimum age 17+. University entrance qualifications needed.

Duration and time of placements: Very flexible, with departures year round and varying lengths of placement.

Cost: Placements are self-funded and the fee charged includes insurance, food, accommodation and overseas support. 3-month placements cost between £995 and £2,295, excluding travel costs.

Volunteering

The current British government strongly supports the ethos of volunteering and is pouring large sums of money into grand schemes to encourage volunteering at all levels, especially among the young. The newest initiative (2003) is to encourage young people from deprived backgrounds to join a volunteer corps who, in exchange for 30 hours a week, will receive a modest allowance of £45. This scheme is partly modelled on the AmeriCorps programme in the US , a kind of 'domestic Peace Corps' as envisioned by President Clinton. Another idea under close scrutiny is to bestow a credit on students who volunteer, including in their gap year, to reduce the costs of university tuition. This is aimed at young people from non-affluent backgrounds who would otherwise find it impossible to justify giving up their time for a worthy cause. At the time of writing (June 2003), it was reported that the Scottish First Minister was proposing a similar ScotsCorps, accompanied by a headline 'School leavers would be funded to have a gap year'. A working group has been set up to find ways of implementing such a volunteering scheme before the end of 2005.

The *Millennium Volunteer* scheme is now well-established. It allows 16-24 year olds to get involved with a range of voluntary organisations in their communities or further afield, with an option to work towards a nationally recognised Certificate in Community Volunteering as part of ASDAN (Award Scheme Development & Accreditation Network; www.asdan.co.uk) Certificate in Community Volunteering; volunteers can log 100 or 200 hours of volunteering with an affiliated organisation in order to earn an award.

Voluntary work can be not only fulfilling and satisfying in itself but can provide a unique stepping stone to interesting possibilities later on. By participating in a project such as digging wells in a Turkish village, looking after orphaned Eskimo children or just helping out at a youth hostel, gap year students have the unique opportunity to live and work in a remote community, and the chance to meet up with young people from many countries. You may be able to improve or acquire a language skill and to learn something of the customs of the society in which you are volunteering. You will also gain practical experience, for instance in the fields of construction, archaeology, museums or social welfare which will later stand you in good stead when applying for paid work. Less tangible but equally marketable benefits include the acquisition of new skills like problem solving, leadership, relationship building, communication skills and self-development generally. Research published recently (based on findings of the recruitment group Reed Executive) showed that three-quarters of employers in business prefer applicants with experience of volunteering.

Although this book is devoted largely to canvassing options abroad, do not discount the possibility of spending some of your gap year in the UK doing something worthwhile away from home. Unlike placements abroad, you are unlikely to be out of pocket at the end of an attachment to British organisations which often pay your travel and living expenses and may even pay an allowance of about £30 a week. A number of such organisations are listed in the Directory later in this chapter.

Community Service Volunteers

Community Service Volunteers (CSV) guarantee a voluntary placement to anyone aged over 16 who commits him/herself to work full-time away from home for at least four months. As many as 2,000 volunteers throughout the UK receive £28 a week in addition to accommodation and meals. Details can be obtained by ringing the Volunteers' Hotline (0800 374991) or on the CSV homepage www.csv.org.uk.

CSV produces oodles of persuasive literature demonstrating how worthwhile a stint as a CSV volunteer can be. **Elizabeth Moore-Bick** volunteered with CSV just after graduating from Cambridge. Studying for a degree in Classics had meant that she had led a fairly rarefied existence and she decided it was time to develop her 'people skills'. Despite initial doubts, she decided to take the plunge and began a placement supporting a woman who had been left paralysed by a car accident 20 years before. Elizabeth and another volunteer provided round-the-clock care:

> *It took me a lot of time to get used to this kind of role. I was really unsure of myself but felt I owed it to Barbara to see the placement through. Volunteering has certainly been a challenge and of course I doubted my ability at times. I felt like I was taking a real leap in the dark. Looking back over the past few months, I'm really proud of myself and I actually get immense satisfaction through volunteering. I won't pretend it's easy, because it isn't. I've had to do a lot of growing up myself as a CSV. I'm having to make real life decisions and take responsibility for another person. I've had to almost give up a part of myself, which is really hard. The best bit is getting things right. It's the simple things that make me feel like I've really achieved something. I'll never look at a person in a wheelchair in the same way again.*

CSV has links with disability services at most British universities and a stint supporting a student might provide a useful initiation as it did for 19 year old **Jo Scluz** who supported three students at Loughborough University for her year between school and university:

> *After finishing A-levels, I wanted to have a break from study and give something back. Being on placement at a university means that everyone is my own age. I've made so many friends. The other students think it is really great that I get to have all the perks of student life without having to do all the study, but of course I've got*

that to look forward to next September when I start my geology course. Being a CSV volunteer has been a crash course in university life.

Note that international volunteers are also welcomed. All overseas CSV volunteers must pay a non-refundable placement fee (£512) before receiving a placement.

European Voluntary Service (EVS)

Thousands of young people aged 18-25 are eligible to take up fully funded placements lasting six but preferably 12 months in Europe or beyond through the EU-funded EVS programme. Full details are available from the *British Council* (see entry for EVS in the *Directory of Specialist Gap Year Programmes*).

The programme is generally regarded as excellent though the usual way in is slightly complicated. After making contact with a national agency, you have to find a sending organisation from the list of youth exchange and other participating voluntary organisations supplied by the EVS department. Alternatively, you can ask a group that you already work or volunteer for (e.g. a youth centre, women's refuge, etc.) to become your sending sponsor. When you have found a sending organisation, they will give you a password to the database of host projects across Europe. These are extremely varied, from conference centres to film workshops, orphanages to environmental projects, though all are socially based with the aim of making contacts across Europe and of benefitting the community.

The programme is open to western European nationals of all social and educational backgrounds. In fact young people from disadvantaged situations are especially encouraged. Participants pay nothing to take part. Both the sending and the host organisations receive some funding from the EU and the volunteers get their travel costs, insurance, board and lodging, language classes, pocket money, orientation and mid-term programme all provided free. There is also a tutor in each project who is available to help with any difficulties and guide the volunteer.

When **Joanne Evans** was an EVS volunteer, she wrote in glowing terms of the programme from her placement at Internationale Haus Sonnenberg, a conference centre in a scenic part of Germany.

Volunteering Abroad

Time spent in a Ghanaian orphanage, an orangutan rehabilitation centre or working with street children in Central America can be a wonderfully liberating release from the exam struggle, whether at school or university, a welcome break before entering the next fray, the search for a job.

In the Newsletter of the Daneford Trust, Rosna Mortuza from Tower Hamlets wrote about her decision to leave the tramlines:
I first considered volunteering abroad at an accountancy recruitment fair in my final year at university. Whilst surrounded by the investment bankers, stockbrokers and consultants of the future, I realised that getting into the city was not a journey I wanted to embark on. Instead I found myself referrring to the stories of my peers who had taken gap years in India, South Africa and Cuba, which sounded like exciting, adventurous and romantic experiences that I wanted a taste of too. More importantly, volunteering offered me something challenging without always having to be competitive and under pressure. And the more I planned my trip with the Daneford Trust, the more it apealed to me as something that was going to be in lots of ways unstructured, unpredictable and unassessed.
I'm not sure exactly why I chose to volunteer in Bangladesh. It seemed a natural choice in order to make use of being bilingual in Bengali/Sylheti and I felt I would be able to interact on a more comfortable and effective level as a volunteer. On returning, I am aware I have not changed the world or indeed a tiny place called

Sylhet. What I'm certain of is that volunteering allows you to extend experiences beyond your own reality, giving a more grounded sense of self and others.

The spirit to help others may be willing but the cash supplies may be weak. While charities in the UK might be able to cover their volunteers' basic costs, this is almost never the case abroad. We have already seen how expensive specialist gap programmes can be. The organisations listed in this chapter do not specialise in gap year students and the initial outlay of joining one of these organisations will normally be less than for the high profile specialist agencies. As a consequence they may not be so geared up for integrating volunteers as young as 18 which is not normally a problem if the volunteer does not carry unreasonable expectations.

Most voluntary jobs undertaken abroad will leave the volunteer seriously out-of-pocket, which can be disillusioning for those who think that a desire to help the world should be enough. After participating in several prearranged voluntary projects in the United States, **Catherine Brewin** did not resent the fee she had paid to *Involvement Volunteers*:

The whole business of paying to do voluntary work is a bit hard to swallow. But having looked into the matter quite a bit, it does seem to be the norm. While it may be a bit unfair (who knows how much profit or loss these voluntary organisations make or how worthy their projects?), most people I've met did seem to feel good about the experience. The group I was with did raise the odd comment about it all, but did not seem unduly concerned. However I should mention that most were around 18 years old and their parents were paying some if not all the costs.

Sources of Information

For information specifically about youth volunteering in the UK, the government-funded *National Youth Agency* (17-23 Albion St, Leicester LE1 6GD; 0116 285 3700; www.nya.org.uk) offers advice and publishes an annual free newspaper called *Volunteer Action* with useful listings of residential and non-residential placements. The website of the National Centre for Volunteering in Bristol (www.volunteering.org.uk) has a listing of UK agencies that send volunteers abroad, as well as disseminating a great deal of other information about volunteering generally.

Worldwide Volunteering for Young People (7 North Street Workshops, Stoke sub Hamdon, Somerset TA14 6QR; 01935 825588; www.www.org.uk) has developed an authoritative search-and-match database of volunteering opportunities for 16-35 year olds which is available individually on-line and by subscription (on-line or CD) for schools, colleges, universities, careers offices, volunteer bureaux, etc.

The revolution in information technology has made it easier for the individual to become acquainted with the amazing range of possibilities. Some superb websites feature a multitude of links to organisations big and small that can make use of volunteers. For example www.idealist.org (from Action Without Borders) is an easily searchable site that will take you to the great monolithic charities like the Peace Corps as well as to small grassroots organisations in Armenia, Tenerife or anywhere else. It lists 20,000 organisations in 150 countries. Another impressive site is one from AVSO, the Association of Voluntary Services Organisations, in Belgium (174 rue Joseph II, 2000 Brussels; www.avso.org) which is supported by the European Commission. The Polish-based Alliance of European Voluntary Service Organizations (www.volunt.net/alliance) has a good search engines for voluntary work. Check also www.timebank.org.uk or the Japan based Go M.A.D. (www.go-mad.org) which has links to unusual voluntary projects worldwide.

Another smaller site is www.eVolunteer.co.uk which includes small British and international grassroots organisations while the UK-based oneworld.net lists vacancies primarily of interest to aid professionals.

The World Service Enquiry of the respected charity Christians Abroad (Bon Marché Centre, Suite 233, 241-251 Ferndale Road, London SW9 8BJ; 0870 770 3274;

wse@cabroad.org.uk/ www.wse.org.uk) provides information and advice to people of any faith or none who are thinking of working overseas, whether short or long term, voluntary or paid. Their World Service Enquiry Guide 2003 is available for a suggested donation of £3 plus 44p stamp; it contains a useful listing of organisations in the UK and overseas, and details how and where to begin a search for work abroad. Working Abroad (formerly known as VWIS, the Voluntary Work Information Service) (59 Lansdowne Place, Hove, Sussex BN3 1FL; ☎/fax 01273 211406; info@workingabroad.com; www.workingabroad.com) distributes information about current volunteer vacancies online and will also produce a personalised report for enquirers who pay a search fee of £29 for an electronic report or £36 for a printed report.

Students with a church affiliation and Christian faith have a broader choice of opportunities since a number of mission societies and charities are looking for young Christians (see the separate listing in this chapter of Religious Organisations). Whereas some religious organisations focus on practical work, such as working with street children, orphans, in schools, building libraries, etc. others are predominantly proselytising, which will only appeal to the very committed. Christian Vocations (St James House, Trinity Road, Dudley, West Midlands DY1 1JB; 01384 233511; www.christianvocations.org) publishes a directory listing short-term opportunities with Christian agencies. The *STS Directory 2003* (Short-Term Service) is available for £7 including postage.

Avoiding Problems

Bear in mind that voluntary work, especially in the developing world, can be not only tough and character-building but also disillusioning. Misunderstandings can arise, and promises can be broken just as easily in the context of unpaid work as paid work. If you are in any doubt about an organisation you are considering working for, ask for the names of one or two past volunteers whom you can contact for an informal reference. Any worthy organisation should be happy to oblige.

Carina Strutt's experiences in Central America are uncommon, but worth bearing in mind when considering joining a privately-run project sight unseen. Before going to study in Plymouth, she signed up for an environmental project in Costa Rica where she spent most of her time painting T-shirts for the owners who wanted the task done in time for their holiday in Australia. Worse, they treated the local people with scant respect.

Other organisations are even more sinister. At the time of writing, the Danish founder of the notorious Humana-Tvind organisation and seven others are standing trial for a massive charity fraud and the trial is expected to continue until October 2004. Humana-Tvind operates under many names worldwide including One World Volunteer Institute and Humana People to People (both in Scandinavia) and the Institute for International Co-operation & Development (USA). Invariably the organisation requires volunteers to pay large upfront fees for training and placement. Details are available on the website www.tvindalert.com. Humana-Tvind has had its charitable status removed by the British Charity Commission.

Workcamps

Voluntary work in developed countries often takes the form of workcamps which accept unskilled short-term labour. Workcamps are an excellent introduction to travelling for 16 to 20 year olds who have never before been away from a family type social structure. As part of an established international network of voluntary organisations they are not subject to the irregularities of some privately run projects. As well as providing gap year and other volunteers with the means to live cheaply for two to four weeks in a foreign country, workcamps enable volunteers to become involved in what is usually useful work for the community, to meet people from many different backgrounds and to increase their awareness of other lifestyles, social problems and their responsibility to society.

Within Europe, and to a lesser extent further afield, there is a massive effort to co-ordinate workcamp programmes. This means that the prospective volunteer should apply in the first instance to an organisation in his or her own country (see entries later in this chapter for *International Voluntary Service (IVS), UNA Exchange, Concordia, Quaker Voluntary Action* and *Youth Action for Peace.* The vast majority of camps take place in the summer months, and camp details are normally published in March/April with most placements being made in April/May. Understandably, these organisations charge £4-£6 for a printed copy of their international programmes though a great deal of information is available online. It is necessary to pay a registration fee (usually £80-£130 for overseas camps), which includes board and lodging but not travel.

Many projects are environmental and involve the conversion/reconstruction of historic buildings and building community facilities. Interesting projects include building adventure playgrounds for children, renovating an open-air museum in Latvia, organising youth concerts in Armenia, constructing boats for sea-cleaning in Japan, looking after a farm-school in Slovakia during the holidays, helping peasant farmers in central France to stay on their land, excavating a Roman villa in Germany, forest fire spotting in Italy, plus a whole range of schemes with the disabled and elderly, conservation work and the study of social and political issues. It is sometimes possible to move from project to project throughout the summer, particularly in countries such as France or Morocco where the workcamp movement is highly developed.

Archaeology

Taking part in archaeological excavations is another popular form of voluntary work especially among gap year students planning to study a related subject at university. Volunteers are almost always expected to make a contribution towards their board and lodging. Also, you may be asked to bring your own trowel, work clothes, tent, etc. (see entry for *Archaeology Abroad* and the country chapters, especially Israel and France). *Archaeology Abroad* makes Fieldwork Awards of £100-£200 and scholarships to selected candidates joining an archaeological excavation listed in the April or November issues (to which applicants must be subscribers).

For those who are not students of archaeology, the chances of finding a place on an overseas dig will be greatly enhanced by having some digging experience nearer to home. Details of British excavations looking for volunteers are published in *Briefing* which comes out with the magazine *British Archaeology* from the Council for British Archaeology (see UK entry).

Anthony Blake joined a dig sponsored by the University of Reims and warns that 'archaeology is hard work, and applicants must be aware of what working for eight hours in the baking heat means!' Nevertheless Anthony found the company excellent and the opportunity to improve his French welcome.

Conservation

People interested in protecting the environment can often slot into conservation organisations abroad. One enterprising traveller in South Africa looked up the 'green directory' in a local library, contacted a few of the projects listed in the local area and was invited to work at a cheetah reserve near Johannesburg in exchange for accommodation and food.

For a directory of opportunities in this specialised area, consult the 2003 edition of *Green Volunteers: The World Guide to Voluntary Work in Nature Conservation* published in Italy and distributed by Vacation Work Publications in Europe (£10.99 plus postage). Related titles from the same publisher are *Working with the Environment* and *Working with Animals.* Also look at the website for the Ecovolunteer Programme of wildlife and conservation holidays worldwide (www.ecovolunteer.org.uk).

To fix up a short conservation holiday, contact *BTCV* (British Trust for Conservation Volunteers) which runs a programme of international projects in most European countries as well as North America, Ecuador, Nepal and many others. Costs vary from £275 though most two or three week trips cost upwards of £500 excluding airfares. Details can be checked on www.btcv.org.uk.

The international system of working-for-keep on organic farms is another good way of visiting unexplored corners of the world cheaply (see entry for *World Wide Opportunities on Organic Farms/WWOOF*). Some have described WWOOFing as the new kibbutz volunteering. Of the several thousand WWOOF members in the UK about half are aged 18-25.

Several organisations assist scientific expeditions by supplying fee-paying volunteers, in addition to *Earthwatch* (entry below). For details of scientific expedition organisations which use self-financing volunteers, see entries for *Biosphere Expeditions* (below) and *Coral Cay Conservation, Greenforce, Trekforce* and *Frontier* in the *Directory of Specialist Gap Year Programmes*.

Developing Countries

Commitment, no matter how fervent, is not enough to work for an aid organisation in the developing world. You must be able to offer some kind of useful training or skill. However if you are travelling in underdeveloped countries and take the time to investigate local possibilities, you may discover wildlife projects, children's homes, special schools, etc. in which it will be possible to work voluntarily for a short or longer time. You may simply want to join your new Vietnamese, Sri Lankan or Ecuadorian friends wherever they are working. You may get the chance to trade your assistance for a straw mat and simple meals but more likely the only rewards will be the experience and the camaraderie.

Directory of Voluntary Placements in the UK

L'ARCHE

10 Briggate, Silsden, Keighley, West Yorkshire BD20 9JT. ☎ 01535 656186. Fax: 01535 656426. E-mail: info@larche.org.uk. Website: www.larche.org.uk.
Programme description: L'Arche is a worldwide network of communities where assistants help people with learning disabilities to live in a congenial atmosphere. The aim is to provide a real home, with spiritual and emotional support.
Destinations: Kent, Liverpool, Inverness, Lambeth, Bognor Regis, Brecon, Edinburgh and Preston.
Number of placements per year: 190-200.
Prerequisites: Assistants need an ability and willingness to live communally.
Duration and time of placements: Generally 12 months, although shorter and longer stays are sometimes acceptable.
Selection procedures and orientation: Enquirers are sent an information pack along with a searching application form. They are invited to visit the community, meet the members and have an informal interview with house leaders/assistants/co-ordinators. All assistants work for a probationary period and receive a one-to-one induction with the community leader.
Cost: Assistants must pay their own travel costs and personal insurance. Free board and lodging are provided and a modest allowance is paid.

THE BLACKIE

Great Georges Community Cultural Project, Great George Street, Liverpool L1 5EW. ☎ 0151-709 5109. Fax: 0151-709 4822. E-mail: staff@theblackie.org.uk.
Long-established community arts venue hosting playschemes, workshops, games, arts and crafts, disabled workshops, etc. set in a former church in inner-city Liverpool.
Programme description: Volunteers are needed to work and play with the children and adults on the schemes. The jobs are shared so that everyone contributes to the cleaning, repairs, administration and playing. Volunteers live in single-sex, shared rooms, with a

shared lounge, bathroom and kitchen. Volunteers bring sleeping bags.
Destinations: Inner-city Liverpool.
Number of placements per year: About 100.
Prerequisites: No specific skills or qualifications are required.
Duration and time of placements: 4 weeks minimum.
Selection procedures and orientation: A fully detailed letter is required about the person applying.
Cost: Volunteers contribute about £20 a week for food costs.

BRAENDAM FAMILY HOUSE
Thornhill, Stirling, FK8 3QH, Scotland. ☎ 01786 850259. Fax: 01786 850738. E-mail: braendam.house@care4free.net. Website: www.braendam.org.uk.
Since 1966 this organisation has been offering short holidays for disadvantaged families. Situated in a peaceful environment, the children can play safely and parents can rest.
Programme description: Volunteers are needed to help with the running of the house. They are required to play with the children, drive house vehicles, encourage families to participate in outdoor activities, organise and take part in games, art, crafts and group work and help with domestic duties.
Destinations: Braendam Family House set in seven acres of its own grounds.
Number of placements per year: 7 volunteers at a time.
Prerequisites: Drivers are preferred, as is some experience of children. Volunteers must be enthusiastic but patient.
Duration and time of placements: 6-12 months.
Selection procedures and orientation: Telephone interviews are sufficient. Volunteers receive a staff pack and induction training on arrival. Fortnightly training is given.
Cost: £40 is paid towards travel costs and board and lodging are free. Weekly spending money of £32 is paid to each volunteer.
Contact: Brian Guidery, Manager.

BREAK
Davison House, 1 Montague Road, Sheringham, Norfolk NR26 8WN. ☎ 01263 822161. Fax: 01263 822181. E-mail: office@break-charity.org. Website: www.break-charity.org.
Break was established in 1968 to provide a range of specialist care services for children, adults and families with special needs. This includes holidays, short breaks and respite care at two holiday centres on the North Norfolk coast, day care for adults with learning disabilities, children's homes and a family assessment unit for families in crisis.
Programme description: Volunteers help at the two holiday centres with the personal care of the guests, including dressing, feeding, toiletting, bathing and getting about and participate in their recreational programme including trips out to local attractions. Stress is placed on the importance of respecting the dignity of guests and promoting their independence. Volunteer accommodation is provided in the centres with shared common room and bedrooms.
Destinations: At two centres on the Norfolk coast, the Sandcastle at Hunstanton and Rainbow in Sheringham.
Number of placements per year: 30 (maximum 10 at any one time).
Duration and time of placements: 3-11 months with flexible start dates.
Selection procedures and orientation: References and police checks required but not interviews. Induction and on-the-job training are given. Volunteers are able to take part in some basic training courses.
Cost: No costs are involved in joining the programme. Free board and lodging and out-of-pocket expenses (currently £45 per week) are provided. Travel costs within the UK are reimbursed.
Contact: Barbara Bajormee, Residential Volunteer Co-ordinator.

BTCV

British Trust for Conservation Volunteers, 36 St. Mary's Street, Wallingford, Oxfordshire OX10 0EU. ☎ **01491 839766 or 01491 821600. Fax: 01491 839646. E-mail: information@btcv.org.uk. Website: www.btcv.org.uk.**
BTCV is a charity established to protect the environment through practical action. With more than 150 offices, thousands of volunteers can take part in a wide range of short environmental projects.
Programme description: Volunteers help with projects such as tree-planting, repairing footpaths and dry stone walls, creating community gardens and recycling materials.
Destinations: In the UK (see BTCV entry in 'Directory of Voluntary Placements Abroad' for details of their International Programme).
Number of placements per year: 600 working holidays a year are organised.
Prerequisites: Energy and enthusiasm needed; no experience necessary.
Duration and time of placements: Mostly 1 week or short weekend breaks.
Selection procedures and orientation: Programmes can be booked on the website or by phone. Full training is given by qualified leaders during the programme.
Cost: All are priced differently depending on whether simple, standard or superior accommodation is offered. Week-long projects cost £60-£115 inclusive of food, accommodation and training.

CATHEDRAL CAMPS

16 Glebe Avenue, Flitwick, Bedfordshire MK45 1HS. ☎ **01525 716237. E-mail: admin@cathedralcamps.org.uk. Website: www.cathedralcamps.org.uk.**
Programme description: Volunteers help to renovate and carry out routine maintenance of parish churches and Cathedrals throughout the UK. Jobs may include cleaning roof voids, conserving marble memorials, washing and painting interior and exterior walls, making detailed records of monuments and helping with gardening activities.
Duration and time of placements: 1 week workcamps, from 6pm Wednesday to noon the following Wednesday.
Selection procedures and orientation: For a volunteer's first camp, a letter of recommendation is required from a Head Teacher, Senior Tutor or a person in a position of authority who is not related to the applicant. All training needed is given on the course.
Cost: Volunteers are asked to contribute £60 towards board and lodging; the full costs are £150 so any extra contributions would be welcomed. Many local Education Authorities award grants to Cathedral Camp volunteers. A limited number of bursaries is available to volunteers who would be otherwise unable to afford a camp.

CHILDREN'S TRUST

Tadworth Court, Tadworth, Surrey KT2D 5DU. ☎ **01737 357171. Fax: 01737 373848. E-mail: c-trust@netcomuk.co.uk. Website: www.thechildrenstrust.org.uk.**
The Children's Trust is a charity which looks after children with long-term special needs, whether physical, learning or behavioural.
Programme description: Volunteers are needed to help with the care, treatment and education of children with exceptional needs and profound disabilities, acting as a friend. Volunteers are often a great help with outings and feeding.
Prerequisites: People aged 18 and over planning to go into the caring professions such as nursing, teaching, medicine and social work are preferred.
Duration and time of placements: July to September or 6-12 months minimum is required.
Selection procedures and orientation: Interviews are held only if the applicant lives locally. Application forms must be completed and references provided. There is a 2-week training period. Volunteers are supported by nurses, therapists, teachers and the Volunteer Department throughout their stay.
Cost: Accommodation is provided free of charge. A subsistence allowance of £51 per week is paid. Additional travel expenses within the UK are paid.

Contact: Rachel Turner.

CSV (COMMUNITY SERVICE VOLUNTEERS)
237 Pentonville Road, London N1 9NJ. ☎ 0800 374991/020-7278 6601. E-mail: volunteer@csv.org.uk. Website: www.csv.org.uk.
CSV is the largest voluntary placement organisation in the UK. It guarantees a voluntary placement to anyone aged 16+ who commits him or herself to a minimum of 4 months volunteering.
Programme description: CSV volunteers help people throughout Britain in a huge range of social care projects, e.g. working with the homeless or helping the disabled to live independently in their homes, and at the same time learn new skills. CSV volunteers are full-time and live away from home anywhere within Britain.
Number of placements per year: 1,500-2,000.
Prerequisites: No specific qualifications are needed. Other nationalities can participate provided they are over 18 and are able to pay the non-refundable placement fee of £512 (details from international@csv.org.uk).
Duration and time of placements: 4-12 months, beginning at any time of the year.
Selection procedures and orientation: Volunteers receive regular supervision and back-up support from their local CSV office. No one is rejected.
Cost: CSV volunteers receive £28 per week living allowance; food, accommodation and travel expenses are also provided.

COUNCIL FOR BRITISH ARCHAEOLOGY
Bowes Morrell House, 111 Walmgate, York YO1 9WA. ☎ 01904 671417. Fax: 01904 671384. E-mail: info@britarch.ac.uk. Website: www.britarch.ac.uk.
The CBA works to promote the study and safeguarding of Britain's historic environment, to provide a forum for archaeological opinion and to improve public knowledge of Britain's past. The *Briefing* insert in Council's regular magazine *British Archaeology* appears five times a year giving details of fieldwork projects and excavations throughout Britain which accept volunteers and/or offer training courses. The magazine is published in February, April, June, August, October and December. An annual subscription costs £23 but it also forms part of an individual membership package which is available for £27 with extra benefits. Full-time students can join for £16. Information is also published on the CBA website. Readers should apply directly to the projects listed on the website rather than to the CBA.
Contact: Dr. Mike Heyworth.

EARTHWATCH EUROPE
267 Banbury Road, Oxford OX2 7HT. ☎ 01865 318838. Fax: 01865 311383. E-mail: info@earthwatch.org.uk. Website: www.earthwatch.org/europe.
International environmental charity whose mission is to promote the conservation of the world's natural resources and cultural heritage by supporting scientific field research and education.
Programme description: Various environmental projects such as monitoring endangered species.
Destinations: Throughout the UK (and worldwide, see entry in next section).
Duration and time of placements: Average duration is two weeks though project length varies from 2 days to one month.
Selection procedures: No special skills required.
Cost: Membership is £25 per annum, £15 for students, £30 for Europe. UK prices start at £120 for a short project, e.g. monitoring mammals in a nature reserve, conducting a study of basking sharks or tracking dinosaurs along the coast of Yorkshire.

FESTINIOG RAILWAY COMPANY
**Harbour Station, Porthmadog, Gwynedd, North Wales LL49 9NF. **

01766 512340. Fax: 01766 514576. E-mail: info@festrail.co.uk. Website: www.festrail.co.uk.
The world's oldest independent railway company. The narrow gauge trains follow a 13½ mile route through Snowdonia National Park. The Welsh Highland Railway (Caernarfon) is being rebuilt from Caernarfon to Porthmadog.
Programme description: Volunteers are required to help with the maintenance and running of the railway. Work might be in the Commercial sections, Locomotive Operating, Mechanical Departments or Civil Engineering. Skilled and unskilled workers can work in the Buildings, Parks and Gardens area.
Prerequisites: Minimum age 16. All volunteers must be fit.
Selection procedures and orientation: Training is given where necessary.
Cost: Limited self-catering hostel accommodation is provided for regular volunteers, for which a small charge is made; food is extra. Camping space and a list of local accommodation are available.
Contact: Volunteers Resource Manager.

HESSE STUDENT SCHEME
Aldeburgh Festival, Aldeburgh Productions, Snape Maltings Concert Hall, Snape, Saxmundham, Suffolk IP17 1SP. ☎ 01728 687100. Fax: 01728 687120. E-mail: enquiries@aldeburghfestivals.org. Website: www.aldeburgh.co.uk/news/hesse.htm.
Programme description: Volunteers assist in the day-to-day running of the Aldeburgh Festival of Music and the Arts in June and prepare for the Hesse Students Concert. Duties include selling programmes, helping backstage, conducting shuttle buses, page turning and assisting Aldeburgh staff. Students are also expected to devise and perform a concert as part of the programme of free events.
Number of placements per year: 2 sets of 12 students are chosen for each half of the Festival.
Prerequisites: Ages 18-25. Must be a music lover. Also willing to help with the general running of the Aldeburgh Festival and have a cheerful disposition and a professional approach.
Duration and time of placements: One week during the Festival which runs over the middle two weeks in June.
Cost: Volunteers receive a grant to cover the cost of bed and breakfast accommodation and tickets to selected Festival events.
Contact: Hannah Brewer, Education Officer (hannahb@aldeburghfestivals.org).

INDEPENDENT LIVING ALTERNATIVES
Trafalgar House, Grenville Place, London NW7 3SA. ☎/fax: 020-8906 9265. E-mail: mail@I-L-A.fsnet.co.uk. Website: www.I-L-A.fsnet.co.uk.
Volunteers are required to provide support for people with disabilities, to enable them to live independently in their own homes. Placements are suitable for gap year students. The work involves helping clients get dressed, go to the toilet, drive, do the housework, etc. Volunteers receive £63.50 per week plus free accommodation, usually in the London area but also in Cumbria. ILA offers a chance to learn about disability issues and see London at the same time. No qualifications are required, except good English. Vacancies arise all year round.

LOSANG DRAGPA CENTRE
Buddhist College and Meditation Centre, Dobroyd Castle, Pexwood Road, Todmorden, West Yorkshire OL14 7JJ. ☎ 01706 812247. Fax: 01706 818901. E-mail: info@losangdragpa.com. Website: www.losangdragpa.com.
In return for 35 hours' work per week, volunteers receive food, accommodation and teaching on Buddhism. The day begins at about 9am. In the evenings volunteers can participate in meditation classes and on weekends volunteers can explore the surrounding countryside.

MADHYAMAKA BUDDHIST CENTRE
Kilnwick Percy Hall, Pocklington, York YO42 1UF. ☎ 01759 304832. Fax: 01759 305962. E-mail: info@madhyamaka.org. Website: www.madhyamaka.org.
Visitors may offset the cost of a stay by working, which involves construction in the ongoing restoration and expansion programme for the house or working in the extensive grounds. Free dormitory accommodation and vegetarian meals provided. At the weekends and in the evenings visitors may attend evening meditations and teachings.

MANJUSHRI MAHAYANA BUDDHIST CENTRE
Conishead Priory, Ulverston, Cumbria LA12 9QQ. ☎ 01229 584029. E-mail: info@manjushri.org.uk. Website: www.manjushri.org.uk.
Working holidays for volunteers. 35 hours of work (e.g. cooking, gardening, decorating, office work) per week in exchange for a free stay. Applications can be made online or call for an application form.

MILLENNIUM VOLUNTEERS
MV Unit, Room E4b, Department for Education and Skills, Moorfoot, Sheffield S1 4PQ. ☎ 0800 917 8185. E-mail: millennium.volunteers@dfee.gov.uk. Website: www.millenniumvolunteers.gov.uk.
Programme description: UK-wide initiative provides volunteering opportunities for young volunteers in the UK aged 16-24. Volunteers contribute time to a range of voluntary organisations, from their local Citizens Advice Bureau to joining a conservation project organised by BCTV (see entry). Scheme is run in conjunction with CSV (see entry above).
Destinations: Throughout the UK.
Number of placements per year: Unlimited.
Prerequisites: Ages 16-24.
Duration and time of placements: Variable.
Cost: Out-of-pocket expenses covered.

THE NATIONAL TRUST
Long Term Volunteering, 33 Sheep St, Cirencester, Glos. GL7 1RQ. ☎ 01285 651818. Fax: 01285 657935. E-mail: volunteers@nationaltrust.org.uk. Website: www.nationaltrust.org.uk/volunteers.
Programme description: Volunteer placements for people taking a break from education or work. Work might include working alongside a warden or forester with countryside management, assisting house staff with running and conserving historic buildings, gardening, archaeology, education or promotion.
Destinations: Throughout the UK.
Prerequisites: Minimum age 18. Enthusiasm, common sense and adaptability are as important as experience or qualifications.
Duration and time of placements: 3-12 months, though normal minimum is 6 months. Minimum 21 hours per week.
Selection procedures and orientation: Applications accepted year round.
Cost: No wages. Self-catering accommodation available in most regions.

ROYAL SOCIETY FOR THE PROTECTION OF BIRDS (RSPB)
The Lodge, Sandy, Bedfordshire SG19 2DL. ☎ 01767 680551. Fax: 01767 692365. E-mail: volunteers@rspb.org.uk. Website: www.rspb.org.uk/vacancies.
Residential Voluntary Wardening Scheme operates on 35 sites around the UK and provides the opportunity to gain practical experience of the day-to-day management of an RSPB reserve by living and working on the reserve as a volunteer. The work varies from season to season and from reserve to reserve but can include practical management tasks, work with visitors, survey/monitoring work or habitat management. Ornithological knowledge is less important than enthusiasm, an interest in conservation and a willingness to work as

part of a team.
Duration and time of placements: 1-4 weeks (Saturday to Saturday only). Long-term placements available by agreement.
Prerequisites: Minimum age 16 (18 on some sites).
Cost: Accommodation is provided. Volunteers need to organise and pay for their own travel to and from the reserve, and to provide and cover the cost of their own food during their stay.
Contact: Kate Tycer, VW Scheme Development Officer (Youth & Volunteers).

SHAD
SHAD Wandsworth, 5 Bedford Hill, Balham, SW12 9ET (020-8675 6095. E-mail: shadwand@aol.com. Website: www.shad.org.uk).
SHAD (Support and Housing Assistance for people with Disabilities) enables tenants with physical disabilities to live in their own homes. Volunteers are needed to act as the tenants' arms and legs under their instructions.
Duration and time of placements: Minimum 3-4 months, year round.
Work is on a rota basis: volunteers can expect a minimum of 4 days off a fortnight. A shift system is worked by volunteers allowing plenty of free time to explore London.
Prerequisites: No experience is necessary and support is guaranteed.
Selection procedures and orientation: This is an excellent opportunity to gain good work experience in a friendly and supportive environment. Full lifting training and induction are provided.
Payment: Volunteers receive an allowance of at least £60 a week, free accommodation and expenses.

THE SIMON COMMUNITY
PO Box 1187, London NW5 4HW. ☎ 020-7485 6639. E-mail: thesimoncommu nity@yahoo.co.uk. Website: www.thesimoncommunity.org.
The Simon Community is a community of homeless people and volunteers. They run two residential projects, an office and conduct outreach via meeting homeless people one-to-one and through 4 weekly soup runs.
Programme description: Workers are first assigned to residential work, and become involved in the varied tasks involved in the running of community.
Destinations: London.
Prerequisites: Minimum age 19.
Duration and time of placements: Minimum time is 3 months although longer stays preferred.
Cost: None. Volunteers receive free room and board as well as weekly pocket money.

TOC H
The Stable Block, The Firs, High St, Whitchurch, Aylesbury, Bucks HP22 4JU. ☎ 01296 642020. Fax: 01296 640022. E-mail: info@toch.org.uk. Website: www.toch.org.uk.
Programme description: Toc H organises community projects throughout the UK such as conservation and children's playschemes.
Number of placements per year: Over 500.
Prerequisites: Minimum age 16.
Duration and time of placements: Between 2 and 14 days including weekend projects.
Selection procedures and orientation: Interviews not necessary, only written applications.
Cost: Standard registration fee is £20.

TREES FOR LIFE
The Park, Findhorn Bay, Forres, Scotland IV36 3TZ. ☎ 01309 691292. Fax: 01309 691155. E-mai: trees@findhorn.org. Website: www.treesforlife.org.uk.

Programme description: Volunteers needed to restore the native Caledonian Forest in Scotland. Details of different work tasks and locations on website or in brochure.
Destinations: Scottish Highlands.
Prerequisites: No special skills required. Should be fit since projects take place in remote areas accessible by foot.
Duration and time of placements: work weeks start each Saturday from mid-March to early June and from the beginning of September until the end of October.
Cost: £65 (£33 unwaged) includes vegetarian food, accommodation in hostels, bunkhouses or Highland bothies and transport from Inverness.
Contact: Paul Kendall, Work Week Co-ordinator.

WATERWAY RECOVERY GROUP LTD
PO Box 114, Rickmansworth, Herts. WD3 1ZY. ☎ 01923 711114. E-mail: enquiries@wrg.org.uk. Website: www.wrg.org.uk.
Programme description: Opportunities for week-long voluntary workcamps (Canal Camps) restoring derelict and abandoned canals in Britain.
Destinations: Camp locations listed on website.
Prerequisites: For ages 17-70. No skills needed.
Duration and time of placements: 1 week camps mostly between April and October.
Cost: £35 per week for board and lodging plus spending money.

WINGED FELLOWSHIP TRUST
Angel House, 20-32 Pentonville Road, London N1 9XD. ☎ 020-7833 4579 ext 116. Fax: 020-7278 0370. E-mail: admin@wft.org.uk. Website: www.wft.org.uk.
Provides breaks for people with disabilities and their carers.
Programme description: Volunteers are recruited to help at holiday centres for people with disabilities.
Destinations: Centres in Southampton, Southport, Bridgford and Chigwell.
Prerequisites: Minimum age 16 (17 at Sandpipers in Southport). No experience necessary.
Duration and time of placements: Minimum 1 week between February and November.
Selection procedures and orientation: Trained care staff are always around and induction training and ongoing support are given.
Cost: None. All board, lodging and travel to centres is paid.
Contact: Flavia Hernandez, Volunteer Bookings Officer.

WWOOF UK
World Wide Opportunities on Organic Farms, PO Box 2675, Lewes, East Sussex BN7 1RB. E-mail: hello@wwoof.org. Website: www.wwoof.org.
Helps people interested in organic farming to exchange their manual labour for a chance to stay on farms throughout the UK and Ireland. See entry in 'Directory of Voluntary Placements Abroad'.

WORCESTERSHIRE LIFESTYLES
Woodside Lodge, Lark Hill Road, Worcester WR5 2EF. ☎ 01905 350686. Fax: 01905 350684. E-mail: worcslifestyles@btinternet.com. Website: www.worcestershire-lifestyles.org.uk.
Programme description: Full-time volunteers are recruited to act as the arms and legs of people with physical disabilities and/or sensory impairment, to enable them to live independently in their own homes. Duties may include personal care, domestic tasks and sharing leisure interests.
Destinations: Herefordshire & Worcestershire.
Number of placements per year: 100 volunteer workers are required to assist with 30 service users.

Prerequisites: A good level of English is required. Volunteers must be honest, caring and adaptable.
Duration and time of placements: From 4 months.
Selection procedures and orientation: Applicants must make a written application and UK residents are invited to interview. One week's induction is given, with new volunteers shadowing an existing worker.
Cost: None. Free accommodation and a weekly allowance are provided. Travel expenses within UK are covered.
Contact: Nicola Boho, Volunteer Dept.

Directory of Voluntary Placements Abroad

AFRICAN LEGACY
46A Ophir Road, Bournemouth, Dorset BH8 8LT. ☎/fax: 01202 554735. E-mail: explore@africanlegacy.info. Website: http://apollo5.bournemouth.ac.uk/consci/africanlegacy/index.htm.
Non-profit-making organisation with academic affiliations.
Programme description: Study and preservation of archaeology, ecology, wildlife and cultural landscapes of Nigeria.
Destinations: Nigeria, e.g. Sukur Cultural Area (now a World Heritage Site), Okumu National Park, etc. May expand to Ghana in the future.
Prerequisites: Volunteers join 2-week adventure training course to learn Rapid Survey Technology on-the-job. Candidates must be able to 'wade through undergrowth or plod through soft sand in the hot sun all day and still keep smiling'.
Duration and time of placements: 2-52 weeks depending on funding.
Cost: Volunteers must find their own funding.
Contact: Dr. Patrick Darling, Director.

AMERISPAN
PO Box 58129, Philadelphia, PA 19102, USA. ☎ 800-879-6640 or 215-751-1100. Fax: 215-751-1986. E-mail: info@amerispan.com. Website: www.amerispan.com.
Specialist Spanish-language travel organisation with great expertise in arranging language courses, voluntary placements and internships throughout South and Central America.
Programme description: Many choices of volunteer placement and internships. Some come with free accommodation. A typical programme would be a 1-month language programme followed by 1-6 month volunteer placement in health care, education, tourism/marketing or social work.
Cost: Application and placement fee $350 includes travel insurance.

ARCHAEOLOGY ABROAD
31-34 Gordon Square, London WC1H 0PY. Fax: 020-7383 2572. E-mail: arch.abroad@ucl.ac.uk. Website: www.britarch.ac.uk/archabroad.
Established in 1972 and based at University College London.
Programme description: Provides information about archaeological fieldwork outside the UK in its publication *Archaeology Abroad* published in April and November.
Destinations: Worldwide.
Number of placements per year: 700-1,000.
Prerequisites: In some of the overseas digs, directors may prefer those with some experience. Much of the fieldwork involves physical labour and so volunteers need to be

fit and healthy.
Duration and time of placements: From 2 weeks upwards.
Selection procedures and orientation: Applications from people with a definite interest in the subject are preferred. Training is generally offered to those with no excavation experience.
Cost: Annual subscription to the magazine costs £14 (£17/€45 in Europe, £20/$55 elsewhere). Fieldwork Awards available towards cost of joining excavation projects listed in *Archaeology Abroad*.

ATD FOURTH WORLD
48 Addington Square, London SE5 7LB. ☎ 020-7703 3231. Fax: 020-7252 4276. E-mail: atd@atd-uk.org. Website: www.atd-uk.org.
ATD (All Together for Dignity) began in Paris in 1957 and has since expanded with branches in 27 countries across five continents working with disadvantaged communities experiencing long-term poverty.
Programme description: Volunteers can join in with street workshops in the most disadvantaged areas in Europe. The aim is to create a festival atmosphere as part of a fight against poverty and social deprivation. Longer attachments undertake projects such as running a street library in Madrid and Guatemala, youth work in Marseille, etc.
Destinations: France, Belgium, Netherlands, Switzerland and Spain in the summer.
Prerequisites: Volunteers must be over 18 and prepared to stay for the duration of the workshops.
Duration and time of placements: 1 and 2 week workshops and summer projects. Also 3, 6, 9 and 12 month placements.
Cost: £50/€76 weekly contribution for board and lodging. Travelling is at the volunteers' own expense. Health and accident insurance must also be obtained.

ATLANTIC WHALE FOUNDATION
St. Martins House, 59 St Martins Lane, Covent Garden, London WC2H 4JS. ☎ 020-7240 5795. Fax: 020-7240 5795. E-mail: edb@huron.ac.uk. Website: www.whalefoundation.org.uk.
Programme description: Whale and dolphin conservation and research in the Canary Islands of Spain.
Destinations: Tenerife with satellite programmes in La Gomera and El Hierro (Canary Islands).
Prerequisites: Knowledge of European languages is useful. For qualified divers, there is also a marine habitat survey in Tenerife for which a surcharge is payable.
Duration and time of placements: 2-8 weeks from a number of start dates between June and October.
Number of placements per year: 150.
Cost: £100 a week includes half board accommodation, project transfers, all training and funds the projects in Tenerife.
Contact: Ed Bentham.

AZAFADY
Studio 7, 1A Beethoven St, London W10 4LG. ☎ 020-8960 6629. Fax: 020-8962 0126. E-mail: mark@azafady.org. Website: www.madagascar.co.uk.
Programme description: Pioneer Madagascar programme allows volunteers to work with a grassroots organisation tackling deforestation and extreme poverty.
Destinations: Southeast Madagascar.
Number of placements per year: 10-12 per group, 4 groups per year.
Prerequisites: Enthusiasm and cultural sensitivity. Training given. Volunteers learn basic Malagasy and gather skills relevant to working in the fields of development, conservation and sustainable livelihoods. Minimum age is 18, average is 22; all welcome.
Duration and time of placements: 10 weeks starting in January, April, July and October.

Shorter placements available by arrangement.
Cost: Successful applicants pay for pre-project costs such as flight, insurance and visa and are required to raise a minimum donation of £2,000 (different for non-UK applicants). Applicants are provided with extensive fundraising resources and advice.
Contact: Mark Jacobs, Managing Director.

BIMINI BIOLOGICAL FIELD STATION
9300 SW 99 St, Miami, FL 33176-2050, USA. ☎/fax: 305-274-0628. E-mail: sgruber@rsmas.miami.edu; sharklab@batelnet.bs. Website: www.miami.edu/sharklab.
Shark research station in the Bahamas.
Programme description: Active research on lemon sharks in the field. Studies consist of genetics, behaviour, telemetry-tracking, etc. Volunteers perform all tasks including research, maintenance and cooking.
Duration and time of placements: Minimum 1 month.
Number of placements: About 20 per year (5-7 volunteers at any one time).
Prerequisites: Must speak English, have a biological background and an interest in sharks.
Selection procedures and orientation: Applications via e-mail accepted year round. Two academic references must be submitted.
Cost: US$575 per month to cover meals and housing on Bimini.
Contact: Prof. Samuel H. Gruber, Director.

BIOSPHERE EXPEDITIONS
Sprat's Water, Nr Carlton Colville, The Broads National Park, Suffolk NR33 8BP. ☎ 01502 583085. Fax: 01502 587414. E-mail: info@biosphere-expeditions.org. Website: www.biosphere-expeditions.org.
Programme description: Biosphere Expeditions is a non-profit-making organisation offering hands-on wildlife conservation expeditions to all who seek adventure with a purpose. Volunteers with no research experience assist scientific experts.
Number of placements: 200-300.
Destinations: Worldwide, e.g. 2003 animal monitoring projects included monkeys in the Peruvian Amazon, snow leopards among others in the Altai Republic of Central Asia, steppe wolves in the Ukraine and cheetahs in Namibia.
Duration and time of placements: 11 days to 2 months, starting year round.
Prerequisites: No special skills or fitness required to join and no age limits whatsoever.
Cost: £990–£1,250 (excluding flights). Expedition contributions vary depending on the expedition. At least two-thirds of contributions benefit local project directly.
Contact: Michelle Bell, Operations Manager.

BTCV
British Trust for Conservation Volunteers, International Development Unit, 36 St. Mary's Street, Wallingford, Oxfordshire OX10 0EU. ☎ 01491 839766. Fax: 01491 839646. E-mail: information@btcv.org.uk. Website: www.btcv.org.uk.
BTCV is a charity established to protect the environment through practical action. There are more than 150 offices within the organisation, allowing over 5,000 volunteers to take part in a wide range of environmental projects.
Programme description: Volunteers help with projects in an expanding range of countries such as tree-planting, repairing footpaths and dry stone walls, creating community gardens and recycling materials. The international programme offers working holidays which incorporate various assignments, such as turtle monitoring in Thailand, wolf-tracking in Slovakia and reducing human impact on primates in Kenya.
Destinations: International programmes are offered in destinations in Europe, North America, Africa and Asia. Newest destinations are Ecuador, Latvia, Kenya and Kamchatka (Eastern Siberia). (See 'Directory of UK Voluntary Placements' for information on BTCV's

work in Britain).
Number of placements per year: Over 4,000.
Prerequisites: Energy and enthusiasm only requirements. No experience necessary.
Duration and time of placements: Usually a fortnight but variable.
Selection procedures and orientation: Programmes can be booked on the website or by phone. Full training is given by qualified leaders during the programme. Some international programmes may require a little experience.
Cost: From £275 depending on destination but usually more, e.g. £475 for a fortnight in Albania, £740 for 3 weeks in India inclusive of food, accommodation and training but not international travel.

CACTUS LANGUAGE
4 Clarence House, 30-31 North St, Brighton BN1 1EB. ☎ 0845 130 4775. Fax: 01273 775868. E-mail: enquiry@cactusenglish.com. Website: www.cactusenglish.com.
Cactus volunteer programmes in Latin America are designed for people who would like to spend some time out helping people whilst experiencing diverse cultures and learning Spanish (see entry in *Directory of Language Courses*).
Programme description: Wide range of social, healthcare, educational or conservation placements in Peru, Guatemala, Mexico, Bolivia and Ecuador. Examples include working at a hatchery for Leatherback turtles on Guatemala's Pacific Coast, helping in an orphanage for girls in Cusco, Peru and teaching English in a school in Oaxaca, Mexico.
Destinations: Peru, Guatemala, Mexico, Bolivia and Ecuador.
Prerequisites: All volunteers take a language course in the destination country to bring their Spanish to the required level before the placement. Minimum age 18 for some projects or higher for others. Specific prerequisites may apply depending on the chosen placement.
Duration and time of placements: Combination language and volunteer programme in Latin America lasts 8 or 12 weeks: 4-week language course followed by volunteering. Extensions possible.
Selection procedures and orientation: Potential volunteers must fill out a registration form (available online) and have an interview before being accepted. All travel needs can be arranged (flights, insurance and visas). Volunteers are looked after by ground operators in the destination country.
Cost: From £739 for 8 weeks in Guatemala to £1,939 for 12 weeks in Costa Rica. Include registration and volunteer placement fees, 4-week general Spanish language course of 20 lessons per week, course materials and accommodation during volunteer placement.

CAMPHILL COMMUNITIES
The Association of Camphill Communities, Gawain House, 56 Welham Road, Malton, North Yorkshire YO17 9DP. ☎ 01653 694197. Fax: 01653 600001. E-mail: info@camphill.org.uk. Website: www.camphill.org.uk.
The Camphill movement, founded in 1940 by Dr Karl König, a Viennese paediatrician, encompasses therapeutic communities in 20 countries, e.g. residential special schools or centres providing further education and training for youngsters with learning difficulties.
Programme description: Volunteers or co-workers help to run the communities, often teaching or otherwise supporting those with disabilities, helping with chores, therapy, in the gardens or in the workshops.
Destinations: 90 communities worldwide.
Number of placements per year: Average of about 10 volunteers are admitted to each centre.
Prerequisites: No specific qualifications are required, although volunteers need to be enthusiastic, interested in people, approachable and have sufficient grasp of the local language.
Duration and time of placements: Usually around 12 months.

Selection procedures and orientation: Prospective volunteers may apply to and request further information directly from the communities. Most offer formal induction and foundation courses geared to the specific tasks.

Cost: None. Short-term volunteers (up to 12 months) are provided with accommodation, food and a modest amount of pocket money.

CENIT (CENTER FOR THE WORKING GIRL)

Calle Huacho 150 y Jos Peralta, Quito, Ecuador. ☎ +593 2-265 4260. Fax: +593 2-265 4260. E-mail: contact@cenitecuador.org. Website: www.cenitecuador.org.

Programme description: CENIT relies heavily on volunteers from all over the world to work in projects such as early childhood intervention, creative projects in primary schools and drop-in tutoring centres mainly in south Quito.

Number of placements: 80, usually for short periods. Longer term volunteers preferred.

Duration and time of placements: Minimum 1 month. Placement depends on the amount of time committed and level of Spanish.

Prerequisites: Most volunteers are aged 18-26. Should be outgoing and (for some projects) willing to work with children who have suffered severe neglect or abuse.

Cost: One time administrative fee $50. Volunteers are responsible for finding (and funding) their own accommodation, though advice on homestays and hostels can be given.

Contact: Byron Salvatierra, Volunteer Co-ordinator.

CENTRO CAMUNO DI STUDI PREISTORICI

25044 Capo di Ponte, Valcamonica, Brescia, Italy. ☎ 0364 42091. Fax: 0364 42572.Website: www.rockart-ccsp.com.

Programme description: Students can learn about rock art, archaeology and anthropology through apprenticeships and voluntary work. Experience can also be gained concerning how an international research centre is run, how to edit and produce books and how to run conferences and exhibitions.

Destinations: Italy and France, Egypt, Morocco, Israel, Jordan and China.

Number of placements: 12-15.

Prerequisites: Those with skills in Information Technology, translation, editing, publishing and specific aspects of archaeology, art history and anthropology are preferred. Individuals must be motivated and competent in English, French or Italian.

Duration and time of placements: Up to a year; minimum period is 3 months.

Selection procedures and orientation: Telephone interviews permissible.

Cost: Volunteers must meet their own living costs, but accommodation is available.

CHALLENGES WORLDWIDE

13 Hamilton Place, Edinburgh EH3 5BA. ☎ 0131-332 7372. Fax: 01674 820372. E-mail: helen@challengesworldwide.com. Website: www.challengeswor ldwide.com.

Scottish charity organising volunteer placements overseas in projects run by local governments, NGOs or community groups to address issues such as environmental/ conservation challenges, human rights, rural development, poverty alleviation and social development.

Programme description: Individual placements tailored to the skills and interests of the volunteer.

Destinations: Bangladesh, Belize, Ecuador, Tasmania and several Caribbean Islands, with plans to extend further into Asia and Africa (see website for current situation).

Number of placements per year: 60-70.

Prerequisites: Minimum age 18 though average is late 20s. Some placements are general and require only enthusiasm and commitment; others require specific skills or experience such as media, IT/web design, architecture, engineering, research, business/ finance, social care and teaching.

Duration and time of placements: 3 or 6 months. Rolling recruitment with no group departures.

Selection procedures and orientation: All applicants must attend a one-hour face-to-face interview and briefing in the UK. Placement Leaders act as in-country mentors throughout placement.

Costs: Volunteers must fundraise a minimum contribution of £1,650 for 3 months, or £2,650 for 6 months.

Contact: Helen Tirebuck, Head of Recruitment.

CONCORDIA
Heversham House, 20-22 Boundary Road, Hove, East Sussex BN3 4ET. ☎/fax: 01273 422218. E-mail: info@concordia-iye.org.uk. Website: www.concordia-iye.org.uk.

Small not-for-profit charity committed to international youth exchange since 1943.

Programme description: International volunteer projects worldwide. Projects range from nature conservation, renovation, construction and archaeology to social work including working with adults and children with learning or physical disabilities, children's playschemes, youth work and teaching.

Destinations: Europe (East and West), Africa, the Middle East, Southeast Asia and Japan, Latin America and the USA.

Prerequisites: Aged 16-30 and resident in UK. No experience or specific skills needed though enthusiasm is essential.

Duration and time of placements: 2-4 weeks, mainly between June and September.

Cost: Registration fee approximately £90 plus travel. Board and accommodation are free of charge.

Contact: Helen Bartlett, International Volunteer Co-ordinator.

COSMIC VOLUNTEERS
PO Box 11895, Philadelphia, Pennsylvania 19128, USA. ☎ 215-508-2468. E-mail: info@cosmicvolunteers.org. Website: www.cosmicvolunteers.org.

Recently set up volunteer placement company.

Programme description: Volunteering, internships, language study and specialist travel programmes in five developing countries. Volunteer programme includes teaching, medicine, orphanages, journalism, social work, IT, law, HIV/AIDS, business, environment, organic farming, turtle and bird conservation.

Destinations: Nepal, India, Costa Rica, Ecuador and Ghana.

Number of placements per year: 200.

Prerequisites: for all ages (16-60) with average about 25. Must have open mind and be fluent in English. Medical placements available only to health professionals and trainees.

Duration and time of placements: 1 week to 2 years.

Selection procedures and orientation: Applicants accepted year round.

Costs: Application fee $25. Placement fee of $475 for India, Nepal and Costa Rica, plus daily charge to host family: $10-$17 in Costa Rica, $6 in India and $4 in Nepal. Placement fee is $675 per month in Ghana. Optional language classes available in all relevant languages for $5 an hour.

Contact: Scott Burke, Founder.

CROSS-CULTURAL SOLUTIONS
US Head Office: 800-380-4777. UK Information Office: 0845 458 2781. E-mail: info@crossculturalsolutions.org. Website: www.crossculturalsolutions.org.

See website for US and UK postal addresses.

See entry in Directory of Specialist Gap Year Programmes.

CULTURAL CUBE LTD
16 Acland Road, Ivybridge, Devon PL21 9UR. ☎ 0870 742 6932. Fax: 0870 742 6935. E-mail: info@culturalcube.co.uk. Website: www.culturalcube.co.uk.

Programme description: Mediates between selected voluntary organisations around the world and potential volunteers. Current projects include summer workcamps and unpaid internships in Armenia, work experience in Australia and the USA, English language counsellors in Brazil and summer conservation project in Italy.
Prerequisites: Various age limits.
Duration and time of placements: Workcamps last a couple of weeks; internships in Armenia last 1-6 months; teacher programme in Brazil lasts 12-48 months, though shorter placements are available. (See country chapters for further particulars.)
Cost: Placement fees approximately £230 excluding airfares for shorter placements; £1,000 for a 12-month internship in Australia and £1,490 for hospitality internship in the USA.
Contact: Tim Swale-Jarman, Director.

DAD INTERNATIONAL UK
Romania Project Office, Icamilpetrescu, 5725 Pascani Iasi, Romania. ☎ +40 232 718 286. Fax: +40 232 760 231. E-mail: dad@dad.ro or camps@dad.ro. Website: www.dad.ro.
Programme description: British and EU students and young people help organise and run activity camps for Romanian children. The volunteers' main efforts are in teaching conversational English to the students and in taking part in fun and recreational activities.
Duration and time of placements: Programmes last roughly 8 days each and volunteers are expected to work for two programmes, i.e. 16 days, plus another 6-8 days holiday time. Camps are held over 3 months of summer.
Number of placements per year: 30-120 (depending on programme schedule).
Prerequisites: Minimum age 17. Must be EU national. Volunteers must show that they are capable of conversing, reading and writing English with ease. Any creative skill in music, drama, dance, art or anything else relevant is an advantage as the children respond highly to these skills. A basic knowledge of general recreational activities is also desirable, though not essential.
Cost: Volunteer must pay for flights, taxes, administration fees and spending money. Accommodation provided in comfortable lodgings with all modern conveniences. Set meals are available three times a day in the communal canteen.
Contact: Nick Haywood, Head of Enquiries & Volunteer Information Department.

EARTHWATCH EUROPE
267 Banbury Road, Oxford OX2 7HT. ☎ 01865 318838. Fax: 01865 311383. E-mail: info@earthwatch.org.uk. Website: www.earthwatch.org/europe.
International environmental charity which recruits over 4,000 volunteers a year to assist professional, scientific field research expeditions around the world.
Programme description: Various environmental projects such as monitoring turtles in Costa Rica, studying the carnivores of Madagascar and investigating Roman remains near Pompeii.
Destinations: Worldwide including the UK (see entry above).
Number of placements per year: Thousands.
Duration and time of placements: Average duration is two weeks though project length varies from 3 days to 3 weeks.
Cost: Prices range from £465 to discover artefacts in a mammoth cave in the USA to £2,000 for helping to study the cheetah in northern Namibia. Prices quoted in Earthwatch brochures do not include airfares. Membership is £25 per annum, £15 for students.

ECOLOGIA TRUST
The Park, Forres, Moray, Scotland IV36 3TZ. ☎ 01309 690995. Fax: 01309 691009. E-mail: gap@ecologia.org.uk. Website: www.ecologia.org.uk.
The Trust promotes creative change in Russia through youth, ecology and education.
Programme description: Volunteer programme ideal for gap year students at the Kitezh

Children's Community for orphans in western Russia. (See chapter on Russia for first-hand accounts.)
Destinations: Kaluga, Russia.
Number of placements per year: 15.
Prerequisites: Minimum age 17; most are 17-25. No specific skills needed though any of the following would be useful: some knowledge of Russian, TEFL, experience working with children (sports, arts and crafts, music, drama), building, cooking and gardening. An interest in children and a willingness to participate fully in the life of the community are essential.
Duration and time of placements: 1-3 months; additional months are at the discretion of the Kitezh Council.
Selection procedures and orientation: Introductory questionnaire required to apply. Police check in country of residence required. Extensive preparatory materials are sent including feedback from previous volunteers. Informal orientation given on arrival and ongoing support including email contact with Ecologia Trust and weekly meeting for volunteers.
Cost: 1 month costs £540, 2 months £695 (includes consular visa fee) plus airfare (from £260 depending on time of year) and insurance.
Contact: Liza Hollingshead, Director.

EQUINOCCIAL SPANISH SCHOOL
Reina Victoria 1325 y Lizardo Garcia, Quito, Ecuador. ☎/fax: +593-2-256 4488. E-mail: service@ecuadorspanish.com. Website: www.ecuadorspanish.com/en/voluntarywork.
Programme description: Language school (see entry) arranges unpaid environmental or community work with partner organisations (see website). Projects involve working in nature reserves, community work helping children, teaching, etc.
Destinations: Community work is generally in Quito.
Duration and time of placements: Minimum 2 weeks starting any time; open-ended. School suggests programme for gap year comprising 2 months of studying basic Spanish, a month of studying an academic subject like ecology and finally environmental voluntary work in a reserve.

EUROPEAN VOLUNTARY SERVICE (EVS)
Connect Youth International, The British Council, 10 Spring Gardens, London SW1A 2BN. ☎ 020-7389 4030. Fax: 020-7389 4033. Website: www.britishcouncil.org/education/connectyouth/programmes/eyp/evs.htm.
Programme description: EVS gives young people aged 18-25 the opportunity to spend time in a European country (including Eastern Europe) and beyond, as full-time volunteers on a social project, e.g. working with children with special needs. Volunteers do not have to pay for their placement. Further details in the 'Directory of Specialist Gap Year Programmes'.

FBU (FUNDACION BRETHREN Y UNIDA)
Avenida Granda Centena Or4-290 y Barón de Carondelet, 3° pisa, Casilla 17-03-1487, Quito, Ecuador. ☎/fax: 2-244 0721. E-mail: info@fbu.com.ec. Website: www.fbu.com.ec.
Programme description: 1-week introduction to agro-ecology at hacienda followed by individual homestay in Ecuador where volunteers speak Spanish and work with the family, local *campesinos* and community members in a variety of tasks.
Number of placements: 15 a month.
Destinations: 3 areas of Ecuador.
Prerequisites: Committed to learning and participating in cultural exchange. Should have basic level of Spanish, though Spanish classes can be arranged at the hacienda.
Duration and time of placements: 1 week minimum; no maximum.

Selection procedures and orientation: Deadline for applications 2 weeks before start date.
Cost: $130 for first week, $315 per month.
Contact: Stuart Franklin, Programme Co-ordinator.

FUNDACION JATUN SACHA
Eugenio de Santillán N34 248 y Maurián, Casilla 17 12 867, Quito, Ecuador. ☎ 2-432240/2-432246. Fax: 2-453583. E-mail: volunteer@jatunsacha.org. Website: www.jatunsacha.org.
Foundation manages six Biological reserves in Ecuador. Jatun Sacha Biological Station is a 2,000 hectare tropical rainforest reserve. Others are Jatun Sacha in the Amazon, Guandera in the Highlands, Bilsa and Congal in Esmeraldas, Tito Santos in Manabi and the Galapagos Islands.
Programme description: Volunteers and interns participate in research, education, community service, station maintenance plant conservation and agroforestry.
Destinations: Amazonian Ecuador.
Number of placements per year: 500 on different projects.
Prerequisites: Minimum age 16 (with parental authorisation); average 23.
Duration and time of placements: Minimum 15 days at 5 reserves and 30 days at Jatun Sacha, year round. Majority stay for 1 month, and some stay 3-6 months.
Cost: $35 application fee plus reserve fees (including lodging and meals) of $350 per month.
Contact: Gabriela Cadena, Volunteers/Interns Co-ordinator.

GLOBAL ACTION NEPAL (GAN)
Baldwins Eastlands Lane, Cowfold, West Sussex RH13 8AY. ☎ 01403 864704. Fax: 01403 864088. E-mail: info@gannepal.org. Website: www.gannepal.org.
Non-profit-making development charity.
Programme description: CITE programme (Clinic for the Improvement of Teachers of English) aims to develop the skills of Nepalese English teachers. Volunteers watch lessons and give advice and support, hold workshops and improve the standard of spoken English among the local teachers.
Destinations: Various locations in Nepal.
Number of placements per year: 16 in each of two separate programmes.
Prerequisites: All nationalities with fluent English. Must be highly motivated and keen. TEFL background useful but not necessary.
Duration and time of placements: 6 months. First programme begins September 15th, the second December 1st.
Selection procedures and orientation: Applications should be submitted at least 4-5 months before proposed start date. Telephone interviews acceptable. Volunteers are given extensive training before their placement and support throughout. Training covers 3 weeks of instruction in Nepali and TEFL followed by 2 weeks of independent round Nepal, 5 weeks of practice teaching in schools while being helped and observed by GAN staff, a further week of training and final 12 weeks in placement.
Cost: £1,850 including return airfare from London, visa fee, insurance and training (including accommodation and food). Price can be adjusted if volunteer wants to make own travel arrangements. After training, pairs of volunteers live with Nepali families.
Contact: Chris Sowton, Programme Director (UK).

GLOBAL VOLUNTEER NETWORK
PO Box 2231, Wellington, New Zealand. ☎ +64 4-569 9080. Fax: +64 8326 7788. E-mail: info@volunteer.org.nz. Website: www.volunteer.org.nz.
Organisation started in 2000/2001 by New Zealand former volunteer.
Programme description: Volunteers recruited for a variety of educational, environmental and community aid programmes in many countries. Projects include English teaching,

environmental work, animal welfare, health and sanitation and cultural homestays.
Destinations: China, Ecuador, Ghana, Nepal, Romania, Russia, Thailand and Uganda.
Duration and time of placements: 2 weeks to 12 months depending on the placement.
Applications accepted year round.
Number of placements per year: 500.
Prerequisites: Minimum age 18 (average 19–23). No special skills or qualifications needed in most cases. All nationalities placed, although projects in China and Russia accept only Australians, Canadians, Europeans, Irish, British, American and New Zealand.
Cost: US$250 application fee covers administration, marketing and programme information. Programme fees vary from US$350 to US$600 per month and cover: administrative charges, training, accommodation and meals during training and placement, transport for volunteers and supervision.
Contact: Colin Salisbury, Executive Director.

GREENPEACE
Canonbury Villas, London N1 2PN. ☎ 020-7865 8100. Fax: 020-7865 8200/ 1. E-mail: info@uk.greenpeace.org. Website: www.greenpeace.org.uk.
Greenpeace has offices around the world and volunteer participation is sometimes welcomed locally. The Public Information Unit at the above address can send a Greenpeace worldwide address list. Greenpeace in the UK regrets that it is unable to offer internships or work experience, nor does it offer sponsorships.

HABITAT FOR HUMANITY
11 Parsons Street, Banbury, Oxon OX16 5LW. ☎ 01295 220188. Fax: 01295 264230. E-mail: globalvillage@hfhgb.org. Website: www.habitatforhumanity.org .uk.
Christian housing ministry with positions for people to help build simple decent houses in over 80 countries.
Programme description: Volunteers fill many vital staff positions at the US headquarters of Habitat for Humanity in Americus, Georgia. Opportunities in construction, information systems, childcare, human resources, maintenance, Campus Chapters and Youth Programmes, donor response, marketing, communications and development. HFH also organises International Global Village trips for people who are interested both in travel and volunteer work experience. These trips are designed to promote cross-cultural understanding and to raise awareness of the problems of substandard housing which exist worldwide.
Destinations: Africa and the Middle East; Europe, the Commonwealth of Independent States and Canada; Asia-Pacific; and Latin America and the Caribbean.
Prerequisites: Requirements vary according to the position; selection is competitive. Volunteers must be at least 18.
Duration and time of programmes: The headquarter volunteer positions must be taken for at least a month. The Global Village trips last 1-4 weeks.
Selection procedures and orientation: Application forms must be sent in. Preparation is organised through Americus staff.
Cost: Volunteers must cover the costs of travelling to Americus. Volunteers who serve in America for at least a month will receive furnished housing with paid utilities, and a weekly stipend for food and necessities. Anyone serving for a year or more will receive health insurance.
Contact: To request an application form for volunteer work at the headquarters, applicants need to write to Volunteer Recruitment, HR Department, Habitat for Humanity, 121 Habitat Street, Americus, GA 31709, USA. More information about Global Village trips can be obtained by phoning 912-924 6935 or e-mailing GV@habitat.org.

ICEYOM
International Centre for Education Youth Orientation and Mobilisation, c/o Cameroon Vision Trust, PO Box 1075, Limbe, South West Province, Republic of Cameroon. ☎ +237 755 4762. E-mail: iceyom@yahoo.co.uk.
Programme description: Placements for all kinds of voluntary service including hospitality, conservation, community service and fundraising.
Number of volunteers per year: 100.
Destinations: Throughout Africa, especially Cameroon.
Prerequisites: Minimum GCSEs or high school graduation.
Duration and time of placements: Minimum 6 months, maximum 2 years with option to extend.
Selection procedures and orientation: Applications accepted year round.
Cost: £200/$350. Projects normally provide accommodation, holiday schemes, in-country transport and some allowances depending on placement.
Contact: Ms. Rosemary Olive Mbone Enie, Executive Director (Cameroon Vision Trust) & ICEYOM Co-ordinator.

ICYE: INTER-CULTURAL YOUTH EXCHANGE
Latin American House, Kingsgate Place, London NW6 4TA. ☎/fax: 020-7681 0983. E-mail: info@icye.co.uk. Website: www.icye.co.uk.
ICYE is a non profit-making international exchange organisation. Also arranges voluntary placements on the European Voluntary Service scheme and short-term placements that last 1-3 months.
Programme description: Students spend a year abroad with a host family and undertake voluntary work placements, for example in drug rehabilitation, protection of street children and ecological projects. The average number of hours a student is expected to work is 35-40 per week.
Destinations: Bolivia, Brazil, Costa Rica, Honduras, Colombia, Mexico, Mozambique, Ghana, Nigeria, Kenya, South Korea, Taiwan, India, Japan, Uganda, New Zealand plus Europe.
Number of placements per year: Approximately 600 exchanges in over 30 countries.
Prerequisites: Applicants must be aged between 18 and 30 (25 for Europe) and must have a commitment to intercultural learning and the principles of ICYE.
Duration and time of placements: The exchange year begins around the end of July and lasts 12 months. For a 6-month programme it is possible to start in January or July.
Selection procedures and orientation: Recruitment starts in September and continues till May for the July departure. There is an information/selection meeting where more information about the organisation can be obtained. A short interview will be held to find out about the applicant. If the applicant joins the scheme, he or she will be sent a contract to sign and return with a cheque for £200. An application form and certificate of health will then be sent to be filled in for the organisation, the International Office and the Housing Committee. One last preparatory meeting will take place before departure to finalise details and receive more information.
Cost: 12 months costs £3,250, covering travel costs, board and lodging, pocket money, insurance, work placement and administration costs. 6-month placements cost £2,850. Places on the European programme are fully funded by the European Commission.
Contact: Marlis Haase, Programme Co-ordinator.

INFO NEPAL (Inside Nepal Friendship Organization)
PO Box 19531, Paknajol, Thamel, Kathmandu, Nepal. ☎ 1-4425210. E-mail: info@infonepal.org. Website: www.infonepal.org.
NGO formed in 2000, affiliated with the Social Welfare Council.
Programme description: Customised volunteer programme to allow volunteers to make a contribution to the country while gaining experience of Nepal's language and culture. Nepali cultural and language training is followed by short placements in schools

and communities across Nepal. Volunteers teach English, raise awareness about environmental issues and sanitation (especially among children of displaced ethnic tribes), develop income generation programmes, provide primary health care education and so on.

Duration and time of placements: 2 weeks to 5 months.
Cost: Range from approximately $250 for the first 2 weeks which includes intensive language and cultural training, $50 per fortnight thereafter. Volunteers live and eat with their host families.
Contact: Naresh Raj Ghimire (Asim), Director.

INTERNATIONAL VOLUNTARY SERVICE
Old Hall, East Bergholt, Colchester CO7 6TQ. ☎ 01206 298215. Fax: 01206 299043. E-mail: ivs@ivsgbsouth.demon.co.uk. Website: www.ivs-gb.org.uk. IVS North: Castlehill House, 21 Otley Road, Headingley, Leeds LS6 3AA (0113-230 4600/0113-230 4610/e-mail: ivsgbn@ivsgbn.demon.co.uk) and IVS Scotland: 7 Upper Bow, Edinburgh EH1 2JN (0131-226 6722/fax 0131-226 6723/e-mail: ivs@ivsgbscot.demon.co.uk).
IVS is the UK branch of Service Civil International with links with over 40 countries around the world. Its mission is to promote peace, justice and international understanding through voluntary work.
Programme description: Programme of workcamps published each April for £4. Workcamps bring volunteers together to work on projects such as renovating community buildings, campaigning about contentious issues, working with people with disabilities, contributing to ecological work or working on women's or cultural camps. Volunteers live and work together, sharing responsibilities such as cooking and cleaning.
Destinations: In 45 countries from Europe, the former Soviet Union, USA, Australasia and North Africa.
Number of placements per year: About 300. One workcamp group consists of between 6 and 20 members.
Prerequisites: IVS is open to everyone, although those under 18 must have parental consent for a placement. Volunteers with a disability are encouraged to apply, although certain projects will not be accessible for some disabilities.
Duration and time of placements: 2-4 weeks, mainly between June and September.
Selection procedures and orientation: Having applied, volunteers must pay a registration fee.
Cost: In 2003 the cost of registration on workcamps outside the UK was £135 (£105 for students and low-waged) which includes £30 membership of IVS. Volunteers must make their own travel and visa arrangements.

INVOLVEMENT VOLUNTEERS ASSOC. INC (IVI)
PO Box 218, Port Melbourne, Victoria 3207, Australia. ☎ +61-3-9646 9392. Fax: +61-3-9646 5504. E-mail: ivworldwide@volunteering.org.uk. Website: www.volunteering.org.au. UK office: IVUK, 7 Bushmead Ave, Kingskerswell, Newton Abbot, Devon TQ12 5EN (01803 872594; ivengland@volunteering. org.au). German office: IVDE, Volksdorfer Strasse 32, 22081 Hamburg (+49 41269450; ivgermany@volunteering.org.au).
Involvement Volunteers was established in 1988 with the aim of making volunteering available to people wanting to assist and learn from volunteer experiences.
Programme description: IVI arranges short-term individual volunteer placements worldwide. Projects are concerned with conservation, the environment, animal welfare, social and community service, education and childcare.
Destinations: Argentina, Australia, Austria, Bangladesh, Botswana, Cambodia, China, Ecuador, England, Estonia, Fiji, Finland, Latvia, Lebanon, Malaysia (Sabah), Mongolia, Namibia, Nepal, New Zealand, Poland, Samoa, South Africa, Spain, Sri Lanka, Thailand, Togo, Turkey, Ukraine, USA, Vietnam, Venezuela and Zambia.

Prerequisites: Anyone can volunteer, provided they are 18 or older.
Duration and time of placements: 2 weeks to one year.
Cost: Programme fees start at A$280, but fee for many international projects is about A$600.

JOURNEYS END
PO Box 93, Dereham, Norfolk NR9 1WE. E-mail: caroline@journeysend.com.py. Website: www.journeysend.com.py.
Programme description: New voluntary scheme set up by an English woman in Paraguay. Naranjo Community Projects include teaching English classes in various locations and helping in a daycare centre.
Destination: Naranjo Valley, Paraguay, 2 hours east of Asuncion. Naranjo is a disadvantaged subtropical region.
Prerequisites: All welcome, minimum age 18. Must be fit enough to walk or cycle to teaching venues.
Duration and time of placements: 3-6+ months.
Selection procedures and orientation: Application forms will be sent in exchange for a large s.a.e. from the above UK address or via email. Application fee of £150.
Cost: $825 for 3 months, $1,295 for 6 months. Extra months can be added on for $275 or $145. Includes basic camp accommodation.
Contact: Caroline Revell.

THE KAREN HILLTRIBES TRUST
Midgley House, Heslington, York YO10 5DX. ☎ 01904 411891. Fax: 01904 430580. E-mail: enquiries@karenhilltribes.org.uk. Website: www.karenhilltribes. org.uk.
Programme description: Volunteer placements for teaching and also installing water systems in Thailand. Volunteers live with host families, often the village headman.
Destinations: Upland and hill communities of Northwest Thailand.
Number of placements per year: about 20.
Prerequisites: Candidates should be team players, with maturity and a genuine interest in helping the Karen people. No TEFL qualification required.
Duration and time of placements: 6 months or longer, starting October or January.
Selection procedures and orientation: Interviews held in York or London or by phone if necessary. Pre-departure briefings, meetings with past volunteers, training weekend and continuing support given. Paid manager in Thailand.
Cost: £1,250 (from April 2004). Advice given on fund-raising and sponsorship (also on website).
Contact: Penelope Worsley, Director.

LAJUMA RESEARCH & ENVIRONMENTAL EDUCATION CENTRE
PO Box 522, Louis Trichardt 0920, South Africa. ☎/fax: +27 15-593 0352. E-mail: lajumalodge@yahoo.com. Website: www.Lajuma.co.za.
Programme description: Students participate in field projects in a private nature reserve in the Northern part of South Africa. Areas of research are the socio-biology of primates (5 species); resource partitioning in a groundwater forest; and the dynamics of vegetation islands in a montane grassland area. Students either assist with projects or do their own project on a plant or animal of their choice.
Number of placements per year: 35.
Duration and time of placements: Standard 2 months.
Prerequisites: All nationalities. Students should have an interest in the environment.
Cost: US$8 per day (meals excluded). Accommodation in a metal roof building with limited hydro-electricity, hot showers, flush toilets, gas stove, fridge, washing machine, etc.
Contacts: Ian and Retha Gaigher, Owners.

MA'ON SAN SIMON HOME FOR DISABLED PEOPLE

Maa'le Zee'v 9, PO Box 8447, Gonen, Jerusalem 91083, Israel. ☎ +972-2-6792188 or +972-2-6793416. Fax: +972-2-6792188. E-mail: ofra_gur@hotmail.com. Website: none.

Home for disabled adults, located in southwest Jerusalem and run by Greek monastery.

Programme description: Volunteers primarily assist the residents with daily needs by providing physical care and moral support. Activities include helping out of bed, showering, using the toilet, dressing/undressing, and serving food. Volunteers also accompany residents to the supermarket, bank, clinic, hospital, park and outings.

Duration and time of placements: 3 months minimum to 1½ years maximum.

Prerequisites: Previous experience with disabled people preferred but not essential. Medical insurance, certificate of good health and 2 recommendations required.

Remuneration: Pocket money $100 a month in addition to housing, 2 meals a day and laundry.

Contact: Ofra Gur-Ary, Social Worker & Volunteers Co-ordinator.

MONDOCHALLENGE

Galliford Building, Gayton Rd, Milton Malsor, Northampton NN7 3AB. ☎ 01604 858225. Fax: 01604 859323. E-mail: info@mondochallenge.org. Website: www.mondochallenge.org.

Programme description: Volunteers of all ages including some in their gap year (pre- and post-university) are sent to villages in a number of countries, mainly to teach.

Destinations: Nepal, India (Darjeeling region and Ladakh), Sri Lanka, Tanzania (Arusha, Longido and Pangani regions), Kenya, Gambia and Chile (Monte Grande).

Number of placements per year: 200 including 60 to Tanzania.

Prerequisites: All nationalities accepted. Minimum qualification is A-level or equivalent in subjects to be taught. Must be able to cope with remote posting and to relate to people of other cultures.

Duration and time of placements: Normally 3 months but flexible with start dates throughout the year.

Cost: £800 for 3 months. Board and lodging in local family homes costs an extra £15 (approximately) per week.

Contact: Anthony Lunch, Director.

NATIONAL MEDITATION CENTER

Rt 10, Box 2523, Jacksonville, TX 75766, USA. ☎ 903-589-5706. E-mail: emc@nationalmeditation.org. Website: www.nationalmeditation.org.

Programme description: Volunteer placements in the Philippines June and December. Also cultural tours and unpaid internships. Preferably for small groups rather than individuals.

Destinations: Philippines mainly.

Number of placements per year: 1,000.

Duration and time of placements: 2-4 weeks.

Cost: $850-$3,250 excluding airfares.

Contact: Amie Hughes.

THE ORANGUTAN FOUNDATION

7 Kent Terrace, London, NW1 4RP. ☎ 020-7724 2912. Fax: 020-7706 2613. E-mail: info@orangutan.org.uk. Website: www.orangutan.org.uk.

Programme description: Volunteers are involved with hands-on conservation projects in the tropical forests of Indonesian Borneo. Volunteers follow and observe orangutans in the wild.

Number of placements per year: 50-60.

Duration and time of placements: Normally 6 weeks, though visa changes may reduce this to 3-4 weeks. 4 teams of about 12 going out in 2004 in May, June, August and

October.
Prerequisites: Participants must be at least 18 and be members of the Orangutan Foundation. They must work well in a team, be fit and healthy and adaptable to difficult and demanding conditions.
Selection procedures and orientation: Prospective volunteers are interviewed in person or by telephone. Pre-departure briefing day is held.
Cost: Volunteers must pay for and arrange their own travel to Borneo and will have to pay a fee to cover the cost of National Park fees (US$5 per day) plus food and accommodation. Volunteer accommodation is basic, either sleeping on the floor in a communal room or in hammocks in the forest. Another way to become involved is through the Red Ape Challenge whereby anyone who fundraises £3,000 for the Foundation is given an in-depth 12-day tour of orangutan and forest conservation projects.
Contact: Cathy Whibley, Volunteer Co-ordinator.

QUAKER VOLUNTARY ACTION (QVA)
Friends Meeting House, 6 Mount St, Manchester M2 5NS. ☎/fax: 0161-819 1634. ☎ (UK only): 0845 456 0353. E-mail: mail@qva.org.uk. Website: www.qva.org.uk.
Programme description: Short-term volunteer projects abroad.
Destinations: UK including Northern Ireland, Europe including Eastern Europe and Turkey, Japan and the USA.
Duration and time of placements: Mostly 2-3 weeks.
Cost: Registration fee £80 (£60 students) plus transport costs.

RIGHT TO PLAY
111 Gordon Baker Road, Suite 505, Toronto, Ontario M2H 3R1, Canada. ☎ 416-498-1922. Fax: 416-498-1942. E-mail: recruitment@righttoplay.com. Website: www.righttoplay.com. For office addresses in Norway and the Netherlands, see website.
Canadian NGO (formerly called Olympic Aid) that is committed to improving the lives of disadvantaged children and their communities through Sport for Development.
Programme description: Teams of volunteer coaches are sent into communities to implement sport and play programme known as 'SportWorks', sometimes combined with health education programme (e.g. to teach the importance of vaccination, HIV/AIDS prevention and physical fitness)
Destinations: Angola, Benin, Ethiopia, Eritrea, Ghana, Guinea, Tanzania, Uganda, Kenya, Mali, Mozambique, Sierra Leone, Zambia, Pakistan, Thailand and Belize.
Prerequisites: Minimum age is 18 though most volunteers are older. Strong sporting background with experience in coaching and leadership development. Looking for volunteers who have previous experience of implementing projects overseas.
Duration and time of placements: 6½-month or one-year placements, normally starting in March, May, September and November. Shorter placements may be available depending on needs.
Remuneration: Charity pays for training expenses, in-field accommodation and transport and health insurance costs up to US$500 per 6-month period. Also pays an honorarium of US$4,000 per 6-month period.
Contact: Volunteer Services Officer.

SAVE THE EARTH NETWORK
PO Box CT 3635, Cantonments-Accra, Ghana. ☎/fax: 233-21-667791. E-mail: ebensten@yahoo.com.
Programme description: Variety of voluntary positions as English or maths teachers in orphanages, foster homes, primary and junior secondary schools for underprivileged children; in tree-planting, agro-forestry and rainforest conservation projects; primary health care, HIV/AIDS education and youth work. Volunteers mostly work side-by-side with staff and other volunteers.

Destinations: Accra or seven villages within 25 mile radius of the capital. Conservation and rural projects 30-60 miles from Accra.
Duration and time of placements: 4 weeks to 1 year.
Cost: US$300 for 4 weeks, $530 for 8 weeks and $750 for 12 weeks; includes food and accommodation with host families.
Contact: Eben Mensah, Development Director.

SOCIAL DEVELOPMENT GROUP
Surkhet Road Banke, Nepalgunj, Nepal. ☎ 81-523196. E-mail: lokendra77@hotmail.com or businessgroup@wlink.com.np.
Programme description: Work with orphaned children, helping with childcare, teaching and with community farming needs. Opportunity for total immersion in Nepali culture.
Destinations: Nepalgunj is about 12 hours outside Kathmandu.
Number of placements: Up to 6 at one time.
Prerequisites: All welcome. Need compassion for children.
Duration and time of placements: Flexible.
Selection procedures and orientation: Contact at least one month before start date.
Cost: $50 a week, $90 USD for 2 weeks, $125 for 3 weeks $180 for 4 weeks.
Contact: Lokendra Bahadur Chand, Managing Director.

SPORTS COACHES OUTREACH (SCORE)
2nd Floor, Satbel Centre, 2 de Smit Street, Greenpoint (PO Box 4989, Cape Town, 8000), South Africa. ☎ 21-4183140. Fax: 21-4181549. E-mail: info@score.org.za. Website: www.score.org.za.
In operation since 1991 implementing sports and community development programmes.
Programme description: SCORE is a South African NGO which uses volunteers to teach PE and coach and train children, youth and adults in poor communities in a variety of sports. Volunteers either live in a programme house or with a local family.
Destinations: Rural and urban locations throughout South Africa: Western Cape, Eastern Cape, Northern Cape, Mpumalanga Province, Limpopo Province and North-West. Some volunteers work in Namibia and Zambia as well.
Number of placements per year: 40.
Prerequisites: Minimum age 20 unless volunteer has specialist background. Volunteers should have skill, experience, enthusiasm, creativity and an ability to adjust to other cultures. Variety of nationalities accepted including British and North American.
Duration and time of placements: Students: 6 or 12 months; graduates: 12 months. Starting in July or January.
Selection procedures & orientation: Applications for January intake should be submitted by 15th September, and for July intake by 15th March.
Cost: Fee of $1,200 covers health insurance, room, board, transport within South Africa, orientation and back-up but not international airfares. Airfares are covered for EU citizens. Volunteers receive nominal monthly stipend.
Contact: Willem Vriend, Head of Recruitment and Training.

STUDENT ACTION INDIA
c/o HomeNet, Office 20, 30-38 Dock Street, Leeds LS10 1JF. ☎ 07071-225 866. Fax: 0870 135 3906. E-mail: info@studentactionindia.org.uk. Website: www.studentactionindia.org.uk.
Programme description: Arrange voluntary attachments to various Indian non-governmental organisations. Grassroots development projects such as teaching children in urban slums, working with women in income generation schemes and working with deaf and blind children.
Destinations: India with projects in New Delhi, Bangalore, Mumbai, Indore and rural placements.
Prerequisites: Anyone with energy and enthusiasm. No upper age limit.

Duration and time of placements: 2-month summer placements or year-out 5-month placements from September.

Selection procedures and orientation: University recruitment talks/careers fairs take place in January and February (see website). Application deadline 30th March; interviews held end of April. Pre-departure training over one weekend plus 1 week training on arrival. Sessions led by recently returned volunteers include Hindi training.

Cost: £475 for summer (covers placement, training and accommodation); £950 for 5 months. Flights, insurance, visa and subsistence costs are extra.

Contact: Ruth Bergan, UK Co-ordinator.

SUDAN VOLUNTEER PROGRAMME
34 Estelle Road, London NW3 2JY. ☎/fax: 020-7485 8619. E-mail: davidsvp@aol.com. Website: www.svp-uk.com.

Programme description: SVP works with undergraduates and graduates who are native English speakers and who wish to teach English in Sudan. Teaching tends to be informal in style, with only 4-5 hours of contact a day. Volunteers can plan their own teaching schemes, such as arranging games, dramas, competitions and tests for assessing skills learned by the students.

Destinations: Sudan, mostly in and around Khartoum.

Prerequisites: SVP is not at present able to accept pre-university volunteers so should be undergraduate or graduate. TEFL (Teaching English as a Foreign Language) certificate and knowledge of Arabic are helpful but not obligatory. Volunteers must be in good health and be native English speakers. It is preferred that volunteers have already had experience of travelling in developing countries.

Duration and time of placements: Around 3 months from early September, late December or late June.

Selection procedures and orientation: Application forms must be completed and sent with a £5 fee. Two referees are also required. Prior to departure, selection interviews, orientation and briefings take place. Volunteers are required to write a report of their experiences and to advise new volunteers.

Cost: Volunteers must raise the cost of the airfare to Sudan (currently £585 for ticket valid for 12 months) plus £60 (cost of the first 3 months insurance) plus any travel costs to selection interviews and briefings. SVP covers living expenses, accommodation and insurance beyond the initial 3 months.

Contact: David Wolton.

TANZED
80 Edleston Road, Crewe, Cheshire CW2 7HD. ☎ 01270 509994. E-mail: enquiries@tanzed.org. Website: www.tanzed.org.

Charity that recruits teachers to work alongside Tanzanian teachers in rural government primary schools.

Programme description: The aim is to improve the level of English language teaching by the Tanzanian teachers.

Destinations: Morogoro region of Tanzania.

Number of placements per year: 12-20.

Prerequisites: Teachers and graduates with teaching qualification able to commit to 12 months working and living with the local community at grassroots level.

Duration and time of placements: Minimum 1 year; departures in January and September.

Cost: £1,750 to cover airfare, insurance, training in Morogoro and some administrative costs. Volunteer teachers receive living expenses on a local scale of 80,000 Tz shillings per month.

Contact: Zoe Johnson, Administration.

UNA EXCHANGE

United Nations Association, Temple of Peace, Cathays Park, Cardiff CF10 3AP, Wales. ☎ **029-2022 3088. Fax: 029-2066 5557. E-mail: info@unaexchange.org. Website: www.unaexchange.org.**

Non-political and non-religious organisation which aims to promote international understanding and community development through international voluntary projects.

Programme description: Volunteers from the UK travel overseas to work on short-term projects of benefit to local communities. These include renovation, environmental/ conservation, archaeological and cultural projects as well as projects working with refugees, the elderly and people with special needs. The main volunteer programme covers countries in Europe, North America, North Africa and East Asia. The North-South Programme enables volunteers to work in sub-Saharan Africa, Latin America and Southeast Asia.

Destinations: Projects in over 60 countries worldwide including off-the-beaten-track countries like Belarus, Macedonia, Azerbaijan, South Korea, Mongolia and Namibia.

Prerequisites: Most projects are for volunteers aged 18+ although a few in Europe accept volunteers from 15. Older volunteers also welcome.

Duration and time of placements: Usually 2-3 weeks though longer term volunteering is possible.

Selection procedures and orientation: Volunteers on the North-South Programme are required to participate in a training weekend in Cardiff. Training is available for volunteers on other UNA Exchange programmes.

Cost: £100-£160 registration fee covers food and accommodation. Some projects require additional fees.

Contact: Katja Baerwald, Office Co-ordinator.

LA UNION SPANISH SCHOOL

1A Avenida Sur No. 21, Antigua, Guatemala. ☎**/fax: (502) 832-7337. E-mail: launion@conexion.com. Website: www.launion.conexion.com.**

Organisation for sharing Spanish language and Guatemalan culture run by a group of experienced Guatemalan Spanish teachers.

Program description: Voluntary placements in a day-care centre (for the children of single impoverished mothers), in a hospital, in a home for elderly people and in schools.

Number of participants: 100.

Duration of courses: Flexible from 1 or 2 weeks to many months.

Qualifications offered: Desire to do socially beneficial work.

Cost: None, though volunteers pay for their accommodation.

Accommodation: Homestays with full board cost $60 a week.

Contact: Juan Carlos Martinez, General Director.

VILLAGE EDUCATION PROJECT (KILIMANJARO)

Mint Cottage, Prospect Road, Sevenoaks, Kent TN13 3UA. ☎ **01732 459799. E-mail: info@kiliproject.org. Website: www.kiliproject.org.**

This organisation was set up in 1994 and is run by an ex-London lawyer, who is one of the few Europeans to be given permission to teach in Tanzanian government primary schools. The Central Ministry of Education and Culture are in full support of the work of the charity.

Programme description: Volunteers teach English as a foreign language in two primary schools in the Marangu area. Class sizes range between 17 and 40 and good textbooks and some teaching aids are available for each class. Extra periods are assigned where volunteers can read with the children or conduct art, sport or other extra-curricular activities.

Destinations: Marangu, Tanzania.

Number of placements per year: 8-12 UK students.

Prerequisites: Good spoken English and an outgoing personality are required. Art/sport/

music skills are an advantage.

Duration and time of placements: 8-9 months, starting in January.

Selection procedures and orientation: On receipt of an application, an interview is arranged. Pre-departure training is given, including preparing for work, using the textbooks and basic Swahili. A project leader in Tanzania meets the students and helps them settle in. Local staff are always on hand to support volunteers.

Cost: £2,000 must be paid to the charity. Additional costs include living expenses, medical insurance and initial entry visas (currently £38).

Contact: Katy Allen, Trustee and Project Leader.

VOLUNTEER NEPAL 2002

Jhaukhel 4, Bhaktapur, Nepal. ☎ 1-661 3724. E-mail: volunteer_ nepal2000@yahoo.com Website: www.geocities.com/volunteer_nepal2002.

Affiliated to non-profit making HELP Nepal.

Programme description: Placements for volunteers in schools, colleges and universities. Volunteers help with sports, music, extracurricular activities, English teaching and other administrative and social welfare work.

Number of placements per year: 100.

Destinations: Kathmandu Valley near the historic city of Bhaktapur.

Prerequisites: Minimum age 18.

Duration and time of placements: 2 weeks to 5 months, starting January, April, August and November.

Selection procedures and orientation: No interviews needed.

Cost: $600 includes pre-service training, language instruction, homestay and meals, trekking, rafting, jungle safari and volunteering.

Contact: Anish Neupane, Director and Principal of Nabin School in the village of Duwakot.

WILD AT HEART

47 Old Main Rd, Suite 7a, Cowell Park, Hillcrest, Kwa-Zulu Natal, 3610 South Africa. ☎ 31-765 2947. Fax: 31-765 7245. E-mail: billy@wah.co.za. Website: www.wah.co.za.

Working with wildlife at rehabilitation centres, national parks and private game reserves in Botswana, Namibia and South Africa.

Programme description: Gap Year programme consists of 12 weeks in Botswana including 8 weeks at a private game farm, then 16 weeks in South Africa consisting of 4 weeks at National Park East Coast, 4 weeks on Zululand Elephant & Lion project and 12 weeks in Zululand National Parks. Also place volunteer fruit pickers on farms near Cape Town.

Destinations: Possible destinations include Okavango, Kruger National Park, Hluluwe National Park, Chobe National Park, Victoria Falls.

Prerequisites: Ages 18-35.

Duration and time of placements: Gap Year Programme is 6-9 months. Fruit-picking Volunteer Work Experience programme runs from September to May.

Selection procedures and orientation: All welcome.

Cost: Weekly charge on Gap Year programme is €245, so total is €6,860. Volunteer fruit-pickers near Cape Town pay US$150 for meals and accommodation in 5-bedroom house near town of Tulbagh.

Contact: Billy Fourie, Director.

WILDERNESS TRUST

The General's Orchard, The Ridge, Little Baddow, Essex CM3 4SX. ☎/fax 01245 221565. E-mail: info@wilderness-trust.org. Website: www.wilderness-trust.org.

Campaigning organisation dedicated to the preservation of wilderness and wild areas.

Programme description: Conservation volunteer work in various parts of South Africa and new programme planned for arctic Norway. Work in South Africa includes collecting scientific data, helping with the general administration and running of a small game reserve, general maintenance and game counts. Conservation courses and Certified Game Ranger course available plus chance to join 5-day wilderness trail (see *Directory of Expeditions*).

Destinations: South Africa and Lotofen Islands (Norway).
Number of placements per expedition: open-ended.
Prerequisites: Must be at least 16. Most programmes open to all except one in Eastern Cape of South Africa where places are reserved for students with scientific interest or in pursuit of career in biology/conservation.
Duration and time of placements: 6 weeks to 3 months. Most placements are from June to September.
Cost: Average £2,000 for 3 months excluding airfares.
Contact: Jo Roberts, Director.

WORLDwrite
The WORLDwrite Volunteer Centre, Millfields Lodge, 201 Millfields Road, Clapton, London E5 0AR. ☎/fax: 020-8985 5435. E-mail: world.write@btconnect.com. Website: www.worldwrite.org.uk.
International voluntary youth project and educational charity to encourage links between young people across the globe.
Programme description: Range of cross-cultural visits and exchange programmes, e.g. production of educational videos about Ghana and Brazil, computer and film school appeals for Ghana, investigative research programmes on sustainable development, international summits and workshops.
Destinations: Ghana and Brazil (2003/4).
Prerequisites: No specific skills needed but a passionate commitment to equality for all.
Duration and time of placements: Flexible but key programmes overseas commence in July/August.
Selection procedures and orientation: No application forms or CVs wanted. Interested people should become acquainted with the work of WORLDwrite and preferably visit WORLDwrite's London Volunteer Centre.
Contact: Ceri Dingle, Director of Volunteers.

WWOOF (WORLD WIDE OPPORTUNITIES ON ORGANIC FARMS)
PO Box 2675, Lewes, East Sussex BN7 1RB. ☎ 01273 476286. E-mail: hello@wwoof.org. Website: www.wwoof.com.
National WWOOF co-ordinators compile a list of their member farmers willing to provide free room and board to volunteers who help out and who are genuinely interested in furthering the aims of the organic movement.
Programme description: Visitors are expected to work around 6 hours per day in return for free accommodation. Visitors have the opportunity to learn all about the organic growing of crops and food.
Destinations offered: Worldwide.
Number of placements per year: Limited to the jobs available and amount of help required by farmers.
Prerequisites: Nothing specific required except must be over 18, prepared to work hard and interested in organic growing and environmental issues.
Duration and time of placements: Anything from a few days upwards.
Selection procedures and orientation: A stamped, addressed envelope needs to be sent to WWOOF for a brochure and application form.
Cost: WWOOF UK membership costs £15 online or £20 if a printed version of the WWOOF Independents Host List is required, i.e. hosts in countries where there is no national WWOOF organisation. Countries which have national WWOOF organisations have to be joined separately (UK, Denmark, Finland, Sweden, Germany, Switzerland,

Austria, Italy, Slovenia, Australia, New Zealand, Canada, Ghana, Ivory Coast, Togo, Japan and Korea (some mentioned in country chapters).

YOUTH ACTION FOR PEACE (YAP)
8 Golden Ridge, Freshwater, Isle of Wight PO40 9LE. ☎ 01983 752577. Fax: 01983 756900. E-mail: yapuk@ukonline.co.uk. Website: www.yap-uk.org.
Programme description: Worldwide opportunities for unskilled short term voluntary service working with local communities for lasting peace, sustainable development, social justice and protection of the environment.
Destinations: worldwide coverage (Africa, Asia, Latin America, North America, Europe, Eastern Europe and the Middle East).
Number of placements per year: 70-100 outgoing.
Prerequisites: Normally none though language skills are required for some countries. Must speak English. Minimum age 18, though there are some teenage camps for students aged 14-17.
Duration and time of placements: Camps normally last 2-3 weeks. Longer stays are available in some countries.
Selection procedures & orientation: List of projects published in April in directory form and on website. Application forms used for selection. Training compulsory for some countries.
Cost: Registration fee of £95 plus membership fee of £10 (unwaged) or £25 (waged). An extra fee of £50 for training weekend for those going to Southern Countries.
Contact: Colin Clarke.

YOUTH FOR DEVELOPMENT
317 Putney Bridge Road, London SW15 2PN. ☎ 020-8780 7500/7212. Fax: 020-8780 7300. E-mail: yfd@vso.org.uk. Website: www.vso.org.uk/volunt/pdd.
VSO initiative aimed at young people aged 18-25 who have experience of community work, and undergraduates between second and third years of study.
Programme description: Past placements include work in education, health, social and youth work, and business.
Prerequisites: Participants must demonstrate a long-term interest in international development or have experience of volunteering or community work.
Duration and time of placements: 10-12 months.
Selection procedures & orientation: Volunteers take responsibility for arranging their own placement which is identified with the support of YfD staff and VSO programme offices worldwide. Volunteers also complete a project which makes a practical contribution to raising awareness of global development issues.
Cost: Volunteers must raise £700 for their placement.
Contact: Dove Estor, Programme Officer.

Directory of Religious Organisations

BMS WORLD MISSION
PO Box 49, Baptist House, Didcot, Oxon. OX11 8XA. ☎ 01235 517647. Fax: 01235 517601. E-mail: missionteams@bmsworldmission.org. Website: www.bmsworldmission.org.
Programme description: Action Teams enable young people to spend 6 months living and working alongside BMS missionaries or a partner organisation involved in church work, community development work, basic TEFL teaching, youth and children's work, drama and music outreach.
Destinations: Asia, Europe, Africa, Central and South America.

Number of placements per year: 50.
Prerequisites: Aged between 18 and 25. Must be a committed Christian with support from their local UK church. Health clearance required.
Duration and time of placements: 10 months including 6 months overseas and a 2-month tour of UK churches upon return to share experiences and inspire others for mission. Alternatively, Summer Teams run in July and August for 3-5 weeks (ages 18 upwards) and tailor-made placements for between 3 months and 2 years (graduates only).
Selection procedures & orientation: Interviews are held over a weekend at BMS International Training Centre in Birmingham. A 1-month period of training and preparation follows. Debriefing is given on return.
Cost: Approximately £3,200 for Action Team programme and £800-£1,200 for Summer Teams. Cost includes flights, accommodation and living expenses overseas, insurance, visas and training.
Contact: Jo Legg-Bagg, Mission Teams Administrator.

CAREFORCE
35 Elm Road, New Malden, Surrey KT3 3HB. ☎/fax: 020-8942 3331. E-mail: enquiry@careforce.co.uk. Website: www.careforce.co.uk.
Established in 1980, Careforce enables Christians to serve in areas of need in the UK and Ireland.
Programme description: A year designed for committed Christians in their gap year is spent in the UK working as volunteers with churches and Christian projects amongst vulnerable and needy people.
Number of placements per year: 150.
Prerequisites: Ages 17-30. No specific qualifications are required except commitment to Christianity.
Duration and time of placements: Usually 11/12 months.
Selection procedures and orientation: Interviews are essential, first locally and then at the site of the potential placement. Orientation takes place in the first fortnight of the placement. An induction course for all volunteers is also held within the first month.
Cost: None. All volunteers receive a weekly allowance of £30 per week. However, on acceptance, volunteers are asked to raise some financial support to help cover Careforce central costs.

THE CHURCH MISSION SOCIETY
Partnership House, 157 Waterloo Road, London SE1 8UU. ☎ 020-7928 8681. Fax: 020-7401 3215. E-mail: info@cms-uk.org. Website: www.cms-uk.org.
Programme description: The 'Encounter' programme is a 3-5 week mission over the summer for 18-30 year olds. Participants have the opportunity to travel with a group of Christians and share in the lives of Christians of another culture. 'Make a Difference UK' is a 6-18 month placement suitable for gap year students in a multicultural inner city area of Britain. Volunteers are placed with a local community-based church and can be involved in anything including youth and children's work, running a café, befriending the homeless, environmental issues or sports and arts projects. The international 'Make a Difference' programme is for people who are 21+ and who may choose to volunteer in a variety of programmes, for example as a youth worker in Georgia, a nursing assistant in Nepal, a hostel warden in Pakistan, teaching in Uganda or working with the deaf and blind in Lebanon.
Destinations: Africa, Asia, Eastern Europe, the Middle East and Britain.
Prerequisites: Volunteers must be British Christians who are involved in their local church, interested in learning about mission and sensitive to other cultures.
Selection procedures and orientation: 'Encounter' participants must attend 2 preparatory weekends and a debriefing on their return. 'Make a Difference' participants must have 2 interviews. Successful candidates attend a 10-day residential training course and attend a debriefing on their return.

Cost: Volunteers must be self-financing, though CMS can advise on fundraising and grants.
Contact: Alexandra Gough, Experience Programmes Team.

CRUSADERS
Smithfield House, Crescent Road, Luton, Beds. LU2 0AH. ☎ 01582 589850. Fax: 01582 721702. E-mail: crusoe@crusaders.org.uk. Website: www.crusaders.org.uk.
This interdenominational Christian organisation was founded nearly 100 years ago and now runs over 400 clubs for young people.
Programme description: CRUSOE Overseas Challenge is a close knit team dedicated to reaching young people for Christ. Projects may involve painting an orphanage or building a church, working with children in a holiday club or working with street children.
Destinations: Work with youth organisations and ministries worldwide including Europe and in a developing country in South America, Central America, Africa or Asia. Destinations vary from year to year.
Number of placements per year: Approximately 100.
Prerequisites: Applicants must be committed Christians, aged 16-20, in good health and prepared to work hard.
Duration and time of placements: 2-4 week placements in summer.
Selection procedures and orientation: Each project begins with a selection weekend in February. Each team arranges an orientation in the UK. There is also a debriefing weekend in September.
Cost: Maximum £1,500 for world projects depending on destination, £550 for Europe projects. Applicants are encouraged to raise the money through sponsorship.
Contact: Rachel King, CRUSOE Administrator.

INTERSERVE
325 Kennington Road, London SE11 4QH. ☎ 020-7735 8227. Fax: 020-7820 5950. E-mail: ontrack@isewi.org. Website: www.interserveonline.org.uk.
Interserve exists to serve poor and marginalised people, and to help build up the local national church.
Programme description: School leavers and graduates can take part in Interserve's gap year programme which makes individual placements in teaching English, teaching missionary children, work with special needs care, general children's work and administrative support.
Destinations: Asia, the Gulf, the Middle East and North Africa.
Number of placements per year: About 80.
Prerequisites: Applicants must be 18 or over, committed Christians, with a willingness to be flexible and to serve others.
Duration and time of placements: 2-12 months beginning any time of the year. Applications must be made 4-5 months before the intended departure.
Selection procedures and orientation: Interviews are essential, although they are informal. The applicant attends an orientation/training weekend before departure. On-going advice and assistance is available in the country and a debriefing occurs on return home.
Cost: £10 application fee, £300 placement fee, plus £20 per month after 3 months; placement fee includes selection and screening, medical clearance, orientation and training, debriefing and pastoral care. Additional costs are flights, visa, immunisation, insurance and board and lodging (paid locally).
Contact: Brigitte Testet (brigitte@isewi.org) or Rachel Morton (rachel@isewi.org).

JESUIT VOLUNTEER COMMUNITY
23 New Mount St, Manchester M4 4DE. ☎ 0161-832 6888. Fax: 0161-832 6958. E-mail: staff@jvc.u-net.com. Website: jesuitvolunteers-uk.org.

Programme description: Full-time volunteering in a range of demanding social projects in the UK e.g. homeless hostels, drug rehabilitation, drop-in centres, victim support. Also run shorter summer programmes.
Destinations: Inner city Liverpool, Manchester, Glasgow and Birmingham.
Prerequisites: Ages 18-35. Must be prepared to work hard and interested in pursuing spirituality in the modern world.
Duration and time of placements: 10 months from beginning of September or shorter summer attachments.
Cost: None. Programme is fully funded. Volunteers are given an allowance equivalent to unemployment benefit (about £55 a week).

JUST YOUTH
61 Leicester Rd, Salford M7 4DA. ☎ 0161-792 1714. Fax: 0161-792 0435. E-mail: Justyouth@tesco.net.
Programme description: Specifically targets gap year students and also offers graduate sponsorship in Christian youth work.
Destinations: Community in Salford run by the Spiritans (a Catholic order).
Number of placements per year: 3.
Prerequisites: Volunteers for the Gap Year placements must be willing and able to witness to their Christian faith.
Duration and time of placements: Minimum 1 year.
Contact: Kevin Buchanan, Senior Youth Worker.

LATIN LINK STEP PROGRAMME
175 Tower Bridge Road, London SE1 2AB. ☎ 020-7939 9000/9014. Fax: 020-7939 9015. E-mail: stride.uk@latinlink.org. Website: www.latinlink.org.
Programme description: Self-funded team-based programme working on small-scale building projects and church work in Latin America for committed Christians only.
Destinations; Argentina, Bolivia, Brazil, Ecuador, Mexico and Peru.
Number of placements per year: 150.
Prerequisites: Minimum age 17 years for 7-week to 6-month Step 7 Programme; minimum age 18 for 6-month to 2-year Stride programme. Volunteers must have an active Christian faith. Applicants need to be flexible, have initiative and be open to learn. Knowledge of Spanish or Portuguese is not essential but it is a great help. It is suggested that volunteers attend evening classes to prepare for the project.
Duration and time of placements: Spring projects run from March to July and summer ones July to August/September (7 weeks).
Cost: From £2,000 in total; details on application.

OASIS TRUST
115 Southwark Bridge Road, London SE1 0AX. ☎ 020-7450 9000. Fax: 020-7450 9001. E-mail: enquiries@oasistrust.org. Website: www.oasistrust.org.
In operation for 18 years.
Programme description: Practical projects run alongside local Christian groups and churches. Activities include youth and children's work, drama, music and projects with slum-dwellers.
Destinations: Brazil, Peru, Portugal, France, Germany, Romania, India, Kenya, South Africa, Tanzania, Uganda, Zimbabwe and Mozambique.
Number of placements per year: 250.
Prerequisites: Minimum age 18. Applicants should be committed Christians and in sympathy with the aims of the Oasis Trust.
Duration and time of placements: Long-term placements are 6-10 months starting in September and March; short-term are 6 weeks starting in July or 2 weeks throughout the year.
Cost: From £3,000 for long-term projects; approximately £1,000 for 6-week projects and

approximately £950 for a two-week placement.

SALESIAN VOLUNTEERS

Ingersley Road, Bollington, Macclesfield SK10 5RW. ☎ 01625 575405. Website: www.salesians.org.uk.

Programme description: Gap year scheme for living and working in a Catholic residential community with other volunteers providing outdoor education programme for at-risk youth. Charity also has links with institutes in Hong Kong and China and recruits English teachers (must be graduates).

Prerequisites: Ages 18-30.

Duration and time of placements: September to July.

Selection procedures and orientation: Accredited leadership training given.

Cost: None. Weekly allowance is paid.

SCRIPTURE UNION

207-209 Queensway, Bletchley, Milton Keynes MK2 2EB. ☎ 01908 856193. Fax: 01908 856012. E-mail: elizabethf@scriptureunion.org.uk. Website: www.scriptureunion.org.uk.

Programme description: Activities vary depending on the country but generally include working with children and young people, and teaching about Jesus in camps and schools. Participants live with local families or in Scripture Union Centres.

Destinations: Summer placements of 1-3 weeks in Hungary, Ukraine, Slovakia, Romania and Croatia. 6-month placements in Australia, Peru, France, India and South Africa.

Number of placements per year: 30 short-term, 35 longer-term.

Prerequisites: Ages 18-25. Christian faith essential.

Duration and time of placements: 1-3 weeks in summer, 6 months longer-term.

Selection procedures and orientation: Interviews are essential. Advice and preparation are given in the UK, including an orientation weekend. Pastoral support is given to participants both overseas and in the UK.

Cost: Flights and living costs vary depending on the country and length of placement. The 1-3 week placement costs £100-£300; the 6-month placement costs £2,000-£3,000.

Contact: Elizabeth Fewkes, International Relations.

SOUTH AMERICA MISSION SOCIETY (SAMS)

Unit 9, Prospect Business Park, Langston Road, Loughton, Essex IG10 3TR. ☎/ fax: 020-8502 3504. E-mail: persec@samsgb.org. Website: www.samsgb.org.

Programme description: SAMS is working in various projects run by the Anglican church which has placements for committed Christians who wish to work as self-funding volunteers, particularly in English teaching and work with underprivileged children.

Destinations: Peru, Bolivia, Brazil, Paraguay, Uruguay, Argentina and Chile.

Number of placements per year: 10-12.

Prerequisites: Volunteers must be completely self-funding and must be committed Christians with the backing of their local church. Knowledge of Spanish or Portuguese very useful.

TEARFUND

100 Church Road, Teddington, Middlesex TW11 8QE. ☎ 0845 355 8355. Fax: 020-8943 3594. E-mail: enquiry@tearfund.org. Website: www.tearfund.org.

Programme description: 4-month overseas programme 'Transform Teams' for small teams or shorter summer teams to work mainly with children and the vulnerable. Charity fights against global poverty.

Destinations: Transform teams to Kenya, Burkina Faso, South Africa, Rwanda, Uganda, Ghana, Zambia, Malawi (soon), Lebanon, Thailand, India, Armenia, Brazil, Dominican Republic and (soon) Nicaragua.

Duration and time of placements: 4-month placements start in late March.

Cost: 4-6 week summer teams cost £1,250-£1,650.
Contact: Jennie Marshall, Enquiries Officer.

TIME FOR GOD
2 Chester House, Pages Lane, Muswell Hill, London N10 1PP. ☎ 020-8883 1504. Fax: 020-8365 2471. E-mail: recruit@timeforgod.org. Website: www.timeforgod.co.uk.
One of the longest established Christian gap year programmes.
Programme description: Gap year sponsored by 9 Christian denominations. Placements include but are not limited to inner city projects with the homeless and disadvantaged, caring for children with special needs, assisting the ministry team in a Church, children's and youth work, youth retreat centres, drug and alcohol rehabilitation centres and other areas.
Number of placements per year: 150.
Destinations: Thailand, Netherlands, Belgium, Sweden, France, Germany, Denmark and Hungary (fee £1,050); Australia (£1,500), Ghana (£3,000), Argentina (£4,000); Guatemala and Philippines (£5,000). Also UK.
Prerequisites: Ages 18-25. Must be open and sympathetic to the Christian faith.
Duration and time of placements: 10-12 months from September or January.
Cost: Volunteers must fund-raise for overseas placements (amounts as above). Fees include orientation and re-entry training, ongoing training and support while in placement, accommodation, food expenses and pocket money.
Contact: Elaine Hornsby or Glyn Mewton, Recruitment & Development Team.

THE TOYBOX CHARITY
PO Box 660, Amersham, Bucks, HP6 6HY. ☎ 01494 432591. Fax: 01494 432593. E-mail: ange@toybox.org. Website: www.toybox.org.
The Toybox Charity is a Christian organisation established in 1992 to alleviate the plight of street children in Latin America working in the poorest communities to break the cycle of poverty. It runs a comprehensive rescue plan for former street children, with street team, hostel, day centre and family-style homes.
Programme description: 'Gap Year Challenge' consists of 3½ months in Guatemala working with street children, including language training, followed by 8 months raising awareness of the plight of the street children throughout the UK, at schools, churches, interest groups, etc. involving drama, speaking and exhibitions. 12-month 'Gap Year Experience' takes place in the head office in Amersham, building computer and communication skills and being a vital part of the UK team. Can specialise to some extent in design/website work or work with the media. A 2-week visit to Guatemala is encouraged.
Destinations: Guatemala (and UK).
Prerequisites: Minimum age 18. May consider 16 year olds for Gap Year Experience. British nationals only. A desire to learn and invest whatever skills you have in helping make a difference to the street children.
Duration and time of placements: Full year programme (September to August).
Selection procedures and orientation: For Gap Year Challenge: 1 week pre-departure orientation plus 1 week orientation in Guatemala, followed by 3 weeks of Spanish tuition. 2 weeks of presentation training at the start of the UK section of the gap year.
Cost: Around £3,000.
Contact: Angela Murray, Speaker and Gap Year Co-ordinator.

WORLD EXCHANGE
St Colm's International House, 23 Inverleith Terrace, Edinburgh EH3 5NS. ☎ 0131-315 4444. Fax: 0131-315 2222. E-mail: we@stcolms.org.
World Exchange is managed by a number of British Churches and development agencies and draws on the Church's extensive network of international contacts to allow people to

work as volunteers in various places around the world.

Programme description: World Exchange sends volunteers to work with community organisations and projects. Work may be in the community, working with apprentices in skilled trades and agriculture, in education related projects or in health projects.

Destinations: Worldwide, including Malawi, Sudan, India, Pakistan, Lebanon and Kiribati.

Prerequisites: Volunteers must be flexible and adaptable. Minimum age 18.

Duration and time of placements: 10-12 months.

Selection procedures and orientation: World Exchange finds suitable placements for individual applicants. It also provides a training and support package.

Cost: Volunteers are expected to contribute £2,500+ for a one-year placement.

WORLD VISION UK

599 Avebury Boulevard, Milton Keynes, Bucks. MK9 3PG. ☎ 01908 841007. Fax: 01908 841001. E-mail: studentchallenge@worldvision.org.uk. Website: www.worldvision.org.uk.

Christian outreach organisation whose motto is 'Serve the poor in Jesus' name'.

Programme description: Student Challenge programme takes place each summer to various countries.

Destinations: 2003 destinations were Zambia, Ghana and Armenia.

Number of placements per year: Minimum of 5 per team; otherwise the trip does not take place.

Prerequisites: Strong Christian commitment. Ages 18-30.

Duration and time of placements: 4-6 weeks in summer.

Selection procedures and orientation: Interviews take place in March.

Cost: £900-£1,400 including airfares.

WYCLIFFE BIBLE TRANSLATORS

Wycliffe Centre, Horsleys Green, High Wycombe, Bucks. HP14 3XL. ☎ 01494 682256. Fax: 01494 682300. E-mail: chris_oldham@wycliffe.org. Website: www.wycliffe.org.uk.

Programme description: Skills-based voluntary work abroad. Flexible programme with opportunities in IT, home-schooling, accountancy, design, etc.

Destinations: Worldwide.

Prerequisites: Minimum age 18 though for separate linguist-based programme, most candidates are post-university.

Duration and time of placements: Up to 1 year skills-based voluntary year abroad; graduate programme designed as a year programme, though can be longer than the 9-month field placement following 4-month training period.

Cost: Maximum £3,000 for living costs, medical insurance, airfares, etc. on skills-based One-One programme. £7,000-£8,000 for Graduate programme.

Contact: Chris Oldham, Recruitment & Applications.

YEAR FOR GOD

Holmsted Manor, Staplefield Road, Cuckfield, West Sussex RH17 5JF. ☎ 01444 472727. Website: www.holmsted.org.uk.

Gap Year Programme of Youth with a Mission (see next entry) for young Christians to devote 12 months to 'radical discipleship' in one of several countries. In 2003 the destination countries were Uganda, Poland, Albania, Costa Rica and Tanzania. Cost is £3,000-£4,000.

YOUTH WITH A MISSION

Highfield Oval, Harpenden, Herts. AL5 4BX. ☎ 01582 463216. Fax: 01582 463213. E-mail: enquiries@oval.com. Website: www.ywam-england.com.

Founded in 1960, Youth With a Mission is an international, missionary movement of

Christians. It has currently more than 8,500 members.

Programme description: Volunteers can spend a 'Year for God' in which the first part will be spent caring for street children, teaching them to read and helping them with various other practical activities. The second part will be completing a Disciple Training School course in preparation for the next two months of outreach.

Destinations: Albania, Brazil, Bolivia, Colombia, Estonia, Kazakhstan and Uganda.

Number of placements per year: 200.

Prerequisites: Volunteers must be Christian and support the YWAM mission statement.

Duration and time of placements: 5-10 months.

Selection procedures and orientation: Enquiry weekends are run for interested applicants. Interviews are not always required. Participants receive cultural orientation, language training and Biblical discipleship.

Cost: Fees vary from £1,700 to £3,000 for the 5 months to longer periods.

Contact: Clair Gorman, Head of Public Relations and Communications.

A Year Off for North Americans

No tradition has developed in the US or Canada for high school graduates to take a year out before proceeding to university. The expression gap year is almost never used in North America. Americans of course flock to Europe clutching their rail passes and their *Let's Go* guidebooks but they tend to do it merely as summer sightseers. Once they get to university many students find that there is an International Study adviser who encourages them to sign up for a semester or a shorter course abroad (normally in the company of lots of other Americans). But relatively few venture off independently to do an expedition or voluntary placement. Of those that do, many gravitate south to Latin America where there are many language and volunteer programmes geared to American expectations.

Yet a trend has been emerging. It may have started with an article published by the Admissions Office of Harvard University which has had wide circulation entitled 'Time Out or Burn Out for the Next Generation' which argues strenuously for having a break from the intense pressures affecting students trying to get into the top universities. (The article can be read online at http://adm-is.fas.harvard.edu/timeoff.htm). More recently, a special edition of *Newsweek* included an article 'The Lure of the Gap Year' and at a session of New England College Admissions Counselors in 2003, one session was on Gap/Interim Years. One of the speakers was Tim Ellis, director of Global Quest (listed later in this chapter), who called his hand-out 'The Next Thing to Do: Why Deferring College May

Make Sense' in which he wrote:

Too many bright, motivated students are heading off to college without a second thought. It doesn't make sense. The typical student, who follows his peers to college because it's 'the next thing to do' faces a risk of aimlessness, burnout, or even drop-out. The more mature, and often more successful, student takes time to discover his or her passion. The U.S. Department of Education reports that more than 30% of college freshmen do not return for their sophomore year. It's a shocking statistic, but the fact is that they were just not clear about WHY they were going. Colleges recognize this problem. Simply put, they know that the student who does something worthwhile between high school and college will likely arrive energized and ready to learn. Colleges seek students who actively choose higher education, rather than just coasting into it like many of their peers.

Parents sometimes worry that if a student steps off the usual track they will lose their momentum. This may be true for a few, but in my forty years of educating teen-agers, my observation is that this is just not the case, particularly for those students who do sit down and make a plan of action. A structured semester or year of travel, volunteering, or work, nearly always inspires a desire to learn more. Parents and students can avoid this uncertainty altogether by deferring entrance for a year... Students can pursue the normal application process in their senior year and then, in May, send a deposit to the college of their choice with a request to defer entrance to the following fall.

Elisabeth Weiskittel is one young American who decided that she did not want to go straight to college:
I was the only person in my graduating high school class to take a gap year or probably even to consider doing it. My friends, after blinking and looking shocked for a minute, thought it was a great idea but, like the adults, shook their heads and said, 'Oh, you'll never be able to go back to finish college.' My family was used to the idea because I had first brought it up in my sophomore year of high school, and they approved wholeheartedly. I knew that I was going to need a break from school, and I've always loved to travel. The only reason not to go was that I would be a year behind my high school classmates, and a year older than my new classmates at college. But I decided that that wasn't so terrible an idea.

I had already applied to college during my senior year of high school, which is the normal time, and had been accepted at several. When I chose one, I included a letter saying that I was planning to take a year off. The college wrote back saying I had permission, and that they would hold my space in the upcoming class the following year. Deciding where to go turned out to be more difficult than deciding to go.

Elisabeth ended up doing courses in Oxford (see introduction to chapter 'Courses') and in Florence plus an internship in Hawaii (see chapters on 'Italy' and 'USA' respectively) and had a very full and productive year out. Although she admits the year was expensive, it wasn't as expensive as a year at college would have been and summarises the way in which she has benefitted:

Now that I am at college, I realise that being a year older than my friends at college is completely unimportant. Most of my friends from high school are graduating college next year, but I am smirking because they have to go look for jobs while I can sit back for another two years and relax. The year also changed my perspective on education, and has made all the studying I do in college seem worthwhile, since I can see where it fits into the world picture. My gap year also gave me the most obvious of benefits, which was a year to relax and let my brain regenerate. The downside of the year occurred during the first few days of each new experience, when I didn't know anybody and was nervous about being in an unfamiliar place where I didn't know what was going to be expected of me. Italy was the worst adjustment because of the language impediment. Another difficult part was when I started college in the fall. Suddenly my movements became restricted again. I couldn't go off on weekend trips or drop everything and go to a museum, because I had reading to do. All things taken together, it was the best year of my life. If I could do it again the only thing I would do differently is to try to make more Italian friends.

Catherine Leopold wasn't too happy with the colleges that had offered her a place and so decided to take a year out. After a stint doing voluntary work in Kent, she did the *John Hall Pre-University Programme* in Italy (see 'Directory of Art Courses') where she found that she was taking the course more seriously than some of the mainly British participants, many of whom were from very privileged backgrounds. Catherine really enjoyed the chance to engage in some of the course's peripheral activities like learning Italian and taking classes in photography, and feels that many other Americans could benefit from taking a year off to mature and expand horizons before going on to university. What some describe as a 13th year programme may be particularly worthwhile for students who are relatively young when they graduate from high school and who might benefit from a structured programme that gives them the space to mature, to learn to manage their time and be independent, and to have a chance to appreciate how sheltered and privileged a background they have had.

The two most important student exchange organisations in the US are *CIEE* and *InterExchange Inc.* (addresses listed below). CIEE runs work abroad programmes for students in France, Germany, Ireland and other countries. Participants are given visas which allow them to work at any job for the time allowed. CIEE has offices in Paris, Berlin and other cities which will help with the job hunt. *InterExchange* can place au pairs in Europe, arrange teaching assistantships in Bulgaria, Belgium and Spain and fix up internships or short-term work in selected countries.

Of course many Americans taking a gap year do not leave the shores of their country. Some who may be undecided about the next step may join AmeriCorps, the national service programme instituted by President Clinton in 1993 which has been described as a domestic Peace Corps. In exchange for 1,700 hours of community service over a 10-month period AmeriCorps volunteers receive a $4,725 education voucher and a living allowance averaging $7,200. The Federal Work Study programme is another scheme that encourages a volunteering culture with monetary rewards: financial assistance is given to students who work in community service positions during term-time or while on holiday, e.g. working with deprived children to raise literacy rates. The Labour government in the UK is attracted to such incentives and is considering introducing a similar scheme in Britain.

Advisory Services

One of the most useful periodicals available to students and adults considering a gap year at any stage of their lives is the bi-monthly magazine *Transitions Abroad,* (PO Box 745, Bennington, VT 05201, USA) which contains practical information on alternatives to mass tourism including ways in which to live, study, work and travel which allow you to get to know your host country. Annual subscriptions (six issues) cost $28 within the US and they also maintain a very active website on www.TransitionsAbroad.com.

Companies that maintain databases of opportunities (mostly unpaid) and offer personalised consultations to fee-paying clients (often young people aged 16-25) attempt to match them with a suitable work, volunteer or study placement abroad:

Taking Off, PO Box 610104, Newton Highlands, MA 02461 (617-424-1606; Tkingoff@aol.com; www.takingoff.net). Gives clients access to a database with 3,000+ options worldwide. The owner (Gail Reardon) charges $900 for short-term consultations and a flat fee of $1,800 for ongoing personalised assistance.

Center for Interim Programs, PO Box 2347, Cambridge, MA 02238 (617-547-0980; www.i nterimprograms.com). $1,900 fee for 24 months.

LEAPNow, PO Box 1817, Sebastopol, CA 95473 (707-829-1142; www.leapnow.org). Structured programme called LEAPYear for Americans aged 17-20 in South and Central America that can count as college credit.

Horizon Cosmopolite, 3011 Notre Dame Ouest, Montreal, Quebec, Canada H4C 1N9 (514-935-8436; www.horizon.cosmpolite.com). Database of 1,600 opportunities.

World Wide Volunteer Services (WWVS), PO Box 3242, West End, NJ 07740 (732-571-3215; worldvol@aol.com; www.wwvs.org). Individually arranged multi-cultural experiences and internships in a variety of settings around the world. Application fee $50 plus placement fee $200.

The Quaker Information Center (1501 Cherry St, Philadelphia, PA 19102; 215-241-7024; www.quakerinfo.org) collates a great deal of information about volunteering which can be accessed on-line or by post for a $10 contribution ($12 if outside the US). The information, which is updated sporadically, covers what they aptly call a 'smorgasbord' of opportunities ranging from weekend workcamps through to two-year internships with aid agencies. The packet can be ordered by sending $10 or $12 if outside the USA.

Many of the placement organisations to which candidates will be referred offer what are basically volunteer vacations, i.e. two or three week service programmes in developing countries for a substantial fee.

KEY US ORGANISATIONS

Of the thousands of organisations large and small throughout North America which are involved with student exchanges and assisting young people to undertake worthwhile projects abroad, here is a small selection of important ones.

Accent, 870 Market St, Suite 1026, San Francisco, CA 94102 (800-869-9291; info@accentintl.com). Pre-college summer in Florence, Madrid, Paris and London.

Accord Cultural Exchange, 750 La Playa, San Francisco, CA 94121 (415-386 6203/fax 415-386-0240). Family placements in France, Germany, Spain, Austria and Italy. $1,200 placement fee ($750 for summer positions).

Adelante Abroad, 601 Taper Drive, Seal Beach, CA 90740; 562-799-9133; info@adelanteabroad.com; www.adelanteabroad.com. Various internships, volunteering and semester placements in Spain (Bilbao, Madrid and Seville), France, Costa Rica and Mexico. Fees from $1,750 for one month.

AFS International Youth Development, National Service Center, 198 Madison Avenue, 8th Floor, New York, NY 10016; 800-AFS-INFO; http://usa.afs.org. Full intercultural programme lasting 4/6-12 months in 54 countries for volunteers aged 18-29. Most programmes include language training prior to volunteer placement, homestay accommodation and participation in local voluntary projects.

Agriventure, International Agricultural Exchange Association, No. 105, 7710-5 Street SE, Calgary, Alberta T2H 2L9, Canada (canada@agriventure.com). Details of the international farm exchange may be found in the chapter 'Work Experience'.

AIPT – Association for International Practical Training, 10400 Little Patuxent Parkway, Suite 250, Columbia, Maryland 21044-3510 (410-997-3069; www.aipt.org). US citizens who have been offered a full-time position in their field of study or experience in the UK may apply for a work permit through the AIPT but must submit their dossier to the National Council for Work Experience (www.work-experience.org) who forward it to the Overseas Labour Service in Sheffield. The cost of the working visa to the candidate is $250 plus £295 to the employer and the processing time is 8-10 weeks.

Alliances Abroad Group, 2423 Pennsylvania Avenue, NW, Washington, DC 20037 (202-467-9467; 1-888-6-ABROAD; www.allianceabroad.com). Arranges teaching placements in Spain, China and Ecuador, volunteer placements in Costa Rica and South Africa, work in the UK and Australia, and internships in Brazil.

AmeriSpan PO Box 58129, Philadelphia, PA 19102 or 117 S 17th St, Suite 1401, Philadelphia, PA 19103 (800-879-6640 or 215-751-1100; fax (215) 751-1986; info@amerispan.com; www.amerispan.com). Language training organisation which arranges internships lasting 2 weeks to 6 months in many Spanish-speaking countries.

Amity Volunteer Teachers Abroad (AVTA), Amity Institute, 3065 Rosecrans Place, Suite 104, San Diego, CA 92110 (619-222-7000; 619-222-7016; www.amity.org). Provides voluntary teaching opportunities in Latin America (Argentina, Peru, Mexico, Brazil, Venezuela and Dominican Republic), Africa (Senegal and Ghana) and Europe (Spain and Italy). Participants must be graduates over the age of 21, and stay for between three and ten months (and for Latin America and Spain have a knowledge of Spanish).

Au Pair Canada, 15 Goodacre Close, Red Deer, Alberta, Canada T4P 3A3 (☎/fax 403-343-1418; aupaircanada@shaw.ca). France, Holland, Switzerland, Germany and Italy.

Au Pair in Europe, PO Box 68056, Blakely Postal Outlet, Hamilton, Ontario, Canada L8M 3M7 (905-545-6305/fax 905-544-4121; aupair@princeent.com; www.princeent.com). Au pairs placed in Austria, Australia, Belgium, Bermuda, Denmark, England, Finland, France, Germany, Greece, Holland, Iceland, Italy, Japan, New Zealand, Norway, Russia, Spain, Sweden and Switzerland. Registration fee is charged.

British American Education Foundation, PO Box 33, Larchmont, NY 10538 (914-834-2064; study@baef.org; www.baef.org). Offers students from North America the opportunity to spend a gap year in a British boarding school following the normal Sixth Form curriculum. Cost approximately $30,000.

BUNAC USA, PO Box 430, Southbury, CT 06488 (800-462-8622; www.bunac.org). Administer Work in Britain Program which allows full-time college students over the age of 18 to work in Britain for up to six months. BUNAC also operates a number of other programmes for US students and young people including Work in Ireland, Work Australia (up to 4 months), Work New Zealand (up to 12 months), Work Canada and Volunteer South Africa.

Camp Counselors & Work Experience USA, 2330 Marinship Way, Suite 250, Sausalito, CA 94965 (www.campcounselors.com). Work Experience programmes in Australia/New Zealand, internships in Brazil and summer camp counsellors in Russia and Croatia.

CDS International Inc, 871 United Nations Plaza, 15th floor, New York, NY 10017-1814 (212-497-3500; info@cdsintl.org). Practical training internships for American students or recent graduates mainly in Germany but also in Turkey, Argentina, Ecuador and Switzerland.

CIEE – Boston: 3 Copley Place, 2nd Floor, Boston, MA 02116 (toll-free 1-888-268-6245). CIEE-Portland: 7 Customn House Street, 3rd Floor, Portland, ME 04101. Toll-free 800-40-Study; 207-553-7600. Fax: 207-553-7699. E-mail: info@councilexchanges.org. Website: www.ciee.org). Work Abroad programme for students and recent graduates (within 6 months) to Germany, France, Ireland and Canada. Non-students also eligible for Canada and New Zealand, and university graduates for China and Thailand. Participants must be students for the study programmes but not for the Work, Volunteer or Teaching programmes and are given visas which allow them to work at any job for the time allowed. Most programme fees start $350-$450. CIEE has a network of offices worldwide which will help with the job hunt. CIEE also arranges for volunteers to go to 800 International Volunteer Projects in 32 countries. Their directory of opportunities is posted on the website from April and costs $12. Placement fee is $300 for most overseas workcamps.

Cross-Cultural Solutions – 1-800-380-4777; info@crossculturalsolutions.org/ www.crossculturalsolutions.org. Volunteer projects in Central America, South America, Africa, Asia and Eastern Europe.

Cultural Embrace, 1304 Hollow Creek Drive, Suite B, Austin, TX 78704; 523-428-9089). Jobs in British pubs for students and people within six months of graduating. Volunteer teaching throughout Latin America. Culinary courses in Italy.

Dynamy, 27 Sever St, Worcester, MA 01609 (508-755-2571; info-email@dynamy.org). Internship year for 30-40 people aged 17-22; Outward Bound expedition, community service and optional college credit. Tuition for 9-month programme is $11,950 plus housing $4,700; scholarships are available.

Earthwatch Institute, 3 Clocktower Place, Suite 100, PO Box 75, Maynard, Massachusetts

01754 (1-800-776-0188; www.earthwatch.org). International environmental charity which recruits over 4,000 volunteers a year to assist professional, scientific field research expeditions around the world. Prices range from $250 to $2,000 excluding air travel to location.

EIL (Experiment in International Living), PO Box 595, 63 Main St, Putney, VT 05346 (www.usexperiment.org). Programmes lasting 3-5 weeks include some language training.

ELTAP (English Language Teaching Assistant Program), University of Minnesota-Morris, Morris, Minnesota 56267 (320-589-6406; kissockc@mrs.umn.edu; www.eltap.org). Placement programme open to undergraduates, graduate students or as a non-credit certificate option for other adults. Participants sent to 25 countries on all continents for 4-11 weeks throughout the year. $300 placement fee, plus course fee and travel. Accommodation and board provided by host schools.

Explorations in Travel Inc, 2458 River Road, Guildford, VT 05301 (802-257 0152; www.volunteertravel.com). International volunteers for rainforest conservation, wildlife projects, etc. in Ecuador, Costa Rica, Belize, Guatemala, the Dominican Republic, Puerto Rico, Mexico, Nepal and Australia. Other placements in animal shelters, on small farms and in schools. Placement fees start at around $800.

Foundation for Sustainable Development, 59 Driftwood Court, San Rafael, CA 90490 (415-482-9366; info@fsdinternational.org; www.interconnection.org/fsd). Summer and longer term internships for anyone over 18 in the field of development in Bolivia, Costa Rica, Peru, Ecuador, Nicaragua, Tanzania and Uganda. The orientation for the African programmes includes a week's intensive language training whereas for all of the Latin American programmes (except Ecuador) volunteers must speak conversational Spanish.

Global Citizens Network, 130 N Howell St, St. Paul, MN 55104 (800-644-9292; www.globalcitizens.org). Teams of paying volunteers are sent to rural villages in Kenya, Nepal, Mexico, Guatemala, Peru, Tanzania, Arizona and New Mexico; programme fee is $650-$1,950 plus airfares.

Global Experiences, PO Box 396, Arnold, MA 21012 (410-703-1738; admin@globalexperience.com). Range of internships for young professionals of all nationalities. Work placements lasting 1-12 months may be in TESOL (training course offered by Global Experiences), graphic design, business, marketing IT, fashion, etc. and may be located in Italy (Rome, Milan, Florence, Sorrento, Genoa, Naples), Australia (Sydney, Brisbane, Melbourne, Great Barrier Reef), China, Thailand, France and Spain (more coming soon). Prices from $600-$6,000.

Global Quest (Thailand), 195 Montsweag Road, Woolwich, Maine 04579 (207-443-5451/fax 207-443-2551; tellis@gquest.org/ www.gquest.org). 12-week programme for pre-university gap year students and high school seniors in Thailand including home stay, study of Thai language and culture, environmental issues, etc. Semester fee is $12,000. Organisation hoping to start up in other host countries and also would welcome British gap year students.

Global Routes, 1 Short St, Northampton, MA 01060 (www.globalroutes.org). Offers 12-week voluntary internships to students over 17 who teach English and other subjects in village schools in Kenya, Costa Rica, Ecuador, Ghana and Thailand. Participation fee $3,550 for the summer and nearly $4,000 for the spring and autumn (excluding airfares). **Ben Clark** from the US participated in this programme between high school and college:

Previous to my arrival at the Essabba Secondary School in the western provinces, there was no English teacher for the Form 1 students. My school was relatively well off and had most of the appropriate tools needed for learning (text books, notebooks, classrooms, etc.). I was surprised at the ease with which I was inserted into the school as teacher. They simply asked my co-intern and me what subjects we were best at, so I chose to teach English and math. It was a challenge for someone with no experience to manage a class of 37, particularly considering the students' dif-

ferent skill levels. Some of the kids were my age, and it was hard at first to earn the respect and trust of my class. Another problem I encountered was that of corporal punishment. In Kenya, caning is something that a lot of the schools practise as punishment for the students' bad behaviour. If students came in late, failed to do assignments or misbehaved, they were either sent to the Deputy Headmaster or sent out to do manual labour in the field. I chose not to apply these punishments and as a result many of my students did not do the homework that I assigned. The class was also too big for me to go around the room every day and check if each student had done their work. My host family is what I miss most about my time in Kenya.

Global Service Corps, 300 Broadway, Suite 28, San Francisco, CA 94133 (www.glob alservicecorps.org). Co-operates with grass-roots organisations in Thailand and Tanzania and sends volunteers and interns for two or three weeks or longer.

Global Volunteers, 375 E Little Canada Road, Little Canada, Minnesota 55117, USA (651-482-0915/toll-free 1-800-487-1074; email@globalvolunteers.org; www.globalvolun teers.org). Non-profit voluntary organisation that sends 1,500 paying volunteers a year to scores of projects lasting from one to three weeks in Africa, Asia, the Caribbean, the Americas and Europe. Service programmes cost between $500 (for projects in the US) and $2,395 excluding airfares, with some student discounts.

Go Global, International Volunteer Programme, International YMCA, 5 West 63rd St, 2nd Floor, New York, NY 10023 (212-727-8800; sprogram@ymcanyc.org; www.ymcainternat ional.org/GOGlobal/home.htm). Progressive volunteer programmes to YMCAs and other organisations around the world. Work normally consists of camping, childcare, sports instruction, health and environmental education, community development or English teaching. Programmes are available in Africa, the Middle East, Europe, South America, the Pacific, Southeast Asia, Eastern Asia and the Indian Sub-continent.

Habitat for Humanity, 121 Habitat St, Americus, GA 31709 (912-924-6935 ext 2489; www.habitat.org). Ecumenical Christian housing ministry building simple decent houses in partnership with low-income families in over 100 countries. Short-term opportunities may be available locally in the communities where Habitat works (see website for locations).

ICADS, Apartado 300-2050 San Pedro Montes de Oca, San José, Costa Rica (506-225 0508; icads@netbox.com; www.icadscr.com). The well regarded programmes of the Institute for Central American Development Studies combine study of the Spanish language and development issues with structured internships in Costa Rica and Nicaragua lasting a semester ($7,900) or a summer ($3,600).

ICYE: Inter-Cultural Youth Exchange, Fraternitas, 2-13 Belgravia Ave, Toronto, Ontario M6E 2M4, Canada (www.icye.org/canada). International exchange organisation (note there is no US representation) that sends students to spend a year abroad with a host family and undertake voluntary work placements, after a one-month orientation including intensive language study. Placements mainly in Bolivia, Brazil, Costa Rica, Honduras, Colombia and Mexico.

Institute for Cultural Ecology, PO Box 991, Hilo, Hawaii 96721 (808-640-2333; www.cultural-ecology.com). Academic internships in Fiji, Thailand and Hawaii working on marine biology projects, environmental advocacy or custom-designed projects in student's major. 4, 8 or 12 weeks. Sample fees: $1,895 for 4 weeks, $3,850 for 12 weeks, e.g. reef mapping on the Fiji coast.

InterExchange Inc, 161 Sixth Avenue, New York, NY 10013 (212-924-0446; info@interexchange.org/ www.interexchange.org). Teaching assistantships in Bulgaria, Belgium and Spain; au pair placements in France, Germany, Netherlands, Spain; farm work in Norway; volunteering in Russia, South Africa and Peru; internships in Belgium, the UK, France and Costa Rica; work and travel in Australia. Fees from $350-$1,100.

Interlocken, Center for Experiential Learning, Interlocken Way, Hillsborough, NH 03244 (603-438-4659; www.interlocken.org/syp/byp). Bridge Year Program for high school graduates structured into two 16-week terms to work on strengthening life skills, outdoor adventures and travel.

International Co-operative Education, 15 Spiros Way, Menlo Park, CA 94025 (415-323-4944; www.icemenlo.com). Places more than 400 students each summer in jobs in Germany, Switzerland, Belgium, Finland, Japan and Singapore. Their placement fee is $600 in addition to an application fee of $200.

i-to-i, 8 E 1st Avenue, Suite 104, Denver, CO 80203 (800-985-4864; usa@i-to-i.com). US office of British company i-to-i (see 'Directory of Specialist Gap Year Programmes').

Kibbutz Aliya Desk, 633 Third Ave, 21st Floor, New York, 10017 (212-318-6130; kibbutzdsk@aol.com). Volunteer placement service for Israeli kibbutzim.

Living Routes, 79 South Pleasant St, Suite 302, Amherst, MA 01002 (413-259-0025; fax 413-259-1256; programs@LivingRoutes.org/ www.LivingRoutes.org). College programmes lasting 3 or 15 weeks based in eco-villages around the world that help students gain the knowledge, skills and inspiration to build a sustainable lifestyle. Current programmes in India, Scotland, Australia, Senegal and North America. Plans to start programmes in Europe, Brazil, Sri Lanka and Israel. $1,500-$2,700 or $10,750 excluding flights.

MOGPA/Intern in Asia, 2345 Rice St, Ste 200, St. Paul, MN 55113 (651-481-0583/fax 651-481-0592; recruiter@interninasia.com or info@mogpa.com/ www.InternInAsia.com). Helps US college students and recent graduates to obtain 6-12 month professional work assignments in China and Japan. Minimum age is 20. Quotas are often filled well in advance.

Mountbatten Internship Programme, 50 East 42nd Street, Suite 2000, New York, NY 10017-5405 (www.mountbatten.org). Reciprocal programme places American students in London so that they can acquire practical training in business for 12 months.

NRCSA – National Registration Center for Study Abroad, Box 1393, Milwaukee, WI 53201 (414-278-0631; inquire@nrcsa.com; www.nrcsa.com). Website has links to study and volunteering or career-focussed internship programmes in Latin America plus Spain, France and Germany.

Operation Crossroads Africa, 34 Mount Morris Park, New York, NY 10027 (212-289-1949; www.igc.org/oca). 7-week summer projects in Africa and Brazil.

Pacific Challenge, PO Box 3151, Eugene, Oregon 97403 (541-343-4124; HQ@pacificchallenge.org; www.pacificchallenge.org). 2-month experiential travel programmes through New Zealand, Australia, SE Asia, Nepal, China and Tibet. Fees $4,000-$6,000.

Peace Corps, 1111 20th St NW, Washington, DC 20526 (1-800-424 8580/ www.peacecorps.gov). Sends volunteers on two-year assignments to 70 countries (see end of this listing).

Rotary Youth Exchange, One Rotary Center, 1560 Sherman Ave, Evanston, IL 60201 (847-866-3000; youthexchange@rotaryintl.org; www.rotary.org). Short-term and longer exchanges for 8,000 secondary school students aged 15-19 organised through worldwide network of Rotary clubs. Older students (aged 18-25) may participate in short-term New Generations Exchanges. Rotary is looking for people who have been involved in their communities and are potentially strong cultural ambassadors.

SCI-IVS (Service Civil International-International Voluntary Service), 5474 Walnut Level Road, Crozet, VA 22932 (☎/fax 206-350-6585; info@sci-ivs.org; www.sci-ivs.org).

Teaching and Projects Abroad, 19 Cullen Drive, West Orange, NJ 07052 (973-324-2688; info@projects-abroad.org). US office of British company of the same name (see 'Directory of Specialist Gap Year Programmes').

Travel CUTS, 45 Charles St E, Suite 100, Toronto, Ontario M4Y 1S2, Canada. Administers the SWAP (Student Work Abroad Program) for Canadian students to the UK, Ireland, France, Germany, Australia, New Zealand, South Africa and Japan.

University Research Expeditions Program (UREP), University of California, One Shields Ave, Davis, CA 95616 (530-752-0692; www.urep.ucdavis.edu). Programme of short research expeditions suspended at present.

Volunteers for Peace, 1034 Tiffany Road, Belmont, Vermont 05730 (802-259-2759; vfp@vfp.org; www.vfp.org). Annual membership $20. VFP publishes an up-to-date

International Workcamp Directory with over 2,400 listings in 90 countries, available from mid-April. Registration for most programmes is $200.

Where There Be Dragons, PO Box 4651, Boulder, CO 80306 (800-982-9203; www.wheretherebedragons.com). 6-week summer programmes including homestays and service work in the Far East, Southeast Asia and Turkey. Cost from $6,000. Also 12-week semester in China and India.

Wildlands Studies, 3 Mosswood Circle, Cazadero, CA 95421 (707-621-5665; www.w ildlandsstudies.com). 27 conservation projects in the US (including Alaska and Hawaii), Belize, Thailand and Nepal.

WISE – Worldwide International Student Exchange, PO Box 1332, Dyersburg, TN 38025 (731-287-9948; wise@wisefoundation.com). Academic year abroad (ages 15-18) in Germany, Austria, Denmark, Japan and Brazil for 5 or 10 months.

WorldTeach Inc., Center for International Development, Harvard University, 79 John F Kennedy Street, Cambridge, MA 02138 (617-495-5527/800-4-TEACH-0; www.worldteach.org). Non-profit organisation that places several hundred paying volunteers as teachers of EFL or ESL in countries which request assistance. Currently, WorldTeach provides college graduates for 6 or 12 months to Costa Rica, Ecuador, China, Namibia, Mexico and the Marshall Islands.

Youth Challenge International, 20 Maud St, Suite 305, Toronto, Ontario M5V 2M5, Canada (416-504-3370; www.yci.org). Teams of volunteers carry out community development projects lasting 5,6 or 10 weeks in Costa Rica, Guyana, Philippines etc.

The first organisation that American volunteers think of is the *Peace Corps* (1111 20th St NW, Washington, DC 20526; 1-800-424 8580/202-692-1800; www.peacecorps.gov) which sends both skilled and unskilled volunteers on two-year assignments to 77 countries.

Kristie McComb was posted to Burkina Faso till 2003 and gradually concluded that the Peace Corps programme places less emphasis on development than on cultural exchange, i.e. sharing American culture with the host country nationals and then sharing the culture of your host country with Americans on your return:

The cool thing for Americans is that you don't have to be qualified in anything to be accepted by the Peace Corps. There are many generalist programmes where you can learn what you need to know once you get there through the three-month pre-service training. I would encourage interested parties to be honest about what they can and cannot tolerate since not all volunteers are sent to live in mud huts. In a world changed by terrorism it is comforting to know how much of an active interest the US government takes in the safety and well being of its citizens abroad. However some people might find this stifling and not adventurous enough. How well PC keeps tabs on volunteers in any given country depends on the local PC leadership but, regardless, you are still in a high profile group of well locatable people. Risk reduction is the buzz word in Washington these days.

Overall I am happy with my experience though I am often frustrated by the inertia, the corruption and bureaucracy that makes me question whether anything will ever change. But you do gain a lot by (if nothing else) witnessing poverty on a regular basis. You quickly learn to recognise the difference between a problem and an inconvenience and to see how lucky we are as Americans to have some of the 'problems' we have.

Anyone considering the Peace Corps might look at a website created by a returned volunteer (www.peacecorpsonline.org/crossroads).

LANGUAGE COURSES FOR NORTH AMERICANS

At a time when broad-minded Americans may find themselves wanting to try to dispel accusations of insularity and supremacy, going abroad to learn or improve a foreign language may have special appeal. Classroom learning has its place. But it is axiomatic that the fastest progress will be made when you are forced to use a language in every-day situations both at home and work. Programmes that combine structured study of a language or culture with volunteering are arguably a paradigm of the kind of foreign travel experience that can more than justify taking a year out before proceeding to college. Many organisations both international and local can arrange such placements, often in conjunction with a homestay to maximise exposure to the language.

Using a mediating agency simplifies the process of choosing a language school since they tend to deal with well-established schools and programmes on the ground. These agencies also provide a useful back-up service if something goes wrong. An effective search engine for locating courses is provided by the Institute of International Education on www.iiepassport.org which makes it easy to search by country and programme. Another recommended site is www.worldwide.edu. Here are some language course providers and agents of possible interest to North Americans planning a gap year.

ALLIANCE FRANCAISE OF WASHINGTON
2142 Wyoming Avenue NW, Washington, DC 20008. ☎ (202) 234-7911. Fax: (202) 234-0125. E-mail: alliance@francedc.org. Website: www.francedc.org.
Courses offered: Various French classes for beginners and experienced speakers. Courses may be intensive week-long courses, or ongoing evening classes. Private or group tuition.
Duration of courses: Flexible start dates year round.
Qualifications offered: Generally recreational. Some courses are specialised (e.g. literature, cooking, business, legal French). TCF and TEF offered starting in September 2003.
Cost: From $125.

CENTER FOR CULTURAL INTERCHANGE
17 N. Second Avenue, St. Charles, IL 60174. ☎ (630) 377-2272. Fax: (630) 377-2307. E-mail: info@cci-exchange.com. Website: www.cci-exchange.com.
Courses offered: Language courses in Ecuador, France, Germany, Mexico, Italy and Spain. Independent homestay programme in 20 countries. High school semester or year abroad in Australia, France, Germany, Ireland, the Netherlands and South Africa.
Duration of courses: 2 weeks to 10 months.
Qualifications offered: A certificate is awarded indicating course work completed.
Cost: from $800 depending on type of programme and length of stay.
Other Services: Internships can be arranged lasting 1-3 months.
Accommodation: With host families.

CULTURAL EXPERIENCES ABROAD
1400 E Southern Ave, Suite B-108, Tempe, AZ 85282. E-mail: info@gowithcea.com. Website: www.gowithcea.com.
Courses offered: Language courses (beginners to advanced) offered through European universities.
Destinations: French offered in Paris, Grenoble, Dijon and Aix-en-Provence; Italian in Florence, and Spanish in Alicante, Barcelona, Granada, Madrid, Seville, Guadalajara (Mexico) and San José (Costa Rica).

EDUVACATIONS
1431 21ˢᵗ St NW, Ste. 302, Washington, DC 20036. ☎ 202-857-8384. Fax: 202-462-8091. E-mail: Eduvacate@aol.com. Website: www.eduvacations.com.
Travel company specialising in customised language courses combined with sports, art instruction, etc. throughout Europe, Latin America, the Caribbean, Russia, the US, etc.
Cost: Minimum $900 for one week including course, meals and accommodation.
Contact: Mary Ann Puglisi, President.

LANGUAGES ABROAD.COM
413 Ontario St, Toronto, Ontario M5A 2V9, Canada. ☎ **(416) 925-2112. Fax: (416) 925-5990. E-mail: info@languagesabroad.com. Website: www.languagesabroad.com.**
Courses offered: Language immersion programmes worldwide including Europe, South Pacific, Asia, Latin America and the Middle East.
Duration of courses: 2-36 weeks.
Qualifications offered: Possibility of studying towards D.E.L.E. (Spain), C.I.L.S. (Italy), D.E.L.F. and D.A.L.F. (France) and Kleines and Grosses Sprachdiplom (Germany).
Cost: Courses start at $600 for a 2-week programme. 8 weeks in Florence with apartment would cost $3,285.
Accommodation: In apartments with other students, with a host family or in private or hotel accommodation.

LANGUAGE LIAISON
4 Burnham Parkway, Morristown, NJ 07960. ☎ **800-284-4448. E-mail: learen @languageliaison.com. Website: www.languageliaison.com.**
Courses offered: Total immersion language/culture study programmes and leisure learning courses. Language courses can be combined with a diverse variety of options including art, cuisine, golf and skiing.
Duration of courses: Programmes last from 1 week to 1 year, beginning every week of the year.
Qualifications offered: Some courses lead to certificates, others offer the chance to take the D.E.L.F. exam.
Accommodation: Students stay with families as a homestay.

LANGUAGE LINK
PO Box 3006, Peoria, IL 61612-3006. ☎ **800-552-2051/309-692-2961. E-mail: info@langlink.com. Website: www.langlink.com.**
Represents 15 Spanish language schools in Spain and Latin America, viz. La Janda of Vejer de la Frontera, Eureka of Madrid, International House Barcelona, Academia Hispanica Cordoba, Lacunza of San Sebastian and CLIC of Seville in Spain; Proyecto Linguistico Francisco Marroquin in Antigua (Guatemala), Intercultura of Heredia and ILISA of San José in Costa Rica; Spanish Language Institute of Cuernavaca, Becari of Oaxaca and el Bosque del Caribe de Cancun (Mexico); Academia de Espanol Quito (Ecuador); Amauta of Cusco, Peru; ILEE of Buenos Aires, Cordoba and Bariloche (Argentina).
Courses offered: All levels of instruction for any length of time.
Cost: Starting at $90 for one week's tuition and $65-$175 per week for accommodation.
Contact: Kay Rafool, Director.

LANGUAGE STUDIES INTERNATIONAL (LSI)
1706 Fifth Avenue, San Diego, CA 92101. ☎ **619-234-2881. Website: www.lsi.edu.**
Courses offered: Spanish in Spain or Mexico, French in France, Italian in Italy and German in Germany or Switzerland.
Duration of courses: 2-50 week intensive courses year-round.

LEXIA INTERNATIONAL
23 South Main Street, Hanover, NH 03755, USA. ☎ 800-775-3942 or 603-643-9898. Fax: 603-643-9899. E-mail: info@lexiaintl.org. Website: www.lexiaintl.org.
Courses offered: Overseas academic programmes, which include intensive language study, civilisation course, research methodology course, academic research project, elective course, internships and community service projects.
Destinations: Argentina, China, Cuba, Czech Republic, England, France, Germany, Hungary, Italy, Poland, South Africa and Thailand.

Number of placements per year: 500.
Duration of courses: semester or academic year.
Prerequisites: Minimum age 17; average 19-20. All nationalities. Must have strong interest in international educational experience and be a good student (minimum B average).
Qualifications offered: All students receive college-level credit.
Selection procedures and orientation: Deadline for fall and academic year is June 15th; deadline for spring intake, November 15th; deadline for summer, April 15th.
Accommodation: Homestays, dorms and apartments.
Contact: Ned Quigley, Director of University Relations.

NATIONAL REGISTRATION CENTER FOR STUDY ABROAD
PO Box 1393, Milwaukee, WI 53201. ☎ 414-278-0631. E-mail: info@nrcsa.com. Website: www.nrsca.com. Also Washington DC office: 202—338-5927.
Courses offered: Full language and culture immersion and other courses offered at 125 language schools and universities in 43 countries. Varying lengths of stay. Gap year students studying at a university may be able to apply the credit to their subsequent university.
Other services: Many schools offer an option to participate in volunteer work, career-focused internships or adventure travel programmes.

POINT3 LANGUAGE CENTER
404 rue St-Pierre, Bureau 201, Montréal, Québec H2Y 2M2, Canada. ☎ (514) 840-7228. Fax: (514) 840-7111. E-mail: info@point-3.com. Website: www.point-3.com.
Courses offered: French, English, Spanish and Japanese (see entry in 'Directory of Courses').

STUDY GROUP
301 East Las Olas Boulevard, Fort Lauderdale, FL 33301. ☎ 954-522 8810. Fax: 954-522 6955. E-mail: infousa@studygroup.com. Website: www.studygroup.com or www.language-study.com.
Affiliated to Languages Plus (established in 1982). Member of Global Work Experience Association (GWEA) so internships can be organised following on from language courses.
Courses offered: French, Spanish, Italian and German courses in 8 European cities.

TALKING TRAVELER
620 SW 5th Ave, Suite 625, Portland, OR 97204. ☎ 503-274-1776 or 800-274-6007. Fax: 503-274-9004. E-mail: info@talkingtraveler.org. Website: www.talkingtraveler.org.
Non-profit organisation.
Courses offered: Full immersion language and culture courses for adults worldwide. Links with schools in various Italian, Spanish, French, German, Mexican and Costa Rican cities.
Duration of courses: Classes start each Monday of the year for intermediate level students at most schools. Most schools have a 2-week minimum stay. 4 hours of classes per day in classes of 4-12 students.
Contact: Reno J. Tibke, Programme Co-ordinator.

UNIVERSITY STUDIES ABROAD CONSORTIUM
University of Nevada, USAC/323, Reno, NV 89557-0093. ☎ 775-784-6569. Fax: 775-784-6010. E-mail: usac@unr.edu. Website: http://usac.unr.edu.
Courses offered: Spanish, Basque, Chinese, Danish, French, German, Japanese, Hebrew, Italian, Czech, Thai and Twi languages, plus art history, anthropology, business, communications, literature, history, political science, ecology, environmental studies,

education, economics and tourism.
Duration of courses: Month, summer, semester or year long programmes.
Qualifications offered: The programmes are university accredited.
Accommodation: In apartments, residence halls and homestays.

WE STUDY ABROAD

12 Via Florencia, Mission Veijo, CA 92692. ☎ 949-951-0686 or 877-299-4024. Fax: travelstudy@yahoo.com. Website: www.westudyabroad.com.
Travel Study Programme.
Courses offered: Spanish, French, Italian, English.
Duration of courses: Short-term, summer, semester and full year.
Qualifications offered: Undergraduate merit with some institutions overseas.
Other services: Internships, jobs and volunteer projects can be provided.
Contact: Steve Tash.

Paid Seasonal Jobs

The fastest way to save money is of course to live at home and find a job which pays more than the national minimum wage and has scope for working lots of overtime. Vast number of students register with a local temp agency like Blue Arrow and request as many hours as possible. But there may come a time when you can't stand the sight of the same old high street or the same old work mates, and want a complete break while still earning. Depending on the time of year, you may be able to arrange a short sharp change of routine by, say, working at Aviemore in the Cairngorms over Christmas or going to pick grapes in France or Switzerland. The possibilities are so numerous that this chapter can only skim the surface. For much more comprehensive listings of seasonal jobs, look at the annual directories of *Summer Jobs in Britain* and *Summer Jobs Abroad* (price £9.99 each from Vacation Work) and *Work Your Way Around the World* (£12.95).

While opening up an enormous range of possibilities, the internet can be a bewildering place to job-hunt. A host of websites promises to provide free on-line recruitment services for travellers. These include the excellent non-commercial free Jobs Abroad Bulletin (www.payaway.co.uk), www.summerjobseeker.com (for jobs in the tourist industry), www.gapwork.com, www.anyworkanywhere.com, www.jobsmonkey.com (especially for

North America), http://jobs.escapeartist.com, www.hotrecruit.co.uk (which has a section on 'Crazy Jobs') and so on. Justjobs4students.co.uk has a section on 'Year Out' jobs. Because many are in their infancy, they often seem to offer more than they can deliver and you may find that the number and range of jobs posted are disappointing. But everywhere you look on the internet potentially useful links can be found. A surprising number of company home pages feature an icon you can click to find out about jobs.

Working for a local employer abroad is arguably one of the best ways of getting inside a culture, though the kind of job you find will determine the stratum of society which you experience. The student who spends a few weeks picking fruit in Canada will get a very different insight into North American culture from the one who looks after the children of a Texan millionaire. Yet both will have the chance to participate temporarily in the life of a culture and get to know one place well.

Most gap year students looking for holiday jobs abroad will have to depend on the two industries that survive on seasonal labour: tourism and agriculture. School leavers and their parents will probably feel happier with a pre-arranged job, possibly with a British tour operator, but that does limit the choice. Like job-hunting in any context, the competition for seasonal work will be hard to beat unless you are available for interview. If looking for farm work or a berth on a transatlantic yacht, a visit to a village pub frequented by farmers or yachties is worth dozens of speculative applications from home.

The other major fields of paid overseas employment for students are au pairing (see separate chapter) and English teaching (discussed below and also in the relevant country chapters). The more unusual and interesting the job the more competition it will attract. For example it is to be assumed that only a small percentage of applicants for advertised jobs actually get the chance to work as underwater photographic models in the Caribbean, history co-ordinators for a European tour company or assistants at a museum bookshop in Paris. Rather than try to fill one of these rare but interesting vacancies, you can perhaps invent your own bizarre job, like busking on the bagpipes or delivering croissants to holidaymakers in ski resorts.

TOURISM

Hotels, restaurants, pubs and campsites from Cannes to Canada depend on transient workers. Anyone with some home-town restaurant experience and perhaps some knowledge of a second language should be able to fix up a summer job in a European resort.

If you secure a hotel job without speaking the language of the country and lacking relevant experience, you will probably be placed at the bottom of the pecking order, e.g. in the laundry or washing dishes. Even the job of dish-washer, stereotyped as the most lowly of all jobs with visions of the down and out George Orwell as a *plongeur* washing dishes in a Paris café, should not be dismissed too easily. Simon Canning saved enough money in five months of working as a dish-washer in an Amsterdam office block to fund a trip across Asia. Benjamin Fry spent a highly enjoyable few weeks washing dishes at the Land's End Hotel in Alaska and earned more per hour than he could have in Britain. And **Sean Macnamara** was delighted with his job as dish-washer in a French hotel near Chamonix:

> *After a brief interview I was given the job of dish-washer. The conditions were excellent: £300 per month plus private accommodation and first class meals, including as much wine as I could drink. I earned my keep, though, working six days a week from 8am to 10pm with three hours off each afternoon. I was the only foreigner and was treated kindly by everyone. Indeed I can honestly say I enjoyed myself, but then I was permanently high on the thought of all that money.*

Even if the job is fairly grim, you will probably collect some good anecdotes as **S. C. Firn** did in an upmarket restaurant in Oberstdorf in the Bavarian Alps:

I had to peel vegetables, wash dishes, prepare food, clean the kitchen and sometimes serve food. Everything was done at a very fast pace, and was expected to be very professional. One German cook, aged 16, who didn't come up to standard, was punched in the face three times by the owner. On another occasion the assistant chef had a container of hot carrots tipped over his head for having food sent back. During my three months there, all the other British workers left, apart from the chef, but were always replaced by more.

So if you can't stand the heat...

Applications

The earlier you decide to apply for seasonal hotel work the better are your chances. Hotels in a country such as Switzerland recruit months before the summer season, and it is advisable to write to as many hotel addresses as possible by March, preferably in their own language. A knowledge of more than one language is an immense asset for work in Europe. If you have an interest in working in a particular country, get a list of hotels from their tourist office in London and write to the largest ones (e.g. the ones with over 100 rooms). If you know someone going to your chosen country, ask them to bring back local newspapers and check adverts. Enclose international reply coupons and try to write in the language of the country.

On the other hand you might not be able to plan so far ahead, or you may have no luck with written applications, so it will be necessary to look for hotel work once you've arrived in a foreign country. All but the most desperate hoteliers are far more willing to consider a candidate who is standing there in the flesh than one who writes a letter out of the blue. One job-seeker recommends showing up bright and early (about 8am) to impress prospective employers. Perseverance is necessary when you're asking door to door at hotels since plenty of rejections are inevitable.

Hotels represent just one aspect of the tourist trade, and many more interesting venues exist for cooking and serving, including luxury yachts, prawn trawlers, holiday ranches, safari camps and ski chalets. People with some training in catering will find it much easier to find a lucrative job abroad than most. Of course, there are opportunities for the unskilled. You might find a job cooking hamburgers in a chain such as McDonalds or Burger King, which can be found from Tel Aviv to Toronto. (Bear in mind that the *Oxford English Dictionary* now includes the coinage 'Mcjob' to refer to any form of dead-end, low-paid employment; yet one in eight Americans will work for Uncle Ronald at some point in their lives.) When applying for jobs which are not seasonal, you should stress that you intend to work for an indefinite period, make a career of fast food catering, etc. In fact staff turnover is usually very high. This will also aid your case when you are obliged to badger them to give you extra hours.

A good way of gaining initial experience is to work for a large organisation with huge staff requirements like *PGL Travel* in Britain and *Village Camps* on the continent. Since they have so many vacancies (most of which pay only pocket money), the chances of being hired for a first season are reasonably good.

Mark Warner is a leading tour operator with Resort Hotels located around the Mediterranean and Aegean, and Chalethotels in top ski resorts in the Alps. They recruit staff to work in Greece, Turkey, Corsica, Sardinia and Italy for the summer season and in Austria, France and Italy for the ski season. Positions are open for chefs, restaurant and bar staff, nursery nurses and children's activity leaders, watersport, tennis and aerobic instructors, pool attendants, customer service and shop staff, ski hosts and many others. Employees are provided with a competitive package including full board, medical insurance, travel expenses, use of watersport and activity facilities (summer) and ski pass, skis and boots (winter). More information can be obtained by ringing 020-7761 7300 or visiting www.markwarner-recruitment.co.uk.

Campsite Couriers

British camping holiday firms (addresses below) hire large numbers of people to remain on one campsite throughout Europe for several months. *Holidaybreak* alone recruits up to 2,000 campsite couriers and children's couriers for the self-drive camping brands Eurocamp and Keycamp. The courier's job is to clean the tents and caravans between visitors, greet clients and deal with difficulties (particularly illness or car breakdowns) and introduce clients to the attractions of the area or even arrange and host social functions and amuse the children. All of this will be rewarded with on average £90-£100 a week in addition to free tent accommodation. Many companies offer half-season contracts April to mid-July and mid-July to the end of September.

The massive camping holiday industry generates winter work as well. Brad Blanchisserie is a French-registered company in Sautron, Nantes which cleans and repairs tents and bedding on behalf of many of the major companies. Staff (who need not speak French though it is an advantage) are needed between September and May. A wage of €55 a day plus gite accommodation is provided (so having your own transport is an advantage). Their UK office is at Abbey Lakes Hall, Orrell Road, Wigan WN5 8QZ (01695 632797; info@bradint.co.uk).

Short bursts of work are available in the spring (about three weeks in May) and autumn (three weeks in September) to teams of people who put up and take down the tents at campsites, known as *montage* and *démontage*. Sometimes the camping tour operators contract out this work to specialist firms like Mark Hammerton Travel (90-94 High St, Tunbridge Wells, Kent TN1 1YF; 01892 525456; enquiries@markhammerton.co.uk) who pay their crews nearly £100 a week in addition to all expenses.

Some camping holiday and tour operators based in Britain are as follows (with the European countries in which they are active):

Canvas Holidays, East Port House, 12 East Port, Dunfermline, Fife KY12 7JG (01383 629018; www.canvasholidays.com). Mainly France but also Germany, Austria, Switzerland, Italy, Luxembourg and Spain.

Club Cantabrica Holidays Ltd, 146/148 London Road, St. Albans, Herts. AL1 1PQ (01727 866177; www.cantabrica.co.uk). France, Austria, Greece (Corfu), Italy and Spain (including Majorca).

Eurocamp, Overseas Recruitment Department (Ref TGY/03) – 01606 787525; www.hol idaybreakjobs.com. Operate 200 campsites in most European countries. Telephone applications from October. Interviews held in Hartford, Cheshire over the winter. Also trade under Holidaybreak, Hartford Manor, Greenbank Lane, Northwich, Cheshire CW8 1HW (same telephone number).

Eurosites Recruitment/Airtours plc, The Globe Centre, St. James Square, Accrington, Lancs. BB5 0RE (www.eurosites.co.uk). Campsite and children's reps for France, Spain, Italy, Germany and Holland.

Haven Europe, HR Dept, 1 Park Lane, Hemel Hempstead, Herts. HP2 4YL (01442 203970; www.haveneurope.com). Courier and children's courier staff for France, Spain and Italy.

Holidaybreak, see Eurocamp.

Keycamp Holidays, Overseas Recruitment Department (Ref TGY/03), Hartford Manor, Greenbank Lane, Northwich, CW8 1HW (01606 787525/e-mail: www.holidaybreakjob s.com). France, Italy, Spain, Germany.

Solaire Holidays, 1158 Stratford Road, Hall Green, Birmingham B28 8AF (0121-778 5061; www.solaire.co.uk). France, Spain.

Be warned that an offer of a job may be more tentative than it seems as Karen Martin describes:

Before we left in May, we had both been interviewed for the job of campsite courier. We got the jobs and signed the contracts, and our rough start date was the 7th of July. They did not make the position clear that an offer 'subject to terms and condi-

tions' means that it is possible that a week before the start date you can be told that there is no longer a job due to lack of customers, which is what happened to us. We really felt let down.

Successful couriers make the job look easy, but it does demand a lot of hard work and patience. Occasionally it is very hard to keep up the happy, smiling, never-ruffled courier look, but most seem to end up enjoying the job.

Alison Cooper described her job with Eurocamp on a site in Corsica as immensely enjoyable, though it was not as easy as the clients thought:
Living on a campsite in high season had one or two drawbacks: the toilets and showers were dirty, with constant queues, the water was freezing cold, the campsite was very very noisy and if you're unfortunate enough to have your tent in sunlight, it turns into a tropical greenhouse. Of course we did get difficult customers who complained for a variety of reasons: they wanted to be nearer to the beach, off the main road, in a cooler tent with more grass around it, etc. etc. But mostly our customers were friendly and we soon discovered that the friendlier we were to them, the cleaner they left their tents.
I found it difficult at first to get used to living, eating, working and socialising with the other two couriers 24 hours a day. But we all got on quite well and had a good time, unlike at a neighbouring campsite where the couriers hated each other. Our campsite had a swimming pool and direct beach access, though nightlife was limited. The one disco did get very repetitive.

Despite all this, she sums up by highly recommending that others who have never travelled or worked abroad work for a company like Eurocamp which provides accommodation, a guaranteed weekly wage and the chance to work with like-minded people.

Caroline Nicholls' problems at a campsite in Brittany included frequent power failures, blocked loos and leaking tents:

Every time there was a steady downpour, one of the tents developed an indoor lake, due to the unfortunate angle at which we had pitched it. I would appear, mop in hand, with cries of 'I don't understand. This has never happened before.' Working as a courier would be a good grounding for an acting career.

She goes on to say that despite enjoying the company of the client families, she was glad to have the use of a company bicycle to escape the insular life on the campsite every so often. Some companies guarantee one day off-site which is considered essential for maintaining sanity. The companies do vary in the conditions of work and some offer much better support than others. For example a company for which Hannah Start worked ignored her pleas for advice and assistance when one of her clients had appendicitis.

The big companies interview hundreds of candidates and have filled most posts by the end of January. But there is a very high dropout rate (over 50%) and vacancies are filled from a reserve list, so it is worth ringing around the companies as late as April for cancellations. Despite competition, anyone who has studied a European language and has an outgoing personality stands a good chance if he or she applies early and widely enough.

Activity Holidays

Many specialist tour companies employ leaders for their clients, whether children or adults, on walking, cycling, watersports holidays, etc. Any competent sailor, canoeist, diver, climber, rider, etc. should have no difficulty marketing their skills in the UK and abroad. See entries for *Acorn Adventure, 3D Education & Adventure Ltd,* and *PGL Travel* for example.

If you would like to do a watersports course with a view to working abroad, see the entries for *Flying Fish* and *UK Sailing Academy* in the 'Directory of Sport & Activity Courses'. They offer training as instructors in windsurfing, diving, dinghy sailing and yachting, followed by a job recruitment service.

Ski Resorts

The season in the European Alps lasts from about Christmas until late April/early May. Between Christmas and the New Year is a terrifically busy time as is the middle two weeks of February during half-term. Because jobs in ski resorts are so popular among the travelling community, wages can be low; so many gap year and older students are (or become) such avid skiers that in their view it is recompense enough to have easy access to the slopes during their time off. One of the best ways to improve your chances of being hired is to do a catering course, some of which specialise in ski chalet cooking (see 'Directory of Cookery Courses').

Specialist ski recruitment websites can be extremely helpful. The superb Natives.co.uk posts current vacancies on behalf of a selection of the major operators and also includes detailed resort descriptions, links to seasonal workers' email addresses. Try also Free Radicals (www.freeradicals.co.uk), findaskijob.com (part of www.voovs.com and requires that you register your CV) and www.skiconnection.co.uk, all of which aim to be one-stop shops for recruitment of winter staff for Europe and North America, and the smaller Ski Staff (www.skistaff.co.uk) to whom you can send your CV (jobs@skistaff.co.uk).

The new edition of *Working in Ski Resorts* (Vacation Work, 2003; £11.95) contains many addresses of ski companies and details of the job hunt in individual European and North American resorts. In response to the thousands of enquiries about alpine jobs that the Ski Club of Great Britain receives, it distributes *The Alpine Employment Fact Sheet*; send £3 and an s.a.e. to the Ski Club GB, 57-63 Church Rd, Wimbledon SW19 5SB; 0845 45 80783; www.skiclub.co.uk). The Club also takes on intermediate skiers over the age of 22 with extensive experience of on- and off-piste skiing to work as ski reps in 43 European and North American resorts. Ski reps work for between one and three months after doing a two-week training course in Tignes in December (which costs £1,000 including airfares).

Either you can try to fix up a job with a British-based ski tour company before you leave (which has more security but lower wages and tends to isolate you in an English-speaking ghetto), or you can look for work on the spot.

In the spring preceding the winter season in which you want to work, ask the ski tour companies listed below for an application form. Their literature will describe the range of positions they wish to fill. These may vary slightly from company to company but will probably include resort representatives (who may need language skills), chalet girls (who must be able to cook to a high standard), cleaners, odd jobbers and ski guides/instructors. An increasing number of companies are offering nanny and crèche facilities, so this is a further possibility for the suitably qualified.

Here are some of the major UK companies. Some have a limited number of vacancies which they can fill from a list of people who have worked for them during the summer season or have been personally recommended by former employees. So you should not be too disappointed if you are initially unsuccessful.

Inghams Travel & Bladon Lines, 10-18 Putney Hill, London SW15 6AX (020-8780 8803/4400; www.inghams.co.uk/general_pages/job.html). 450 winter staff including reps, chalet staff, hostess/cleaners, *plongeurs* and maintenance staff for resorts in France, Italy, Austria, Switzerland, Norway, Andorra, USA, Canada, etc. Perks include free ski pass, ski and boot hire, meals, accommodation and return travel from the UK.

Crystal Holidays, King's Place, Wood St, Kingston-upon-Thames W4 5RT (020-7420 2081; www.shgjobs.co.uk). Part of Thomson Travel Group. 2,000 overseas staff in more than 100 ski resorts in Europe and North America (visa required). Resort reps, chalet staff and qualified nannies for France, Austria and Italy.

Esprit Holidays, 185 Fleet Road, Fleet, Hants. GU51 3BL (01252 618318; www.esprit-holidays.co.uk). Resort reps, chalet hosts and (especially) nannies for France, Austria,

Italy and Canada.

First Choice/Skibound, 1st Floor, London Road, Crawley, W Sussex RH10 2GX (Recruitment hotline 01293 588585; skijobs@firstchoice.co.uk). 750 winter staff from EU employed in France, Italy, Austria, Canada, etc.

NBV Leisure Ltd., 72 New Bond St, London W1Y 9DD (020-7629 4453; www.nbvleisure.com). Expanding company with catered chalet holidays in France and ski holidays in Austria and Switzerland.

Neilson Overseas Personnel, Locksview, Brighton Marina, Brighton BN2 5HA (0870 241 2901; skijobs@neilson.com/ www.neilson.com). Part of Thomas Cook Group. Resorts in Andorra, Austria, Bulgaria, Canada, France and Italy among others.

PGL Travel Ltd, Ski Department, Alton Court, Penyard Lane, Ross-on-Wye, Herefordshire HR9 5GL (01989 767311; skipersonnel@pgl.co.uk). School group operator with rep and snowboard instructor vacancies for 1-3 weeks during peak school holidays especially February half-term. Reps must be reasonable skiers with knowledge of French, Italian or German.

Powder Byrne, 250 Upper Richmond Road, London SW15 6TG (020-8246 5310; www.powderbyrne.com). Upmarket company operating in Switzerland, France, Austria. Compulsory 1-week training course in Switzerland for full-season staff.

Simply Ski, 12-42 Kings House, Wood St, Kingston upon Thames W4 5RT (020-7420 2083; www.shgjobs.co.uk). Part of Thomson Travel Group. Chalet and other staff needed in Austria, France and Switzerland.

Ski Gower, 2 High St, Studley, Warks. B80 7HJ (01527 851420/fax 01527 857236). Reps and evening programme organisers for school trips to Switzerland and Poland.

Ski Total, 3 The Square, Richmond, Surrey TW9 1DY (020-8948 6922; www.skitotal.com). France, Austria, Switzerland and Canada.

Skiworld, 3 Vencourt Place, London W6 9NU (020-8600 1654; www.skiworld.ltd.uk). Chalet holidays in all the major European and North American resorts.

Travelclass, www.travelclass.co.uk. Ski reps, guides and instructors for school groups in Austria, France, Italy and Switzerland.

A classic job for the gap year is as a 'chalet girl'. The number of chalets in the Alps has hugely increased over the past decade with the biggest areas of expansion for British holidaymakers being Méribel, Courchevel and Val d'Isère in France, Verbier in Switzerland and St Anton in Austria. Clients in chalets are looked after by a chalet girl or (increasingly) chalet boy. The chalet host does everything (sometimes with an assistant) from cooking first-class meals for the ten or so guests to clearing the snow from the footpath (or delegating that job). She is responsible for keeping the chalet clean, preparing breakfast, packed lunches, tea and dinner, providing ice and advice, and generally keeping everybody happy.

Although this sounds an impossible regimen, many chalet girls manage to fit in several hours of skiing in the middle of each day. The standards of cookery skills required vary from company to company depending on the degree of luxury (i.e. the price) of the holidays. In most cases, you will have to cook a trial meal for the tour company before being accepted for the job or at least submit detailed menu plans. Average pay for a chalet host starts at about £75 a week, plus perks including accommodation, food and a ski pass. Recruitment of the 1,000+ chalet girls needed in Europe gets underway in May so early application is essential.

If you wait until you arrive to look for a ski resort job, be prepared for lots of refusals. You will almost certainly have to fund yourself for some weeks before anything crops up (and of course there is no guarantee that anything will). Arrive as early as you can (say early November) so that you can get to know people and let them get to know your face. Apply directly to hotels, equipment rental agencies, tourist offices, etc. If you miss out on landing a job before the season, it could be worth trying again in early January, since workers tend to disappear after the holidays.

If you are already a good skier and interested in qualifying as an instructor, contact BASI, the *British Association of Snowsport Instructors,* or one of the gap year instructor courses such as *Ski Le Gap, Peakleaders* or the *International Academy* (see 'Directory of Sports Courses'). The recent explosion in snowboarding has resulted in an ongoing worldwide shortage of instructors.

FARM WORK

Itinerant workers have traditionally travelled hundreds of miles to gather in the fruits of the land, from the tiny blueberry to the mighty watermelon. Living and working in rural areas is often a more authentic way of experiencing another culture than working in the tourist industry. The availability of harvesting work in Europe has been greatly reduced by the large numbers of Slovaks, Poles, Albanians, etc. who have moved into every corner of Europe trying to earn the money their own struggling economies cannot provide.

To find out which farmers are short of help, check www.pickingjobs.com, which is strongest on the UK and Australia or, if already on the road, ask in the youth hostel, campsite or local café/pub. (According to one experienced traveller, this is great for people who are good at meeting prospective employers in pubs, unlike him who just gets drunk and falls over.) The great advantage of job-hunting in rural areas rather than in cities is that people are more likely to know their neighbours' labour requirements and often are more sympathetic and helpful in their attitudes. **Adam Cook** interrupted a cycling tour of the South of France to look for fruit-picking work:

Faced with having to decide between hurrying north to catch up with the cherries and going south to meet the first peaches, I decided to go south. It took ten good days of asking everywhere, cafés, bars, post offices, grocery shops – one of the best places I found to look as the owners very often know who is picking what and where.

Picking fruit may not be as easy as it sounds. If you are part of a large team you may be expected to work at the same speed as the most experienced picker, which can be both exhausting and discouraging. Having even a little experience can make the whole business more enjoyable, not to mention more financially worthwhile if you are being paid piece work rates. The vast majority of picking jobs are paid piece work (with the notable exception of grape harvests in Europe), though a minimum level of productivity will be expected, particularly if you are being given room and board.

Anyone with a farming background could consider placing an advert in a farmers' journal or small town newspaper in your favoured destination. Something might work, along the lines of: '19 year old Briton taking a year out before university seeks farm work. Willing to exchange labour for board and lodging and chance to get to know the country.' The usual caution must be exercised when considering any replies. If possible, talk to your prospective employer on the telephone and ask them for a reference. Always try to obtain the terms of employment in writing.

Experienced grooms, riding instructors and stable staff may consider registering with an equestrian agency like *World of Experience Equestrian Employment Agency* (52 Kingston Deverill, Warminster, Wilts. BA12 7HF; ☎/fax 01985 844102) or *International Exchange Program* (see entry in 'Directory of Specialist Gap Year Programmes'). For people with relevant experience, these agencies have vacancies in dozens of countries in Europe and worldwide which pay between £80 and £300 a week plus free accommodation.

Some European countries have programmes whereby young people spend a month or two assisting on a farm, e.g. Norway and Switzerland (see country chapters). A farming background is not necessary for participating in these schemes, though of course it always helps. The work-for-keep exchange on organic farms known collectively as World Wide Opportunities on Organic Farms (WWOOF) is described in the chapter on Volunteering. **Mike Tunnicliffe** joined WWOOF in New Zealand to avoid work permit hassles and his experience is typical of WWOOFers' in other countries:

My second choice of farm was a marvellous experience. For 15 days I earned no money but neither did I spend any, and I enjoyed life on the farm as part of the family. There is a wide variety of WWOOF farms and I thoroughly recommend the scheme to anyone who isn't desperate to earn money.

TEACHING ENGLISH

The English language is the language which literally millions of people around the world want to learn. There are areas of the world where the boom in English language learning seems to know no bounds, from Ecuador to China, Lithuania to Vietnam. People who are lucky enough to have been born native speakers of English find their skills universally in demand, though it is far easier to land a teaching job in a language school once you have a university degree.

As is obvious by the programme descriptions of the major gap year placement agencies in an earlier chapter, a high percentage of all gap year volunteer placements revolve around teaching English to young children, in secondary schools and to adult learners. Placement organisations like *Teaching Abroad* and *i-to-i* specialise in this field.

One of the best sources of information about the whole topic of English teaching (if I may be permitted to say so) is the 2003 edition of *Teaching English Abroad* by Susan Griffith (Vacation-Work, £12.95) which covers in great detail training courses, recruitment agencies and lists individual language schools around the world.

Your chances of gaining employment in a gap year are much stronger if you have undergone some training, preferably the four-week certificate course (see chapter on Courses for further information).

Job-hunting

Printed advertisements have been largely replaced by the internet, though it is probably still worth checking ads in Tuesday's *Guardian* between February and June. Most advertisers are looking for teachers who have some training or experience but in some cases, a carefully crafted CV and enthusiastic personality are as important as EFL training and experience.

For schools, a website advert offers an easy and instantaneous means of publicising a vacancy to an international audience. People looking for employment can use search engines to look for all pages with references to EFL, English language schools and recruitment. CVs can be e-mailed quickly and cheaply to advertising schools, who can then use e-mail themselves to chase up references. This presupposes a degree of IT awareness which the majority of gap year students are sure to have. The internet has very quickly taken over as the primary means of recruitment.

Arguably it has become a little too easy to advertise and answer job adverts online. At the press of a button, your CV can be clogging up dozens, nay, hundreds of computers. But everywhere you look on the internet, potentially useful links can be found, many of them leading to Dave Sperling's ESL Café (www.eslcafe.com) which so expertly dominates the field that it is hard to see how others can compete (though dozens try). 'Dave' provides a mind-boggling but well-organised amount of material for the future or current teacher including accounts of people's experiences of teaching abroad (but bear in mind that these are the opinions of individuals). It also provides links to specific institutes and chains in each country.

Native speaker teachers are nearly always employed to stimulate conversation rather than to teach grammar. Yet a basic knowledge of English grammar is a great asset when pupils come to ask awkward questions. The book *English Grammar in Use* by Raymond Murphy is recommended for its clear explanations and accompanying student exercises.

Most schools practise the direct method (total immersion in English) so not knowing the language shouldn't prevent you from getting a job. Some employers may provide nothing more than a scratched blackboard and will expect you to dive in using the 'chalk and talk' method. If you are very alarmed at this prospect you could ask a sympathetic colleague if you could sit in on a few classes to give you some ideas. Brochures picked up from tourist offices or airlines can be a useful peg on which to hang a lesson. If you're stranded without any ideas, write the lyrics of a pop song on the board and discuss them.

Whatever the kind of teaching you find, things probably won't go as smoothly as you would wish. After a year of teaching English in Italy, **Andrew Spence** had this sensible advice:

Teaching is perhaps the best way there is of experiencing another country but you must be prepared for periods when not all is as it should be. The work is sometimes arduous and frustrating, or it can be very exhilarating. Be prepared to take the very rough with the fairly smooth.

Directory of Paid Seasonal Jobs in the UK

3D EDUCATION & ADVENTURE
Osmington Bay, Shortlake Lane, Weymouth, Dorset DT3 6EG. ☎ 01305 836226. Fax: 01305 834070. E-mail: admin@3d-jobs.co.uk. Website: www.3d-jobs.co.uk.
3D is a specialist provider of multi-activity and educational courses for young people aged 7-18.
Employment available: Staff are required to work with children as multi-activity staff (teaching anything from mountain biking to kayaking), field studies instructors or IT instructors. Alternatively, there are less energetic non-activity roles working in the kitchens, restaurants, linen rooms, shops, bars and security.
Destinations: 11 coastal centres across the UK comprising 3 of their own residential Education and Adventure centres on the South Coast of England and 8 Pontin's Holiday Villages along the UK coastline.
Number of placements per year: 750 seasonal vacancies.
Prerequisites: Any sports coaching awards or national governing body awards are advantageous; however jobs and training are available for people with lots of energy and a desire to work with children. If applying for a non-activity role, some previous experience would be welcome. Field studies instructors must be doing a relevant degree course. All applicants must have lots of enthusiasm, energy and social skills and must enjoy working in a friendly team atmosphere.
Duration of employment: At least 12 weeks.
Selection procedures and orientation: Applicants can telephone 01305 836226 for a recruitment pack between September and May. Or alternatively, visit www.3d-jobs.co.uk where they can apply on-line. All instructor positions require the satisfactory completion of a training/assessment programme immediately prior to work commencing. In addition all staff will need to undergo a full criminal records disclosure check (www.disclosure.gov.uk).
Wages: All staff are paid at least the minimum wage, with all training provided free. A small charge is made for accommodation and food if living on-site.
Contact: Darren McLean, HR Planning Manager.

ANGLO CONTINENTAL PLACEMENTS AGENCY
Dial Post House, Dial Post, Near Horsham, W. Sussex RH13 8NQ. ☎ 01403

713344/55. Fax: 01403 713366. E-mail: sharon@anglocontinental.fsnet.co.uk.
Website: www.anglocontinentalplacements.co.uk or www.anglocontinentalcaterin g.co.uk.
Agency established 1993.
Employment available: Agency which places chefs, waiters, waitresses, chamber staff, kitchen porters, receptionists and nannies.
Destinations: All over England, Scotland and Wales (and also Spain).
Prerequisites: Previous work experience not essential but must have references in English.
Duration of employment: Minimum 6 months.
Wages: All positions are live-in.
Contact: Sharon Wolfe, Owner.

ARDMORE ADVENTURE LTD

Berkshire College, Hall Place, Burchetts Green, Maidenhead, Berkshire SL6 6QR. ☎01628 826699. E-mail: dos@theardmoregroup.com. Website: www.ardmore.org.uk.
This organisation runs multi-activity and English language courses for overseas children aged 8-17 at residential centres throughout Britain.
Employment available: Group leaders are required to run a range of sports, drama and art/craft activities. Positions are available for EFL teachers, teaching assistants, overseas work experience placements and more senior posts.
Destinations: Residential centres around the UK.
Prerequisites: Experience with children for group leaders. Applicants aged 20 or over are preferred. Teaching assistants must be native English speakers.
Duration of employment: 2-8 weeks during June, July and August.
Wages: From £50 per week salary is paid for group leaders. Limited accommodation

available.

AVIEMORE HIGHLANDS HOTEL
Aviemore Mountain Resort Ltd, Aviemore, Inverness-shire PH22 1PJ. ☎ 01479 810771. E-mail: personnel@aviehighlands.demon.co.uk.
Employment available: Temporary live-in positions as receptionists, bar, waiting, housekeeping and kitchen staff.
Destinations: Scottish resort of Aviemore.
Prerequisites: Good communication skills, bright, enthusiastic, well-presented and ambitious.
Duration of employment: Vacancies fit in with school/university vacations (Christmas, Easter, summer).

BARRACUDAS SUMMER ACTIVITY CAMPS
Bridge House, 27 Bridge St, St Ives, Cambridgeshire PE27 5EH. ☎ 01480 497533. E-mail: jobs@barracudas.co.uk. Website: www.barracudas.co.uk.
Children's Multi-Activity Day Camps.
Employment available: Group co-ordinators, activity instructors (fencing, archery, tennis, art, drama, etc.), lifeguards and senior positions are all required to help run the centres.
Destinations: Greater London, Middlesex, Essex, Berkshire, Surrey, Kent, Norfolk and Cambridgeshire.
Number of placements per year: 340 altogether.
Prerequisites: Lifeguards require the RLSS Pool Lifeguard Award. Activity instructors need relevant qualifications for their sport/s. Experience of working with children and fluent English are also necessary.
Duration of employment: 4-6 weeks.
Selection procedures and orientation: Training courses leading to National Governing Body qualifications are organised prior to the camps. Barracudas meet the full cost of these courses, which include accommodation, meals and examination fees for all staff that work a full season.
Wages: Wages between £140 and £180 per week for instructors and group co-ordinators.

BELL BROTHERS NURSERIES LTD
West End, Benington, Boston, Lincolnshire PE22 0EE. E-mail: info@bellsplants.co.uk. Website: www.bellsplants.co.uk.
Employment available: Temporary glasshouse operatives to work alongside permanent staff in large modern nursery. Duties include pricking out plants, labelling products and collating orders. Much of the work is mechanised.
Number of placements per year: 5-10.
Prerequisites: No previous experience necessary, however an interest in horticulture and/or relevant qualifications would be an advantage.
Duration of employment: 3 months initially. May be extended subject to performance.
Wages: Variable according to job undertaken. 10-25 hours of overtime generally available. Shared accommodation provided in a house in village. Rent is payable and deducted from wages each week.
Selection procedures and orientation: No deadline for applications. Interviews not essential. Only email applications will be considered. All successful applicants will be required to sign an employment contract detailing their terms and conditions of employment.
Contact: Sally Hooper, Personnel Manager.

CAMBRIDGE PASSENGER CRUISERS
Riverboat Georgina, PO Box 401, Cambridge CB4 3WE. E-mail: info@georgina.co.uk. Website: www.georgina.co.uk.

The *Georgina* is a passenger cruiser on the River Cam.
Employment available: Crew positions serving food and drink and taking the boat through the locks.
Number of placements per year: 5-6.
Prerequisites: Minimum age 18; proficient in English. Full training given.
Duration of employment: May to September. Part-time work also available through the winter.
Wages: £5 per hour plus tips.
Contact: Nick Bennett, Operations Manager.

CLACHAIG INN
Glencoe, Argyll PH49 4HX, Scotland. ☎ 01855 811252. Fax: 01855 811679. E-mail: jobs@glencoescotland.com. Website: www.glencoescotland.com.
Employment available: General assistants, mainly bar work, serving food/drinks, and housework. Also assistant chefs. Website includes detailed jobs section.
Prerequisites: Minimum age 18. Smart and presentable, enthusiastic and able to work well as part of a team. Best suited to those who enjoy outdoor pursuits.
Duration of employment: Minimum 3 months but preference given to those able to work longer. 40-50 hours per week, 5 days per week.
Wages: Approx £4 per hour. Chefs earn £5/£6+. Accommodation available in single or twin rooms, some with cooking facilities. Meals are available in hotel for those not self-catering.
Selection procedures and orientation: Phone interviews.
Contact: Guy and Edward Daynes, Partners.

EF LANGUAGE TRAVEL
EF House, 36-38 St Aubyn's, Hove, Sussex BN3 2PD. ☎ 01273 822777. Fax: 01273 729561.
Employment available: Group leaders and teachers are required. Activity organisers are also recruited to plan activity programmes.
Destinations: All around the UK.
Number of placements per year: 650 nationwide and 40 activity organisers.
Prerequisites: Activity organisers must have previous organisational experience.
Duration of employment: At least 3 weeks between late May and late August. Staff work flexible hours, 7 days a week.
Wages: Salaries vary depending on region and experience. Both residential and non-residential staff are required.

FACILITIES MANAGEMENT CATERING LTD (FMC)
All England Lawn Tennis & Croquet Club, Church Road, Wimbledon, London SW19 5AE. ☎ 020-8947 7430/020-8947 7430. Fax: 020-8944 6362. E-mail: resourcing@fmccatering.co.uk. Website: www.fmccatering.co.uk.
Employment available: Casual bar, waiting, chef, management work at Wimbledon, plus many other prestigious sporting events. 2,500 people employed annually.
Destinations: Nationwide with a few opportunities abroad (e.g. for the Paris Air Show).
Prerequisites: Minimum age 18. Good social skills, self-confidence, outgoing personality and ability to use initiative.
Duration of employment: Wimbledon lasts about a fortnight (late June/early July). Other assignments last from 1 day to 6 weeks.
Selection procedures and orientation: phone interviews sufficient for some jobs.
Wages: Variable. Food and uniform provided. For Wimbledon subsidised accommodation is available in Kingston University halls of residence.
Contact: Alison Gray, Human Resources Manager.

FULLER, SMITH & TURNER PLC
The Griffin Brewery, Chiswick Lane South, Chiswick London W4 2QB. ☎ 020-8996 2000. Fax: 020-8996 2013. E-mail: recruitment.manager@fullers.co.uk. Website: www.fullers.co.uk.
Employment available: Fixed term positions in this pub group.
Destinations: Mainly London area but elsewhere in the UK.
Prerequisites: Minimum age 18. No skills needed since training given.
Wages: Bar staff are paid £4-£5 an hour. Wages for assistant managers and chefs are discussed at interview. Some jobs are live-in with meals included; some are live-out.

G's MARKETING LTD
Hostel Office, Barway, Ely, Cambs. CB7 5TZ. ☎ 01353 727314.
Employment available: Packing salad and vegetable crops.
Prerequisites: Must be fit and willing to work hard.
Duration of employment: Production operatives needed between October and the end of April.
Wages: Piece work rates; employer claims earnings average £180 per week.
Contact: Sharon Gudgeon, Hostel Recruitment Officer.

HARRODS LTD
Recruitment Centre, 11 Brompton Place, Knightsbridge, London SW1X 7XL. ☎ 020-7893 8793. Website: www.harrods.com.
Sales staff, clerical staff and selling support staff are required to work August-January and to cover the Christmas and January sale. Applicants must be a minimum of 16 years old, be eligible to work in the UK, and based within the London region. Fluent English is essential.

HF HOLIDAYS
Imperial House, Edgware Road, London NW9 5AL. ☎ 020-8905 9556. Fax: 020-8205 0506. Email: info@hfholidays.co.uk. Website: www.hfholidays.co.uk.
Non-profit making organisation which owns 19 country house hotels based in National Parks for individuals and families on walking and special interest holidays.
Employment available: Walk leaders plus assistant managers, general assistants, kitchen porters, assistant chefs and deputy chefs are required.
Destinations: Throughout the UK.
Prerequisites: Experience is not necessary for some positions.
Duration of employment: Jobs are offered for the season lasting from March to November and also at Christmas and New Year.
Selection procedures and orientation: Applications should be made to the Recruitment and Training Department.
Wages: Wages range between £80 and £215 per month plus full board and lodging. Walk leaders receive travel expenses and free room and board.

KIDS KLUB
The Lodge, Finborough Hall, Stowmarket, Suffolk IP14 3EF. ☎ 01449 742700. Fax: 01449 742701. E-mail: info@kidsklub.co.uk. Website: www.kidsklub.co.uk.
Kids Klub runs activity holidays for children aged 6-17 in 7 centres in Hertfordshire, Suffolk and Nottinghamshire.
Employment available: Activity supervisor, instructors, EFL teachers and general assistants are required.
Number of jobs: 80 per year.
Prerequisites: No experience for Activity Supervisor or General Assistants as full training is given. Instructors must hold a current National Governing Body award; EFL teachers must hold a TEFL qualification or a PGCSE.

Duration of employment: All positions are for 6 days a week. Season runs from Easter to October with extra staff taken on at Easter and summer. Minimum period of work is 4 weeks.

Selection procedures and orientation: All applicants welcome. An interview with all applicants is required. Applications can be made at any time of the year.

Wages: Salary plus room and board and training opportunities are provided.

Contact: Rob Buckland, Operations Manager.

KINGSWOOD GROUP

11 Prince of Wales Road, Norwich, Norfolk NR1 1BD. ☎ 01603 284284. Fax: 01603 284250. E-mail: jobs@kingswood.co.uk. Website: www.kingswood.co.uk.

The Group operates 6 year-round educational activity centres in Staffordshire, Norfolk, the Isle of Wight, Lake District and North Wales.

Employment available: Activity, IT and environment studies instructors, chefs, cooks, catering assistants, drivers and domestic assistants are required to work at the camps.

Prerequisites: All applicants must have a keen interest in working with children. Chefs need City and Guilds 706 I and II; drivers require P.S.V./P.C.V. qualifications; managers, chefs and drivers must be over 21.

Duration of employment: 3-8 month contracts, 5½-6 days per week.

Selection procedures and orientation: Training for catering assistants, activity/IT/ environmental studies instructors and domestic assistants is provided.

Wages: Sports instructors are paid £250 per month net; environmental instructors are paid £728 per month gross.

OPTIONS TRUST

4 Plantation Way, Whitehill, Bordon, Hants. GU35 9HD. ☎ 01420 474261. E-mail: hcil@pvm.ndo.co.uk.

Registered charity.

Employment available: This organisation is run by disabled people who require help with washing, dressing, moving around, household tasks and driving about.

Destinations: Mainly the South of England.

Prerequisites: Applicants need to be physically fit, reliable, able and willing to listen and carry out instructions, enjoy a varied routine and have a sense of humour. A driving licence is essential.

Duration of employment: 6 months or more.

Selection procedures and orientation: Once an application form is returned to the Co-ordinator, details will be passed on to members who need staff at this time. The individual employer will then contact the applicant, ask for references, arrange interviews and discuss the possibility of offers.

Wages: Salaries vary among employers. However, in all cases, board and lodging are provided in the home of the employer.

PGL TRAVEL LTD

Alton Court, Penyard Lane, Ross-on-Wye, Herefordshire HR9 5GL. ☎ 01989 767833. Fax: 01989 768769. E-mail: pglpeople@pgl.co.uk. Website: www.pgl.co.uk/people.

PGL Travel runs activity holidays for children, usually involving lots of outdoor activities.

Employment available: Group leaders, activity instructors, catering staff, support staff, overseas couriers and administrators.

Destinations: Various locations around the UK, France and Spain.

Number of jobs: Over 2,500 per year.

Prerequisites: Qualifications are not necessary except in certain activity positions. PGL training is available for most jobs and the company will help candidates obtain the relevant qualifications. Experience of working with children is also helpful.

Duration of employment: The minimum period is usually 6-8 weeks. The centres are open between February and early November.

Selection procedures and orientation: As soon as an application form is received, a decision will be made as to whether the applicant can be offered a position. Nominated referees will be contacted. If an applicant is only available for the summer, it is better to apply earlier. The earlier a worker is available, the better their chances of being offered employment.

Wages: Workers are paid between £50 and £85 per week on top of free board and lodging.

SEASONAL STAFF UK

Old Mining College, Queen St, Chasetown, Staffs. WS7 8QH. ☎ 01543 675707. Fax: 01543 672046. E-mail: admin@seasonalstaff.co.uk. Website: www.seasonalstaff.co.uk.

Employment available: Live-in hotel, country inn and pub work throughout the UK and holiday islands for students, graduates, young professionals and working holidaymakers.

Prerequisites: Ages 18-28. EU national or with working holiday visa.

Duration of employment: Variable.

Wages: Minimum wage or higher. Overtime opportunities to increase earnings. All positions include accommodation and meals on duty (and often off-duty meals as well).

Selection procedures and orientation: Applications accepted year round. Application form can be downloaded from website. No experience required provided candidate is presentable and prepared to learn.

Contact: Phil Edrop, Proprietor.

YOUTH HOSTELS ASSOCIATION

National Recruitment Department, PO Box 11, Matlock, Derbyshire DE4 2XA. ☎ 01426 939216/07626 939216. E-mail: recruitment@yha.org.uk. Website: www.yha.org.uk.

Seasonal assistant wardens are required to help run the YHA's 240 youth hostels in England and Wales.

Employment available: Assistants undertake various duties including catering, cleaning and reception work.

Number of placements per year: 400.

Prerequisites: Minimum age 18. Experience in one or more of the relevant duties is essential, as are enthusiasm and excellent customer service.

Duration of employment: Work is available for varying periods between February/March and October.

Wages: Basic monthly salary of £370 plus free accommodation and food.

Selection procedures and orientation: All posts are subject to a face-to-face interview at applicant's expense, at the hostel where the vacancy arises. Interviews may be called at short notice. Most recruitment takes place between December and May.

Directory of Paid Seasonal Jobs Abroad

ACORN ADVENTURE LTD

22 Worcester St, Stourbridge DY8 1AN. ☎ 01384 446057. E-mail: topstaff@ac ornadventure.co.uk. Website: www.acorn-jobs.co.uk.

Outdoor adventure camps for schools, youth groups and families in Europe and the UK.

Employment available: 300 seasonal work opportunities for activity instructors, catering staff, administrators and drivers between mid-April and September.

Destinations: France (Ardèche and Northern France), Italy (the Alps) and Spain (Costa

Brava), Wales and the Lake District.
Wages: All staff receive an on-site living allowance (minimum £50) plus an end-of-contract bonus and (if applicable) a qualification bonus.
Application procedure: Application enquiries welcome all year round.
Contact: Ben Keen, Recruitment & Training Co-ordinator.

APPELLATION CONTROLEE
Ulgersmaweg 26C, 9731 BT Groningen, Netherlands. ☎ 050-549 2434. Fax: 050-549 2428. E-mail: project2@bart.nl. Website: www.apcon.nl.
Employment available: Seasonal picking jobs arranged with farmers.
Destinations: France, Denmark, England and the Netherlands.
Number of placements per year: 500-1,000.
Prerequisites: Minimum age 18. Must be in good health and physical condition. Must have EU passport/identity card or valid working permit.
Duration of employment: 2 weeks to 6 months. Hours of work mainly between 5 and 10 per day depending on weather and amount of ripe fruit, 5 or 6 days per week. Grape-pickers work 7 days a week, 8 hours a day.
Selection procedures and orientation: Interviews not necessary.
Wages: At least national minimum wage or piece work by kilo, normally £25-£40 a day.
Contact: Itziar van Breemem.

CANVAS HOLIDAYS
East Port House, 12 East Port, Dunfermline, Fife KY12 7JG. ☎ 01383 629018. Website: www.canvasholidays.com.
Employment available: Camping tour operator which employs a large number of campsite couriers and children's couriers for its European campsites.
Destinations: France, Germany, Austria, Switzerland, Italy, Luxembourg and Spain.
Prerequisites: Minimum age 18 or 19 depending on destination. Good working knowledge of relevant language preferred but not essential.
Duration of employment: April to October with some high season positions available.
Application procedure: Applications from September.
Wages: Tented accommodation, uniform and travel to and from Britain provided.

CLUB CANTABRICA HOLIDAYS LTD
146/148 London Road, St. Albans, Herts. AL1 1PQ. ☎ 01727 866177. Fax: 01727 843766. Website: www.cantabrica.co.uk.
Employment available: Camping tour operator which employs campsite couriers.
Destinations: France, Italy, Austria, Spain (including Majorca) and Greece (Corfu).
Prerequisites: Minimum age 21. Good working knowledge of relevant language an advantage.
Duration of employment: May to October.
Application procedure: Applications before end of December. Interviews held in January/February.
Wages: From £75-£100 a week plus end-of-season bonus.

R J CORNISH & CO PTY LTD
RMB 2024 Cottons Road, Cobram, Victoria 3644, Australia. ☎ +61 3 5872 2055. Fax: +61 3 5872 1054. E-mail: jobs@rjcornish.com. Website: www.rjcornish.com.
Employment available: Casual fruit picking work in the months of January (starting mid to late), February and March. Pickers needed for pears and peaches, also some apples at the end of the above season.
Number of jobs per year: 600.
Prerequisites: Minimum age 18. Must be prepared to work in hot conditions and to undertake heavy lifting of ladders and bags of fruit. Must have legal right to work in

Australia.
Duration of employment: Normal maximum would be 7 weeks; most people work a week or two. Hours of work are normally 7am-4pm Sunday to Friday.
Selection procedures and orientation: Applications accepted from December. Interviews not necessary since jobs are mainly fixed up over the internet.
Wages: Piece work rates paid according to how many bins of fruit picked. Barrack-style accommodation provided. (See website for further information).
Contact: Doug McKean, Office Manager.

EQUITY TOTAL SKI
Dukes Lane House, 47 Middle Street, Brighton BN1 1AL. ☎ 01273 886901. Fax: 01273 203212. Website: www.equity.co.uk/employment.
Employment available: Winter resort staff (reps, ski companions, chalet, bar and housekeeping staff, plongeurs, night porters, handymen, etc.).
Destinations: Austria, France and Italy.
Number of placements per year: 200+.
Prerequisites: EU nationality essential.
Duration of employment: Some jobs start October-December; others December-May.
Wages: Accommodation, board, ski pass, insurance, uniform and transport to the resort provided.
Selection procedures and orientation: Application form on website. Applications begin to be processed from May onwards.

EUROCAMP HOLIDAYS
Overseas Recruitment Department (Ref TGY/03), Hartford Manor, Greenbank Lane, Northwich, CW8 1HW. ☎ 01606 787525. Website: www.holidaybreakjo bs.com.
Employment available: Family camping tour operator that employs summer season campsite and children's couriers. See entry for *Holidaybreak* below.

GOAL-LINE SOCCER INC.
PO Box 1642, Corvallis, OR 97339, USA. ☎ 541-753-5833. Fax: 541-753-0811. E-mail: info@goal-line.com. Website: www.goal-line.com.
Employment available: Qualified football coaches are required to teach football to American children and play exhibition games against local teams. Coaches stay with American families and are able to participate in recreational activities such as golf and water skiing.
Destinations: USA, especially west coast states of Washington and Oregon.
Number of placements per year: 26.
Prerequisites: Coaching certificates from recognised national soccer associations are required. Applicants must be over 21. J-1 visas available through BUNAC.
Duration of employment: 5 weeks, starting at the beginning of July and running to mid-August. Additional weeks may be available.
Selection procedures and orientation: Applicants must commit themselves by mid-March. Interviews are conducted 2-3 times a year in the UK. Prior to coaching, staff receive a 4 day Pre-Camp Orientation at Oregon State University.
Wages: Flights to the USA, the J-1 visa (arranged through BUNAC) and a registration fee of approximately £200 must be paid. Coaches are paid a wage of $300+ per week.
Contact: Tom Rowney, Director.

HAVEN EUROPE
HR Dept, 1 Park Lane, Hemel Hempstead, Herts. HP2 4YL. ☎ 01442 203970 (Recruitment hotline). E-mail: joel.metcalfe@bourne-leisure.co.uk. Website: www.uk.haveneurope.com.
Employment available: Family camping tour operator which employs summer season

campsite and children's couriers.
Destinations: France, Spain and Italy.
Prerequisites: Minimum age 18. Knowledge of relevant language not essential.
Duration of employment: April till early September.
Wages: Accommodation, insurance and uniform provided plus wage. Travel expenses paid from home on successful completion of contract.

HOLIDAYBREAK
Overseas Recruitment Department (Ref TGY/03) ☎ **01606 787525. Website: www.holidaybreakjobs.com.**
Employment available: Camping tour operator which employs a large number of campsite couriers and children's couriers in Europe for the self-drive camping brands: Eurocamp and Keycamp.
Destinations: Austria, Belgium, France, Germany, Italy, Spain, Switzerland, Netherlands and Croatia.
Prerequisites: Minimum age 18. Must have UK or EU nationality. Some working knowledge of relevant language preferred.
Duration of employment: Minimum period is April/May to September.
Application procedure: Applications accepted from September/October. Interviews held in Hartford Cheshire between October and April.
Wages: Competitive salary plus tented accommodation, uniform and travel to and from Britain provided.

EXSPORTISE LTD
PO Box 402, Godstone, Surrey RH9 8YQ. ☎ **01883 744011. Fax: 01883 744066. E-mail: simon@exsportise.co.uk. Website: www.exsportise.co.uk.**

Employment available: Staff for sports holidays: coaching, administration, lifeguarding, nursing, management.
Number of placements per year: 60-70.
Prerequisites: Sports coaches must be qualified. Lifeguards must hold a current NPLQ.
Duration of employment: 1-7 weeks in July/August.
Wages: Unpaid work experience for those under 19. Qualified staff earn £150-£500 per week.

IAN MEARNS HOLIDAYS
Tannery Yard, Witney St, Burford, Oxon. OX18 4DP. ☎ 01993 822655. Fax: 01993 822650. E-mail: karen@ianmearnsholidays.co.uk.
Tour operator offering self-drive family camping holidays.
Employment available: Campsite reps and montage/demontage assistants.
Destinations: France.
Number of placements per year: About 50.
Prerequisites: Must be healthy and able to work without supervision.
Duration of employment: Minimum 10 weeks between March and October. People available to start work in March especially in demand.
Wages: £400 per month plus end-of-contract bonus.
Selection procedures and orientation: Applications with CV from 1st October. Interviews held in Burford.
Contact: Karen Mearns.

GUATENANNIES
89J Victoria Drive, Wimbledon, London SW19 6PT. ☎ 07985 026019. Also: Calle San Luquitas 3, Antigua 03001, Guatemala; 502-591 2979. E-mail: guatenannies@yahoo.com.
Employment available: Placement of English-speaking nannies with Guatemalan families. Nannies must speak English and perform some domestic duties as agreed in standard contract, e.g. looking after the children, perhaps 1 hour a day of English conversation practice, some cleaning. In exchange nannies received board and lodging and up to $50 a month.
Number of placements per year: 10 in first year of operation.
Prerequisites: Minimum age 18 (provided they have enough maturity to handle challenging conditions in a developing country). Must be responsible, flexible, strong, outgoing and fun individuals who seek to immerse themselves in a different culture. Must speak fluent English.
Duration of employment: 1-3 months usually but can be extended to a year.
Selection procedures and orientation: Application should be made 2-3 months in advance, though not always necessary. Interviews not necessary. Successful candidates must do a one-week basic Spanish course on arrival.
Wages: Up to $50 a month with free accommodation and food (3 meals a day except over weekends).
Contact: Valerie Lefebvre, Director.

INTERNATIONALE HAUS SONNENBERG
Clausthalerstr. 11, D-37444 St Andreasberg, Germany. ☎/fax: 05582-944100. E-mail: Sonnenberg@tu-clausthal.de. Website: www.tu-clausthal.de.
International conference centre in Harz Mountains National Park (3km from nearest village).
Employment available: Jobs in the domestic department. Duties include dining hall and kitchen, cleaning rooms and conference rooms. Also shorter work periods possible as a conference assistant in Education Team.
Number of placements per year: 6.
Prerequisites: Ideal age is 18 between school and university. Basic knowledge of

German needed, though good chance to improve German. Must be willing to work in all areas of the Housekeeping Department.

Duration of employment: 6-12 months (12 months preferred).

Wages: From €700 (gross) per month. Full insurance provided. Private room in personnel house costs €140 per month.

Selection procedures and orientation: Applicants should send a CV and covering letter anytime. Interviews not necessary.

Contact: Frau Schmidt or Frau Smy (Heads of Housekeeping). See chapter on Germany for a first-hand account.

JOBS IN THE ALPS

17 High Street, Gretton, Northants NN17 3DE. ☎ 07050 121648. Fax: 01536 771914. E-mail: enquiries@jobs-in-the-alps.com. Website: www.jobs-in-the-alps.com.

Agency which arranges summer and winter jobs in hotels and restaurants in alpine resorts.

Employment available: Waiters, buffet staff, kitchen staff, chambermaids, porters and receptionists for first-class hotels, family hostels, etc. Limited amount of au pair work also available.

Destinations: Switzerland, France and Germany.

Number of placements per year: 250.

Prerequisites: Applicants must have a good knowledge of French or German (e.g. A-level) and be EU passport holders. Restaurant or pub work experience preferred.

Duration of employment: Applicants must be prepared to sign a contract for the whole winter season, i.e. December to Easter. Summer contracts more flexible, i.e. 2-4 months between April and November.

Selection procedure and orientation: Applications should be submitted by 15th September for the winter, April 15th for the summer. Interviews are held in the weeks just before and after these deadlines. There is an agency fee of £30 plus £20 per month of the contract up to a maximum of £110. All workers are visited by a representative during the season.

Wages: £450-£500 a month net for a five-day week in France and Switzerland; £350-£400 in Germany. Board and keep are free and most staff benefit from discounts on ski passes.

Contact: Alan Mullins, Proprietor.

KEYCAMP HOLIDAYS

Overseas Recruitment Department (Ref TGY/03), Hartford Manor, Greenbank Lane, Northwich, CW8 1HW. ☎ 01606 787525. Website: www.holidaybreakjobs.com.

Employment available: Family camping tour operator that employs summer season campsite and children's couriers. See entry for *Holidaybreak* above.

Duration of employment: April-July, July-October or March-October.

MERISKI

1st Floor, Carpenters Buildings, Carpenters Lane, Cirencester, Gloucestershire GL7 1EE. ☎ 01451 843100. Fax: 01285 651685. E-mail: hr@meriski.co.uk. Website: www.meriski.co.uk.

Méribel specialist with 12 chalets in this top French resort.

Employment available: Chalet chefs and cooks, qualified nannies and drivers. Also chalet operations managers, guest services managers, maintenance staff, etc.

Number of placements per year: 45.

Prerequisites: Minimum age 23 (except for nannies). Must hold an EU passport.

Duration of employment: Full winter season.

Selection procedures and orientation: Applications accepted from May. Training and

management support offered throughout the season.
Wages: Usual ski perks.
Contact: Louise Reuter, HR Co-ordinator.

PERFECT WAY
E-mail: info@perfectway.ch. Website: www.perfectway.ch.
In operation since 1995.
Employment available: Au pair agency making placements in Swiss, American and other international families in Switzerland.
Destinations: Switzerland.
Number of placements per year: 100-200.
Prerequisites: Ages 18-29. Candidates must have common sense, be honest and have good manners. 2 references required. EU nationals need no seasonal work permits (from Jun 2004).
Duration of employment: 6-18 months.
Selection procedures & orientation: Some families fly candidates in for interview; otherwise telephone contact.
Wages: At least SFr700 per month plus other perks.
Contact: Karin Schatzmann, Owner (speaks English, German and Swedish).

PRO EXCEL
10281 Frosty Court, Suite 100, Manassas, VA 20109. ☎ 703-330-2532. Fax: 703-330-6850. Website: www.proexcel.com.
Soccer education organisation operating in the USA (formerly Britannia Soccer).
Employment available: Soccer coaching opportunities.
Destinations: Nationwide throughout the USA.
Number of placements per year: 200 summer coaches plus 50 coaches on 9-month contracts. Recruit specifically in the UK.
Prerequisites: U.E.F.A. coaching qualification, plus coaching and teaching experience needed. Must also have playing background and dynamic personality.
Duration of employment: Variable between June and August for summer positions.
Selection procedures & orientation: Interviews and coaching sessions held in most UK locations. Briefing provided on arrival in the USA. J-1 visa arranged through BUNAC.
Wages: $100-$300 a week. Homestay accommodation and transport provided (including upfront airfares).

SNOWLINE/VIP
Collingbourne House, 140-142 High St, Wandsworth, London SW18 4JJ. ☎ 020-8870 4807. Fax: 020-8875 9235. E-mail: recruitment@snowline.co.uk. Website: www.snowline.co.uk/jobs or www.valdisere.co.uk.
Employment available: Positions available: Chalet host, ski host/driver, concierge/driver and driver/handyman.
Number of placements per year: 140.
Prerequisites: Minimum age 21. Chalet hosts need previous catering experience; ski hosts need about 20 weeks of ski experience and a driving licence for 3 years.
Duration of employment: Mid-November to end of April or early May.
Selection procedures and orientation: Online applications welcomed until the beginning of November which is the deadline. Interviews are essential.
Wages: Details on application. Package includes a full area ski pass, travel to and from the Alps and ski hire if needed.
Contact: Jo Pain, Personnel Manager.

SPECIALIST HOLIDAYS GROUP
Kings Place, 12-42 Wood St, Kingston upon Thames, Surrey KT1 1SH. ☎ 0870 888 0028. E-mail: overseasrecruitment@s-h-g.co.uk. Website: www.shgjobs.co.uk.

The Specialist Holidays Group and TUI UK employ 10,000 staff with 13 leading tour operators including Crystal Holidays (www.crystalholidays.co.uk), Thomson Ski, Lakes & Mountains (www.thomson-ski.com) and Simply Travel (www.simply-travel.com).
Employment available: Resort representatives, chalet hosts, chalet assistants, catering staff, hotel chefs, hotel assistants, maintenance staff, kitchen/night porters and nannies.
Destinations: Many European, American and Canadian destinations.
Prerequisites: Qualified and unqualified staff are recruited. Flexible and friendly attitude needed plus a good understanding of customer requirements and the ability to work within a busy team. All employees must be aged 18 and over. Overseas reps should be over 21 and able to communicate in Spanish, Portuguese, Italian or French.
Duration of employment: Winter season is November to April; summer season is May to September or sometimes March to November.

SUNSHINE AU PAIR AGENCY
128 rte du Moulin-de-la Ratte, 1236 Cartigny (Geneva), Switzerland. ☎ 022-756 82 03. Fax: 022-756 82 00. E-mail: info@au-pair-sunshine.ch. Website: www.au-pair-sunshine.ch.
Employment available: Au pair agency placing European and other nationalities in Swiss families.
Number of placements per year: Around 50.
Prerequisites: Ages 17-30. Must be trustworthy, honest and have some experience and interest in children.
Duration of employment: 6-18 months.
Selection procedures & orientation: Interviews held if possible; otherwise serious references.
Wages: SFr500-730.
Contact: Mrs. Laurence de Rham, Director.

TORRENS VALLEY ORCHARDS
Forreston Rd, Gumeracha, South Australia, Australia. ☎ +61 8-8389 1405. Fax: +61 8-8389 1406. E-mail: tvo@hotkey.net.au. Website: www.tvo.com.au.
Large orchard just south of the Barossa Valley wine region, with access to Adelaide via a daily bus (30 minutes, A$5).
Employment available: Range of orchard work including cherry picking and packing (December/January), pear picking and packing (Feb-Sept), tree planting and training, pruning, maintenance and office work.
Number of placements per year: 500, usually about 20 at one time.
Prerequisites: Travellers must be over 18.
Duration of employment: Minimum 2 weeks, up to several months. Normal hours are 8 per day, 5 days per week. During cherry harvest, pickers may work up to 12 hours per day, 7 days a week.
Selection procedures and orientation: Interviews not necessary; most recruitment conducted over internet.
Wages: Normal daily minimum of A$50 (after tax and accommodation deductions). Up to $1,000 for key personnel during cherry season. Accommodation in hostel-like conditions.
Contact: Tony Hannaford, Owner.

VENUE HOLIDAYS
1 Norwood St, Ashford, Kent TN23 1QU. ☎ 01233 649950. Fax: 01233 634494. E-mail: jobs@venueholidays.co.uk. Website: www.venueholidays.co.uk.
Family run camping tour operator.
Employment available: Campsite couriers and other jobs.
Destinations: France, Spain, Italy.
Prerequisites: Must be outgoing, fit and able to work hard in difficult conditions. Minimum age 18. Knowledge of a language useful but not essential.

Duration of employment: Minimum 2 months between March and October.
Wages: £100 per week.

VILLAGE CAMPS
rue de la Morache, 1260 Nyon, Switzerland. ☎ 022-990 9405. Fax: 022-990 9494. E-mail: personnel@villagecamps.ch. Website: www.villagecamps.com.
Employment available: Counsellors, sports instructors, TEFL teachers and general domestic and administrative staff needed for multi-activity centres and language camps for international children in Europe. Also hire up to 100 ski counsellors and other staff for the winter season in the Swiss Alps.
Number of jobs: 300.
Destinations: Switzerland (Anzère, Leysin), Austria (Zell-am-See), England and France.
Prerequisites: Candidates must have experience of working with children, while instructors must be qualified in canoeing/kayaking, gymnastics, arts and crafts, climbing, tennis, soccer, archery, golf or swimming. Knowledge of any European language or Japanese, Korean, Russian or Arabic is a distinct advantage.
Wages: Staff receive room and board, accident and liability insurance and an expense allowance of €240 a week (plus a ski pass in the winter).

WORLDNETUK
Emberton House, 26 Shakespeare Road, Bedford MK40 2ED. ☎ 0845 458 1550/1. E-mail: info@worldnetuk.com. Website: www.worldnetuk.com.
Programme description: Nannies and au pairs placed in ski and summer resorts in Europe and in the USA via the Au Pair in America programme (see 'Directory of Specialist Gap Year Programmes'). Place counsellors on American summer camps and other exchange programmes in the US.
Destinations: USA, France, Corsica, Spain, Balearics, Turkey, Italy, Sardinia, Greece, Austria, Switzerland.
Prerequisites: *Nanny/Childcare Programme USA* – 18-26 year olds with childcare training, NNEB, BTEC National Diploma in Nursery Nursing or NVQ Level III. Full clean driving licence. Departures every month on 12-month programme. Opportunity to travel at end of year.
Au Pair Programme USA – 18-26 year olds with 200 hours childcare/babysitting. Full clean driving licence. Departures every month. Opportunity to travel at end of year.
Ski/Summer Resort Nannies – Applicants must be qualified/experienced in childcare to work either in activity clubs, crèches or with individual families. No age limit. Applicants must be available for either the full summer or ski season (some shorter term placements sometimes available).
Contact: Elizabeth Elder.

Au Pairing

Gap year students who choose to become au pairs are generally looking for an affordable way to improve their knowledge of a country's language and culture. For several generations, female school leavers have been flocking to the Continent, and more recently to the United States and even Australia, attracted by the safe and stable environment which a family placement can provide. When the au pair arrangement works well, it is ideal for young, under-confident and impecunious students who want to work abroad. Occasionally, young men can find live-in jobs, but the number of families and therefore agencies willing to entertain the possibility of having a male au pair is still painfully small.

The terms au pair, mother's help and nanny are often applied rather loosely, since all are primarily live-in jobs concerned with looking after children. Nannies may have some formal training and take full charge of the children. Mother's helps work full-time and undertake general housework and/or cooking as well as childcare. Au pairs are supposed to work for no more than 30 hours a week and are expected to learn a foreign language while living with a family. Although the term au pair is used in the American context, the hours are much longer and there is no language learning element for British au pairs (see chapter on the USA).

One of the great advantages of these live-in positions generally is that they are relatively easy to get (at least for women over 18). After proving to an agency or a family that you are reasonably sensible, you will in the majority of cases be able to find a placement, though it is much easier and quicker in some countries than others, e.g. easy in France, Austria, Italy and Israel, but more difficult in Scandinavia and Portugal. Furthermore au pairs can usually benefit from legislation which exempts them from work permit requirements.

The minimum age can be a stumbling-block for some school leavers who are not yet 18. The majority of agencies prefer to accept applications only from candidates over 18, as Camilla Preeston discovered:
I had decided even before I had finished school that I would take a year off between school and university, and au pairing seemed like the perfect way to do this. Being seventeen and a half made things much more difficult in the beginning though I sent off endless letters to agencies in Britain and overseas. Most flatly replied that I was too young, though a couple said that they would try anyway. I eventually had success with a foreign agency. The reason they didn't turn me away may have been because the fee they levy is paid upfront before a family is found. By the time they had found me a family in Calais, four months of my year off had already gone by and I was almost ready to give up. I immediately accepted the offer, perhaps a little hastily. However, had I refused it, I might not have found another family willing to accept me due to my age, and it was the first family offer I had received in the four months I had been trying.

Camilla's youth did not prevent her from coping with what turned out to be a difficult situation in which she was expected to accept a lot of responsibility for the children (including a newborn baby) and the running of the household, while the mother was away for five days and two nights a week.

The standard length of au pair stay is for one academic year, typically September to June. Summer stays can also be arranged to coincide with the school holidays and there is some inevitable turn-over at Christmas when homesick au pairs go home to their families and then decide not to return. The advantage of a summer placement is that the au pair will accompany the family to their holiday destination at the seaside or in the mountains; the disadvantage is that the children will be your responsibility for more hours than they would be if they were at school, and also most language classes will close for the summer. Make enquiries as early as possible, since there is a shortage of summer-only positions.

Anyone interested in finding out about all aspects of live-in childcare should consult *The Au Pair & Nanny's Guide to Working Abroad* (Vacation-Work, £12.95).

PROS AND CONS

The relationship of au pair to family is not like the usual employer/employee relationship; in fact the term au pair means 'on equal terms'. The Home Office leaflet on au pairs in Britain uses the terminology 'hostess' and 'hospitality'; a copy may be obtained from the Immigration & Nationality Directorate, Lunar House, 40 Wellesley Road, Croydon CR9 2BY; enquiry line 0870 606 7766; www.ind.homeoffice.gov.uk (then search `Au Pair'). Therefore the success of the arrangement depends more than usual on whether individuals hit it off, so there is always an element of risk when living in a family of strangers. The Council of Europe guidelines stipulate that au pairs should be aged 18-27 (though these limits are flexible), should be expected to work about five hours a day, five days per week plus a couple of evenings of babysitting, must be given a private room and full board, health insurance, opportunities to learn the language and pocket money. The standard pocket money paid to au pairs in Europe is usually in the neighbourhood of £40-£50 a week, though it can be more, for example in Switzerland.

Once you have arrived in the family, it is important to clarify immediately what your hours and duties will be, which day you will be paid, whether you can expect a rise and how much notice either party must give if they wish to terminate the arrangement. This gets everyone off to a business-like start. But no matter how well-defined your duties are, there are bound to be occasions when your extra services will be taken for granted. It may seem that your time is not your own. So the standard working hours can soon turn into an unofficial string of 14 hour days. Whether you can tolerate this depends entirely on your disposition and on the compensating benefits of the job, e.g. free use of car and telephone, nice kids, good food, lots of sunshine, etc.

Gillian Forsyth's au pairing experience in Bavaria was a great success:

I had no official day off or free time but was treated as a member of the family. Wherever they went I went too. I found this much more interesting than being treated as an employee as I really got to know the country and the people. In the evenings I did not have to sit in my room, but chatted with the family. Three years later we still keep in close contact and I have been skiing with them twice since, on an au pair/friend basis.

If you do not have such a friendly arrangement with your family, you may feel lonely and cut off in a foreign country. Many au pairs make friends at their language classes. Some agencies issue lists of other au pairs in the vicinity.

Most au pairs' duties revolve around the children. For some, taking sole responsibility for a child can be even more alarming than cooking for the first time. You should be prepared to handle a few emergencies (for example sick or lost children) as well as the usual excursions to the park or collecting them from school. The agency questionnaire will ask you in detail what experience you have had with children and whether you are willing to look after newborn infants, etc., so your preferences should be made known early. You must also be prepared to hurt the children's feelings when you leave. **Nicky Parker** left a family in Majorca after just nine weeks and reported, 'I could only feel guilty and sad at the distress caused to the children by yet another in a long line of people whom they had learned to love, leaving them forever.'

APPLYING

It simplifies matters to use the services of an au pair or domestic agency (listed below). The most established agencies in the UK belong to the Recruitment and Employment Confederation (36-38 Mortimer St, London W1N 7RB; www.rec.org.uk). A good source of jobs for people with some childcare experience is the kind of tour operator which caters for families. *Nannies Abroad* (address below) offers childcare positions across Europe with reputable tour companies in a range of European seasonal resorts. Applicants need to have at least one year's full time experience in childcare to apply. The season lasts 17 weeks during which time nannies do not work more than 48 hours a week (on average). Accommodation is provided as well as a food allowance, free uniform, free travel at the start and end of the season, use of ski and other sports equipment, ski pass plus a weekly wage of £80-£120.

In the first instance check some up-to-date websites such as www.nannyjob.co.uk which has links to more than 80 au pair agencies in the UK. It is advisable to make contact with several agencies to compare terms and conditions. If your requirements are very specific as regards location or family circumstances, ring around some agencies and ask them to be blunt about their chances of being able to fix you up with what you want. Some provide a follow-up and travel service as well as placement.

For many years, British au pair agencies sending girls abroad were allowed to charge girls a placement fee of up to £40 plus VAT, provided they used the services of a mediating agent abroad. This allowable maximum remained unchanged for at least 15 years and most agents said that they could barely break even on the transaction given the time involved in finding a placement. New regulations on employment agencies have made it illegal to charge an applicant for finding him or her a job as a nanny, mother's help or au pair either in the UK or abroad, which has had the inevitable result that some agencies have stopped bothering making outgoing placements. Much of the matching of au pairs and families now takes place online.

Sometimes information about your family is scant, so make an effort to communicate with the family by phone, e-mail or letter before the job begins. The alternative to using an agency is to arrange something on your own. One way of doing this is to answer or place advertisements in *The Lady* (39/40 Bedford St, London WC2E 9ER) published each Tuesday. However far fewer advertisements find their way into print than was the case ten years ago.

Agencies

Arguably there is too little regulation in the world of au pair agencies, and things can go wrong in even the most tightly controlled programmes. Many leading au pair agencies and youth exchange organisations in Europe belong to IAPA, the International Au Pair Association (c/o FIYTO, Bredgade 25H, 1260 Copenhagen K, Denmark), an international body trying to regulate the industry. The IAPA website (www.iapa.org) has clear links to its member agencies around the world.

Agencies that specialise in one country are mentioned in the country chapters. The following UK au pair and/or nanny agencies all deal with a number of European countries:

Academy Au Pair & Nanny Agency, 42 Milsted Road, Rainham, Kent ME8 6SU (☎/fax 01634 310808; www.academyagency.co.uk). Place nannies in Australia as well as France, Belgium, Netherlands, Denmark, Germany, Italy and Spain.

Almondbury Agency, 4 Napier Road, Holland Park, London W14 8LQ (☎/fax 01288 359159; www.aupair-agency.com).

A-One Au Pairs & Nannies, Top Floor, Union House, Union St, Andover, Hampshire SP10 1PA (01264 332500; info@aupairsetc.co.uk). Some outgoing placements but mainly places incoming au pairs in the UK.

The Au Pair Agency, 231 Hale Lane, Edgware, Middlesex HA8 9QF (020-8958 1750; elaine@aupairagency.com). Mainly France, Spain (including Majorca), Italy and Germany.

Au Pair and Student Placement Agency, Nation House, The Stable Block, Milwich Road, Stafford ST18 0EG (01889 505544; www.internationalaupair.com).

Au Pair Connections, 39 Tamarisk Road, Wildern Gate, Hedge End, Southampton SO30 4TN (01489 780438; www.aupair-connections.co.uk). France, Spain, Italy.

A.Z.E. Au Pairs, 5 Vanguard Road, Priddys Hard, Gosport PO12 4FE (0870 165 6900; uk@aze.biz).

Bloomsbury Bureau, 37 Store St, London WC1E 7PN (020-7813 4061; bloomsburo@aol.com).

Childcare International Ltd., Trafalgar House, Grenville Place, London NW7 3SA (020-8906 3116; www.childint.co.uk).

Childcare Solution & Worldnet UK, Emberton House, 26 Shakespeare Road, Bedford MK40 2ED or Avondale House, 63 Sydney Road, Haywards Heath, W Sussex RH16 1QD (0845 458 1550/1; www.worldnetuk.com or www.thechildcaresolution.com). Seasonal nannies placed in European resorts, among other placements.

Edgware Agency, 1565 Stratford Road, Hall Green, Birmingham, W. Midlands B28 9JA (0121-745 6777; www.100s-aupairs.co.uk). Solihull Au Pair Agency is part of the same organisation and operates from the same address (0121-733 6444; solihull@100s-aupairs.co.uk).

IEC International Exchange Centre, 35 Ivor Place, London NW1 6EA (020-7724 4493; www.isecworld.co.uk). Au pair placements in Denmark, France, Germany, Netherlands, Norway and the USA.

Janet White Agency, 67 Jackson Avenue, Leeds LS8 1NS (0113-266 6507; www.janetwhite.com).

Jolaine Agency, 18 Escot Way, Barnet, Herts. EN5 3AN (020-8449 1334; aupair@jolaine.prestel.co.uk).

Nannies Abroad, Abbots Worthy House, Abbots Worthy, Winchester SO21 1DR (01962 882299/fax 01962 881888; www.nanniesabroad.com).

Nanny & Au Pair Connection, 62 Alexandra Road, Bolton BL6 4BG (01204 694422; www.aupairs-nannies.co.uk).

People & Places, Trewornan, Wadebridge, Cornwall PL27 6EX (01208 812652).

Problems Unlimited Agency, 177a Cricklewood, Broadway, London NW2 3HT (02-8438 9938; info@krsa.prinex.co.uk).

Quick Help Agency, 307A Finchley Road, London NW3 6EH (020-7794 8666; www.quickhelp.co.uk).

South Eastern Au Pair Bureau, 39 Rutland Avenue, Thorpe Bay, Essex SS1 2XJ (☎/fax 01702 601911).

Worldnet UK, see Childcare Solution above.

UK & Overseas Agency Ltd, Suite 21-23 Kent House, 87 Regent St, London W1R 7HF (020-7494 2929; www.nannys.co.uk).

Courses

After the rigours and stresses of sitting A-levels, many school leavers aspire to spend the following 15 months reading nothing more challenging than *Backpack* by Emily Barr about an obnoxious young Londoner who gradually comes to appreciate the joys of extended travel in Asia (while narrowly escaping murder by a serial killer). But after a decent recovery period has elapsed after exams, the idea of studying something either for fun or with a view to your future at university or in a career may come to seem more bearable. Some universities require preparatory work in a particular subject, for example some art colleges require students to do a foundation course. Whatever course is embarked on, extra qualifications and skills are viewed favourably by universities and potential employers, and students will gain practical knowledge for use at university and in later life.

Several new course providers, principally Objective Team and The Knowledge Gap have begun offering short preparatory courses for gap year students embarking on expeditions and world travel. See entries for Gap Year Preparation Courses on page 280.

RANGE OF COURSES

Depending on how you have decided to divide up your gap year, you may find yourself spending a good chunk at the beginning trying to earn money in a less-than-stimulating workplace like a supermarket or chain store. If most of your friends have gone off to university or travelling, you may have the leisure to take a course locally (see section below). This can provide an ideal chance to learn the basics of word processing, get your driving licence, obtain a life-saving qualification or sports instructor certificate, etc.

If you go abroad later in the year with no pre-arranged placement, it is a good idea to take documentary evidence of any qualifications you have earned in case you have the chance to work as an office temp in Sydney, drive a van for a charity in the Balkans or spend a week cooking on a private yacht.

The long established educational consultancy *Gabbitas* offers one-to-one advice on options of interest to gap year students and can also recommend suitable courses in areas such as business, secretarial and computer skills, cookery and catering, as well as foreign language courses in the UK and abroad and American universities. Gabbitas also offers extensive guidance on university entry and careers. Contact Gabbitas Educational Consultants, Carrington House, 126-128 Regent St, London W1 5EE (020-7734 0161; admin@gabbitas.co.uk/ www.gabbitas.co.uk).

The current government is keen to disseminate information about training and education opportunities nationwide. Although many of its initiatives are aimed at adult learners, some may be of use to gap year students including the National Grid For Learning (www.ngfl.gov.uk). The NGFL web portal brings together a vast and growing collection of sites that support education and lifelong learning including a large number of resources for parents and students assembled by the Department for Education & Skills.

The National Organisation for Adult Learning (NIACE), Renaissance House, 20 Princes Road West, Leicester LE1 6TP (0116 204 4200; www.niace.org.uk) distributes information about vocational training courses throughout the UK, including language courses in both private and public educational institutions. You should be able to consult this at your local careers office.

Learndirect (0800 100 900; www.learndirect.co.uk) is a government-financed helpline that tries to provide advice and information about any aspect of training courses available in your area plus careers and funding. The helpline is open 9am to 9pm Monday to Friday and 9am to 12 noon on Saturday.

Language Courses

The gap year is an ideal opportunity for students to brush up on a barely-remembered GCSE language or even start from scratch with a new language. Most employers will view this as a very constructive allocation of time, and anyone with competence in another language has an advantage in many job hunts. Even people who are not planning to study modern languages at university should consider the advantages of getting to grips with one of the main European languages. Evening language classes offered by local authorities usually follow the academic year and are aimed at hobby learners. Intensive courses offered privately are much more expensive. If you are really dedicated, consider using a self-study programme with books and tapes (which start at £30), correspondence course or broadcast language course, though dedication is required to make progress. Hold out a carrot to yourself of a trip to a country where your target language is spoken. Even if you don't make much headway with the course at home, take it with you since you will have more incentive to learn once you are immersed in a language.

Although many people have been turning to the web to teach them a language, many conventional teach-yourself courses are still on the market, for example from Berlitz (020-7518 8300), the BBC (08700 100222), Linguaphone (0800 282417; www.linguaphone.co.uk) and Audioforum (www.audioforum.com). All of them offer deluxe courses with refinements such as interactive videos and of course these cost much more (from £150). Linguaphone recommends half an hour of study a day for three months to master the basics of a language.

If you are interested in an obscure language and don't know where to study it, contact the CILT Library (020-7379 5110; www.cilt.org.uk) which has a certain amount of documentation on courses especially in London.

A more enjoyable way of learning a language (and normally a more successful one) is by speaking it with the natives. Numerous British companies represent a range of language schools abroad offering in-country language courses. They are very familiar with differences between schools, qualifications, locations, etc. and what is most suitable for clients. *CESA Languages Abroad, Caledonia Languages Abroad, Cactus Language, Euro-Academy* and *Language Courses Abroad*, among others, all have wide-ranging programmes abroad in Europe and beyond. These agencies also provide a useful back-up service if the course does not fulfil your requirements in any way. See the first 19 entries of the 'Directory of Language Courses' later in this chapter. For agencies in the USA and Canada, see the chapter 'Gap Years for North Americans'.

> **Of course it is also possible to book a course directly with a language school abroad which is the route that Annabel Iglehart from Edinburgh chose in her post-university gap year:**
> *I completed my university degree in July 2002 and am taking a year (or two) out to gain new skills and participate in interesting activities around the world. After working in a variety of jobs at home, I went to Salamanca to do a three-month intensive Spanish language course with Mester. I planned and paid for my course and accommodation directly through Mester and this saved me a lot of money; it was by far the most economical way to organise the trip. The course was fantastic. The classes were fast-paced and the teachers excellent. I lived with a Spanish family for a while and then moved to a flat with other students. I met loads of people with whom I am still in touch.*

While learning a language at secondary school, you normally have two hours of classes a week which works out at about 80 hours a year. While doing an eight-week intensive course, you might have 240 hours, the equivalent of three years of school instruction plus you will be speaking the language outside the classroom, so progress is normally very quick.

Literally thousands of language schools around the world would like your business, so care needs to be taken in choosing one that suits individual needs. Possible sources of language school addresses on the web are www.languageschoolsguide.com (part of www.goabroad.com), www.language-learning.net (listing 6,500 schools in 90 countries), www.language-schools-directory.com; and http://language.shawguides.com. After considering the obvious factors like price and location when choosing a language school, also try to find out the average age and likely nationalities of your fellow learners, how experienced and qualified the staff are, whether there will be any one-to-one tuition and whether the course concentrates on oral or written skills, whether there are extracurricular activities and excursions included in the fee, and generally as much as you can. One key factor is whether or not a school prepares its students for exams. If they do and you are there only for the fun of it, you may find that lessons are not suitable.

Whereas some language schools run purely recreational courses, others offer some kind of qualification. Some schools are instantly recognised such as the Alliance Française and the Goethe Institute. At the other end of the spectrum, some schools offer nothing more than a certificate outlining the period of study and perhaps the level of language reached or work covered in the course, which may be of limited value if you ever need to show proof of language attainment.

When choosing a school, it may be worth finding out whether they have any external validation. For example EAQUALS is a pan-European association of language training providers which aims to promote and guarantee quality of teaching. To become a member, institutes have to adhere to a strict Code of Practice and submit to inspection every three years. At present EAQUALS has 83 members (www.eaquals.org) though a third teach English in the UK. Similarly, in France some schools are given recognition by bodies such as the Paris Chamber of Commerce and Industry and the Ministry of National Education.

Serious language schools on the continent usually offer the possibility of preparing for one of the internationally recognised exams. In France, the qualification for aspiring language learners is the D.E.L.F. *(Diplôm Elémentaire de Langue Français)* while the Spanish counterpart is the D.E.L.E. *(Diploma de Español como Lengua Extranjera)* both of which are recognised by employers, universities, officialdom, etc. The D.E.L.E is split into three levels: *Certificado Inicial de Español, Diploma Básico de Español* and the *Diploma Superior de Español.* Most schools say that even the Basic Diploma requires at least eight or nine months of study in Spain. A prior knowledge of the language, of course, allows the student to enrol at a higher level and attain the award more quickly. No single qualification in Italy is as dominant as the D.E.L.E. or the D.E.L.F. Typical of Italian exams is C.I.L.S. *(Certificato di Italiano come Lingua Straniera)* which was established by Siena University and is authorised by the Italian Ministry of Foreign Affairs.

Recreational language courses are offered by virtually every school and are preferred by most gap year students. Some programmes are much more structured than others, so students need to look for flexible courses which allow them to progress at their own rate. Many people agree that the fastest way to improve fluency is to have one-to-one lessons, though of course these are more expensive than group classes. Usually a combination of the two works best.

Another factor that can impede progress is if you are in the midst of your compatriots. A class in which many languages are represented is more likely to use the target language rather than slip into English. Even if you get to spend a lot of time in the company of locals, you may be expected to help them improve their English. One wily young woman studying French in Bordeaux during her gap year arrived at a solution to this problem:

The only real frustration of my time so far has to be coming across French people who wish to improve their English. They respond to your attempt in French with their own attempt in English. However I have developed a cunning solution. I provide them with a quick explanation that I am in fact Icelandic or Russian and we are soon back on track.

Increasingly, major language schools are offering work experience placements to their 'graduates'. Many belong to the newly formed Global Work Experience Association (GWEA) described in the chapter on Work Experience. Many language courses abroad combine language tuition with cultural and other studies. While learning Spanish in Andalucia you can also take lessons in Flamenco dance; while studying Italian in Florence, you can also take drawing classes, and so on. The possibilities are endless. Living with a family is highly recommended especially for beginners since it usually forces you to speak the target language from the beginning. Many agencies (like *Gala Spanish in Spain*) offer a programme whereby you are placed with a family who have children roughly your age.

Another possibility is to forgo structured lessons and simply live with a family. Several agencies arrange paying guest stays which are designed for people wishing to learn or improve language skills in the context of family life. Try *En Famille Overseas* (4 St Helena Road, Colchester CO3 3BA; 01206 546741; www.enfamilleoverseas.co.uk) which specialises in France and charges a fee of £35 on top of the fee payable to the family. *EIL*, a non-profit cultural and educational organisation, offers short-term homestay programmes in 30 countries (287 Worcester Road, Malvern, Worcestershire WR14 1AB; 01684 562577; www.eiluk.org).

TEFL Training

In some cases, a preparatory course in Teaching English as a Foreign Language (known as TEFL, pronounced 'teffle') is required by year out placement agencies or individual language schools, whereas in others a willingness to communicate is sufficient.

If you are entertaining the idea of teaching English in your gap year, the best way to outrival the competition and make the job-hunt (not to mention the job itself) easier is to do a TEFL training course of which there is an enormous choice in the UK. Two standard recognised qualifications will improve your range of job options. The best known is the Cambridge Certificate in English Language Teaching to Adults (CELTA) administered and awarded by the University of Cambridge Local Examinations Syndicate (ESOL Examinations, 1 Hills Road, Cambridge CB1 2EU; 01223 553355; esol@ucles.org.uk/ www.cambridgeESOL.org/teaching). The other is the Certificate in TESOL (Teaching English to Speakers of Other Languages) offered by Trinity College *London*, 89 Albert Embankment, London SE1 7TP (020-7820 6100/fax 020-7820 6161; info@trinitycolle ge.co.uk/ www.trinitycollege.co.uk). Both are very intensive and expensive, averaging £850-£950. These courses involve at least 100 hours of rigorous training with a practical emphasis (full-time for four weeks or part-time over several months). Most centres expect applicants to have the equivalent of university entrance qualifications, i.e. three GCSEs and two A-levels, but some admit only university graduates.

A list of the 250+ Cambridge Certificate centres both in the UK and abroad offering the CELTA course can be found on the UCLES website as above or requested from UCLES in exchange for a large s.a.e. Here is a small selection:

Ealing, Hammersmith & West London College, Gliddon Road, London W14 9BL (020-8563 0063). £745.
International House, 106 Piccadilly, London W1V 9FL (020-7518 6999). Also offer course at IH Newcastle.
Regent Language Training, 90 Banbury Road, Oxford OX2 6JT (01865 515566; oxford@regent.org.uk). Centres also in London and Edinburgh; www.regent.org.uk.
St. Giles Educational Trust, 51 Shepherd's Hill, Highgate, London N6 5QP (020-8340 0828; www.tefl-stgiles.com). Also offer course at Brighton school.
Stanton Teacher Training, Stanton House, 167 Queensway, London W2 4SB (020-7221 7259; www.stanton-school.co.uk). £698.

Centres offering the Trinity College Certificate include:
Grove House Language Centre, Carlton Avenue, Greenhithe, Kent DA9 9DR (01322 386826; EFL@grovehouse.com). £875.
Inlingua Teacher Training & Recruitment, Rodney Lodge, Rodney Road, Cheltenham, Glos. GL50 1HX (01242 253171; training@inlingua-cheltenham.co.uk). Can help place successful candidates in posts in inlingua schools in Spain, Italy, Germany, Russia, Poland, etc.
The Language Project, 27 Oakfield Road, Clifton, Bristol BS8 2AT (0117-927 3993; www.l anguageproject.co.uk). £1,050. Also offer short Introduction to TEFL/TESL.
Oxford House College, 28 Market Place, Oxford Circus, London W1W 8AW (020-7580 9785; www.oxfordhousecollege.com). 4-week Trinity course offered in Barcelona and Prague.
A number of other centres offer TEFL courses in the UK and abroad which vary in duration and price. Note that taking a TEFL course in a non-English speaking country provides a head start when looking for a job in that country. Among the best known are the British Council and International House offering the CELTA in many cities from Madrid to Sydney, but there are other independent providers of TEFL training abroad:
Global Vision International (GVI), Nomansland, Wheathampstead, St. Albans, Herts. AL4 8EJ (01582 831300/fax 01582 834002; info@gvi.co.uk/ www.gvi.co.uk). Intensive weekend TEFL courses held monthly at the London School of Economics. Course will enable prospective volunteer teachers to survive in the classroom. £175 non-residential.
ITC International TEFL Certificate Prague, Kaprova 14, 110 00 Prague 1, Czech Republic (☎/fax 2-2481-7530/2481-4791; US fax: 1-877-682-6515; info@itc-training.com/ www.itc-training.com). Internationally-recognised 4-week TEFL Certificate courses in Prague, Barcelona and Madrid. Sessions held year-round on a monthly basis.

Trainees need not have prior teaching experience; the course includes supervised teaching practice with foreign students. The total cost of €1,280 includes registration, course manual, immediate job guarantee in Eastern Europe, lifetime job assistance and employment contacts worldwide. City tour, survival Czech or Spanish lessons, cultural orientation and welcome dinner also included. Job workshop and career counselling during and after course. On-site EFL school with job opportunities for graduates. Housing and work visa advice available.

i-to-i, Woodside House, 261 Low Lane, Horsforth, Leeds LS18 5NY (0870 333 2332; info@i-to-i.com/ www.teflcourses.com). 40-hour weekend TEFL training courses across the UK or a 40-hour online version, including grammar modules, CD-ROM and teaching worksheets, and TEFL Toolkit of teaching activities for any classroom. Courses cost £195 and can be combined into an 80-hour Extended TEFL qualification for £295. Free taster TEFL course on-line at www.onlinetefl.com. i-to-i are accredited by the Open and Distance Learning Quality Council for TEFL and can also arrange for trainees to go on ambitious volunteer placement programme in a range of countries (see 'Directory of Specialist Gap Year Programmes').

Prague TEFL & Prague Schools, Na Sekyrce 1392/2, 160 00 Prague 6, Czech Republic (info@tefl.cz or info@pragueschools.co.uk/ www.tefl.cz). Offers Prague TEFL certificate course 10 times per year and assists graduates in finding teaching opportunities worldwide. Fee is $1,520 inclusive of all accommodation and meals; $1080 course only. Trainees must be at least 18 and have completed secondary school.

Teaching Abroad, Gerrard House, Rustington, West Sussex BN16 1AW (01903 859911/ fax 01903 785779; info@teaching-abroad.co.uk/ www.teaching-abroad.co.uk). TEFL taster course and volunteer preparation offered by International English TEFL in Arundel Sussex, in association with the placement agency Teaching Abroad. Short intensive weekend courses and 4-day weekday courses. 2-day residential course costs £265; 4-day non-residential course in London costs £455.

TEFL International, PO Box 396, Arnold, Maryland 21012, USA (410-703-1738; admin@teflcourse.com/ www.teflcourse.com. Offers 4-week proprietary certificate every month in six countries: Thailand, China, Spain, Italy, France and USA. They claim to have a large network of job placement, often straight out of the course. Graduates can access the job placement service for life. The course costs $1,590 in Asia, $1,690 in Europe.

After finishing A levels, **Sam James** and **Sophie Ellison** from Yorkshire decided to spend their gap year in Barcelona if possible. They both signed up to do the Trinity Certificate in TESOL course at Oxford House in their destination city, deciding that this would give them the introduction they needed, and it worked (see *Spain* chapter).

IT and Business Skills Courses

Colleges of Further Education and private colleges offer a wealth of courses that many Gap Year students might choose to pursue, possibly with a view to earning money quickly for a planned placement or expedition later in the year. IT and Business skills courses (the preferred name for outmoded and sexist sounding 'Secretarial Courses') can prove very useful for finding well-paid temporary work before and during university. Note that the government has been pouring significant funding into vocational training and that tuition charges are non-existent for candidates under 19 undertaking a full-time course. Students over the age of 19 may also be eligible for free vocational training though they normally have to pay exam entry fees where relevant, up to about £150.

A good source of institutes offering such courses is the prestigious British Accreditation Council for Independent Further and Higher Education (BAC). Links to its 110 member colleges can be found on its website (www.the-bac.org). About a third of its member institutions offer Business and Professional training courses while a slightly higher percentage operate as independent sixth-form colleges which specialise in tutoring candidates for A-level retakes.

A variety of qualifications can be gained to impress future employers. A range of general and specialist certificates and diplomas are offered by OCR (combination of the Oxford & Cambridge exam board with Royal Society of Arts), Pitman (now overseen by City & Guilds) and LCCI (London Chamber of Commerce and Industry).

The basic qualifications are:

BTEC (Business and Technology Education Council) (www.edexcel.org.uk) run courses in media studies, graphic design, health studies, public services, etc. as well as IT.

Oxford Cambridge & RSA (www.ocr.org.uk) specialise in secretarial and administrative qualifications.

London Chamber of Commerce & Industry (www.lccieb.org.uk) grants a Diploma in Secretarial Administration and a Private Secretary's Diploma.

Pitman (www.pitmanqualifications.com) now part of City & Guilds. Has long offered secretarial skills courses such as typing, computer skills and shorthand.

Information on courses in London can be obtained from the *Floodlight* directories produced by the Association of London Government and sold by newsagents and bookshops (www.floodlight.co.uk). *Part-time Floodlight in London* appears in the first week of July (price £6.50 including postage); *Summertime Floodlight* is published ten days before Easter (£5) and *Full-time Floodlight* comes out in the early autumn (£7.50).

Outdoor Pursuits and Sports Courses

A recognised qualification in any sport will make it very easy to pick up work later in your gap year and find enjoyable holiday jobs throughout your university career. Skilled sportsmen and women can often find gainful employment in their area of expertise whether instructing tennis locally or joining a scheme to coach soccer in the USA or South Africa (see country chapters). Numerous multi-activity centres in Britain and Europe recruit staff to lead and instruct and offer their own pre-season training, sometimes free of charge.

A structured way of acquiring skills and qualifications during your sporting gap year is to participate in the Duke of Edinburgh Award scheme (described in the chapter on Expeditions). This can lead to a qualification in a variety of activity and sporting areas, including expedition skills.

A life-saving qualification allows you to work as a lifeguard, though there are different qualifications for pool and beach lifeguarding (check www.lifeguards.org.uk). The Swimming Teachers' Association (01922 645097; www.sta.co.uk) recommends the National Aquatic Rescue Standard as a professional lifeguarding qualification.

Further afield, diving instructors work at Red Sea resorts, mountain leaders are hired to guide groups in the Himalayas, trainee parachutists find work packing parachutes in the US and Competent Crew get positions on ocean-going yachts. The best starting place for acquiring the necessary training and certification is the governing body of the sport that interests you which will be able to point you towards instructors' courses in the UK and beyond. See entries for the *British Association of Snowsport Instructors* which offers a 10-week course aimed specifically at gap year students, and the *Royal Yachting Association* below. Others include the British Canoe Union (0115 982 1100; www.bcu.org.uk), the British Mountaineering Council (0161-445 4747; www.thebmc.co.uk) and the British Horse Society (0870 120 2244; www.bhs.org.uk). The Mountain Leader Training England (MLTE; www.mltb.org) offers certificates at different levels e.g. Walking Group Leader, Rescue and Emergency Care, Single Pitch Award Training, etc., many of which are offered by the Edale Youth Hostel (01433 670302).

Many companies and youth training organisations run expedition and related courses at varying levels. For example the *Brathay Trust* (see entry in *Directory of Expeditions*) based in the Lake District offer occasional weekend winter climbing courses for less than £100. You can start gently with an Introduction to Bushcraft weekend where you learn basic survival skills from TV survival expert Ray Mears; details of their range of courses from Woodlore Ltd, PO Box 3, Etchingham, East Sussex; 01580 819668; www.raymears.com). Then you might graduate to a climbing course in the Welsh mountains, for instance at the Plas y Brenin National Mountain Centre (Capel Curig, Gwynedd; 01690 720214; www.pyb.co.uk); a 5-day residential course will cost from £400. The most ambitious courses are run by companies like Jagged Globe based in Sheffield (www.jagged-globe.com) which runs ice climbing and other courses in Scotland, the Alps and Canada.

Many multi-activity youth holiday companies run their own training programmes for leaders and instructors, normally to work a summer season in their network of camps and holiday schemes in the UK and abroad. For example Junior Choice Adventures offer training over two or three weeks leading to seasonal employment with them (www.travelclass.co.uk). The cost of training is £345 but this may be reimbursed on successful completion of a contract.

More advanced qualifications are available. For example Newbury College offer an Adventure Travel Guide course (01635 550066; www.adventuretravelguide.co.uk). There are global shortages of qualified instructors in several sports including watersports and snowboarding.

Cookery Courses

A short cookery course can prove immensely useful in finding temporary employment both at home and abroad. (It can also put you in a class of your own when you come to share a house with friends at university.) A catering certificate opens up many appealing employment options in ski resorts, private villas or private yachts. For further information on this subject, consult *The Good Cook's Guide to Working Abroad* by Katherine Parry (Vacation Work, £11.95). The recruitment website www.voovs.com has a useful listing of cookery courses; click on 'Voovs Links'.

The private courses are expensive, but some students (and their parents) decide to splash out in order to acquire such an instantly recognised qualification as *Cordon Bleu* or *Tante Marie*. Most further education colleges in the UK offer catering courses with NVQ (National Vocational Qualification) or C&G awards though generally speaking these are not attended by students planning to go on to university. A Basic Food Hygiene Certificate can be acquired in half a day or even on-line (course costs from £35) and is useful for picking up casual work in restaurants to help fund your gap year.

Creative Arts Courses

While the vast majority of school leavers have no fixed idea what they want to pursue, a few may already have developed a leaning towards one of the creative arts or another vocation. They may want to pursue this interest in their gap year before heading to university, though more usually this kind of course is taken post-university. Examples might be fashion (the London College of Fashion runs summer courses in London and Paris), furniture design (the Chippendale International School of Furniture in Scotland runs courses) or gardening. A useful source of information might be the book *Creative Futures: A Guide to Courses and Careers in Art, Craft and Design* by Tony Charlton, published by the National Society for Education in Art and Design. The book costs £15 including postage and can be ordered via www.nsead.org.

A gap year can provide a useful space in which to pursue one of the creative arts, as reported by Kirsty on the gapyear.com message board:

I spent my gap year doing an art foundation course. My friends were trying to persuade me to go travelling with them, and I felt a bit square staying in England, but I had always wanted to study art. I was good at art at school, but got on really badly with the teacher. I got a place at Camberwell Art School and managed to take out a career development loan to fund it. My parents eventually agreed that it was something worthwhile and they agreed to help support me. I rented a room in a shared house that I found through the newspaper. The course was fantastic - I discovered that sculpture is my thing - and I had a really good time in London. I have now decided to go on to do a fine art degree, rather than English as I planned. I'm so pleased I didn't bow to peer pressure and go off travelling.

Study Programmes

Erasmus, the European Community Action Scheme for the Mobility of University Students, is a programme that enables students to get financial assistance for 3-12 months study in any of 29 European countries. This is normally taken as part of a recognised degree course, e.g. third year university year abroad for language students but is open to anyone who has completed at least one year at a British university. In fact there is not a full take-up of UK students. The programme is administered in the UK by the Socrates-Erasmus Council (R & D Building, The University, Canterbury, Kent CT2 7PD; erasmus@ukc.ac.uk). The official European Union website with full details is at http://europa.eu.int/comm/education/erasmus.html.

An Erasmus grant covers tuition fees at the host university and provides a contribution towards the extra costs which arise from studying abroad, but it does not cover all living expenses. Anyone interested in taking part in the Erasmus programme ought to look for universities which participate in the Erasmus exchange. This information is contained in *Experience Erasmus* published every July by ISCO Publications (12A Princess Way, Camberley, Surrey GU15 3SP; 01276 21188; sales@careerscope.info); the price is £13.95 plus £2 postage. Note that knowledge of a foreign language is helpful but not essential in the Netherlands and Scandinavia where whole courses are given in English.

Conclusion

While some students spend part of their year out cramming to improve their A-level grades, others are in the fortunate position to be able to sign up for courses at these same colleges just for fun, as was the case with **Elisabeth Weiskittel** from the United States:

I decided to begin my gap year in Oxford, England. I chose it because I had been before and loved it there, and because I spoke the language and had family friends, which would make the initial transition easier. My original plan was to get a job in England and work all autumn, but I discovered that Americans can't get a three-month visa unless they are matriculated college students. I had been accepted, but I had not yet gone to college so I was ineligible.

So I went with my alternative plan, which was to enroll in one or two classes somewhere. After doing some research on the internet with my family, we sent away for a few brochures and eventually settled on the Oxford Tutorial College (12 King Edward Street, Oxford OX1 4HT; fax 01865 793233/ www.oxtutor.co.uk). The college gave me a letter saying I had enrolled and that my fees were paid in full, which I had to show at Immigration to get me into the country. I enrolled in two classes: Shakespeare and the History of Art. I went to my classes, but very little reading was required and minimal simple assignments. I spent most of my time sightseeing and spending time with the friends I made. There's a 24 hour bus service between Oxford and London, and so I spent many days in London. I also spent weekends in Dublin and Paris. I had an internship with the Museum of Modern Art in Oxford, which the Oxford Tutorial College had arranged for me. I went in one afternoon a week and helped in the archives. It was very low-key and enjoyable. The whole time in Oxford was wonderful.

Italy attracts more than its fair share of gap year students wanting to broaden their minds and learn more about art and architecture, following in the footsteps of the privileged English men and women who took the Grand Tour of the Continent two hundred years ago. But there is more to be studied during a gap year than Renaissance art and architecture. The courses listed in this chapter and others mentioned throughout the book might never have occurred to you but might inspire you to try something different, from studying photography or folk culture in Greece to learning practical conservation skills while studying Spanish in Guatemala, from a course in Thai massage to the care of wildlife in South Africa.

DIRECTORIES OF COURSES

Language Courses

The following entries represent a tiny proportion of language schools worldwide. Of key interest are the first 19 entries which are for companies mainly in the UK which represent a selection of language schools. Using an agency simplifies the selection process. Schools and agencies of interest to North Americans are listed in the chapter *A Year Off for North Americans*.

AMERISPAN
PO Box 58129, Philadelphia, PA 19102, USA. ☎ 800-879-6640 or 215-751-1100. Fax: 215-751-1986. E-mail: info@amerispan.com. Website: www.amerispan.com.
Specialist Spanish-language travel organisation with great expertise in arranging language courses, voluntary placements and internships throughout South and Central America.
Courses offered: Wealth of options throughout South and Central America. Has recently begun to offer other languages in other countries, e.g. French in Montreal and Quebec, French in Nice and Paris, German in Frankfurt, Italian in Florence plus Chinese, Japanese, Arabic, Russian and Thai.
Accommodation: mostly homestays.

Your essential guide to the best language courses abroad

We can help you...

- **Improve your language skills**
- **Expand your horizons**
- **Have a fantastic time**
- **Immerse yourself in the culture**
- **Meet like-minded people**

All ability levels catered for
Start dates offered all year
Languages for Life courses: 8, 12, 16 wks
Minimum course duration: 2 wks
Expert tuition at quality colleges
Accommodation arranged
Support and advice always available
Excursions and activities offered

FRENCH - SPANISH
GERMAN - ITALIAN
and others...

www.cesalanguages.com
telephone 01209 211 800

languages abroad
CESA

YEAR OUT
GROUP
FOUNDER MEMBER

Other services: Unpaid volunteer placements in Costa Rica, Bolivia, Brazil, Chile, Mexico, Guatemala, Ecuador, Argentina and Peru (see entry in 'Directory of Voluntary Placements').

CACTUS LANGUAGE
No 4 Clarence House, 30-31 North St, Brighton BN1 1EB. ☎ 0845 130 4775. Fax: 01273 775868. E-mail: enquiry@cactuslanguage.com. Website: www.cactuslanguage.com.
Courses offered: Spanish (Spain and Latin America), French, Italian, Chinese, Russian, Japanese, Portuguese (Portugal and Brazil), German (Germany and Austria), Arabic, Turkish, Danish, Dutch, Swedish, Thai and Indonesian. Combined language learning with overland safaris, round-the-world travel, volunteer placements (see entry), skiing in the Alps, work placements in Europe, etc.
Duration of courses: from 1 hour to 1 year.
Qualifications offered: D.E.L.E. preparation offered in Spain, D.E.L.F. offered in France, Goethe exams in Germany and Austria; Cambridge, IELTS in UK and worldwide.
Cost: Sample prices: 1-week budget General Course (20 lessons) in Salamanca £119, 2-week Individual Course (20 lessons per week) in Antigua, Guatemala including host family and meals £369.
Accommodation: Choice of full-board host family, half-board host family, bed and breakfast, student residence, budget hotels, luxury hotels and private/shared apartments.

GAP YEAR language programmes worldwide: Spanish in Spain, Cuba, Costa Rica, Peru, Ecuador, Mexico, Bolivia and Argentina; French, German, Italian, Russian in Europe; Portuguese in Portugal and Brazil. Italian/French/German + skiing; Italian + art history/literature/archeology. Courses from 1 week to 1 year. All levels, all year round. Accommodation and cultural activities included.

Volunteer work placements in Germany, Peru, Costa Rica, Brazil, Bolivia and Ecuador.

Càlédöñiâ
LANGUAGES ABROAD

The Clockhouse, Bonnington Mill
72 Newhaven Road, Edinburgh EH6 5QG
Tel: 0131 621 7721/2
info@caledonialanguages.co.uk
www.caledonialanguages.co.uk

CALEDONIA LANGUAGES ABROAD
The Clockhouse, Bonnington Mill, 72 Newhaven Road, Edinburgh EH6 5QG. ☎ 0131-621 7721/2. Fax: 0131-621 7723. E-mail: info@caledonialanguages.co.uk. Website: www.caledonialanguages.co.uk.
Caledonia was established in 1994 and offers independent advice and information on language courses in Europe, Latin America and Russia.
Courses offered: Language courses for general interest, exam revision, language and culture. These can often be combined with special interest courses such as walking, cooking, diving and skiing. There are also opportunities to participate in volunteer work programmes in Latin America (see entry in 'Directory of Specialist Gap Year Programmes'). Two or more language programmes can be taken consecutively in different countries to give a long term Gap Year trip.
Duration of courses: 1 week to a year.
Cost: 6-week programme of 3 weeks of Spanish tuition in Sucre, Bolivia and 3 weeks voluntary work would cost from £1,220 including accommodation.
Accommodation: Students can stay with local host families or in residential accommodation, although Caledonia recommends the former.

CESA LANGUAGES ABROAD
CESA House, Pennance Road, Lanner, Cornwall TR16 5TQ. ☎ 01209 211800. Fax: 01209 211830. E-mail: info@cesalanguages.com. Website: www.cesalanguages.com.

Founding member of Year Out Group (www.yearoutgroup.org).

Courses offered: Beginner, intermediate and advanced courses in French (Cannes, Nice, Montpellier, Tours, Bordeaux, Paris or, for a more exotic option, Guadeloupe), Spanish (Seville, Nerja, Salamanca, Malaga or Madrid in Spain, plus Mexico, Costa Rica or Ecuador), German (Berlin, Lindau, Munich, Cologne or Vienna in Austria), Italian (Florence, Rome and Siena), Portuguese, Japanese, Russian, Greek and Arabic (in Morocco).

Duration of courses: 2-24 weeks with possibility of studying in more than one location during a year-out programme. At least one start date per month year round.

Qualifications offered: D.E.L.E. preparation offered in Spain. D.E.L.F., Alliance Francaise and CCIP exams in France. Full range of Goethe exams offered in Germany and Austria.

Cost: Languages for Life 16-week course in Seville or Madrid costs from £2,287 including shared apartment accommodation and 20 hours tuition for week. A 12-week course in Nice costs £2,172.

Accommodation: Options include student apartments or residences, on-campus accommodation, host families, sole-occupancy apartments and hotels.

CHALLENGE EDUCATIONAL SERVICES
101 Lorna Road, Hove, East Sussex BN3 3EL. ☎ 01273 220261. Fax: 01273 220376. E-mail: enquiries@challengeuk.com. Website: www.challengeuk.com.

Courses offered: French language courses in private language schools and Universities throughout France. Courses can be for any age and ability, in preparation for examinations or purely recreational. Junior programmes are offered in the summer (and Easter) which combine language tuition with sports, cultural and social activities. In addition to the short courses, Challenge offer a specially designed Gap Year opportunity which consists of studying at a French university for a term or full academic year. This programme requires a high level of French.

Duration of courses: From one week to a full academic year.

Qualifications offered: Students may study towards the D.E.L.F. or D.A.L.F.; University courses may offer the opportunity to sit the Certificat or Diplomes de Langue Francaise.

Cost: Academic Year at a French University would cost around £7,000 including residential accommodation.

CIEE
Language Study Abroad Programme, 52 Poland Street, London W1F 7AB. ☎ 020-7478 2020. Fax: 020-7734 7322. E-mail: infouk@councilexchanges.org.uk. Website: www.ciee.org.uk.

CIEE UK offers study, work and teaching abroad programmes for Britons.

Courses offered: Courses at language schools in 23 destinations across France, Spain, Italy, Germany and Latin America, aimed at gap year students, undergraduates and young professionals.

Duration of courses: Standard and intensive courses are offered for 2-16 weeks throughout the year. Applications should be submitted at least one month before start date.

Cost: Sample course prices: 2 weeks in Nice £350 including tuition.

Accommodation: Self-catering apartment, student residence or host family with bed and breakfast.

DON QUIJOTE
2-4 Stoneleigh Park Road, Epsom, Surrey KT19 0QT. ☎ 020-8786 8081. Fax: 020-

8786 8086. E-mail: info@donquijote.co.uk. Website: www.donquijote.co.uk.
Courses offered: Intensive (20 lessons a week) and Super Intensive (30 lessons a week) courses for all levels throughout Spain: Barcelona, Granada, Madrid, Malaga, Puerto de La Cruz (Tenerife), Salamanca, Seville and Cusco (Peru). Also available is 'Spanish for Life' (12 weeks and longer) and in Cusco a 'Spanish Study and Volunteer Work Programme'.
Duration of courses: 1–40 weeks.
Qualifications: Students will receive a Don Quijote certificate of attendance and level attained at the end of the course and are also encouraged, but not obliged, to take the D.E.L.E. examination (Spanish for Foreigners).
Cost: From £394 for 2 weeks intensive course and single room lodging in a self-catering student flat. Spanish for Life courses start at £1,813 for 12 weeks including student flat accommodation.
Accommodation: Homestay, residence and flats.
Follow-up: Further courses can be arranged, particularly to specialise in business Spanish and including an internship placement programme in Madrid and Barcelona. Private tuition is available at all schools.

EF INTERNATIONAL LANGUAGE SCHOOLS
74 Roupell Street, London SE1 8SS. ☎ 08707 200735. Fax: 08707 200767. E-mail: languages.gb@ef.com. Website: www.ef.com.
Courses offered: Foreign language courses at privately owned and EF schools in France, Germany, Italy, Spain, Ecuador, China and Russia.
Duration of courses: 2–52 weeks, beginning every week.
Qualifications offered: DELE (Spain), DELF (France), business, culture, music, university classes.
Cost: Depending on the destination, £650–£900 for a 2-week period. This price includes accommodation, tuition, course materials and meals.
Accommodation: Host families or student residence.
Other services: EF has its own Travel Service and tailor-made student insurance. Its Language Travel division employs group leaders and activity organisers for summer work in the UK (see 'Directory of Paid Seasonal Jobs').

EIL CULTURAL & EDUCATIONAL TRAVEL
287 Worcester Road, Malvern, Worcestershire, WR14 1AB. ☎ 0800 018 4015. Fax: 01684 562212. E-mail: info@eiluk.org. Website: www.eiluk.org.
Non-profit cultural and educational organisation, offers short-term homestay programmes in more than 20 countries (see entry in 'Directory of Specialist Gap Year Programmes').

EN FAMILLE OVERSEAS
4 St Helena Road, Colchester CO3 3BA. ☎ 01206 546741. Fax: 01206 546740. E-mail: marylou_toms@btinternet.com. Website: www.enfamilleoverseas.co.uk.
Arranges homestays in France, Germany, Italy and Spain with or without language tuition (see entry in 'Directory of Specialist Gap Year Programmes').

EURO-ACADEMY LTD
67-71 Lewisham High St, London SE13 5JX. ☎ 020-8297 0505. Fax: 020-8297 0984. E-mail: enquiries@euroacademy.co.uk. Website: www.euroacademy.co.uk.
Courses offered: French, Italian, German, Portuguese, Spanish, Russian and Greek. Opportunities for homestays, individual tuition, vacation courses, intensive courses (for students wishing to make considerable progress in a short time), and long-term courses specially aimed at gap year students. Also arrange work experience in France and Germany (see 'Directory of Work Experience').
Duration of courses: 4–12 weeks.
Qualifications offered: Some destinations offer the chance to prepare for the D.E.L.F./ D.A.L.F./D.E.L.E. exam (France and Spain) and Paris Chamber of Commerce certificate;

also Kleine Deutsche and Sprachdiplom can be obtained in Germany.
Accommodation: Bed and breakfast, rooms in private homes, with families, in student residence or in flat shares.

EUROCENTRES UK
56 Eccleston Square, London SW1V 1PQ. ☎ 020-7834 4155. Fax: 020-7834 1866. E-mail: vic-info@eurocentres.com. Website: www.eurocentres.com. ☎ 020-7834 4155. Fax: 020-7834 1866.
Courses offered: All levels of Spanish in various centres.
Other services: Excursions (e.g. to the Costa Brava and Dalí Museum), Spanish films, language and cultural courses and gastronomy courses available.
Accommodation: With family or in hotels.

EUROLINGUA
61 Bollin Drive, Altrincham WA14 5QW. ☎/fax: 0161-972 0225. Website: www.eurolingua.com.
Courses offered: Variety of language courses worldwide. Work experience placements also possible (see entry).
Duration of courses: 1-4 weeks.
Cost: Standard fees throughout Europe: one-to-one tuition while living in tutor's home for a week costs €850 for 10 hours and €1,335 for 20 hours. To participate in a group programme, fees are €248 for 15/20 lessons in a week and €992 for 4 weeks (tuition only).
Accommodation: Host families (for one-to-one programme), homestays or studio apartments. Approximate prices are €165 for one week's half-board homestay up to €644 for 4 weeks. A studio apartment (when available) will cost €400 per month.

GALA SPANISH IN SPAIN
Woodcote House, 8 Leigh Lane, Farnham, Surrey GU9 8HP. ☎/fax: 01252 715319.
Operating since 1993 and run by an ex-Director of Studies of a Spanish language school, Gala offers an information, advisory and placement service for students of any level from age 16.
Programmes offered in a number of Spanish cities: Homestays, with or without Spanish language courses. Also offered hotel work experience (see *Directory of Work Experience*).
Language courses: From 2 weeks to 9 months duration.
Cost: A minimum placement fee of £25 is required. Cost of course and accommodation varies according to location and time of year. Sample prices of family stay with half-board would be £733-£930 for 4 weeks, £2,020-£2,538 for 12 weeks; or with self-catering

residence £620-£1,025 for 4 weeks, £1,625-£2,882 for 12 weeks.
Accommodation: With families or in student self-catering accommodation. Courses also offered in South America. Arrangements can also be made for 16/17 year olds to spend one or more terms in a senior Spanish school in Madrid while living with a family.
Contact: Anne Thomas, Proprietor.

IALC (INTERNATIONAL ASSOCIATION OF LANGUAGE CENTRES)
PO Box 798, Canterbury CT1 2WX. ☎ 01227 769007. Fax: 01227 769014. E-mail: info@ialc.org. Website: www.ialc.org.
Language school association with 81 members in 20 countries.
Courses offered: Hundreds of programmes available ranging from short general language courses to specialised courses combining language with culture, cookery, dance, art, etc. Some IALC schools offer work and study combinations.
Accommodation: Most schools offer a choice of family stay, hall of residence, guesthouse or flat-share.
Application procedures: Canterbury office is not a booking office. People can access individual member schools through IALC website.
Contact: Rebecca Willis or Jan Capper.

INTERNATIONAL LINKS
145 Manygate Lane, Shepperton, Middlesex TW17 9EP. ☎/fax: 01932 229300. Fax: 01932 222294. E-mail: internatlinks@aol.com.
Courses offered: Language courses with homestays in Spain.
Duration of courses: 1-4 week homestays with 2 hours individual language tuition per day.
Cost: £370 for a week's full board homestay and tuition.
Other services: Advice on cheap travel given.
Contact: Eve Moody, Principal.

LANACOS
64 London Road, Dunton Green, Sevenoaks, Kent TN13 2UG. ☎ 01732 462309. E-mail: languages@lanacos.com. Website: www.lanacos.com.
Language agency run by linguists.
Courses offered: Language courses in more than 200 locations: Spanish in many Spanish and Latin American cities; French in Paris, Nice, Annecy, Savoie Bordeaux, St. Malo, Brittany, Belgium and Montréal; German in Salzburg, Berlin, München, Tyrol Münster, Cologne, Bavaria and Hamburg; Italian in Rome, Florence, Milan, Tuscany, Siena, Sicily, Orvieto, Rimini and Pisa; Portuguese in Lisbon, Porto, Faro and Brazil; Greek in Athens, Crete and Thessaloniki; and Japanese in Tokyo and Osaka.
Duration of courses: 2+ weeks.
Cost: From £394 for a fortnight in Granada to £2,433 for 12-week academic course in Paris.
Accommodation: Homestays with full or half board, B&Bs, single or shared apartments.
Contact: Martin Pickett, Director.

LANGUAGE COURSES ABROAD LTD
67 Ashby Road, Loughborough, Leicestershire LE11 3AA. ☎ 01509 211612. Fax: 01509 260037. E-mail: info@languagesabroad.co.uk. Website: www.langua gesabroad.co.uk.
Parent company, Spanish Study Holidays Ltd., is a member of FIYTO (Federation of International Youth Travel Organisations) and ALTO (Association of Language Travel Organisations).
Programme description: In-country language courses in Spanish, French, German, Italian, Portuguese and Russian, sometimes in preparation for work experience placements (see entry in 'Directory of Work Experience').

Prerequisites: Minimum age 16 or 18, average age 18-26.
Duration and time of placements: 1-40 weeks.
Accommodation: Shared self-catering student apartments, private studio apartments, host families, student residences or hotels.

S.I.B.S. LTD
Beech House, Commercial Road, Uffculme, Devon EX15 3EB. ☎ 01884 841330. Fax: 01884 841377. E-mail: trish@sibs.co.uk. Website: www.sibs.co.uk.
Language consultancy which arranges language courses abroad for clients.
Courses offered: For business and pleasure in France (Avignon, Biarritz, Bordeaux, Ferrieres, Hyères, Lisieux, Monlezun, Montpellier, Nice, Paris, Spa, Tours), Italy (Bagno Di Romagna, Florence, Milan, Ravenna, Rome, Siena); Germany (Berlin, Frankfurt, Munich, Wiesbaden); Austria (Kitzbühel, Vienna); Portugal (Faro, Libson, Porto) Japan (Nagano, Osaka, Spa Niveze, Tokyo, Yokohama); Spain (Alicante, Barcelona, Benalmadena, El Puerto De Santa Maria, Granada, Gran Canaria, Madrid, Nerja, Salamanca, Seville, Valencia); Greece (Athens, Hania, Thessaloniki); Russian (Moscow, St. Petersburg); Argentina, Ecuador and Mexico.
Cost: From £200 per week including accommodation.
Other services: Variety of courses and locations can be combined with cultural subjects, work experience, etc.
Contact: Patricia Cooper, Director.

VIS A VIS
2-4 Stoneleigh Park Road, Epsom KT19 0QT. ☎ 020-8786 8021. Fax: 020-8786 8086. E-mail: info@visavis.org. Website: www.visavis.org. German office: Münsterstrasse 111, 48155 Münster (info@carpe.de).
Courses offered: Courses for all levels in French at schools in France (Paris, Annecy, Antibes, Montpellier, Nice, Royan and Vichy), Belgium (Brussels) and Canada (Montréal). Many activities and excursions available in all locations.
Duration of courses: From 2 weeks onwards.
Cost: Prices start at £428 (2003) for a 2-week course (20 lessons a week) plus single room half-board accommodation with a family in Annecy.
Qualifications: Some courses prepare students for official language diplomas, such as the D.E.L.F. and the more advanced level (D.A.L.F.). These can be worked towards at the student's own pace.
Accommodation: Student flats and halls of residence are available for those wishing to mingle with other students. Host families also accommodate students which allows the student an insight into French culture.

Language Schools Abroad

ACADEMIA DE ESPANOL QUITO
Marchena Street 0e1-30 and 10 Av. de Agosto, PO Box 17-15-0039-C, Quito, Ecuador. ☎ 2-2553-647/2554-811. Fax: 2-2506-474. E-mail: academiaquito@ andinanet.com. Website: www.academiaquito.com.ec.
Courses offered: Spanish language courses, with the teaching programme split into five levels. Around 45 hours are needed to complete each level.
Duration of courses: From 1 week, all year round. Flexible starting dates: pre-booked classes may start on any day of the week.
Qualifications offered: All students receive a transcript which records final marks in courses.
Cost: Private Spanish classes cost $7 per hour. Accommodation in a host family is $22 per day, including breakfast and dinner.

Accommmodation: With a host family in a private bedroom and bathroom, with laundry service. Morning and evening meals included.
Contact: Virginia Villamar, Director.

ACADEMIA HISPANO AMERICANA
Mesones 4, 37700 San Miguel de Allende, GTO, Mexico. ☎ **415-152 0349/ 152 4349. Fax: 415-152 2333. E-mail: info@ahaspeakspanish.com. Website: www.ahaspeakspanish.com.**
Courses offered: Intensive Spanish and related subjects.
Duration of courses: 12 4-week sessions per school year. Normal stay 2 weeks in Intensive Course. 35 hours of lessons and activities per week.
Cost: One-to-one tuition costs $600 for 2 weeks (5 hours per day); group tuition costs $300 for 2 weeks, $450 for one session (4 weeks).
Accommodation: Homestays cost from $252 for 2 weeks, on a shared room basis, including 3 meals if booked separately.
Contact: Pauline Hawkins, Director.

ACADEMIA SUPERIOR DE ESPANOL SIMON BOLIVAR
Calle Leonidas Plaza 353 y Roca, Quito, Ecuador. ☎ **2-236688.** ☎**/fax: 2-504977. E-mail: info@simon-bolivar.com. Website: www.simon-bolivar.com.**
Affiliated to Columbus Travel Ltd.
Courses offered: Individual or group lessons.
Duration of courses: 1-52 weeks.
Qualifications offered: US credits are offered.
Cost: US$140 per week for individual lessons; $100 per week for lessons in pairs. (20 hours per week).
Accommodation: Homestay, apartments or hostels; from $105 per week homestay.
Other services: Links with volunteer programmes via New Horizons, Av. 6 de Diciembre 2130 y Av. Colón Edificio Antares, Primer piso, Oficina 107, Quito (PO Box 17-07-9463); ☎/fax 2-2542-890; info@voluntariosecuador.org.

ACCADEMIA BRITANNICA TOSCANA
Via Pietro da Cortona 10, Arezzo, Italy. ☎ **0575-21366. Fax: 0575-300426. E-mail: italcors@ats.it. Website: www.etr.it/accademica_britannica.**
Courses offered: Intensive Italian language courses at 6 levels.
Duration of courses: 40 hours of lessons over 2 weeks. Ideal minimum 4 weeks, but 1 week also possible.
Cost: €150 for 1 week, €279 for 2, €387 for 3 and €475 for 4 weeks. Further weeks cost €116 each. Individual lesson costs €28.
Accommodation: Host family or apartment. Family accommodation costs €77 per week in shared room, €103 in single room.
Qualifications offered: Recognised exams are available in June and December. All courses receive a registered descriptive certificate.

ACCADEMIA DEL GIGLIO
Via Ghibellina 116, 50122 Florence, Italy. ☎**/fax: 055-230 2467. E-mail: info@adg.it. Website: www.adg.it or www.italyhometuition.com.**
Courses offered: Italian courses for foreigners plus art and art history courses (see below). Intensive classes or one-to-one tuition.
Duration of courses: 1, 2, 4, 8, 12 or more weeks. 4 hours of classes a day, more on one-to-one programme.
Qualifications offered: Students sit a written exam at the end of each month to determine whether they are ready to move to the next level. Language certificates available.
Cost: 1-week intensive course costs €145, 8 weeks costs €810. Enrolment fee of €41.
Accommodation: All kinds of accommodation can be arranged from single room in a

family for €26 a day half-board to €750 for 4 weeks in a self-catering flat sharing kitchen and other facilities. School located in a peaceful area of the city centre.
Other services: Visits and social activities included in the price.
Contact: Lorenzo Capanni, Assistant Director.

ACCADEMIA ITALIANA
Piazza Pitti 15, 50125 Florence, Italy. ☎ 055-284616/211619. Fax: 055-284486. E-mail: modaita@tin.it. Website: www.accademiaitaliana.com.
Courses offered: Italian language and culture courses, drawing and painting, textile design, fashion design, interior design and graphic arts. Language courses can be taken alongside other courses.
Duration of courses: From one month to the whole gap year, beginning in either September or January.
Qualifications offered: Students are awarded diplomas for completion of basic, intermediate and advanced level courses.
Accommodation: Housing is arranged in apartments shared with other students or in families, residences, hotels or pensions.
Follow-up: Exchanges are possible with universities in Italy and abroad with which Accademia Italiana maintains links. It also participates in the Leonardo da Vinci programme.

ACTE-CHALLENGE
10 square Adanson, 75005 Paris, France. ☎ 1-42 17 07 06. Fax: 1-42 17 06 66. E-mail: actechallenge@club-internet.fr. Website: www.actechallenge.fr.
Member of the Office National des Garantie des Séjours et Stages Linguistiques (www.loffice.org), FIYTO and Maison de la France.
Courses offered: Language courses in Paris, Nantes, Angers, Poitiers, Perpignan and Antibes.
Duration of courses: 1 week to 8 months in Paris, 2 weeks to 9 months at the other destinations.
Accommodation: Homestays with families or student/youth residences.

ALLIANCE FRANCAISE
101 Boulevard Raspail, 75270 Paris Cedex 06, France. ☎ 1-42 84 90 00. Fax: 1-42 84 91 00. E-mail: info@alliancefr.org. Website: www.alliancefr.org.
Alliance Française has 1,000 language centres in 129 countries, including in the UK (see next entry), where students can study French in their own country.
Courses offered in Paris: French language courses at 5 levels with a choice of shared or individual classes at the school in Paris. Students have the chance to study general French or specialised French, e.g. French for tourism, hotel work or secretarial.
Duration of courses: From 2 weeks onwards. Session consists of 16 days of instruction over one month, 4 hours of lessons a day.
Qualifications: Various French diplomas can be awarded including Paris Chamber of Commerce & Industry and the Ministry of National Education. Normally test can be sat after 128 hours (i.e. two sessions).
Cost: 16-day intensive session (as above) costs €584 plus annual enrolment fee of €50.
Accommodation: Provided on demand in student residence or in studios.

ALLIANCE FRANCAISE DE LONDRES
1 Dorset Square, London NW1 6PU. E-mail: info@aflondon.org.uk. Website: www.alliancefrancaise.org.uk.
Courses offered: French language courses for all levels. Daytime, evening or Saturday courses. Short intensive courses and revision courses available.
Duration of courses: 2-12 weeks; 2½-15 hours per week throughout the year.
Qualifications offered: Course certificates, preparation for D.E.L.F./D.A.L.F. and Paris

Chamber of Commerce examinations.
Accommodation: None available.

ALPHA SPRACHINSTITUT AUSTRIA
Schwartzenbergplatz 16/ Canovagasse 5, 1010 Vienna, Austria. ☎ **+43 1-503 69 69. Fax: +43 1-503 69 69-14. E-mail: info@alpha.at. Website: www.alpha.at.**
Courses offered: German as a foreign language.
Duration of courses: 2 weeks to one year; intensive or evening courses.
Qualifications offered: Institute is an examination centre for German Language Diploma of the Goethe Institute, Austrian Language Diploma (OESD) and the European Language Certificate. German intensive courses follow Goethe Institute system to highest level diploma (on behalf of Ludwig Maximilians University Munich). Also offer exams in Business German.
Cost: From €400 upwards.
Accommodation: Private families, apartments, student hostels.
Contact: Verena Kogler, Course Consultant.

AMILI
Selva Alegre 1031 y La Isla, Ecuador. ☎ **+593 2-222 6947. Fax: +593-2-250 0669. E-mail: info@amili.org/amili@amili.com. Website: www.amili.com.**
Courses offered: Spanish courses and internships in Ecuador (see *Directory of Work Experience*).
Duration of placements: Minimum 2 months up to 6 months (since foreigners require no visa for stays of less than 6 months).
Cost: $200 placement fee includes transfer from airport to host family. Language lessons cost $6 an hour (20 hours a week).
Accommodation: Accommodation with host families costs $12 per day including full board.
Contact: Patricia Fernández (Internship Consultant), Patricio Fernández (General Co-ordinator).

ATHENS CENTRE
48 Archimidous St, 116 36 Athens, Greece. ☎ **210-701 2268. Fax 210-701 8603. E-mail: athenscr@compulink.gr. Website: www.athenscentre.gr.**
Courses offered: Modern Greek.
Duration of courses: 3, 4, 7 or 10 weeks throughout the year. Summer courses held on island of Spetses.
Qualifications offered: Serious courses with certificate given at end.
Accommodation: Hotels, pensions, apartment sub-lets and studios.
Cost: €580.
Contact: Rosemary Donnelly, Director.

ATRIUM
Istituto di Lingua e Cultura Italiana, Piazza Papa Giovanni XXIII, 3, 61043, Cagli (PU), Italy. ☎**/fax: 0721 790321. E-mail: atrium@info-net.it. Website: www.istitutoatrium.com.**
Courses offered: Italian language courses.
Duration of courses: Monthly sessions year-round. Courses range from 2 weeks to 12 months.
Qualifications offered: Possible CILS examination.
Cost: about €200 for 1 week (including 20% VAT), €450 for 4-week standard course plus €75 one-time registration fee.
Accommodation: Homestay, apartments, hotels, bed and breakfasts, etc. The latter charges from €105 per week.
Contact: Donna Galletta.

BRIDGE-LINGUATEC INTERNATIONAL
915 S. Colorado Blvd, Denver, CO 80246, USA. Toll-free in the US and Canada: 1-800-724-4210. ☎ 303-777-7783 ext 19. Fax: 303-777-7246. E-mail: studyabroad@bridge-linguatec.com. Website: www.bridge-linguatec.com.
Language schools in Chile, Argentina and Brazil. Chile: Los Leones 439, Providencia, Santiago. Argentina: Av. Eduardo Madero 1020, Planta Baja 1106, Buenos Aires. Brazil: Rua da Ajuda 35, Sobreloja 201, 20040-000 Rio de Janeiro.
Courses offered: Spanish courses in Chile, Argentina, Costa Rica and Spain plus Portuguese in Brazil. Special interest courses also available.
Duration of courses: Minimum 1 week private and 2 weeks group starting every Monday year round.
Accommodation: Homestays and aparthotels available.
Other services: Many students who come to study Spanish earn some money by English teaching (though this is mainly for university graduates). Bi-weekly and weekend excursions and special workshops related to Latin American culture are also offered. Some students who come to study Spanish become English teachers after completing their language course (if they are university graduates and if there is a demand).

THE BRITISH INSTITUTE OF FLORENCE
Piazza Strozzino, Piazza Strozzi 2, 50123 Florence, Italy. ☎ 055-26 77 82 00. Fax: 055-26 77 82 22. E-mail: info@britishinstitute.it. Website: www.britishinstitute.it.
Courses offered: Language tuition among many other courses (see entry in 'Specialist Gap Year Programmes'). Special arrangements regarding length of course, number of hours and course content can be made.
Duration of courses: 2 days to 1 year.
Cost: Tuition fees vary according to length and intensity of the course chosen. For example a 4-week Italian Language course costs from €430 (£280) approximately, and a 3-day History of Art course costs €230 (£145).
Accommodation: Can be arranged in local homes, *pensione* and hotels starting at €22 (£14) a day.

BWS GERMANLINGUA
Bayerstr. 13, D-80335 Munich, Germany. ☎ 89-59 98 92 00. Fax: 89-59 98 92 01. E-mail: info@bws-germanlingua.de. Website: www.bws-germanlingua.de.
Courses offered: German language courses, standard (20 lessons per week), intensive (25 lessons) or one-to-one.
Duration of courses: 2-48 weeks. Minimum 1 week for a tailor-made course.
Cost: €390 for 2 weeks to €6,720 for 48 weeks. Prices higher for intensive courses (from €450) and one-to-one (€340 for 1 week with 10 lessons).
Accommodation: With a German family (€140 per week); in a flat shared with students (€120 per week) or in a studio (€160).
Contact: Florian Meierhofer.

CAFFE ITALIANO CLUB
Largo Antonio Pandullo 6, 89861 Tropea, Italy. ☎ 0963-603284. Fax: 0963-61786. E-mail: info@caffeitalianoclub.net. Website: www.caffeitalianoclub.net.
Courses offered: Italian crash courses; special courses for the hotel and tourism industry; individual crash courses in business Italian; Italian for fashion and style. Courses are given to small groups of a maximum of 4-6 students.
Duration of courses: Usually 1-8 weeks, but it is possible to stay longer. Courses begin every Monday all year round.
Qualifications offered: Opportunity to work towards the C.I.L.S. examination.
Cost: 8-weeks conversation course costs €670; 8-weeks main course costs €1,205; 8-

weeks intensive course costs €2,387. 10% discount on course fees From November to March. Registration fee of €100 includes the transfer from and to the airport/train station at Lamezia Terme or 2 excursions from the weekly programme.

Accommodation: Accommodation is extra at €950 for 8 weeks in a single room (shared flat) or €1,365 in a single room apartment. Generally in holiday flats situated in the centre of Tropea, with a sea or mountain view. Flats usually have one, two or three rooms, kitchen and a terrace or balcony.

Sports & Other Activities: The school offers sea surfing, sailing, diving, tennis and riding as well as excursion programmes in Calabria and Sicily. Further courses are available in watercolour painting, history of art and cookery.

CALES (CENTER FOR ARABIC LANGUAGES AND EASTERN STUDIES)

PO Box 29107, Azzumar St, Sana'a, Yemen. ☎ +967-1-292090. ☎/fax: +967-1-281700. E-mail: cales@ust.edu. Website: www.y.net.ye/cales.

Courses offered: Arabic language and Yemeni culture for foreigners at centre in heart of Old Sana'a next to the *souk* (market).

Duration of courses: short courses by the month or full academic year.

Qualifications offered: University credit may be available.

Cost: 80 hours per month (4 hours a day, 5 days a week) costs $360 for shared tuition, $580 for private lessons.

Accommodation: $100 per month for a single room, $75 in a shared room.

Contact: Jameel, Director.

CAMPUS AUSTRIA

Wiener Internationale Hochschulkurse, Universitaet Wien, Ebendorferstrasse 10, A-1010 Vienna. ☎ 01-4277 24102. **E-mail: info@campus-austria.at. Website:**

www.campus-austria.at.
Courses offered: Huge range of German language courses offered by 16 language schools throughout Austria, all described in brochure of Campus Austria. Some courses lead to Goethe Institut qualifications or the Austrian Diploma for German as a Foreign Language (OESD).
Duration of courses: Normally two or more weeks, year round with choice of holiday courses and youth programmes.
Cost: Prices vary, but approximately €10 per 45-minute lesson or €360 per fortnight excluding accommodation.
Contact: Mag. Sigrun Inmann-Trojer.

CAVILAM
1 av.des Célestins, BP 2678, 03206 Vichy Cedex, France. ☎ 4-70 30 83 83. Fax: 4-70 30 83 84. E-mail: info@cavilam.com. Website: www.cavilam.com.
Courses offered: Intensive French courses at all levels.
Duration of courses: Minimum 1 week year round. Long-term intensive courses (37 weeks) specially suited for a gap year.
Qualifications offered: In-house certificate or preparation for exams including D.E.L.F., D.A.L.F., TEF and TCF.
Cost: Price for 37-week course is €5,600. Intensive courses cost €215 per week plus €49 registration fee; summer courses for juniors cost €1,275 for 2 weeks.
Accommodation: Can be arranged. Family accommodation costs €22.50 per day, half board; furnished studio costs from €17 per day.
Contact: Christine Barge, Service des Relations Extérieures.

CEDIC ARGENTINE SPANISH LEARNING CENTRE
Reconquista 715, Piso 11 E, 1003 Buenos Aires, Argentina. ☎/fax: 11-4312 1016/4315 1156. E-mail: spanish@cedic.com.ar. Website: www.cedic.com.ar.
Courses offered: Spanish language in groups or individually. 10 or 20 hours a week.
Duration of courses: 2-4 weeks per level.
Cost: US$240 for 40-hour group course. Private lessons cost $9 per hour.
Other services: accommodation arranged with nearby families or student residences.
Contact: Susana Bernardi.

CHINESE LANGUAGE CENTER
The Chinese University of Hong Kong, Fong Shu Chuen Building, Shatin, NT, Hong Kong. ☎ +852-2609 6727. Fax: +852-2603 5004. E-mail: clc@cuhk.edu.hk. Website: www.cuhk.edu.hk/clc and www.cuhk.edu.hk/clc/sum03.htm.
Largest tertiary Chinese language learning centre in Hong Kong. Runs New Asia Yale-in-China programme.
Courses offered: Full-time Cantonese and Putonghua courses.
Duration of courses: autumn, spring and summer semesters.
Cost: HK$23,700 per term apart from summer term (HK$17,325).
Accommodation: Hostel available in summer term.
Contact: Eddie Sin, Executive Assistant.

CIAL CENTRO DE LINGUAS
Av. da República, 41-8°E, 1050-187, Lisbon, Portugal. ☎ +351-21-794 04 48. Fax: +351-21-796 07 83. E-mail: portuguese@cial.pt. Website: www.cial.pt.
Courses offered: Full Portuguese language and culture course in six stages, with 60 hours of language tuition for every stage.
Duration of courses: 4 weeks for each course, with new courses every month.
Qualifications: Possibility of qualifying for the Diploma of Portuguese as a Foreign Language.
Cost: 4-week course will cost €840.

Accommodation: With families in individual rooms with breakfast included.
Contact: Dr. Renato Borges de Sousa, Administrator.

CIS (CENTRO DE INTERCAMBIO SOLIDARIDAD)
Mélida Anaya Montes Language School, Boulevard Universitario No. 4, Colonia El Roble, San Salvador, El Salvador. ☎/fax: +503 226-2623. E-mail: cis@netcomsa.com. Website: www.cis-elsalvador.org.
Courses offered: Spanish classes and political-cultural programme. Social justice oriented volunteer opportunities also available teaching English, working with human rights and in community service.
Duration of courses: Classes start every Monday. Any number of weeks can be booked.
Qualifications offered: Recreational courses.
Cost: US$100 per week for 4 hours of morning classes. $25 per week for afternoon political-cultural programme, plus admin fee of $12.50 per week for first 4 weeks, plus $25 one-time application fee.
Accommodation: Homestays with breakfast and dinner cost $60 a week. Alternatives in guest houses or shared flats can be arranged.
Contact: Jennie Busch.

CLE (CENTRE LINGUISTIQUE pour ETRANGERS)
7-9 Place Châteauneuf, 37000 Tours, France. Fax: 2-47 05 84 61. E-mail: info@cle.fr Website: www.cle.fr
Courses offered: French language courses, plus additional classes such as wine tasting.
Duration of courses: Up to 24 weeks.
Qualifications offered: Students are prepared for the D.E.L.F. examinations from October till June. The units needed to pass the D.E.L.F. diploma can be taken in an examination centre in the Tours area or in the student's home country. A certificate of achievement is also awarded to students.
Cost: 12-week course will cost no more than €3,070.
Accommodation: Homestay with half board or in rented apartments or studios.
Contact: Herve Aubert, Director.

CLIC INTERNATIONAL HOUSE
C/ Albareca 19, 41001 Seville, Spain. ☎ 095-450 21 31. Fax: 095-456 16 96. E-mail: clic@clic.es. Website: www.clic.es.
Courses offered: Spanish intensive courses year round. Junior programme during summer.
Duration of courses: Minimum 2 weeks.
Qualifications offered: Recreational.
Cost: From €270 (tuition only).
Accommodation: Choice of sharing flat with young Spaniards, CLIC IH halls of residence, living with Spanish family or living independently in flats.

COLLEGIUM PALATINUM
CH-1854 Leysin, Switzerland. ☎ 024-493 03 03. Fax: 024-493 03 00. E-mail: acs-schiller-cp@bluewin.ch. Website: www.american-college.com.
Part of Schiller International University, The American College of Switzerland.
Courses offered: Language courses combined with sport or recreational activities. Opportunity to study a university level course for 3 hours a week.
Duration of courses: Monday-Friday year round except at Christmas.
Qualifications offered: Courses are recreational but certificates of attendance and attainment may be awarded. College credits are awarded for completion of the combination course.

Cost: SFr370 per week. Obligatory activities fee and municipal tax at SFr55 and SFr30 respectively per week. Room and board SFr480 per person per week in a single room or SFr430 per person in a double. Cost of acquiring a Swiss residency permit and medical insurance must be borne by student.
Accommodation: In student residence.

COSTA RICA SPANISH INSTITUTE (COSI)
PO Box 1366-2050 San Pedro, San José, Costa Rica. ☎ 506-234 1001. Fax: 506-253 2117. E-mail: office@cosi.co.cr. Website: www.cosi.co.cr.
Courses offered: Spanish language classes. Students can choose between San José and a beach programme where classes are held in Manuel Antonio National Park. Outdoor activities such as hiking, boat trips, snorkelling, ocean kayaking and boogie boarding.
Duration of courses: 1-16 weeks or longer.
Cost: $345 per week for 20 hours group tuition plus a homestay. The beach programme costs $440 per week for group tuition plus homestay. Prices include tuition, cultural programme, airport pick-up, books and materials. Where the price includes a homestay, this covers a private room, breakfast, dinner and laundry service.
Accommodation: Homestay or hotel.

DID DEUTSCH-INSTITUT
Hauptstrasse 26, 63811 Stockstadt am Main, Germany. ☎ 6027 41770. Fax: 6027 417741/42. E-mail: office@did.de. Website: www.did.de.
Accredited by EAQUALS; certified by ISO 9001.
Courses offered: Short and long-term intensive German language courses year round in Berlin, Frankfurt and Munich. Summer programmes in many more cities throughout Germany. Tuition in small classes or on individual basis.
Duration of courses: 1 week up to 12 months.
Qualifications offered: Diploma examinations at the end of each course level, under supervision of the German Language Society, Wiesbaden.
Accommodation: Choice of homestays with German families; guesthouses and apartments also available.
Other services: Internships and high school year are also offered.

ECO-ESCUELA DE ESPANOL & BIO-ITZA
Calle Centromerica, Ciudad Flores, Petén 17001, Guatemala. ☎/fax: (502) 926-3202. E-mail: ecomaya@guate.net. Website: www.ecomaya.com.
Courses offered: Students learn Spanish in Guatemala's Petén region. Students accepted at all levels. All lessons are one-to-one with a certified teacher. Intense individual attention focuses on reading, writing, conversation and comprehension skills. In addition to personal language training, interested students are encouraged to participate in daily conservation and community development projects organised by the school, such as developing an interpretive nature trail, environmental education and restoration of public schools and libraries. Opportunities for knowledge exchange with local naturalists, midwives, chicle harvesters, etc. who can teach about traditional cooking and local recipes.
Duration of courses: Courses are offered at weekly intervals, starting every Monday throughout the year. Students may stay as long as they wish.
Cost: $175 per week including 20 hours of private Spanish instruction, lodging with a local famiily for 7 days and 3 meals a day.
Accommodation: Students stay with a host family within walking distance of the school. Accommodation is modest but comfortable. Students generally have their own rooms but share a bathroom and shower with the family.

EQUINOCCIAL SPANISH SCHOOL
Reina Victoria 1325 y Lizardo Garcia, Quito, Ecuador. ☎/fax: +593-2-256 4488. E-mail: service@ecuadorspanish.com. Website: www.ecuadorspanish.com.

Courses offered: One-to-one tuition combined with classes of up to 4 in Quito, Cuenca or other locations. Other options include academic and social studies in Spanish. Spanish also taught in the jungle, on the coast and in the rainforest aimed at travellers looking for adventure.
Duration of courses: 20 hours per week is standard though can be adjusted. Courses arranged in modules of 1 week.
Qualifications offered: Students who take more than 100 hours of Spanish classes earn a certificate from the Ecuadorian Ministry of Education.
Cost: $112 for standard one-week course in Quito. $6.80 per hour for private tuition.
Accommodation: Can be arranged with middle-class Ecuadorian families, in hostals and hotels. Price from $15 a day.
Other services: Voluntary work programme (see 'Directory of Voluntary Placements Abroad').

LA ESCUELA DE IDIOMAS D'AMORE
PO Box PO 67-6350, Quepos, Costa Rica. ☎/fax: (506) 777-1143. E-mail: damore@sol.racsa.co.cr. Website: www.escueladamore.com. Contact numbers in Wisconsin (☎/fax 262-367-8598) and California (☎/fax 310-435-9897).
Founded in 1992. Original beach school and campus in Costa Rica.
Courses offered: Intensive Spanish immersion for anyone over 18. Located near Manuel Antonio Beach and National Park with on-campus butterfly farm.
Duration of courses: 2, 3, or 4 weeks Monday to Friday.
Cost: Courses with homestay cost $980 for 2 weeks, $1,325 for 3 weeks and $1,690 for 4 weeks.
Contact: David D'Amore, Director.

ESTUDIO SAMPERE
Lagasca 16, 28001 Madrid, Spain. ☎ 91-431 4366. Fax: 91-575 9509. E-mail: jmanuel@sampere.es. Website: www.sampere.es.
Member of IALC (see entry earlier in this section).
Courses offered: Spanish language and culture.
Duration of courses: 12, 16 and 24 weeks starting the first Monday of every month (except December).
Qualifications offered: Courses leading to D.E.L.E. Certificates of the Ministry of Education and Instituto Cervantes are offered.
Cost: €110 per week.
Accommodation: Homestay and student rooms from €90 per week.
Contact: Juan M. Sampere, Director.

EXPERIENCIA CENTRO DE INTERCAMBIO BILINGUE
Leyva 200, Colonia Las Palmas, Cuernavaca, Morelos, Mexico. ☎ 777-312 65 79. E-mail: experiencia@experienciacuernavaca.com. Website: www.experiencia.com.mx.
Courses offered: Spanish immersion classes. Excursions are offered on Saturdays at no extra charge. There is also an evening cultural exchange between Mexican students studying languages at the school.
Duration of courses: Year round classes beginning each Monday; students may stay for as many weeks as desired.
Qualifications offered: Certificate of completion.
Cost: $160 per week and discounts for 4 or more weeks of study. $100 registration fee required. Accommodation available in houses/dorms.

EXPERIMENT PARIS
89 rue de Turbigo, 75003 Paris, France. ☎ 1-44 54 58 03. Fax: 1-44 54 58 01. E-mail: incoming@experiment.france.org. Website: www.experiment.france.org.

French counterpart of EIL in UK (see 'Directory of Specialist Gap Year Programmes').
Courses offered: Serious language courses offered at universities (e.g. universities of Nantes, Poitiers and Angers). Also internships.
Duration of courses: Summer courses, 1 semester or 1 academic year.
Cost: From €5,000 per semester including accommodation.
Accommodation: Private rooms in student residences.
Contact: Anne Blassiau, Incoming Programmes Manager.

FOREIGN STUDENT SERVICE
Oranje Nassaulaan 5, 1075 AH, Amsterdam, Netherlands. ☎ 020-671 5915. Fax: 020-676 0555. E-mail: ucn@antenna.nl. Website: www.antenna.nl/ucn/fss/fss.html.
FSS provides information about the various courses which can be taken in Holland. It offers a survey of schools and institutions which organise Dutch language courses for foreigners, leading to Dutch educational levels MAVO, HAVO or VWO.

GLS SPRACHENZENTRUM BERLIN
Kolonnenstr. 26, 10829 Berlin, Germany. ☎ 30-78 00 89/0. Fax: 30-787 41 92. E-mail: germancourses@gls-berlin.com. Website: www.german-courses.com.
Courses offered: Language courses offered year round at all levels, starting every Monday. Central location near Brandenburg Gate and New Reichstag.
Duration of courses: 20, 30 or 40 lessons per week for any number of weeks. International mix in classes of about 8.
Cost: Sample price for 2 weeks German language course with 20 weekly lessons, activity programme and self-catering single room is €620.
Accommodation: Shared apartments, bed and breakfast, host family or budget hotels available through accommodation service. Single rooms on adult courses; double or multi-bedded for junior summer programmes.
Other services: Extended sightseeing programme in and around Berlin. GLS runs an internship programme combining a language course of at least 4 weeks with a work experience placement in a Berlin-based company (seee *Directory of Work Experience*).
Contact: Dorothee Robrecht, Director of Marketing.

GOETHE INSTITUT
Headquarters in Munich, Germany. Website: www.goethe.de. UK address: 50 Princes Gate, London SW7 2PH; 020-7596 4000. E-mail: german@london.goethe.org.
Courses offered: German language at all levels in dozens of locations in Germany and worldwide. All course details and institute addresses are on website. Summer courses offered in four locations including Heidelberg and Lake Constance.
Duration of courses: Variable.
Qualifications offered: The Goethe Institut administers its own language exams at all levels, e.g. the ZdaF, KDS and GDS.

IMAC
Instituto Mexico-Americano de Cultura, A.C., Bi-Cultural Courses, Donato Guerra No. 180, Col. Centro. Guadalajara, Jalisco, C.P. 44100 Mexico. ☎ 33-3613 1080. Fax: 33-3613 4621. E-mail: spanish-imac@imac-ac.edu.mx. Website: www.spanish-school.com.mx.
Member of GWEA (Global Work Experience Association).
Courses offered: Spanish to students from around the world. Group classes and private tutoring.
Duration of courses: Minimum 1 week. New classes start every week so flexible start dates.
Qualifications offered: Transferable credits for US schools and colleges.

Cost: 4 hours of tuition a day costs $194 per week, $517 for 4 weeks. Private lessons cost $100 a week for 1 hour a day. Discounts offered for longer stays. Free unlimited internet, e-mail and multimedia lab.
Accommodation: Homestay programme costs $98 per week, including 3 meals a day. Hotel accommodation available at a discounted rate.
Contact: Alberto Garcia.

INSTITUTO ALLENDE
Ancha de San Antonio 20, San Miguel de Allende Gto, Mexico 27700. ☎ 415-152 0226/152 0173. Fax: 415-152 4538. E-mail: iallende@instituto-allende.edu.mx. Website: www.instituto-allende.edu.mx.
Incorporated into the University of Guanajauto since 1950.
Courses offered: Spanish courses at various levels of intensity. Conversational involves 50 minutes a day, semi-intensive 2 hours a day; intensive 6 hours a day and total impact (one-to-one). Other courses in painting, drawing, photography and many others (see entry for Art Courses).
Duration of courses: 4 weeks normal minimum for group courses. Others may be shorter.
Qualifications offered: Academic credits available at US universities, e.g. one after 15 hours of Spanish classes.
Cost: $470 for intensive 4-week course, $250 for semi-intensive, and $125 for conversation. Total impact costs $13 an hour.
Accommodation: Family homestays cost $22 a day including 3 meals.
Contact: Guillermo Engelbrecht, Dean of Enrolment.

INSTITUTO CHAC-MOOL
Privada de la Pradera 108, Colonia Pradera, Cuernavaca, Morelus, Mexico. ☎ 777-317 1163. Toll-free from US: 1-888-397-8363. E-mail: spanish@chac-mool.com. Website: www.chac-mool.com.
Courses offered: Spanish immersion classes. Courses offered at 10 levels. When a student's ability falls between 2 levels, one-to-one instruction can be arranged to bring the student up to the higher level.
Duration of courses: Classes begin each Monday year round.
Qualifications offered: Certificate of completion.
Cost: $180 per week; slightly higher June-September. Discounts for enrolling for 5 weeks or longer. $100 registration fee required.
Accommodation: With Mexican families; $17-$24 per day.
Contact: Deana and Julia Najera, Owners.

INSTITUTE OF MODERN SPANISH
Mérida, Yucatan, Mexico. Toll-free from US: 1-877-463-7432. Fax: 775-213-0406. E-mail: 4merida@modernspanish.com. Website: www.modernspanish.com.
Courses offered: Spanish language and conversation for all ages and ability levels; Mexican and Mayan culture classes.
Duration of courses: Any number of weeks, beginning every Monday. Recommended minimum 2 weeks. 4, 5, 6, or 8 hours per day.
Qualifications offered: Transcripts are offered which can be used for college credit at many American colleges and universities.
Cost: From $300 for course plus full room and board with Mexican host families selected by the school.
Accommodation: Homestays or hotels.

INSTITUTO INTERNACIONAL EUSKALDUNA
PO Box 195545, San Juan, Puerto Rico 00919-5545. ☎ 787-281-8013. Fax: 787-274-8291. E-mail: study@spanishinpuertorico.com. Website: www.spanishinpuertorico.com.

Courses offered: Spanish (and English).
Duration of courses: Starts every Monday. Flexible duration. Recommended minimum 1 month. Long-stay course lasts 3 semesters. Minimum age 18. Average age 34.
Qualifications offered: University credit given by certain US universities.
Accommodation: Homestay with local family, half-board or just lodging.
Other services: Arrangement possible whereby students give English classes in exchange for Spanish so that accommodation would be only expense. Extracurricular activities offered.
Contact: Sacha Delgado, Director.

INTERCULTURA LANGUAGE & CULTURAL CENTRE
PO Box 1952-3000, Heredia, Costa Rica. ☎ (506) 260-8480. US ☎ 800-205-0642. Fax: (506) 260-9243. E-mail: info@interculturacostarica.com. Website: www.interculturacostarica.com.
Courses offered: Spanish language, literature and culture, Latin dance, cooking, music and lectures on feminism, indigenous peoples, ecology, intercultural communication and Costa Rican customs. Language courses are eligible for US college accreditation. Intensive Spanish courses in colonial town of Heredia or at the beach in Playa Sámara.
Duration of courses: 1 week to 1 year. Average duration is 1-2 months.
Cost: US$1,125 per month and $275 per week after 4 weeks, including all classes and homestay with breakfast and dinner.
Other services: Intercultura often hosts students between secondary school and university for up to a year. Voluntary work can be arranged if requested.
Contact: Laura Ellington, Director.

INTERNATIONAL CENTER FOR HELLENIC AND MEDITERRANEAN STUDIES (DIKEMES)
College Year in Athens, PO Box 17176, 100 24 Athens, Greece. ☎ 210-7560 749. Fax: 210-7561 497. E-mail: programs@dikemes.gr. Website: www.cyathens.org. US office: PO Box 390890, Cambridge, MA 02139 (617-868-8200; fax 617-868-8207; info@cyathens.org).
Courses offered: College Year in Athens in autumn and spring semesters as well as various summer courses, e.g. a study tour of the major archaeological sites of Crete and mainland Greece. Two tracks offered: Ancient Greek Civilisation including three levels of ancient Greek language, and East Mediterranean Studies including study of modern Greek at two levels.
Duration of courses: Full year course divided into two semesters (Sept-Dec and Jan-May). Summer courses last 3 or 6 weeks in May/June.
Cost: Approx £2,000 for summer courses; Year in Athens costs $10,800 per semester.
Accommodation: Self-catering shared flats in Athens with study bedrooms and communal kitchen, or air-conditioned hotel. Choice of hotel or self-catering studio apartment for summer courses on the island of Paros.

INTER-SEJOURS
179 rue de Courcelles, 75017 Paris, France. ☎ 1-47 63 06 81. Fax: 1-40 54 89 41. E-mail: marie.inter-sejours@libertysurf.fr. Website: http://asso.intersejours.free.fr.
Courses offered: Language courses as part of a homestay in Paris (and French students placed abroad).
Duration of courses: Minimum 1 week up to 34 weeks, with starting dates at specific times throughout the year.
Qualifications offered: Opportunity to work towards the D.E.L.F. examination and the *Certificat Pratique de Français*.
Cost: Examples of price in Paris: 30 lessons in 2 weeks would cost €610. A standard course with 20 lessons over 2 weeks costs €440.

Accommodation: Accommodation and breakfast with a host family costs €160 per week either in Paris or the suburbs. Same arrangement with half board would cost €175. Prices including breakfast from €219 per week.
Contact: Marie-Helene Pierrot, Director.

KOINE
Via Pandolfini 27, 50122 Florence, Italy. ☎ 055-213881. Fax: 055-216949. E-mail: info@koinecenter.com. Website: www.koinecenter.com.
Courses offered: Italian language for foreigners offered year round in Florence, Lucca and Bologna, and from spring through autumn at schools in Cortona and Orbetello.
Duration of courses: 1 week to 6 months.
Qualifications: Certificate C.I.L.S. from Siena University.
Cost: €495 for a month's tuition plus €375 for a month's basic accommodation without use of kitchen. 2-week homestay from €235, 3 weeks for €315.
Accommodation: With an Italian family.

LORENZO DE' MEDICI
Via Faenza 43, 50123 Florence, Italy. ☎ 055-287360. Fax: 055-239 8920. E-mail: info@lorenzodemedici.it. Website: www.lorenzodemedici.it.
Courses offered: Group or individual Italian language courses. Customised courses for special needs. Youth language programme, from scratch to proficiency.
Duration of courses: From 1 week.
Cost: Group tuition costs from €170 for one week, €590 for one month. 5 hours of private tuition cost €140.
Other services: Possible to combine language course with art course (see entry for *The*

Art Institute of Florence). Extracurricular activities offered weekly.
Contact: Margherita Rulli, Registrar.

MALACA INSTITUTO
Calle Cortada 6, 29018 Málaga, Spain. ☎ +34 952-29 3242. **Fax:** +34 952-29
6316. **E-mail: espanol@malacainstituto.com. Website: www.malacainstituto.com.**
Courses offered: A variety of Spanish language and culture classes are offered, from
standard beginner to preparation for university entrance. Gap-year students normally take
courses of between 16 and 36 weeks. Hispanic Studies programme is especially suitable.
In addition, a range of short courses includes Spanish + Dance, Commercial Spanish and
General Intensive Spanish, Summer Courses and one-to-one tuition.
Duration of courses: Hispanic Studies Term I – 16 weeks; Term II – 20 weeks. Academic
Year – 36 weeks.
Qualifications offered: Students can work towards the D.E.L.E. examinations or Spanish
university entrance if their level of language is suitably advanced.
Cost: 2-week intensive course would cost €328; 16-week D.E.L.E. examination preparation
would costs €2,298 including lessons, materials required, introductory party, a tour of
Malaga, Flamenco and Salsa lessons, use of swimming pool and accident insurance.
Additional costs are airfare, accommodation, excursions, medical insurance and external
examination fees. 4 weeks of accommodation costs €244 in Student Apartments, €621
with host family on a half-board basis, and €540 at Club Hispanico.
Accommodation: All types with single and twin rooms.

MESTER SPANISH COURSES
Vázquez Coronado 5, 37002 Salamanca, Spain. ☎ 923-21 38 35. **Fax:** 923-21
38 41. **E-mail: mester@mester.com. Website: www.mester.com.**
Courses offered: Spanish at all levels offered in Granada, Malaga, Salamanca, Seville
and Tenerife and on specific dates in Barcelona, Leon, Madrid and Valencia.
Duration of courses: 1-40 weeks starting every Monday. 40-week Academic Year course
includes language classes (including business Spanish) and Spanish culture. Participants
need not know much Spanish before starting in September
Qualifications offered: Some courses are recreational; others lead to D.E.L.E. and
Certificate of Business Spanish (exam fees extra).
Cost: From €138 (for a no-frills week-long course of two lessons of conversation and two
of grammar);
Accommodation: Full range including homestays, student flats, university residences
and (in Granada and Salamanca only) independent apartments. Tenerife accommodation
is in flats and residential complex 12 minutes from two beaches.
Contact: Saturnino Pérez López-Arias.

MOSCOW INSTITUTE FOR ADVANCED STUDY
**Lebyazhii Pereulok 8, Building 1, Moscow, Russia 119019. US office: 156 W 56th
St, 7th Floor, New York, NY 10019.** ☎ 212-245-0461. **Fax:** 212-489-4829. **E-
mail: info@mifas.org. Website: www.studyabroad.com/moscow.**
Courses offered: Intensive Russian language courses, history, literature, political science,
art and culture. Internships also organised (see 'Directory of Work Experience').
Duration of courses: 2 months in summer, 3½ months in autumn and spring semesters.
Cost: $6,800-$7,800 all-inclusive (excluding airfares) in autumn and spring, $4,500 in
summer.
Accommodation: Dormitory or homestay.
Contact: Johanna Brownell, Administrative Director.

OIDEAS GAEL
Foras Cultuir Uladh, Gleann Cholm Cille, Co Donegal, Ireland. ☎ 073-30248. **Fax:**
073-30348. **E-mail: oideasgael@eircom.net. Website: www.Oideas-Gael.com.**

Courses offered: Irish language lessons at all learning levels. Separate cultural activity courses in (for example) pottery, set dancing, landscape and culture, marine painting, archaeology, hill walking and folklore, flute playing and Bodhran playing.
Duration of courses: From 1 week.
Qualifications offered: Recreational only.
Cost: From £90.
Accommodation: Choice of host family, self-catering and on-campus accommodation.

OLE SPANISH LANGUAGE SCHOOL
Mariano Escobedo No. 32, Col. Centro, C.P. 76000, Querétaro, Qro., Mexico. ☎ 442-214 4023. Fax: 442-214 2628. E-mail: info@ole.edu.mx. Website: www.ole.edu.mx.
Courses offered: Spanish immersion programmes open at all levels and for all ages. Intensive group programmes, one-to-one and cultural classes. Special junior and senior programmes.
Duration of courses: Courses start every Monday all year round; minimum stay 1 week, no maximum.
Qualifications offered: School offers certificate for each level completed. Academic credit available.
Cost: From $115 per week. Additional costs include $60 registration fee and course books at $24 each.
Accommodation: It is preferred that students stay with families in the nearby area, costing $150 per week for a single room with 3 meals per day. Other accommodation options available are apartments, pensions, cabins and hotels.
Other services: School arranges recreational, extracurricular and cultural activities, city tours, field trips and weekend trips.
Contact: Miss Karina Ayala, Director.

POINT3 LANGUAGE CENTER
404 rue St-Pierre, Bureau 201, Montréal, Québec H2Y 2M2, Canada. ☎ (514) 840-7228. Fax: (514) 840-7111. E-mail: info@point-3.com. Website: www.point-3.com.
Courses offered: French, English (intensive, semi-intensive, semi-private and private) Spanish, Japanese (semi-private, private). Group Learning Vacation Programs, TOEFL Preparation Courses, ESL and North American Business & Communication Skills.
Duration of courses: 2 weeks to 1 year.
Cost: Sample price for 36 weeks of Intensive French: C$6,653 for tuition, $100 registration fee, $150 accommodation application fee, $740 for 4 weeks homestay including 2 meals a day or $650 for 4 weeks in a student residence, $75 airport pick-up fee.
Accommodation: Homestay (French, English or bilingual), student residences, furnished apartments.
Contact: Yuriko Nadeau.

THE PROBA INTERNATIONAL EDUCATIONAL CENTRE
PO Box 109, Lappeenranta, Fin 53101, Finland. ☎ +007-812-234 5024. Fax: +007-812-346 2758. E-mail: info@studyrussian.spb.ru. Website: www.studyrussian.spb.ru.
Courses offered: Russian language courses, courses at teachers' homes, Study & Work and volunteer programmes in St. Petersburg, Russia. Cultural programme including a weekly excursion or theatre visit.
Duration of courses: From 2 weeks (20 lessons per week) in groups of 4. Semester-long courses also available, 5 months from September, January or May. Language course followed by 4 or 8 weeks volunteering in hospitals, kindergartens, summer camps or teaching English in schools.
Qualifications offered: An examination can be taken at the end of the semester course and there is the possibility of obtaining a Diploma in the Russian language.

Cost: 4-week course followed by 4 weeks of volunteering costs US$2,100; 8-week course followed by 8 weeks volunteering costs $2,850. Semester course costs from $5,000. Cost includes accommodation and visa support but not airfares.
Accommodation: Single room in a Russian host family home near the city centre or at least close to an underground station. Possible alternatives in a hotel or hostel (on request).
Contact: Mr. Slava Oguretchnikov, Director General.

PROYECTO ESPANOL
C/ García Morato 41, 03004 Alicante, Spain. ☎ 965-23 06 55. Fax: 965-14 53 30. E-mail: info@proyecto-es.com. Website: www.proyecto-es.com.
Courses offered: Intensive Spanish language courses in Alicante and Granada. A cultural and language exchange is also organised.
Duration of courses: From 2 weeks to 6 months.
Qualifications offered: A certificate is offered upon completion of the course.
Accommodation: Students can stay in a family with full or half board or in an apartment shared with other students.

RUTA DEL SOL SPANISH SCHOOL
Tarqui 231 & 12 de Octubre, Quito, Ecuador. ☎/fax: 2-554612. E-mail: rutade lsol33@hotmail.com. Website: www.rutasolacademy.com.
Courses offered: Spanish and Quechua language courses.
Duration of courses: 12-week Spanish course, 10-week Quechua course.
Qualifications offered: Recreational courses for travellers plus others lead to diploma of Ministerio de Educacion del Ecuador.
Cost: One-to-one lessons cost $5 for Spanish, $10 for Quechua.
Accommodation: Homestay with Ecuadorian families costs $13 a day.
Other services: Teaches Andean culture and has a gallery of naïf Ecuadorian art.
Contact: Jorge Tasiguano and Guiovana Camino.

RYUKOKU UNIVERSITY JAPANESE CULTURE & LANGUAGE PROGRAM
67 Tsukamoto-cho, Fukakusa, Fushimi-ku, Kyoto 612-8577, Japan. ☎ 75-645 7898. Fax: 75-645 2020. E-mail: ric@rnoc.fks.ryukoku.ac.jp. Website: www.ryukoku.ac.jp/english/english1.
Courses offered: Intensive Japanese language programme.
Duration of courses: One year: 2 semesters April-August and September-February.
Qualifications offered: Recreational.
Accommodation: 4 dormitories for foreign students.
Other services: Classes offered on Japanese culture including theatre, religion and business.

IL SILLABO
Via Alberti 31, 52027 San Giovanni Valdarno (AR), Italy. ☎ 055-912 3238. Fax: 055-942439. E-mail: info@sillabo.it. Website: www.sillabo.it.
Courses offered: Italian language and literature courses, cooking, drawing, painting and history of art.
Duration of courses: 2-40 weeks.
Qualifications offered: C.I.L.S.
Cost: From €220 for 1 week intensive instruction (20 hours).
Accommodation: Single or shared apartments, host family, hotel. Sample price €285 for a fortnight's single room with breakfast.
Other services: Internships in tourism-related companies and restaurants are available after course. Can search for other kinds of placement on request.
Contact: Anna Paola Bosi, Director.

SOCIEDAD HISPANO MUNDIAL
San Anton, 72 (Edif. Real Center), 18005 Granada, Spain. ☎ 958-01 01 72. Fax: 958-01 01 73. E-mail: info@shm.edu. Website: www.shm.edu.
Courses offered: Spanish language courses in Granada, in Almuñecar on the coast and Guadix (Spanish and horsebackriding). Combination programmes in more than one centre can be arranged. All courses include a free programme of social and cultural activities (e.g. flamenco, monuments, tapas tour, Spanish cooking, literature workshop).
Duration of courses: Normally 1 month but any length from 1 week to a year. Language courses offered year round. Specialised courses last a minimum of 2 weeks.
Cost: 4-week course costs €450-€750 plus accommodation with host families, in hostels, student residence or shared flats.
Other services: Opportunity to sit D.E.L.E. exams. Excursions in and around Granada and Andalucia arranged and also to Morocco. Extra activities provided: ceramics, hiking, diving, sailing, etc.
Contact: José Antonio Ruiz Cantero, Director.

SOCIETY FOR CO-OPERATION IN RUSSIAN AND SOVIET STUDIES (SCRSS)
320 Brixton Road, London SW9 6AB. ☎ 020-7274 2282. Fax: 020-7274 3230. E-mail: ruslibrary@scrss.org.uk. Website: www.scrss.org.uk.
Courses offered: Russian language courses in Moscow and St Petersburg with possibilities for homestays. There is also a centre in London which organises lectures, and advises on visits and exchanges, as well as providing a library, language centre and visual aids collection.
Duration of courses: 1 week to 10 months.
Qualifications offered: Certificates of completion.
Cost: 2 weeks on a language course at Moscow University, staying in double room hostel accommodation would cost £480. 10 months in St Petersburg living with a family would cost £4,873 (excluding airfares and insurance).
Accommodation: Homestays, bed and breakfasts or hostels..

TERRE DES LANGUES
32 bis, rue de Clocheville, 37000 Tours, France. ☎ 2-4731 13 00. Fax: 2-47 64 20 81. E-mail: france@terredeslangues.com. Website: www.terredeslangues.com.
Courses offered: Summer courses in Paris, Tours, Cannes and Nice. Semester and year-long programme including high school and homestay placement at large range of schools throughout France.
Duration of courses: 4 months (term), 6 months (semester) and 9 months (year).
Cost: €2,560 for 4 months (September-December), €3,300 for 6 months (January-June) and €3,950 for full academic year.
Accommodation: Homestay.
Contact: Pascal La Vigoureux, Director.

UNIL COURS DE VACANCES
BFSH2, University of Lausanne, CH-1015 Dorigny, Switzerland. ☎ 21-692 30 90. Fax: 21-692 30 85. E-mail: CoursDeVacances@vac.unil.ch. Website: www.unil.ch/cvac.
Courses offered: French for all levels from elementary.
Duration of courses: Minimum 3 weeks; maximum 12 weeks. Intensive 6-week courses for beginners between July and September.
Qualifications offered: Courses are serious but no diploma at the end, only an *attestation*.
Cost: SFr500 per 3 weeks, SFr1,100 for 6 weeks.
Accommodation: List of suitable accommodation given on website or can be fixed up via tourist office (www.lausanne-tourisme.ch/Hotels.F_Pensio.htm).

LA UNION SPANISH SCHOOL

1A Avenida Sur No. 21, Antigua, Guatemala. ⬚/fax: (502) 832-7337. E-mail: launion@conexion.com. Website: www.launion.conexion.com.

Organisation for sharing Spanish language and Guatemalan culture run by a group of experienced Guatemalan Spanish teachers.

Courses offered: One-to-one lessons. Placements can be made on voluntary projects after study (see entry).

Duration of courses: Minimum 1-2 weeks.

Cost: 4 hours of morning tuition for 5 days costs $95; 25 hours for $105, 30 hours for $115 and 35 hours for $125. Afternoon sessions cost less, e.g. 20 hours for $70 and 25 hours for $80.

Accommodation: Homestays cost $60 a week.

Contact: Juan Carlos Martinez, General Director.

UNIVERSITE DE PERPIGNAN

Centre Universitaire d'Etudes Françaises, 52 av. de Villeneuve, 66860 Perpignan-Cedex, France. ☎ 4-68 66 60 50. Fax: 4-68 66 03 76. E-mail: ue@univ-perp.fr. Website: www.cuefp.com.

Courses offered: French courses at all levels.

Duration of courses: Offered year round. Semester courses October-January, February-May or full year October-May.

Qualifications offered: D.E.L.F., D.A.L.F, etc.

WIENER INTERNATIONAL HOCHSCHULKURSE

Universität, A-1010 Vienna, Austria. ☎ 1-405 12 54-0. Fax: 1-405 12 54-10. E-mail: wihok@univie.ac.at. Website: www.univie.ac.at/WIHOK.

Courses offered: German courses.

Duration of courses: 13 weeks, beginning either in October or March. 15 lessons per week, 5 days a week.

Qualifications offered: A certificate is awarded for regular attendance and for passing the final examination.

Cost: The course fee per semester is €580, plus a registration fee of €20 (valid for one year).

Art, Design, Drama & Film Courses

Art & Design

ACADEMIA DEL GIGLIO

Via Ghibellina 116, 50122 Florence, Italy. ☎/fax: 055-230 2467. E-mail: info@adg.it. Website:www.adg.it.

Courses offered: Art and art history courses in addition to Italian language courses described above. Fresco workshop available over 4 weeks.

Duration of courses: Mainly one or two week courses with 14 hours of tuition per week.

Cost: 1-week course costs €181, 2 weeks costs €336. Enrolment fee of €41.

Accommodation: All kinds of accommodation can be arranged from single room in a family for €26 a day half-board to €750 for 4 weeks in a self-catering flat sharing kitchen and other facilities.

Other services: Visits and social activities included in the price.

Contact: Lorenzo Capanni, Assistant Director.

ART HISTORY ABROAD

26 De Laune St, London SE17 3UU. ☎ 020-7277 4514. Fax: 020-7740 6126.

E-mail: info@arthistoryabroad.com. Website: www.arthistoryabroad.com.
Founding member of the Year Out Group.
Programme description: Unique programme that looks to broaden participants' sense of self as well as cultural and intellectual horizons. Tuition in art, history, Italian sociology, architecture, politics, philosophy, economics, music, poetry, theology, literature and classics. 6 weeks of travel throughout Italy including Venice, Verona, Florence, Siena, Naples and Rome plus at least 6 other cities. All tuition is on-site and in groups of no more than 8.
Duration and time of programme: 6-week course offered 3 times a year (Autumn, Spring and Early Summer) and 2-week course offered in July/August.
Cost: £5,100 for the Autumn, Spring and Early Summer courses and £2,100 for the shorter Summer course. Fee for 6-week course includes drawing classes, materials, Italian conversation classes and private visit to the Vatican Museum.
Accommodation: Shared rooms in hotels in the city centres.

THE ART INSTITUTE OF FLORENCE LDM
Via Dell'Alloro 14R, 50123 Florence, Italy. ☎ 055-283142. Fax: 055-289514. E-mail: info@lorenzodemedici.it. Website: www.lorenzodemedici.it.
Courses offered: Fresco restoration, graphic arts, painting and drawing, printmaking, photography, video production, interior design, sculpture, ceramics, jewellery, fashion design, art history. All classes conducted in English.
Duration of courses: 1 month in summer, semester or year long.
Qualifications offered: Certificate programme.

THE ART SCHOOL – ART UNDER ONE ROOF
Via Pandolfini 46R, 50122 Florence, Italy. ☎/fax: 055-247 8867. E-mail: arte1@arteurope.it. Website: www.arteuropa.org.
School located a 5-minute walk from the Ponte Vecchio in the centre of Florence in a 14th century palazzo.
Courses offered: Core areas are painting and drawing, figurative sculpture, boutique and interior design, fresco and decorative techniques, ceramics and other electives.
Duration of courses: 13-14 weeks in a semester. Also 2-semester Academic Year Foundation Programme suitable for post-A level candidates.
Accommodation: Single or shared rooms with use of kitchen facilities.
Other services: Language courses also offered. Other electives included in the programme are jewellery-making, mosaics, painting restoration, furniture restoration, Renaissance and Baroque art history. Studio art summer courses held in Paris and the south of France.

CAMBRIDGE SCHOOL OF ART AND DESIGN
Round Church Street, Cambridge CB5 8AD. ☎ 01223 314431. Fax: 01223 467773. E-mail: enquiries@catscollege.com. Website: www.cambridgeartschool.c om or www.ceg-uk.com.
Pre-university study programmes in art, design and media.
Courses offered: Art foundation course and portfolio courses. Subject options include painting and drawing, sculpture, art of architecture, ceramics, metal work, fashion, textiles, graphics and illustration, photography and video. Also offer drama courses (see separate entry below).
Duration of courses: One year for the foundation course and one term for the portfolio courses.
Qualifications offered: The art foundation course offers a diploma on completion; the portfolio course is recreational.
Cost: Approx £3,830 per term.
Accommodation: Hostels, family or self-catering.

CENTRAL ST MARTINS COLLEGE OF ART AND DESIGN
Southampton Row, London WC1B 4AP. ☎ 020-7514 7015. Fax: 020-7514 7016. E-mail: shortcourse@csm.linst.ac.uk. Website: www.csm.linst.ac.uk/shortcourse.
Courses offered: Fashion Folio, Graphic Design Portfolio Course and a wide range of evening, weekend and vacation courses. Summer school courses are also run July-September.
Qualifications offered: None; most courses are suitable for post-university gap students. Drawing for Portfolio Preparation open to those under 18.
Accommodation: Halls of residence near the college are available for summer courses.

CHIPPENDALE INTERNATIONAL SCHOOL OF FURNITURE
Myreside, Gifford, East Lothian EH41 4JA. ☎ 01620 810680. Fax: 01620 810701. E-mail: info@chippendale.co.uk. Website: www.chippendale.co.uk.
Courses offered: Non-residential professional course in furniture design, making and restoration.
Duration of courses: 30 weeks commencing each October.
Qualifications offered: Internationally recognised qualification.
Cost: £10,450.
Contact: Anselm Fraser, Principal.

INSTITUTO ALLENDE
Ancha de San Antonio 20, San Miguel de Allende Gto, Mexico 27700. ☎ 415-152 0226/152 0173. Fax: 415-152 4538. E-mail: iallende@innstituto-allende.edu.mx. Website: www.instituto-allende.edu.mx.
Incorporated into the University of Guanajauto since 1950.
Courses offered: Painting, drawing, sculpture, ceramics, etching, jewellery, batik, weaving, photography and art history as well as Spanish language.
Duration of courses: 2 weeks minimum.
Qualifications offered: Academic credits available at US universities, e.g. one after 15 hours of Spanish classes.
Cost: $470 for intensive 4-week course, $250 for semi-intensive, and $125 for conversation. Total impact costs $13 an hour.
Accommodation: Family homestays cost $22 a day including 3 meals.
Contact: Guillermo Engelbrecht, Dean of Enrolment.

JOHN HALL PRE-UNIVERSITY COURSE
12 Gainsborough Road, Ipswich, Suffolk IP4 2UR. ☎ 01473 251223. Fax: 01473 288009. E-mail: info@johnhallpre-university.com. Website: www.johnhallpre-university.com.
Courses offered: A pre-university course covering art, art history, architecture, music, opera, literature, history and Italian cinema. Introductory week in London including the museum and commercial art world is followed by six weeks in Venice where daily lectures and visits (including a private visit to San Marco) are combined with practical classes in life-drawing and photography, with optional Italian classes and visits to Palladian villas in the Veneto. The extensions of a week in Florence and five days in Rome continue the study of history, art, music and architecture on-site and include private visits to the Uffizi, the Accademia, the Keats Shelley Museum, the Vatican and Sistine Chapel.
Duration of courses: 1 week London, 6 weeks Venice. Extensions: 1 week Florence, 5 days Rome. Offered annually from late January.
Qualifications: Interest and enthusiasm.
Cost: 1 week London and 6 weeks Venice: £5,800; Florence £795, Rome £770. Travel to and from Italy, entrances, accommodation including breakfast and dinner in Italy, are included in fees. Accommodation in London not included.
Contact: Clare Augarde, Secretary.

THE JOHN HALL PRE-UNIVERSITY COURSE

London VENICE Florence Rome

- entirely different from any other cultural programme in Italy

January to March annually for Students of the Arts and Sciences.
Lectures/on-site visits given by a team of writers, artists,
musicians and university lecturers.
Art History, Music, Architecture, Conservation, History,
Opera, Literature, Design, Cinema.
Visits include Padua, Ravenna, Villas and gardens near
Venice, Florence and Rome.
Private visit to the Vatican Museums and Sistine Chapel.
Classes: Life Drawing, Photography, Italian Language.

**Information from: The Secretary,
12 Gainsborough Road, Ipswich IP4 2UR
Tel: 01473-251223   Fax 01473-288009**
email: info@johnhallpre-university.com   www.johnhallpre-university.com

LONDON COLLEGE OF FASHION
20 John Princes St, London W1G 0BJ. ☎ 020-7514 7566. Fax: 020-7514 7490. E-mail: dali@lcf.linst.ac.uk. Website: www.lcf.linst.ac.uk.
Courses offered: Intensive short evening and day courses in all fashion-related subjects.
Duration of courses: 3-5 days or 4-10 weeks. Courses commence October, January and May. Summer School June-September.
Qualifications offered: Certificate of Attendance.
Cost: Prices range from £205 to £2,225.
Other services: Help can be given finding accommodation.
Contact: DALI Office.

STEVE OUTRAM TRAVEL PHOTOGRAPHY WORKSHOPS
D.Katsifarakis Street, Galatas, Chania 73100, Crete, Greece. ☎ 28210-32201. Fax: 28210-28210. E-mail: mail@steveoutram.com. Website: www.steveoutram.com.
Courses offered: Photo Workshops held annually in Western Crete, Lesbos and Zanzibar. Maximum 8 people (of mixed ability).
Duration of courses: 9-14 days.
Cost: US$2,050 per person, excluding travel.
Accommodation: Renovated hotels with character.

STUDIO ART CENTERS INTERNATIONAL (SACI)
Palazzo dei Cartellone, Via Sant'Antonino 11, Florence 50123, Italy. ☎ 055-289948. E-mail: info@saci-florence.org. Website: www.saci-florence.org.

Courses offered: Studio art, art history, Italian language at all levels and Italian culture courses in Florence.
Duration of courses: Semester courses September-December or January-April. Summer courses May-June and June-July.
Qualifications offered: The post baccalaureate programme is a one-year programme taken between completion of an undergraduate degree and a master's degree. Aimed at students who did not major in art or do not have enough of a background in art to pursue an MA or Master of Fine Art. All undergraduate courses can be taken for university credit.
Cost: Tuition is $8,250 per fall semester, $3,300 for late spring or summer. Plus housing costs of $3,000 and $2,300 respectively.
Accommodation: Furnished apartments throughout Florence.
Contact: Karl Baisch, Co-ordinator.

Drama & Film

CAMBRIDGE ARTS & SCIENCES (CATS)
Round Church Street, Cambridge CB5 8AD. ☎ 01223 314431. Fax: 01223 467773. E-mail: drama@catscollege.com. Website: www.ceg-uk.com.
Pre-university study programmes in art, design and media.
Courses offered: Drama foundation course in association with RADA. Training and experience in acting and theatre production.
Duration of courses: One academic year.
Qualifications offered: The course aims to help students to attain entry to drama degree programmes at university.
Cost: Approx £3,830 per term.
Accommodation: Hostels, family or self-catering.

GREEK DANCES THEATRE
8 Scholiou Street, Plaka, 105 58 Athens, Greece. ☎ 210-324 4395. Fax: 210-324 6921. E-mail: mail@grdance.org. Website: www.grdance.org.
Courses offered: Short courses for foreigners in Greek folk dance and folk culture in conjunction with evening performances in outdoor theatre near the Acropolis.
Duration of courses: 1 week between May and September. 4 hours of instruction every afternoon.
Cost: €110. Volunteers must fund their own stay in Athens.

LONDON ACADEMY OF PERFORMING ARTS
Saint Matthew's Church, St Petersburgh Place, London W2 4LA. ☎ 020-7727 0220. Fax: 020-7727 0330. E-mail: admin@lapadrama.com. Website: www.lapadrama.com
Courses offered: Summer School for Shakespearean Acting. Course is for amateurs or professionals who wish to update their Shakespearean skills.
Duration of courses: 4 weeks.
Cost: £850.
Accommodation: None is provided.
Follow-up: Possibility of further training.
Contact: Brian Parsonage Kelly, Administrative Director.

NEW YORK FILM ACADEMY
100 E 17th St, New York, NY 10003. ☎ 212-674-4300. Fax: 212-477-1414. E-mail: film@nyfa.com. Website: www.nyfa.com.
Courses offered: Film-making including writing, producing, directing and editing film in New York, London (King's College) and Universal Studios (LA).
Duration of courses: One year course starting in July or September. Short 4 and 8-week

courses also available.
Cost: $25,000 tuition for full year course about $4,000 extra for film, processing and production expenses.
Contact: Juhi Shareef, Director of Student Affairs.

ROYAL OPERA HOUSE EDUCATION
Covent Garden, London WC2E 9DD. ☎ 020-7212 9410. Fax: 020-7212 9441. E-mail: education@roh.org.uk. Website: www.royaloperahouse.org.
Courses offered: 'Behind-the-Scenes' course at the Royal Opera House, primarily for 18-22 year olds.
Duration of courses: 5 days in April, offered annually.
Qualifications offered: Purely recreational.
Other services: Work placements/internships also offered (see entry in 'Directory of Work Experience').
Contact: ROH Education.

THE SCHOOL OF THE SCIENCE OF ACTING
67-83 Seven Sisters Road, London N7 6BU. ☎ 020-7272 0027. Fax: 020-7272 0026. E-mail: find@scienceofacting.org.uk. Website: www.scienceofacting.org.uk.
Courses offered: 1 year Acting course. The aim of the course is for the students to understand the basic laws of good acting and to become competent professionals. Students study the syllabus through lessons in theory and a series of assessed exercises. In addition students have classes in the study of Voice, Movement, Dance and other subjects including histories of Art, Music, Psychology and Philosophy. Students take part in the Directing students' exercises, exam days and the Edinburgh Festival. This accumulated knowledge and experience lead to the presentation of two end-of-course plays.
Duration of courses: 1 year of 4 terms.
Qualifications: Certificate of merit issued by the school.
Cost: Average £2,350 per term.
Accommodation: Not provided but help given with finding it.
Contact: Johan Aksell, Administrator.

UNIVERSITY OF DETROIT MERCY THEATRE COMPANY
8200 W Outer Drive, Box 94, Detroit, MI 48219, USA. ☎ 313-993-6463. Fax: 313-993-6465. E-mail: beeraj@udmercy.edu. Website: http://theatre.udmercy.edu.
Courses offered: Study and perform classical drama in amphitheatres in Greece. 3 weeks of movement, voice and acting workshops and classes in Greek myth, drama and classical culture. 1 week touring performance of a fully mounted comedy and tragedy.
Duration of courses: 4-week programme from early June. 6 hours college credit available (though not required).
Prerequisites: Minimum age 16, average 20. Auditions necessary but they need not be face-to-face. If unable to attend auditions in Detroit, Chicago or New York, applicants can send a tape with a comic and a serious monologue and a song, as well as a resumé and 8 X 10 photo. Must be English-speaker (any nationality). Applications should be submitted in February though possible to apply until April. Primarily looking for acting ability but spots for singers, dancers and technicians too.
Accommodation: Private rooms in one-time boys' boarding school on the island of Spetses. While touring, students stay in double rooms in hotels.
Contact: Dr. Arthur Beer, Program Director.

YEAR OUT DRAMA COMPANY
Stratford-upon-Avon College, Alcester Road, Stratford-upon-Avon, Warks. CV37 9QR. ☎ 01789 266245. Fax: 01789 267524. E-mail: yearoutdrama@strat-avon.ac.uk.

Founding member of Year Out Group.
Courses offered: Challenging, intensive, practical Drama course specific to Gap Year students. Led by experts in professionally equipped performance spaces. Students benefit from working with theatre professionals on varying disciplines including Acting Techniques, Voice, Movement, Directing, Text Study and Performance. Students perform annually at the Edinburgh Fringe Festival.
Duration of courses: September to July, split into three terms.
Cost: £4,000 for the year which includes all production costs, travel and tickets for frequent theatre trips. Accommodation costs are extra.
Accommodation: Students can live in halls of residence, with landladies or in shared houses.
Follow-up: Students are given help with auditions and UCAS applications. The Company has strong support from The Royal Shakespeare Company and other working professionals.

Business Skills Courses

CAVENDISH COLLEGE
35-37 Alfred Place, London WC1E 7DP. ☎ **020-7580 6043. Fax: 020-7255 1591. E-mail: learn@cavendish.ac.uk. Website: www.cavendish.ac.uk.**
Member of British Accreditation Council.
Courses offered: Art & Design (foundation), Business Studies, Travel and Tourism, Secretarial training and Hotel Management.
Duration of courses: Majority are 6 or 9 month foundation courses.
Qualifications offered: General foundation courses with possibilities for HNDs in Business Studies.
Follow-up: Suitable background for going on to foundation academic and vocational courses for university entrance.

GSC BUSINESS & SECRETARIAL COLLEGE
17 Chapel St, Guildford, Surrey GU1 3UL. ☎ **01483 564885. Fax: 01483 301896. E-mail: mail@g-s-c.co.uk. Website: www.g-s-c.co.uk.**
Member of BAC.
Courses offered: Full-time, part-time and one-day courses in the following subjects: Computing & Information Technology, Business & Administration, such as PA Diploma, Private Secretaries' Diploma, Legal Secretaries Certificate or Diploma, Business Administration and Shorthand. Online learning courses also available.
Duration of courses: Flexible start dates on many courses. Full-time courses run 15-24 weeks. Range of 1-day IT courses available. Touch Typing and Computing start at any time. Other start dates are variable. Business Secretarial and Marketing run for less than 15 weeks. LCCI run for 21+ weeks.
Cost: As in literature from GSC. For example, intensive secretarial and administrative course lasting 15 weeks costs £2,990.
Other services: Students can take an additional language or a Business/Language course.
Contact: Victoria Alexander (Principal), Cheryl Dunn (Centre Manager).

KUDOS TRAINING LIMITED
Suite 10, The Sanctuary, 23 Oakhill Grove, Surbiton, Surrey KT6 6DU.
☎ **020-8288 8766. Fax: 020-8288 8764. E-mail: jvev@kudostraining.org.**
Website: www.kudostraining.demon.co.uk.
Courses offered: One-term full-time intensive course leading to Privatate Secretary's

Diploma or Executive Secretary's Diploma which are professional qualifications of the London Chamber of Commerce & Industry (Educational Development International). Subjects include Business Administration, Communication for Business, Principles and Practice of Management, Audio/Touch Typing. Subject to demand, Pitmans shorthand is also offered.

Qualifications offered: LCCI as above.

Cost: Approximately £800 per term (12-week terms). Government grants may be available to reduce cost.

Accommodation: Can be arranged; accommodation always provided during weekend intensive courses and examination periods.

Follow-up: Further courses can be taken at the school or by distance learning. Most of the students from Kudos Training have no difficulty finding suitable employment which makes it useful training for a gap year.

Contact: Mrs. Elaine Howard, Principal.

OXFORD BUSINESS COLLEGE
Kings Mead House, Oxpens Road, Oxford OX1 1RX. ☎ 01865 791908. Fax: 01865 245059. E-mail: enquiries@oxfordbusinesscollege.co.uk. Website: www.oxfordbusinesscollege.co.uk.

Courses offered: Career Skills courses which include a paid work placement, combining training and experience. 3, 6 and 9 month professional qualifications from CIM for those planning a marketing career to enhance earning potential. Business qualifications for employment or for university entrance.

Duration of courses: 6 weeks to 9 months with flexible start dates.

Qualifications offered: Pitman, Chartered Institute of Marketing (CIM), Institute of Commercial Management.

Accommodation: Shared houses near college are available through the Accommodation Office. Host family accommodation can be arranged if preferred.

Follow-up: Many courses include optional work placement arranged by the college recruitment service which allows students to earn for college or travel funds as part of their course. Also encourage graduates to apply for the Mountbatten Internship Programme in New York (see USA chapter).

OXFORD MEDIA AND BUSINESS SCHOOL
Rose Place, Oxford OX1 1SB. ☎ 01865 240963. Fax: 01865 242783. E-mail: courses@oxfordbusiness.co.uk. Website: www.oxfordbusiness.co.uk.

Courses offered: 6-week Gap 'Life Skills' course is a total immersion in taught and practised IT skills designed to help people make the most of their Gap Year. Intensive tuition builds a broad base of job-related skills in Microsoft IT and communication skills; essential project work to tight deadlines simulates a temping assignment in terms of prioritising, time management, working in teams, and production quality; all of these are part of the Course Assessment. The school also offers Business Studies, Marketing and Fashion Studies.

Duration of courses: 9 months except for 6-week Gap Course.

Qualifications offered: ABE (Association of Business Executives) Diploma, CIM (Chartered Institute of Marketing) Stage I & II (Professional Level), ECDL.

Cost: Variable (consult website).

Accommodation: Shared houses within walking or cycling distance or host families in the locality.

Follow-up: Specialist in-house recruitment service, Careers Direct, helps the students in the transition from trainee to successful interviewee. Students can also be matched with an international student at the sister school of English for language exchange.

QUEEN'S BUSINESS & SECRETARIAL COLLEGE
24 Queensberry Place, London SW7 2DS. ☎ 020-7589 8583. E-mail:

info@qbsc.ac.uk. Website: www.qbsc.ac.uk.
Courses offered: Short modular courses of 1-6 weeks cover specific IT and Business Skills. Intensive IT and Business Skills, Executive and Personal Assistant, Marketing, PR and Advertising with IT and Business Skills courses.
Duration of courses: 1, 2 or 3 12-week terms, starting September, January or April.
Qualifications offered: OCR, LCCI and Pitman examinations.
Cost: From £2,750 for 1 term course. Short courses: 1 week £280-£320; 4 weeks £1,020-£1,175; 6 weeks £1,395-£1,595.
Accommodation: The College does not provide accommodation.
Follow-up: Career Preparation and job search skills are an important part of each course. The College has a strong relationship with a number of London recruitment agencies and is constantly approached by companies looking for well-trained staff. Work experience is an integral part of the 2 and 3 term courses and students on the shorter courses can be assisted in finding placements.
Contact: Corinne Bickford/Lucy Napper.

ST JAMES'S & LUCIE CLAYTON COLLEGE
4 Wetherby Gardens, London SW5 0JN. ☎ **020-7373 3852. Fax: 020-7370 3303. E-mail: information@sjlccollege.co.uk. Website: www.sjlccollege.co.uk.**
Course description: Most popular course for gap year students is the One Term Pre/Post University Course. 12-week course provides a platform from which students acquire the essential skills and confidence required to gain competitive temping rates. In addition to the core skills of keyboarding, IT and Teeline Shorthand, the course includes seminars in a range of personal development areas including assertiveness, interview techniques and self-defence. Also offers an introduction to marketing, public relations a hands-on creative advertising course and many others
Duration of courses: 12 weeks (one term) most suitable for gap students but many other options including short keyboarding and IT courses. Term courses start in September, January, April and July. Short courses start every Monday throughout the year.
Qualifications offered: CIPD Certificates in Personnel Practice, Training Practice and Management.
Cost: £180 + VAT for one week keyboard course up to £2,770 + VAT for a 12-week one-term course.
Follow-up: Free careers service, CV advice and interview techniques. Work experience forms an integral part of the longer courses. Many students at the end of their training are placed directly by associated recruitment consultancy.

Cookery Courses

APICIUS COOKING SCHOOL
Via Guelfa 85, 50123 Florence, Italy. ☎ 055-26 58 135. Fax: 055-26 56 689. E-mail: info@apicius.it. Website: www.apicius.it.
Courses offered: Professional programmes in culinary arts (at beginners, intermediate and advanced levels), wine expertise, hotel management, bakery and pastry, food packaging and design, etc. Non-professional classes in Italian cooking and wine appreciation.
Duration of courses: From short 1-week to year-long courses.
Qualifications offered: 1-year Diploma in culinary arts suitable for year out students.
Cost: Semester (professional course) is €5,240. Recreational courses from €105.
Other services: Opportunity to combine courses with Italian language and art. Professional programmes include 10 hours a week internship in local restaurants, wineries and hotels.
Contact: Gabriella Ganugi (President) and Valentina Monacò (Admissions Director).

BALLYMALOE COOKERY SCHOOL
Shanagarry, Co. Cork, Ireland. ☎ 21-46 46 785. Fax: 21-46 46 909. E-mail: info@cookingisfun.ie. Website: www.cookingisfun.ie.
Situated on organic farm by the coast with access to excellent ingredients.
Courses offered: 3-month Certificate in Cookery course. Range of short courses also offered.
Duration of courses: Certificate course starting each January and September. Short courses given between April and July, including two 1-week introductory courses in July.
Qualifications offered: Students who pass written and practical exams at end of course are awarded the Ballymaloe Cookery School Certificates of Food and Wine.
Cost: €6,995 for Certificate course excluding accommodation. 1-day course costs €185, 2½-day course €400 and 5-day Intro course €695.
Accommodation: Self-catering student accommodation in converted farm cottages costs €85 per week in twin room and €105 in single (2004 prices). Nightly charges for short courses are €25 shared, €32 single.
Contact: Susan Fahy, Secretary.

CHALET CUISINE
Chalet Gene Di Ver, Les Allues, Meribel 73550, France. ☎ 6-32 89 84 21. E-mail: info@chaletcuisine.com. Website: www.chaletcuisine.com.
Courses offered: Cookery and Chalet Management.
Duration of courses: 6 days, 7 nights. Offered once a month between June and November or at other times on request.
Cost: £499 including meals and transfer. (No-frills flights available from London for £50.)
Accommodation: Full accommodation provided in chalets.
Follow-up: Help given in finding a job in the ski industry.
Contact: Chris Dixon, Owner.

COOKERY AT THE GRANGE
The Grange, Whatley, Frome, Somerset BA11 3JU. ☎/fax: 01373 836579. E-mail: info@cookery-grange.co.uk Website: www.cookery-grange.co.uk.
Courses offered: An intensive, hands-on cookery course.
Duration of courses: 4 weeks, offered 8 times per year.
Qualifications offered: Basic Food Hygiene Certificate. A certificate of attendance is also given and a letter of recommendation can be written for future employers, on request.
Cost: £2,390-£2,790.
Accommodation: Mainly twin rooms, although some single rooms are available for a

supplementary payment. Accommodation has a Games Room with a pool table, CD player, TV and video plus a tennis court.

Follow-up: The course equips students for working in ski chalets, on yachts, in shooting/ fishing lodges, working for outside catering companies, cooking for families at home or abroad and for a host of other cooking opportunities.

LE CORDON BLEU CULINARY INSTITUTE
114 Marylebone Lane, London W1V 2HH. ☎ **020-7935 3503. Fax: 020-7935 7621. E-mail: london@cordonbleu.net. Website: www.cordonbleu.net.**
Institute has branch in Paris and many other cities.

Courses offered: Le Cordon Bleu Essentials Course covers both basic and complex recipes, from traditional meals to vegetarian and ethnic recipes. The course includes an overnight trip to Paris.

Duration of courses: 4 weeks.

Qualifications offered: Le Cordon Bleu Essentials Course certificate.

Cost: about £2,000, including all ingredients, uniform and trip to Paris.

Accommodation: A list of accommodation agencies, hostels and hotels is available from the Admissions office. They are selected according to proximity to the school.

Follow-up: Le Cordon Bleu has strong links with some of the top ski companies, many of whom recruit directly from the school. The course is ideal for those wishing to work on yachts or find employment during their Gap Year or school and university holidays.

EDINBURGH SCHOOL OF FOOD AND WINE
The Coach House, Newliston, Edinburgh EH29 9EB. ☎ **0131-333 5001. E-mail: info@esfw.com. Website: www.esfw.com.**

Courses offered: Courses for aspiring cooks of all levels from basic to 'cordon bleu' standard cookery.
Duration of courses: 6-month Diploma, 5 Week Intensive and Chalet Cooks, 1 Week Summer Survival, 1 Day Courses.
Qualifications offered: Certified by the British Accreditation Council (BAC).
Cost: £70.50 for 1 day course; £365 for 1-week course; £2,000 for 4-week course; £2,500 for 5-week course; £8,500 for Diploma course.
Accommodation: Assistance always offered.
Follow-up: The School works closely with ski companies and agencies, offering opportunities in the UK and abroad.

FOOD OF COURSE COOKERY SCHOOL
Middle Farm House, Sutton, Shepton Mallet, Somerset BA4 6QF. ☎ 01749 860116. Fax: 01749 860765. E-mail: louise.hutton@foodofcourse.co.uk. Website: www.foodofcourse.co.uk.
Lou Hutton is a professional cook who has run her own catering business and has over 16 years teaching experience.
Courses offered: 4-week Foundation Cookery Course is ideal for gap year students who want to work in chalets, lodges and galleys, or simply to broaden their culinary expertise. This intensive hands-on course teaches classic and modern methods moving on to more complex recipes. Students are given Basic Food Hygiene Course tuition and examination whilst on course. Guest cooks and visits to local markets are organised throughout the course. For the experienced cook the 5-day intensive New Food Course introduces new tastes and timesaving recipes.
Cost: 4-week Foundation Course £2,450: 5-day New Food Course £720. Included in the costs are all meals, accommodation and equipment. A comprehensive recipe file is provided, together with useful food charts and tips. Single room supplement £50 per week.
Accommodation: In twin guest rooms with en-suite bathrooms and comfortable student sitting room with TV/DVD.
Follow-up: Graduates of the course can be put in touch with ski companies and employment agencies.
Contact: Lou Hutton, Principal.

GABLES SCHOOL OF COOKERY
Bristol Road, Falfield, Glos. GL12 8DL. ☎ 01454 260444. Fax: 01454 261821. E-mail: FranWinston@msn.com. Website: www.thegablesschoolofcookery.com.
Specialists in training chalet hosts.
Courses offered: 4-week cookery courses ideal for working in chalets or on yachts as well as providing lifelong cookery skills. Students gain experience in operational first-class

restaurant kitchen.
Duration of courses: 4 weeks available year round.
Prerequisites: Minimum age 17; average ages 18-25.
Qualifications offered: School certificate equivalent to NVQ 2/3.
Cost: £2,395 inclusive.
Accommodation: three-star accommodation in twin rooms with ensuite bathrooms.
Follow-up: School aims to find positions for all graduates.
Contact: Fran Winston, Principal.

KILBURY MANOR COOKERY COURSES
Colston Road, Buckfastleigh, Devon TQ11 0LN. ☎ 01364 644079. Fax: 01364 644059. E-mail: suzanne@kilbury.co.uk. Website: www.kilbury.co.uk.
Courses offered: Tailor-made courses for beginners to advanced, amateurs or professionals. An intensive, hands-on approach to cooking.
Duration of courses: To suit individuals. Standard is 2-night stay with 12 hours cooking.
Cost: £325 per person for one-on-one tuition, fully inclusive; £185 per person for a group of four.
Accommodation: In one of three bedrooms at the Manor Farmhouse where the courses are held, with en suite and colour television.
Contact: Suzanne Lewis.

LEITHS SCHOOL OF FOOD AND WINE
21 St. Albans Grove, London W8 5BP. ☎ 020-7229 0177. Fax: 020-7937 5257. E-mail: info@leiths.com. Website: www.leiths.com.
Courses offered: Basic Certificate in Practical Cookery, designed for Gap Year students and suitable for anyone wishing to assist in chalets, villas and lodges. Longer alternative course offered: Beginners' Certificate in Food and Wine. Both courses comprise demonstrations and practical cooking, including meat, fish and vegetable preparation, pastries, puddings and sauces.
Duration of courses: Basic Certificate lasts for 4 weeks full-time in September. Beginners' Certificate 10 weeks October-December.
Qualifications offered: Basic Certificate in practical cookery. Beginners' Certificate in Food and Wine.
Cost: 4 weeks £1,955 for the course, plus extra fees of around £150 for various extras such as cookery books, clothing and an equipment wallet. 10 weeks £4,350 plus extras.
Follow-up: The company also runs Leiths List, an agency for cooks, which helps to place ex-students in suitable careers.

THE MANOR SCHOOL OF FINE CUISINE
Old Melton Road, Widmerpool, Nottinghamshire NG12 5QL. ☎/fax: 01949 81371.

Courses offered: Cookery courses covering basics and more advanced creative skills suitable for those embarking on a career in the culinary profession.
Duration of courses: 5-day Beginners' Foundation Course and 4-week Certificate Course, Monday to Friday.
Qualifications offered: A graded certificate on successful completion.
Cost: Beginners' course costs £525 residential, £450 non-residential. Certificate course costs £2,350 with accommodation, £2,000 without.
Accommodation: Students stay in the 17th Century Manor, site of the cookery school.
Follow-up: A letter of recommendation may be issued for future employment. Skills learned are ideal for careers in chalet cooking, yachts, directors' dining rooms, outside catering, hotels and shooting lodges.

MIRANDA HALL – CHALET COOKS
Old School, Hambleton, Oakham, Rutland LE15 8TJ. ☎ 01572 723576. E-mail: chaletcooks@hall.vispa.com. Website: www.hall.vispa.com/chaletcookscourse.
Courses offered: Chalet cooks courses. Candidates under 21 train as chalet assistants. Every menu has a built-in vegetarian version for speed and ease. Instruction given on coping with varied diets, crisis management and a course on wine in addition to high altitude cake recipes, canapés and interesting breakfasts that every chalet cook needs. Students are given the chance to cook a three-course meal and cakes every day.
Duration of courses: 5 days, Monday to Friday, offered last two weeks of October and possibly November.
Qualifications offered: Certificate recognised by more than 30 chalet companies with which owner is in touch.
Cost: £495 inclusive of accommodation.
Accommodation: Fully residential (Manor House, Hambleton).
Contact: Miranda Hall, School Owner/Lecturer.

THE MURRAY SCHOOL OF COOKERY
Glenbervie House, Holt Pound, Farnham, Surrey GU10 4LE. ☎ 01420 23049. Fax: 01420 23049. E-mail: KMPMMSC@aol.com Website: www.cookeryschool.net.
Courses offered: Cookery certificate courses.
Duration of courses: Certificate course lasts 4 weeks; Chalet Chef course lasts 1 week. Held in January, March, July and September.
Qualifications offered: The Certificate Course is accredited by major ski chalet operators, yacht catering agencies and by major companies offering retraining schemes. The Chalet Chef course is approved by major ski holiday operators.
Cost: £1,500 for a 4-week course. Chalet chef course costs £395.

Accommodation: Local bed and breakfasts are available at £25 per night.
Follow-up: The courses are designed for people wanting to work in ski chalets or on yachts.
Contact: P Murray.

NATIVES.CO.UK
39-43 Putney High St, London SW15 1SP. ☎ **08700 463355. Fax: 0845 127 5048. E-mail: info@natives.co.uk. Website: www.natives.co.uk/skijobs/cookery.**
UK's leading website for finding jobs in ski and summer resorts.
Courses offered: Cookery courses offered at a girls' school in Surrey or in Rutland. Practical cookery courses designed for winter staff and taught by seasonal workers who know what the job involves and can share hands-on experience.
Duration of courses: 1 week, 4 times a year (July, August, October).
Prerequisites: Minimum age 21.
Qualifications offered: Course is recognised through the industry. Participants receive Alpine Cooking Advice Manual.
Cost: £379-£495 including 4 nights accommodation.
Other services: Also conduct half-day job workshops (cost £11.99) once a month for ski resort work.
Follow-up: Guaranteed job through natives.co.uk for those who pass.
Contact: Vicky Brown, Recruitment Manager.

ROSIE DAVIES
Penny's Mill, Nunney, Frome, Somerset BA11 4NP. ☎ **01373 836210. Fax: 01373 836018. E-mail: info@rosiedavies.co.uk. Website: www.rosiedavies.co.uk.**
Courses offered: A cookery course beginning with essential skills and basic techniques but moving on to more complex aspects. Part of the course will include the specialist skills needed to cook in a chalet or on board a yacht.
Duration of courses: 4 weeks.
Qualifications offered: Certificate of completion and a Basic Hygiene Certificate.
Cost: £2,450 including accommodation.
Accommodation: Twin bedded rooms with toilet/shower room and sitting area with TV/video.
Follow-up: Ideal for becoming chalet hosts and yacht cooks.

TANTE MARIE SCHOOL OF COOKERY
Woodham House, Carlton Road, Woking, Surrey GU21 4HF. ☎ **01483 726957. Fax: 01483 724173. E-mail: info@tantemarie.co.uk. Website: www.tantemarie.co.uk.**
UK's largest independent cookery school, accredited by the BAC.

Courses offered: Variety of practical courses suitable for gap year students. Cordon Bleu Certificate course (11 weeks) offers a formal qualification useful for students who wish to work in ski chalets and on yachts as well as gaining temporary employment during university vacations. The Essential Skills course (4 weeks) is a good foundation though there is no formal qualification. Beginners Course lasts 1 or 2 weeks and is a basic introduction to cookery.
Duration of courses: Essential Skills course offered in July, September, October, January and April; Cordon Bleu Certificate course begins September, January and April. Beginners course offered in mid-July.
Qualifications offered: Internationally recognised qualifications including Cordon Bleu Diploma and Certificate.
Cost: £1,800 for Essential Skills, £4,250 for Certificate Course and £450 for 1-week Beginners or £775 for 2-week Beginners.
Accommodation: With homestay families arranged via the school
Follow-up: Essential Skills course recognised by many ski operators. Tante Marie offers employment advice and has good industry contacts.
Contact: Gill Hurst.

LA VIEILLE FORGE
4 Rue de Burguet, Berlou, 34360 Herault, France. ☎ 4-67 89 48 63. E-mail: holidays@la vieilleforge.com. Website: www.lavieilleforge.com/chalet_courses.
Courses offered: Chalet cookery courses offered in the Languedoc region of France. Classes for up to 3 participants.
Duration of courses: 3½ days Monday-Thursday between August and November.
Cost: £499 inclusive of all meals, accommodation and return flight from Montpellier, Carcasonne or Nimes.
Accommodation: Own guest house.
Contact: John McFetridge (☎ 0871 717 4278), Director of Winter Adventure Company, 53 High Street, Crail, Fife KY10 3RA; www.winteradventure.co.uk).

Sport & Activity Courses

BASE CAMP GROUP
Howick, Balls Cross, Petworth, West Sussex GU28 9JY. ☎ 01403 820899. Fax: 01403 820063. E-mail: contact@basecampgroup.com. Website: www.basecampgroup.com.
Programme description: Gap Snowsports Programme in the Alps and Rockies whereby students learn about and improve at skiing and snowboarding and have the chance to obtain a recognised ski or snowboard instructor's qualification. Chance to improve skiing and riding (off-piste, freestyle, racing, etc.). Also chance to improve spoken French and take first aid course, avalanche course, ski and snowboard tuning clinics and go on a variety of trips.
Destinations: Meribel (France), Verbier (Switzerland) and Whistler (Canada).
Duration and time of placements: 11-week intensive programme from beginning of January.
Qualifications offered: BASI qualifications are accepted in France, Austria, Italy and the UK.
Number of placements per year: 100.
Prerequisites: Some skiing/snowboarding experience recommended.
Costs: £5,500-£5,800 excluding insurance. Includes accommodation throughout, mostly in four-person flats.

Contact: Fergie Miller, Marketing Director.

BLUE DOG ADVENTURES
Amwell Farm House, Nomansland, Wheathampstead, St. Albans, Herts. AL4 8EJ. ☎ 01582 831302. Fax: 01582 834002. E-mail: info@bluedogadventures.com. Website: www.bluedogadventures.com
Courses offered: Programme of adventure internships includes sail training on Canada's largest tallship, scuba DiveMaster training in the Caribbean and Guanacaste (Costa Rica), PADI scuba courses on tropical island of Roatan, Honduras, and whitewater raft and kayak guide training in Morocco and Turkey.
Duration of courses: 1-3 months.
Prerequisites: Adventure Internships have various skill requirements.
Cost: 15 weeks on board the Canadian *Empire Sandy* in EarthShip sail training programme costs £2,435/$3,950; 31 weeks costs £4,680/$7,600.
Accommodation: Almost always included. Participants are met at the local airport upon arrival, and returned to the airport at the end of the adventure.
Contact: Jenna Troy, Adventure Co-ordinator.

BRITISH ASSOCIATION OF SNOWSPORT INSTRUCTORS (BASI)
Glenmore, Aviemore, Inverness-shire PH22 1QU. ☎ 01479 861717. Gap hotline: 01479 861409. Fax: 01479 881718. E-mail: basi@basi.org.uk. Website: www.basi.org.uk.
BASI runs training and grading courses throughout the year in five disciplines: Alpine Skiing, Snowboarding, Telemark, Nordic and Adaptive. BASI also publishes the *BASI News* in which job adverts for ski and snowboard instructors appear.
Courses offered: BASI Ski Gap Year course offered over 10 weeks leading to the first level ski or snowboard instructor's qualification. Courses take place from January to March in Europe (e.g. Aosta, Nendaz, Andorra) and the USA.
Prerequisites: Minimum age 16. Must demonstrate confidence in parallel skiing at preselection in the UK.
Cost: £3,800-£4,000.
Contact: Carol Clark, Gap Co-ordinator.

CANADIAN ASSOCIATION OF SNOWBOARD INSTRUCTORS
60 Canning Crescent, Cambridge, Ontario N1T 1X2, Canada. ☎ 519-624-6593. Fax: 519-624-6594. E-mail: info@casi-acms.com. Website: www.casi-acms.com.
Courses offered: Levels 1 to 4 Snowboard Instructor; Levels 1 to 3 Freestyle Coach; Levels 1 to 3 Race Coach.
Duration of courses: Level 1 Instructor and Coach – 3 days; Level 2 Instructor – 4 days; Level 3 Instructor and Level 2 Coach – 5 days; Level 4 Instructor – 7 days.
Qualifications offered: All CASI courses are certification courses.
Cost: Level 1 Instructor and Coach – C$250; Level 2 Instructor – C$325; Level 3 Instructor and Level 2 Coach – C$400; Level 4 Instructor – C$550.
Contact: Dan Genge, Executive Director & CEO.

DEUTSCH-INSTITUT TIROL
Am Sandhügel 2, 6370 Kitzbühel, Austria. ☎ 53-56 712 74. Fax: 53-56 723 63. E-mail: dit@kitz.netwing.at. Website: www.deutschinstitut.com.
Courses offered: German language combined with ski and snowboard instruction specially designed for gap year students.
Duration of courses: 12 weeks from end of September to just before Christmas. Course includes 8 weeks intensive German tuition at DIT in Kitzbühel interspersed with 8 3-day weekends skiing/snowboarding on the glacier at Kaprun. Also 7-day trip to Eastern Europe.
Qualifications offered: Preparation for Austrian ski/snowboard instructor exams.

Cost: €8,000 (£5,525) inclusive of everything except travel to Kitzbühel and insurance.
Accommodation: Half-board accommodation in Kitzbühel; full board in Kaprun.

FLYING FISH
25 Union Road, Cowes, Isle of Wight PO31 7TW. ☎ 0871 250 2500. Fax: 01983 281821. E-mail: mail@flyingfishonline.com. Website: www.flyingfishonline.com.
Flying Fish trains watersports staff and arranges employment for sailors, divers, surfers and windsurfers (see programme details in 'Directory of Specialist Gap Year Programmes').
Courses offered: Professional Diving training, International Yacht Training and Sail and Board Sports Instructor training programme. There is a specially organised modular scheme for Gap Year students offering training followed by work experience and a period of employment in Australia or Greece.
Duration of courses: Courses last from 2 weeks to 4 months. Training takes place in the UK at Poole Harbour in Dorset, in Australia at Sydney or the Whitsunday Islands, and in Greece at Vassiliki. Courses come with a 'professional' option where trainees take part in a period of work experience as an instructor.
Qualifications offered: Flying Fish courses lead to qualifications from the Royal Yachting Association (RYA), Professional Association of Dive Instructors (PADI), the Australian Yachting Federation (AYF) and Surfing Australia (SA).
Cost: Prices range from £790 for 2-weeks Windsurf Skillbuilder course in Greece to 17-week Dive Instructor Professional Traineeship in Sydney for £8,580.
Accommodation: Varies according to course and destination but always provided.
Follow-up: Possibility of extended employment after short work experience placements in the Mediterranean, the Caribbean or Australia. Qualifications gained can be used after the year out in holiday periods to gain extra cash.

THE INTERNATIONAL ACADEMY
St Hilary Court, Copthorne Way, Culverhouse Cross, Cardiff CF5 6ES. ☎ 02920 672500. Fax: 02920 672510. E-mail: info@international-academy.com. Website: www.international-academy.com.
Courses offered: Instructor training in outdoor activities that lead to internationally recognised qualifications. All training in line with governing bodies. Locations worldwide. Outdoor pusuits include skiing, snowboarding, whitewater rafting and diving. Courses allow people to turn their hobbies into a career or make the most of their Gap Year while training in exotic places like Whistler (British Columbia, Canada), Sunshine Coast (Queensland, Australia) and the Seychelles.
Duration of courses: 4-12 weeks.
Cost: £3,950-£7,950. Sample 12-week course with ski instruction and accommodation and board costs between £6,350 and £6,950 in Mammoth and Lake Tahoe (California), Stowe (Vermont) and Whistler, Lake Louise and Tremblant (Canada).
Contact: Cath Lewis, Operations Director.

NONSTOPSKI
1A Bickersteth Road, London SW17 9SE. ☎/fax: 020-8772 7852. E-mail: info@nonstopski.com. Website: www.nonstopski.com.
Courses offered: Ski and Snowboard Instructor Courses in Fernie, British Columbia, Canada. Training in mountain safety, avalanche awareness. Winter survival skills, first aid and ski and snowboard maintenance. Evening classes in French, Spanish, TEFL and cookery can also be taken.
Number of participants: 70 on 11-week course.
Duration of courses: 3-week course from late December to mid-January. 11-week programme runs from mid-January to early April.
Prerequisites: Minimum age 18 (about half of participants are gappers).
Qualifications offered: Internationally recognised CSIA (Canadian Ski Instructor

Alliance) and CASI (Canadian Association of Snowboard Instructors). Also CAA (Canadian Avalanche Association) Recreational Avalanche 1 certificate and St. John's Ambulance Basic first aid certificate. Freestyle and race coach qualifications can also be obtained. **Cost:** £2,999 for 3-week course includes accommodation, most meals, lift pass and all tuition. £5,800 for 11-week course includes flights, and weekend trips as well as the above.

Accommodation: Twin rooms in houses for 4-10 people with equipped kitchens, comfortable living rooms and cable TV.

Other services: Work experience may be arranged with local ski school and contacts with other ski schools for instructing jobs, provided candidate has working visa.

Contact: Rupert Taylor, Operations.

OUTWARD BOUND
Watermillock, Penrith, Cumbria CA11 0JL. ☎ 01768 485014. Fax: 01768 486983. E-mail: enquiries@outwardbound-uk.org. Website: www.outwardbound-uk.org.

Courses offered: Outdoor multi-activity courses at three centres in UK (Aberdovey in Wales, Loch Eil in Scotland and Ullswater in the Lake District) plus many abroad. Activities include mountaineering, canoeing, rock climbing, abseiling and in-grounds activities such as zip wire, trapeze and high ropes courses. See entry for *Outward Bound Global* in Directory of Expeditions.

Duration of courses: 1-2 weeks.

Qualifications offered: Recreational or possibility of NVQ key skills.

Cost: Financial assistance available.

Accommodation: Shared, single-sex rooms. There is usually at least one night away from the centre.

PEAK LEADERS
Mansfield, Strathmiglo, Fife KY14 7QE, Scotland. ☎ 01337 860079. Fax: 01337 868176. E-mail: info@peakleaders.com. Website: www.peakleaders.com.

Gap year ski and snowboard instructor courses in the Canadian Rockies and Argentina, and Jungle Expedition Leader Programmes with diving and sailing in Sumatra.

Courses offered: Ski and Snowboard instructor courses in Canada, Argentina and New Zealand. Course includes structured programmes of mountain safety, first aid, avalanche awareness and leadership. Courses held in the Canadian Rockies, Bariloche in Patagonia and Queenstown, New Zealand. Also Jungle Expedition Leader courses in the remote Riau archipelago of Indonesia. Diving, sailing and wakeboard modules are available.

Duration of courses: 3 Snowsport courses per year lasting 9 weeks: June–September in the southern hemisphere, January-March in the northern hemisphere. Jungle training with diving and sailing in Indonesia lasts 6 weeks in September/October (see entry for JET Asia in *Directory of Courses* for further details).

Qualifications offered: 5 internationally recognised qualifications: instructor, leader, mountain safety and avalanche awareness. Indonesian course can confer Jungle Expedition leader, first aid and PADI Open Water Diver. Both offer an introductory award in Team Leading, validated by the Institute of Leadership & Management (www.i-l-m.com).

Cost: £5,950 inclusive for Argentina and New Zealand, £5,650 for Canada. Indonesian trip costs £2,950 excluding flight to Singapore.

Other services: On winter courses, extras offered like skidoo driving, backcountry training, Spanish and French language, field trips to Argentine Patagonia and Chile. Work experience and advice on job opportunities worldwide.

Contact: David Hughes, Director.

PERFORMANCE YACHTING SAILING SCHOOL
Mayflower Marina, Ocean Quay, Richmond Walk, Plymouth, Devon PL1 4LS. ☎ 01752 5659023. Fax: 01752 569256. E-mail: info@performanceyachting.co.uk.

Website: www.performanceyachting.co.uk.
Contact: Carole Newman, Manager.
Courses offered: Sailing courses from beginner to Yachtmaster Ocean commercial endorsement. 14-week Fast Track course from beginner to Yachtmaster offshore attracts some gap year students.
Duration of courses: 5 days to 16 weeks. Courses run all year round. Fast Track starts February, May and September, with some flexibility.
Qualifications offered: All courses lead to RYA certification.
Cost: £370 for 5-day course, £6,800 for the Fast Track Course or £7,700 for extended 16-week which includes the Ocean theory and the MCA proficiency in medical care.
Accommodation Onboard for all practical courses. For Theory courses accommodation is at a nearby B & B.
Contact: Carole Newman.

PLAS MENAI
The National Watersports Centre, Caernarfon, Gwynedd, Wales. ☎ 01248 670964. Fax: 01248 670964. E-mail: plas.menai@scw.co.uk. Website: www.plasmenai.co.uk.
Courses offered: Professional Watersports Instructor Training and work experience programme.
Duration of courses: 26 weeks.
Qualifications offered: All courses lead to national governing body qualifications which allow graduates to become multi-qualified and teach a range of outdoor activities such as dinghy sailing, kayaking, climbing, cruising and windsurfing.
Cost: from £6,350 including full-board and accommodation in single rooms in shared house.
Follow-up: Graduates go on to teach at centres across the UK, abroad or to join a paid work experience programme.
Contact: Suzanne Creasey, Marketing Manager.

ROYAL YACHTING ASSOCIATION
RYA House, Ensign Way, Hamble, Southampton SO31 4YA. ☎ 0845 345 0374. E-mail: info@rya.org.uk. Website: www.rya.org.uk.
The RYA is the governing body for sailing and motor boating in the UK. It's the best starting place for any information about courses at every level for sailing or power boating.
Courses offered: First level is Competent Crew plus other advanced certificates.
Cost: £280-£400 for 5-day course.

SKI-EXP-AIR & EXP-AIR-GUIDE
770 Colonel Jones, Ste. Foy, Québec GIX 3K9, Canada. ☎ 418-654-9071. Fax: 418-654-9071. E-mail: info@ski-exp-air.com. Website: www.ski-exp-air.com & www.exp-air-guide.com.
Courses offered: Ski-Exp-Air is a ski and snowboard school located in Québec City serving an international clientele. Exp-Air-Guide is an Outdoor Adventure Guiding school which takes clients to the rivers and lakes surrounding Québec City to teach techniques for organising a wilderness trip. Course includes fast water and sea kayaking, canoe-camping and trekking.
Duration of courses: 3 months.
Cost: £6,400 for Ski-Exp-Air; £6,900 for Exp-Air-Guide. Discounts for early booking (before July 1st for ski and snowboard, before January 1st for wilderness programme).
Accommodation: College campus lodgings with private rooms.
Contact: Luc Fournier, Director.

SKI LE GAP
220 Wheeler St, Mont Tremblant, Quebec J8E 1V3, Canada. ☎ +001-819-429-

6599 or freephone from England 0800 328 0345. Fax: +001-819-425-7074.
E-mail: info@skilegap. Website: www.skilegap.com.
Programme description: Ski and Snowboard instructor's programme operating since 1994 specifically designed for gap year students from Britain. The course combines ski/snowboard instruction with French conversation lessons plus other activities such as igloo-building, dogsledding, extreme snowshoeing, and trips to Montreal, Quebec City and Ottawa.
Destinations: Quebec, Canada.
Number of placements per year: 200.
Prerequisites: All nationalities. Must be passionate about skiing, but all levels of ability accepted from beginners to expert.
Duration and time of placements: 3-month and 1-month placements from November.
Selection procedures and orientation: Places are reserved on a first-come, first-served basis so early reservations are advised.
Cost: £5,600 plus tax (£400) for 2004 for 3-month course. Price includes return London-Montreal airfare but not medical insurance or ski equipment. £2,600 for 1-month course excluding flights.
Contact: Amelia Puddifer, Programme Director.

SPORT AFRICA EXPERIENCE
**Guardian House, Borough Road, Godalming, Surrey GU7 2AE. ☎ 01483 860560.
E-mail: info@SportAfrica.org. Website: www.SportAfrica.org.**
Courses offered: Aspiring sportsmen and women can train and improve their sport in South Africa at the International Academies of Cricket, Rugby, Golf or Scuba. You will also have the chance to visit game reserves as part of the experience of being in Africa.
Duration of courses: 8 weeks for rugby, 8 weeks cricket, 4 weeks golf and 9-38 days scuba.
Prerequisites: Ideal for school leavers with dreams of developing their sport but who haven't been picked up by a county side and who want some excellent coaching and facilities in a good climate to take their game up to the next level.
Cost: Contact Sport Africa Experience for particulars. Part of costs are donated to the Sports Trust of South Africa and the Born Free Foundation to maintain the Big Cat Sanctuary.
Accommodation: Normally 3-star hotel.

UK SAILING ACADEMY
**West Cowes, Isle of Wight PO31 7PQ. ☎ 01983 294941. Fax: 01983 295938.
E-mail: info@uksa.org. Website: www.uksa.org.**
Courses offered: Windsurf, Dinghy, Kayak and Kitesurf Instructor Training, and Professional Crew and Skipper training courses. 2-week Jump Start or Mile Building course may be of interest to less experienced sailors.
Duration of courses: 12-17 weeks or a combination of courses over a year.
Qualifications offered: Beginners to Watersports Instructor/Yachtmaster.
Cost: £4,795 (Instructor training) to £8,495 (Crew & Skipper training).
Accommodation: Shared with 2 or 3 others.
Other services: On-site careers service to help with job placement. 700+ companies use UKSA for recruitment.

Gap Year Preparation

THE KNOWLEDGE GAP LIMITED
**Pitt Farmhouse, Chevithorne, Nr Tiverton, Devon EX16 7PU. ☎ 0117-974 3217.
Fax: 0117-974 3436. E-mail: info@kgap.co.uk. Website: www.kgap.co.uk.**

Courses offered: 2½ day residential gap year preparation and safety course which focuses on providing students with an appropriate mindset prior to departing on their year off. The course tries to instil an acknowledgement that preparation is valuable, that all cultural differences should be respected but also trains the candidate to avoid situations in which he or she must relinquish control to a stranger. Practical advice given on essential 'before you go activities', what to take, risks associated with accommodation and all types of transport. A qualified paramedic also provides a half day's training of first aid focusing on Road Traffic Accidents.

Duration of courses: 2½ day courses offered twice a week, i.e. Sunday afternoon to Wednesday midday, and Wednesday afternoon to Saturday midday. Offered between July and January only.

Cost: £350 per person (to maximum of 15) including hostel accommodation.

Contact: Henry Gordon Clark, Founder.

OBJECTIVE TEAM LTD

Bragborough Lodge Farm, Braunston, Daventry, Northants NN11 7HA. ☏ 01788 899029. Fax: 01788 891259. E-mail: office@objectiveteam.com. Website: www.objectivegapsafety.com.

Courses offered: One-day pre-gap year safety and security awareness training. Course includes a special section from a recently returned gapper and a separate briefing for female travellers.

Duration of courses: Course runs most weeks, usually Wednesdays though this can be flexible. Can be done on other premises, e.g. schools or offices.

Cost: £150 for an individual attending a course in London or Edinburgh.

Special features: The company runs safety training courses for travellers ranging from gap year travellers to journalists covering conflict zones. In all training they try to ensure input from the practitioners meaning that when conducting a gap year course they have a special section from a recently returned gapper and a separate briefing for female travellers.

Contact: Charlie McGrath, Director.

Miscellaneous Courses

ACHILL ARCHAEOLOGICAL FIELD SCHOOL

Achill Folklife Centre, Dooagh, Achill Island, Co. Mayo, Ireland. ☏ 98-43564. Fax: 98-43595. E-mail: achill-fieldschool@iol.ie. Website: www.achill-fieldschool.com.

Courses offered: Introduction to Irish archaeology, excavation methodology, landscape and architectural surveying. Emphasis on hands-on participation.

Duration of courses: 2 6-week modules between June and August. 1-week introductory course available.

Qualifications offered: Academic credit possible.

Cost: €595/$640 for 1 week, €2,200/$2,350 for 4 weeks, €2,700/$2,950 for 6 weeks, and €3,950/$4,250 for 12 weeks.

Accommodation: Modern self-catering houses and apartments.

AFRICAN ECO GAP

PO Box 704, Harrismith 9880, South Africa. ☏ +27 5862 30026. Fax: +27 5862-22955. E-mail: walkabout@internext.co.za.

Courses offered: African Ecology and Conservation course covers the basic elements of field guiding, 4 X 4 bush driving, foot safari in 'big five' country (with elephant, buffalo, rhino, lion and leopard), as well as experiencing an array of trees, grasses, birds, reptiles

and insects, located in South African wilderness areas.
Number of participants: 30.
Duration of courses: 28 days.
Prerequisites: For gap year students plus graduates in biology, zoology, anthropology and veterinary science.
Qualifications offered: Constitutes the practical module of the 2-year South African Game Rangers Diploma Course.
Cost: £835 excluding flights, visas and insurance.
Accommodation: Bush camp with tents or thatched huts.
Contact: Peter and Penny Schofield.

CHILCOTIN HOLIDAYS GUEST RANCH
Gun Creek Road, Gold Bridge, B.C., VOK 1PO, Canada. ☎/fax: (250) 238-2274. E-mail: adventures@chilcotinholidays.com. Website: www.chilcotinholidays.com/guidetraining.
Courses offered: Wilderness Guide Training for Adventure Tourism taught by a licensed Guide Outfitter. Provides participants with a working knowledge and practical skills for packhorse trips, ranch adventures, fishing, hunting, wildlife viewing and photo safaris. Modules cover guiding on horseback, horse handling, mountain riding, horse packing and shoeing, driving a team, backcountry living, wildlife habits, etc.
Duration of courses: 1 and 2 week graduated modular training programme. Short but intense modules offered in June, July and August.
Qualifications offered: Graduates receive a certificate, an apprenticeship logbook and job opportunity listing.
Cost: 1-week programme C$1,397; 2-week programme $2,450.
Accommodation: Ranch tent cabins and some high alpine camping.
Follow-up: Skills learned are required by a professional guide in adventure tourism. Suitable graduates can be assisted with employment with one of 400+ outfitters in the region.
Contact: Candra French.

CONSTANCE SPRY
Moor Park House, Moor Park Lane, Farnham, Surrey GU9 8EN. ☎ 01252 734477. Fax: 01252 712011. E-mail: info@constancespry.com. Website: www.constancespry.com.
Courses offered: Flower arranging, floristry and hospitality courses.
Duration of courses: 1 day to 20 weeks.
Qualifications offered: Professional courses lead to qualifications; the diploma course in Floristry Management is accredited by Middlesex University.
Cost: From £41.50 to £12,278 (including accommodation and VAT).
Accommodation: Provided in single and double bedrooms with washbasins and shared bathrooms.

EMERSON COLLEGE
Forest Row, East Sussex RH18 5JX. ☎ 01342 822238. Fax: 01342 826055. E-mail: mail@emerson.org.uk. Website: www.emerson.org.uk.
International adult education centre and community based on the work of Rudolf Steiner.
Courses offered: The Orientation Programme is aimed specifically at 18-21 year olds and gives the opportunity to spend a 6-9 week volunteer placement abroad in the second term. The course focuses on historical and contemporary cultural issues, group dynamics and the community and self development. Practical activities include drawing, painting, sculpture, drama, music, pottery, metal work, weaving, environmental work and building. Career development activities will be offered throughout the year. Other courses are run in puppetry, storytelling and creative writing, sculpture and organic agriculture.
Duration of courses: Mid-September to June.
Qualifications offered: Certificate of Completion.

Cost: £4,300 for tuition, £2,070 for accommodation (meals extra) plus £300-£700 during overseas placement.
Accommodation: Single room accommodation on campus is available for half the students. The rest live with host families in the village of Forest Row.
Contact: Ethan Friedman.

ICA:UK
PO Box 171, Manchester M15 5BE. E-mail: vsp@ica-uk.org.uk. Website: www.ica-uk.org.uk.
Courses offered: Short courses are offered for the orientation, training and preparation of prospective volunteers and a few placements are offered each year by local development organisations worldwide. There is an introductory orientation weekend for volunteers to explore the issues related to volunteering. Prospective volunteers are then guided through a process of preparation and training. The Volunteer Foundation Course consists of 3 days in September and 9 days in October. At this time participants are informed of placements currently available, and supported to apply for and negotiate the placement of their choice. Recent placements have included work in community projects in Bangladesh, Burkina Faso, Chile, Ghana, Guatemala, India, Mexico, Nepal, Peru, Portugal, Uganda and the USA.
Duration of courses: 1 weekend plus 3+9 days for the Volunteer Foundation Course certificate.
Cost: The initial weekend costs £90 (£60 concessions) and the Volunteer Foundation Course costs £990 (with concessions of up to £400 off).
Accommodation: Weekend courses are residential.
Follow-up: Many of the previous participants have gone on to work for volunteer groups and development agencies.
Contact: Angeline Attenborough, Ghee Bowman.

JET ASIA (JUNGLE EXPEDITION TRAINING)
c/o Turi Beach Resort, Batam Island, Indonesia. E-mail: info@jet-asia.com. Website: www.jet-asia.com.
JET Asia Jungle programme specifically for gap year students offered in conjunction with Peak Leaders UK Ltd (see entry). Batam Island is 30 minutes from Singapore.
Courses offered: Students undertake First Aid Training, Jungle Expedition Training, Jungle Survival, a 10-day Jungle expedition, Sailing, Diving (PADI) Certification, wakeboarding, waterskiing and golf, in addition to receiving an award from the Institue of Leadership and Management.
Duration of courses: 6 weeks in September/October. 8-day Emergency Survival course offered in February and November for advanced level expedition leaders.

JST YOUTH LEADERSHIP @ SEA SCHEME
Jubilee Sailing Trust, Hazel Road, Woolston, Southampton SO19 7GB. ☎ 023-8044 9108. Fax: 023-8044 9145. E-mail: info@jst.org.uk. Website: www.jst.org.uk.
For more information about the Jubilee Sailing Trust, see entry in 'Directory of Expeditions'.
Courses offered: Leadership course on a sea voyage to develop communication, leadership and team skills.
Prerequisites: Ages 16-25.
Selection procedures and orientation: By written application; mark form with 'Youth Leadership @ Sea' and enclose short personal statement.
Cost: The JST Youth Leadership @ Sea Scheme offers young people aged 16-25 up to £300 towards the cost of any voyage (prices start from £495).

OPERATION NEW WORLD LTD
4 Eccleston Square, London SW1V 1NP. ☎ 020-7931 8177. E-mail: al@operati

onnewworld.co.uk. Website: www.operationnewworld.co.uk.
Educational charity providing self-help programmes for unemployed young people.
Courses offered: Personal development and environmental studies for unemployed people aged 18-25.
Duration of courses: Weekend training in outdoor skills, following by 12 weeks part-time environmental studies course and then 2 weeks abroad working on a field studies project where trainees can put their new skills into practice. Recent destinations have been the Parc Naturel Regional on the coast of Corsica and on remote Swedish islands.
Cost: None.
Contact: Anne Leonard, Director.

ROYAL HORTICULTURAL SOCIETY
RHS Garden, Wisley, Woking, Surrey GU23 6QB. ☎ 01483 224234. Fax: 01483 211750. E-mail: timhu@rhs.org.uk. Website: www.rhs.org.uk.
The RHS serves to encourage and improve the science, art and practice of horticulture. Also offers an (over-subscribed) opportunity to volunteer student gardeners to work alongside experts for 1-4 months. Applicants must have completed a course of study in Vocational Horticulture.
Courses offered: Wisley Diploma in Practical Horticulture. Specialist one-year option certificates.
Duration of courses: 1 or 2 year courses starting September. Work is available year round.
Prerequisites: Ages 19-35. Candidates should have some horticultural training and a year's experience.
Cost: Trainees are paid £10,300 for the year.
Accommodation: Room, communal lounge and food are supplied.
Contact: Tim Hughes, Horticultural Training Officer.

VISITOZ
Springbrook Farm, MS 188, Goomeri, 4601 Queensland, Australia. ☎ 07-4168 6106. Fax: 07-4168 6155. E-mail: info@visitoz.org. Website: www.visitoz.org. UK Contacts: Will and Julia Taunton-Burnet, Visitoz, Grange Cottage, Shipton Road, Ascott under Wychwood, Oxfordshire OX7 6AY; ☎ 01993 832238/ 831972; fax 01993 830927; Mobiles 07966 528644 or 07771 992352; jules@visitoz.org or julesmltb@aol.com.
Courses offered: Training in all aspects of working on a rural property or in rural hospitality with guaranteed work in Australia afterwards. Instruction in tractor driving, horse riding, sheep and cattle work, fencing and chainsaw work OR bar and kitchen work, waitressing and hospitality work, drive-in bottle shop, roadhouse and housekeeping work.
Duration of courses: 5 days followed by 3-month jobs throughout rural Australia.
Cost: £595 includes airport pick-up, 3-day beachside jet lag recovery weekend, course and follow-up jobs for the duration of the visa.
Other services: Offers all successful candidates with working holiday visas the chance to fill one of 300 vacancies with some of the 950+ employers all over Australia who pay a minimum $300 per week after tax plus free board and accommodation. (Youth wages apply in some cases for those under 20 years of age.) Higher wages are available for top quality tractor drivers, chefs and cooks.
Contact: Dan and Joanna Burnet in Australia; Will and Julia Taunton-Burnet in UK.

WILDERNESS EXPERTISE
The Octagon, Wellington College, Crowthorne, Berkshire RG45 7PU. ☎ 01344 774430. Fax: 01344 774480. E-mail: info@wilderness-expertise.co.uk. Website: www.wilderness-expertise.co.uk.
Part of Expertise Consultancy Group. Wilderness Expertise was founded in 1995 and aims to provide the logistics, planning and safety systems for group travel of 6 or more

people anywhere in the world.
Courses offered: Expedition preparation course covers money and emergencies, basic first aid, insurance, language and cultural differences, keeping in touch with home. Also offer Remote Emergency Care first aid courses.

WORLD CHALLENGE EXPEDITIONS
Black Arrow House, 2 Chandos Road, London NW10 6NF. ☎ 020-8728 7222. E-mail: welcome@world-challenge.co.uk. Website: www.world-challenge.co.uk.
Programmes described in 'Directory of Specialist Gap Year Programmes' and 'Directory of Expeditions'.
Courses offered: Leadership Challenge offers 2 different adventure and skills courses based in the UK. Courses seek to raise motivation through developing skills in leadership, team building, decision making and problem solving.
Duration of courses: 4, 7 and 10 days.

PART III

Gap Year Opportunities
listed by Country

Europe

Worldwide

EUROPE

Benelux

Netherlands

The Dutch language is studied by so few students at university that the Netherlands does not attract very many gap year students. However for those who want to experience the country's liberal traditions of tolerance, longer term stays are better than just a brief sightseeing trip to Amsterdam.

Most Dutch people speak excellent English so a knowledge of Dutch is generally not essential for voluntary or seasonal work. The Netherlands has the lowest rate of unemployment it has had for 20 years so paid work is available. It may be worth spending a few months working to save for further travels. The Dutch have some of the most progressive laws in the world to minimise exploitation of workers. The minimum wages are very good for those over 23 but are less for younger workers.

Au Pairing

Since Dutch is not a language which attracts a large number of students, au pairing in the Netherlands is not well known; however there is an established programme for those interested and able to stay at least six months. Working conditions are favourable in that pocket money of €250-€340 is paid per month in addition to health insurance costs. The main agencies are reputed to offer solid back-up, guidance on contacting fellow au pairs and advice on local courses. The agency with the largest incoming au pair programme is *Travel Active* (PO Box 107, 5800 Venray; 0478-551900/info@travelactive.nl) which places au pairs aged 18-30 as well as sending Dutch young people abroad on various work exchanges.

Another important agency is *Activity International,* Steentilstraat 25, 9711 GK Groningen, or PO Box 7097, 9701 JB Groningen (050-31 30 666/fax 31 31 633; www.activityinternational.nl). Activity International annually places between 300 and 500 au pairs in the Netherlands for whom it organises meetings and trips as well as family placements. **Jill Weseman** was very pleased with the service Activity International provided and also with her experiences as an au pair in a village of just 500 people 30km from Groningen:

> After graduation I accepted an au pairing position in Holland, mainly because there is no prior language requirement here. I really lucked out and ended up with a family who has been great to me. Though the situation sounds difficult at best – four children aged 1½, 3, 5 and 7, one day off a week and a rather remote location in the very north of Holland – I have benefitted a great deal. The social life is surprisingly good for such a rural area.

The newest agency is Debora Aupair Services (Ipestrjitte 27, 9051 St. Stiens; 058-257 2760; info@aupair-services.nl; www.aupair-services.nl) established in 2002 which claims to have good contacts with the immigration service and so can offer assistance with visa applications for non-EU au pairs. Try also the House o Orange Au Pairs, Noordeinde 134b, 2514 GP The Hague (070-324 5903; www.house-o-orange.nl).

Voluntary Work

If you are in the Netherlands you might make enquiries of the Dutch workcamps organisation *SIW/Stichting Internationale Vrijwilligersprojekten* (Willemstraat 7, 3511 RJ Utrecht; 030-231 7721; www.siw.nl); otherwise apply through affiliated workcamp organisations at home, e.g. IVS, Quaker Voluntary Action and UNA Exchange (see 'Directory of Voluntary Placements Abroad'). Archaeological and building restoration camps are arranged by *NJBG (Nederlandse Jeugdbond voor Geschiedenis,* Prins Willem Alexanderhof 5, 2595 BE Den Haag; fax 070-335 2536; www.njbg.nl) whose website includes a small section in English.

Working on Boats

A little known opportunity for people who can communicate in German or Dutch is to work on one of the 250 *Platbodems,* traditional sailing boats that cruise the waters of Ijsselmeer and Waddensea off the north coast of the Netherlands in spring, summer and autumn. They cater mainly to school groups and are staffed by a skipper and one mate *(maat)* one of whose jobs is to offer simple instruction to the guests though he or she must also help the skipper on watch, carrying out repairs and so on. Even without any background in sailing, **Felix Fernandez** was offered ten jobs after adding his CV to the databank *(vacature bank)* of job-seekers and ended up working the summer season on the two-masted ship *Citore*:

> I didn't have sailing experience before. The first week of sailing was a nightmare because of my lack of experience but I got through and now there is no problem. It is normal to work seven days a week with one day off a month. You have to be prepared to work around 70 hours a week. Having little privacy is also something one has to get used to. Nevertheless there are many advantages of the job and I met a lot of people who have returned for several seasons.

Opportunities for Paid Work

The *Centra voor Werk en Inkomen or CWI (the Dutch equivalent of Jobcentres formerly known as Arbeidsbureau)* may be a useful source of paid employment. **Neil Datta** decided he wanted to spend part of his gap year in the Netherlands before applying to study medicine. He simply enquired at his local Jobcentre which passed on details of a heavy labouring job registered through EURES, the Europe-wide employment service. Although the work itself was unexciting, he greatly enjoyed being based in small-town Holland especially during the winter carnival in February (comparable to Mardi Gras). Furthermore he was able to save enough money to fund a big trip to Southeast Asia afterwards.

A small private Dutch agency is active in this field as well. *Appellation Controlee* (Ulgersmaweg 26C, 9731 BT Groningen; 50-549 2434; www.apcon.nl) arranges seasonal picking jobs in the Netherlands lasting two weeks or more between early June and late September (see entry in 'Directory of Paid Work'.) Farmers will normally pay the minimum wage of about €4.70 (net). The fee charged by the agency for arranging the work is €89, equivalent to more than half a week's work.

Another youth-oriented agency which may be of interest is the JoHo Company (which stands for Jobs & Holidays) with offices in Amsterdam, Rotterdam, Leiden and Groningen. See their website www.joho.nl for contact details and the services they offer. If in Rotterdam, it is also worth visiting the youth information bureau Use It on the west side of the station (www.use-it.nl) though it is not involved in job-finding.

Both in cities and the country, many employers turn to private employment agencies (*uitzendbureaux* – pronounced 'outzend') for temporary workers. Therefore they can be a very useful source of temporary work in Holland. They proliferate in large towns, for example there are about 250 in Amsterdam alone, though not all will accept non-Dutch-speaking applicants. *Uitzendbureaux* deal only with jobs lasting less than six months.

Most of the work on their books will be unskilled work such as stocking warehouse shelves, factory or agricultural work, etc. Among the largest *uitzendbureaux* are Randstad with about 300 branches (www.randstad.nl), Unique (www.uniquemls.com), Manpower (www.manpower.nl), Creyf's Interim and Tempo Team.

The largest employer of seasonal work is the bulb industry, though Dutch agriculture employs thousands of short-term helpers. The European Employment Service (EURES) looks beyond Dutch borders to recruit EU young people to fill hundreds of seasonal jobs in the agricultural and horticultural industries, with many jobs available in greenhouses, flower and tree nurseries, bulbs packing houses, strawberry farms and so on. Because of the unpredictability of working hours, employers guarantee 25 hours of work a week, though more hours will be available most of the time. The minimum hourly wage before tax is €7.48 and simple accommodation will be provided at a cost of up to €30 a week. Those who work for at least six weeks will have their travel expenses reimbursed up to a maximum of €225. Application should be made via the EURES office in the Hague (+31-70-338976).

Hordes of young travellers descend on the area between Leiden and Haarlem without a pre-arranged job; it is easier to find openings in the early spring and through the autumn than in high summer. Traditionally, itinerant workers congregate on big campsites, where the seasonal regulars will advise newcomers. Excellent earnings are possible with employers who offer a lot of overtime (paid at a premium rate). But the work is hard and boring and the area attracts hardened long-term travellers looking to save money for further travels.

In this richly agricultural land, other opportunities present themselves for students looking for outdoor work. The area around Roermond (about 50km southeast of Eindhoven and north of Maastricht in the province of Limburg) is populated by asparagus growers and other farmers who need people to harvest their crops of strawberries, potatoes and vegetables, especially in the spring. Elsewhere, the area of Westland between Rotterdam, the Hook of Holland and Den Haag is well known for tomato production; the whole region is a honeycomb of greenhouses.

Dutch hotels and other tourist establishments occasionally employ foreigners, especially those with a knowledge of more than one European language. A few tour operators like *Holidaybreak* employ British young people as staff at their camps for the summer season. In **Adam Skuse's** year off before university, he almost succeeded in finding hotel work but not quite:

One very useful resource I found was the website www.visitholland.com, where I got a list of hotels and then systematically emailed them all asking for a job. Most had no vacancies, a couple told me to call them when I was in Amsterdam, and one actually arranged an interview with me. But even the knockbacks were pleasant. Quite a few offered to buy me a drink anyway. Alas, I never managed to find the hotel in time, ran out of funds and am now back in Blighty. I had plans for my gap year, but just ended up sitting around on the dole.

This is exactly what this book is meant to help you prevent.

Those setting their sights higher than work in hotels or campsites, fields or greenhouses, may find it difficult to find work without fluent Dutch. Urban Dutch people have such a high degree of competence in English after they finish their schooling that there is not much of a market for EFL teaching. Berlitz in Amsterdam (Rokin 87-89; 020-622 13 75) employ about 60 freelancers who have done the compulsory ten-day Berlitz training course.

Courses & Information

For general information about studying in the Netherlands, contact the Foreign Student Service (FSS), Oranje Nassaulaan 5, 1075 AH Amsterdam (fax 020-676 0555; ucn@antenna.nl) for their publications including *Non-University Dutch Language Courses in the Netherlands.* They also publish an *Expat Survival Guide* in English (€4.95). JoHo mentioned above can advise on language and culture courses in the Netherlands (71-516 1277). Nuffic (the Netherlands Organization for International Co-operation in Higher Education) publishes *Study in the Netherlands,* a comprehensive catalogue in English of courses available, mostly for post-graduates, which can be requested by writing to Nuffic at PO Box 29777, 2502 LT The Hague (www.nuffic.nl). English is used as the medium of instruction on a variety of courses in the Netherlands.

Regulations

If you intend to stay in the Netherlands for more than three months, the first step is to acquire a sticker in your passport from the local aliens police (*Vreemdelingenpolitie*) or Town Hall, normally over-the-counter. They will expect you to provide a local address. The passport should then be taken to the local tax office to apply for a *sofinummer* (social/ fiscal number). To turn the initial sticker into a residence permit *(Verblijfsvergunning* or *verblijfskaart)* after three months, you will have to show a genuine work contract or letter of employment from an employer (not an agency) and pay a fee. The contract will have to show that the legal minimum wage and holiday pay are being paid and the proper tax and deductions are being made.

If you feel that you are not being treated fairly by an employer or landlord, you can get free legal advice from any branch of YIPs (Youth Information Points) or you can make enquiries at any CWI employment office.

Information on working and living in the Netherlands is available on the Dutch Embassy website (www.netherlands-embassy.org.uk/econfaq_eng.htm) and no longer in booklet form. The Consular Department in London (38 Hyde Park Gate, SW7 5DP) has information regarding rules for aliens and how to apply for visas and residence permits, also on its website (www.netherlands-embassy.org.uk/consul_eng.htm).

Belgium

Belgium's proximity to Britain and its distinctive culture make it worth considering for a gap year experience. Its population of just over 10 million can be broadly divided between the French-speaking people of Wallonia in the south (about 42% of the total population) and those who speak Flemish (which is almost identical to Dutch) in the north.

Work Experience

The large number of multinational companies, attracted by the headquarters of the European Union in Brussels, have a constant and fluctuating demand for bilingual office workers. High flyers who would like to work for the European Commission as administrators, translators, secretaries, etc. must compete in open competitions held at regular intervals; the London office of the European Commission (see entry in 'Directory of Work Experience Abroad') can send application forms. The Commission runs a five-month *stagiaire* programme whereby graduates from member countries take up short-term training positions mostly in Brussels. Applications must be postmarked not later than 31st August for positions starting in March and 1st March for positions starting in October. They should be addressed to the Traineeships Office, Directorate General for Education & Culture, European Commission, 200 Rue de la Loi, 1049 Brussels, Belgium (02-295 39 93).

One company which arranges work experience placements for students of French or German is M.B. Language asbl (41 rue Henri Bergé, 1030 Brussels, Belgium; 02-242 27 66; macbaron@chello.be). Most linguistic and cultural exchanges last two weeks though longer ones may be possible. The programme is designed for European students aged 16-18 heading into the upper sixth. The placement fee is €450 or €475 depending on the time of year (more expensive in summer).

People who live in the south-east of England can make use of EURES Crossborder HNFK based at South Kent College (Maison Dieu Road, Dover CT16 1DH; 01304 244356) which assists people looking for jobs in Belgium, especially in West-Vlaanderen and Hainaut (western Belgium). Two bilingual Euro-Advisers can put job-seekers in touch with network partners on the continent and can also give advice and information about living and working conditions.

Look for opportunities as a seasonal guide with one of the coach tour companies which run tours of scenic and historic Belgium. Venture Abroad (Rayburn House, Parcel Terrace, Derby DE1 1LY; www.ventureabroad.co.uk) employs reps, including students with a background in scouting or guiding, for its programme in Belgium.

For more casual opportunities, the best way to find out about short-term general work is to visit a branch of the Belgian employment service in any town. A special division called T-Interim (in the Flemish part) or Trace (in French-speaking Belgium) specialises in placing people in temporary jobs. Most jobs obtained through T-Interim or Trace offices will be unskilled manual ones though they may also be able to help students who have done an office skills course at the beginning of their gap year to find well-paid temporary office jobs, provided they can function in French.

Though understated, Belgium's tourist industry flourishes and some UK tour operators employ Britons. Young people's hostels often give free accommodation in exchange for duties. Try for example the lovely town of Bruges.

Americans can apply through Interexchange in New York (address as for au pairs above) to be placed in a summer job, internship or teaching position in Belgium. Applicants over 18 with a working knowledge of French (or Dutch) can be placed in companies or organisations for between one and three months. The programme fee is $700 and the application deadline is late April; full details on the website (www.interexchange.org).

Teaching English

The casual EFL teacher will have trouble finding work in Belgium where there is a great deal of competition from highly qualified expatriates. Prolinguis runs summer language courses for teenagers and employs native speaker teachers (Institut de Langues, 228 Place de l'Eglise, 6717 Thiaumont; 63-22 04 62; www.prolinguis.be). **Philip Dray** from Ireland worked for them one summer:

I was employed in a freelance capacity to work 90 days between April 5th and September 15th. The salary was the equivalent of £60 a day and I had a sort of hotel room in a building that housed the students' dorms. For my keep I had to check the dorms twice a week, which was not too bad since most of the kids were co-operative. The work was grammar-based but with some emphasis on games and role play.

Au Pairing

Anyone who wishes to be an au pair in Belgium will find it harder than it used to be. The government has brought in stringent requirements that families pay a very high wage for only 20 hours of work: €400 a month for au pairs from the EU, €450 for non-EU au pairs. These changes have forced several Belgian agencies to cancel their incoming programme, though Stufam (Vierwindenlaan 7, 1780 Wemmel; 02-460 33 95; aupair.stufam@pi.be) and the Catholic organisation Services de la Jeunesse Feminine (29 rue Faider, 1050 Brussels; 02-539 35 14; or rue de Dave, 174, 5100 Namur; 081-30 91 35) still make placements inside Belgium.

Voluntary Work

The Flemish association of young environmentalists called *Natuur 2000* (Bervoetstraat 33, 2000 Antwerp; 03-231 26 04; http://home.planetinternet.be/~n2000) organises summer conservation workcamps open to all nationalities. The sizeable registration fee covers accommodation, food, insurance and local transport. Those interested in participating in residential archaeological digs for three weeks in July should contact *Archeolo-j* (Avenue Paul Terlinden 23, 1330 Rixensart; 02-653 8268/fax 02-673 40 85; www.skene.be). There is a charge for membership in the Society and camp expenses are €520 for 22 days.

Courses & Information

A few UK-based language course agencies send candidates to Belgium to learn French including *Vis-à-Vis*. A number of language schools advertise in the English language weekly magazine *The Bulletin*. Its address is 1038 Chaussée de Waterloo, 1180 Brussels (02-373 99 09); the magazine is published on Thursdays and can be bought from newsstands. *Newcomer* is a bi-annual publication (available from the above address for €2.50) which is aimed at new arrivals in Belgium and carries useful sections called 'Getting to Grips with the Red Tape' and 'Job-Seekers' Guide'.

The Federation Infor Jeunes Wallonie-Bruxelles is a non-profit making organisation which co-ordinates 12 youth information offices in French-speaking Belgium. The Brussels branch is at rue Van Arteveld 155, 1000 Brussels; 02-514 41 11). These can give advice on work as well as leisure, youth rights, accommodation, etc. Their headquarters are in Namur (081-71 15 90) though much of their information is published on their website www.inforjeunes.be. A related organisation also with a useful site is www.bruxelles-j.be. Among Infor Jeunes' services, they operate holiday job placement offices (Service Job Vacances) between March and September.

Regulations

The usual rules apply to EU nationals coming to work or live in Belgium: EU nationals arriving in Belgium to look for work and who intend to stay for a period of three months or more should register within eight days at the local Town Hall where the *administration communale* will issue either a temporary *certificat d'immatriculation* valid for three months or the one year certificate of registration (*certificat d'inscription au registre des étrangers* – CIRE).

Luxembourg

If Belgium is sometimes neglected, Luxembourg is completely by-passed. Yet it is an independent country with an unemployment rate of less than 2%, and a number of useful facilities for foreign students. The national employment service *(Administration de l'Emploi)* or ADEM at 10 rue Bender, L-1229 Luxembourg (352-478 53 00; www.etat.lu/ADEM/adem.htm) operates a *Service Vacances* for students looking for summer jobs in warehouses, restaurants, etc. To find out about possibilities, you must visit this office in person, although EU nationals looking for long-term jobs may receive some assistance from EURES counsellors. The *Centre Information Jeunes* (CIJ), 26 Place de la Gare/Galerie Kons, 1616 Luxembourg (26 29 32 00; www.cij.lu) also runs a holiday job service between January and August for students from the EU.

With a population of less than 400,000, job opportunities are understandably limited, but they do exist especially in the tourist industry. Even the Embassy in London at 27 Wilton Crescent, London SW1X 8SD (020-7235 6961) maintains that 'seasonal jobs are often to be found in the hotels of the Grand Duchy of Luxembourg' and will send a list of the 250+ hotels in exchange for an A4 envelope and a 50p stamp. Wages are fairly good in this sector, often about £500 per month after room and board.

Opportunities for gap year work experience may be available since many multinational companies are based in Luxembourg, some of whom may regard a knowledge of fluent English in addition to a local language as an advantage. Addresses of potential employers can be obtained from the Luxembourg Embassy who on receipt of an s.a.e. will send lists of British and American firms, as well as of the largest local companies.

France

Near destinations have been somewhat eclipsed in recent years by the more exotic far-flung gap year destinations like Nepal and Peru, but there is still plenty of glamour to be found in good old France. Your ambition may be to get to know Paris, to spend the winter in a French ski resort, to live with a provincial family as an au pair or a paying guest or simply to improve your schoolboy/girl French by conversing with the natives. All are worthy aims for occupying part of your gap year.

Sources of Information

The *Agence National pour l'Emploi* or ANPE is the national employment service of France, with dozens of offices in Paris and 600 others throughout the country. Their website www.anpe.fr now carries lots of recruitment information in English. According to the site, it is looking to recruit a colossal 35,000 pickers, e.g. 9,000 grapepickers for Bordeaux, 6,000 apple pickers for Limousin and so on. Other vacancies are also recorded on the regional sites (see www.anpe.fr/contacts for links by département). For example the ANPE in Narbonne (ANPE, BP 802, 29 rue Mazzini, 11108 Narbonne Cedex) has seasonal hotel vacancies from May to September.

One of the 32 regional offices of the *Centres d'Information Jeunesse* (CIJ) may be of use to the newly arrived gap year traveller. They can advise on cheap accommodation, local jobs, the legal rights of temporary workers, etc. The main Paris branch is CIDJ *(Centre d'Information et de Documentation Jeunesse)* whose foyer notice board is a useful starting place for the job or accommodation seeker in Paris. It can also provide booklets and leaflets on such subjects as seasonal agricultural or resort work, the regulations that affect foreign students in France, language courses and so on. To obtain their catalogue, send four international reply coupons to CIDJ at 101 Quai Branly, 75740 Paris Cedex 15 (01-44 49 12 00/www.cidj.asso.fr). Most leaflets cost €3.50 and booklets €9. Note that their web pages do not cover employment.

Once you know you are going to stay longer than three months, you should apply for a *carte de séjour* (residence permit) at the local police station *(préfecture)* or town hall *(mairie)*. This requires a huge battery of documents and sometimes delays of months.

COURSES & HOMESTAYS

A good transition between the A-level classroom and a holiday or job in France is an intensive French language course in Britain (see entry for *Alliance Français* in London or try the Institut Français attached to the French Embassy, 14 Cromwell Place, London SW7 2JR). An even better one would be a French course abroad. If you want to select a course on your own, request the list *Cours de Français pour Etrangers* from the Service Cultural section of the French Consulate (21 Cromwell Road, London SW7 2DQ) or from CIDJ mentioned above. It is easier to rely on one of the UK companies to arrange a course on your behalf (see 'Directory of Language Courses').

The British Council manages several student exchanges with France including the Charles de Gaulle Bursary Trust which bequeaths up to £800 on 17-19 year olds who submit an impressive proposal of what project they want to pursue or study for up to a month. For details, contact the Bureau's Belfast office on 028 9024 8220 ext 241 and plan to apply by the end of January.

Hundreds of British students do an exchange year in Paris. For example about 1,300 British students participate in the Erasmus European student exchange, though this scheme is open to undergraduates not school leavers. Several hundred more attach themselves to the *British Institute* in Paris (11 rue de Constantine, 75340 Paris Cedex 07), and of course the *Sorbonne* is a magnet for students wanting to take language and civilisation courses.

For a range of standard language courses, look at the brochure from *Vis-à-Vis* which specialises in French language courses. It offers two-week courses in Paris starting at not much more than £300 (20 hours a week tuition) and in Annecy for less than £200 (20 lessons a week). *EIL* in Malvern also arranges homestay, language courses and high school placements in France (see entries for its French counterpart *Experiment Paris* in the 'Directory of Work Experience' and the Directory of Language Courses'). On the Schools Programme offered by *AFS Intercultural Programmes UK* (Leeming House, Vicar Lane, Leeds LS2 7JF; 0113-242 6136; info-unitedkingdom@afs.org) students aged 15-18 spend an academic year or term living with a French family and attending the local school.

During her gap year, **Lucinda Capel** was as pleased with the extracurricular activities on the course in Bordeaux which *CESA* fixed up for her as she was with the lessons:

Day to day life in Bordeaux is definitely a fun experience. There is something to satisfy everyone in this city: pubs, bars and night clubs (with DJs from London sometimes). Then there are the museums, historic architecture, vineyard visits, wine tastings, go-karting and trips to the cinema and theatre.

I came over to Bordeaux to work on my French. I'm writing this half way through the 12-week course and I am glad to say it's a case of, so far, so very, very good. Everybody I have met has been really amazed at just how quickly they have picked the language up, even the beginners. The combination of the lessons in the morning and meals with the French family in the evening provide you with a total immersion in the French language and culture that allows you to learn continuously without even being aware of it. The classes are streamed according to ability but it is very flexible. During the first few days, you may move classes until you are comfortable with the pace.

One problem is the food served up nightly by my host family. It is simply too good and I have had to join a gym. Gym life in Bordeaux is a cultural experience in its own right. Having done it, I don't recommend it unless you wish to be outshone by the femme Bordelaise who, whilst being twice your age, are superbly flexible. You need a strong sense of self to survive that ordeal.

Obviously the gym and the DJs didn't provide too many distractions since she passed all four units of her D.E.L.F. exam.

A rough estimate of how much a 20-hour course will cost per week would be €220-€260 plus a further €150-€170 to stay with a host family. Obviously prices are higher in Paris. The prestigious *Alliance Française* offers four hours a day over 16 days in a month for €584. For details of courses in France in the 'Directory of Language Courses', see entries for *ACTE Challenge, Alliance Française, Experiment* and *Interséjours* in Paris, *CLE* and *Terre des Langues* in Tours, *Cavilam* in Vichy and the *Université de Perpignan*. Another major provider is the Eurolingua Institute (5 rue Henri Guinier, 34000 Montpellier; www.eurolingua.com/French_in_Montpellier.htm) which arranges work placements too. Bookings can be made through their UK office (☎/fax 0161-972 0225).

Some language schools double as au pair agencies such as *Inter-Séjours* and *Institut Euro'Provence,* 69 rue de Rome, 13001 Marseille; euro.provence@wanadoo.fr) which makes a language course much more affordable. A cheap way to have a base in France from which to improve your knowledge of the language is to participate in a work exchange, for example the one offered by the Centre International d'Antibes, a French language school on the Côte d'Azur. Up to 50 summer volunteers do administrative or domestic work in exchange for board and lodging and/or French tuition. Details of the scheme are available from CIA, 38 boulevard d'Aguillon, 06600 Antibes (04-92 90 71 70; admin@cia-france.com).

For listings of 200 language schools, see *The Complete Guide to Learning French in France: From Short Study Holidays to Gap Year Breaks* published in 2002 by Summersdale Publishers (£8,99).

WORK EXPERIENCE

Work experience placements are referred to as *stages* in France and are widely available through a number of organisations. British students enrolled in courses in France who are interested in gaining work experience might find the local CROUS office helpful. The Centres Régional des Oeuvres Universitaires et Scolaires operate a service called *Service de Liaison Etudiante* which has links with local employers.

Euro-Academy Ltd (67-71 Lewisham High St, London SE13 5JX; 020-8297 0505; enquiries@euroacademy.co.uk) has an Internship Department that can fix up unpaid work experience placements in a number of French cities for a minimum of a month. The only exception is its Brittany programme which allows for students with a reasonable knowledge of the language to be placed in a business in Dinan for two, three or four weeks. Placement fees start at £30 per week (for a 12-week stay) but accommodation at £25-£30 a night makes this option quite pricey.

Horizon HPL (Signet House, 49/51 Farringdon Road, London EC1M 3JB; 020-7404 9192/fax 020-7404 9194; Horizonhpl.London@btinternet.com/ http://perso.club-internet.fr/horizon1) is an Anglo-French training organisation which offers packages lasting between two and 12 months combining language tuition and live-in hotel work placements and company placements all over France. The wages are on a trainee scale, from £50 per week plus accommodation, while the package fee is £240. Horizon's office in France is at 22-26 rue du Sergent Bauchat, 75012 Paris (01-40 01 07 07/fax 01-40 01 07 28) while the Dublin office is at 3 Lower Abbey St, Dublin 1 (01-8745 002).

The long established Club des 4 Vents (1 rue Gozlin, 75006 Paris; france@cei4vents.com) has a variety of workplace openings for young people over 17 who have an intermediate standard of French (see Work Experience entry for C.E.I.).

PAID OPPORTUNITIES FOR YEAR OUT STUDENTS

The best areas to look for work in the tourist industry of France are the Alps for the winter season, December-April, and the Côte d'Azur for the summer season, June-September, though jobs exist throughout the country. The least stressful course of action is to fix up work ahead of time with a UK campsite or holiday company in summer or ski company in winter. For example First Choice (1st Floor, London Road, Crawley, W Sussex RH10 2GX; 01293 588528; overseas.recruitment@firstchoice.co.uk) hires people from the age of 18 to work in hotels in the Alps and Normandy. Staff must have EU nationality but need not have relevant experience.

One important feature of working for a French employer in France is that you should be paid at least the *SMIC (salaire minimum interprofessionel de croissance)* or national minimum wage. There are slightly different rates for seasonal agricultural work and full-time employees; at present the basic SMIC is €6.83 per hour gross or €1,154.27 per month based on a working week of 39 hours. These are adjusted annually to take account of inflation.

Campsites and Holiday Centres

British camping tour operators hire an army of language students to staff their network of campsites throughout France. These companies offer holidaymakers a complete package providing pre-assembled tents and a campsite courier to look after any problems which arise. Since this kind of holiday appeals to families, people who can organise children's activities are especially in demand. In addition to the Europe-wide companies like *Eurocamp* and *Canvas* (see 'Directory of Paid Seasonal Jobs'), the following all take on campsite reps/couriers and other seasonal staff for France:

Carisma Holidays, Bethel House, Heronsgate, Chorleywood, Herts. WD3 5BB (01923 284235; personnel@carisma.co.uk).

Fleur Holidays, 4 All Hallows Road, Bispham, Blackpool FY2 0AS (01253 593333;

employment@fleur-holidays.com).

International Life Leisure, Kerry House, Kerry St, Leeds LS18 4AW (0113 205 0292; overseasemployment@frenchlife.co.uk).

Ian Mearns Holidays, Tannery Yard, Witney St, Burford, Oxon. OX18 4DP (01993 822655; karen@ianmearnsholidays.co.uk). People able to start work in March especially in demand.

Select France, Fiveacres, Murcott, Kidlington, Oxford OX5 2RE (01865 331350; selectfrance@sol.co.uk).

Venue Holidays, 1 Norwood St, Ashford, Kent TN23 1QU (01233 629950; www.venueholidays.co.uk). Website carries job information.

The best time to start looking for summer season jobs from England is between September and February. In most cases candidates are expected to have at least A-level standard French, though some companies claim that a knowledge of French is merely 'preferred'. It is amazing how far a good dictionary and a knack for making polite noises in French can get you.

The massive camping holiday industry generates winter work as well. Brad Blanchisserie is a French-registered company in Sautron, Nantes which cleans and repairs tents and bedding on behalf of many of the major companies. Staff (who need not speak French though it is an advantage) are needed between September and May. A wage of €55 a day plus gite accommodation is provided (so having your own transport is an advantage). Their UK office is at Abbey Lakes Hall, Orrell Road, Wigan WN5 8QZ (01695 632797; info@bradint.co.uk).

Outdoor activity centres are another major employer of summer staff, both general domestic staff and sports instructors. Try the companies mentioned in the introductory section *Working in Tourism* such as *Acorn Adventure* and *PGL.*

One of the most interesting and varied opportunities is offered by the specialist independent company *French Encounters* (see entry in 'Directory of Work Experience'). They hire gap year students with a knowledge of French for the period February to May. Staff work with groups of British children on field study holidays based at chateaux in rural Normandy, after undergoing a fortnight's intensive training in presentation skills, first aid and the French language.

Eighteen-year-old **Juliette Radford** summarised this part of her gap year with enthusiasm:

It might seem strange for a potential medic to have spent 3½ months of a Gap Year in France. By the end of the season, you will not only have gained the patience of a saint (and a warped sense of humour) and lost all traces of self-consciousness and shame, but you will also have acquired an extensive repertoire of French folk songs. I'm more independent, more confident and can cope in crises. I found I could manage and supervise all sorts of different people and I've practised tact and patience. I've been given the opportunity to use my initiative in lots of ways. Thanks to the people I have been working with, I have had one of the best times of my life, despite how hard we have had to work.

For work in an unusual activity holiday, contact Bombard Balloon Adventures, Chateau de LaBorde, 21200 Beaune (03-80 26 63 30; www.bombardsociety.com/jobs) who hire hot-air balloon ground crew for the summer season May to October. The job requires excellent physical fitness and strength, a cheerful personality, clean-cut appearance and year-old clean driving licence.

Ski Resorts

France is the best of all countries in Europe for finding jobs in ski resorts, mainly because it is the number one country for British skiers, 200,000 of whom go there every year. The main problem is the shortage of worker accommodation; unless you find a live-in job you will have to pay nearly holiday prices or find a friend willing to rent out his or her sofa. If trying to fix up a job from Britain, there are agencies which arrange for young people with a very good knowledge of French to work in ski resorts. Alpotels (part of *Jobs in the Alps*) carry out aptitude tests on behalf of employers in various alpine resorts and match suitable candidates with prospective employers who pay a net salary of approximately £500.

Another agency is *UK Overseas Handling* (UKOH, PO Box 2791, London W1A 5JU; 020-7629 3064; cv@ukoh.co.uk) which specifically welcomes gap year students to fill seasonal and annual vacancies in hotel and restaurant chains, ski chalets and beach resorts in France. Specialist ski recruitment websites can be invaluable for tracking down jobs in French resorts including Natives.co.uk, freeradicals.co.uk, findaskijob.com and skistaff.co.uk. Hardworking students on a gap year are also courted by a French company that manages hotels and villas in the French Alps: Eurogroup Vacances, 1091 Avenue de la Boisse, 73000 Chambéry (04-79 62 36 63; www.eurogroup-vacances.com). According to the Employment section of their website, staff are needed for hotel and tourist properties in winter and summer.

If you attempt to find work in a ski resort on your own, success is far from guaranteed and competition for work is increasing. Val d'Isère attracts as many as 500 ski bums every November/December, many of whom hang around bars or the ANPE (Jobcentre) for days in the hope that work will come their way. If looking for work in Val, try Radio Val which broadcasts from next door to the tourist office. Job vacancies are announced in the morning (mostly babysitting and kitchen portering) and then posted in French outside the studio. The earlier you try for these, the better your chances.

Writing in the *Ink Pellet* (an arts magazine for teachers), Nico Stanford described a success story:

> *I'd finished my A-levels and was determined to take a gap year with a snowboard and loads of snow. My parents went on at me to 'go through a tour operator and do washing up' or something equally dull. When I got to France in late November with no job, two flatmates, 20 loo rolls and enough savings for ski pass and flat but no food, it was snowing, so we immediately set about the important business of getting out onto the slopes. The job hunting was intermittent and unsuccessful and, as money ran out, I could almost here the 'I told you so' from my father.*
>
> *About a month after we arrived, with desperation setting in, I went to a local bar and was told about a job going at the local radio station translating and reading the weather in English, so French was essential. Off I went, feeling very grateful for my French A-level, and the guys at the station were so desperate (the girl had quit suddenly after less than a month) that they hired me on the spot at pretty good pay… I went on to have a wonderful time which was financed by a fascinating hands-on experience in the media and I feel ready to cope with and enjoy university life to the full in October.*

It should be noted that British tour operators in France are waging an ongoing battle with employment inspectors especially in British-dominated resorts like Méribel. The French object to the long hours and low wages paid to staff recruited in the UK, far less than their French counterparts in the tourist industry have to pay French staff. If the French authorities get their way, jobs for young ski-loving Britons would be much harder to come by.

Having accommodation provided by your employer is a very valuable perk. The UK company Seasons on Snow (Unit 1a, Franchise St, Kidderminster DY11 6RE; 08700 111360; info@seasonsonsnow.com/ wwwseasonsonsnow.com) specialises in renting out affordable accommodation to young skiers and snowboarders for the whole season, some of whom take lessons, others work and others just ski. Through this company you can book a bed in a multi-bedded chalet in Tignes, Morzine-Avoriaz or Serre Chevalier starting at £73 a week if you stay for the whole season. Packages cost from £2,200 for full season including accommodation, return flights and insurance but not the lift pass (£290 in Serre Chevalier, £439 in Tignes). Long stay accommodation is available in Les Arcs from Planet

Subzero (20 Woodsyre, London SE26 6SS; info@planetsubzero.com).

Yachts

A few months on the Riviera would be hard for someone taking a gap year to fund unless some means of earning was to be found. Yachts may provide the answer. It is not impossible to penetrate the world of yacht owners and skippers in glamorous resorts like Antibes and St Tropez. It is essential to start looking early, preferably the beginning of March, since by late April most of the jobs have been filled. Boats frequently take on people as day workers first and then employ them as crew for the charter season if they like them. Deckhands on charter yachts are paid a weekly wage, usually around £100 which can sometimes be doubled with tips from big-rollers. The charter season ends in late September (convenient if you're returning to university) when many yachts begin organising their crew for the trip to the West Indies.

Kevin Gorringe headed for the south of France in June with the intention of finding work on a private yacht. His destination was Antibes, where so many British congregate, and he began frequenting likely meeting places like the Gaffe Bar and the Irish bar as well as the agencies like Adrian Fisher and Blue Water. He recommends using the services of The Office (La Galerie du Port, 8 Blvd d'Aguillon, 06600 Antibes; 04-93 34 09 96; theoffice@wanadoo.fr) which for a small fee can be used as a contact point for potential employers. (Several yacht crewing agencies are housed in the same building including Peter Insull's Crew Agency; www.insull.com.) Competition will be fierce, so doggedness together with charm and a good measure of luck will be needed for success. Look tidy and neat, be polite and when you get a job work hard. The first job is the hardest to get, but once you get in with the community of yachties, people will help you move onto other boats.

Grape-Picking

Although the French tourist industry offers many seasonal jobs, there are even more in agriculture: approximately 100,000 foreign workers are employed on the grape harvest alone. The timing of the *vendange* in late September/early October is not very convenient for gap year travellers. Farmers almost always provide some sort of accommodation, but this can vary from a rough and ready dormitory to a comfortable room in his own house. Obviously it is easier for the owner of a small vineyard with a handful of workers to provide decent accommodation than for the owner of a chateau who may have over a 100 workers to consider. Food is normally provided, but again this can vary from the barely adequate to the sublime: one picker can write that 'the food was better than that in a 5-star hotel, so we bought flowers for the cook at the end of the harvest', while another may complain of instant mashed potatoes or of having to depend on whatever he or she can manage to buy and prepare. When both food and accommodation are provided there is normally a deduction of one or two hours' pay from each day's wage.

The work itself will consist either of picking or portering. Picking involves bending to get the grapes from a vine that may be only three and a half feet tall, and filling a pannier which you drag along behind you. The panniers full of grapes are emptied into an *hotte*, a large basket weighing up to 100lb which the porters carry to a trailer.

The first few days as a *cueilleur/cueilleuse* or *coupeur* (picker) are the worst, as you adjust to the stooping posture and begin to use muscles you never knew you had. The job of porter is sought after, since it does not require the constant bending and is less boring because you move around the vineyard.

The demand for pickers in all regions is highly unpredictable. Whereas there is usually a glut of pickers looking for work at the beginning of the harvest (early to mid-September), there is sometimes a shortage later on in the month. Harvests differ dramatically from year to year; a late spring frost can wreak havoc. The element of uncertainty makes it very difficult for farmers to make any fixed commitment in advance.

The best plan is to find out whether the local ANPE (Jobcentre) knows of likely vacancies (www.ANPE.fr). For example the ANPE in Orange (282 Allée Auvergne

Roussillon, 84106 Orange Cedex; 4-90 51 64 23) was trying to round up pickers for Chateauneuf-du-Pape for the 2003 season.

If you fix up a job directly with a farmer well in advance of the harvest, it is a good precaution to phone at regular intervals to remind the farmer you still intend to take up the job. If you are hunting in person, ask around in hostels and villages, follow up leads, check the CIJ and university notice boards, ask at the regional Syndicat d'Initiative (tourist office). As usual, the village bar is often the hub of activity during the *vendange* as **Keith Flynn** found to be the case in Chateauneuf de Pape (which incidentally is where the famous system of *appellation controlée* was invented):

> One of the easiest ways of finding work is to go to the one and only bar in town across from the tourist office. All the workers go there in the evening and a lot of the bosses, so just ask everybody. There were at least 30 or 40 pickers in town in the middle of September and more arriving; yet everybody seemed to have plenty of work.

Work on Farms

Although the *vendange* may produce the highest concentration of seasonal work, there are tremendous opportunities for participating in other harvests and with far less competition for the available work. France is an overwhelmingly rural country. One additional way of finding harvesting work is to ask at the fruit and vegetable markets where farmers gather daily to watch their farming co-operative sell their produce at the height of the season.

> **Through the European agency Appellation Controlée (see entry in 'Directory of Paid Seasonal Jobs Abroad'), Karen Martin and Paul Ansell found work castrating maize in the Loire Valley:**
> While we were in Amsterdam we looked on the internet and found a Dutch agency (www.apcon.nl) who mediate between workers and farmers in England, Denmark, Holland and France. They charged a fee of £60 and got us work doing maize castration on a farm where two people had dropped out (God bless 'em). We made our way by hitching from Angers and were greeted by the farmer Bernard and his wife Merielle with lovely cherry wine. They speak little English but it was not an obstacle. You camp on the farm for a pound a day and have good facilities.

The proprietors cooked barbecues for them, washed clothes and were generally very hospitable and Karen and Paul were delighted to be invited back soon afterwards for a month's apple picking which allowed them to save £1,000 between them. Karen thinks that they were among the first non-French workers here but the farmer expressed interest in hosting more foreign young people at this farm which is about 20 miles east of Angers; contact Earl le Chêne du Mensonge, Hye, Bernard, Porteau, 49350 Les Rosiers sur Loire; 02-41 51 90 27.

English Teaching

A more realistic possibility than finding employment with a language school is to offset the high cost of living in Paris by doing some tutoring which sometimes shades into au pairing. Language exchanges for room and board are commonplace in Paris and are usually arranged through advertisements (in the places described below in the section on Paris) or by word of mouth. **Kathryn Kleypas** studied the notice board at the American Church to good effect:

> I contacted a family from the notice board and was invited to come over to their home for an interview and to meet the three children to whom I would be teaching English every day. I was not asked if I had any teaching experience, yet was offered the position which involved 18 hours of English teaching/conversation in exchange for room,

board and pocket money. My family took me with them to the seaside near Bordeaux in July and to their castle near Limoges during August.

University students and recent graduates who would like to spend a year as an English language *assistant* in a French primary or secondary school should contact the British Council at assistants@britishcouncil.org or www.languageassistant.co.uk. They also have placements as *lecteurs/lectrices* at teacher training colleges. Altogether they place about 1,000 students aged 20-30 to work 12 hours a week. *Assistants* are paid about £550 a month.

Occasionally pre-university students are accepted in this capacity. For example an education authority in the Vendée offers a year's work experience teaching English in French primary schools or acting as an assistant in the local lycée. The only requirements are that you be aged 18-25, have an A-level in French and have some experience of living in France. In exchange for 20 hours of teaching a week between the end of September and the end of May, you receive free board and lodging with a local family and a monthly allowance of €260-€300. Details are available from the Syndicat Mixte Montaigu-Rocheservière, 35 avenue Villebois Mareuil, 85607 Montaigu Cedex (02-51 46 45 45/fax 02-51 46 45 40).

AU PAIRING

Au pairing has always been a favoured way for young women in their gap year to improve their French and, increasingly, for young men too. The pocket money for au pairs in France is linked to the minimum wage (SMIC) and is currently €260-€290 per month. Most British agencies with an outgoing programme deal with France (see list in introductory chapter on Au Pairing) but applying directly through a French agency is commonplace. The most established agencies are members of UFAAP, the Union Francaise des Associations Au Pair, an umbrella group set up in 1999, based at present at Butterfly et Papillon listed below. Their member agencies are included on their website http://ufaap.tripod.com. While some agencies charge nothing, others do charge a registration fee which can be steep (€160+). Here are some agencies to contact:

Alliance Francaise, 55 rue Paradie, 13006 Marseille (04-91 33 28 19; info@alliancefrma rseille.org).

L'Arche, 53 rue de Gergovie, 75014 Paris (☎/fax 01-45 45 46 39).

Association Familles & Jeunesse, 4 rue Masséna, 06000 Nice (04-93 82 28 22; info@afj-aupair.org; www.afj-aupair.org). Places more than 300 au pair girls and boys, mainly in the South of France plus the French Riviera and Corsica.

Association Mary Poppins, 4 place de la Fontaine, 38120 Le Fontanil (04-76 75 57 33; Mary.Poppins@wanadoo.fr; http://assoc.wanadoo.fr/marypoppins.aupair).

Butterfly et Papillon, 5 avenue de Genève, 74000 Annecy (04-50 46 08 33; aupair.france @wanadoo.fr).

Euro Pair Services, 13 rue Vavin, 75006 Paris (01-43 29 80 01; europairservices@wana doo.fr).

France Au Pair - Eurojobs, 6 Allée des Saules, BP 29, 17420 Saint Palais sur Mer (05-46 23 99 88; contact@eurojob.fr; www.eurojob.fr).

Institut Euro'Provence, 69 rue de Rome, 13001 Marseille (04-91 33 90 60; euro.proven ce@wanadoo.fr; http://perso.wandadoo.fr/euro.provence). Largest au pair agency in southern France.

Inter-Séjours, 179 rue de Courcelles, 75017 Paris (01-47 63 06 81; http://asso.intersejou rs.free.fr).

Office Universitaire International/O.U.I., Au-Pair Européa, B.P. 5050, 20 rue Victor Micholet, 83091 Toulon Cedex (4-94 62 83 83; au-pair@wanadoo.fr). Second agency in Lille: 24 rue Arago, 59130 Lambersart (☎/fax 2-30 00 97 42). Placements throughout France (including the Riviera and Corsica) and also overseas French départements (Antilles, Réunion).

Oliver Twist Association Aquitaine Au Pair, 50 avenue de la California, 33600 Pessac (05-57 26 93 26; oliver.twist@wanadoo.fr).

Soames Paris Nannies, 6 route de Marlotte, 77690 Montigny sur Loing (01-64 78 37 98/ fax 01-64 45 91 75; Soames.Parisnannies@wanadoo.fr).

The French American Center in Montpellier (4 rue St. Louis, Montpellier 34000; 04-67 92 30 66) arranges au pair placements for Americans aged 18-25 with families in the Languedoc region. It also offers some internships in local businesses.

By law, families are supposed to make social security payments to the local URSSAF office on the au pair's behalf, though not all do and you might want to enquire about this when applying. Au pairs in or near Paris should receive the *carte orange* (monthly travel pass) which is worth about €45.

Quite a few foreigners are too hasty in arranging what seems at the outset a cushy number and only gradually realise how little they enjoy the company of children and how isolated they are if their family lives in the suburbs (as most do). Unless you actively like small children, it might be better to look for a free room in exchange for minimal babysitting (e.g. 12 hours a week). **Matt Tomlinson** went into his au pair job with his eyes open:

I'd heard too many horror stories from overworked and underpaid au pair friends to be careless, so chose quite carefully from the people who replied to my notice on the upstairs notice board of the British Church (just off the rue de Faubourg St Honoré). My employers were really laid back, in their mid-20s so more like living with an older brother and sister. The little boy was just over two whilst the little girl was three months old, and they were both completely adorable. On the whole it was great fun. Baking chocolate brownies, playing football and finger-painting may not be everybody's idea of a good time but there are certainly worse ways to earn a living (and learn French at the same time).

VOLUNTARY WORK

France has as wide a range of opportunities for voluntary work as any European country, and anyone who is prepared to exchange work for subsidised board and lodging should consider joining a voluntary project. The majority of short-term projects last two or three weeks during the summer and cost between €7 and €17 a day. Many gap students join one of these to learn basic French and make French contacts as well as to have fun. All workcamp associations in Britain can arrange for you to join camps in France (see 'Directory of Voluntary Placements Abroad').

Archaeology

A great many archaeological digs and building restoration projects are carried out each year. Every May the Ministry of Culture (Direction de l'Architecture et du Patrimoine, Sous-Direction de l'Archéologie, 4 rue d'Aboukir, 75002 Paris; 01-40 15 77 81) publishes a national list of summer excavations throughout France requiring up to 5,000 volunteers which can be consulted on its website (www.culture.gouv.fr/fouilles). Most *départements* have *Services Archéologiques* which organise digs. Without relevant experience you will probably be given only menial jobs but many like to share in the satisfaction of seeing progress made.

Anthony Blake describes the dig he joined which the History Department of the University of Le Mans runs every summer:

Archaeology is hard work. Applicants must be aware of what working 8.30am-noon and 2-6.30pm in baking heat means! That said, I thoroughly enjoyed the working holiday: excellent company (75% French so fine opportunity to practise French), weekends free after noon on Saturday, good lunches in SNCF canteen, evening meals more haphazard as prepared by fellow diggers. Accommodation simple but adequate.

Unskilled volunteers are charged a small contribution for their board and lodging. For example every July M. Louis Roussel (28 rue du Bourg, 21000 Dijon; malain_ gam@hotmail.com) takes 20 volunteers to work on a Gallo-Roman site outside Dijon; volunteers contribute a modest €15 per week. Further north the Service Archéologique of the Musée de la Chartreuse (191 rue St-Albin, 59500 Douai; 03-27 71 38 90/fax 03-27 71 38 93; arkeos@wanadoo.fr; http://arkeos.org) carries out summer digs on a Mérovingian abbey and mediaeval town. The registration fee here is €22.87 for two weeks.

Conservation

France takes the preservation of its heritage *(patrimoine)* very seriously and there are numerous groups both local and national engaged in restoring churches, windmills, forts and other historic monuments. Many are set up to accept foreign volunteers, though they tend to charge more than archaeological digs:

APARE, Association pour la Participation et l'Action Régionale, 41 cours Jean Jaurès, 84000 Avignon (04-90 85 51 15; www.apare-gec.org). An umbrella organisation which runs a total of 20 work sites in southern France. Cost of €113 for three weeks.

Club du Vieux Manoir, Ancienne Abbaye du Moncel, 60700 Pontpoint (03-44 72 33 98). Board and lodging cost €13 per day.

REMPART, 1 rue des Guillemites, 75004 Paris (01-42 71 96 55/fax 01-42 71 73 00; Minitel 3616 REMPART; www.rempart.com). Similar to the National Trust in Britain, in charge of 140 endangered monuments around France. Most projects charge €7 per day plus €40 for membership and insurance. Registration must be done by post.

La Sabranenque, Centre International, rue de la Tour de l'Oume, 30290 Saint Victor la Coste (04-66 50 05 05; www.sabranenque.com). Approximately €230 per fortnight. US applicants should contact Jacqueline Simon, 124 Bondcroft Drive, Buffalo, NY 14226 (716-836-8698).

UNAREC (Etudes et Chantiers), Délégué International, 3 rue des Petits Gras, 63000 Clermont-Ferrand (04-73 31 98 04; www.unarec.org). Hundreds of international volunteers for short-term conservation projects and longer-term professional training. €115 fee includes accommodation and insurance for 2-3 week workcamps.

Try to be patient if the project you choose turns out to have its drawbacks, since these organisations depend on voluntary leaders as well as participants. Judy Greene volunteered to work with a conservation organisation and felt herself to be 'personally victimised by the lack of organisation and leadership' or more specifically by one unpleasantly racist individual on her project. Tolerance may be called for, especially if your fellow volunteers lack it.

If you would like to survive in rural France, communal living is a possibility. Roberta Wedge enjoyed several months at the 'bleakly beautiful' Le Cun de Larzac Peace Centre (Route de Saint-Martin, 12100 Millau; 05-65 60 62 33) and says that they need work-for-keep volunteers in the summer to look after visitors, tend the gardens, preserve the fruit, etc. **Robert Abblett** moved from one such community to another – with mixed results:

From the Australian WWOOF list, I found the address of Les Courmettes. This was my favourite WWOOF for it was situated on a plateau 800 metres above the Côte d'Azur. I spent a wonderful August here in a most peaceful place, camping and swinging in my hammock, contemplating life and exploring the top of the nearby mountain naked. On my days off I would go swimming in some of the most beautiful rivers and swimming holes with the other volunteers. I would work four days washing up followed by three days off. My French really helped me enjoy the experience.

PARIS

Like all major cities in the developed world, Paris presents thousands of ways to earn your keep, while being difficult to afford from day to day. Unless you are very lucky, you will have to arrive with some money with which to support yourself while you look around.

Expatriate grapevines all over Paris should prove helpful for finding work and accommodation. Many people find their jobs as well as accommodation through one of the city's many notice boards *(panneaux)*. The one in the foyer of the CIDJ near the *métro* stop Bir-Hakeim has already been mentioned as being good for student-type jobs such as extras in movies, but sometimes there are adverts for full-time jobs or *soutien scolaire en Anglais* (English tutor). It is worth arriving early to check for new notices.

The other mecca for job and flat-hunters is the American Church at 65 Quai d'Orsay (01-40 62 05 00; *métro* Invalides). Official notices are posted on various notice boards inside and out; the cork board in the basement is a free board where anybody can stick up a notice. Obviously it is necessary to consult the notices in person; they are not available by phoning the church or on the internet.

Although the notice board at the *Alliance Française* is for the use of registered students of French, you may be able to persuade a student to look at the adverts for you, many of which are exchanges of room for some babysitting and/or teaching. The notice board is in the annex around the corner at 34 rue de Fleurus.

The famously eccentric English language bookshop *Shakespeare and Company* at 37 rue de la Bûcherie in the fifth *arrondissement* has a large notice board, but is more useful as a place to chat to other expats about work and accommodation. The shop operates as a writer's guest house. If you are prepared to write a short account of yourself, you can stay free for up to a week, assuming there is space. The elderly American expat owner George Whitman (grandson of Walt) still hosts weekly Sunday open house for aspiring *literati* and also hires English-speaking staff to clean, run errands and work behind the till.

> When **Claire Judge** was in her last year at school she decided she would like to work at Shakespeare and Company during the summer:
> *I wrote to them saying I would like to work for a month in July/August, and they replied on a post card saying they would give me a place to stay for an hour's work a day. When I wrote asking if my specific date of arrival was all right, they didn't reply and a second attempt failed too.*

This might have defeated most 17 year olds, but Claire decided to go to Paris anyway to check it out and ended up being given a room overlooking Notre Dame in exchange for two hours of working in the shop and cleaning per day.

Most expat places like WH Smith's Bookshop near the Place de la Concorde and the Virgin Megastore on the Champs Elysées distribute the free bilingual newsletter *France-USA Contacts* or *FUSAC* (www.fusac.org) which comes out every other Wednesday. It comprises mainly classified adverts which are best followed up on the day the paper appears. An advert in *FUSAC* costs US$20 for 20 words, and can be sent before your arrival (franceusa@aol.com).

Disneyland Paris

The enormous complex of Disneyland Paris, 30km east of Paris at Marne-la-Vallée, has 5,800 hotel rooms and an entertainment centre as well as the theme park, employing about 12,000 people in high season both on long-term and seasonal contracts. Seasonal positions are from March or May to September with a minimum availability of 15th June to 31st August. 'Cast members' (Disneyspeak for employees) must all be over 18, have a conversational level of French and preferably a third European language. The majority of jobs are in food and beverage, housekeeping, merchandising and custodial departments, though one of the best(?) jobs is as a Disney character. Further details are available from Service du Recruitement-Casting, Disneyland Paris, BP 110, 77777 Marne-la-Vallée Cedex 4 (01-49 31 19 99; dip.casting.fr@disney.com; http://disneylandparis.com/uk/employment/index.htm). For all jobs the well-scrubbed look is required (though they do now tolerate neatly trimmed facial hair), and of course they are looking for the usual friendly, cheerful and outgoing personalities. The monthly gross starting wage is €1,119-€1,315 from which deductions are made for social security (about €160). Staff accommodation costs €230 per month and travel expenses are reimbursed on completion of a contract.

Germany

Students who have studied German at school and may intend to pursue those studies in higher education should consider spending at least part of their gap year in Germany, either doing a language course or a work experience placement, as an au pair or a volunteer. Even if you are not planning to specialise in modern languages, German can be combined with many commercial and other subjects to make you ultimately very employable. The economic powerhouse of Europe can absorb a great many foreign students in various capacities. Despite the current high level of unemployment, it is possible to arrange paid work experience independently, though easier with the help of a teacher or contact.

The stereotype of the obsessively efficient and hard-working German is found by many gap year students to have a basis in truth but is not the whole truth. Institutionally, Germany can be inflexible and rule-bound, but individual Germans can be helpful and humorous.

Placement Organisations

GAP Activity Projects offer a variety of placements in Germany lasting 6-12 months departing September, January and February, with some date flexibility. Most positions are voluntary and in the field of caring, e.g. working in hospitals, schools for children with disabilities and residential homes for the elderly. Normally accommodation and pocket money are provided which means that the outlay for this programme is less than for most others, i.e. about £1,000.

Interspeak (Stretton Lower Hall, Stretton, Cheshire SY14 7HS; 01829 250641/ www.interspeak.co.uk) can arrange short and longer term traineeships (internships or *stages)* for students in hotels and on farms in the region of Franconia (around Nuremburg) and Munsterland (Munster and Hamm). These 'maxi-stages' last 4-24 weeks; the placement fee starts at £300 and board and lodging may need to be paid for.

EIL (287 Worcester Road, Malvern, Worcs. WR14 1AB; 0800 018 4015; www.eiluk.org) arranges homestay, language courses and high school placements in Germany.

It is possible to use the Federal Employment Service from outside Germany. The *Zentralstelle für Arbeitsvermittlung* (Central Placement Office) has an international department *(Auslandsabteilung)* for dealing with applications from German-speaking people abroad. Details and application forms are available from ZAV, Villemombler Str. 76, 53123 Bonn (0228-713-0; fax 0228-713 1111; www.arbeitsamt.de/zav). All applications from abroad are handled by this office. The Zentralstelle has a special department which finds summer jobs for students of any nationality, because this is felt to be mutually beneficial to employers and employees alike. Students who wish to participate in this scheme should contact ZAV before March. Students must be at least 18 years old, have a good command of German and be available to work for at least two months. Work is available in hotels and restaurants, as chamber staff and kitchen helpers in hospitals, and in agriculture. The Zentralstelle assigns jobs centrally, according to employers' demands and the level of the candidate's spoken German. For example those with fluent German may be found service jobs while those without will be given jobs such as chambermaids or dishwashers. If you decline the first job offered by ZAV, you cannot be sure that they will offer another.

The UK agency *Jobs in the Alps* (www.jobs-in-the-alps.com) carries out aptitude tests on behalf of German hoteliers looking for about 50 English-speaking staff (with EU nationality) for the summer and winter seasons. The Bloomsbury Bureau (37 Store St, London WC1E 7BH; 020-7813 4061; bloomsburo@aol.com) recruits up to 40 general assistants for hotels mainly in Bavaria. Applicants must be EU citizens and have a knowledge of German. A net wage of $360 on top of free room and board is promised in exchange for working a 45-hour week.

The IJAB (International Youth Exchange) in Bonn has a EuroDesk which administers European student exchanges (Heussallee 30, 53170 Bonn; 0228-95 06 208; www.eurodesk.de). The website www.prabo.de, available in English, describes itself as the leading free internship database for companies, students and anyone else who is looking for an internship in Germany. If you function in German try www.praktikum.info or the job search site www.jobware.de.

The Happy Hands working holiday scheme places language and gap year students from the UK and the rest of Europe in the field of rural tourism. Participants are given weekly pocket money of €51 and full board and lodging with families on farms or in country hotels. In return they look after children and/or horses and farm animals. The preferred stay is three to six months though a two-month commitment is also allowed; details available from Happy Hands, Römerberg 8, 60311 Frankfurt; 069-293733; Anne.Gleichen@t-online.de; www.workingholidays.de. An agency registration fee from €230 is charged.

Special Schemes for Americans

CIEE in the US administer two programmes in Germany. American students who have studied German for at least two years at college can work for up to three months between mid-May and mid-October or students who can fix up a career-related internship can work for up to six months at any time of year. CIEE's office in Germany can be found at Oranienburger Str. 13-14, 10178 Berlin (030-28 48 59-0; InfoGermany@councilexchange s.de; www.councilexchanges.de).

InterExchange in New York can place full-time students in German resorts during the summer provided they have intermediate German. Applications must be in by the middle of February.

Six-month internships for American students or recent graduates in business, engineering or technical fields are available through CDS International Inc. (871 United Nations Plaza, 15th Floor, New York, NY 10017-1814; 212-497-3500; www.cdsintl.org). If needed, the first month can be spent at an intensive language course in Cologne, after which participants undertake a paid internship which they have secured previously with the help of the InWEnt (www.inwent.org) formerly the Carl Duisberg Gesellschaft e.V. (CDG), the partner organisation of CDS International. Longer placements of 12-18 months are also available.

Seasonal Work

As well as trying the Zentralstelle beforehand, you can try to fix up a summer job ahead of time by sending off speculative applications. This worked for **Dean Fisher,** an engineering apprentice who decided to take a break from what was turning out to be a discouraging job hunt at home. He went to wash dishes in Berchtesgaden on the Austrian border:

> I spent 2½ months working in a very orderly and efficient kitchen on the top of a mountain in the Kehlsteinhaus (Eagle's Nest) with the most amazing view I've ever seen. I actually enjoyed the work even though it was hard going. I met loads of good people and learned a lot of German.

Get hotel addresses from tourist office brochures or the web.

Recommended areas to try for a summer job are the Bavarian Alps (along the border

with Austria), the shores of Lake Constance, the Bohmer Wald (along the Czech border), the Black Forest (in south-west Germany), and the seaside resorts along the Baltic and North Seas. One employer on the Baltic coast hires a number of foreign students as general assistants, food and beverage staff, child carers and sports instructors at a coastal campsite/golf and holiday park. The hours are long and you must be able to speak German but the wages are good. Apply in the spring to Camping Wulfener Hals, Riechey Freizeitanlagan GmbH, 23769 Wulfen/Fehmarn (04371 8628-0/www.wulfenerhals.de).

Although few British tour companies operate in Germany, ski jobs can be found on-the-spot in resorts like Garmisch-Partenkirchen (which also has hotels and services for the American Army) on the Austrian border 50 miles southeast of Munich, and the spa resort of Oberstdorf in the mountains south of Kempten.

The *Internationales Haus Sonnenberg,* a conference centre in the Harz Mountains (see 'Directory of Paid Seasonal Jobs') not only pays a wage to young people willing to work in the domestic department while improving their German, but it includes them in many of the conference excursions and activities. **Joanne Evans** wrote enthusiastically from the centre where she was doing her year as a fully funded European Volunteer (see EVS in 'Directory of Specialist Gap Programmes' and further programme details in chapter on Voluntary Work):

I was looking for an interesting way to spend my university year abroad and arranged through EVS to work at Sonnenberg where I had worked on the domestic staff twice before. Speaking from person experience, I can say that the German members of staff are very patient on the language side of things, and will go to great lengths to make themselves understood. The working relationships between all the departments here is very close and there is always someone to speak to if there are problems like homesickness. Out of my wages I pay DM280 a month for a furnished well-heated room and shared kitchen, living room and bathroom. The house is good fun with the German 'Zivis' (young men doing civilian service rather than the army) living downstairs and domestic staff ('praktikanten') and EVS volunteers upstairs.

If you are looking for a congenial place to stay in Berlin before a placement or just on your travels, A & O Hostels has three hostels in Berlin with a fourth opening March 2004 (www.aohostels.com).

Work Experience

Work placements can be organised in a wide range of sectors including tourism, trade, telecommunications, marketing and banking depending on timing and availability. Most internships are organised in conjunction with an intensive language course. Normally an upper intermediate level of language ability is required for work experience to be successful. Most are unpaid or are rewarded only with a subsistence wage. Board and lodging will generally be provided only in the tourism sector.

DID-Deutsch Institute is a major language course provider (see 'Course Directory') which can also arrange two to six month internships following their language courses in Berlin, Frankfurt, Munich and Wiesbaden; the processing fee for an unskilled work placement is €300 while a qualified internship placement will cost €415 in addition to the preceding language course (e.g. €1,609 for 8 weeks). Similarly *GLS (Global Language Services)* combines a minimum 4-week language course with an internship in a Berlin-based company of 4, 8 or 12 weeks. Host companies want their trainees to speak German to at least an intermediate level.

Astur GmbH (Sturmiusstrasse 2, 36037 Fulda; 661-92802-0; info@astur-gmbh.de; www.astur-gmbh.de/work_1.html) organises linguistic stays in about 50 cities and towns around Germany with work experience placements lasting four or eight weeks for EU nationals. An excellent standard of German is required to work in a German company, normally in industry, sales, marketing, administration, accountancy, tourism, law, translation or computers. Astur also arrange hotel experience placements for which candidates need an intermediate standard of German after a compulsory pre-placement language course.

Euro-Academy's Internship Department matches students' area of interest with work placements in companies in Munich, Berlin and Frankfurt. Participants do a 4-week German course first which together with the placement fee costs £950. Accommodation can be arranged separately with a host family for £125 per week (bed and breakfast) or £160 (half-board).

Eurolingua (61 Bollin Drive, Altrincham WA14 5QW; ☎/fax 0161-972 0225; www.eurolingua.com) offers a German Language and Work Experience programme in Berlin, Cologne, Munich, Radolfzell, Saarbrücken, Dortmund, Hanover and Mannheim. Trainees are not paid. Eurolingua will try to match internships with requests for specific fields such as marketing, banking, insurance, travel and tourism, graphic design, social services, political organisations, and communication technologies. Candidates must do a minimum 4-week German language course to ensure they are at Intermediate standard before undertaking a 4-week internship or longer.

The Brussels-based linguistic and cultural exchange agency M.B. Language Asbl (41 rue Henri Bergé, 1030 Brussels, Belgium; 2-242 27 66/ macbaron@chello.be) arranges short placements in Hamburg for students aged 16-18 studying German; the placement fee for a two week summer placement and homestay is €475.

Graduates with a background in economics or business who can speak German have a reasonable chance of finding teaching work in a German city, since most of the demand comes from companies. A TEFL Certificate has less clout than relevant experience when looking for freelance English teaching work. University students and recent graduates who would like to spend a year as an English language assistant in a German secondary school should contact the British Council at assistants@br itishcouncil.org or www.languageassistant.co.uk. Altogether they place about 300-400 students aged 20-30 to work 12 hours a week. *Assistants* are paid about £500 a month. A few secondary schools in Germany (including the former East) employ native English speakers as *Helfers* (junior assistants) at boarding schools. These posts are normally reserved for students who apply through the *British Council* (10 Spring Gardens, London SW1A 2BN). To be eligible for posts starting in August/ September or occasionally early summer, you must be aged 18-20, have A-level or equivalent German and have a guaranteed place at a university (not necessarily to study German).

A list of opportunities to live and work in Germany can be found in the Jobs section of the British Council-hosted British German Youth portal The Voyage (www.the-voyage.com). Among the listings are work experience placements, au pairing and voluntary work. They suggest links (among others) to Eurostage (www.eurostage.org/de/accueiluk.htm).

School leavers with a particular field of interest can try to pursue it in their gap year in Germany. For example **Robin Lloyd** from Hampshire had always been interested in car design. With an A-level in German and a place at Bristol University to do a German and engineering degree, he wrote to a number of motor car manufacturers in Germany only to be told that he was too young and that they accepted only students already embarked on a university-level engineering degree. The one exception was BMW in Munich which runs a scheme for young trainees and who provided Robin with a pleasant flat on his own and enough wages to support himself in Munich for nine months. Although he found the formal protocol of German industry a little hard to swallow, he greatly enjoyed Munich and quickly developed a social life based on the city's Irish pubs. If you intend to look for a placement with a company, take evidence of any qualifications and some good references *(zeugnisse)* which are essential in Germany.

Philip Oltermann organised two work placements for himself, both in the German media, helped by the fact that he was born and had spent time living in Hamburg where both the magazines were located:

I had read both magazines before when in Hamburg and got their addresses from the Yellow Pages. I phoned them up about a year before I started my year off and asked about the possibility of doing a work experience, then wrote an application soon after. They were both relatively small publications, one of them a sort of free city-mag with a focus on local politics and culture, the other the local Hamburg section of Germany's most alternative (and poorest) newspaper. This however turned out to be a big bonus in both cases, as I got to do a lot of independent work, i.e. doing research, taking pictures, writing larger articles and reviews, instead of just making coffee, as it seems to be the custom at bigger publishers.

Au Pairing

Most UK au pair agencies have partner agents in Germany who make family placements. Some, like the Bloomsbury Bureau (address given above in the section on jobs in tourism), specialise in Germany. Au pairs must have some knowledge of German and experience of childcare and those from outside the European Union must be aged 18-24.

Among the longest established agencies is the non-profit Roman Catholic agency IN VIA with branches throughout Germany (Ludwigstr. 36, 79104 Freiburg (0761-200208; www.invia.caritas.de). Its Protestant counterpart is affiliated to the YWCA: Verein für Internationale Jugendarbeit (Goetheallee 10, 53225 Bonn; 0228-698952; www.vij-Deutschland.de). VIJ has 23 offices in Germany and places both male and female au pairs for a preferred minimum stay of one year. Pocket money of €215 net per month is promised.

With the de-regulation of employment and recruitment agencies that took place in Germany in March 2002, dozens of private agents have popped up all over Germany, many of them members of the newly formed Aupair Society (www.au-pair-society.org) which carries contact details for its nearly 50 members. Commercial au pair agencies do not charge a placement fee to incoming au pairs.

Au Pair Interconnection, Staufenstr. 17, 86899 Landsberg am Lech (08191-941378; www.aupair-interconnection.de).

Au Pair in Deutschland, Baunscheidtstr. 11, 53113 Bonn (0228-957300; www.gijk.de). Part of GIJK, a cultural exchange organisation, which is also involved in holiday job and internship placements for German young people. Has an informative brochure in English. Applications must be made through a partner agency in your home country.

Perfect Partners Au Pair Agency, Am Sonnenhugel 2, 97450 Arnstein (09363-994291; www.perfect-partners.de).

The monthly pocket money for an au pair in Germany starts at €200 a month. Some families offer to pay for a monthly travel pass or even cover your fare home if you have stayed for the promised period of nine months, typically up to €150. In return they will expect hard work which usually involves more housework than au pairs normally do, as Maree Lakey found during her year as an au pair in Frankfurt:

I found that Germans do indeed seem to be obsessed with cleanliness, something which made my duties as an au pair often very hard. I also found that from first impressions Germans seem to be unfriendly and arrogant, however once you get to know them and are a guest in their home, they can be the most wonderful and generous people. The Germans I met were sincerely impressed by my willingness to learn their language and at the same time genuinely curious about life in Australia, my home country.

It is possible for non-EU citizens to become au pairs through one of the above organisations provided they are not older than 24. A special au pair visa must be obtained before leaving the home country, a process which requires an *Annahmebestätigung* or official confirmation of placement.

VOLUNTARY WORK

Countless opportunities exist throughout the vast nation of Germany for undertaking voluntary work whether in environmental protection or in community service. The green movement in Germany is very strong and many organisations concentrate their efforts on arranging projects to protect the environment or preserve old buildings.

All the major workcamp organisations send people of all ages on short-term projects mostly in the summer. It is also possible to apply direct to an indigenous voluntary organisation such as:

Other German workcamp organisations to try are:

Internationale Begegnung in Gemeinschaftsdiensten (IBG), Schlosserstrasse 28, 70180 Stuttgart (0711-649 11 28/ www.workcamps.com). Publish a booklet in English of their projects in both eastern and western Germany.

Mountain Forest Project (Bergwald Projekt e.V.), Hauptstr. 24, 7014 Trin, Switzerland (081-630 4145; www.bergwaldprojekt.ch). One-week forest conservation projects in the alpine regions of southern Germany. Basic knowledge of German is useful since the foresters conduct the camps in German. Hut accommodation, food and insurance are provided free though participants must pay an annual membership fee of SFr50/ €30.

Norddeutsche Jugend im Internationalen Gemeinschaftsdient (NIG), Gerberbruch 13A, 18055 Rostock (0381-492 2914/ www.campline.de). Range of environmental and social projects in northeastern Germany.

Offene Häuser (Open Houses), Goetheplatz 9B, 99423 Weimar (03643-502390; info@openhouses.de/ www.openhouses.de). Volunteers restore historic buildings year round; contribution of €25-€40 per week. Website in English.

Pro International, Bahnhofstr. 26A, 35037 Marburg/Lahn (06421-65277; www.pro-international.de). Social projects published in English (booklet and website). Application fee €65.

Vereinigung Junger Freiwilliger (VJF), Hans-Otto-Str. 7, 10407 Berlin (030-428 506 03; office@vjf.de). Camps take place in the former East Germany. Registration fee for applicants who apply directly is €220-€250.

There are some longer term possibilities as well. Internationaler Bund (IB), Freier Träger der Jugend-, Sozial- und Bildungsarbeit e.V., Burgstrasse 106, 60389 Frankfurt am Main (069/9 4545-0; Info@internationaler-bund.de) takes on young people for a period of six or twelve months in various social institutions such as hospitals, kindergartens, homes for the elderly or disabled people. In some German states, young people may also work on ecological projects. Volunteers are paid pocket money plus full board and accommodation.

The Australian voluntary organisation Involvement Volunteers Association Inc. (IVI) has an office in Germany: IV Deutschland, Volksdorfer Strasse 32, 22081 Hamburg (+49-412 69450; ivgermany@volunteering.org.au). Those who wish to volunteer to work on organic farms should contact the German branch of WWOOF (Willing Workers on Organic

Farms), Postfach 210 259, 01263 Dresden (info@wwoof.de). Membership costs €18 which gives access to about 160 farm addresses.

COURSES AND HOMESTAYS

The main language provider is the government-funded *Goethe Institut* which has centres in London, Manchester, York and Glasgow as well as in nearly 20 German cities and towns. A list of addresses in Germany with full course details offered by each one is available from the website www.goethe.de or from the Goethe Institut in London (50 Princes Gate, London SW7 2PH; 020-7596 4000; german@london.goethe.org). The Goethe Institut administers language exams at all levels, leading to internationally recognised certificates such as the ZdaF, KDS and GDS. **Rosanne Curling** decided to spend eight weeks in the first part of her gap year learning German at the Goethe Institut in Dresden. The cost for the intensive course plus self-catering accommodation was £1,300.

Although I had learnt German to GCSE level, I soon discovered that I could read and write much better than I could listen and speak, which meant that initially communication proved difficult. However I soon became accustomed to the 'Sachische' dialect and was able to differentiate the words, even if I could not understand them. It also took time to become accustomed to having lessons conducted entirely in German, as opposed to in England, where at least the grammar was explained in English. However in a class combining an Egyptian, a Japanese, a Ukrainian, a Pole, an American, a Cantonese and me, the only language common to all was German. This was a huge advantage of this course: the chance to meet a whole range of personalities from around the world and make great friends from a Venezuelan opera singer to an Italian voluntary worker.

As well as enjoying the facilities of Dresden – the parkland, musical culture, hockey club – its location and Germany's fantastic public transport system allowed for many weekend excursions to Berlin, Prague, Leipzig and Weimar. On one trip I visited Buchenwald Concentration Camp which brought home the horrors of war in a way that sitting in a history class simply could not.

All the major language course agencies like *CESA, EF, Caledonia, En Famille, Euro Academy* and *Euroyouth* run extensive programmes in Germany. Among the most popular destinations for year-out language students are Munich, Heidelberg and Freiberg, though less picturesque places will be cheaper. It might be worth noting that the purest German is spoken in the north, but even if you are living in Bavaria where there is a pronounced accent, the teaching will be of standard German.

Dialogue Sprachinstitut, Bahnhofplatz 1b, 88131 Lindau (08382 944600; info@dialogue.com/ www.dialogue.com) has a selection of courses followed by *stages* (internships) for those who achieve a satisfactory level of German. Fees are from €579 for a 4-week course plus homestays starting at €140 per week (out of season and sharing a room) and rising to €180 (single room in summer).

See also entries for *BWS Germanlingua, GLS* and *DID (Deutsch in Deutschland)* in the 'Directory of Language Courses'. The average cost for a full-time two-week course is normally around €400 for tuition alone, €600-€650 with accommodation. A range of German language courses is available at private language schools through *EIL, CIEE* and a number of others. Alternatively you can stay with a private home tutor which costs from £540 per week through *Challenge*. Junior summer programmes are also available, combining language tuition with sport, social and cultural activities.

One of the great educational institutions of Germany is the *Volkshochschulen (VHS)* or folk high schools which can be found in nearly every town of the republic. In addition to offering 'German for Foreigners', it offers a range of evening classes in drama, handicrafts, sport and so on, all at subsidised prices. Most bookshops sell the prospectus of courses available for terms beginning in September and January. **Emma Colgan** was delighted with the *Volkshochschule* which she attended in Hamburg twice a week and also enjoyed the international make-up of the classes:

> *Our class resembled a United Nations meeting… Naturally the lessons were con- ducted in German and helped me to maintain my written German. At the end of the course in May, I sat the Mittelstufe Prüfung II as set by the Goethe Institut and passed with 'gut'. Unfortunately nobody seems to have heard of this exam in England.*

Nevertheless Emma was pleased with her achievement, since the *Volkshochschulen* courses are primarily designed for enjoyment.

The German Academic Exchange Service *(Deutscher Akademischer Austausch Dienst* or DAAD) with headquarters in Bonn has offices in London (34 Belgrave Square London SW1X 8QB; 020-7235 1736) and New York (871 United Nations Plaza, New York, NY 10017; 212-758-3223; fax 212-755-5780; daadny@daad.org/ www.daad.org). It assists people enrolled full-time at an institute of higher education to study or do research in Germany. The London office publishes a list of summer language and music courses in Germany.

Academic Associates International can arrange for young people to spend September-June or January-June at a German *Gymnasium*. The German education system is very rigorous so participants will have to be prepared for intensive studies. It might be worth looking at a 200-page book called *Studying and Working in Germany: A Student Guide* by Peter James and David Kaufman from the University of Newcastle (2002, £12.99).

Greece

Two decades ago, Greece was probably as popular a destination for student travellers between school and university as Australia or Thailand is now. Although many young people do want to spend time relaxing on a Greek island, fewer consider longer-term possibilities in Greece during their gap year. Anyone planning to read classics or archaeology at university will be attracted to the great sites of Greek antiquity as well as to the beautiful scenery and climate, friendly and carefree people, memorable wine and food. Anyone interested in picking up casual work to support a long stay should consult the book *Work Your Way Around the World* which has detailed information about work on the harvest of grapes, oranges, olives, etc. and advice for finding work in resorts.

AU PAIRING & TEACHING

Living with a Greek family is one of the best ways of organising an extended stay. Yet au pairing hours tend to be longer in Greece than elsewhere, partly because there is no expectation that a gap year student will need time off to study the language. The Nine Muses Agency accepts applications from young Europeans and American women for au pair positions and can also place candidates after arrival in Athens. Contact the agency at PO Box 76080, 171 10 Nea Smyrni, Athens; 210-931 6588; ninemuses@ninemuses.gr). The owner Kalliope Raekou prides herself on her after-placement service, meeting regularly with au pairs at coffee afternoons. There is no fee to au pairs.

> Among her satisfied au pairs is **Riitta Koivula** who, from an unsatisfactory situation on Kos, moved with Popy Raekou's help to a much better one in Athens:
> *I started my work as an au pair on Kos when I was 19. At first I was so excited about my new family and the new place since I had never been to Greece before and I loved the sun and the beach. I lived in a small village called Pili where almost*

> no one spoke English. But soon I got tired of the village because winter came, tourists left and it wasn't so warm to spend time on the beach any more. I also got tired of the family. The three little girls didn't speak English and they were very lively. The working hours were also terrible: 8 to 12 in the morning and then 4 to 10 in the evening every day except Sundays. I was very homesick on Kos and decided I wanted things to change. So I went to Athens in November and was soon given a new family. I fell in love with Athens and its people right away. My new family was the best and we are still very close. I met other au pairs and one Finnish au pair became my best friend. I learned so many things, even to read and write and speak Greek because we took Greek lessons during the spring with Popy. I have many happy memories of Athens and friends who are still dear to me.

Mig Urquhart arrived in Athens on a Friday, got the English daily, the *Athens News* on Saturday, had an interview on Sunday and started a live-in job a week later, even though she had hoped to avoid that option. She would have preferred an English teaching job but hadn't done a training course and lacked the confidence to bluff. At that time of year (September) few jobs seemed to be around that didn't require a knowledge of Greek. Live-in jobs of course cut out the hassle and cost of finding accommodation. Although Mig liked the children and the father well enough, she didn't enjoy being treated more like a servant than a member of the family by the mother.

Thousands of private language schools called *frontisteria* are scattered throughout Greece creating a huge demand for native English speaker teachers. Unfortunately for gap year students, all but the dodgiest schools will expect to see a university degree (which is a government requirement for a teacher's licence). The basic gross hourly wage is currently €5.76 gross (€485 net). Earnings can be increased substantially by compulsory bonuses at Christmas and Easter and holiday pay at the end of the contract.

Chains of schools may be worth approaching with your CV. The two main ones are *Strategakis ISDN Language Schools* (24 Proxenou Koromila St, 546 22 Thessaloniki; 031-264276; stratken@compulink.gr) and the *Omiros Association* (52 Academias St, 106 79 Athens; 01-36 22 887).

University graduates who fancy the idea of taking a gap year teaching English in Greece after graduation should be aware that agencies exist to match graduates with 10-month vacant posts. Interviews are carried out in Greece and the UK during the summer for contracts starting in September. These agencies are looking for people with at least a BA and normally a TEFL certificate (depending on the client *frontisterion's* requirements). The following undertake to match EU nationals with *frontisteria* and do not charge teachers a fee:

Anglo-Hellenic Teacher Recruitment, PO Box 263, 201 00 Corinth (☎/fax 27410-53511; jobs@anglo-hellenic.com/ www.anglo-hellenic.com). Dozens of posts in wide choice of locations for university graduates from the UK, preferably with a CELTA or Trinity TESOL.

Cambridge Teachers Recruitment, 17 Metron St, New Philadelphia, 143 42 Athens (☎/ fax 210-258 5155). Interviews conducted in UK in summer by Andrew MacLeod-Smith (macleod_smith_andrew@hotmail.com). One of the largest agencies, placing 75 teachers per year in vetted schools. Applicants must have a degree and in most cases a TEFL Certificate, a friendly personality and conscientious attitude.

NET (Native English Teachers), 72 Windsor Road, Worthing, West Sussex BN11 2LY. ☎ 01903 218638. Small agency.

After completing a PhD in classics at Cambridge but before landing a job, **Jamie Masters** decided to go to Crete to teach English and play music for a year. He arrived in Heraklion in October, when it was too late to register with agencies:

> I advertised (in Greek) in the Cretan newspapers, no joy. I lowered my sights and started knocking on doors of frontisteria. I was put onto some guy who ran an English-language bookshop and went to see him. Turned out he was some kind of

lynch-pin in the frontisterion business and in fact I got my first job through him. Simultaneously I went to something which roughly translates as the 'Council for owners of frontisteria' and was given a list of schools which were looking for people. The list, it turned out, was pretty much out of date. But I had insisted on leaving my name with the Council (they certainly didn't offer) and that's how I found my second job.

OTHER GAP YEAR OPPORTUNITIES

Seasonal Work

The Sani Beach Holiday Resort on the Halkidiki peninsula near Thessaloniki (www.saniresort.gr) employs a large number of hospitality industry trainees for a minimum of five months on what they describe as a 'training wage' (63077 Kassandra, Halkidiki; 23740-31231; hrdtrain@saniresort.gr).

Seasonal jobs can be arranged from the UK. Mark Warner (020-7761 7300) run several resort hotels in Greece which require British staff who are paid anything from £50 per week depending on the position in addition to full board and accommodation, use of watersport facilities and flights. Other possibilities are Olympic Holidays (1 Torrington Park, Finchley, London N12 8NN; 020-8492 6742; www.olympicholidays.co.uk) who are always on the lookout for outgoing EU nationals over 20; Golden Sun Holidays (Mason's Drive, 1-3 Valley Drive, Kingsbury, London NW9 9NG; 020-8206 4733; www.goldensun.co.uk) which employ 150 overseas representatives to work in Greece or Cyprus for three months or more between April 1st and October 31st; and Pavilion Tours (Lynnem House, 1 Victoria Way, Burgess Hill, West Sussex RH15 9NF; 0870 241 0425; www.paviliontours.com) which need watersports instructors for children.

Tour operators seem to be more interested in finding the right attitude rather than experience when recruiting reps, as **Debbie Harrison** discovered:
Last summer I worked as a holiday rep on the island of Kos. I was introduced to Golden Sun by an English friend who had worked for them before. Despite the fact that I had no qualifications or relevant experience, had never been to Greece and had never even been on a package holiday, I was offered a job on the island I wanted immediately at the end of my interview. Perhaps this had something to do with the fact that it was mid-March, less than a month before training began and they obviously still had positions to fill. However Golden Sun (and I assume other tour operators) do hire reps as late as May or June to help out with the extra workload of high season. Six or seven months is a long time to stay in one place. One of the reasons I stuck it out to the end was so I'd get my £100 deposit refunded. As a rep my wages were about £300 per month on top of accommodation. The youngest full-time rep was an 18 year old who had just finished a college course in Tourism, and at the other end of the scale, one of my colleagues was 28 and had resigned from her position at an advertising agency to work in the sun for a bit.

Another possibility is Sunsail International (The Port House, Port Solent, Portsmouth, Hants. PO6 4TH; 02392 222308; www.sunsail.com) though they are looking to recruit staff who are over the age of 20. Sailing Holidays Ltd (105 Mount Pleasant Road, London NW10 3EH; 020-8459 8787; www.sailingholidays.com) look to hire flotilla skippers and hostesses, boat builders and marine engineers for their upmarket holiday programme in the Greek and Dalmatian islands. The specialist tour operator Setsail Holidays (The Business Centre, 140 Station Rd, Redhill, Surrey RH1 1ET; 01787 764443; www.setsail.co.uk) recruits a similar range of staff for the full seven-month season in the eastern Med.

The internet is bound to turn up further possibilities such as the Heart Rock Bar on Kos (094-552 5217 or 094-969500) whose website allows you to register interest in a job (www.heartrock.gr). As always, young people, especially young women, considering a job overseas found over the internet, should go cautiously and should ask to be put in touch with one or two previous student workers before accepting.

Many gap year travellers stop a while in one place and swap some labour for free hostel accommodation. They enjoy the hostel atmosphere and the camaraderie among hostel workers, and regard the job as a useful stop-gap while travel plans are formulated, often based on the advice of fellow travellers. Anyone who sticks at it for any length of time may find themselves 'promoted' to reception; in this business a fortnight might qualify you for the honour of being a long-term employee. The work is easy-come, easy-go, and is seldom secure even when you want it to be. The popular and cheap Hotel Festos near Syntagma Square in Athens (18 Fillelinon St, 105 57 Athens; 01-323 2455; consolas@hol.gr/ www.consolas.gr) employs casual staff itself and passes on job-seekers to other places when it is full. Jill Weseman describes the 1,000-bedded Pink Palace on Corfu (066-53103) as a cross between a Club Med for backpackers and an American summer camp, though others are less complimentary, reporting that in the crowded high season, brawls and trouble erupt almost nightly. The hostel employs an army of foreign workers as bartenders, cooks, receptionists, etc. Michel Falardeau, a more mature traveller from Quebec, picked up work there at the end of 2001 even though November is the quiet season, and found that the wage (all the employees got less than €10 a day) was not much and everybody spent their money partying.

It is sometimes worth checking the Situations Vacant column of the English daily *Athens News* (9 Christou Lada, 102 37 Athens; 210-333 3404/8; an-classified@dolnet.gr). You can check the classified ads on the internet (www.athensnews.gr).

Another interesting possibility for people over 21 with experience of nursing, catering or maintenance is at the holistic holiday centre on the island of Skyros in the northern Aegean. A number of 'work scholars' help with cleaning, bar work and domestic and maintenance duties in exchange for full board and accommodation and £40 a week. The minimum stay is three months from May or August. The main perk is that workers are allowed to participate in the multitude of courses and workshops on offer including windsurfing, music, theatre and yoga. Details are available from *Skyros*, 92 Prince of Wales Road, London NW5 3NE (020-7267 4424; www.skyros.com).

In past summers, volunteers have been recruited to row a 170-oared trireme, a reconstruction of a ship used by the ancient Greeks, now berthed at Poros. Unfortunately the hull of the *Olympias* was badly damaged by Mediterranean shipworm a few years ago and repairs have been slow. However as of mid-2003 they are underway and the possibility of sea trials in the summer of 2004 or 2005 were being investigated, though not in time for the Athens Olympics. Interested people can make contact with members of the Trireme Trust through the website www.atm.ox.ac.uk/rowing/trireme).

Conservation and Archaeology

Conservation Volunteers Greece (15 Omirou St, 145 62 Kifissia, Athens; 210-623 1120; cvgpeep@otenet.gr; http://users.otenet.gr/~cvgpeep) is a non-profit organisation promoting intercultural exchanges and nature and heritage conservation. Projects include work in protected landscapes, conservation of traditional buildings and work on archaeological sites. Applications should be sent to a partner workcamp organisation in your country (e.g. UNA Exchange in the UK). The participation fee for people applying directly is €120 for two or three weeks.

A UK conservation charity Earth, Sea and Sky (PO Box 308, Lincoln LN4 2GQ; anna@earthseasky.org) recruits volunteers to carry out a coastal clean-up for the benefit of wildlife in the newly designated National Marine Park in the Ionian island of Zakynthos. The sustainable tourism charity is run by a British woman married to a Greek man from Zakynthos.

Organisations involved in the protection of sea turtles actively use volunteer helpers. Archelon is the Sea Turtle Protection Society of Greece (Solomou 57, 104 32 Athens; ☎/ fax 210-523 1342; www.archelon.gr) which carries out research and conservation on the loggerhead turtle on Zakynthos, Crete and the Peloponnese. A free campsite is provided for those who stay at least a month; volunteers will need at least £6 a day for food plus pay a registration fee of €70.

Conservation Koroni (Poste Restante, Koroni 240 04, Messinias; fax 27250-22779) has in the past taken on volunteers in phases between mid-May and mid-October to spend a couple of hours each day working to clean up the beach and surrounding habitats of the loggerhead turtle near Koroni in the Peloponnese. No wage is paid and the cost of accommodation for one month is about €170. Bears are even more threatened than marine turtles. Arcturos accepts short-term volunteers at its bear protection centre (Victor Hugo 3, 546 25 Thessaloniki; 2310-55 59 20; arcturos@arcturos.gr).

Nineteen year old Giles Standing became a subscriber to *Archaeology Abroad* at the beginning of his gap year and won one of their Fieldwork Awards to participate in a research dig on the Peloponnese and wrote an account of his experiences for the *Archaeology Abroad Bulletin*:

> On this particular dig, we were lucky enough to be staying and working in a beautiful rural part of Greece, deep in the heartland of the Peloponnesian countryside with its towering hills and ancient olive groves. We worked there Monday to Friday each week, with weekends left free for relaxing or taking trips to other archaeological sites. After years of being interested in ancient sites, it was an incredible experience for me to see Corinth, Delphi and the Acropolis at close quarters. I will not forget the first time I glimpsed the main body of the Parthenon through the massive columns of the Propylaia, truly a remarkable and humbling experience.
>
> I was working on a farm track which was cut in half, running parallel to a field of lemons and another of grapes. We were investigating a target detected last year with GPR. Unfortunately the equipment was incorrectly calibrated and it became clear that this could not possibly be a Classical Greek site as the objects were far too close to the present-day surface level. Digging on the exposed road was surprisingly tough with the hottest part of the day reaching well into the 90s/30s on a daily basis. We worked roughly a seven-hour day with afternoons off to recuperate and we would meet later for dinner at a taverna on the beach.

Giles was the only Briton among Americans, all of whom had paid a large sum to join. The current costs are $460/€460 per week; further details are on www.geoprobe.org/helike/volunteers.html.

Courses

Enjoyable as it is to master the Greek alphabet and learn simple greetings with which to befriend the locals, not many gap year students want to make a formal study of modern Greek. Any that do should enquire about courses in Athens, Thessaloniki and Crete such as those lasting between three and ten weeks offered by the *Athens Centre* (48 Archimidous St, 116 36 Athens, Greece; 210-701 2268/ www.athenscentre.gr).

Alternatively, the *International Centre for Hellenic and Mediterranean Studies* in Athens (PO Box 17176, 100 24 Athens; www.cyathens.org) offers semester and summer courses in Athens. It runs regular courses in language and civilisation from its premises next to the Olympic Stadium and from a secondary location on the island of Paros. This college has traditionally concentrated on the American market though other nationalities are accepted as well (see entry in 'Directory of Language Courses').

The Aegean Center for the Fine Arts (Paros 84400, Greece; 22840-23 287; studyart@aegeancenter.org) has been offering fine arts courses to individuals in small groups for almost 40 years at its centre on the Cycladic island of Paros. Students can create their individual curriculum with the help of artists in residence choosing from among the visual arts (photography, print making, painting and drawing) and literary arts (creative writing, literature, voice). One student said that she felt as though she had spent a whole semester on a film set rather than real life. The 14-week session from early March costs about €7,500; application should be made up to two years in advance. The website (www.aegeancenter.org) gives details.

Anyone interested in Greek folk culture might wish to contact the *Greek Dances 'Dora Stratou' Theatre* (8 Scholiou Street, Plaka, 105 58 Athens; 01-324 4395; http://users.hol.gr/~grdance) which runs courses and workshops on traditional dance and theatre between May and October. The organisation puts on a series of summer performances at the outdoor theatre on Philopappou Hill in Athens and takes on about ten unpaid foreign student volunteers to help look after the large costume collection and assist at performances.

A North American drama programme takes place in Greece every summer. See the entry for the *University of Detroit Mercy Theatre Company* in the 'Directory of Drama Courses'. Participants in the 4-week performing course must audition before acceptance.

Purely recreational courses in painting and photography can also be found. Steve Outram's travel photography courses in western Crete (see entry) are aimed more at photographers wanting to learn enough to take saleable photos. Unfortunately such courses tend to be expensive, e.g. more than $2,000 for one week.

Italy

Italy has always been a favourite destination for young people wanting to expand their cultural horizons. In the 18th century, the Grand Tour of Europe, which was considered to be an essential part of the education of young men of good breeding or fortune, was centred on Italy; and generations of educated people journeyed between the great artistic centres of Venice, Florence and Rome. Although their modern-day equivalents are seldom accompanied by a private tutor, many now do enrol in courses which will help them to appreciate the art and civilisation of ancient Rome and Renaissance Italy.

Italy is still a remarkably welcoming country and Italians are capable of breathtaking generosity and hospitality, with no expectation of anything in return. Some first-time visitors mistakenly expect Italy to be poor and backward in some respects but instead they find the most cultivated and sophisticated people in the world, not to mention the best-dressed.

SPECIALIST GAP YEAR PROGRAMMES

Two exclusive cultural programmes in Italy maintain the tradition of the Grand Tour and are still aimed at young people of fortune since they are expensive. *Art History Abroad* and the *John Hall Pre-University Interim Course* both provide a superb introduction to European art and culture on their spring courses. Both are aimed at school leavers who may be planning to go on to university to study art history or who may just have an independent interest in Western history and civilisation.

John Hall offers courses in Italy for non-specialists on European civilisation, especially the visual arts and music, including architecture, conservation, opera, design, literature and Italian cinema. Practical options include Italian language, drawing, painting and photography. The spring course consists of an introductory week in London followed by six weeks in Venice where accommodation, meals, lectures, visits and classes are included in the price of £5,800 with optional extra periods in Florence and Rome. A recent participant describes the ambitious range of subjects covered:

It's hard to believe all the things we did in a relatively short space of time: making friends, visiting some of the most beautiful places in the world, and learning more than we ever thought possible about a huge range of topics, from Titian to Tate

Modern, Massacio to Mozart, Palladian villas to Peter Lauritzen, Byron to Bellini and everything in between.

Art History Abroad offers six-week programmes in spring and autumn (October to early December) plus a two-week course in the summer. Their programme involves travel around Italy so that students are introduced to a broad spectrum of Italian life. **Richard Sherrington** participated in the Art History Abroad Gap Course in 2002 and clearly enjoyed escaping from the classroom between school and taking up a place to read Biology at Oxford:

> *I now enjoy, and have studied close up, many of the wonders of European creativity. We were taught by charismatic tutors, some university graduates, some professional artists and other well established art historians. There was not one classroom session, no test nor exam; the course didn't need them. The whole AHA experience defined enthusiasm for me.*

Similarly positive feedback has been received about the John Hall Pre-university Course in Venice:

> *There is no way that any lists or itineraries can begin to tell you all of what you will experience on this trip. The course is naturally many different things to different people. It's not just an incredibly well-situated introduction to the history of western culture, it concerns far more. As the name suggests, it does a fantastic job of bridging the gap between school and university and so serves as an insight into a variety of lecturing styles and also living in close quarters with lots of people on a day-to-day basis. But most importantly, it's a chance to consistently combine large doses of business and pleasure.*

The *British Institute of Florence* has developed a varied and interesting programme specifically for gap year students. Most stay for two to three months though some stay for a whole year to do A-level Italian or art history. To help structure and justify taking her gap year in Italy, **Katherine Wratten** enrolled in an A-level course at the British Institute of Florence for 2002/3:

> *There are so many opportunities for young people today and, in an ever-shrinking world, the chance of a gap year between school and university is becoming a reality for more than just a fortunate few. Last year I left school one of these lucky individuals and chose to begin my adventure along the cobbled streets of Florence. Unable to justify coming to Florence for just a holiday, I decided to study the Italian language and to do a one-year Italian A Level course, which would give me a goal and boost my UCAS points.*
> *Leaving home, language and culture for a foreign country was a daunting prospect and students at the British Institute have to adapt to an entirely new existence, which requires learning new social and practical skills. However, the Institute had taken this difficult aspect of our adventure into account creating a cosy, friendly and informative base for students to come and go as they please. Throughout our stay, and especially during the first two weeks, every effort was made to ensure that each of us was integrating into both school and social life with added lessons, conversation exchanges, and evening outings.*
> *Learning another language has always been an ambition of mine after I failed so abysmally at French GCSE, and what better place to learn than in the country itself. The teaching at the Institute has been, and continues to be, outstanding. Conversational Italian is reinforced by regular meetings with the Italian students studying English at the Institute. There is so much happening everyday, with courses and talks on an incredibly diverse range of topics, plus excursions to Rome, Venice and*

the opera. Some weeks my feet have barely touched the ground, although there have also been times when I have been able to lie back, take it easy and enjoy the view. And what a glorious view!

Courses at the British Institute of Florence (www.britishinstitute.it) can combine language tuition with other subjects such as life drawing, opera and cookery, while accommodation is with selected families or in student flats. The Institute accepts other nationalities as well as British. American students might also be interested in the study abroad semester and foundation year programmes offered by *Art Under One Roof* or the *Studio Art Centers International* both in Florence and both with entries in the 'Directory of Art Courses'. The Aegean Center for the Fine Arts based in Greece (Paros 84400, Greece; 284-23 287; studyart@aegeancenter.org) has been offering autumn courses in fine arts for many years at its centre in the Tuscan city of Pistoia before moving on to Paros (see chapter on Greece). Students study and practise the visual arts of their choice and are taken on excursions to Venice and Rome. The inclusive cost is €8,000 for 14 weeks from early September. Application should be made up to two years in advance; see www.aegeancenter.org for details.

COURSES & HOMESTAYS

The specialist gap year programmes originating in the UK are mentioned earlier in this chapter. Italian is one of the easiest and most satisfying languages to learn, especially if you already have some knowledge of a Latin-based language. Many courses combine Italian language lessons with art history, cuisine, etc. For example *Accademia Italiana* in Florence offers courses in design (fashion, furniture, graphic, textile, etc.) with language, while Linguadue (Corso Buenos Aires 43, 20124 Milan; 02-2951 9972; linduemi@tin.it) and Linguaviva (Via Fiume 17, 50123 Florence; 055-28 00 16; info@linguaviva.it) offers a range of courses on Italian culture and language plus organises internships. The *Accademia del Giglio* in Florence offers Italian courses for foreigners plus art and art history courses.

Caledonia Languages Abroad offers a wide range of courses throughout the country, with schools in the main cities like Florence and Rome and in smaller lively university cities like Siena and Bologna.

An excellent source of Italian language school listings is the website www.it-schools.com. The US site www.iiepassport.org also has many leads. Serious courses often work towards the *Certificazione di italiano come lingua straniera* (C.I.L.S.) exam of the University of Siena which is divided into four levels. For Italian language schools in the 'Directory of Language Courses', see entries for the *Koinè Center* in Florence, *Il Sillabo*, *Accademia Britannica Toscana* in Arezzo which has a special pre-college Italian course, the *Caffe Italiano Club* in Tropea on the western side of Italy's toe, and *Atrium* in Cagli.

Three related schools offer Italian, art and cookery in Florence (or a combination). See entries in the 'Directory of Courses' for *Lorenzo de' Medici, The Art Institute of Florence* and the *Apicius Cooking School*. A starting price for one week's intensive study would be €150 and €450 for four weeks. Accommodation in one of the major cities would cost a further €500+ a month bed and breakfast with a host family. Needless to say, courses in central Florence or Venice will be more costly than ones in more obscure towns.

On the Schools Programme offered by *AFS Intercultural Programmes UK* (Leeming House, Vicar Lane, Leeds LS2 7JF; 0113-242 6136; info-unitedkingdom@afs.org) students aged 15-18 spend an academic year or term living with an Italian family and attending the local school.

TEACHING

Hundreds of English language schools around Italy employ native English speakers though the majority are not suitable for gap year students unless they have acquired a qualification in Teaching English as a Foreign Language. But some do manage to find openings, despite their lack of a TEFL certificate. After **P. Penn** left his selling job, he went to Turin to find TEFL work and he succeeded without any experience whatsoever. But this is certainly the exception. **Natalia de Cuba's** experience is more typical: she could not persuade any of the language schools in the northern town of Rovereto where she was based to hire her without qualifications. So she decided to enrol in the Cambridge Certificate course run by International House in Rome (Viale Manzoni 22, 00185 Rome). She found the month-long course strenuous but not terribly difficult, and worth the fee (which now stands at €1,500). Job offers come into IH from all over Italy and no one seems to have a problem getting a job immediately after the course.

Several Italian-based chains of language schools might be worth a try. Recruitment is normally carried out by the individual schools, but the administrative offices should be able to provide a list of addresses. The British Institutes (Via Leopardi, 8, 20123 Milan; 02-439 0041; www.britishinstitutes.org) group has nearly 200 member schools; email addresses can be searched on their website or you can pick up a leaflet listing them from the youth travel bureau CTS (also represented in most cities). Oxford Schools hire up to 30 teachers for their 15 schools in northeast Italy (Via S. Pertini 14, Mirano 30035 Mirano, Venice; ☎/fax 041-570 23 55; www.oxforditalia.it).

As in other European countries, summer camps for unaccompanied young people usually offer English as well as a range of sports. The organisation called A.C.L.E. Summer Camps (Via Roma 54, 18038 San Remo, Liguria; ☎/fax 0184-506070; www.acle.org) advertises in the UK for more than 150 young people who must be 'fun-loving, energetic and have high moral standards' and with a genuine interest in children, to teach English and organise activities including drama for one, two or three months. The promised wage is €800 per month plus board, lodging, insurance, bonus and travel between camps within Italy. However summer staff must enrol in a compulsory three-day introductory TEFL course for which a deduction of €150 is made from earned wages.

Another organisation that hires native English speakers to work at summer language camps is Smile (Via Vigmolese 454, 41100 Modena; ☎/fax 059-363868).

AU PAIRING

Most European au pair agencies deal with Italy, so you should have no trouble arranging a job with a family. **Angie Copley** describes her experiences after arranging a family through a specialist agency (now closed):

I wrote to Au Pairs Italy and before I knew it they had found me a family in Sardinia. I couldn't believe it was so easy. All I had to do was pay for a flight out there and that was that. When I arrived, the family met me and took me to their house. Some house. It wasn't just a house but a castle where the Italian royal family used to spend their holidays. What was even better was that the family had turned it into a hotel, the best possible place for meeting people. I ended up having the best summer of my life in Sardinia. Once I picked up the language I went out, met lots of people, had beach parties. My work involved not much more than playing with their two-year old boy all day and speaking English to him. Basically it was one big holiday.

Summer-only positions are readily available. Most Italian families in the class which can afford live-in childcare go to holiday homes by the sea or in the mountains during the summer and at other holiday times which did not prove as idyllic as it sounds for **Jacqueline Edwards**:

My first job as an au pair in Italy was with a family who were staying in the middle of nowhere with their extended family. It was a total nightmare for me. I could just about say hello in Italian and couldn't understand a word of what was going on. After three weeks I was fed up, homesick and ready to jump on the next plane to England. But a few days later we moved back to town (Modena) and from then on things improved dramatically. I was able to go out and meet other au pairs and nannies at the park, etc. and we all socialised together. I ended up learning Italian quite well, making lots of friends (partly through my language school, which was free) and visiting most of the Italian cities. The only part that I didn't like in that job was going away with the family to their holiday houses for skiing, etc. You end up working twice your usual hours for the same pay, have no social life as you don't have any friends there, can't go skiing as you are minding the baby and then they tell you to cheer up because you're on holiday.

The average monthly wage for au pairs is in the range €250-€280 and for mother's helps from €300. Wages are slightly higher in the north of Italy than central and southern parts of the country because the cost of living is higher. The demand for nannies and mothers' helps able to work 40+ hours is especially strong since a high percentage of families in Italy have two working parents.

Most staff at Italian agencies speak English and welcome applications from British au pairs. Make sure first that you won't be liable to pay a hefty registration fee. Try any of the following:

ARCE (Attivita Relazioni Culturali con l'Estero), Via XX Settembre 20/124 16121 Genoa (010-583020; fax 010-583092; arceita@tin.it). Long established agency which makes placements free of charge throughout the country.

Au Pair International, Via S. Stefano 32, 40125 Bologna (051-267575/238320; www.aupair-international.com). Member of IAPA. No placement fee.

Aupairitaly.com, Via Demetrio Martinelli 11/d, 40133 Bologna (051-383466; www.aupairitaly.com).

Au Pairs Recruitment, Via Gaeta 22, 10133 Turin (329-211 6277; annaparavia@paravia.it).

The English Agency, Via Pigafetta 48, 10129 Turin (011-597458; info@theenglishagency. com). No placement fee is charged.

Euroma, Viale B Buozzi 19 AA, int 3, 00197 Roma (06-806 92 130). €129 fee.

Europlacements Italy, Via Felica Cavallotti 15, 20122 Milan (02-760 18 357; euro@posta2000.com).

Intermediate SNC, Via Bramante 13, 00153 Rome (06-57 47 444; www.intermediateonli ne.com). €200 fee. Intermediate has its own language school in the Aventino district of Rome.

Jolly Italian Au Pair Agency, Via Giovanni XXIII 20, 36050 Monteviale (VI); ☎/fax 0444-552426; www.goldnet.it/~jolly]. Au pair agency accepts all nationalities.

Mix Culture Roma, Via Nazionale 204, 00184 Rome (06-4788 2289; mixculture@tiscalin et.it).

PAID OPPORTUNITIES FOR GAP STUDENTS

Working in Italy is something of a hit and miss situation and if you can't speak a word of Italian, you will be at a distinct disadvantage. Contacts are even more important in Italy than in other countries. **Louise Rollett**, for example, first went out as a paying guest to a town near Bologna with *EIL* and then extended her stay on a work-for-keep basis as an English tutor. **Dustie Hickey** went for treatment to a doctor in Milan who immediately offered to pay her to tutor his children in English.

The language school already mentioned *Il Sillabo* north of Arezzo provides internships to people who have studied Italian intensively with them for at least eight weeks, so far in restaurants and a flower shop. The unpaid work period will be 4-12+ weeks and interns will receive free board and lodging and back-up from the agency which charges an enrolment fee of €155.

You are not expected to speak Italian if you work for a British tour operator; in fact German is probably more sought after than Italian because of the high number of German tourists in Italy. Try any of the major campsite tour companies like *Canvas, Holidaybreak, Eurosites, Keycamp* or *Haven Europe* who are looking primarily for people over 18 with customer service skills. The smaller Venue Holidays (1 Norwood St, Ashford, Kent TN23 1QU; www.venueholidays.co.uk) employs summer season reps at campsites on the Venetian Riviera, Lake Garda and in Tuscany.

A knowledge of Italian would of course be needed by anyone hoping to work in an Italian hotel. For example a small hotel group on the Lago d'Orta employs chamber, kitchen and dining room staff who speak English but know some Italian; applications to the Hotel Giardinetto, Via Provinciale 1, Pettenasco; 0323 89118; hotelgiardinetto@tin.it).

Winter Resorts

Crystal Holidays, part of the Thomson Travel Group (King's Place, Wood St, Kingston-upon-Thames W4 5RT; 020-7420 2081; www.shgjobs.co.uk) hire resort reps and chalet staff for work in the Italian Alps as well as staff for summer holidays. The Ski Department of PGL Travel Ltd (Alton Court, Penyard Lane, Ross-on-Wye, Herefordshire HR9 5GL) offers some jobs as ski reps, leaders and ski/snowboard instructors to fully qualified skiers, especially for short periods during half-term and Easter holidays.

If you haven't fixed up a job with a UK tour operator, job openings can be found on-the-spot in the winter resorts of the Alps, Dolomites and Apennines. Many are part-time and not very well paid, but provide time for skiing and in many cases a free pass to the ski-lifts for the season. During her gap year before going to Nottingham University, **Jaime Burnell** from Hungerford was not very thrilled with her job with a British ski tour operator near Trento:

The initial honeymoon period of thinking I was extremely clever for getting work with a British tour company ended quickly when I was hit with the bombshell that I was to be put in the smallest resort on the programme. Quite frankly the work is only bearable when the nightlife and skiing are great so working in a resort where the nightlife was non-existent and the clients were therefore miserable, is it really surprising that two 18 year olds were unhappy and decided to quit? The whole skiing scene relies on the fun you have outside work. No fun at night, then all you have is a boring life which just happens to be in a ski resort.

Things looked up enormously when she travelled independently to Sauze d'Oulx to look for work:

I cannot recommend enough winter work in Sauze d'Oulx. I arrived on the 14th of January. Everyone tells you that the turnover is high but that is an understatement. Going out every night you couldn't be sure who would be behind the bar that day.

Jaime goes on to offer one more nugget of information which proves once and for all that blondes really do have more fun:

The best investment you can make in Italy is a bottle of blonde hair dye. My tips tripled.

Other Jobs in Tourism

As throughout the world, backpackers' haunts like hostels and campsites often employ travellers for short periods. While planning her escape route from a less-than-satisfactory summer au pairing job in Naples, Jacqueline Edwards asked in the Sorrento youth hostel about job possibilities and a few weeks later moved in to take over breakfast duties in exchange for free bed and breakfast.

VOLUNTARY WORK

Many Italian organisations arrange summer work projects which are as disparate as selling recyclable materials to finance development projects in the Third World to restoring old convents or preventing forest fires. Here is a selection of voluntary organisations which run working holidays. In some cases, it will be necessary to apply through a partner organisation in your home country:

Abruzzo National Park, c/o National Parks Office, Viale Tito Livio 12, 00136 Rome (06-3540 3331; post@pna.it). Volunteers carry out research and protection of flora and fauna in remote locations. Further details are available by contacting the local park offices in Pescasseroli (011-39-0863-91955) or Villetta Barrea (011-39-0864-9102; fax 011-39-0864-9132).

AGAPE, Centro Ecumenico, 10060 Prali (Torino) (0121-807690; www.agapecentroecume nico.org). Volunteers help run this ecumenical conference centre in the Alps.

CTS, Dipartimento per la Conservazione della Natura, Via A. Vesalio 6, 00161 Rome (06-4411 1476; ambeinte@cts.it).

Emmaus Italia, Via Castelnuovo 21/B, 50047 Prato (0574 541104). Social and community workcamps.

International Building Companions (Soci Costruttori), Via Smeraldina 35, 44044 Cassana, Ferrara (0532-730079; www.iboitalia.org). Renovation projects in deprived communities listed on website.

LIPU, Lega Italiana Protezione Uccelli, Via Trento 49, 43100 Parma (02-2900 4366; www.lipu.it). Long-established environmental and bird conservation association which publishes a catalogue of summer projects (and a short summary in English). Volunteer camps cost approximately €150 per week.

Mani Tese, P. le Gambara 7/9, 20146 Milan (02-407 5165; www.manitese.it). International campaigning organisation raises funds for projects in developing countries and hosts study camps for which a basic knowledge of Italian is needed.

La Sabranenque, Centre International, rue de la Tour de l'Oume, 30290 Saint Victor la Coste, France (04-66 50 05 05; www.sabranenque.com). French-based organisation uses voluntary labour to restore villages and monuments in Altamura (inland from Bari in Southern Italy) and Gnallo (Northern Italy). The cost of participation is €160 or €240 for ten days.

Servizio Civile Internazionale, Via San Martino della Bataglia 6, 00185 Rome (06-848 800715; www.serviciocivile.it).

Jesce Conservation Project, c/o Cultural Cube, 16 Acland Rd, Ivybridge, Devon PO21 9UR (www.culturalcube.co.uk). Summer workcamps to clear weeds and rubbish from neglected Roman site along the Appian Way. Food costs are €20 a day plus an application fee.

WWF Italia, Servizio Campi, Via Po 25/C, 00198 Rome (www.wwf.it/ENG/holiday/camps). A few environmental conservation camps, though the emphasis is on holidays. Sample 9-day fire-watching camps in Sicily cost €233.

Willing Workers on Organic Farms (WWOOF), c/o Bridget Matthews, 109 Via Casavecchia, 57022 Castegneto Carducci (LI); 0565-765001 (info@wwoof.it; www.wwoof.it). WWOOF volunteers in Italy must join the national association at a cost of €24 for insurance purposes.

Volunteers can also join archaeological camps. The national organisation Gruppi Archeologici d'Italia is the umbrella group for regional archaeological units that co-ordinate 2-week digs (Via Degli Scipioni 30/A, 00192 Rome (☎/fax 06-397 34 449); the website www.gruppiarcheologici.org provides links to regional archaeological offices. The fee for participation is likely to be about £150 per week.

There are also archaeological camps which volunteers can join. The national organisation Gruppi Archeologici d'Italia is hard to track down but was last heard of at Via Degli Scipioni 30/A, 00192 Rome (06-397 33 786/fax 397 34 449; www.gruppiarcheologic

i.org). Another possible source of information is Archeoclub d'Italia, Via Sicilia 235, 00100 Rome (06-488 1821/fax 428 81 810). The fee for participation is likely to be about £150 per week.

Malta

Although small in area (30km by 15km), Malta has much of interest. The student and youth travel organisation NSTS (220 St Paul St, Valletta VLT 07; 246628/www.nsts.org) markets English courses in conjunction with sports holidays for young tourists to Malta. NSTS run weekly vacation courses from June to August, which might take on a water sports enthusiast on a work-for-keep basis.

The Malta Youth Hostels Association (17 Triq Tal-Borg, Pawla PLA 06; ☎/fax 356-693957; myha@keyworld.net) can put volunteers aged between 16 and 30 to work for a minimum of 21 hours a week in exchange for free accommodation and breakfast. Jobs to be done include administration, decorating, building, etc. The minimum period of work is a fortnight and the maximum is three months. A good faith deposit and application fee must be paid; the deposit will be forfeit if the volunteer works less than the prescribed number of hours. MYHA obtains work permits for participants, a process that takes up to three months. Send three IRCs for details.

Russia & Eastern Europe

While Russia has been wrestling with its political and economic demons, the more stable Central European states of Hungary, Poland, the Czech Republic and Slovakia have steadily moved towards the west to the point where they have been accepted into the European Union. From May 2004 Hungary, Poland, the Czech Republic, Slovakia, Slovenia, Estonia, Latvia and Lithuania will join the EU (with a possibility that Romania and Bulgaria might join in 2007). However there may be reciprocal transitional controls on the free movement of labour (which is likely to be much more in one direction than another given that the rates of unemployment in Poland and Slovakia, for example, are hovering around 18% at present).

During the heady days immediately after the various Communist governments fell (when gap year students were aged about five), thousands of young Westerners flocked to Prague, Budapest and Kraków. Many of them supported themselves for short and longer periods by teaching English to a population which clamoured for access to the English-language media and culture. Things have settled down now and there has been a mild backlash in some quarters against what has been seen as a selling out to the West, especially in the major capitals which have been swarming with foreigners (especially Americans) since 1990.

ENGLISH TEACHING

Several English-teaching schemes are described in this chapter suitable for a gap before or after university. Most participants will be sent to small provincial towns and industrial cities rather than to the glamorous capitals. In Russia, the Baltic states of Latvia, Lithuania and Estonia and the other (no-longer-newly) independent states of the old Soviet Union, the English teaching situation is more fluid. Native speakers can still arrange some kind of teaching, often on a private basis, but with no guarantee of earning a living wage from it.

Placement Organisations

The vast majority of opportunities in Russia and Eastern Europe are for English-teaching volunteers. While commercial EFL recruitment agencies are involved with filling vacancies in Eastern Europe with certificate-holding teachers, educational charities and year out placement organisations send volunteer teachers. For example *GAP Activity Projects* send TEFL volunteers to Hungary, Poland, Romania and Russia for 5-6 months; and *Teaching Abroad* to Russia and the Ukraine. GAP volunteers must do a short TEFL training course before departure. A Teaching Abroad package of up to three months teaching in Moscow costs £1,395 (without travel) or £895 in Kiev. They also offer work experience in various fields, e.g. animal care, journalism and medicine.

With *Travellers* (7 Mulberry Close, Ferring, West Sussex BN12 5HY; ☎ 01903 502595; fax 01903 500 364; www.travellersworldwide.com), paying volunteers teach conversational English in Russia and the Ukraine. Work experience placements are available in the Ukraine only, in journalism, law, medical care and veterinary medicine. Karate placements are also available. Prices start at £895 for 3 months teaching in Kiev (excluding international travel).

Services for Open Learning (SOL) (North Devon Professional Centre, Vicarage St, Barnstaple, Devon EX32 7HB; 01271 327319; sol@enterprise.net) is a non-profit organisation which annually recruits about 30 graduates to teach for a year in state schools in most Eastern and Central European countries (Belarus, Croatia, Czech Republic, Hungary, Romania and Slovakia).

BUNAC co-operates with the English language organisation Language Link to place post A-level (and older) students in one-year teaching positions in Russia after they complete a four-week Certificate in TEFL. The total programme cost is £1,500 including the course, placement and travel.

IEC (International Exchange Center) in London runs programmes in what it still refers to as the former Soviet Union, i.e. summer camp counsellor and longer term teaching for people over 19.

The youth exchange company *CCUSA* runs a Summer Camp Russia Programme whereby teacher/counsellors are placed on youth camps in Russia lasting four or eight weeks between mid-June and mid-August. Participants must be between the ages of 18 and 35, have experience working with children and/or abroad, and have an interest in learning about the Russian language and culture. Camps are widely scattered from Lake Baikal in Siberia to the shores of the Black Sea. The programme fee of £699 includes round-trip travel from London to Moscow, visa, travel insurance, orientations on arrival and room and board. In the UK contact CCUSA at Green Dragon House, 64-70 High St, Croydon CR0 9XN (020-8688 9051; www.ccusaweusa.co.uk/ccrussia/programme.html) or in the US: 2330 Marinship Way, Suite 250, Sausalito, CA 94965 (1-800-449-3872; www.campcounsellors.com). From summer 2003, CCUSA are setting up a new venture in Croatia, a language camp for European teenagers for which English-speaking counsellors will be needed; details from www.campcalifornia.com.

The *Anglo-Polish Universities Association* (93 Victoria Road, Leeds LS6 1DR) organises summer teaching placements in Poland on which British-educated native speakers spend four or eight weeks in July and August at holiday language camps sponsored by Polish colleges. A detailed information pack is available from APASS at a cost of £3 plus envelope and 41p stamp from mid-March. An administrative fee is charged. Reports have been received that placement details are not finalised until not long before departure, so be prepared to endure some suspense.

Some gap year students are enterprising enough to arrange teaching jobs with indigenous organisations like one of the following:

Akademia J. A. Komenskeho, Trziste 20, Mala Strana, 118 43 Prague 1, Czech Republic (2-5753 1476; www.akademie.cz). It actively welcomes gap year students to teach at one of 50 adult education centres and schools throughout the Czech Republic.

English School of Communication Skills/ESCS, ul. Sw. Agnieszki 2, 31-068 Kraków, Poland (☎/fax 012-422 85 83; personnel@escs.pl). Private language teaching organisation which runs short-term holiday courses staffed by native speakers.

International Exchange Center, 2 Republic Square, 1010 Riga, Latvia (fax +371 783 0257; info@iec.lv). Invites young people with a TEFL qualification to work at summer language camps in Russia, Ukraine, Belarus and a few in Latvia. Registration fee is £85.

Svezhy Veter Travel Agency, 426076 Izhevsk Pushkinskaya 154, 426000 Izhevsk, PO Box 2040, Russia (3412-512500/fax 3412-752268; www.sv-agency.udm.ru). Native speakers needed to teach evening course (15 hours a week) at Secondary School No. 27 in Izhevsk in exchange for homestay with meals and visa support (which costs $34-$132 depending on how far in advance you apply). Application fee is less than $100.

> **Koober Grob from Chicago was impressed with this arrangement she'd tracked down on the internet, and found lots of scope for initiative:**
> *I corresponded with Vladimir Bykov (the teacher I would eventually work with) for seven months before I went to Izhevsk. The students and I would discuss various topics such as domestic violence, cooking, nature, war or even manure and chocolate-covered ants. There was never any pretence in any of the classes. Eventually I started a theatre club for teenagers at a local school and then accompanied a six–week school trip around Siberia helping students individually with their English. The students were all so motivated, respectful and friendly. I only spent $600 for the three-month period that I was in Russia since Russia is very inexpensive and my students and friends paid for most of my expenses.*

Year-out students often end up providing conversational English practice for the older classes in secondary schools, which means they are teaching people nearly the same age as they are, as happened to **Trudie Darch** who spent a year teaching in Hungary through GAP:

> *I had been there three weeks and with very little notice I was told that I'd be teaching on my own for one whole week. This was the scariest thing that had happened so far. Virtually unprepared, I walked into a classroom full of 18 year olds (I was 19) and had to teach. The first lesson was not very good and I had some difficulties getting them to listen to me. It was hard to get over the fact that these were my students not people who were supposed to be my friends. However I overcame this and learnt that to be a more professional teacher, I had to distance myself from trying to be their friend. The school was basic, the food was interesting (pasta and icing sugar was one I hated) and my accommodation left a lot to be desired. But even the bad things I wouldn't swap because they taught me a lot.*

Obviously the experience was not too off-putting since on her return she went off to Lancaster University to start a teaching course.

Helen Fagan did not have to work to gain her pupils' respect in her GAP placement in a remote Hungarian village:

> *Arriving at the children's home where I was to teach is one of my most treasured and vivid memories. As we pulled up outside this very grand old building, the young-est boy from my group met me with a bunch of flowers and a kiss. As I proceeded down the stairs, all 50 children were holding small bunches of flowers which they presented to me individually with a kiss, a traditional Hungarian welcome. The low point of my placement in Hungary was definitely the day I had to leave.*

COURSES & HOMESTAYS

Ironically the study of Russian has been in sharp decline since Russia abandoned Communism and decided to throw in its lot with western capitalism. Compared to the heady 1960s, few schools and universities offer Russian. However there is still a contingent that want to be able to communicate in the language of Tolstoy, undaunted by reports of escalating crime.

The big language agencies like *Caledonia, CESA, EF* and *Euro-Academy* all offer Russian courses in Russia, particularly St Petersburg. The London office of the *Society for Co-operation in Russian and Soviet Studies* (www.scrss.org.uk) can arrange courses and homestays lasting as long as you like. Sample courses include a three- or four-week summer course in Moscow for £836/£977 excluding airfares and a Russian Christmas and New Year course lasting two weeks for £880 including flights on Aeroflot. SCRSS can also arrange 'Russian at Home' whereby you live in your tutor's home and receive 15 hours of individual tuition a week; the weekly price is £600 excluding airfares. Look also at the programmes offered by the Finnish-based *Proba International Education Centre* and the *Moscow Institute for Advanced Study* (entries in 'Directory of Language Courses'). Proba offers a combined language study with voluntary work lasting two to five months for US$2,100-$5,000, while MIFAS arranges post-language course internships with high level companies and organisations, provided the applicant has reached a high enough standard of spoken Russian.

Eighteen year old **Kathryn Emmett** wanted to gain a good basis in Russian and really wanted to get to know the country, so she booked a ten-week course in St Petersburg through *CESA Languages Abroad* with which she was delighted:

> I was really impressed with how much Russian I could learn in 2½ months. I certainly got to see the many faces of Russia just by going out for a drink and shopping. It was the normal things that made it unforgettable like going to a kiosk to buy a beer. The excursions were a good way of getting to know other students as well as going to places a bit further afield that at the beginning I didn't have the courage to do alone.
>
> The teaching staff were brilliant. I still don't know how they got me from absolute beginner who panicked at the utterance of any Russian word to being quite comfortable with the language. I'd tell everyone to go to Russia as long as they don't mind giving up a few creature comforts (like baked beans).

Kathryn reports that many a friendship with her fellow students blossomed over the topic of food.

VOLUNTARY WORK

The vast region of Eastern Europe is a hive of workcamp activity during the summer, so if a short-term group voluntary project appeals to you at all, contact the main UK workcamp organisations listed in the 'Directory of Voluntary Placements Abroad', all of which have partners in Eastern Europe. In many cases the projects are a pretext for bringing together young people from East and West in an effort to dismantle prejudice on both sides. Often discussion sessions and excursions are a major part of the three- or four-week workcamps and some volunteers have been surprised to find that their experiences are more like a holiday, with very little work expected. The people of Eastern Europe are repeatedly praised for their generosity and hospitality.

Some preparation is recommended by all the recruiting organisations and participants are encouraged to get some workcamp experience closer to home first and to attend orientations. The registration fee is normally higher than for Western Europe, say £130-

£150. Projects vary from excavating the ancient capital of Bulgaria to organising sport for gypsy children in Slovenia. There is also a high proportion of much-needed environmental workcamps.

The Christian voluntary organisation Aid to Russia and the Republics (PO Box 200, Bromley, Kent BR1 1QF; 020-8460 6046/www.ARRC.org.uk) sends volunteers to various locations throughout the former Soviet Republics from Armenia to Tajikistan, where volunteers assist with church-organised social projects, e.g. orphanages, centres for people with disabilities and work with street children. Most placements last between three weeks and three months, though gap placements last up to a year. Living conditions can be rough but volunteers (who need to be tolerant though not necessarily practising Christians) will be given a warm welcome. Volunteers pay an admin fee of £50 in addition to their accommodation and meals (£200 per month so as not to leave the host community out of pocket), visa costs (£25-£50), insurance and travel (e.g. £380 to Moldova, £625 to Armenia).

Many international voluntary schemes are particularly active in the region including the fully funded *European Voluntary Service* and its agencies like *Inter Cultural Youth Exchange (ICYE)* whose 'Eastlink' programme this year sent volunteers aged 18-25 to Latvia, Estonia, Poland and the Russian Federation from January to August; the volunteers incurred no expense.

Kitezh Children's Community for orphans in Kaluga, 300km south of Moscow, has close links with the *Ecologia Trust* in Scotland (see entry in 'Directory of Voluntary Placements Abroad'). The Trust specifically recruits students in their gap year to spend on average two months at Kitezh and provides extensive preparatory information, down to profiles of the resident children. The joining fee is £540 for one month, £695 for two months, including visa fee but not airfares to Moscow. Many recent volunteers have found Kitezh a friendly, welcoming and relaxing place to spend some time, among them **Sarah Moy**:

> *When I first arrived it was hard to work out what was expected of me, what my role was meant to be. Kitezh life is so different from the rest of the world that it took a while to know where you could go, how to get involved in work/play with the children, etc. I worked in the kitchen and garden and also painted a radiator which I appreciated. I felt very much a part of the community and enjoyed sharing my talents (but would have liked to have taught more English). I lived in the computer room so went to bed with people playing war games and woke up with people demanding to play; result – no privacy. But I was expecting that, so it wasn't too bad. Living as families is great as it makes you really feel a part of Kitezh. And the food is great considering the circumstances. Apart from the obvious benefits of improving Russian and learning more about Russian culture and people, I gained much from the slower pace of life. I was very impressed by the idea of people who have made a career out of genuinely caring and giving. I learnt more about a rural way of life and appreciated being reminded how many luxuries we have here. Altogether it was a fantastic experience.*

Romania

The orphanages and special schools of Romania continue to need voluntary input more than a decade on from the fall of Ceaucescu who neglected the needs of his citizens so abominably. Of the many charities which were formed to help the children of Romania, the Nightingales Children's Project operates a full-time volunteer programme. Each year about 120 volunteers spend from one to six months (average three) working at an orphanage in Cernavoda, 80km from the Black Sea resort of Constanta. Volunteers work with children, some of whom are disabled and have special needs, some with the HIV virus. Accommodation is shared with eight volunteers in a flat; volunteers contribute £2.50 a day to cover their rent and food. Further information is available from Nightingales Children's Project, 11 Colin Road, Preston, Paignton, Devon TQ3 2NR (☎/fax 01803 527233).

Writing in her college magazine, Emma Hoskison reminisced about her time spent with the orphans of southeast Romania:

During my Gap Year I spent the summer working for the Nightingales in Romania. Every day we went to the state-run orphanage and spent the morning and evening with our 'salons', groups of about 8 children of varying ages from 6 months to 10 years who had been neglected or abandoned due to some physical disability or financial reason (few of them were truly orphans). Many of the children did not speak and social interactions were minimal, so we used activities and games to stimulate their speech and learning. The charity provided many exciting toys and resources for the children. I tried hand printing once and they seemed more interested in throwing the paint around the room and over me! After every session, all the toys were locked away to prevent the nurses taking them home, such is the poverty there. Several children had mobility problems, so much time was spent walking around the grounds or in the playground; the swings were a great favourite with some. The time I spent in Romania was extremely challenging both emotionally and physically, yet it was the most rewarding experience of my Gap Year. I met some amazing people who have devoted years of their lives to the children's welfare and I often think of how my little friends are growing up, picturing their smiley faces.

Although conditions are much better than they were in the early years, the work can still be emotionally very draining. One gap year student who spent time in a Romanian orphanage suffered recurring nightmares for a long time after going on to university at Cambridge.

Another orphanage that uses regular voluntary assistance is run by an American couple Bruce and Sandy Tanner whose Tanner Romania Mission is a well respected organisation. They recruit their volunteers who are expected to stay between 3 and 12 months primarily through the *Global Volunteer Network* in New Zealand (see entry in 'Directory of Voluntary Placements Abroad').

DAD International UK has been actively recruiting volunteers to work and teach on summer language camps (see entry in 'Directory of Voluntary Placements Abroad'; www.dad.ro). British-Romanian Connections (PO Box 86, Birkenhead, Merseyside L41 8FU; 0151-645 8555/512 3355) runs an English club in Piatra-Neamt where new graduates and others are welcome to volunteer.

A completely different kind of placement is available at the Stefan cel Mare Horse Riding Centre in Transylvania through *Blue Dog Adventures* (see 'Directory of Work Experience'). Volunteers, who must have extensive experience working with horses, spend three weeks marking trails and training young horses to be used for equestrian tourism, and then spend the final week trail riding. The cost is £70.

TRAVEL

The Trans-Siberia rail journey persists in capturing the imagination of adventurous travellers. Note that booking this journey through an agent can more than double the price. On Ben Spencer's gap year in 2003, he and his friends started in China and decided to buy the various legs of the journey locally which meant that they got from Beijing to Moscow for £200 each. They greatly enjoyed being the only foreigners out of hundreds of friendly Russians (one of whom came to their rescue when Ben's friend left his wallet containing $400 in the toilet and it was returned to him). They disembarked a couple of times, i.e. in Ulaan Bator, Mongolia for five days, Irkutsk for five days and Ekaterinburg for two days, so that the longest single stretch was 51 hours.

A recommended specialist for independent travel in Russia is Findhorn EcoTravels, 66 The Park, Findhorn, Morayshire IV36 3TZ (01309 690995; gtravel@ecologia.org.uk). They can also arrange homestays.

Scandinavia

Not every gap year traveller wants to hit the trail to the tropics. The Scandinavian countries of Denmark, Sweden, Finland, Norway and Iceland exercise their own fascination and can be visited as part of an Inter-rail tour of Europe or separately. Substantial student discounts are available from DFDS Scandinavian Seaways (www.dfdsseaways.co.uk) on their ferry routes to Denmark and Sweden.

One way of getting away from the notoriously high cost of living and of travel in this region is to join one of the organised schemes described in this chapter for example working on a Norwegian farm or on a Swedish commune. Alternatively you can try to find work on your own, though this will be a challenge.

As the demand for English-speaking au pairs has been increasing in Denmark, Sweden and Norway, a growing number of young women over 18 are being placed with families for 10-12 months. A good chance of quick placement is through the au pair agency Exis in Denmark (Postbox 291, 6400 Sønderborg; 74 42 97 49/fax 74 42 97 47; info@exis.dk). Another possibility is the Scandinavian Au-Pair Center, Saturnusgatan 240, 26035 Ödråkra (42-20 44 02; www.aupair.se).

Even Iceland offers some prospects to someone who wants to spend part of their year out in the role of au pair. Vista X Change (Bankastraeti 10, 101 Reykjavik, Iceland; 562 2362/fax 562 9662; www.vistaxchange.is) is a leading exchange agency in Iceland, the only agency certified to bring foreign au pairs to Iceland (and British au pairs are always welcome). The Au Pair in Iceland programme accepts au pairs aged 18-26 for periods of 9-12 months starting in August/September or for 6, 8 or 12 months from January. Families undertake to reimburse half the cost of your flights if you stay 6-9 months and all your travel expenses if you stay 9-12 months. The minimum rate of weekly pocket money in Iceland is kr6,500 (£50) plus extra pay for babysitting beyond 30 hours a week. The partner agency in Iceland promises close supervision, opportunities to meet other au pairs and hiking and riding trips offered at a discount.

American young people should make contact with the American-Scandinavian Foundation (Exchange Division, 58 Park Avenue, New York, NY 10016; 212-879-9779/fax 212-249-3444; trainscan@amscan.org/ www.amscan.org) which places about 30 American trainees aged 21-30 each summer in the fields of engineering, chemistry, computer science and business in Scandinavia, primarily Finland and Sweden. It also has a year-long English teaching programme in Finland. Summer assignments usually last 8 to 12 weeks, though longer placements are also possible. The ASF can also help 'self-placed trainees', i.e. those who have fixed up their own job or traineeship in a Scandinavian country, to obtain a work permit.

Denmark

Denmark has the highest average wage of any EU country (90 Danish kroner equivalent to £8/€12) and a dropping rate of unemployment (5.1%), though the rate is still high among people aged 16-24 in Copenhagen. Work exists on farms and in factories, offices and hotels: the main problem is persuading an employer to take you on in preference to a Danish speaker. Any job-seeker in Copenhagen should take advantage of the youth information centre Use It, Rädhusstraede 13, 1466 Copenhagen K (33 73 06 20/ www.useit.dk). Their primary function is to help newcomers find affordable accommodation but they also distribute an excellent free booklet *Working in Denmark* in almost faultless English which has information about red tape procedures and some realistic tips for those trying to find a job or study Danish. It covers everything from the hours and locations where busking is permitted to how to register for a social security number. If requesting the booklet before arrival, send two IRCs and an s.a.e. Newly arrived job-seekers can visit Use It to consult their files, newspapers and *fagboden* (Yellow Pages) and to check their notice board for lift-shares (there is no jobs board).

Copenhagen, the commercial and industrial centre of the country, is by far the best place to look for work. It is also the centre of the tourist industry, so in summer it is worth looking for jobs door to door in hotels, restaurants and the Tivoli Amusement Park. Among the largest employers of casual staff in Denmark are newspaper distribution companies. Typically, papers must be collected from a local depot at midnight and delivered by 7am. The job is much easier if you have invested in a second-hand bicycle (from kr200) or a wagon. To get a job as an *omdeler* or 'paper boy/girl', contact one of the distribution offices listed in the *Yellow Pages* under the heading 'Aviser Distriktsblade' such as A/S Bladkompagniet, Dag Hammarskjölds Allé 13, 2100 Copenhagen Ø (35 27 71 06; bladko mpagniet@bladkompagniet.dk).

Another possibility is to contact VHH (the Danish equivalent of WWOOF) to obtain a list of their 30 or so member farmers, most of whom speak English. In return for three or four hours of work per day, you get free food and lodging. Always phone or write before arriving. The list can be obtained only after sending £5/US$10/€10 to Inga Nielsen, Asenvej 35, 9881 Bindslev (www.wwoof.dk).

Many young Europeans end up picking strawberries in Denmark in the summer, although the strength of the pound against the kroner means that potential earnings are not as high as they once were. Pickers get paid between 5.40kr and 7.25kr per kilo and can expect to pick not much more than 5 kilos an hour when they start out. Worker shortages between mid-June and the end of August mean that several schemes recruit pickers in Britain; for example Earth Work Ltd (8 Beauchamp Meadow, Redruth, Cornwall TR15 2DG; 01209 219934) hires 200 strawberry pickers for its holdings on Samsø. Applications are invited from EU nationals before June 1st ready for a 12th or 26th June start date. Other contacts for strawberry picking work include the Groningen-based agency *Appellation Controlee* (with an entry in the 'Directory of Paid Seasonal Jobs'), *IEC* the International Exchange Center in London and the Danish youth travel and exchange organisation Exis mentioned above in the context of au pairs. You can also apply directly, of course, for example to Else Lysgaard & Ingvar Jørgensen (Alstrup 2, 8305 Samsø; 86 59 03 45; www.else-ingvar.dk) or to Alstrup Frugtplantage (Alstrupvej 1, Alstrup, 8305 Samsø; elicc@samso.com).

Finland

Finland offers short-term paid training opportunities. The International Trainee Exchange programme in Finland is administered by CIMO, the Centre for International Mobility (PO Box 343, 00531 Helsinki, Finland; +358 1080 6767; http://finland.cimo.fi); their website is in English. British students and graduates who want on-the-job training in their field (agriculture, tourism, teaching, etc.) lasting between one and 18 months should apply directly to CIMO. Short-term training takes place between May and September, while long-term training is available year round. Applications for summer positions must be in to CIMO by the middle of February.

To join WWOOF Finland, send US$10 or FIM50 plus two IRCs and an s.a.e. to Anne Konsti, Partala Information Services for Organic Agriculture, Huttulantie 1, 51900 Juva (15-321 2380; amkonsti@hotmail.com).

In case you've heard of the Finnish Family Programme whereby young people spent some months living with a family, helping with the children and speaking English, note that the programme (once organised by CIMO) came to an end in 2000. It is now open only to foreign students studying the Finnish language at foreign universities.

The University of Helsinki Language Centre offers Finnish courses for foreigners who are not enrolled as students at the University of Helsinki. New courses begin in September and January, and usually last for a whole term. Shorter intensive courses are also available in the summer. Further information of tuition fees, etc. is available from the University of Helsinki Language Centre, Language Services, P.O. Box 33, 00014 University of Helsinki (+358-9-1912 3234). Finnish courses for foreigners are also available from the Open University of the University of Helsinki (www.avoin.helsinki.fi) and the Helsinki Summer University (www.kesayliopistohki.fi).

Norway

Atlantis Youth Exchange at Kirkegata 32, 0153 Oslo (☎/fax 22 47 71 79; post@atlantis-u.no/ www.atlantis.no) runs an excellent 'Working Guest Programme' which allows people aged between 18 and 30 of any nationality to spend two to six months in rural Norway (Americans and other non-Europeans may stay for no more than three months). The only requirement is that they speak English. In addition to the farming programme open to all volunteers, placements in family-run tourist accommodation are available to European nationals.

Farm guests receive full board and lodging plus pocket money of at least NOK825 a week (£70) for a maximum of 35 hours of work. The idea is that you participate in the daily life, both work and leisure, of the family: haymaking, weeding, milking, animal-tending, berry-picking, painting, house-cleaning, babysitting, etc. A wardrobe of old rugged clothes and wellington boots is recommended.

After receiving the official application form you must send off a reference, two smiling photos, a medical certificate confirming that you are in good health and a registration fee of £100+ (which differs between countries and agencies) for stays of up to three months and kr2,500 (£200) for longer stays. British applicants are asked to apply through *Concordia* (see 'Directory of Voluntary Placements Abroad') and Americans through InterExchange (161 6th Avenue, New York, NY 10013; 212-924 0446; www.interexchange.org).

Atlantis will try to take into account individual preferences and preferred part of the country. There are about 400 places (for all nationalities), so try to apply at least three months before your desired date of arrival. If they are unable to place you, all but NOK250 will be refunded.

Robert Olsen enjoyed his farm stay so much that he went back to the same family another summer:

The work consisted of picking fruit and weeds (the fruit tasted better). The working day started at 8am and continued till 4pm, when we stopped for the main meal of the day. After that we were free to swim in the sea, borrow a bike to go into town or whatever. I was made to feel very much at home in somebody else's home. The farmer and his daughter were members of a folk dance music band, which was great to listen to. Now and then they entrusted me to look after the house while they went off to play at festivals. Such holidays as these are perhaps the most economical and most memorable possible.

Atlantis also runs a programme for 200 incoming au pairs who must be aged 18-30 and willing to stay at least six months but preferably 8-12 months. The first step is to write to Atlantis or check the information on its website www.atlantis.no. Atlantis charges a sizeable registration fee, a quarter of which is non-refundable if the placement doesn't go ahead. The majority of families are in and around Oslo, Bergen or the other cities in southern Norway, although applicants are invited to indicate a preference of north, south, east or west on their initial application. Virtually all employers will be able to communicate in English.

The pocket money for au pairs in Norway is at least NOK3,000 per month which sounds generous until you realise that it could be taxed at 25%-30% (depending on the region), leaving a net amount of NOK1,800-NOK2,200. Atlantis can advise on possibilities for minimising tax by obtaining a *frikort* which entitles you to a personal allowance of NOK30,100. Au pairs are also given a travel card worth NOK400 a month.

Anyone interested in learning Norwegian should find out about the International Summer School offered at the University of Oslo. Americans can obtain details from a partner college in the US: St Olaf College, Northfield, MN 55057-1098.

Sweden

Unfortunately Sweden has no equivalent of CIMO or Atlantis. However several agencies do make au pair placements in Sweden (see introduction to this chapter). The Swedish Migration Board has an information sheet 'Facts About Work Permits for Au Pair Employment' on its website (www.migrationsverket.se). The minimum 'salary' stipulated is SEK3,500 a month (currently £250). Two domestic agencies that send many Swedish au pairs abroad will try to place British and other nationalities as au pairs in Sweden: Au-Pair World Agency Sweden (Box 356, 461 27 Trollhättan; www.interteam.se/au-pair.html) and Swede Au Pair (Nämndemansvägen 32, 64332 Vingaker; swedeaupair@swipnet.se). Swedish language courses are available at the Uppsala International Summer School (www.uiss.org).

WWOOF is now represented in Sweden: Andreas Hedren, Hunna, Palstorp, 340 30 Vislanda (0470-75 43 75) which so far has about 20 host farms.

Stifelsen Stjärnsund (77071 Stjärnsund; 0225-80001/fax 80301; www.stdi.w.se) is located amongst the forests, lakes and hills of central Sweden. Founded in 1984, the community aims to encourage personal, social and spiritual development in an ecologically sustainable environment. It operates an international working guest programme throughout the year, but is at its busiest between May and September when most of the community's courses are offered. Carpenters, builders, trained gardeners and cooks are especially welcome. First-time working guests pay SEK500 (less than £40) for their first week of work and if the arrangement suits both sides it can be continued with a negotiable contribution according to hours worked and length of stay. Enquiries should be made well in advance of a proposed summer visit.

Spain & Portugal

SPAIN

At the beginning of the 21st century, the popularity of Spanish studies continues to increase in Britain and beyond. It is possible to take short intensive courses in all the major Spanish cities, and bear in mind that it is also possible (and usually cheaper) to study Spanish in Latin America.

Spain has never lost its pre-eminent position as a favourite destination for British holidaymakers, and gap year students are no exception. Many book themselves on cheap packages to the Canaries, Ibiza and the Balearic Islands or any of the Costas as a good place to unwind after exams or after rigorous travels in developing countries. With an explosion in cheap and flexible flights from various UK airports with no-frills airlines like easyJet and MyTravelLite it is now possible to fly very easily to one of many Spanish cities. However the cost of living is relatively high and opportunities for picking up a job to fund further travels are not very numerous.

The demand for native speakers of English to teach remains strong, but unqualified and inexperienced 18 year olds will have difficulty finding a position during the academic year (with exceptions; see below). They might have more luck at summer language camps. It is always worth checking the English language press in Spanish resorts and cities for the sits vac columns which sometimes carry adverts for live-in babysitters, bar staff, etc. If you can arrange to visit the Spanish coast in March before most of the budget travellers arrive, you should have a chance of fixing up a job for the season. The resorts then go dead until late May when the season gets properly underway and there may be jobs available.

Courses and Homestays

Two UK language course agencies which specialise in Spain are *Don Quijote* (2-4 Stoneleigh Park Road, Epsom, Surrey KT19 0QT; 020-8786 8081; www.donquijote.co.uk)

and *Gala Spanish in Spain* (Woodcote House, 8 Leigh Lane, Farnham, Surrey GU9 8HP; ☎/fax 01252 715319). All the major agencies like *CESA, Caledonia, En Famille* and *Euroyouth* plus *International Links* are active in Spain. Intensive summer courses arranged by Euroyouth in Madrid, Salamanca and El Puerto are aimed at anyone over 17. *International Links* (01932 229300; internatlinks@aol.com) arranges homestays and language tuition in Spain and is one of the few companies to send students to Puerto de Santa Maria, a resort favoured by Spanish holidaymakers near Cadiz.

Longer courses will work out cheaper per week. It normally saves money (but not time) to book directly with the school in Spain, as **Annabel Iglehart** from Castle Douglas in Scotland did with Mester (see 'Directory of Language Courses':

I completed my University degree last July and am taking a year (or two) out to gain new skills and participate in interesting activities around the world. I didn't take a year out before I went to University and because of this I think that I am making the most of my opportunities now. As soon as my exams finished I got straight down to organis-ing my year out. I worked for two months in a variety of jobs in Edinburgh and then went to Salamanca, Spain to do a three-month intensive Spanish language course with Mester. The course was fantastic. The classes were fast paced and the teach-ers excellent. I met loads of people who I am still in touch with now, the social events organised by the school being a lot of fun and there was something for everyone. I lived with a Spanish family for a while and then moved to a flat with other students, something I had arranged before I headed out there. Mester is a company in Spain that provides excellent courses in Spanish, for any number of weeks and in a variety of cities in Spain. I'm afraid I cannot remember exactly how much it cost but it was roughly £1,300 for three months. I had an intensive course (five hours of tuition a day), stayed for three weeks with a Spanish family and the rest in a self-catering flat. The costs are calculated according to the type of course (there are many to choose from) and the class of accommodation. The schools seem to be a lot less busy in winter time (when I was there, September to December) and so this can mean that classes are smaller, but not always. Classes are never more than ten people I am told.

Lynn Thomas chose an intensive 12-week course in Malaga, booked through CESA:
I picked CESA out of a book and handed over a lot of money. It could easily have been a disaster, but it was one of the best experiences of my life. I did not just learn Spanish; I learned a lot about life in Spain and made friends in more countries than I care to list, friendships that will continue.

Bruno Williams was equally satisfied with his Barcelona experience organised though Gala Spanish in Spain, at least according to his mother:

He had a splendid time with the family with whom he stayed, so much so that he is arranging an exchange this summer with the boy nearest his age. It all went very well, and he loved Barcelona. It improved his Spanish by leaps and bounds, and he reports very good marks from Edinburgh where he has started a degree in French and Spanish.

Living with a family usually forces you to speak more Spanish from the beginning. Homestays can often lead to longer-lasting friendships and subsequent exchanges arranged on a private basis.

Another Gala client, **Paul Emmett,** was pleased at how much progress in Spanish he was able to make during his five months at *CLIC* in Seville (see entry in 'Directory of Language Courses'). Having done no formal Spanish before arriving, he passed the D.E.L.E. Basico and, on the strength of that, was allowed to do Spanish as a subsidiary subject in his first year at the University of Birmingham. Paul was pleased to discover that his standard of Spanish was better than many of the students on the Honours course. The youth exchange organisation *Relaciones Culturales Internacionales* at Calle Ferraz 82, 28008 Madrid (91-541 71 03; spain@clubrci.es), places native English speakers (who must join the Club for €16) with families who want to practise their English in exchange for providing room and board; they also arrange voluntary work for English assistants on summer language/sports camps.

Two other agencies involved in making this sort of live-in placements are GIC, Pintor Sorolla 29, Apdo. 1080, 46901 Monte Vedat, a suburb of Valencia (gic@eremas.net) and Castrum, Ctra. Ruedas 33, 47008 Valladolid (983-222213; info@castrum.org). The latter makes placements in Castille and Leon whereby participants undertake to spend three or four hours a day teaching English to members of the family and to enrol in a Spanish course (minimum five hours a week).

These live-in arrangements are useful for Americans and other non-European nationals who will find it very difficult to obtain a work permit. For example InterExchange (161 Sixth Avenue, New York, NY 10013; www.interexchange.org) and Alliances Abroad (2423 Pennsylvania Ave NW, Washington, DC 20037; 202-467-9467; www.allianceabroad.com) arrange Teach in Spain programmes whereby young American women live with a family in exchange for speaking English and providing 15 hours of tutoring a week.

The non-profit Instituto Cervantes (www.cervantes.es) is now the largest worldwide Spanish teaching organisation, with headquarters in Madrid and a network of centres around the world (comparable to the Alliance Francaise for French). It also has centres in London (020-7235 0359) and Manchester (www.centros.cervantes.es). For language institutes in Spain, check the 'Directory of Language Courses for the *Málaga Instituto* (Calle Cortada 6, 29018 Málaga), *Sociedad Hispano Mundial* in Granada, *Proyecto Espanol* in Alicante, *CLIC International House* in Seville and *Estudio Sampere* in Madrid and *Mester* throughout Spain.

A family-run business in the West Midlands, Pyrenean Holidays, organises language courses in conjunction with walking and other activity holidays (0121-711 3428; www.pyr eneanexperience.com).

Most language schools prepare interested students for the D.E.L.E. Spanish language exams. For further information on courses, contact the library of the Spanish Institute in London (102 Eaton Square, London SW1W 9AN; 020-7235 0324) or check the online listing of Spanish courses in Spain on the website of the Hispanic and Luso Brazilian Council (Canning House, 2 Belgrave Square, London SW1X 8PJ; 020-7235 2303; www.canninghouse.com/spanish_courses.htm).

Of course many other things can be studied in Spain apart from language. Learning some of the traditional dances is the aim of some gap year travellers who have the chance to learn Sevillanas, Malagueras, the Pasadoble or even the very difficult Flamenco.

Anyone interested in learning to sail or participating in a tall ships voyage in this part of the Mediterranean should request the brochure from the *JST Y. L. @ Sea* or the *Sail Training Association,* youth charities that run adventure sail training courses lasting between one and two weeks. Between November and May, square riggers sail around the Spanish islands of the Canaries off the northwest coast of Africa and also to the Azores (the Portuguese islands in the middle of the Atlantic Ocean). These winter sun voyages are available to 16-19 year olds or 18-69 year olds (see 'Directory of Expeditions'.

Opportunities For Paid Work

Year out students have successfully found (or created) their own jobs in highly imaginative ways. One of the most striking examples is a 19-year-old student who wrote to the address on a Spanish wine label and was astonished to be invited to act as a guide around their winery for the summer. **Tommy Karske** returned home 'knowing a lot about wine and believing that anything is possible'.

Many yachts are moored along the Costa del Sol and all along the south coast. It might be possible to get work cleaning, painting or even guarding these luxury craft. There are also crewing possibilities for those with no time constraints and outgoing personalities.

A good starting point for finding out about seasonal job vacancies in Ibiza is the website of the Queen Victoria Pub in Santa Eulalia (www.ibizaqueenvictoria.com) which posts jobs and accommodation both on its site and on the pub notice board which anyone can drop by and consult (though it is more polite to buy a drink while consulting the board). The Queen Vic itself employs a large number of European fun-seekers as well. Two other websites worth checking are www.balearic-jobs.com which covers the Balearic Islands of Ibiza, Mallorca and Minorca, and www.gapwork.com.

A more conventional form of employment is with a British tour company such as *Canvas Holidays, Eurocamp* or *Keycamp Holidays* (see 'Directory of Paid Seasonal Jobs'). *Haven Europe* needs Spanish-speaking couriers and children's staff to work at mobile home and tent parks from early May to the end of September.

Acorn Adventure (22 Worcester St, Stourbridge, West Midlands DY8 1AN; 01384 378827) hires seasonal staff for their watersports and multi activity centre near the resort of Tossa de Mar on the Costa Brava. RYA qualified windsurfing and sailing instructors, BCU qualified kayak instructors and SPSA qualified climbing instructors are especially in demand, for the season April/May to September.

Some language schools can arrange work experience placements (mostly unwaged) in Spanish firms; see entries for Don Quijote, Euro-Academy, Euro-Practice, Gala Spanish in Spain, Interspeak and Language Courses Abroad in the 'Directory of Work Experience'. ONECO Global Training in Seville is a member of the Global Work Experience Association and can fix up unpaid internships in many fields; its website www.oneco.org gives extensive details of the kind of positions available and also the reasonably priced language courses if offers. Refer also to the list of au pair agencies below, some of which arrange internships. The Californian company Adelante LLC (601 Taper Drive, Seal Beach, CA 90740; 562-799-9133; www.adelantespain.com) places interns in Bilbao, Madrid and Seville.

English Teaching

The great cities of Madrid and Barcelona act as magnets to thousands of hopeful teachers. Opportunities for untrained native speakers of English have all but disappeared in respectable language academies. However some determined students have obtained a TEFL Certificate at the beginning of their gap year and gone on to teach.

> **After A levels, Sam James and his girlfriend Sophie Ellison headed off to Barcelona to do the four-week Trinity Certificate course which they found demanding but passed. Then they did the rounds of the language schools:** *Though tedious, this did work and we doubt we would have found work any other way. Job availability didn't seem that high in Barcelona when we were looking in October and we both accepted our only job offers. (Our age may have put off some employers.) Most schools seem to have recruited in September, so October was a bit of a lean month. I got my job by covering a class at two hours notice for a teacher who had called in sick. When this teacher decided to leave Barcelona, I was interviewed and offered her classes on a permanent basis. I got the job permanently about a fortnight after handing out CVs. Sophie was asked to her first interview after about three weeks of job-hunting. She was selected but then had to wait for several more weeks while her contract was finalised.*
>
> *The conventional wisdom says that the beginning of summer is the worst time to travel out to Spain to look for work since schools will be closed and their owners unobtainable. However Sam James handed round his CV again in May (when his hours were cut) and was given some encouragement. He thinks that because so few teachers look for work just six weeks before the end of the academic year, employers are sometimes in need of replacements. With so many no-frills cheap flights on the market, it might be worth a gamble.*

Sam James had to teach a variety of age groups in Barcelona during his gap year and, despite the problems, ended up enjoying it:

The children I taught were fairly unruly and noisy. The teenagers were, as ever, pretty uninterested in learning, though if one struck on something they enjoyed they would work much better. Activities based on the lyrics of songs seemed to be good. They had a tendency to select answers at random in multiple choice exercises. On the other hand they were only ever loud rather than very rude or disobedient. The young children (8-12) were harder work. They tended to understand selectively, acting confused if they didn't like an instruction. Part of the problem was that the class was far too long (three hours) for children of that age and their concentration and behaviour tended to tail off as the time passed.

Sam James blamed his lack of job security and bitty hours on Barcelona's popularity, 'the result of the great supply of willing teachers here keeping working conditions down and making it hard to exert any leverage on an employer when one is so easily replaced.' For this reason other towns may answer your requirements better. There are language academies all along the north coast and a door-to-door job hunt in September might pay off. This is the time when tourists are departing so accommodation may be available at a reasonable rent on a nine-month lease.

Without a TEFL qualification, the best chance of a teaching job in Spain would be on a summer language camp. Some pay a reasonable wage; others provide little more than free board and accommodation. **Glen Williams** describes his summer job at a summer language camp in Izarra in the Basque Country:

The children learned English for three hours in the morning with one half hour break (but not for the teacher on morning snack duty trying to fight off the hordes from ripping apart the bocadillos). Then we had another three or four hours of duties ranging from sports and/or arts to shop/bank duty. For many of us, inexperienced with dealing with groups of kids, there were a few problems of discipline.

Au Pairing

Au pair links between Spanish agencies and those in the rest of Europe have been increasing partly because Spanish is gaining popularity as a modern foreign language. Young people can often arrange to stay with Spanish families without having to do much domestic or childcare duties by agreeing to help with English tuition. In addition to the British au pair agencies making placements throughout Europe (listed in the introductory chapter on Au Pairing), you may deal directly with established Spanish agencies. The pocket money for au pairs at present is €54 a week.

ABB Au Pair Family Service, Via Alemania 2, 5°A, 07003 Palma de Mallorca (971-752027; abbaupair@ono.com).

B.E.S.T., Calle Solano 11, 3°C, Pozuelo de Alarcón, 28223 Madrid (☎/fax 91-518 7110; www.inglespain.com). Au pair placements for Americans and Europeans; fee $500. B.E.S.T. also organises internship and work-study programme for young women for varying fees.

Centros Europeos Galve, Calle Principe 12-6°A, 28012 Madrid (91-532 7230; ccprincipe@inicia.es). Mainly places au pairs in the Madrid, Valencia, Alicante and Pamplona areas.

Easy Way Association, C/ Gran Via 80, Planta 10, oficina 1017, 28013 Madrid (91-548 8679; www.easywayspain.com). Also makes hotel and restaurant placements.

Experiment Spain, Fernández de los Rios 108, 1° izda, 28015 Madrid (91-549 3368; eilspain@retemail.es).

G.I.C. Au Pairs, Pintor Sorolla 29, 46901 Monte Vedat-Valencia (☎/fax 96-156 5837). Founding member of the International Au Pair Association.

Instituto Hemingway de Español, Bailén 5, 2°dcha, Bilbao 48003 (94-416 7901; www.insti

tutohemingway.com). Accepts Europeans, Americans, Canadians and Japanese. Also makes placements in local companies.

Interaupair/Horizon hpl, Puente de Deusto 7-5° Dpto. 1, 48014 Bilbao (94-475 4746; interaupair@euskalnet.net).

Interclass, C/ Bori I Fontestá 14, 6° 4°, 08021 Barcelona (93-414 2921; www.interclass.es).

Planet Au Pair, C/Los Centelles 45-6-11, Valencia 46006 (96-320 6491). €60 a week for au pairs, €90 for au pairs plus.

Relaciones Culturales, Calle Ferraz 82, 28008 Madrid (91-541 71 03; spain@clubrci.es). Annual membership in Club de RCI of €16.

S & C Asociados, Avda. Eduardo Dato 46, 2°B, 41005 Seville (☎/fax 95-464 2447; idiomas@supercable.es). Most positions in southern Spain.

Voluntary Work

The Sunseed Trust, an arid land recovery trust, has a remote research centre in southeast Spain where new ways are explored of reclaiming deserts. The centre is run by both full-time volunteers (minimum five weeks) and working visitors (minimum one week, preferably two) who spend half the day working. Weekly charges for working visitors are £63-£98 according to season and for full-time volunteers £42-£84; students and those on unemployment benefit get a discount. Typical work for volunteers might involve germination procedures, forestry trials, hydroponic growing, organic gardening, designing and building solar ovens and stills, and building and maintenance. Living conditions are basic and the cooking is vegetarian. The address of the centre is Apdo. 9, 04270 Sorbas, Almeria (☎/fax 950-552770; www.sunseed.org.uk).

The *Atlantic Whale Foundation* (St. Martins House, 59 St Martins Lane, Covent Garden, London WC2H 4JS; www.whalefoundation.org.uk) runs hands-on whale and dolphin conservation and research projects in the Canary Islands in which volunteers can participate for a fee of £100 a week.

For short voluntary projects, workcamps are the obvious solution. The major workcamp organisations recruit for environmental and other projects in Spain. The co-ordinating workcamp organisation in Spain is the government-run *Instituto de la Juventud* (José Ortega y Gasset 71, 28006 Madrid; fax 91-401 8160) which oversees 150 camps every year.

PORTUGAL

Portugal is seen by gap year students mainly as a place in which to relax and have fun rather than spend a large part of their gap year. There is a long and vigorous tradition of British people settling in Portugal, and the links between the two countries are strong so, with luck, you might be able to chase up a contact to provide initial accommodation and orientation. If you want to extend your stay, ask members of the expatriate community for help and advice. A good idea is to scan the advertisements in the English language press or place an ad yourself. The long-established English-language weekly *Anglo-Portuguese News* (Apartado 113, 2766-902 Estoril; 21-466 1551; apn@mail.telepac.pt) carries job adverts.

If your chosen language is Portuguese, one of the best known language schools is *CIAL Centro de Linguas* in Lisbon which offers a well-structured series of courses, normally 15 hours a week for four weeks. Students are billeted in family homes both in Lisbon and Faro. *Euroyouth* can organise a summer homestay with language course in Lisbon, Oporto and Faro, with an associate school in Oporto. *CESA* and *Euro Academy* also include Portugal in their programmes and you can study the language at International House in Lisbon (portuguese@ihlisbon.com).

According to some British backpackers, all you need for a working holiday is to fly to Faro with a tent and hitch a lift to Albufeira where any number of bars and restaurants might hire you for the season. Wages are not high, but accommodation is cheap. If you are aiming a little higher and know some Portuguese, it would be worth contacting the British-Portuguese Chamber of Commerce (*Camara de Comércio Luso-Britanica*) in Lisbon (Rua da Estrela 8, 1200-669 Lisbon; 21-394 2020; www.bilateral.biz).

Switzerland & Austria

SWITZERLAND

Every winter a small army of gap year students migrates to the Alps to spend the winter season working and skiing at a Swiss or Austrian ski resort. One of the disadvantages of spending any time in Switzerland is the very high cost of living. But of course this goes with high wages which can be earned by people willing to work hard in hotels in the summer season as well as the winter.

Although Switzerland is not yet a member of the European Union, it is moving in the direction of integration. Since the Bilateral Agreement between Switzerland and the European Union on the free movement of persons came into effect in June 2002, Switzerland has been undergoing a huge shift in its immigration and employment policy. The category of seasonal worker was abolished. The system is now more in line with the rest of Europe so that EU job-seekers can enter Switzerland for up to three months (extendable) to look for work. If they succeed they must show a contract of employment to the authorities and are then eligible for a short-term residence permit, valid for up to one year and renewable. The idea is that the free movement of labour will be introduced step by step. Until June 2004, quotas of foreign workers in each canton will remain in place. But from 2007, Switzerland may opt for unfettered movement of workers.

Hitherto the visa issue has loomed large and the regulations fairly strictly enforced. According to **Joseph Tame** from Herefordshire, who spent eight months working at a hotel near Grindelwald when he was 18, there was no question of anyone working without a permit. With a residence permit you become eligible for the state insurance scheme and the minimum gross wage (more than £1,300 a month). The Swiss are very *korrect* in regulating employment and foreigner workers will have many deductions made from their earnings. (Switzerland must be about the only country in which au pairs pay tax.) Students staying longer than four weeks must obtain Swiss medical insurance unless they can prove that their cover is as extensive as the Swiss. Few students head for Switzerland to study German though it is possible (see entries for *UNIL Vacation Courses* at the University of Lausanne and *Collegium Palatinum* in the 'Directory of Language Courses'). While it is true that many Swiss and Austrian people speak a dialect of German, language schools teach *Hoch Deutsch*. Austria in particular has been trying to build up its German language tourism and is worth considering (see below).

The cost of living in Switzerland is very high. One way of keeping costs down is to investigate the network of mountain, forest and city hostels run by Nature Friends International with headquarters in Vienna (www.nfhouse.org). Most are very inexpensive and are 'green' in their sympathies.

Work Experience

Trainee exchanges between Switzerland and a number of other countries including the UK and US will continue unchanged for the next year or two. For British trainees the old Swiss/UK Trainee exchange agreement will provide the easiest route to a working permit for Switzerland at least until 2004/5. Permits for temporary trainee placements *(stagiaires)* can be obtained from the Swiss Federal Aliens Office (BFA), Sektion Auswanderung und Stagiaires, Quellenweg 15, 3003 Bern (031-322 42 02; swiss.emigration@bfa.admin.ch; www.swissemigration.ch/elias.en (in English). This office can also send addresses of co-operating partner organisations. The trainee position arranged must be in the vocational field of the applicant, who must be aged 18-30. The UK exchange agreement allows up to 400 young Britons to gain work experience in Switzerland for up to 18 months after completing their studies. Information in the first instance should be requested from the Overseas Labour Service of the Department of Employment, W5, Moorfoot, Sheffield S1 4PQ.

The Swiss Farmers' Union runs a programme for international trainees in agriculture. Participants who want to work for 3, 4, 6, 12 or 18 months must have at least two years' practical experience or relevant training and be able to speak some English, French or German. Further details are available from Agroimpuls, c/o Farmers' Union, Laurstrasse 10, 5201 Brugg, Switzerland (056-462 51 44; www.agroimpuls.ch).

Paid Work in the Tourist Industry

Provided you have a reasonable CV and a knowledge of languages (preferably German), a speculative job hunt in advance is worthwhile. The *Swiss Hotel Guide* provides detailed entries in English on 2,500 hotels including the proprietor's name and can be ordered via www.swisshotels.ch for €15. The Swiss Hotel Association has a department called Hoteljob which runs a placement scheme (in the German-speaking part of Switzerland only) for registered EU students from the age of 18 who are willing to spend three to four months doing an unskilled job in a Swiss hotel or restaurant between June and September. Excellent knowledge of the German language is essential. Member hotels issue a standard contract on which salary and deductions are carefully itemised. From the gross salary of SFr2,790 or SFr3,100, the basic deduction for board and lodging (for any job) is SFr900 and a further 12-15% is taken off for taxes and insurance. Tips for waiting staff can bring net earnings back up to the gross. Application forms are available from the Swiss Hotel Association, Monbijoustrasse 130, 3001 Bern (031-370 43 33/fax 031-370 43 34; www.hoteljob.ch). The deadline for applications is 20th April.

The *Jobs in the Alps Agency* (see entry in 'Directory of Paid Seasonal Jobs') places waiters, waitresses, chamber staff, kitchen assistants and porters in Swiss hotels, cafés and restaurants in Swiss resorts, 200 in winter, 150 in summer. Wages will be higher if you work for a Swiss employer than if you are hired by a British tour operator.

Swiss hotels are very efficient and tend to be impersonal, since you will be one in an endless stream of seasonal workers from many countries. The very intense attitude to work among the Swiss means that hours are long (often longer than stipulated in the contract): a typical working week would consist of at least five nine-hour days working split shifts. Whether humble or palatial, the Swiss hotel or restaurant in which you find a job will probably insist on very high standards of cleanliness and productivity.

Most ski tour operators mount big operations in Switzerland, such as *Mark Warner, Crystal Holidays* and *Ski Total* (see chapter 'Paid Seasonal Jobs'). A Swiss specialist On-the-Piste Holidays (2 Oldfield Court, Cranes Park Crescent, Surbiton KT5 8AW; recruit@otp.co.uk) operates in Anzère, Nendaz, Villars and Zermatt. The main disadvantage of being hired by a UK company is that the wages will be on a British scale rather than on the much more lucrative Swiss one. A Swiss company that has been advertising for resort staff and ski instructors recently is Viamonde, Route de Founex 7, Commugny 1291 (022-776 8401).

Most people go out and fix up their jobs in person, sometimes with the help of the tourist office. In some resorts the tourist office keeps a list of job-seekers which local hoteliers and other employers can consult when they need to, usually well in advance of the start of the season. The most promising time to introduce yourself to potential employers is

April/May for the summer and early September for the winter. November is a bad time to arrive since most of the hotels are closed, the owners away on holiday and most have already promised winter season jobs to people they know from previous seasons or ones who approached them at the end of the summer season.

Sometimes it is necessary to escape the competition from all the other gap year and other job-seekers by moving away from the large ski stations. Joseph Tame's surprising tip is to go up as high as possible in the mountains. After being told by virtually every hotel in Grindelwald in mid-September that they had already hired their winter season staff, he despaired and decided to waste his last SFr40 on a trip up the rack railway. At the top he approached the only hotel and couldn't believe it when they asked him when he could start. Although at 18 he had never worked in a hotel before, they were willing to take him on as a trainee waiter, give him full bed and board plus £850 a month. At first he found the job a little boring since there were few guests apart from Japanese groups on whirlwind European tours. But things changed at Christmas and New Year when he had to work three shifts a day, which was rewarded in the end by an increase in pay.

Summer Camps

The Swiss organisation *Village Camps* advertises widely its desire to recruit staff for their multi-activity centres and language camps for children in Anzère and Leysin. They also hire up to 100 ski counsellors and other staff for the winter season. Jobs are available for EFL teachers, sports instructors and general domestic staff. For jobs with Village Camps, room and board are provided as well as accident and liability insurance and an allowance which amounts to pocket money. An application pack is available from Village Camps, rue de la Morache, 1260 Nyon (022-990 9405/fax 022-990 9494; personnel@villagecamps.ch).

Another possible employer is the Haut-Lac International Centre (1669 Les Sciernes; 026-928 4200; info@haut-lac.ch/ www.haut-lac.ch) which employs teacher/monitors of any nationality for both their summer and winter camps for teenagers. See also the entry for *Institut Le Rosey* in the 'Directory of Work Experience'.

Work on Farms

Young Europeans who are interested in experiencing rural Switzerland may wish to do a stint on a Swiss farm. The *Landdienst* is the Central Office for Voluntary Farm Work which is located at Mühlegasse 13 (Postfach 728), 8025 Zürich (1-261 44 88/fax 1-261 44 32; admin@landdienst.ch). It fixes up farm placements for a minimum of three weeks for young people from Western Europe who know some German or French. Last year about 600 foreign young people were placed through the Landdienst. Workers are called 'volunteers' and can work for up to two months without a work permit. They must pay a registration fee of SFr60.

In addition to the good farm food and comfortable bed, you will be paid at least SFr20 per day worked. Necessary qualifications for participating in this scheme are that you be between 18 and 25 and that you have a basic grounding in French or German. On these small Swiss farms, English is rarely spoken and many farmers speak a dialect which some find incomprehensible.

Most places in German-speaking Switzerland are available from the beginning of March to the end of October and in the French part from March to June and mid-August to the end of October, though there are a few places in the winter too. It is also possible for Britons to apply through *Concordia*, preferably at least a month before you wish to work. The hours are long, the work is hard and much depends on the volunteer's relationship with the family. Most people who have worked on a Swiss farm report that they are treated like one of the family, which means both that they are up by 6am or 7am and working till 9pm alongside the farmer and that they are invited to accompany the family on any excursions, such as the weekly visit to the market to sell the farm-produced cheeses.

WWOOF Switzerland (Postfach 59, 8124 Maur) keeps a constantly updated list of farmers around the country, currently 45. To obtain the list you must join WWOOF at a cost of SFr20/£10/$15/€15 in cash. Details are available on WWOOF's web-site www.wwoof.org/switzerland.

> **Joseph Tame made use of the WWOOF website to fix up a place on a farm in the spring:**
> *I can honestly say that it has been an absolutely fantastic experience. The hours could be thought fairly long by some (perhaps 35 per week) considering there is no money involved, but I absolutely love the chance to work outside in this land that reminds me so much of the final setting in 'The Hobbit.' From our farm your eyes take you down the hillside, over the meadows covered in flowers, down to the vast Lake Luzern below and over to the huge snow-capped mountain Pilatus. It really is paradise here. The family have been so kind, and as I put my heart into learning all that I can about the farm they are only too happy to treat me with generosity. I really feel a part of the family.*

Au Pairs

For those interested in a domestic position with a Swiss family there are rules laid down by each Swiss canton, so there are variations. You must be a female between the ages of 17 and 29 (18 in Geneva) from Western Europe or North America, stay for a minimum of one year and a maximum of 18 months, be in possession of a residence permit and attend a minimum of three hours a week of language classes in Zürich, four in Geneva. Families in most places are required to pay half the language school fees.

Au pairs in Switzerland work for a maximum of 30 hours per week, plus babysitting once or twice a week. The monthly salary varies among cantons but the normal range is SFr700-800.

There are two major au pair agencies. The first is Compagna whose incoming programme is co-ordinated by the Sektion Innerschweiz, Reckenbühlstrasse 21, 6005 Luzern. Compagna charges a registration fee of SFr30-35 plus a further SFr100-150 when a family has been found. For the French part of Switzerland (Geneva and Lausanne), contact Compagna Lausanne (Rue du Simplon 2, 1006 Lausanne; 021-616 29 88/fax 021-616 29 94). The other main agency is Pro Filia which has 15 branches including 32 Av de Rumine, 1005 Lausanne (021-323 77 66) for the French-speaking part, and Beckenhofstr. 16, 8035 Zürich (01-363 55 01/fax 01-363 50 88) for the German part.

Independent agencies also place au pairs such as *Heli Grandjean's Placements Au Pair,* Chemin de Relion 1E, 1245 Collonge-Bellerive (022-752 38 23; grandjean@geneva-link.ch) which is active in the Geneva area. Two others have entries in the 'Directory of Paid Jobs': *Perfect Way* and *Sunshine Au Pair Agency.*

Voluntary Work

The Mountain Forest Project (Bergwald Projekt) publishes its literature and website in English and is very welcoming to foreign volunteers who know some German:

People from overseas travelling in Europe will surely enjoy a week's workcamp with MFP in Switzerland, Germany or Austria. You will learn a lot about alpine forests and nature in general.

For details send two IRCs to MFP, Hauptstr.24, 7014 Trin, Switzerland (081-630 41 45; www.bergwaldprojekt.ch).

AUSTRIA

Like its alpine neighbour, Austria offers a great deal of seasonal employment to gap year students hoping to save some money and do some skiing. Some knowledge of German will be necessary for most jobs apart from those with UK tour operators. There is no shortage of hotels to which you can apply either for the summer or the winter season. The largest concentration is in the Tyrol though there are also many in the Vorarlberg region in western Austria. The main winter resorts to try are St Anton, Kitzbühel, Mayrhofen, St. Johann-im-Pongau which is a popular destination for British holidaymakers creating a demand for English-speaking staff. Wages in hotels and restaurants are lower than in Switzerland, though still reasonable.

If you want to improve your chances of finding work in a ski resort, you could consider joining the annual trip to Club Habitat in Kirchberg in the Austrian Tyrol (Kohlgrub 9, 6365 Kirchberg; 05357 2254; clubhab@kirchberg.netwing.at) for the first three weeks of December. During the trip, participants are given German lessons and lectures on job opportunities and red tape at a cost of about £400 which includes travel and half-board accommodation. It is organised in conjunction with Top Deck Travel (131-135 Earls Court Road, London SW5 9RH; 020-7244 8000; www.topdecktravel.co.uk).

After spending the first part of her gap year doing a German language course in Dresden, **Rosie Curling** decided she needed to consolidate her new skills by working in a German-speaking environment. She chose to head for Lech in Austria, where she had a friend, and within 24 hours of arriving she had a job as a commis waitress:

It would be fair to say that my five months in Austria were a rollercoaster ride of emotions. For the first three weeks I was lonely and homesick, finding the work tough, relations with my colleagues a strain and communication difficult. However after the Christmas period, I began to make friends and enjoy the wonderful skiing and to realise that the work was a means to an end, namely to have some serious fun. Again I was experiencing a new lifestyle, incredibly relaxed, where the major responsibility of the day was deciding where to ski and then where to après ski. Life assumed an idyllic routine. Get up at 8.50am, be the first on the slopes, ski till 11am, work the lunch shift, a couple more hours skiing, a bit more work in the evening, before hitting the night scene. Despite (or possibly because of) all this it was also an incredibly constructive period. For a start I saved £2,500 (to fund a Trans-Siberian railway trip). My German is now almost fluent, although I speak an Austrian dialect; my skiing has improved from a Grade 4/5 to 3a, but most importantly I have made some life-long friends, mainly Austrians and Swedes.

Because Austria is a very popular destination for British skiers, jobs abound with UK tour operators, though most are looking for staff over 21. One possibility for both seasons is First Choice/Skibound (London Road, Crawley, West Sussex RH10 2GX; 01293 588585; overseas.recruitment@firstchoice.co.uk) which hires hundreds of people to work in hotels and resorts in Austria; no qualifications are required because staff are given in-house training, but you must be available to stay for the whole season from May to September.

One of the more unusual casual jobs in Austria was described on a post card from **Fionna Rutledge** written during her gap year:

I thought you might be interested in my summer job in Vienna. I spent two months working for a classical music concert company (Strauss). There are loads of these in Vienna and most of them employ students. I was paid on commission and spent the day dressed up in Mozart costume in the main Vienna tourist spots. Hard work, but a great opportunity to meet people. You have to sell the concert tickets to complete strangers. I earned about £1,300 in six weeks. All you need to do is approach the 'Mozarts' on the street and ask them to introduce you to their boss.

Summer Work

Two organisations that run summer language camps are the similarly named *English for Children* (Salzachstrasse 15/38, 1220 Vienna; 1-958 1972; www.englishforchildre n.cc) and *English for Kids* (A. Baumgartnerstr. 44/A 7042, 1230 Vienna; 1-667 45 79; www.e4kids.co.at) both of which are looking for young monitors and English teachers with experience of working with children and preferably some TEFL background.

The organisation *Young Austria-Ferienhöfe* (Osterreichisches Jugendferienwerk, Alpenstrasse 108a, A-5020 Salzburg; 662-62 57 58-0; office@camps.at) recruit about 30 teachers and monitors to work at summer language and sports camps near Salzburg. Teachers receive about €240 per fortnight and monitors receive €160 in their first year.

For information about WWOOF Austria, contact Hildegard Gottlieb, Einoedhöfweg 48, 8042 Graz (☎/fax 0316-464951; wwoof.welcome@telering.at; www.wwoof.welcom e.at.tf). Membership costs €20/$25 per year plus two IRCs which entitles you to the list of around 130 Austrian organic farmers looking for work-for-keep volunteer helpers.

> **Jakob Steixner, a native of Doren in the Vorarlberg region of Austria, thinks that it should be possible to find work on a mountain farm:**
> *There is one sort of job available to everybody who doesn't mind working long hours in agriculture in Austria and Switzerland (and probably everywhere along the Alps). It's working temporarily on livestock farms in the mountains. It can be quite interesting not only because it involves so many different activities but also you're outside a lot of the time, often in extraordinarily beautiful surroundings. Pay is by the day and might seem very little by European standards (around £20-£30 in my area, but more if you get deeper into the mountains). But you can save a lot as there is nowhere to spend the money and you get free food and accommodation. Depending on your bosses you might have to work quite long hours though, sometimes searching for lost cattle for hours in the pouring rain or hail, 5000ft above sea level, or repairing fences when it's snowing in the middle of July. But that can be quite hilarious when you think about it later.*

The best time to ask around for work is March, well ahead of the season which lasts from June till early September.

Au Pairs

Austria has a well-developed tradition of au pair placement and several well-established and respectable agencies place hundreds of au pairs in Austria each year. Most of the families live in Vienna and Salzburg. The main agency is the Catholic-affiliated *Auslands-Sozialdienst* (Johannesgasse 16, 1010 Vienna; 1-512 7941; office@aupair-asd.at). Most agencies charge an upfront registration fee in the region of one week's pocket money; the minimum pocket money at present is laid down at €58.14. A private agent, Irmhild Spitzer (Sparkassenplatz 1, 7th Floor, 4040 Linz; ☎/fax 732-23 78 14) has a good choice of families throughout Austria both in towns and countryside.

Language Courses and Homestays

Euroyouth arranges homestays with language courses in Graz and suburbs in co-operation with an Austrian organisation Deutsch in Graz (Kalchberggasse 10, A-8010 Graz; 316-833 900/ www.dig.co.at). The organisation *Campus Austria* at the University of Vienna comprises 16 language schools all providing German language training. Some courses lead to Goethe Institute qualifications while others lead to the OESD (Austrian Diploma for German as a Foreign Language). Campus Austria publishes a clear pamphlet of the courses on offer and prices, with contact details of its 16 member schools. One of the schools, the *ActiLingua Academy* (Gloriettegasse 8, A-1130 Vienna; 1-877 67 01/ www.actilingua.com) offers some interesting courses including German and Music (in co-operation with the Vienna Conservatorium) and German combined with work experience in the Austrian tourism industry for between one and twelve months. Most job opportunities are in Vienna, Salzburg or alpine resorts.

The *Anglo-Austrian Society* (46 Queen Anne's Gate, London SW1H 9AU; 020-7222 0366) can provide information about language courses in Austria and exchange visits, as can the *Austrian Cultural Institute* (28 Rutland Gate, London SW7 1PQ; 020-7584 8653). Another language school to try is Alpha Sprachinstitut Austria which runs German courses with cultural programme and homestay all year round (Schwarzenbergplatz 16, A-1010 Vienna; www.alpha.at).

Gifted musicians might be interested in doing some master classes through the organisation Vienna Master Classes (Reisnerstr. 3, A-1030 Vienna; 1-714 8822; www.wiener-meisterkurse.music.at) which accepts performers and listeners in July and August. People of all ages can join 2-week courses with professional musicians in flute, guitar, piano, cello or voice culminating in a concert; the fee to participate is €400 and to audit €190.

WORLDWIDE

Africa

It is difficult to generalise about countries as different from each other as Morocco, Ghana, Kenya and South Africa. Yet the magic contained in the word Africa exercises a powerful attraction for many people about to leave school or university. Many organisations large and small can assist in setting up a placement in Africa, whether a stint of voluntary teaching in a village school, an attachment to a scientific expedition or on a safari.

Because English is the medium of instruction in state schools in many ex-colonies of Britain (e.g. Ghana, Nigeria, Kenya, Zambia, Zimbabwe and Malawi), EFL teachers are less in demand than subject teachers. A number of recognised gap year organisations in the UK arrange placements which usually last six months. Missionary societies have played a very dominant role in Africa's modern history, so young Christians will find a host of opportunities available to them in their gap year.

Conditions can be very tough and many gap students teaching or working in rural Africa find themselves struggling to cope, whether with the loneliness of life in a rural West African village or with the hassle experienced by women in Muslim North Africa. A certain amount of deprivation is almost inevitable; for example volunteers can seldom afford to shop in the pricey expatriate stores and so will have to be content with the local diet, typically a staple cereal such as millet usually made into a kind of stodgy porridge, plus some cooked greens, tinned fish or meat and fruit. Typically the housing will not have running water or electricity which means that showers consist of a bucket and cup and toilets are just a hole in the ground. Local customs can come as a shock, for example being treated with something akin to reverence, even though you may feel yourself to be just a naïve school leaver. But the rewards can also be tremendous and any efforts you put in are bound to be appreciated. When **Amelia Cook** started out teaching in a Ghanaian primary school she was bowled over (not just figuratively) by the curiosity of her class:

Even our first shaky classes using ideas from out own schools were met with great enthusiasm. Once my class of 45 teenage boys (plus many others who had sneaked in at the back) literally knocked me over in their enthusiasm to see what was in my bag of props for that day's lesson.

In the end she was glad that she had chosen a small organisation (AfricaTrust Network) which fulfilled her ambition to be of real benefit to the community and not just on an exotic holiday.

Regional crises also flare up making volunteering potentially risky. For example programmes in Zimbabwe have been severely affected by domestic conflict and most of the sending organisations have put their Zimbabwe projects on hold for the present. Try to research in advance any local issues that may be causing concern. The Foreign & Commonwealth Office runs a regular and updated service; you can ring the Travel Advice Unit on 020-7008 0232/fax 020-7238 4545 or check their website www.fco.gov.uk/travel to get advice about travelling to regions and countries experiencing conflict or instability.

Often the most useful preparation is to talk to someone who has survived and enjoyed a similar placement in the recent past. It is amazing how many volunteers are glad that they gave up their material privileges for a time and lived like the locals. Some even go on to make a career in development work. One year-out student **Rachel Attree** summed up her experience of teaching in East Africa with *Gap Challenge*:

Going to Tanzania has to have been the scariest thing I have done, ever. But as the saying goes, 'Nothing ventured, nothing gained' and this really was the case. Out of a scary daunting experience blossomed a wonderfully rewarding and enriching gift that will stay with me for life. That is not to say that I didn't have any rough times because I did and that was one of the benefits of my trip, learning to cope by yourself with no parents to turn to for support. All in all I have learnt so much about myself and other people and feel that my gap year has let me into a secret that only a special few will ever get to know.

Action against the spread of HIV/AIDS in sub-Saharan Africa is a matter of the utmost urgency and a number of agencies are tackling the issue head on, including the well respected charity SPW (Students Partnership Worldwide). **Juliet Austin** joined SPW after finishing her degree at Sussex University:

The biggest challenge is how to change a continent's sexual practices. The task is enormous. However through SPW I discovered that one answer lies with young people educating other young people, an approach known as peer education. I was recruited to work alongside a counterpart Zimbabwean volunteer and together we used participatory and non-formal methods to promote the development of life skills and positive lifestyles with regard to adolescent sexual and reproductive health. We used drama, role play, discussion groups, debates, poetry writing and recital, poster design, music and dance. Living and working with people from both my own country and Zimbabwe was an incredible experience and so much fun. What struck me most about my stay was the enthusiasm of the local people, coupled with their overwhelming friendliness and support for what we as volunteers were trying to achieve. I have never had a more fun and rewarding experience.

SENDING AGENCIES

In addition to SPW which sends volunteers to Tanzania, Uganda, South Africa and Zambia, the main year-out agencies are all active on the African continent: *Gap Activity Projects* with placements in South Africa, Swaziland, Tanzania and Zambia; *Gap Challenge* active in Tanzania and South Africa; *Project Trust* with Namibia, Egypt, Uganda, Botswana, Lesotho, Mozambique, Niger, Mauritania and Morocco as destinations and *i-to-i* which sends voluntary English teachers to Ghana and Kenya, has community work and conservation placements in South Africa and Kenya and also sends media and advertising volunteers to Ghana.

Sarah Johnson from Cardiff went to Zanzibar (part of Tanzania) with *Gap Challenge* in September to teach English and geography at a rural secondary school:

The expectations which Zanzibari children have from school are worlds away from those of British school children. They expect to spend most of their lessons copying from the blackboard, so will at first be completely nonplussed if asked to think things through by themselves or to use their imagination. I found that the ongoing dilemma for me of teaching in Zanzibar was whether to teach at a low level which the majority of the class would be able to understand, or teach the syllabus to the top one or two students so that they would be able to attempt exam questions, but leaving the rest of the class behind. Teaching was a very interesting and eye-opening experience. I believe that both the Zanzibari teachers and I benefitted from a cultural exchange of ideas and ways of life.

The following organisations also recruit gap year volunteers for Africa, mostly for work in schools and community projects. Most have entries in the 'Directory of Specialist Gap Year Programmes' in the first part of this book. Usually a local allowance or pocket money is paid and housing is provided.

Adventure Alternative, 31 Myrtledene Road, Belfast BT8 6GQ (☎/fax 02890 701476; office@adventurealternative.com/ www.adventurealternative.com). Three-month programmes for gap year students (among others) in Kenya combining 8 weeks of teaching/community work plus climbing, trekking, rafting, safaris and independent travel. Participants teach and work in HIV-education in rural schools.

Africa & Asia Venture, 10 Market Place, Devizes, Wilts. SN10 1HT (01380 729009/fax 01380 720060; av@aventure.co.uk/ www.aventure.co.uk). Places British school leavers as assistant teachers in primary and secondary schools in Kenya, Uganda, Tanzania, Botswana and Malawi, normally for one term. Programme includes in-country orientation course, insurance, allowances paid during work attachment and organised safari at end of four months. The 2003/4 participation fee is about £2,500 plus airfares.

AfricaTrust Networks, Africatrust Chambers, PO Box 551, Portsmouth, Hants. PO5 1ZN (02392 838098; info@africatrust.gi/ www.africatrust.gi) have three or six month residential programmes in Ghana (Cape Coast and inland), Mali (Bamako) for gap year students and others aged 18-25 to work with needy children or for a British animal charity. New programme due to begin in Morocco in 2005.

AFS Intercultural Programmes UK, Leeming House, Vicar Lane, Leeds LS2 7JF (0845 458 2101; info-unitedkingdom@afs.org/ www.afsuk.org). Participants can go to Ghana or South Africa to join community service programme for six months, e.g. working on health, welfare or human rights projects. Volunteers contribute £3,300.

Azafady, Studio 7, 1A Beethoven St, London W10 4LG (020-8960 6629; www.madagascar.co.uk). 10-week Pioneer Madagascar programme allows volunteers to work on a grassroots level trying to combat deforestation and extreme poverty in Madagascar. Fundraising target is £2,000 excluding flights.

BUNAC, 16 Bowling Green Lane, London EC1R 0QH (020-7251 3472; www.bunac.org). Work and travel programmes in Ghana and South Africa. Graduates with some classroom experience are placed in Ghanaian schools for a year from August on the Teach in Ghana programme. The programme fee is approximately £1,300 and participants may receive a local wage. BUNAC also arranges for students and graduates to join three to six month volunteer community service projects in Ghana. Group departures are in January, April, July and October. On-the-ground arrangements are made in Accra by SYTO (Student & Youth Travel Organisation).

Camps International, PO Box 67, Stroud, Glos. GL5 1ZR (01453 767901; www.camps international.com). Gap year safari camps and expeditions in Kenya and Tanzania, where participants undertake a range of wildlife and community projects lasting 2 weeks to 3 months. 28-day Gap adventure costs from £900.

Daneford Trust, 45-47 Blythe St, London E2 6LN (☎/fax 020-7729 1928; dfdtrust@aol.com). Youth education charity that sends students and school leavers resident in London (only) to Namibia, Botswana, South Africa and possibly Zimbabwe for a minimum of 3 but preferably 6-9 months. Volunteers must raise at least £2,000 towards costs for a 3-4 month placement and £4,000 for 6-9 months, with help from the Trust. A couple of years ago **Mariama Conteh** spent time working in a Montessori nursery in rural Namibia which she described colourfully in a *Daneford Trust Newsletter* (issue 41):

> *Despite the fact that I may have been able to afford things that afforded me a more comfortable life, the remoteness of the village of Onayena acted as an equaliser. The closest I could get to fresh food was one hour away and the quickest way to get there was through hitch-hiking, which was not a very reliable method of travelling, yet it didn't take me too long to get into this new pattern of living. There was something very relaxed about it.*

EIL, 287 Worcester Road, Malvern, Worcs. WR14 1AB (0800 018 4015; www.eiluk.org). Run community service and volunteer programmes in Ghana. Prices depend on length of visit.

Gap Sports Abroad (GSA), 39 Guinions Road, High Wycombe, Bucks. HGP13 7NT (☎/fax 01494 769090; info@gapsportsabroad.co.uk). Football, basketball, tennis and boxing coaching placements in Ghana, mostly lasting 3-4 months. Other placements relate to teaching, art and design, media, sports psychology, physiotherapy and medicine. £1,395-£1,755 for three months.

Global Vision International (GVI), Nomansland, Wheathampstead, St. Albans, Herts. AL4 8EJ (01582 831300; info@gvi.co.uk/ www.gvi.co.uk). Placements from 1-12 months. South Africa and Swaziland: wildlife research at Karongwe Game Reserve of South Africa and courses in field guiding and Gap Year Conservation Course. Also Teaching and community development projects, conservation of endangered reptiles. Prices vary from £835 for a 4-week field guide course to £2,450 for a 10-week wildlife research expedition.

Vacancies in Africa with various charities and aid agencies are posted on the internet, for example on www.volunteerafrica.org whose originator, Simon Headington, has set up a new NGO in Tanzania. The *Health Action Promotion Association (HAPA)* works with village projects in the Singida Region of Tanzania. Volunteers may join the project for four, seven or ten weeks for fees (respectively) of £970, £1,390 and £1,810, a large proportion of which is given as a donation to the host programme.

Madventurer, Adamson House, 65 Westgate Road, Newcastle-upon-Tyne NE1 1SG (0845 121 1996; team@madventurer.com). Non-profit-making organisation that arranges summer and 3-month expeditions to Peru, Bolivia, Chile, Tanzania, Togo, Uganda and Kenya that combine voluntary work and adventure travel. The summer fee is from £1,585.

MondoChallenge, Galliford Building, Gayton Rd, Milton Malsor, Northampton NN7 3AB (01604 858225; info@mondochallenge.org). Volunteer teachers including year-out students are sent to projects in 3 African countries. Tanzania (60 volunteers): locations include Longido (teaching in a Maasai village), Arusha (helping in an orphanage, teaching in primary or secondary school near Mt Meru) and Pangani on the coast, teaching adults and children. New programme planned in the Pane Mountains. The Business Development programme in Arusha involves micro-finance and training for small firms. Gambia: teaching in small village near the coast south of Banjul and business development in partnership with the Foresty Department. Kenya: new programme in the Maasai Mara area around Bomet, teaching in secondary schools with accommodation on-site.

Caroline Fowle, a volunteer for MondoChallenge in Pangani, found the whole environment idyllic:
We were teaching the most adorable little kids and working just a few hundred yards from the beach. Miles of golden sand in all directions and the lovely Pangani River winding out from the interior. The people were so kind to us and it really was the career break I needed.

Quest Overseas, 32 Clapham Mansions, Nightingale Lane, London SW4 9AQ (020-8673 3313; emailus@questoverseas.com/ www.questoverseas.com). 12-week Africa programme with departures from January to April. 6-week voluntary conservation work in Swaziland or a community development project in Tanzania followed by a 6-week expedition throughout Mozambique, Botswana and Zambia. £3,470 excluding flights and insurance. It was contact with the wildlife in Botswana which proved the highlight for **Claire Grew** who joined a Quest Overseas trip in 2003:

Having not even intended to take a gap year, I think I must've had one of the best going. It was ace living in the community seeing so much of Africa and so much game. We were very lucky in Chobe to see absolutely everything, including a leopard and a huge herd of buffalo. For me the best part had to be watching the elephants crossing the river, trunks sticking out of the water... We managed to fit in a phenomenal amount of activities, and the group was so good, I loved every minute.

Sudan Volunteer Programme, 34 Estelle Road, London NW3 2JY (☎/fax 020-7485 8619; davidsvp@aol.com). Needs volunteers to teach English in Sudan for about three months from early September, late December or late June. Undergraduates and graduates are accepted but not pre-university; TEFL certificate and knowledge of Arabic are not required. Volunteers pay for their airfare (currently £585). Local host institutions pay for insurance and living expenses in Sudan; most are in the Khartoum area.

TANZED, 80 Edleston Road, Crewe, Cheshire CW2 7HD (01270 509994; enquiries@tanzed.org/ www.tanzed.org). Charity that recruits graduates to teach in rural government primary schools in the Morogoro region of Tanzania. Fundraising target £1,750 to cover airfare, insurance, training and partial administrative costs.

Trade Aid Tanzania, Burgate Court, Burgate, Fordingbridge, Hants. SP6 1LX (01425 657774; tradeaid@netcomuk.co.uk). Recruits both gap year volunteers and professionals to work at schools and eco-tourism projects in and around Mikindani in Tanzania.

Teaching Abroad, Gerrard House, Rustington, West Sussex BN16 1AW (01903 859911/fax 01903 785779; info@teaching-abroad.co.uk). Work placements in Ghanaian schools. Also programme in French-speaking Togo and South Africa.

The Leap Overseas Ltd (Windy Hollow, Sheepdrove, Lambourn, Berks. RG17 7XA; 0870 240 4187; info@theleap.co.uk). New company arranges 3-month voluntary placements in the field of eco-tourism in game parks and conservation zones in Kenya, Tanzania, Malawi, Botswana, Namibia, South Africa and Zambia. £1,950-£2,100 excluding travel.

Travellers, 7 Mulberry Cottage, Ferring, W Sussex BN12 5HY (01903 502595; www.travellersworldwide.com). Teaching placements (English, French, drama…) in Ghana, Kenya and South Africa. Conservation volunteering placements (with elephants, seahorses, lions, wild dogs, whales, dolphins, sharks and crocodiles) in South Africa and Kenya. Work experience in law, journalism, TV, veterinary medicine, etc. available in Ghana and South Africa. Placements start at £1,095 for one month teaching in South Africa (including food and accommodation but not flights).

VAE Teachers Kenya, Bell Lane Cottage, Pudleston, Nr. Leominster, Herefordshire HR6 0RE (01568 750329; vaekenya@hotmail.com/ www.vaekenya.co.uk). 6 month gap year placements teaching in rural schools in the central highlands of Kenya. Inclusive fee of £3,000.

A past volunteer with VAE is **Robert Breare** who was a client of *Gap Enterprise* and it is on their website (www.gapenterprise.co.uk) that his story is told:

I thought I had it sorted: eighteen, House Captain, A-Levels under my belt, a place at Oxford and four months wages to travel on. In Kenya Njoroge thought that he had it sorted: eighteen, primary school exams finished, hands and feet calloused by a lifetime in the fields, but already in debt for his first two children's school fees. Njoroge became a good friend as I taught his children for six months in my year off, cramming eight children to a desk around a torn section of exercise book. Forty perpetually grinning children, driven by a desire to learn, were undeterred by wind driving through the crumbling mud walls...

Robert returned to university and set about raising £30,000 to help build a new school for the 600 children in that community in the Central Highlands of Kenya and went on to co-found the charity Harambee Schools Kenya (www.hsk.org.uk).

Village Education Project (Kilimanjaro), Mint Cottage, Prospect Road, Sevenoaks, Kent TN13 3UA (01732 459799). Gap year programme which sends about 8 UK students each year to help teach EFL and other subjects in village primary schools in Tanzania for an academic year (8-9 months). Fee is £2,000.

WORLDwrite, WORLDwrite Volunteer Centre, Millfields Lodge, 201 Millfields Road, Clapton, London E5 0AR (☎/fax 020-8985 5435; www.worldwrite.org.uk). International educational charity that organises range of cross-cultural visits and exchange projects in Ghana and South Africa (among others worldwide) e.g. production of educational videos about Ghana, computer and film school appeal for Ghana and research on sustainable development.

Clare Cooper describes the work she did at a children's home in Ghana under the auspices of AfricaTrust Networks:

During the May of my final year of a geography and African and Asian studies degree, I made the decision to have a gap year before getting a 'proper' job or starting postgraduate study. The Dean of my department recommended Africatrust Networks as a reputable organisation looking for volunteers interested in getting some vocational work experience in West Africa. Excited by the prospect of being in Africa after my studies (and ignoring the fact that the volunteer programme cost £1950 plus £500 donation towards the projects, and that I was already over my overdraft limit) I filled in the on-line application and was accepted to join the team leaving for Ghana September 2002.

After the excellent two-week induction in Cape Coast we travelled inland to Kumasi in Central Ghana to meet our host families and begin working. For me the host family experience was a real highlight of my time in Ghana; I became close friends with the older daughters, learnt how to cook the Ghanaian way, pounding fufu in the yard and grinding pepper and beans, suffered the pain of hair extensions, learnt how to carry buckets of water on my head and became the official homework and dissertation proof-reader. My family leant me traditional funeral robes and took me to some family funeral celebrations which were like huge colourful summer festivals complete with DJs and dancing (funerals in Ghana are held every Saturday and are huge social occasions, completely different from British funerals).

Africatrust Networks places volunteers in struggling and under-privileged state-run institutions. Another volunteer and I were placed at Kumasi Children's Home for abandoned and orphaned children. I worked with the younger children teaching simple lessons, singing songs and playing games. I devoted much of my spare time to the severely disabled children in the orphanage. After much debate and discussion with the NGO director and children's home managers I began volunteering at a local special needs school with the view of transferring the children from the orphanage at a later date. By far my happiest day in Ghana for me was the day we transferred the children from the orphanage to the special school. Seeing these once shy and withdrawn boys in new school uniforms, laughing and playing with other children and taking part in lessons and sports was indescribable. It just goes to show that as a volunteer you can change things and 'make a difference', but these changes must come from working alongside members of your host community, in accordance with their cultural methods for getting things done.

Africatrust is unique in the fact that volunteers must each raise £500 to be used as donations towards projects in the institutions in which they're working. Then the volunteers, Ghanaian teachers and managers discuss how best this money can be spent. I soon realised that the best way in which my project money could benefit the largest number of children was to buy craft, tie-dye, leather-work, wood-work and jewellery making materials as well as a number of educational learning aids and recreational toys. In this way the teachers could make the most of their expertise, and many more children could take part. With the remainder of the project money we commissioned a blacksmith to build some swings out of local materials and built a climbing frame and some walk ways to help the children improve their balance and co-ordination.

Volunteering with Africatrust really gave me an insight into Ghanaian culture, people and social institutions. I honestly feel as though my work did actually help people, although maybe not in the ways I first presumed, instead of merely providing an 'exciting African adventure' for foreign volunteers. The dedication and enthusiasm of the project director coupled with the warmth and open friendliness of Ghanaians, make volunteering in Ghana a rewarding, fun and totally unforgettable experience.

Courses and Work Experience

A few of the main language course organisers can arrange Arabic courses in Morocco, for example *Amerispan* and *CESA*; the latter offers beginner and more advanced courses for three or six weeks starting at £482. **Jill Cavanagh** was very happy with the Arabic course which CESA arranged for her in Fez:

> My aim was to gain a basic grounding in Arabic and to learn about Morocco and Islam from being exposed to the culture. I left feeling I had a strong beginning in conversational Arabic. The family I stayed with were very welcoming and supportive. I was invited to join in many family activities and was always offered help with homework, etc. Plus I was fed wonderfully. The downsides are far outweighed by the good aspects of life here. The men aren't that big a deal. Yeah, they hassle you a bit, but you quickly learn how to deal with this, and even though it doesn't go away, you get used to it.

Other courses of possible interest to year-out students revolve around music and dance. For example it is possible to study drumming at the Academy of Music & Art in Kokrobite not far from Accra in Ghana, where private lessons cost just $3 an hour, and also on the Senegalese island of Ile de Goree. The enterprising American charity *Cosmic Volunteers* (see the 'Directory of Voluntary Placements') emphasises language learning in its programmes, no matter how obscure. *African Legacy* (in the same Directory) runs trips for paying volunteers to study and preserve the archaeology, ecology, wildlife and cultural landscapes of Nigeria.

An interesting cross-cultural trip is run from the US to Senegal every summer by Intercultural Dimensions (PO Box 391437, Cambridge, MA 02139-0015; janetid@aol.com). Participants can improve their conversational French while working alongside Senegalese people for three or four weeks. Arrangements can be made to extend the stay for volunteer work, field work or internships to study dance, musical instruments, the Madinka language, etc.

Opportunities to do paid work are very limited in Africa. Ghana has a long tradition of welcoming foreign students to participate in its educational and commercial life. *S & S Human Resources Development* (see 'Directory of Work Experience') arranges practical training and paid and unpaid internships in Ghanaian businesses in Accra, Kumasi, Cape Coast, Tema, Ho and Takoradi.

Workcamps

Short-term workcamps operate in many African countries, mainly to assist with rural development for example installing water supplies or to assist with social welfare, e.g. working in homes for disabled or underprivileged children. You have to finance your own travel and pay a registration fee to cover food and lodging for the three to six week duration of the camp. To find out about the range of workcamps in Africa, it is a good idea to obtain the international list of projects from a sending organisation in your own country, e.g. International Voluntary Service, UNA Exchange or VFP (US).

If you want to arrange a place on an African workcamp before leaving home, you may have to prove to an international organisation that you have enough relevant experience. The workcamp movement is particularly well developed in North Africa especially Morocco which has a number of regional organisations creating green spaces, building communal facilities, etc. If you decide to try to join a project once you are in an African capital like Nairobi, Accra, Freetown or Maseru, it should not be hard to track down a co-ordinating office. Ask at the YMCA or in prominent churches.

Organisations in the US

The African-American Institute (Chanin Building, 380 Lexington Ave, Crn. of 42nd St, New York, NY 10168-4298) is a repository of information for Americans on opportunities in Africa for employment, teaching, aid projects, etc. From the US, try any of these voluntary organisations for short or long-term projects in Africa:

The *Alliances Abroad Group,* 2423 Pennsylvania Avenue, NW, Washington, DC 20037 (202-467-9467; 1-888-6-ABROAD; www.allianceabroad.com) arranges volunteer placements in Ghana and Senegal, as does *Amity Volunteer Teachers Abroad* (AVTA, Amity Institute, 3065 Rosecrans Place, Suite 104, San Diego, CA 92110; 619-222-7000; 619-222-7016; www.amity.org). Amity participants must be graduates over the age of 21, and stay for between three and ten months.

Cross-Cultural Solutions – 800-380-4777; www.crossculturalsolutions.org. Places volunteers for 2-12 weeks in grassroots projects in Ghana and Tanzania.

Operation Crossroads Africa, Inc, PO Box 5570, New York, NY 10027 (212-289-1949; oca@igc.org; http://oca.igc.org/web/index.html). Runs 6-week summer projects in rural Africa staffed by self-financing volunteers from the U.S. and Canada. Inclusive cost is $3,500. The deadline for applications is mid-March.

Traveling Seminars Abroad, Inc, 1037 Society Hill, Cherry Hill, NJ 08003 (609-424-7630). Summer and longer term programs for students and others in village in northern Ghana helping to build Habitat for Humanity homes. Estimated cost for 3-month stay is $1,200.

United Children Fund, P.O. Box 20341, Boulder, CO 80308-3341 (303-469-4339; www.unchildren.org). East Africa aid organisation that places volunteers in Ugandan clinics, schools, farms, etc. for short periods or 6 months. Fees from $820 for 1 week to $6,750 for 6 months, excluding airfares.

Visions in Action, 2710 Ontario Rd., NW, Washington, DC 20009 (202-625-7402; www.visionsinaction.org). 6 and 12 month volunteer positions in Uganda, Zimbabwe, Burkina Faso, South Africa, and Tanzania plus short-term opportunities in Tanzania. Volunteers must have a degree or relevant work experience to fill positions in human rights, journalism, micro-enterprise, social work, health, environment and research. Participation fees are $5,500-$6,600.

World Camp for Kids, 367 Paul Presnell Road, Sugar Grove, NC 28679 (919-967-3303; worldcampforkids@hotmail.com/ www.worldcampforkids.org). Address in Malawi: Box 1866; Lilongwe (+265-991-1377). Volunteers mainly get involved in HIV/AIDS eduction in Malawi, departing January-February and June-August.

WorldTeach Inc, Center for International Development, Harvard University, 79 John F Kennedy Street, Cambridge, MA 02138 (617-495-5527/1-800-4-TEACH-0; info@worldteach.org/ www.worldteach.org). Non-profit organisation that recruits graduates as volunteers to teach English for ten months from late December in Namibia (fee $5,990) or for the summer ($3,990).

YMCA Go Global, International YMCA, 5 West 63rd St, 2nd Floor, New York, NY 10023 (212-727-8800 ext 4439; www.ymcanyc.org). Places volunteers for 3-12 months in Ghana, Gambia, Egypt, Zambia and Mauritius to work in education, youth work and computing. The programme fee is $250.

GRASSROOTS VOLUNTARY ORGANISATIONS

Africa is still very reliant on aid agencies, mission societies and voluntary assistance. The large majority of volunteers in Africa are trained teachers, doctors, nurses, agricultural and technical specialists who have committed themselves to work with mainstream aid organisations like VSO and Skillshare Africa for at least two years. However openings for unskilled volunteers do exist through smaller charities and indigenous organisations. It may be possible to offer your services on a voluntary basis to any hospital, school or mission you come across in your travels, though success is not guaranteed. If you have a useful skill and a letter of introduction from a church or family friend, your way will be made smoother. After leaving school, **Benjamin Fry** travelled to the Jiropa Hospital in the Upper Region of Ghana and persuaded the head of the mission hospital who was an acquaintance of his parents to keep him on for a while. He did odd jobs around the hospital such as cleaning the pharmacy and wards, assembling an incubator imported from Uganda and helping in the orphanage in exchange for his keep.

Till Bruckner is a veteran world traveller who has developed a strong preference for fixing up teaching and voluntary placements independently after arrival rather than with the help of an agency:

My advice to anyone who wants to volunteer in Africa (or anywhere else) is to go first and volunteer second. That way you can travel until you've found a place you genuinely like and where you think you might be able to make a difference. You can also check out the work and accommodation for yourself before you settle down. If you're willing to work for free, you don't need a nanny to tell you where to go. Just go.

However for those who find this prospect daunting (and unless you are a mature and seasoned traveller you probably will), you might like to pursue the middle way which is to make contact with small local organisations in Africa which actively look for volunteers abroad, though be prepared for problems in communication. The following are listed in alphabetical order by country:

International Centre for Education Orientation and Mobilisation, ICEYOM, c/o Cameroon Vision Trust, PO Box 1075, Limbe, Cameroon (see entry in 'Directory of Voluntary Placements Abroad').

CYTFWEA, Charity Youth Travel & Working Experiences Abroad, PO Box MA30, Ho (Volta Region), Ghana. Self-funding volunteers placed in range of development projects run by local NGOs. Two recent volunteers from the UK worked in community eco-tourism at the Ghana Wildlife Societyin Ho and another assisted at the Victoria Memorial School in Ho.

RUSO (Rural Upgrade Support Organisation), c/o University of Ghana, PMB L21, Legon, Accra, Ghana (513149; http://interconnection.org/ruso). International volunteers join tree planting, AIDS awareness education, fish farming and other projects especially in the Kome area of Ghana. The cost to volunteers is $25 per week for stays of 1-3 months or $15 a week if staying 3-6 months.

Save the Earth Network (STEN), Affiliated to WWOOF/FIOH Ghana, P.O. Box CT 3635, Cantonments-Accra, Ghana; +233-21-667791; ebensten@yahoo.com). Volunteer placements with this established NGO last between one and six months and accommodation is provided free. Farm volunteers are placed on organic and traditional farms in Ghana to help with the maintenance and harvesting of crops like maize and cassava. Volunteers are also needed to work in the bicycle repair workshop and in rainforest conservation projects near Accra. The contribution to expenses for projects lasting one to six months varies from $70 to $190 per month.

Sénévolu, Dakar (550 4885; fax 855 7172; www.senevolu.mypage.org). Organisation founded in 2002 to involve foreign young people in local community projects and schools while living with a local family and spending weekends in cultural workshops in drumming, batik, etc. Minimum stay is 4 weeks; fee €525.

CADO (Community Animation & Development Organisation), 108 Kissy Road, PMB 1317, Freetown, Sierra Leone (022-226148/226163; cado@sierratel.sl) whose director Solomon Kargbo wrote in 2003 to say that they are always willing to receive self-funded volunteers.

Future in our Hands (FIOH) Tanzania, PO Box 147, Bunda, Tanzania. Volunteers for conservation and education. FIOH is also active in Kenya (PO Box 4037, Kisumu, Kenya; 03-40522; FIOHK@hotmail.com). Volunteers needed for 5 weeks to 6 months.

AJVPE – Association des Jeunes Volontaire pour le Protection de l'Environment, B.P.

4568, Lomé, Togo (901 2506; enquiries@ajvpe-togo.org; www.ajvpe-togo.org). Summer workcamps last 21 days carrying out projects like tree planting and building a municipal garden in the small town of Agbodrafo.

WWOOF Togo, c/o Prosper Agbeko, B.P. 25, Agou-Gare, Togo (471036). Places volunteers on organic farms, forest projects, etc. in Togo (no recent confirmation). Send 2 IRCs for information before paying registration fee of $25.

SOUTHERN AFRICA

Undaunted by the frightening levels of violent urban crime, many year out and volunteer agencies have programmes in South Africa, the majority of which involve placing volunteers in orphanages or special schools. For example BUNAC runs a volunteer programme in South Africa for a small number of full-time students and recent graduates under the age of 27. The programme fee is approximately £1,150 including processing of a visa, placement, accommodation, return flight to Cape Town, orientation and back-up from the South African Students Travel Service. Group departures for Volunteer South Africa take place monthly.

Gap Challenge send quite a few volunteers to special schools in and around Cape Town. **Laura Foster** from Sussex took up a Gap Challenge placement working in a centre with mentally and physically handicapped children:

At first I was quite apprehensive but after 2 weeks I really settled in and felt welcomed. By the time I left, I felt I had a beneficial influence on some of the children's lives and learnt a lot about myself. It was a great experience.

One of the advantages of being attached to a school is that most gap year volunteers are free to travel during school holidays. Many in South Africa choose to do the Garden Route or explore the Cedarberg mountain range. Post-placement travel destinations include Victoria Falls in Zimbabwe, Botswana (with its Okavango Swamps) and Namibia.

African Conservation Experience (PO Box 9706, Solihull, West Midlands B91 3FF; 0870 241 5816; www.ConservationAfrica.net) sends people to game and nature reserves in southern Africa where they do conservation work with rangers and conservationists and get first-hand experience of animal and plant conservation. The total cost is about £3,600 for 12 weeks (see 'Directory of Specialist Gap Year Programmes').

The Eco Africa Experience (Guardian House, Borough Road, Godalming, Surrey GU7 2AE; 01483 860560; www.EcoAfricaExperience.com) is another specialist gap year programme available on South Africa's game reserves. Over the course of one, two or three months, volunteers participate in a range of conservation activities to support the ongoing work being carried out to protect wildlife (see entry). The price of £3,500 for a 12-week placement includes flights from London.

In addition to offering short wilderness treks, the Wilderness Trust (The General's Orchard, The Ridge, Little Baddow, Essex CM3 4SX; ☎/fax 01245 221565; info@wilderness-trust.org) organises work for conservation volunteers. Participants help with the running of a small game reserve and help with game counts and general maintenance. The average cost is £2,000 for three months excluding flights. Check the Trust's website (www.wilderness-trust.org) for upcoming treks, e.g. to follow Bushmen tracks in November 2003 for people over 16 (cost £320 excluding flights).

In a similar vein, African Eco Gap based in South Africa (walkabout@internext.co.za) has just started to market its four-week eco training courses in a game reserve in South Africa to gap year students. The fee of £2,300 includes return airfares London-Johannesburg, tuition and living expenses in a bush camp (see entry in 'Directory of Miscellaneous Courses').

African Botswana Challenge (Private Bag 0047, Serowe, Botswana; fax +267 430992; admin@abcgap.com; www.abcgap.com). 10-week gap programme in Botswana wilderness areas for 17-25 year olds ending with a one-week safari. Fee is £3,000 including flights from London to Gaborone.

Volunteer sports coaches and organisers over 20 are placed in rural or urban communities for 6-12 months from January or July. Further details of this programme are available from *SCORE/Sports Coaches' OutReach* (2nd Floor, Satbel Centre, 2 de Smit Street, Greenpoint (PO Box 4989, Cape Town, 8000), South Africa; 21-418 3140; info@score.org.za). Suitable candidates must be interested in hands-on development work and willing to live with a host family. Participants receive a nominal monthly stipend but pay an administrative fee of $1,200.

After starting his course in Sports, Exercise and Leisure Studies at the University Of Ulster, twenty-one year old Niall Johnson joined the SCORE programme in South Africa and found it fulfilling on various fronts:
The term of service for volunteers begins with a General Orientation in Paarl, Western Cape which aims to equip the group of mostly European volunteers with the skills to cope with the traumatic transition of moving from a relatively secure Dutch, Norwegian, Finnish lifestyle to the insecurities of Cape Town or a rural African setting...Soon these people from all over Europe and Southern Africa became my best friends and adequately took the place of all those I had left at home. My firm friends from this programme have promised me places to stay for free in their own countries, one of the many benefits to arise from this year.

Professionally, the benefits have been immense... I have been not only teaching PE in three primary schools for up to six hours a day, but I have been teaching teachers how to teach and evaluating their progress together. I have had event management of a kind that cannot be found at home; the major event of my first three months was the Provincial Tournament which was hosted in my own village of Ga-Nchabeleng, Northern Province about 100kms south of Pietersburg. All these experiences are so different in an African setting. These are rural communities with little money around to spare for transport, expensive materials, equipment and manpower. It's a different mindset, the most important facet of which is 'African Time.'

But by the end, it was clear to Niall that his year in South Africa had been the best possible decision for a year-out placement.

Tourism

Cape Town is the tourist capital of South Africa including for backpackers, though jobs are harder to find here than elsewhere. Furthermore the job hunt is made much harder by the competition from a large number of Zimbabwean exiles who are willing to accept low wages.

Although himself at the upper end of 'youth', Roger Blake made extensive use of South Africa's youth hostels and several times was able to extend his stay by working for his keep:

There are more than 100 hostels in South Africa, many of which 'employ' backpackers on a casual basis. Within two weeks of arrival I was at a hostel in George on a work-for-keep basis. Through contacts made here I also sold T-shirts at the beach for a small profit and I did a few days at a pizza place for tips only. Then I was offered a job at a hostel in Oudtshoorn (Backpackers Oasis). They gave me free accommodation and 150 rand a week to run the bar and help prepare the ostrich braai (BBQ) that they have every evening. Also I did breakfasts for fellow travellers which was like being self-employed as I bought all the ingredients and kept all the profit. It was a small but worthwhile fortune after six weeks here.

Although Johannesburg is often maligned as a big, bad, city, it is the earning capital of South Africa with better job possibilities than many other places. Unfortunately some of the inner city areas where backpackers used to congregate and find jobs (Yeoville, Brixton) have succumbed to the crime and grime for which the city is known. Many travellers now prefer the northern suburbs to which hostels like the Ritz have moved (now at 1A North Road, Dunkeld West; ritz@iafrica.com) and Rockey's of Fourways (22 Campbell Road, Craigavon A.H., Sandton; 011-465 4219; www.backinafrica.com), an area of the city in which travellers can often get jobs waiting tables, working on the bar, etc.

Conservation and Wildlife

An increasing number of companies and eco-tourism operations are marketing the South African wilderness to gap year students (and others) as a place to learn skills and see big game. The *African Conservation Trust,* PO Box 310, 3652 Link Hills (031-2601062; info@projectafrica.com/ www.projectafrica.com) is a South African based trust that recruits self-funding volunteers to staff environmental research projects in southern Africa.

A company called Bio-Experience based in Pretoria aims to help South African nature reserves and wildlife rehabilitation centres by arranging for fee-paying international and local volunteers to spend a working holiday assisting them. International volunteers assist with various projects otherwise unaffordable to reserve owners due to a lack of funding. Volunteers can get involved in wildlife feeding and cage cleaning at wildlife centres and invader plant control and game counts at nature reserves located in Gauteng, Warmbaths, Natal, etc. The inclusive participation fee averages $600 a month. Further details are available from Natanya Dreyer (011-964 1900; natanya@cybertrade.co.za).

One of the projects to which Bio-Experience sends foreign volunteers is the seabird conservation organisation, the South African National Foundation for the Conservation of Coastal Birds. SANCCOB requires volunteers to help with the cleaning and rehabilitation of oil-soaked birds since oil pollution is a major problem in the coastal waters of South Africa. Volunteers must fund their own living expenses, e.g. $35+ a day, for at least two weeks. Details are available from SANCCOB, PO Box 11116, Bloubergrant 7443, Cape Town (021-557 6155; www.sanccob.co.za).

Wild at Heart in Kwazulu Natal (see entry in 'Directory of Voluntary Placements Abroad') offers hand-on opportunities to work with species such as lions, cheetah and elephants at wildlife rehabilitation centres in South Africa, Botswana and Namibia. About a thousand volunteers, many without specific skills, are placed in 15 projects every year. See the same directory for details of field projects at *Lajuma Research & Environmental Education Centre* in northern South Africa. *Kwa Madwala Private Game Reserve* has a three-month gap year programme in the Kruger National Park; details are available from UK rep (see entry in 'Directory of Specialist Gap Year Programmes'). Another possibility in this field is *African-Experience* (+27 31-765 47 80; *fax: +27 31-765 47 81; www.african-experience.co.za).*

Alliances Abroad mentioned above place volunteers in South Africa. Students live with local families for 3-8 weeks while volunteering with veterinarians and zoologists, to learn about wildlife in South Africa. Fees begin at $1,400.

In Kenya, the Tsavo Conservation Trust (P.O. Box 48019, Nairobi, Kenya; 02-331191; www.savannahcamps.com/tdc/volunteeropp.html) looks for competent, but not necessarily qualified, volunteers to participate in a variety of conservation and community projects in rural Kenya and contribute US$177 per week to cover costs (2003). The Trust runs the Taita Discovery Centre in the wilds of Kenya where a number of gap year students are placed on organised schemes.

The campaigning Born Free Foundation (3 Grove House, Foundry Lane, Horsham, West Sussex RH13 5PL; 01403 240170; www.bornfree.org.uk) is responsible for vetting applicants for the Eco-volunteer programme at the Colobus Trust's centre on the south coast of Kenya where colobus monkeys and their habitat are being studied. Volunteers (who must be over 22) stay for up to three months and pay $400 a month for accommodation plus about $100 for food and incidentals.

Willing Workers in South Africa places international volunteers in projects related to eco-tourism, skills transfer and social services. WWISA tries to match volunteer requests with projects which are all located along the Garden Route and in the Eastern Cape. Participants pay $380 for the first month, $350 thereafter and, in exchange for working six hours a day, are given free room and board. Details are available from WWISA, PO Box 2413, Plettenberg Bay 6600 (fax 044-534 8958; wwisaafrica@telkomsa.net; www.wwisa.co.za). Another volunteer placement company is AVIVA (Africa Volunteering & Ventures Abroad, PO Box 60573 Flamingo Square, Cape Town 7441; 021-557 5996).

EXPEDITIONS

The African continent hosts a huge variety of scientific and conservation expeditions and most interests can be accommodated, from measuring the height of waterfalls in Lesotho to tracking warthogs in a Ghanaian national park. If by any chance you know someone doing their PhD on a relevant African subject, you might be able to persuade them of your usefulness. But most gap year students will join a more formal expedition, either one organised through a university or the Royal Geographical Society or one set up by an expedition society like BSES or one of the following:

Frontier, 50-52 Rivington St, London EC2A 3QP (020-7613 2422; info@frontierconser vation.org). Volunteers spend 4, 8, 10 or 20 weeks helping in environmental research and conservation expeditions in the forests, savanna and marine habitats of Madagascar and Tanzania. Volunteers must make a contribution of £2,200/£2,450 for 10 weeks or £3,400/ £3,800 for 20 weeks, excluding flights. Participants can choose to qualify for a BTEC Level 3 in Tropical Habitat Conservation.

Greenforce, 11-15 Betterton Street, Covent Garden, London WC2H 9BP (020-7470 8888/fax 020-7470 8889; info@greenforce.org/ www.greenforce.org). Recruits volunteer researchers to join wildlife surveys in Zambia. 10-week duration studying threatened species and habitats. No previous experience needed as training is provided. The cost is £2,550 plus flight.

Raleigh International, 27 Parsons Green Lane, London SW6 4HZ (020-7371 8585; ww w.raleighinternational.org). Leading youth development charity which offers young people the chance to take part in challenging environmental, community and adventure projects as part of 3-month expeditions overseas. Well-established projects in Namibia and Ghana, e.g. working with park rangers to help ease conflicts between communities and wildlife, building schools and becoming part of remote rural communities.

Wind, Sand & Stars, 6 Tyndale Terrace, London N1 2AT (020-7359 7551; www.wind sandstars.co.uk). Organises expeditions for 16-23 year olds every summer to the Sinai Peninsula of Egypt to carry out specific scientific, environmental and historical research. Applications are accepted from September onwards; the cost is from £1,300 excluding flights. It also takes over the logistics of other expeditions to the area including those run by BSES.

After saving most of the £2,400 necessary while working for a pharmaceutical company, **Andrew Roland-Price** joined a *BSES* expedition to the Sinai. The expedition divided into six groups carrying out various scientific tasks and he felt himself fortunate that his group had the most variety. After studying water supplies in the granite desert of west Sinai for two weeks and then in the sandstone desert of east Sinai for two weeks, they carried out an historical and archaeological survey of various sites and a marine biology study of the Red Sea:

For me the highlight of each day was lying around the camp fire, worn out but with a full stomach, chatting to the Bedouin guides and looking up at the stars. Away from the ambient light, the Milky Way was visible, and we saw countless shooting stars and satellites each evening...The highlight came with the viewing of sunrise from the top of Mt. Sinai.

Tom Watkins joined a *BSES* expedition at the other end of the African continent. In the summer before his A-level year, he went to Lesotho and found the experience satisfying in every respect. His group was studying an endangered species of plant, the spiral aloe, which is a national symbol and grows only on steep and remote mountain slopes in that country. In fact there was scope for pursuing non-botanical interests. For example Tom became interested in the history and politics of Lesotho and explored these topics with the help of Libe the local man who was their guide and interpreter and also by getting to know the expatriate Englishman who ran the local museum in Morija and who had written books about the region. By contrast, the assistant leader, who was just finishing an art degree, was more interested in the rock art and the architecture of Lesotho.

But Tom learned that late 20th century culture has penetrated most corners of the globe. He stepped off the six-seater plane in the small town of Mokholong and into the local bar only to find Coca Cola (though it may not have been made under licence), Carling Black label beer and satellite television. The expedition to Lesotho was the first one BSES had run to this country but it was a great success and will probably be repeated since it benefitted the scientists, the locals and the student participants. In fact it was considered a model of its kind and more successful than the one to Morocco that same summer.

Richard Jenson enjoyed his time in Tanzania with Frontier tremendously:
Having narrowed down all the options, I chose to go to East Africa with Frontier, studying the savannah grasslands out there. Like a lot of people, I love the wildlife programmes on TV and the chance to go and track elephants on the African plains was mind-blowing. Of course there was the little matter of raising £2000...I can't imagine a better feeling than when I realised I had reached my target. Having worked so hard, I was determined to have the time of my life. It wasn't difficult. The area we were working in was right next to the Selous Game Reserve, the largest game reserve in the world and it was absolutely incredible. Elephants, giraffes, buffaloes, hippos, you name them, we saw them. It was like our very own mini-safari but without all the other tourists. My personal favourites though are zebras. It was only seeing them in real life that made me realise just how strange a black and white striped horse really is.
I spent a lot of time with the local traditional healers. Many of their children are attracted by the bright lights of the big cities and the healers have no one to pass their knowledge on to. My job was to make a note of all the plants and herbs they use. It was absolutely fascinating, hearing how they deal with rheumatism, headache and malaria. And as for the cure for male impotence involving a razor blade, that is definitely not something to be tried at home. I have so many great memories of Africa that my friends have nicknamed me 'Wiwia' because everything I say starts with 'When I was in Africa'. I have definitely caught the African bug and can't wait to go back. I just wish I could have my gap year all over again.

ADVENTURE TRAVEL

Anyone with a diver's certificate might be able to find work at Red Sea resorts like Sharm el Sheikh and Hurghada. If you aren't sufficiently qualified but want to gain the appropriate certificates, the Red Sea is a good place to train for example with the British-managed firm Emperor Divers (www.emperordivers.com) with dive centres in Hurghada, Sharm El Sheikh, Nuweiba and Soma Bay. Once qualified as an instructor, they might hire you or help you make contact with diving schools worldwide. At local dive centres, you can sometimes get free lessons in exchange for filling air tanks for a sub-aqua club. It is possible to be taken on by an Egyptian operator (especially in the high season November to January); however the norm is to be paid no wage and just earn a percentage of the take. You could also check out http://jobs.red-sea.com.

Overland tour operators make it possible for young travellers to visit remote parts of Africa in relative safety. Some African specialists are:

Absolute Africa, 41 Swanscombe Road, Chiswick, London W4 2HL (020-8742 0226; www.absoluteafrica.com).

Acacia Expeditions, Lower Ground Floor, 23A Craven Terrace, London W2 3QH (020-7706 4700; acacia@afrika.demon.co.uk; www.acacia-africa.com).

Bukima Africa, 15 Bedford Road, Great Barford, Beds. MK44 3JD (01234 871329; www.bukima.com).

Economic Expeditions, 29 Cunnington St, Chiswick, London W4 5ER (020-8995 7707; www.economicexpeditions.com).

Oasis Overland, The Marsh, Henstridge, Somerset BA8 0TF (01963 363400; www.oasisoverland.co.uk). Medium length trips in Africa cost around £100 a week plus about £40 a week local payment.

Phoenix Expeditions, College Farm, Far St, Wymeswold, Leicestershire LE12 6TZ; www.phoenixexpeditions.co.uk).

Truck Africa, www.truckafrica.com.

Young people interested in working as drivers, guides or couriers for an overland company should be aware that couriers are required to have first-hand knowledge of travel in Africa or must be willing to train for three months with no guarantee of work. Requirements vary but normally expedition leaders must be at least 23 and be trained diesel mechanics.

Once again travellers' hostels are a magnet for young travellers, and even in some cases provide opportunities for longer stays by offering a work-for-keep arrangement. It is something that many independent trans-Africa travellers do for the odd week, from the Red Sea to the suburbs of Johannesburg, and is a way to have a break without having to pay for it. Bear in mind that the Tourism Concern report published in 1999, which lambasted gap year travellers for their insensitivity to other cultures, was largely based on research carried out in the backpackers' diving resort of Dahab in Egypt. If your aim is to experience an alien culture, it may be preferable not to move from one backpackers' enclave to the next.

If exploring the African bush always take the necessary precautions proffered by rangers and other old hands, to avoid what happened to a 19 year old gap year student a couple of years ago. When David Pleydell-Bouverie was working at the remote Matusadona National Park in Zimbabwe, he was killed by a pride of lions after he failed to zip up his tent.

While travelling throughout Africa, be prepared for contradictions and aggravations. One trick which might help at border crossings is to carry an official-looking list of addresses, for example of voluntary organisations, to show to suspicious immigration authorities.

Asia

Lumping together places as different as Java and Japan, Singapore and Saigon is a dangerous business. The gap year student who spends six months in Hong Kong because her uncle can arrange a job for her in his export business may have almost nothing in common with the gap year student who teaches at a village school in Nepal. Different corners of the vast continent of Asia beguile individuals for personal and possibly inexplicable reasons. Perhaps a childhood book, acquaintance or memory has bequeathed a longing to visit a faraway and mysterious place. This may not be the kind of reason which cuts much ice with college admissions tutors but it can be what sparks incredible and memorable experiences.

There are dangers in spending time at a young age in a seriously alien country. This is true of Bolivia, Zambia or even Romania but somehow the culture shock which gap year travellers experience in the Indian subcontinent or in a small industrial Chinese town is especially acute. A novelty-seeking foreigner is not really what a struggling village in Bengal or Borneo most needs. Preconceptions about what benefits you will be able to bring are often proved misguided in the first week. **Andy Green** spent some time with a long-established voluntary organisation in India and came to some rather negative conclusions about volunteering in India:

> I did two weeks' worth of workcamps and I feel that I was of no help to Indian society whatsoever. Due to differences in climate, food and culture, it is difficult to be productive. I could have paid an Indian a few pounds to do what I did in two weeks. It was however an experience I'll never forget.

In other words, the experience is bound to benefit you, the gap year traveller, but its value to local people may be questionable. That is not to say that a six-month attachment to a school or orphanage will not be valuable for the local community, but its value might lie in unexpected places.

The climate is not a trivial concern. Although Robert Abblett had carefully planned his trip to India and had the addresses of organic farms where he intended to work, he had not counted on the debilitating heat and decided to enjoy a holiday instead. This is an alternative worth considering, i.e. to make your fortune at home or in a western country, whether as an accountancy trainee in England, chambermaid in Switzerland or tomato picker in Australia, in order to finance months of leisurely travel in the developing countries of Asia.

Of course none of this applies to those Asian countries associated with a 'tiger economy', principally Japan, Taiwan, the Hong Kong Special Administrative Region and Singapore. Despite some economic problems, these countries can provide a variety of opportunities for enterprising young people. Special schemes permit pre- and post-university students to work in these countries, mainly as teachers of the English language.

SENDING AGENCIES

Most of the key gap organisations make placements in a number of Asian countries including *Gap Activity Projects, Gap Challenge, Venture Co's Himalaya Venture, Africa & Asia Venture, Project Trust, Students Partnership Worldwide* and *Teaching & Projects Abroad*. India and Nepal are probably the most popular destinations, though many opportunities also exist in Southeast Asia (especially teaching English in Vietnam) and the Far East.

If you want to spend time in a less well-travelled country of Asia, it will be necessary to sift through the literature of all the relevant organisations to find which ones (if any) offer what you are looking for, for example the *Daneford Trust* has placements in Bangladesh, *Coral Cay Conservation* has projects in the Philippines, Fiji and Malaysia, *Raleigh International* in Sabah-Borneo, *GAP* in Vanuatu and Fiji, *Outreach International* sends people to Cambodia to teach English, computing, art, etc., *i-to-i* has sizeable programmes in Korea, Sri Lanka, Cambodia and Mongolia, and so on.

EXPEDITIONS & CONSERVATION

The mainstream London-based conservation expedition organisers all run projects in Asia. These expeditions are normally open to anyone reasonably fit who can raise the cost of joining (typically £2,500-£3,000):

Coral Cay Conservation, The Tower, 13th Floor, 125 High Street, Colliers Wood, London SW19 2JG (0870 750 0668; info@coralcay.org). Volunteers needed for conservation programmes, e.g. carrying out reef surveys in the Philippines and Fiji. CCC also run a rainforest conservation project on the Philippine island of Negros and reef and rainforest projects in Malaysia. Marine expeditions cost about £2,000 for six weeks.

Frontier, 50-52 Rivington St, London EC2A 3QP (020-7613 2422; info@frontierco nservation.org/ www.frontierconservation.org). Volunteers can spend 4 weeks on the Andaman Islands in the Indian Ocean (£1,600) or 10 weeks in Vietnam (£2,450) helping in environmental research and conservation expeditions. Participants can choose to qualify for a BTEC Level 3 in Tropical Habitat Conservation.

Although **Joanne Roberts** from Newbury wanted to study law not ecology, she hugely enjoyed her six months with Frontier in Vietnam:

It took us three days to get from Hanoi to our work-site right up in the north. We started off in a Bedford truck, then swapped to a 4 wheel-drive once the road dete-riorated. The final ten kilometres were covered on the back of ponies as we went up into the mountains. We really felt like we were going to the end of the world. Every-thing else seemed a lifetime away. Our six months in the mountains were amazing. The work we were doing really made a difference. We weren't building fences or other physical stuff but carrying out proper environmental research work, looking at the different species that lived in the forest and talking to the local people to find out what problems they faced. The people were incredible; they were so friendly, giving us food when they clearly didn't have enough for themselves and offering help. And they were curious. We were the first westerners they had seen in 20 years. Now I'm at university those six months in Vietnam don't seem real.

Global Vision International (GVI), Nomansland, Wheathampstead, St. Albans, Herts. AL4 8EJ (01582 831300; info@gvi.co.uk/ www.gvi.co.uk). Placements from 3 weeks to 1 year. Work on an animal sanctuary in Thailand, teach in China, volunteer in Nepal, work with orangutans in Sumatra. Prices from £595 to £1,100.

Greenforce, 11-15 Betterton St, Covent Garden, London WC2H 9BP (020-7470 8888/ fax 020-7470 8889; info@greenforce.org/ www.greenforce.org). Volunteer researchers are needed to join coral reef survey projects in Fiji and Malaysian Borneo. Training is given in the UK and in the host country. Projects involve studying endangered species and habitats. The cost is £2,750 which includes diving equipment and training but not flights.

Operation Wallacea, Hope House, Old Bolingbroke, Nr Spilsby, Lincolnshire PE23 4EX (01790 763194; www.opwall.com). Volunteer students, divers and naturalists assist with surveys of marine and rainforest habitats on remote islands of Southeast Sulawesi in Indonesia. Dive training can be given. Land surveys for studying birds and mammals also organised. Volunteers stay 2, 4, 6 or 8 weeks. Costs from £875 for 2 weeks to £2,700 for 8 weeks, excluding flights.

The Orangutan Foundation, 7 Kent Terrace, London, NW1 4RP (020-7724 2912/fax 020-7706 2613; info@orangutan.org.uk/ www.orangutan.org.uk). Volunteers join hands-on conservation projects in the tropical forests of Indonesian Borneo for 4-6 weeks. Volunteers must pay a fee to cover the cost of National Park fees (US$5 per day) plus food and basic accommodation, either sleeping on the floor in a communal room or in hammocks in the forest.

Despite the rigours, past volunteers have greatly enjoyed having daily contact with the orangutans and getting to know them by name. The majority of the work undertaken by volunteers is taxing physical work in the construction of patrol posts from which locals and future volunteers can protect the forest and the animals which inhabit it. But sometimes more front-line action is needed, as volunteer Anna Fooks recounts:
Prior to our arrival, Mike (the project manager) thought that we would be building a post and jetty in Beguruh. However, priorities changed at short notice when chainsaws (as I understood it) had been heard in another part of the park close to the research area. It was therefore decided that a patrol of assistants and 30 police be assembled to pinpoint illegal logging sites and nine volunteers were fortunate enough to accompany them on a 15-day patrol camping out in the forest. From a

socio-economic and political standpoint, the experience was invaluable as we got to see logging activity, its subsequent forest destruction and some of the critical problems/dilemmas facing the OFI firsthand. We pinpointed two groups of loggers and Gambor workers and helped to break up one of the logging tracks. I was lucky enough to accompany Togu and a team of assistants when they unearthed the second logging camp and a network of logging tracks which ran for several miles. Visits were made to the second loggers' camp (by this time the 30 police had bailed). We also assisted with 'trail clearing', parangs in hand.

Raleigh International, Raleigh House, 27 Parsons Green Lane, London SW6 4HZ (020-7371 8585; www.raleighinternational.org). Leading youth development charity which offers people aged 17-25 the chance to take part in challenging environmental, community and adventure projects as part of 3-month expeditions overseas. Malaysia is the most recently added destination. Volunteers work with local and international scientists in some of the most remote and inaccessible areas of the world. One of these is called the Maliau Basin, only accessible since the 1970s.

Trekforce Expeditions, 34 Buckingham Palace Road, London SW1W 0RE (020-7828 2275/fax 020-7828 2276; info@trekforce.org.uk/ www.trekforce.org.uk). Organise and run conservation, scientific and community projects in the rainforests of Sarawak and Sabah, East Malaysia. The expeditions last 8 to 17 weeks and offer a week of jungle training followed by seven weeks of conservation teamwork on a challenging project. The longer programmes involve expedition work and then a second phase of teaching English in remote villages, for a further two months. Each expedition's project varies and in the past has included work at an orangutan rehabilitation centre, and construction of wardens' posts in one of the national parks. Help and advice on fundraising are given at introduction days, and initial training is given in the UK prior to departure.

Venture Co, The Ironyard, 64-66 The Market Place, Warwick CV34 4SD (01926 411122/ fax 01926 411133; mail@ventureco-worldwide.com/ www.ventureco-worldwide.com). Their Himalayan Venture incorporates a nine-week expedition to Everest Base Camp as well as participating in community and conservation projects after undergoing cultural orientation in Delhi. Total cost of £4,500 including flights and insurance. Indochina Venture for Career Gap participants only includes working on an aid project with Cambodian children and trekking along the Great Wall of China.

Himalayas

Few gap travellers to Nepal can resist joining a trek in the Himalayas or a river rafting trip. *World Challenge Expeditions* (parent company of Gap Challenge) run a number of trips in Nepal and elsewhere in Asia. Of course it is not necessary to book it ahead with a UK agency. Many indigenous companies in Kathmandu can provide the support for expeditions at much less cost. The average cost for a trekking expedition is US$40 a day which includes permits, porters, food and lodging.

It may be possible to volunteer to work for one of the local companies running rafting trips, according to Rebecca Barber:

When I went on a rafting trip (which are fantastic but expensive by Nepali standards – minimum $200 for ten days), I met a guy who had just done two free trips as 'safety kayaker'. No qualifications were needed apart from being confident of your ability to paddle the river. When in Kathmandu, simply walk into every agency you see and offer to work. You would be unlikely to get full-time or long-term work but as a way of getting a few free trips, living at no expense and getting some great paddling experience, not to mention the chance of future employment, it's ideal.

Caution

So many gap year travellers and other backpackers are wandering around India, Nepal and Thailand that it can be a challenge to get away from them (assuming that is your ambition). Although it is a good idea to try to step off the well-worn path between Goa, Kathmandu and Kho Samui, it may be unwise to stray too far from the beaten track. During his year out, Joel Emond from Bristol was travelling alone in northeast China. Unwittingly he wandered out of a national park mentioned in his guidebook and into North Korea where he was instantly arrested and put in jail. The Korean authorities contacted the British Embassy in Beijing to confirm that Joel was not a spy. Unfortunately, they got his name wrong and requested information about Joe Lemond. After several weeks, someone in Beijing twigged and the problem was resolved but not before Joel had gone on hunger strike in protest at the vile diet of rotten cabbages.

One way of exploring Asia in a protected environment is to join an overland tour such as those offered by *Exodus* (9 Weir Road, London W12 0LT) or *Encounter Overland* (01728 862222) which runs shorter and longer adventures trips in Asia.

TEACHING

Throughout Asia thousands of people of all ages are eager for tuition in English. Native English speakers, whatever their background, are wanted to meet that demand and school leavers can find voluntary placements in a range of countries. It can be a daunting prospect standing in front of a class of eager learners when you are just 18. Most teaching will be of conversational English rather than grammar. Several of the sending agencies insist that you do a short TEFL training course beforehand, for example *i-to-i* offers its own weekend course and *GAP Activity Projects* makes a 5-day course compulsory. **Emma Wolfson**, who went to teach in Vietnam, enjoyed GAP's preparatory course:

> The TEFL course I attended was the first chance I had to meet all the other people going to Vietnam and, in a way, that was the best part about it. However, we had a great teacher, who started our first class by talking at us in Czech, and making us learn the words for hello and goodbye without uttering a word of English. That I can remember this (although sadly not the Czech) makes me realise how important a good teacher is, and therefore how vital it was for us 18 year olds to learn at least the basics in teaching skills. We learnt a little of everything - how to get up in front of a class and not be afraid to open your mouth, ice-breaking games and other lesson fillers, how to plan a lesson and so on.

In the end Emma didn't have much chance to use what she had learned since she found herself teaching trainee cabin attendants for Vietnam Airlines, all older than her. They were chiefly interested in learning phrases like 'Would you like chicken or beef?' and 'the emergency exits are located to the rear'; and they wanted drills in saying 'rice' not 'rye'.

Paid teaching work is available primarily to people who have a university degree. Most commercial language school directors are looking for teachers who are older than 18 and who have finished university. In the case of Korea and Japan, a BA or BSc is virtually essential for obtaining the appropriate visa. Teaching English in Japan is one of the classic jobs for people filling a gap in their lives, but almost all are post-university.

The situation is different on the Indian sub-continent where very few private English language schools exist. Many gap students find themselves attached to schools, sometimes with a rather indeterminate role. The intention may simply be to enrich the lives of children by exposing them to a foreigner as much as to teach them English or anything concrete. **Suzanne Duffin's** placement in India involved teaching very basic English and maths, singing and playing games with the children and mainly giving the children lots of love and affection. She got to know each one very well and really enjoyed helping each child achieve the smallest things like writing his or her name. **Steven Stuart** found himself (under the auspices of *GAP Activity Projects*) teaching in a primary school in the jungles of Sarawak in Borneo. He taught only about two hours of lessons a day but enjoyed leading extracurricular activities like football and badminton clubs and learned a valuable lesson that 'improvisations are all part of the job'. He was pleased to feel he was trusted by the head of the school and never felt anyone peering over his shoulder:

Helping children learn gave a crazy sense of achievement, and having to earn the respect of the village was such a great feeling.

Many other gap year students have found their placements thoroughly rewarding and worthwhile. But some have found themselves attached to schools for privileged children and wonder why they are there. **Rachel Sedley's** main complaint about her placement in Nepal was that she was teaching in a private school for privileged children when she had been led to believe that she would be contributing her time and labour to more needy children. She suspected that she was there partly to boost the prestige of the school and its head. Similarly **Tim Palmer** ended up teaching everything from English literature to Indian history at a very old traditional public school in Darjeeling which he imagined is run along the lines of Eton. So anyone with strong views about the kind of school in which they want to work should find out as many details as possible beforehand.

The vast majority of opportunities are for people to teach English. There follows brief descriptions of the situation in the main countries of Asia, together with contact addresses. More detailed information on teaching English in the countries of Asia is contained in the 2003 edition of *Teaching English Abroad* by Susan Griffith (Vacation-Work Publications, £12.95).

Japan

Japan is an ideal destination for a post-university gap year or two. Thousands of English schools in Tokyo, Osaka and many other Japanese cities are eager to hire *gaijins* (foreigners) to teach. A great many of these are willing to hire native speakers of English with no teaching qualification as long as they have a university degree and preferably some teaching experience. Apart from a few schools which advertise and conduct interviews abroad, most schools recruit their teachers within Japan.

For many years Canadians, Australians and New Zealanders have been eligible to apply for a working holiday visa for Japan. In 2001, the scheme was extended to British citizens aged 18-25 (or up to 30 in restricted circumstances). The working holiday visa allows 400 single young Britons to accept paid work in Japan for up to 12 months. Note that applications are accepted from April and once the allocation of 400 has been filled, no more visas will be granted until April of the following year. So gap year students interested in spending a year in Japan should submit their applications around Easter of their A2 year. Further details are available by ringing 020-7465 6500 or on the embassy website at www.embjapan.org.uk. In May 2003 a Volunteer Visa for Japan was launched which permits British nationals to work for a charitable organisation for up to one year.

The services of the Japan Association for Working-Holiday Makers (www.jawhm.or.jp) with offices in Tokyo, Osaka and Kyushu, are very helpful to people on working holiday visas. Jobs registered with JAWHM are normally in ski resorts, hotels or English schools. The visa specifically prohibits working for employers who might be contravening regulations, especially in the food and entertainment business, a direct result of the tragic murder of the 21-year old British woman Lucie Blackman who was working in a 'hostess bar'.

Those who want to work in Japan but do not succeed in obtaining a working holiday visa must acquire a Japanese sponsor. This can be a private citizen but most teachers are sponsored by their employers. Graduates should investigate the government's flourishing *JET (Japan Exchange & Teaching) Programme*. Anyone with a Bachelor's degree in any discipline who is under 40 (recently raised from 35) and from the UK, US, Ireland, Canada, Australia or New Zealand (plus a number of other countries) is eligible to apply. In Britain details may be obtained from the JET Desk at the Japanese Embassy, 101-104 Piccadilly, London W1J 7JT (020-7465 6668/6670; jet@embjapan.org.uk). Last year more than 1,000 Britons joined the programme (compared to about half that number in 1997). Other nationalities should contact the Japanese Embassy in their country of origin for information and application forms. Applications in Britain are due by early December for one-year placements beginning late July. The annual salary is 3,760,000 yen (equivalent to about £19,000/$32,000) in addition to a free return air ticket if you complete your contract.

A number of the largest language training organisations recruit graduates abroad as well as in Japan. Among the main employers are:

ECC Foreign Language Institute, Kanto District Head Office: 5th Floor, San Yamate Building, 7-11-10 Nishi-Shinjuku, Shinjuku-ku, Tokyo 160-0023 (03-5330 1585; www.ecc.co.jp though the website for job applicants is www.japanbound.com). 500 teachers for 150 schools throughout Japan.

GEOS Corporation, Simpson Tower 2424, 401 Bay Street, Toronto, Ontario M5H 2Y4, Canada (416-777-0109; geos@istar.ca; www.geoscareer.com). UK address: GEOS Language Ltd., St. Martin's House, St. Martin's Le Grand, London EC1A 4EN (020-7397 8405; london@geos.demon.co.uk). One of Japan's largest English language institutions employing 2,000 teachers for 500 schools, all of whom are hired outside Japan. Recruitment campaigns held in UK, Australia, New Zealand and North America.

Interac Co Ltd. Fujibo Building 2F, 2-10-28 Fujimi, Chiyoda-ku, Tokyo 102-0071 (03-3234 7857; www.interac.co.jp/recruit). 500 Assistant Language Teachers in a number of branches.

Nova Group, Carrington House, 126/130 Regent Street, London W1R 5FE (020-7734 2727; www.teachinjapan.com). Employ more than 5,000 in 520 Nova schools throughout Japan. Recruitment in North America via Interact Nova Group, 2 Oliver St, Suite 7, Boston, MA 02109, USA (617-542-5027); and 1881 Yonge St, Suite 700, Toronto, Ontario M4S 3C4, Canada (416-481-6000).

China

Teaching opportunities are mushrooming throughout the People's Republic of China and many schools and institutes are turning to the internet to fill teaching vacancies. Although many posts are open only to university graduates, younger people are also being accepted (albeit at a much lower wage) because of the acute shortage and some gap year agencies are becoming active. For example *GAP Activity Projects* places gap year students in some fairly remote institutes which can cause a degree of culture shock. Ben Spencer visited a friend from his sixth form college who was doing her GAP placement in a middle school (for 13-16 year olds) in Jiangxi, a province considered something of a backwater, but which Rachel was mostly enjoying. Crime was so rare in this city of 300,000 that they were still talking about a bicycle that had been stolen five years before (which brings to mind the brilliant recent film *Beijing Bicycle*). The only aspect of life she minded was the authorities' attempt to curtail her freedoms, e.g. the supervior/mentor tried (without success) to prevent her from joining an aerobics class and from eating at restaurants rather than at the school canteen. She and her GAP partner had been looking forward to travelling during a school holiday but because of the SARS crisis, all leave had been summarily cancelled and everyone was virtually imprisoned in the town.

University graduates will find it extremely easy to find a job at a school, college or private institute in China. *CIEE* in the UK and US run a Teach in China programme for graduates (see below). *BUNAC* (020-7251 3472; www.bunac.org) has entered into a partnership with Language Link (020-7225 1065; www.languagelink.co.uk) to send gap year students and others to teaching posts in China (and Russia). Candidates must first be prepared to obtain an approved 4-week TEFL certificate through Language Link or elsewhere.

With the explosion in opportunities, the job hunt is far more straightforward than it was a few years ago when most teacher applications were for state-run institutes of higher education and had to go through the Chinese Education Association for International Exchange (CEAIE; www.ceaie.edu.cn) or one of its 37 provincial offices. Nowadays there are many private recruiters, foundations or China-linked companies, on and off the internet, eager to sign up native speakers (with or without relevant experience) for an academic year. Many English teaching posts in the Chinese provinces remain unfilled, though aid agencies like VSO and Christians Abroad do their utmost to fill vacancies. The requirements for these two-year posts are not stringent and, in return, teachers get free airfares, a local salary and other perks.

Some of the tried and tested old schemes are still in place and still work. The British Council in co-operation with the Chinese Education authorities refers anyone who has done two years of higher education to schools and universities across China. The normal pay range is 2,500-3,500 Renminbi yuan (RMB) (£185-£260) per month. Details of the scheme are on line at www.britishcouncil.org/education.assistants or can be obtained from the Chinese Links Officer at the British Council (10 Spring Gardens, London SW1A 2BN; 020-7389 4595; fax 020-7389 4426; world.links@britishcouncil.org).

> **Although sheltering under the umbrella of a UK or US-based agency may make some things easier, it is also possible to arrange a teaching post independently, as William Hawkes did in his last year at university:**
> In my final year at Cambridge, I was unsure of what to do next. I did not take a gap year between school and university and by then I was desperate to really get to know a country, learn the language, meet the people, make friends, lead a normal life somewhere interesting without M & S, the Bill, kebabs and Heineken. At that time, my current hot country was China. I spotted an advertisement in the university job opportunities circular for a meeting with officials from the Chinese Embassy about English teaching. I liked what I heard (i.e. working in China sounded stable and foreign teachers were obviously established and familiar there) and after a quick interview to prove that I could speak English, I was handed a long list of universities and colleges which were looking for teachers. I sent faxes to the ten most suitable-looking ones with a letter and CV, and in time received five job offers. I quickly narrowed the choice to two, both offering a good salary in Chinese terms, and chose the Qingdao Chemical Institute in northern China because Mandarin would be prevalent but mostly because a friend of mind had taught there and strongly recommended it.

For the most part having no protective agency caused no problems. The Institute looked after all the red tape and working conditions were favourable - 20 hours a week, the equivalent of £300 a month. Typically a gap year teacher would earn less. William Hawke spent his time very constructively and achieved all that he hoped, learned fluent Mandarin, made friends and got to know China well. His gap year experience put him in a strong position when he applied for a job as an International Officer with the Hong Kong Shanghai Bank, which he got soon after his return.

Depending on experience and qualifications, teachers are designated as foreign teachers (FTs) or foreign experts (FEs). The latter usually requires a post-graduate degree and confers much more status as well as a higher salary, a return airfare, holiday pay and other benefits. Most foreign teachers are expected to teach between 12 and 18 hours a week, which sounds a light load until you find yourself with classes of 50 or even 100 students.

CIEE UK, US and Australia runs a Teach in China programme for graduates. Placements are in secondary and tertiary institutions throughout China for either five or ten months starting in either August or February. Programme includes a seven-day orientation on arrival in Shanghai; programme cost is from £995 plus flights. In the UK, the details of Teach in China may be obtained by ringing 020-7478 2020 or by e-mailing infouk@councilexchanges.org.uk.

The Buckland International Education Group (Buckland ESL Hostel, PO Box 555,

Yanshuo, Guilin 541900; buckland@china.com; www.bucklandgroup.org) advertises on the internet for native speaker teachers of any background either to undertake casual conservation teaching lasting 1-5 months or to accept a contract for a full or half academic year. The organisation even makes a contribution to airfares on completion of a contract and provides visas and accommodation.

Two other UK-based programmes are Project China (01273 775000; fax 08700 523487; scherto@projectchina.org) which sends 30 native speakers to two partner schools in Beijing and one in Shenyang (Northeast China); and Oakland Education Service, 5 Oak Way, Harpenden, Herts. AL5 2NT (01582 713821; oaklands@dial.pipex.com) which sends gap year students to teach in China.

Another possibility is to teach in Hong Kong through the Chatteris Educational Foundation (18/F Honest Motors Building, 9-11 Leighton Road, Causeway Bay, Hong Kong; 2520 5736; www.chatteris.org.hk) which places volunteer English Language Teaching Assistants for nine months. ELTAs can be school leavers, undergraduates or recent graduates, all of whom are assigned accommodation in shared flats and paid a monthly allowance to cover food and pocket money.

Some US-based placement programmes to consider are:

Amity Foundation, 71 Han Kou Road, Nanjing, Jiangsu 210008 (25-332-4607; wwww.am ityfoundation.org). Christian organisation that sends 60-80 people to teach English in China.

China Teaching Program, Western Washington University, High Street Hall 6, Bellingham, WA 98225-9047 (360-650-3753; www.wwu.edu/~ctp). Up to 20 graduates with TEFL accreditation. Placement fee $625.

Colorado China Council, 4556 Apple Way, Boulder, CO 80301 (303-443-1108; www.asiacouncil.org). 20-35 teachers per year placed at institutes throughout China, including Mongolia.

IEF Education Foundation, 18605 E Gale Avenue, Suite 203, City of Industry, CA 91748 (626-965-1995; www.ief-usa.org). Recruits mainly Americans with a BA to spend at least six months teaching English to junior high and high-school aged students in many Chinese cities.

WorldTeach, Centre for International Development, 79 John F Kennedy St, Cambridge, MA 02138 (617-495-5527; www.worldteach.org). Non-profit organisation sends volunteers to teach adults for six months in Yantai and runs Shanghai Summer Teaching Program. Volunteers teach small classes of high school students at a language camp in Shanghai. Volunteers pay about $4,000 for airfares, orientation, health insurance, living expenses and field support.

With an invitation letter or fax from an official Chinese organisation, you should be able to obtain a long term work visa from the Embassy of the PRC in your country. The cost of a multi-entry visa for Britons is £60 for six months, £90 for 12. It is also possible to enter China on a tourist (L) visa and then the Foreign Affairs Office at your institute or equivalent at a private company offering employment will arrange for an Alien Residence Permit (Z visa). Make sure this happens before your visitor visa expires; otherwise you will be liable to a fine and will have to leave the country to change status.

Travellers in China have been approached and invited to teach English as Ben Spencer discovered on his gap year travels in China. After visiting a friend teaching on a placement with GAP Activity Projects, Ben was attracted to the idea of teaching English and came across various possibilities as he travelled. For example in picturesque Yangshuo south of Guilin, Ben became friendly with a language school owner whom he paid for a week of Chinese lessons (two hours a day) and who offered him a job. A contact in Beijing put him on to the GuanYa Education Group (www.sinoed.com) who offered him a job (even though their literature claims that they are looking for university graduates).

For an insight into the complexities of modern China, look at the novel *The Drink and Dream Teahouse* by Justin Hill who did a stint in the provincial town of Yuncheng with VSO straight out of university (and wrote about that in *A Bend in the River*).

The classroom is not always the best place to draw out the students. Extracurricular activities can present a better opportunity for imparting the English language, as **Richard Vincent** found when he spent a year as a Project Trust volunteer in Southern China:

> *Most of the positive aspects of my year were achieved outside the classroom. The good students will always work all the hours god sends. However the less motivated can become motivated to try and learn. In my case, playing football gave lots of students who had been labelled 'dossers' the chance to speak English, and many of them became the best contributors in class. The emphasis should always be on fun and trying to get them to use the English they know.*

Taiwan

The country remains a magnet for English teachers of all backgrounds since it managed to escape the Asian economic crisis. Hundreds of private language institutes or *buhsibans* continue to teach young children, cram high school students for university entrance examinations and generally service the seemingly insatiable demand for English conversation and English tuition.

Many well-established language schools are prepared to sponsor foreign teachers for a resident visa, provided the teacher has a university degree and is willing to work for at least a year. On arrival check the Positions Vacant column of the English language *China Post* and the *China News* though work tends to result from personal referrals more than from advertising.

The following language schools hire on a large scale:

Hesse Educational Organization No. 419, Chung Shan Rd, Sec 2, Chung Ho City, Taipei County 235 (02-3234 6188; www.hess.com.tw). Specialise in teaching children including kindergarten age. 375 Native Speaking Teachers (NSTs) in more than 125 branches. Very structured teaching programme and curriculum. Quarterly intake of teachers in September, December, March and June.

International Avenue Consulting Company, 16F-1 No 499 Chung Ming South Road, Taichung City (04-2375 9800; www.iacc.com.tw). Recruitment agency with links to Canada who hire up to 150 teachers.

Kid Castle Language Schools, Min Chuan Road No. 98, 8F, Hsin Tien City 231, Taipei (02-2218 6996; http://personnel.kidcastle.com). 160 franchise branches throughout Taiwan.

Kojen ELS, 6F, No 9, Lane 90, Sung Chiang Road, Taipei or 12 Kuling St, Taipei (02-2321 9005; www.kojenenglish.com). Employs 200-300 teachers at 19 schools, mostly in Taipei but also Kaohsiung and Taichung. Minimum starting salary for 25 hours per week is NT$52,000 per month (approx. US$1,500).

Korea

Although Korea does not immediately come to mind as a likely destination for British TEFLers, it has been long known in North America as a country which can absorb an enormous number of native speaker teachers, including fresh graduates with no TEFL training or experience. South Korea seems to be making a surprisingly rapid recovery from the severe economic difficulties it suffered at the end of the 20th century and English teachers are still in great demand. The agency *i-to-i* can place large numbers of graduates willing to spend 12 months teaching their native tongue; the cost of the placement is £595 which includes return flights (paid at end of contract) and a job with a monthly salary of £800-£1,000.

Hundreds of language institutes *(hogwons)* in Seoul the capital, Pusan (Korea's second city, five hours south of Seoul) and in smaller cities employ native speaker teachers of English. The majority of these are run as businesses, so that making a profit seems to be what motivates many bosses rather than educating people. Certificates and even degrees are in many cases superfluous.

The English Program in Korea (EPIK) is a scheme run by the Ministry of Education, and administered through Korean embassies in the west to place about 2,000 native speakers in schools and education offices throughout the country. The annual salary (2003/4) is 1.7, 1.9 or 2.2 million won per month (depending on qualifications) plus accommodation, round trip airfare, visa sponsorship and medical insurance. Work starting dates are staggered over the summer with application deadlines falling between April and June. Current information should be obtained from the Education Director, Korean Embassy, 60 Buckingham Gate, London SW1E 6AJ (020-7227 5547/fax 020-7227 5503; http://epik.knue.ac.kr) or contact the office in Korea (82-431 233 4516/7). Note that EPIK does not attract the praise which the JET Programme does; check Dave Sperling's ESL Café website for details (www.eslcafe.com).

ELS International/YBM employs 400-600 native English teachers for English Conversation Centers and other kinds of institute throughout Korea. The central contact address is 55-1 Chongno 2ga, Chongno Gu, 3rd Floor, Seoul 110 122 (202264 7472; www.ybmhr.com).

Thailand

Thailand is one of the most popular destinations for gap year travellers but, until recently, not many of the specialist placement agencies sent young volunteers to this country. However, *i-to-i* and *GAP Activity Projects* have a TEFL programme in Thailand and *AFS* has a flourishing counterpart which runs a year long educational and homestay programme which is undersubscribed. *CIEE* UK, US and Australia runs a Teach in Thailand programme for graduates. Placements are in secondary institutions throughout Thailand for five or ten months starting in August or February. In the UK, details of Teach in Thailand may be obtained by ringing 020-7478 2020 or by e-mailing info@councilexchanges.org.uk.

EIL (287 Worcester Road, Malvern, Worcs. WR14 1AB; 0800 018 4015; www.eiluk.org) arranges volunteer work in Thailand from 6 to 29 weeks in a range of social, environmental and health projects. Global Quest (195 Montsweag Road, Woolwich, Maine 04579, USA; www.gquest.org) specialises in sending American gap year students to study Thai language and culture, environmental issues, etc. for 12 weeks (fee $12,000).

Independent-minded gap year travellers can pick up casual teaching work in Bangkok but wages are low and working conditions not very satisfactory. Finding a list of language schools to approach on arrival will present few difficulties. The best place to start is around Siam Square where numerous schools and the British Council are located or the Yellow Pages which lists dozens of language school addresses.

Another possible source of job vacancies is the English language press, viz. the *Bangkok Post* (with at least five adverts every day) and to a lesser extent the *Nation.* The noisy Khao San Road is lined with expat pubs and budget accommodation, many with notice boards offering teaching work and populated with other foreigners (known as *farangs*) well acquainted with the possibilities. They will also be able to warn you of the dubious schools which are known to exploit their teachers.

Teaching opportunities crop up in branches of the big companies like ECC (Thailand), 430/17-24 Chula Soi 64, Siam Square, Bangkok 10330 (2-253 3312; jobs@ecc.ac.th/ www.eccthai.com) with 40 branches in Greater Bangkok and 20 elsewhere in Thailand. Teachers must have one of the following: a Bachelor's degree, TEFL qualification or a minimum of six months teaching experience.

Tourist destinations like Chiang Mai are attractive to job-hunting teachers. According to Annette Kunigagon, the Irish woman married to a Thai whose Eagle Guest House is a great place to find out about the teaching scene in Chiang Mai (www.eaglehouse.com), 'There are still lots of paid and voluntary English teaching posts in Chiang Mai available; the language schools can't get enough'. Annette's general advice for the job hunt is to dress conservatively and cultivate a reserved manner: 'too many gesticulations and guffawing are not considered polite'. She is developing a volunteer programme called 'Helping Hands Social Projects' by which volunteers teach at a centre for disabled people, school for the blind, etc.

An interesting programme has been introduced by the Youth Hostels Association of

Thailand called 'Giving English for Community Service'. Foreign volunteers with some basic English teaching experience spend three to five months teaching English to classes of low-paid members of the community working in tourism. In exchange for teaching up to four hours a day, they receive all living expenses including travel between the provinces in which they work. Details are available from the Youth Hostels Association, International Community Service Programme, Thai YHA, 25/14 Phitsanulok Road, Si Sao Thewet, Dusit, Bangkok 10300 (02-628 7413-5; bangkok@tyha.org).

Officially you need a work permit for Thailand, but the authorities normally turn a blind eye to trespassers. You will have to leave the country every three months to renew your visa; most choose Penang Malaysia for this purpose and many have done it four or five times. There is a fine of B100 for every day you overstay your tourist visa. With a letter from your school, you can apply for a non-immigrant visa, which is better for teaching than a tourist visa. It too must be renewed by leaving the country every 90 days for a fee of B500.

Thailand is one country where you might like to take a course instead of teach one. Gap travellers have been known to sign up for courses in massage and meditation as well as cookery.

Vietnam

The largest growth area in English teaching has been in those countries which were cut off from the West for many years, viz. Vietnam, Cambodia and Laos, where a number of joint venture language schools have been opened employing native speaker teachers. *Outreach International* (Bartletts Farm, Hayes Road, Compton Dundon, Somerset TA11 6PF; ☎/fax 01458 274957; www.outreachinternational.co.uk) is one of the few organisations with a programme in Cambodia; it sends volunteers aged 18-30 to work for three or more months with local NGOs, for instance to teach English, computing or art to landmine victims or to work in a small orphanage or art and craft centre. These placements are suitable for volunteers wishing to pursue a career in overseas development or aid work. Physiotherapists and older volunteers are needed for some of the projects.

GAP Activity Projects has been increasing the number of students that it sends to Vietnam and has projects in Thailand. **Stephanie Lee** applied late in the day to GAP Activity Projects and didn't get her first choice of Nepal. She knew very little of Vietnam but was eager to accept and quickly began to gather information and to work as much overtime as possible to raise the necessary money in the two months before her placement began in September:

> *I was teaching in a large secondary school just outside central Hanoi. The class sizes were huge, about 45-50, something that at first filled me with fear. The students (aged 13) were so very excited and eager to learn English. We were only contracted to work for 20 hours a week and often we weren't working that much. The working conditions were very good, but the school had no windows, blank walls and toilets like animal sties. I was one of the lucky few who was able to live with a family. Through living with a family, I was really able to learn and understand the culture and customs and have a real family and place to call home for four months. It is impossible to describe how much I fell in love with Vietnam, the people, my students and my family.*

What came after Stephanie's time with Gap in Vietnam turned out to be even more influential:

> *My experiences in Vietnam enabled me to mature, to learn so much and to experience things most people will never know. They completely changed my attitude towards my life and my future. Whilst there, I decided I didn't want to study art after all, but instead became interested in learning Vietnamese. Upon returning home, I gave these ideas serious consideration and re-applied to SOAS to study Southeast*

Asian languages. I am very excited by this new course of study and far more passionate to learn and build with GAP in Hanoi, I purposely chose to travel alone. At first I was anxious, but got off to a great start. It was during my travels in Thailand that I realised that I preferred to involve myself in a community rather than aimlessly roam around. Coincidentally, I met a reporter on a bus who told me of his work with Karenni refugees from Burma seeking asylum in Thailand. I immediately became interested and asked to be taken to one of the camps. Three days later I was flying home to earn some more money, give presentations to Amnesty groups, write letters and articles, etc. Every penny I was given by Rotary, Bristol Uni students and other companies and sponsors (totalling about £1,700) has gone directly to the refugees. I flew back to Asia next year with 355 kilos of basic supplies, clothing, books, educational aids and stationery. I spent a week arranging transportation and clearing customs in Bangkok. I am now living and teaching in Refugee Camp No. 3 in Mae Hong Son and have adjusted to a basic life eating rice and yellow beans and showering with a bucket of brown river water. While I am working here, I am trying to raise people's awareness of the situation inside Myanmar. I have never been interested in politics, but have become so politically active since arriving here. I could never have dreamt of experiencing, learning and doing so much during my year out.

Nepal

Nepal is one of the most promising destinations for gap year volunteers, now that it has regained some stability after the tragic death of the King and his family in June 2001 and the ceasefire announced by the Maoist rebels in January 2003. The years of Maoist insurgency saw a massive 70% decline in the number of visitors and (among many other barbarities) the closure of many village schools. The volunteer placement organisation *MondoChallenge* (see 'Directory of Voluntary Placements Abroad') started in the village of Sermathang where the school was forcibly closed down by the Maoists in July 2001 (temporarily they hope) and the 150 pupils thrown out overnight. Fortunately a certain number were moved to a school in Kathmandu where 30 MondoChallenge volunteers continue to work, as well as around Dhulikhel.

Kate Mitchell from Chelmsford is one of many gappers who has had a wonderful time in Nepal, in her case through *GAP Activity Projects*:

I hadn't been to Asia before and Nepal sounded magical. My placement involved teaching English to children 4-16 years old. From beginning to end my placement was full of new experiences, challenges and fun. Teaching, especially the young children, was the most challenging thing we had to do. But when our little terrors started to string sentences together I felt a huge sense of achievement and pride. We may have walked into our first few lessons thinking that English was all we could teach these children, we were wrong. We could teach them to think for themselves, to share, to respect each other and to use their imaginations too. But as we taught we learnt so much, did so much, saw so much. Everyday was fresh, new and exciting. As the humid heat of summer faded into the chill of winter we realised that Nepal had subtly changed, and so had we.

People who find voluntary openings in Nepal will be faced with a visa problem. Tourist visas (which can be purchased on arrival for $25 cash) are valid for 30 days whereupon they have to be renewed. This is straightforward for the first three months for a fee of $1 a day. A four-month visa can be applied for at the Immigration Office in Thamel, Kathmandu. Normally these will not be granted unless the request is supported by an official organisation like the gap placement agencies which are very active in the country. People who overstay their visas have in the past been fined $4,000 or even put in prison.

An impressive range of non-governmental organisations makes it possible for people to teach in a voluntary capacity including some of the 'Directory of Voluntary Placements Abroad' (see entries for *Global Action Nepal, INFO Nepal, Social Development Group* and *Volunteer Nepal 2002*. No indigenous organisations can afford to bestow largesse on foreigners joining their projects, so westerners who come to teach in a school or a village must be willing to fund themselves. None of the programme fees below includes airfares to Nepal. Of course living expenses are very low by western standards, prompting some young people to bypass the fees charged by many of the gap year agencies. Organising a school placement directly or with a Nepali-based agency is invariably cheaper. If you want to avoid an agency fee you can make direct contact with schools on arrival. Relevant organisations include:

Cultural Destination Nepal, PO Box 11535, Kathmandu (01-426996; cdnnepal@wlink.com.np; www.volunteernepal.org.np). Volunteer service work programme. $650 includes language training and homestay plus $50 application fee. Placements last 2-4 months starting February, April, August and October.

Gorkha District Health & Educational Development Scheme, c/o Joy Leighton, Chairwoman – Fax 01277 841224; info@leighton.org/ www.nepal.co.uk. Charity is always looking for volunteers to teach English and practical subjects to Nepalese school kids for a minimum of three weeks, but a longer time preferred.

Grahung Kalika, Southwestern Nepal, Dol Raj Subedi, c/o Mr. Tara Prasad Subedi, P.O. Box 11272, Kathmandu (1-532674/fax 1-527317; mail@multcon.wlink.com.np). Volunteers are needed to improve the English of both pupils and teachers in local schools in Walling, a municipality in the remote Syangja District of western Nepal (260km west of Kathmandu). Volunteers must have an enthusiastic and inventive approach as resources are basic and teaching conditions challenging. Volunteers stay with local families for the duration of their placements (between August and May) and are asked to contribute Rs4,000 (US$52) plus a monthly fee of Rs3000 (US$40) to the host family for food and accommodation.

Insight Nepal, PO Box 489, Pokhara, Kaski, Nepal (insight@mos.com.np; www.insightnepal.org). 3-month placements for all post A-level and high-school graduate native speakers of English. Non-refundable $40 application fee plus participation fee of $800 ($400 for 4-6 week programme). Full programme includes pre-orientation, placement in a primary or secondary school in Nepal to teach mainly English or in community development projects, a one-week village or trekking excursion and 3 days in Chitwan National Park. Eighteen year old **Giles Freeman** from Australia spent three months with Insight Nepal:

I would advise that applicants do have some teaching practice before coming. Classes easily reach 60 or 80 in many schools, making it necessary for the patient teacher to know what they are doing. With no teaching experience, this proved a little hard, but it's a great challenge. All in all it was extremely rewarding.

Kathmandu Environmental Education Project, P.O. Box 9178, Thamel, Jyatha, Kathmandu (01-259567 www.keepnepal.org). KEEP sends volunteers to different trekking villages in Nepal to teach the English language to lodge owners, trekking guides and porters. Volunteers stay with a mountain family. Volunteers must be totally self-funding. Membership fee £12/$20; logistical support fee US$100.

New International Friendship Club, Post Box 11276, Maharajgunj, Kathmandu, Nepal; (01-427406; fcn@ccsl.com.np). 40 English-speaking university graduates placed in schools or colleges. Volunteer teachers should contribute $150 per month for their keep (unless they become a project expert). Basic Nepalese standard accommodation is provided and Nepali (rice-based) meals.

People's Welfare Committee, GPO 12137, Kathmandu, Nepal (01-412997; jbardewa@wlink.com.np). Volunteer agriculturalists and teachers placed monthly.

RCDP Nepal: Kathmandu Municipality, P.O. Box 14, Kathmandu (1-278305/fax 1-276530; www.rcdpnepal.com). Paying volunteers work on various programmes lasting 2 weeks to 5 months, including teaching English. Volunteers stay with families in villages.

Volunteer & Support Program (VSP) Nepal (PO Box 11969, Kathmandu; 1-488773;

vsp_nepal@yahoo.com). Volunteer jobs in city and countryside. One-off registration fee of $20/€20/20 plus organisation fee of $50/€50 plus $100 per month payable to host family. Run by same man as VWOP (see next entry).

VWOP (Voluntary Work Opportunities in Nepal), PO Box 4263, Kathmandu (fax 1-416144; vwop2000@hotmail.com). VWOP provides voluntary jobs and opportunities in remote areas of Nepal including teaching English in schools, organising community work and being involved in research while living with a Nepali family. Volunteers may also arrange and implement their own programmes/activities which directly help the local community. Qualifications and experience are not essential. The registration fee is US$20, placement fee is $400 and the monthly fee payable to host family is $50.

> **Ruth Woodhouse, a past volunteer with the Gorkha Scheme who went on to Leicester University, gives a colourful account of her volunteering experiences in Gorkha, Nepal:**
> *Over the weeks, I settled into school life. I politely refused the use of a stick and instead set about running my classes with games and activities. This proved quite difficult because of the language barrier and, as far as the children were concerned, the lack of violent discipline meant that things often got out of control. It wasn't long before class 2 screamed in delight at the Hokey-Cokey, class 5 were constructing their own cubes, class 6 were proudly colouring in family trees... With £200 I had raised for having my head shaved (on a geology field trip to Scotland), we managed to buy a hefty amount of equipment for the schools. With more space and more materials the children seemed a little more relaxed and we set about drawing pictures and posters to cover the walls, as I tried to introduce them to the repertoire of the Beatles and, in complete contrast, they taught me traditional Nepali songs and dances. Life in Nepal is so full of hope and joy, any excuse and they'll find something to celebrate.*

Nepal is so welcoming to foreigners that it is quite possible to arrange your own voluntary post simply by becoming known in a village and asking local teachers if you can help out, possibly in exchange for simple accommodation. This is a country to which many travellers flock for rest and relaxation, for eating, drinking and socialising. Tim Palmer is one such gap year traveller who enjoyed Nepal for five weeks (including trekking and rafting) but found it all too easy and soon hankered again for the 'hassle that is India' where he travelled until the last day of his six-month visa.

India

Volunteering in India sometimes takes the form of teaching but more often it involves social projects. Among the many projects supported by the UK-based *Student Action India* (entry in 'Directory of Voluntary Placements Abroad'), teaching assignments and social welfare placements are most common. These last for a summer or five months from September.

Peter Hill returned from India from a successful placement though *Changing Worlds*:

Whether remembering my first attempts at eating rice with my fingers, watching the iron-flat plains stretch beneath me as I climbed a sacred hill barefoot with thousands of pilgrims during a Hindu festival or the exhilaration of my first successful hour as an English teacher, my six months in India remain unforgettable. Changing Worlds found me a voluntary placement in Southern India working with the People's Craft Training Centre, an organisation aiming to instil 'collective self-reliance' among the poor and disabled of their local area. One aspect of the centre's work lies in educating and monitoring the development of children affected by cerebral palsy. Although my time was mainly spent helping in this special school, my role was not strictly defined at all and it was more like working in partnership with a group of friends than being given a list of instructions. I think the clash of cultures was as novel for many locals as it was for me. The welcome I received and the friendships I made reflect the warmth of Indian hospitality; you will rarely be on your own for long. Changing Worlds fully briefed me on India and what to expect at their two-day pre-departure course. I felt welcomed by Krish, the local rep, on arrival in Chennai and felt well looked after during my entire stay in this wonderful country.

An Indian organisation which places graduates on a voluntary basis in educational institutes in South India is *Jaffe International Education Service* (Kunnuparambil Buildings, Kurichy, Kottayam 686549, India; ☎/fax 0481 430470; jaffeint@sify.com). Volunteers teach for short periods in English medium high schools, hotel management colleges, teacher training centres, vocational institutes and language schools in Kerala State and also at summer schools in various locations in India. As with all projects in India, no wage is paid but you are billeted with a family.

Several organisations in the UK send volunteers to teach English or undertake other voluntary work in India. For example *Teaching and Projects Abroad* (Gerrard House, Rustington, Sussex BN16 1AW; 01903 859911) arranges short-term teaching and other workplace assignments in Kerala and Tamil Nadu, South India for between £1,195 and £1,595 excluding flights. *Travellers* (7 Mulberry Close, Ferring, West Sussex BN12 5HY; ☎01903 502595; fax 01903 500364; www.travellersworldwide.com) organises teaching (Brunei, China, India, Sri Lanka, Vietnam), conservation (Brunei, Malaysia, Sri Lanka) and work experience (India, Sri Lanka). Teaching placements concentrate mainly on conversational English. Conservation programme includes working with orangutans, elephants and turtles. Work experience includes law and journalism. Asian placements start at £995 for 3 months teaching in China (excluding flights). *Cross-Cultural Solutions* with offices in the US and UK (www.crossculturalsolutions.org) places volunteers in grassroots projects in the Himalayas and Delhi (as well as Thailand and China).

Few opportunities of any kind exist in the restricted Himalayan state of Sikkim. One exception is a programme run by the *Muyal Liang Trust* at the Demajong Cheoling Academy located near Pemayangtse Monastery. Information about placements as volunteers to teach English or other subjects for up to 60 days is available in the UK from Jules Stewart, 53 Blenheim Crescent, London W11 2EG (020-7229 4772; JJulesstewart@aol.com). There is the possibility of teaching for longer periods in neighbouring Darjeeling. *MondoChallenge* offers 30 Indian placements mainly in the Kalimpong region near Darjeeling in the Himalayan foothills.

For information about teaching Tibetan refugees in Himalayan India, contact the Dharamsala Earthville Institute (DEVI), Dharamsala Mandala, Above Western Travels, Dalai Lama Temple Road, McLeod Ganj, Himachal Pradesh (volunteer@earthville.org / www.earthville.org/devi). They are especially keen to attract computer teachers and people with fund-raising skills for a minimum of six months.

Sri Lanka

As mentioned above, *i-to-i* has volunteer travel placements in Sri Lanka (as well as in Cambodia, China, India, Mongolia, Nepal, Thailand, and Vietnam). To join, you must have a TEFL qualification (i-to-i provide an intensive weekend course which is included in the training and placement fee from £1,195 (excluding travel costs). **Simon Rowland** joined i-to-i's teaching in Sri Lanka programme between school in Cambridge and university in York:

I am based in a private non-profit making English institute in a town called Binginya. The school, which opened 10 months ago, is run by a local school teacher of English. Additional classes were set up on my arrival for teachers and business people as well as children. The teaching is mostly enjoyable; classes are conducted purely in English except when they occasionally communicate in Sinhala, to my disgust and telling off. They are all willing to learn and, I like to think, have mostly improved quite a lot in the three months I've been here. The house I'm living in next to the school is wonderful, as are the meals which are brought to us from another house. The local people are all so friendly and falling over themselves to help me. I'd recommend rural Sri Lanka to anyone and think I've had a unique experience.

Despite reservations about the level of organisational back-up provided in relation to the high cost (for example Simon had no idea where he would be until he arrived in Sri Lanka), he had to conclude that without the UK agency, he would never have been able to have the experience.

MondoChallenge (Galliford Building, Gayton Rd, Milton Malsor, Northampton NN7 3AB; 01604 858225; www.mondochallenge.org) has expanded from its origins at one small village school in Nepal to arrange mainly three-month teaching placements in a number of other countries including Sri Lanka. The teaching takes place in Buddhist temple communities near Kandy (placement fee is £800).

> **Satya Byock taught with MondoChallenge at a temple in Sri Lanka:**
> *I have had an absolutely incredible wonderful time here and don't know how I am going to leave. The temple near Kandy has given me peace of mind that I will be able to carry with me for the rest of my life.*

VOLUNTARY WORK

Many young people who have travelled in Asia are dissatisfied with the role of tourist and would like to find a way of making a contribution. It must be stressed that Westerners almost invariably have to make a financial contribution to cover food and accommodation as well as their travel and insurance.

If you have never travelled widely in the Third World you may not be prepared for the scruffiness and level of disorganisation to be found in some places. Not many 18 year olds would be capable of contributing or benefitting much from a long attachment to a grassroots charity in developing regions. A further difficulty with participating in local voluntary projects (of which there are many) is in fixing anything up ahead of time. Occasionally Asian charities have a representative abroad who can send information about voluntary possibilities but this is unusual.

Indian Subcontinent

Here is a small selection of organisations which can sometimes use paying volunteers. It is possible to become a part-time volunteer at Mother Theresa's children's home in Calcutta (Shishu Bhavan, 78 A.J.C. Bose Road), in the Home for Dying Destitutes at Kalighat and other Homes run by the *Missionaries of Charity* in other Indian cities, but no accommodation can be offered. The work may consist of feeding and caring for orphaned children or the elderly. To register, visit the administrative office at 54A A.J.C. Bose Road, Calcutta 700016. Further information is also available from their London office at 177 Bravington Road, London W9 3AR (020-8960 2644).

Another organisation with a UK base is *Student Action India* (c/o HomeNet, Office 20, 30-38 Dock Street, Leeds LS10 1JF; ☎ 07071-225 866; www.studentactionindia.org.uk) which can arrange attachments to various Indian NGOs for volunteers to spend the summer or five months from September (see 'Directory of Voluntary Placements Abroad').

Indian Volunteers for Community Service (12 Eastleigh Avenue, South Harrow, Middlesex HA2 0UF; www.ivcs.org.uk) sends willing volunteers over 18 on its DRIVE programme (Discover Rural India for a Valuable Experience). Volunteers start with three weeks at Amarpurkashi Polytechnic in Uttar Pradesh learning about development and then join a hands-on project in the region between September and March. The placement fee which includes orientation and training is £160 while living expenses will be £30-£40 a week. The India Development Group (68 Downlands Road, Purley, Surrey CR8 4JF; 020-8668 3161; www.idguk.org) runs a similar six-month programme in Lucknow for 5-10 volunteers over the age of 21, concentrating on appropriate technology to support village life; food and lodging will cost the volunteer about £3 a day.

Dakshinayan (c/o Siddharth Sanyal, F-1169 Ground Floor, Chittarangan Park, New Delhi 110019; ☎/fax 011-262 76645; www.linkindia.com/dax) works with tribal peoples in the hills of Rajamhal and nearby plains. Volunteers join grassroots development projects every month and contribute $250 for a 2-4 week stay plus a $50 admin fee. **Geoffroy Groleau** from Montreal found his way to Dakshinayan via the internet and decided to take a career gap:

The application process is simple and can be conducted fully over the internet. The registration fee which must be provided before setting out for the project is the primary source of revenues for Dakshinayan. So there I was in early March 2002, stepping onto a train from New Delhi heading to Jharkhand. The project provides an opportunity to acquire a better understanding of the myths and realities surrounding poverty in the developing world, and specifically about the realities of rural India. The tribal people of these villages do not need or want fancy houses or televisions, but simply an education for their children and basic healthcare in order to improve the life they have been leading in relative isolation for centuries. It was interesting for me to see that they lead a quiet and simple life based on the rhythm of harvests and seasons, in marked contrast to most westerners. The primary role for volunteers is to teach English for a few hours every day to the kids attending the three Dakshinayan-run schools. I should also mention the numerous unforgettable football games with enthusiastic kids at the end of another sunny afternoon. One should be aware that Dakshinayan is an Indian NGO fully run by local people, which in my view is another positive aspect. But it also means that volunteers will have to adapt to Indian ways.

A community organisation in the Himalayan foothills with the charming acronym *ROSE* (Rural Organization on Social Elevation, Social Awareness Centre, PO Kanda, Bageshwar, Uttar Pradesh 263631) can assist volunteers wishing to work with poor villagers, teaching children, doing office work, carrying out environmental work and organic farming in this village in the Himalayan foothills. Volunteers pay £4 per day for board and lodging. To receive further details send 3 IRCs to the above address. Originally from London, Heather Joiner wrote to say how much she was enjoying her time with ROSE:

I am a volunteer who is currently here working in the tiny school. I am also here at ROSE in order to improve my basic Hindi. In the morning we join the primary school children learning basic reading, writing and counting.

During his year out before attending Bristol University, **Laurence Koe** followed up a lead he'd been given and visited a Catholic monastery in a suburb of Bombay where foreigners were a real oddity. The monks generously gave him their 'deluxe suite' and full board. He tried to repay their hospitality by offering to work but all they wanted was for him to discuss the western way of life with the trainee monks whenever he felt so inclined.

The *Bangladesh Workcamps Association* (289/2 Work Camp Road, North Shahjahanpur, Dhaka 17, Bangladesh; fax 02-956 5506; www.bwca.homepage.com) will try to place you on seven or ten day community development camps between October and February. The participation fee is $20 a day. They publish detailed camp information in English. Applications must be submitted at least by mid-September for autumn camps and by the end of November for January camps, enclosing a non-refundable $25 application fee. BWCA can also accommodate foreign volunteers on a medium-term basis (one to three months or more).

In Sri Lanka short-term and long-term volunteers and interns can be accommodated at *Lanka Jatika Sarvodaya Shramadana Sangamaya* (98 Rawatawatte Road, Moratuwa, Colombo, Sri Lanka; fax 01-647084/ www.sarvodaya.org) to engage in social, economic and technical development activities in villages; and planning, monitoring and evaluation work at the head office in Colombo.

Samasevaya Sri Lanka (Anuradhapura Road, Talawa N.C.P., Sri Lanka; ☎/fax 025-76266) invites volunteers to their rural locations. Volunteers can be used rather loosely for their educational and development programmes, though it is more akin to a cultural exchange. If the volunteer wants to stay past the initial month of their tourist visa, it is sometimes possible to arrange a renewal. The organisation provides simple accommodation in their office complex in Talawa or with local families. They expect a contribution of $90 a month for meals.

Southeast Asia and the Far East

The Wild Animal Rescue Foundation of Thailand (235 Sukhumvit Soi 31, Bangkok 10110 (2-668 0898; www.warthai.org) offers the chance to high-paying volunteers to work with animals, ideally to people with an appropriate background.

Volunteers including gap year students are sent out to northern Thailand each year to work in communities of Karen tribespeople. Details of the programme are available from the *Karen Hill Tribes Trust*, Midgley House, Heslington, Yorks. YO10 5DX (see entry in 'Directory of Voluntary Placements Abroad').

Japan is a famously expensive country in which to travel. One way around it is to join a workcamp. The Japanese workcamp organisation has a reassuring name and acronym NICE: *Never-ending International Work Camps Exchange*. It is probably not worth writing directly to NICE unless you are already in Japan (2-4-2-701 Shinjuku, Shinjuku-ku, Tokyo 160-0022; www.jah.ne.jp/~nice-do) but via one of their corresponding agents such as *Concordia* or *UNA Exchange*.

An unusual opportunity to teach local people is available at a farm in Hokkaido, the most northerly island of the Japanese archipelago, known as Shin-Shizen-Juku (Tsurui, Akan-gun, Hokkaido 085-12; 0154-64 2821), a place well known to the travelling fraternity for a generation. The owner Hiroshi Mine welcomes international travellers who want to conduct conversation classes with local businessmen, farmers, housewives, doctors and children, in exchange for board and lodging but no pocket money. Mr. Mine organises the classes, provides transport and some teaching materials. The place is fairly disorganised, and much depends on the personalities of the other volunteers (often just two or three, up to a maximum of seven); whereas some travellers perceive it to be a good opportunity and enjoy a warm atmosphere and the beautiful surroundings, others find the place bleak and exploitative.

The *Korean International Volunteer Association* organises voluntary placements throughout Korea. Projects include teaching English at an orphanage for at least a month and working in sheltered communities. Details are available from KIVA, 1102 Sekwang B/D, 202 Sejong-ro, Chongro-gu, Seoul 110-050 (02-723 6225; info@kiva.or.kr). More and more workcamps organisations in exotic places are coming to light, most recently the Mongolian Youth Development Centre, Baga Touruu-44, Ulaanbaatar 210648 (976-1-314433; www.owc.org.mn/mydc). The charge for participation works out at about $100 a week.

PAID WORK

Few paid jobs are available to gap year students unless they have a contact in Hong Kong or Singapore, for example, able to arrange a business internship. The flourishing economy of Singapore can absorb some student trainees. The Singapore High Commission (9 Wilton Crescent, London SW1X 8BR) will send a fact sheet which explains that people earning a monthly income of S$2,500 or less need to apply for a Work Permit from the Work Permit Department, Ministry of Manpower, 18 Havelock Road, Singapore 059764 (65-438 5122/ www.gov.sg/mom/ftawp.htm) and those earning more than S$2,500 need to apply for an Employment Pass at the Singapore Immigration & Registration Building, Ministry of Manpower, 5th level, SIR Building, 10 Kallang Road, Singapore 208718 (☎ 65-438 5122 or 2975443; www.gov.sg/mom/fta/ep/ftaep.htm).

Work Experience

Interesting internships for people 18-25 are arranged by a company in Colombo called Volunteer International Projects (148/1B Kynsey Road, Colombo 7; 74-720658; www.vo lunteerinternational.com). They offer a structured programme in the hospitality industry, business, conservation, teaching and so on. Participants pay between £950 and £1,350 for three months (plus travel). Some internship placements are available in the Maldive Islands for people fluent in French.

Homestays

Young people interested in spending their gap year studying at a Japanese high school should investigate *Youth for Understanding* (see 'Directory of Specialist Gap Year Programmes'). This programme is funded by the Japanese government and pays for everything except spending money (£100+ a month) and a school trip taken during the year.

Partly because of the high cost of accommodation and the fascination of the cultures, staying with a Japanese or Korean family is worth considering. The Korean national Tourism Organization publishes a very useful free booklet on the subject; ring 020-7321 2535 or email koreatb@dircon.co.uk to request a copy. It lists seven homestay agencies including Labo Korea (2-736 0521; www.labostay.or.kr), LEX Youth Korea (2-538 9660; www.lex.or.kr) and Alpha Home Stay (62-226 7920; www.home-stay.co.kr). With the average cost of a night's accommodation at about US$35, you probably won't want to spend a prolonged period.

The Japan Homestay Service in Chiba-city (43-266-1926; http://home.att.ne.jp/orange/star/homestay.index.htm) places foreigners with Japanese families for varying charges; the only requirements is 'not to hate Japanese food'. You can combine homestay with language study through programmes such as 'Experience Osaka' marketed by Nelson Research & Consultants for Study Abroad (9-2-8 Tanimachi 603, Chuo-ku, Osaka 542-0012; ☎/fax 6-6762-8858; ex-osaka@mbi.nifty.com). Try also the Hokkaido International Foundation (14-1 Motomachi, Hakodate, Hokkaido 040-0054; www.hif.or.jp/eng) which arranges homestays to provide cultural and language immersion; a two-week programme in August costs 35,000 yen (about £180).

Budding writers under 25 might like to enter the Goi Peace Foundation International Essay Competition for a chance to win a prize of 100,000 yen and a free trip to Japan; details are on the website www.goipeace.org.jp.

Turkey

Turkey is a wonderful country to travel in with a wealth of important historic sites which you will certainly have heard of like Troy and Ephesus. Turkey's currency crisis (£1 equals 2,328,000 Turkish lire at the time of writing) means that the money you've saved from your temping job will go a lot further here than in many other countries.

Turkey is also a good choice of destination for fledgling English teachers though few opportunities are available to pre-university gap year students with no TEFL training or experience. Although Istanbul is not the capital, it is the commercial, financial and cultural centre of Turkey, so this is where most of the EFL teaching goes on.

For short-term opportunities, the Education Department of the youth travel and exchange organisation *Genctur* (Istiklal Cad. Zambak Sok. 15/5, Taksim 80080, Istanbul (212-249 2515; www.genctur.com) organises summer camps for children where English, German and French are taught by native speakers who work for seven hours a day in exchange for free board and lodging. Pocket money of $100-$350 is also given according to experience and skills. Applicants must have some experience of working with children.

Genctur also runs 30 international workcamps. Another organiser of nearly 50 international youth camps is GSM (Genclik Servislieri Merkezi, Youth Services Centre, Bayinder Sok. 45/9, Kizilay 06650, Ankara; www.gsm-youth.org. The fee for joining one of the ten-day camps starts at €60.

On most camps you will have to work reasonably hard in the hot sun (and wear long sleeves and jeans in deference to Muslim customs). **Mary Jelliffe** recounts her experiences in Turkey:

> *I applied to UNA (Wales) quite late (in May/June) and heard from Turkey just one week before my camp commenced in August. My workcamp, which consisted of digging an irrigation canal from the nearby hills to the village, took place in Central Anatolia. I was told that our camp was the most easterly, since the majority are in Western Turkey.*
>
> *Conditions in this remote village were fairly primitive. We lived in a half-built school-room sleeping on the floor and sharing the daily duties of collecting water and sweeping out the scorpions from under the sleeping bags. The Turkish volunteers were a great asset to the camp: through them we could have far more contact with the villagers and learn more about Turkish culture in general. In fact I later stayed in Istanbul and Izmir with two of the women volunteers I'd met on the camp.*

Au pair jobs in Turkey normally involve more tutoring of English than domestic chores. The following agencies make placements in Turkey:

Anglo Nannies London, 2 St. Marks Place, Wimbledon SW19 7ND (020-8944 6677; www.anglonannies.com). Specialises in placing professional English-speaking nannies and teachers in Turkey. Support provided by Istanbul office.

Anglo Pair Agency, 40 Wavertree Road, Streatham Hill, London SW2 3SP (020-8674 3605; www.angloaupairs.co.uk). Nannies and au pairs (approximately 100) for summer or academic year. Qualified nannies earn £200-£300 a week. Agency has office in Istanbul.

ICEP (International Cultural Exchange Programmes), 2 Innes Lodge, Inglemere Road, London SE23 2BD (020-8699 0366; london@icep.org.tr). London office of Turkish organisation with offices in Ankara (Yuksel Cad. 9/10, Kizilay, Ankara; 312-418 4460; www.icep.org.tr) and Istanbul. Au pair in Turkey programme for 3-12 months. Minimum pocket money €200 a month.

One persistent problem is that it is generally not acceptable for young women to go out alone in the evenings. But Turkish families are normally very generous and allow their live-in child carers to share in family life on equal terms, even in their free time and on holidays.

The main Aegean resorts of Marmaris, Kuşadasi and Bodrum absorb a large number of foreign travellers as workers. Other places firmly on the travellers' trail like Antalya on the south coast and Goreme in Cappadocia are also promising. The best time to look is March or early April. Major Turkish yachting resorts are excellent places to look for work, not just related to boats but in hotels, bars, shops and excursions. A good time to check harbourside notice boards and to ask captains if they need anyone to clean or repair their boats is in the lead-up to the summer season and the Marmaris Boat Show in May.

A Turkish company USEH International Training & Education Services arranges internships mainly in the hospitality industry in Istanbul and the Turkish Republic of Northern Cyprus open to college students of business, marketing, finance, hotel administration, etc.; details from USEH, Bagdat Cad. 217/14, Ciftehavuzlar, Kadiköy, Istanbul; 216-478- 3444 (www.useh.org is in English).

The Middle East

Few gap year students are likely to be seriously considering the Middle East at a time when the region is so troubled. In the aftermath of the infamy perpetrated on the US in September 2001 and with increased enmity between Israelis and Palestinians, the taste for travel and employment in the Middle East has been soured and many prospective travellers have (understandably) been put off by fear for their personal security. The Iraqi War has certainly destabilised the area and fanned the flames of Islamic distrust of the West. Perhaps young intrepid travellers can play a small part in diminishing the distrust and tension between the two cultures, bringing people together, allowing individuals on both sides to gain some understanding of the complexity of the world's problems.

Many parts of the Middle East remain reasonably calm and untroubled. For example Yemen has a large and interesting expat community and is a good place to consider studying Arabic (see entry for CALES in the Directory of Courses). The CALES website (www.y.net.y/cales) carries some first-hand accounts, including the following by Elizabeth Muller from Germany:

I studied at CALES for one month. Although it is only a short time, I have learnt a lot there. I want to tell everybody, this is a good school. The teachers are well experienced and the atmosphere is excellent... If you want or need to learn Arabic grammar, you will do so. If you prefer to have more practice of the speaking language they will give you the opportunity to speak a lot to practise the language.

It is a good choice to study in Yemen. Here you can experience the real Arabic life, more than in the Arabic countries on the Mediterranean Sea where the western influence is greater. Yemeni people are really friendly and very open to western people. The school is situated in an authentic building in the old center of Sana'a and this city is marvellous, a real wonder of architecture. In the souq, close to the school, you can practice the Arabic language all the time.

Australia & New Zealand

AUSTRALIA

In response to its phenomenal popularity as a destination for so many young Europeans, Australia has developed a magnificent industry to cater specifically for backpackers. Hostels, both official and private, are full of gap-year travellers and working holidaymakers who will advise newcomers on the best travel deals and adventures, and the places to go to find jobs. Specialist travel offices, employment agencies and even outback farms specifically target the backpacking community, which in Australia includes everybody from people fresh from school to professionals in their 30s.

First-time visitors to Australia are often surprised by the degree to which that far-off continent is an imitation of Britain. Despite their reputation as 'pommy-bashers', most Australians take for granted a strong link with Britain, and this may be one reason why British travellers are so often welcomed as prospective employees especially off the beaten tourist track. On the other hand, in the areas that backpackers have colonised, like certain suburbs of Sydney and certain Queensland islands, they are not at all popular since they have a reputation for 'Ibiza' type behaviour.

Red Tape

Since 2001, the compulsory tourist visa for Australia has not been available free of charge. The paperless visa, the ETA (Electronic Travel Authority), must be obtained via a private agency like Visas Australia or the Australian Immigration Department's website (www.eta.immi.gov.au) which will incur a fee of A$20. The dispensing of visitor visas has in essence been privatised and specialist visa providers can charge a fee of their choice (none of which is passed on to the Australian government). Among the cheaper providers are www.fastozvisa.com (0800 096 4749) which charges £6.50/€11/US$11 and www.evisas.com which charges £13/US$20.

The number of working holiday visas has risen sharply from 33,000 in 1995 to 85,200 in 2002. The visa is for people intending to use any money they earn in Australia to supplement their holiday funds. Working full-time for more than three months is not permitted, though you are now permitted to engage in up to three months of studies or training. Applicants must be between the ages of 18 and 30 and without children. You are eligible for a working holiday visa only once. The working holiday visa is valid for 12 months after entry, which must be within 12 months of issue, and is non-renewable.

Britons can apply to an Australian Consulate or though a private visa agency. In 2002, it became possible to apply for an electronic working holiday visa and the procedure and drawbacks are described below. The High Commission in London is located in Australia House, Strand, London WC2B 4LA (020-7379 4334; www.australia.org.uk) though it is no longer possible to apply in person.

Assuming you are using the traditional paper method, the first step is to get the working holiday information sheet and form 1150 Application for a Working Holiday Makers (WHM) visa from the Department of Immigration (DIMIA) website www.immi.gov.au or a specialist agent like Consyl Publishing (3 Buckhurst Road, Bexhill-on-Sea, East Sussex TN40 1QF; 01424 223111) enclosing an A4 stamped addressed envelope (66p stamp). The non-refundable processing fee in the UK is currently £70.

The second step is to get as much money in the bank as possible. Each application is assessed on its own merits, but the most important requirement is a healthy bank balance. You must have enough money for your return fare, although it is not essential to have a return ticket at the time of entry. You must show evidence of having saved a minimum of A$5,000/£2,000. If your bank statements do not show steady saving, you may have to submit documents showing where the money came from (e.g. sale of a car, gift from a relative).

Now that ticketless flights are well established, paperless visas are now a possibility and are being heavily marketed by the visa agencies who don't like to handle passports. For an e-WHM visa there is no need to provide proof of funds nor do you send in your passport. Your passport isn't physically inspected until you arrive in Australia when you must take it along to an office of the Department of Immigration, a process that may involve hours of waiting around if you go to a busy DIMIA office. Some have concluded that it is preferable to stick to the conventional method. However there may be special circumstances when you will want to use the electronic route, e.g. if you are leaving within a few days or are on the road (though you are not meant to apply if you are already in Australia). You can try to obtain the visa on your own if the link from www.immi.gov.au is working or you can pay an extra fee to a specialist agent like Visas Australia (www.visas-australia.com) or Travellers Contact Point (www.travellers.com.au) to whom you will have to pay an extra £15 or £20. Either way you will have the authorisation within a couple of days.

The Department of Immigration & Multicultural & Indigenous Affairs is a valuable source of all relevant visa information either on its website www.immi.gov.au or in Australia by ringing DIMIA on 131881. The busy office in Sydney is at 88 Cumberland St in the Rocks.

Placement Agencies & Special Schemes

Naturally, Australia is not included as a destination by the gap year organisations which focus on developing countries. However the following do make placements downunder, often in boarding schools, doing conservation work or working on outback properties: *GAP Activity Projects, Gap Challenge, Changing Worlds* and *i-to-i*. For example Gap Challenge arranges three-month jobs on cattle stations or horse ranches while i-to-i can arrange a six-week conservation package through CVA (see below) for a fee of £995 excluding travel. GAP Activity Projects has a big programme in Australia with a contingent of about 100 volunteers, most of whom work in schools. A number of fee-paying schools in Australia have country campuses where pupils spend one year (typically at age 14/15) and where the emphasis is on outdoor activity and developing team spirit. This can become an ideal setting for a year-out student away from home for the first time. Furthermore, some get paid a wage on top of free room and board, usually in the vicinity of $100 a week.

But even similar sounding school placements can be utterly different. For example GAP participant Ben Hartley was assigned to the country campus of a girls' school, 3½ hours drive north of Melbourne. He was a little surprised to learn that he would be assisting with sports like rock climbing and skiing which he had never done, but wasn't too worried about keeping the girls (aged 13-14) in line. In fact, late in his 10-month attachment, four of the girls for whom he was responsible perpetrated the heinous crime of smuggling in a bottle of Bacardi and were caught swigging, for which they were nearly expelled. The high points for Ben, on the other hand, came with the long periods of holiday and travel, which allowed him to spend Christmas in New Zealand, visit Perth, Sydney, the Northern Territory and then Queensland when his family flew out from England in the spring.

At the other end of the country, another GAP volunteer Matt Applewhite spent five months at a progressive school outside Darwin called Kormilda attended by white Australian and Aboriginal children from all over the Northern Territory. When Matt chose Australia, he was not bothered by the fact that Australia was considered a soft option by some of his contemporaries. It didn't always feel like a soft option when he looked at his very full timetable of teaching and supervising.

Matt Applewhite ended up having not only a fascinating but a fulfilling year:
As I walked around Kormilda College for the last time, it seemed that every room, every corner had a memory associated with it. A glimpse of the college canoes awakened the vivid memories of Year 8 Outback camps when by day under the blazing sun we noisily splashed around the leafy billabongs and bushwalked through Crocodile Dundee's back yard. A traditional Aboriginal drawing in the library allowed me to reminisce about my trip to the remote community of Peppimenarti and the way in which the welcoming community allowed me to observe the elders silently weaving traditional baskets, watch the village children learn English in the community school and appreciate their cultural traditions, dignity and warmth. I reflected on all the experiences I'd relished and how lucky I'd been to spend time in this place.
All these priceless memories, all for £1,500 which was his total outlay for eight months.

BUNAC (16 Bowling Green Lane, London EC1R 0QH; 020-7251 3472) features Australia as one of its destination countries. Anyone who is eligible for the working holiday visa may choose to join the BUNAC Work Australia package which costs from £1,500. This includes the group departures, organised three-day stopover, round-the-world flight, visa, orientation on arrival and back-up services. Enquiries about this programme may be made by e-mail to downunder@bunac.org. Similarly *CCUSA* (Camp Counsellors USA) in Croydon has a 12-month Work Experience Downunder programme.

Changing Worlds, 11 Doctors Lane, Caterham, Surrey CR3 5AE (01883 340960/fax 01883 330783; welcome@changingworlds.co.uk/ www.changingworlds.co.uk). Paid placements in hotels in tourist hotspots and on farms throughout Queensland including ones where there are riding opportunities. Voluntary placements in a zoo and on conservation projects. Placements last from three to six months starting in September, January and March.

CIEE UK and USA have an Australian Work and Travel programme. Britons can take part in the working holiday visa scheme for up to 12 months, which includes initial accommodation, post-arrival orientation and lots of job help on arrival at CIEE, Sydney HQ (Level 3, 91 York St, Sydney 2000; 02-8235 7099).

The *Visitoz Scheme*, Springbrook Farm, MS 188, Goomeri, 4601 Queensland, Australia (07-4168 6106; info@visitoz.org) or in the UK: Grange Cottage, Shipton Road, Ascott under Wychwood, Oxfordshire OX7 6AY (01993 832238/831972; jules@visitoz.org). 5-day training in all aspects of working on a rural property or in rural hospitality followed by a guaranteed 3-month paid job in rural Australia. Fee of £595 includes airport pick-up, 3-day beachside jet lag recovery weekend, course and follow-up jobs for the duration of the WH visa.

The *Involvement Volunteers Association Inc* (PO Box 218, Port Melbourne, VIC 3207; 03-9646 9392/ www.volunteering.org.au) arranges short-term (2+ week) or long-term (up to 1 year) volunter placements for individuals worldwide. Placements possible in all the states of Australia (and worldwide) for up to a year. Projects are concerned with conservation, the environment, animal welfare, social and community service, education and childcare. Programme fees start at A$280.

In addition to the gap year specialists, an increasing number of backpacker travel and youth exchange agencies are offering packages that may be of special interest to first-time travellers in their gap year. Some are all-inclusive; others simply give back-up on arrival. Typically, the fee will include airport pick-up, hostel accommodation for the first few nights and a post-arrival orientation which advises on how to obtain a tax-file card, suggestions of employers and so on. Some even guarantee a job. Various perks are thrown in like a telephone calling card and maps.

For example Travellers Contact Point (2-6 Inverness Terrace, Bayswater, London W2 3HX; 020-7243 7887; www.travellers-contact.com.au) operates a free job search centre in connection with recruitment agencies in six offices around Australia and New Zealand. Membership for £25 includes services such as mail forwarding, e-mail and word processing access. They sell a Gap Year Package to Sydney (and Auckland) for £229 and a cheaper arrivals package for £75 which includes your first two nights in Sydney and a working holiday information kit, among other things. In Sydney the TCP office is at Level 7, Dymocks Building, 428 George St, Sydney 2000 (02-9221 8744/fax 9221 3746).

The Backpackers Travel Centre now has two offices in London (Level 1, 171 Earls Court Rd, Earls Court, SW5 9RF; 020-7370 4765; and 415 North End Rd, Fulham Broadway, SW6; 0207-385 2900), both promoting a new Work Australia Programme. The fee of £200 provides the usual soft landing for working holiday makers (see www.workaustralia.net). Similarly Oz Talk Travel in Harrogate (www.oztalk.co.uk) has teamed up with the Travel & Work Company (45 High St, Tunbridge Wells, Kent TN1 1XL; 01892 516164; www.worktravelcompany.co.uk) to create an all-inclusive working holiday package costing £699 and another providing background assistance for independent travellers for £179. Further alternatives include Free Spirit (Brook House, 229-234 Shepherd Bush Rd, London W6 7AN; 020-8742 6042; london@freespirit.com.au) and the WorldWide Club (www.worldwideclub.com).

Work Experience

Increasingly, Australian recruitment agencies are actively looking for people in the UK to fill their clients' temporary vacancies in Australia and are geared up to advise people with working holiday visas. Private employment agencies are very widespread and are a good potential source of jobs for travellers, especially those with office skills, computer, data processing or financial experience. A surprising number positively encourage UK people on working holidays, often by circulating their details to hostel managers. This is more common in Sydney and Melbourne than in Perth where most recruitment agencies are just not interested in working holidaymakers. The offered wages are good too: from

$12 an hour for clerical work, $14 for secretarial and $15 for computer work. This might be an ideal route for a student who has done a secretarial or business skills course at the beginning of their year out.

Cultural Cube Ltd. in Devon (www.culturalcube.co.uk; see entry in 'Directory of Specialist Gap Year Programmes') arranges internships in multinational or medium to big Australian companies. These can be in any field and last from 1 week to 12 months, starting year round. The vast majority are unpaid, however some companies may make a small contribution towards living expenses. Participants usually enter Australia on a student, working holiday or even tourist visa. The fee for arranging this is £440 for a 6-week placement, £1,000 for a year; accommodation and airfares are of course extra.

Anyone with experience of the horse industry should contact the International Exchange Program in the UK (The Old Rectory, Belton-in-Rutland, Oakham, Rutland LE15 9LE; enquiries@iepuk.com) whose Australian partner is Stablemate, PO Box 1206, Windsor, NSW 2756 (02-4576 4444; info@stablemate.net.au). They deal exclusively with placing equestrian and thoroughbred staff but are sometimes able to assist people with limited experience with horses if they want to work as a nanny or general farm assistant. The fee inclusive of airfares is £1,800.

Interesting research projects take place throughout Australia and some may be willing to include unpaid staff looking for work experience. For example a research station in northern Queensland operated by the Australian Tropical Research Foundation (PMB 5, Cape Tribulation, Qld 4873; 07-4098 0063; www.austrop.org.au) welcomes 50 volunteers a year to carry out all sorts of tasks to conserve the rainforest. Volunteers are asked to pay at least $70 a week to cover their food and accommodation. It might be worth trying the *Heron Island Research Station* (Great Barrier Reef, via Gladstone, Qld 4680; www.marine.uq.edu.au/hirs/index.htm) which has been known to offer free accommodation in exchange for about four hours of work a day.

The Australian Institute of Marine Science (AIMS) at Cape Ferguson near Townsville (07-4753 4240; visitor_coord@aims.gov.au/ www.aims.gov.au) runs a Prospective Visitors Scheme which encompasses volunteers; applicants with their own research projects or a scuba diving certificate are especially welcome. Application must be done on-line.

Often the state conservation organisation organises a voluntary programme, as is the case in Western Australia with the Conservation & Land Management Department of CALM (www.calm.wa.gov.au). The programme is open to anyone though it can't provide accommodation in remote places; write to the Volunteer Co-ordinator at CALM for details (Locked Bag 104, Bentley Delivery Centre, WA 6983; 08-9334 0333). For people with a conservation background or relevant skills, CALM also runs an Educational Work Experience Programme, though none of the positions involves working with wildlife.

The gap year programme being developed by *IDP Education Australia* can finish up with a work experience placement (see entry in 'Directory of Specialist Gap Year Programmes'). Anyone under 19 looking to spend a year attending an Australian secondary school should make enquiries of Southern Cross Cultural Exchange (Locked Bag 1200, 3930 Mt. Eliza, VIC 3930; +61 3 9775 4711; scceaust@scce.com.au).

The Job Hunt

If you decide not to organise a placement through an agency, you will be on your own looking for work, along with a huge number of other working holiday makers competing for the same jobs. The glut of travelling workers is especially bad in Sydney and on the Queensland 'Route' between Sydney and Cairns, whereas Melbourne and Adelaide offer better prospects. In addition to asking potential employers directly (which is the method used by most successful job-seekers in Australia), there are four main ways of finding work: Employment National (Jobcentres), private employment agencies, newspaper advertisements and notice boards (especially at travellers' hostels).

Either before you leave Britain or once you are in one of the major cities, get hold of the free booklet *Australia & New Zealand Independent Travellers Guide* published by the London-based travel magazine *TNT* (14-15 Child's Place, London SW5

9RX; www.tntmagazine.com/au). It includes a section on work and some relevant advertisements as well as travel advice. The same company publishes specific monthly magazines for Sydney/NSW, Queensland, Victoria/Tasmania and the Outback, available free at airports, bus and train stations. They carry a certain number of classified ads for job-seekers and a section called 'Finding Work'.

Some charities are perennial advertisers for paid fund-raisers. The most amusing account of earning money this way comes from **Chris Miksovsky**, who earned $12 an hour (but only for four to six hours a week) as a street collector in Brisbane:

My year in Australia ended with a rather fitting and hilarious job, collecting for the Wilderness Society, a sort of Australian Greenpeace, wearing a koala costume. After a brief interview with the Koala Coordinator ('So, Chris, do you have any experience walking around as a big furry animal?'), I found myself in a busy square wearing a full-body fluffy grey koala suit complete with fake felt claws and droopy oversize ears. Actually it works. Takings per hour were about $25 on average. For me, probably the best thing was that you learned to not take yourself so seriously.

If interested contact the Wilderness Society which in Sydney is on Level 2, 64-76 Kippax St, Surry Hills, NSW 2010 (02-9282 9553; sydney@wilderness.org.au); hourly earnings average $15-$20. Another charity that employs travellers as fundraisers is in the same building, i.e. the Australian Quadriplegic Association (02-9281 8214) which pays its collectors a quarter of donations collected, which they estimate will work out to be $50-$100 a day.

As mentioned, the dense network of hostels is a goldmine of information. Gappers find employment in the hostels themselves too. **Stephen Psallidas** describes the proliferation of work:

I've met loads of people working in backpackers' hostels. Typically you work two hours a day in exchange for your bed and a meal. Work may be cleaning, driving the minibus, reception, etc. and is always on an informal basis. I will be jumping on the bandwagon myself soon. I'll be completely shattered from picking tomatoes so I'm going to 'work' in a hostel in Mission Beach, where the owners invited me to work when I stayed there earlier. I'm going to rest up in a beautiful place before continuing my travels, and not spend any of my hard-earned dollars.

One of the most successful groups of non-YHA hostels is VIP Backpackers Resorts of Australia which is especially strong in New South Wales and Queensland. A booklet listing their 146 Australian hostels is distributed far and wide or can be obtained from overseas by purchasing their VIP kit for A$40 (£16 in the UK) which gives $1 off each hostel stay among other discounts; contact VIP Backpackers in the UK: Riverbank House, 1 Putney Bridge Approach, London SW6 3JD; 020-7736 4200; www.vipbackpackers.com). Almost all VIP hostels have notice boards advertising jobs, flats, car shares, etc. and most charge from $20 a night for a dorm bed.

The international hostel group Nomads (www.nomadsworld.com) sells an Adventure Card for $A29 (£15) through specialist travel agents abroad and in Australia. Nomads operate a couple of working hostels (for example in Bundaberg) and sell a Job Package to new arrivals for A$159 (Sydney) or A$189 (Melbourne). They also maintain a database of job vacancies updated weekly accessible by members via telephone.

The Outback

Most of Australia's area is sparsely populated, scorched land which is known loosely as the outback. Beyond the rich farming and grazing land surrounding the largest cities, there are immense properties supporting thousands of animals and acres of crops. Many of these stations (farms) are so remote that flying is the only practical means of access, though having a vehicle can be a great help in an outback job search. **Sandra Gray** describes the drawbacks of spending time on a station:

> *Be warned! Station life can be severely boring after a while. I managed to land myself on one in the Northern Territory with very little else to do but watch the grass grow. If you have to save a lot of money quickly station work is the way to do it since there's nothing to spend it on. But make sure the place is within reasonable distance of a town or at least a roadhouse, so you have somewhere to go to let off steam occasionally.*

Your chances of getting a job as a station assistant (jackaroo or jillaroo) will be improved if you have had experience with sheep, riding or any farming or mechanical experience. Several farmers are in the business of giving you that experience before helping you to find outback work, like the one mentioned above in the Visitoz Scheme.

> **Shaun Armstrong thoroughly enjoyed an outback course in Queensland:**
> *Should any traveller wish to discover an introduction to authentic rural Australia, no better window of opportunity exists than Pat and Pete Worsley's Rocky Creek Station. I braved the five-day jackaroo course with three other travellers. Horsecraft, cattle mustering, ute driving, trail biking (the 'ings' were numerous) and other tasks occupied our days: wonderful hospitality ended each evening. Memorable days. Station placement was arranged afterwards as was transport if needed. I was sorry to leave really. I'd say the course did prepare me for most experiences encountered in the job. For example I was able to muster cattle on horseback with four experienced riders having spent only 15 hours in the saddle. It wasn't easy, but I did it.*

The course fee is $440 including job placement afterwards with one of more than 300 employers, plus ongoing back-up; alternatively you can pay $330 for the course and no job. Rocky Creek is located inland from Bundaberg (Isis Highway MS 698, Biggenden, Qld 4621; 07-4127 1377; www.isisol.com.au/rockycrkfarmstay).

Other farms offer such courses for example Curtis Park Farm in Queensland (www.coombe.com.au) where an intensive four-day farm training course costs $525; and a Jackaroo/Jillaroo course near Tamworth New South Wales costing £167 for five days, available through Oz Talk mentioned above.

Conservation Volunteering

Several organisations give visitors a chance to experience the Australian countryside or bush. The main not-for-profit conservation organisation in Australia is called, predictably enough, Conservation Volunteers Australia (CVA) and it places volunteers from overseas in its 'Conservation Experience' projects, though the charges are quite steep. Sample projects include tree planting, erosion and salinity control, seed collection from indigenous plants, building and maintaining bush walking tracks, etc. Overseas volunteers are welcome to become involved by booking a four- or six-week package which include food and accommodation and some transport at a cost of A$790 and $1,175 respectively (which works out at $28 a day for accommodation, food and transport). Further details are available from the National Head Office, Box 423, Ballarat, Vic 3353 (03-5333 1483; www.conservationvolunteers.com.au). There are volunteer offices in all the states.

Nicky Stead was forced to take a gap year at the last minute and hurriedly enquired about placements through i-to-i. The project that caught her eye was doing conservation work with ATCV (now CVA) in Australia and soon she was saving money for the placement and the flight (£2,000+). She had done a few conservation projects in the Lake District so knew what she was letting herself in for, and this appealed more than teaching. So she signed up for eight weeks based in Adelaide and had a marvellous time:

Going to Australia was the best thing I ever did. Everything worked out as it was meant to. I had no problems at all. We lived in Adelaide but travelled all over South Australia on different projects. We planted trees by a flooded mine shaft, built a fence on the coast of the Great Australian Bight, laid bait to poison foxes in the beautiful Flinders Ranges and weeded on the banks of the huge River Murray. We were well looked after by the managers and team leaders of ATCV; although I never felt I needed their support, it was good to know it was there. They made us work from 8am to 4pm which was not unreasonable, and with a break mid-morning and an hour for lunch it wasn't too strenuous. The fee I'd paid (£1,200) covered food, accommodation (which was often very very basic), transport and training. At the end the estate manager wrote me a great reference.

The other volunteers were all English, doing six months through GAP Activity Projects. My new friends made it for me. We all got on really well and I hope they will be lasting friendships. Leaving them at the end of the two months was definitely the low point of the year. I had to leave a lovely holiday romance with the knowledge that he'd quickly forget me (he didn't) and suddenly I was alone again preparing to travel on to New Zealand, the US and Canada to visit friends.

More ad hoc opportunities may present themselves and cost considerably less:

Daniele Arena from Italy stumbled across a project on the coast of Queensland that appealed to him:
One of the most amazing experiences I had in Oz was the time I was volunteering at the Turtle Rookery in Mon Repos Beach. We could pitch our tent for free, and gave a small contribution of $5 a day for food. The work was to patrol the beach waiting for nesting turtles and, when they come in, to tag and measure them and the nest. This goes on between November and March. I was fortunate enough to get this by chance but normally there's quite a few people who want to do it, so you should probably contact the Queensland Parks & Wildlife Service for info.

World Wide Opportunities on Organic Farms (WWOOF) is very active in Australia and their publicity is distributed by many hostels. WWOOF Australia (Mt Murrindal Co-operative, Buchan, Vic 3885; 03-5155 0218; www.wwoof.com.au) publish an 'Organic Farm & Cultural Experience List' of 1,500+ addresses throughout Australia of organic farmers looking for short or long term voluntary help. The list is sold with accident insurance at a cost of A$50 within Australia, A$60 outside ($55 and $65 respectively for a double membership).

A free internet-based exchange of work-for-keep volunteers can be found at www.helpx.net where about 130 hosts are listed.

Fruit Picking

Many gap year students fund their travels around Australia by migrating between fruit and vegetable harvests. Employment National effectively publicises harvest vacancies online and via the telephone; contact the IMP Go Harvest hotline on 1300 720126. Employment National encourage working holidaymakers to contact their specialist fruit and crop-picking department or of course to call in at any employment office. Note that Australia's first specialist harvesting recruitment agency, the unflinchingly named Grunt Labour Services, has offices in Darwin, Katherine, Kununurra, Childers and Brisbane (www.gruntlabour.com).

In some regions demand for pickers is so strong that farmers publicise vacancies outside their region, as in the case of the Northern Victoria Fruitgrowers' Association Ltd, PO Box 394, Shepparton 3632 (21 Nixon St, Shepparton; 03-5821 5844; www.nvfa.com.au) and the Victorian Peach and Apricot Growers' Association, PO Box 39, Cobram 3644 (03-5872 1729). Several large Australian orchard employers are listed in the 'Directory of Paid Seasonal Jobs' (see *Cornish* in Victoria and *Torrens Valley Orchards* in South Australia).

For detailed information about harvest dates, locations, wages, etc. throughout Australia, see *Work Your Way Around the World* by Susan Griffith (Vacation Work, £12.95).

Although harvesting work is often not hard to *get*, some find it hard to make any money. The apple/pear/grape crates may look quite small at the outset but will soon seem unfillable with mysterious false bottoms. Many eager first-timers do not realise how hard the work will be physically, and give up before their bodies acclimatise. But you should have faith that your speed will increase fairly rapidly and with it your earnings.

The Tourist Industry

Casual catering wages both in the cities and in remote areas are high compared to the equivalent British wage. The casual rate for waiting staff is about $10 an hour, with weekend loadings of time and a half on Saturdays and time and three-quarters on Sundays and holidays. Although tipping was traditionally not practised in Australia, it is gradually becoming more common and waiting staff in trendy city establishments can expect to augment their basic wage to some extent.

Standards tend to be fairly high especially in popular tourist haunts, so inexperienced gap year students have little chance of being hired to work in a restaurant or pub. A common practice among restaurant bosses in popular places from Bondi Beach to the Sunshine Coast is to give a job-seeker an hour's trial or a trial shift and decide at the end whether or not to employ them. Stephen Psallidas was taken aback when he approached a hospitality employment agency in Cairns:

> *I was in Cairns in April and thought I'd have little trouble getting work. But though I had a visa and experience I had no references, having worked as a waiter in Greece, where they wouldn't know a reference if one walked up and said 'Hi, I'm a reference', so I was doomed from the start. The agency told me that if I'd had references they could have given me work immediately. Curses.*

Anyone with experience as a cook or chef will probably find her/himself in demand. One tourist area which is not normally inundated with backpacking job-seekers is the stretch of Victorian coast between Dromana and Portsea on the Mornington Peninsula near Melbourne. Although most jobs don't start until after Christmas, the best time to look is late November/early December.

If exploring Australia is your target rather than earning high wages, it is worth trying to exchange your labour for the chance to join an otherwise unaffordable tour. For example camping tour operators in Kakadu and Litchfield Park have been known to do this; try for example Billy Can Tours.

Diving and Watersports

One of the larger employers is the dive industry. Although not many visitors would have the qualifications which got **Ian Mudge** a job as Dive Master on *Nimrod III* operating out of Cookstown (i.e. qualified mechanical engineer, diver and student of Japanese), his assessment of opportunities for mere mortals is heartening:

> *Anyone wishing to try their luck as a hostess could do no worse than to approach all the dive operators with live-aboard boats such as Mike Ball Water Sports in Townsville, Down Under Dive, etc. 'Hosties' make beds, clean cabins and generally tidy up. Culinary skills and an ability to speak Japanese would be definite pluses. A non-diver would almost certainly be able to fix up some free dive lessons and thus obtain their basic Open Water Diver qualification while being paid to do so. Normally females only are considered for hostie jobs.*

Year-out students who have a sailing qualification might find temporary work instructing. To take just one example Northside Sailing School at Spit Bridge in the Sydney suburb of Mosman (02-9969 3972; www.northsidesailing.com.au/employment_opportunities.htm)

offers casual instructing work during school holidays to travellers who have experience in teaching dinghy sailing. *Flying Fish* run a structured watersports training and recruitment programme in Australia. After yacht and dive training, graduates can be helped to find work in the industry. Many trainees who have completed Professional Dive Training with Flying Fish at the Pro Dive Academy in Sydney go on to work at Pro Dive's network of resorts in Australia and the South Pacific. (See entry for Flying Fish in 'Directory of Specialist Gap Year Programmes'.)

Ski Resorts

Another holiday area to consider is the Australian Alps where ski resorts are expanding and gaining in popularity. Jindabyne (NSW) on the edge of Kosciusko National Park and Thredbo are the ski job capitals, though Mount Buller, Falls Creek, Baw Baw and Hotham in the state of Victoria are relatively developed ski centres too. The best time to look is a couple of weeks before the season opens which is usually around the middle of June. Most successful job-seekers use the walk-in-and-ask method, though as everywhere the internet is playing an increasing role. Check out www.ski.com.au/jobs/jobs.html which has a Jobs Database and links to the resorts and pertinent email addresses like jobs@perisher.com.au or recruitment@thredbo.com.au.

Travelling Fairs

Travelling fairs such as the Melbourne Show are very popular and have frequent vacancies. Although it is partly a case of being in the right place at the right time, you can research likely times and locations. To get a job you need to go to the site and walk around asking for work. Some jobs are paid hourly while others pay a percentage of takings; the latter should be accepted only by those with very outgoing personalities who can draw in the punters. Even if you don't land a job before the show opens, it is worth hanging in there in case of last minute cancellations. You can also get a job dismantling the rides at the end which is very physically demanding work.

Geertje Korf, on a gap year between studying archaeology and taking up a career, was at first thrilled to land a job with a travelling fair but it wasn't all as exciting as she had hoped:

> *The work itself was good enough, helping to build up the stalls and working on the Laughing Clowns game. But the family I got to work for were not extremely sociable company. As a result, when we left a place and headed for the next I would spend time (about a week) until the next show day wandering lonely around incredibly hot and dusty little country towns where there was absolutely nothing to do while the showmen sat in a little circle drinking beer and not even talking to me. Also, the public toilets on the showgrounds were not usually open until showday, never cleaned since the last showday and usually provided some company (at last!) such as frogs, flies and redback spiders. I got paid $200 a week plus the use of a little caravan and evening meals which was not bad.*

Au Pairing

The demand for live-in and live-out childcare is enormous in Australia. Applicants are often interviewed a day or two after registering with an agency and start work immediately. Nanny and au pair agencies are very interested in hearing from young women and men with working holiday visas. A number of au pair agencies place European and Asian women with working holiday visas in live-in positions, normally for a minimum of three months. Not all placements require childcare experience. Try any of the following:

Affordable Au Pairs & Nannies, with offices in Sydney, Melbourne and Brisbane (head office 07-5530 1123; www.nanny.net.au). Charges registration fee of $120 plus placement fee of $330.

Australian Nanny & Au Pair Connection, 404 Glenferrie Road, Kooyong, Melbourne, Vic

3144 (☎/fax 03-9824 8857; www.australiannannies.info).
Dial-an-Angel, Suites 20 & 21, Edgecliff Mews, 201 New South Head Road, Edgecliff, NSW 2027 (02-9362 4225; www.dial-an-angel.com.au). Long established agency with branches throughout Australia. Wages offered $250-$500 per week.
Family Match Au Pairs & Nannies, PO Box 448, Double Bay, Sydney, NSW 1360 (☎/fax 02-9328 2553; www.familymatch.com.au). Place people on working holiday visas. 20-30 hours per week for pocket money of $150-$180 plus all live-in expenses.
People for People, PO Box W271, Warringah Mall, Brookvale, NSW 2100 (02-9972 0488; www.peopleforpeople.com.au). Welcome working holidaymakers for three month summer positions.
Most agencies will expect to interview applicants and check their references before placement. As in America, a driving licence is a valuable asset. As well as long term posts, holiday positions for the summer (December-February) and for the ski season (July-September) are available.
Another possibility is to register with an employment agency that supplies staff to day care centres as Catharine Carfoot did during her year of travelling after university:

One surprisingly successful route to employment was through Select Education (109 Pitt St, Level 19, Sydney 2000). There is plenty of work at the moment. It depends on how you feel about being left in sole charge of (for example) 16 3-4 year olds or 6 babies. I should emphasise that I was never left as the only member of staff in the building even if it felt like that sometimes. Select provides childcare workers for kindergartens, pre-schools, day care or whatever.

Travel

The Australian Tourist Commission's *Traveller's Guide* contains quite a bit of hard information and useful telephone numbers as well as all the advertising; request a copy by ringing 0906 863 3235 (60p a minute).

Your transport problems are by no means over when you land in Perth or Sydney. The distances in Australia may be much greater than you are accustomed to and so you will have to give some thought to how you intend to get around. Even with increased airline competition, flying is costly, though you should look into routes and fares available from Richard Branson's no-frills Virgin Blue (www.virginblue.com.au or 136789) which has launched daily flights from Sydney/Melbourne/Adelaide/Canberra to Brisbane. Substantial discounts are offered by the major domestic airlines to overseas visitors who buy a certain number of domestic flights. There are also other discounts for booking at the last minute, and for travelling at unsocial hours or standby.

If you plan a major tour of the country you might consider purchasing a Greyhound Pioneer coach pass along a pre-set route (☎ 13 20 30; www.greyhound.com.au). Sample prices are A$290 for the nearly 3,000km trip between Sydney and Cairns whereas the all-Australia pass costs $2,333; people with YHA or other cards should be entitled to a 10%-15% discount. If you just want to get from one coast to another as quickly as possible and qualify for the very cheapest deals, you will pay around A$370 one way on the coach or train (excluding berth and meals). A multiplicity of private operators has sprung up to serve the backpacking market such as Oz Experience and Wayward Bus.

Having your own transport is a great advantage when job-hunting in Australia. Some places have second-hand cars and camper vans for sale which they will buy back at the end of your stay, for example Boomerang Cars in Adelaide (261 Currie St, 0414-882559; www.boomerangcars.com.au) or Travellers Auto Barn in Sydney, Melbourne, Brisbane and Cairns (www.traveller-autobarn.com). The price of camper vans starts at $1,000 though you would have to spend $2,000-$3,000 to have more chance of getting a reliable vehicle. Car hire is expensive, but occasionally 'relocations' are advertised, i.e. hire cars which need to be returned to their depots; try a company called Britz Campervans (03-8379 8890; www.britz.com).

Although, arguably behind New Zealand, Australia prides itself on being the land of adventurous activities. For example diving courses are widely available, ranging from about £60 for a one-day introduction to £250 for a six-day course. Any number of agencies, especially in Sydney and Brisbane, offer attractive adventure breaks, e.g. Wanderers Travel at 477 Kent St in Sydney (www.wanderers-travel.com) organises learn-to-surf safaris, dive trips, sky dives, etc.

Conclusion

It is the rare gap year traveller who comes home from Australia disappointed. The Aussies are a fantastically friendly, good-natured and helpful bunch and very easy to socialise with. Many student visitors are struck by what a good standard of living can be enjoyed for not very much money. As Gawain Paling put it so graphically, 'If you're poor in Britain it's the pits; if you're poor in Australia you can have a nice comfortable life'. There is a marvellous range of jobs even if you are unlikely to repeat Sandra Grey's coup of being paid $50 for three hours 'work' testing a sunscreen on her lily-white back, or Jane Thomas's bizarre jobs, one in a sex change clinic, the other in a morgue typing up the labels for dismembered parts of bodies.

NEW ZEALAND

Mothers of prospective gap year students have been known to tell their daughters that the only countries they will be allowed to visit are Canada and New Zealand. Mothers always know which countries are safe and friendly, and they don't come any safer or friendlier than New Zealand. These same mothers probably also have a list of expatriate cousins and old family friends who could be relied on in a crisis. New Zealand may be about as far away from Britain as it is possible to get, yet it makes things very easy for young travellers on a budget.

Most year-out students simply travel around New Zealand rather than work or study. Typically, students earn money in Australia to fund a holiday in NZ which includes the obligatory bungy jump or other adrenalin sport in Queenstown. Other enterprising gap year students get a working holiday visa for New Zealand (see below) and hunt out their own jobs.

Placement Organisations

GAP Activity Projects has been sending year-out students to boarding schools for many years. Because New Zealanders are so fanatical about sport, schools place a strong emphasis on outdoor activities, and GAPpers make ideal helpers. Most of these placements are for a whole year from the end of August, though a few eight-month placements start half-way through the year.

BUNAC has a Work New Zealand programme which provides the usual range of services to students and non-students: group departures, organised 3-day stopover, round-the-world flight, visa, orientation on arrival and ongoing support from their partner International Exchange Programs (IEP) in New Zealand. The package is available for an inclusive fee of about £1,700.

CIEE UK (www.ciee.org.uk) operates a scheme for up to 12 months, which includes initial accommodation, post-arrival orientation and job assistance on arrival. The Work Experience Downunder programme from *CCUSA* (Green Dragon House, 64-70 High St, Croydon CR0 9XN; 020-8688 9051; www.ccusaweusa.co.uk) operates to New Zealand as well as Australia. The application and programme fees come to £375 plus insurance, travel and visas.

Changing Worlds (11 Doctors Lane, Caterham, Surrey CR3 5AE; 01883 340960; www.changingworlds.co.uk) offer paid placements in hotels in the Bay of Islands, Rotorua and Queenstown and also on farms throughout the North Island. Unpaid opportunities exist to work on a tall ship. Changing World's New Zealand placements last three to six months starting in September, January and June.

Global Visions International make placements lasting 4-12 weeks at an Eco-Sanctuary in the Coromandel State Forest Park where volunteers plant trees, create forest tracks and work on alternative energy systems, carry out ecological surveys, control weeds, build bridges, etc. but also have time to explore the area. The fee for a 4-week attachment is £730 excluding travel.

Red Tape

Visitors from the UK need no visa to stay for up to six months. Tourists entering the country may be asked to show an onward ticket and about NZ$1,000 per month of their proposed stay (unless they have pre-paid accommodation or a New Zealand backer who has pledged support in a crisis). In practice, respectable-looking travellers are unlikely to be quizzed at entry.

The UK Citizens' Working Holiday Scheme allows Britons aged 18-30 to do temporary jobs in New Zealand for up to 12 months. When the scheme was introduced in 1993, the quota was 500. That number has now risen (from January 2003) to 9,000 working holiday visas which are granted annually on a first come first served basis starting from September 1st. Although the literature says the quota fills quickly, the increased number means that visas should be available throughout the year (though they may run out in the summer). Information can be obtained from the New Zealand Immigration Service, Mezzanine Floor, New Zealand House, 80 Haymarket, London SW1Y 4TE (fax 020-7973 0370) in person, by phone on 09069 100100 (charged at £1 per minute) or via the internet www.immigration.govt.nz. To apply you need an Application for Work Visa form, your UK passport valid for 28 months beyond the date of application, the fee of NZ$90 (£30), a return ticket or a one-way ticket plus NZ$2,000.

Casual Work

New Zealand is a country where it may be better to take enough money to enjoy travelling, and perhaps supplement your travel fund with some cash-in-hand work, odd jobs or work-for-keep arrangements. Camping on beaches, fields and in woodlands is generally permitted. Hitch-hiking is rewarding. Hire cars can even be free. So many hirers leave their hire cars in Wellington before catching the ferry to the South Island and then in Christchurch, that the major outlets need people to deliver these cars north again to Auckland.

Because New Zealand has a limited industrial base, most temporary work is in agriculture and tourism. As in Australia, hostels and campsites are the best sources of information on harvesting jobs (and there is a wealth of budget accommodation throughout New Zealand). Often local farmers co-operate with hostel wardens who collate information about job vacancies or they may circulate notices around youth hostels, for example, 'Orchard Work Available January to March; apply Tauranga Hostel' so always check the hostel board (bearing in mind that some hostels entice job-seekers with a vague promise of local work simply to fill beds). **Ian Fleming** soon realised how valuable hostels could be in his job hunt:

> *During our travels around the North and South Islands, the opportunity to work presented itself on several occasions. While staying in the Kerikeri Youth Hostel, we discovered that the local farmers would regularly come into the hostel to seek employees for the day or longer. (This was in July, which is out-of-season.) My advice to any person looking for farm work would be to get up early as the farmers are often in the hostel by 8.30am.*

The website of the Budget Backpackers Hostels group includes details of jobs going at its 290 member hostels (www.backpack.co.nz/jobs.html).

Private agencies are also involved in the working holiday market. Auckland Central Travel located in Auckland Central Backpackers (229 Queen St; 09-358 4877 or 357 3996) operate a Job Search service for backpackers (jobs@acb.co.nz; www.acbtravel.co.nz or www.nzjobs.go.to). Registered members have access to vacancy information in the hospitality, construction and temp industries. The ACB also sells a starter pack which includes 12 months registration with Job Search, four nights accommodation on arrival, etc. for $245.

Similarly Travellers Contact Point has an office in Auckland on the Ground Floor of the Dingwall Building at 87 Queen St (09-300 7197; info@travellersnz.com). Their starter pack costs $160. In 2002 the mainstream travel publisher Jason's launched a good website www.destinationdownunder.com with links to 400 hostels and job info. Try also Seasonal Work NZ (www.seasonalwork.co.nz) based in Rotorua, which provides splendidly full details on employers.

Rural & Conservation Volunteering

World Wide Opportunities on Organic Farms or WWOOF NZ is popular and active, with nearly 650 farms and smallholdings on its fix-it-yourself list that welcome volunteers in exchange for food and accommodation. The list can be obtained from Jane and Andrew Strange, PO Box 1172, Nelson (☎/fax 03-544 9890; www.wwoof.co.nz) for a fee of £12/ US$20/NZ$40.

Another organisation matches working visitors with about 190 farmers throughout New Zealand. Farmstays can last from three days to several months. *Farm Helpers in New Zealand* (FHiNZ, 16 Aspen Way, Palmerston North; ☎/fax 06-355 0448; www.fhinz.co.nz) charges NZ$25 for their membership booklet containing all the addresses. The list is updated monthly since the scheme is growing quickly. No experience is necessary and roughly four hours of work a day are requested. The co-ordinator (Warwick Grady) advises that hosts in the Auckland area tend to be oversubscribed, so that it is best to head into the countryside.

The New Zealand Department of Conservation (DOC) carries out habitat and wildlife management projects throughout New Zealand and publishes a detailed Calendar of Volunteer Opportunities (see their website www.doc.govt.nz/community/006~volunteers/index.asp) which lists all sorts of interesting sounding projects from counting bats to cleaning up remote beaches. Most require a good level of fitness and a contribution to expenses, often quite small. The DOC also needs volunteer hut wardens at a variety of locations. Details are available from any office of the Department of Conservation (all addresses are listed on website).

Paul Bagshaw from Kent spent a thoroughly enjoyable week on an uninhabited island in Marlborough Sound monitoring kiwis, the flightless bird whose numbers have been seriously depleted. An ongoing programme removes them from the mainland to small islands where there are no predators:

> *The object of the exercise was to estimate the number of kiwis on Long Island north of Picton. As the kiwi is noctural, we had to work in the small hours. As it's dark, it's impossible to count them so we had to spread out and walk up a long slope listening for their high-pitched whistling call. During the day they hide in burrows and foliage so it is very rare to see one. One night, when we heard one rustling around our camp, my girlfriend went outside with a torch and actually managed to see it. She was so excited that she couldn't speak and resorted to wild gesticulations to describe its big feet and long beak.*
>
> *The island has no water source except rainwater which collects in tanks, all very basic. We lived in tents and prepared our own meals from supplies brought over from the mainland. Our one luxury was a portaloo.*

The New Zealand Trust for Conservation Volunteers was set up in 1999 to match both local and international volunteers with conservation projects of all kinds to counteract the loss of native bush and wildlife. Whereas DOC projects take place only on DOC lands, NZTCV registers projects run by many local and national organisations as well as DOC projects. Details are available on their website www.conservationvolunteers.org.nz (☎/fax 09-415 9336; conservol@clear.net.nz). NZTCV has created a central database on which individuals can register in order to be put in touch with organisations running conservation projects.

The Earthwise Living Foundation (PO Box 108, Thames 2815; voicemail/fax 09-353 1558; www.elfnz.com) places international visitors in a variety of settings including a wilderness ecology and conservation programme lasting 4-14 weeks or a personalised work experience/internship programme in a career field of your choice. Fees are from US$1,950 for a minimum 6-week, maximum 52-week internship to US$3,940 for a 12-week professional development internship. Many of the placements involve living with a local family. Participants must arrange their own visas as appropriate.

Canada

Canada is one of those countries your mum probably won't mind you visiting for part of your gap year (New Zealand is another). It has what mums like in abundance: low crime rate, prosperity, orderliness, polite and friendly natives and an excellent communication system. On the down side, it is expensive (especially compared to Nepal) and bureaucratic (as you will soon discover when you look into obtaining a student Employment Authorization). It is also the country which inspired the writer Saki to say 'Canada is all right, really, but not for the whole weekend'. However most gap students who choose to work or travel in Canada end up disagreeing strenuously with Saki.

Special Schemes

The *British Universities North America Club* or BUNAC provides the easiest route to spending all or part of a gap year in Canada. Their 'Work Canada' programme offers students (including gap year students with a university place and finalists with proof that they will return to the UK) the chance to go to Canada for up to a year and take whatever job they can find. Students on this programme can depart at any time between February and December. The great majority of participants go to Canada without a pre-arranged job and spend their first week or two job-hunting.

'Work Canada' and 'Gap Canada' have slightly different eligibility requirements though you must be a British or Irish passport holder aged 18-29 (under 20 for 'Gap Canada') when applying for the visa and entering Canada. Participants in Gap Canada must be in receipt of a conditional or unconditional offer of a place on a full-time degree level course starting the following September and have attained suitable qualifications to satisfy the offer.

The requirements for Work Canada are that you must be a current full-time university student on a degree level course or equivalent such as HND or a post-graduate level student at a UK college/university in 2003/4. Alternatively you can be a gap year student holding an unconditional university level place. Applicants in their last year of A-levels should contact BUNAC in May for a copy of the Gap Canada brochure and application form. Departures start in September. If you already hold an unconditional offer to study at a university or are a current university level student, you should contact BUNAC for a Work Canada application form. Departures start in February.

Applicants must also have C$1,000 in Canadian funds (or $600 plus either a letter of sponsorship from a Canadian relative or a job offer) and a return ticket. It is no longer compulsory to have a medical examination with a designated doctor unless you want to work in childcare or healthcare; if you do need a medical certificate reckon on paying at least £80 to one of the specified doctors. The BUNAC programme fee is currently £145 and BUNAC insurance (about £141 for four months) is compulsory. Participants can travel independently or on a BUNAC flight costing approximately £500.

The majority of jobs listed in BUNAC's Work Canada *Vital Info Handbook* are in hotels and tourist attractions in the Rockies which is a beautiful part of the world in which to spend a summer or winter season. The huge Banff Springs Hotel alone employs 900 people, and its sister hotels Chateau Lake Louise and Jasper Park Lodge, plus Lake Louise Inn, Inns of Banff Park, Banff International Hotel and Athabasca Hotel in Jasper all have huge staffs. British students have an edge over their Canadian counterparts in this sphere of employment since they don't have to return to university until mid to late September rather than the beginning of September.

Changing Worlds and *Gap Challenge* send gap year students to work at hotels and ski resorts in the Rocky Mountain resorts in and around Banff. This is one of the few examples of specialist gap organisations arranging paid seasonal work for school leavers, as distinct from voluntary work. The minimum stay is six months with departures in November for the winter season and March for the summer. The cost of Changing World's programme (which is always popular and fills up about six months in advance) is £1,895 excluding staff accommodation which is deducted directly from wages at a rate of between $6 and $12 a day.

In order to obtain the student exchange working visa, participants must have an unconditional offer from a college or university on a degree or HND course, before they depart which, as with BUNAC, is not usually available until A-level results are published in mid-August, which in some cases doesn't leave much time to complete the paperwork. The jobs are the usual hotel jobs like housekeeping, waiting on tables and bartending. Hours are long in high season, up to 50 a week, but can drop when client numbers go down or when the snows come late, e.g. 20 hours a week which cuts into earnings. Workers earn about $9 an hour before tips and in some cases are given a free or reduced price ski pass.

Jennie Cox from Derbyshire was unsure about what she wanted to do at the end of her degree at Durham University so consequently decided to take a year out for some time to think and to have a break before going into full-time employment. She applied to Gap Challenge in October and attended a two-day selection course in December. After completing a skills training course the following July she left for Canada in September. On her return she described her seven months away.

> *I had graduated from university and was unsure of what career to take so I not only wanted to take time out to have a think, but wanted to go somewhere different and have some new experiences. I had previously been on an expedition to Tanzania with Gap Challenge and was impressed with the organisation, so when I heard about a long-term arrangement in Canada through them, I was keen to go. I always wanted to go to Canada and had heard much about the country from friends and family. It's renowned for its friendly people; and Banff, in particular, looked beautiful. I was especially keen to ski and snowboard which influenced my decision. My placement involved housekeeping at Banff Park Lodge and general room cleaning, making beds, etc.*
>
> *Overall I had an amazing time in Canada, and I certainly couldn't have asked for a more beautiful placement than the one I had in Banff. To wake up to vast snow-capped mountains each morning was such a luxury, that we had to be careful not to take it for granted. At times, of course, the work could be hard and exhausting, but you had to remind yourself why you were there: young friendly people to meet, lots of places to visit and days up on the slopes snowboarding, topped off by a pint of Canadian lager at night – who could ask for more? I've come back feeling relaxed, happy and refreshed and full of some great memories. Now I just have to find a job.*

CIEE UK (52 Poland Street, London W1F 7AB; 020-7478 2020/www.ciee.org.uk) operates an Internship Canada programme on which British and Irish students undertake work experience in Canada for up to one year. Participants must be enrolled in full-time further or higher education, including gap students with a confirmed place at college and those due to graduate. Interns must find their own work placements in their field of study, often with advice from their tutors. The programme fee is from £200 and insurance is compulsory.

Several schemes designed for gap year students who want to ski or train to be ski instructors in Canada are described below under the heading Skiing.

For many years the Frontier Club in the north of England has been signing up members (currently £22 a year) and inviting them to join various trips and work projects, usually lasting a fortnight. The Club owns two sites in Canada which volunteers can stay at free of charge with a choice of self-catering or contributing to a food kitty. One site is in northern Ontario, the other is in the Selkirk Mountains of British Columbia where volunteers are engaged in turning an old 15-mile packhorse trail into a hiking trail (www.pan4gold.com). A brochure can be requested online at www.work4travel.co.uk or in exchange for an s.a.e. sent to 58 Manchester St, Heywood OL10 1DL (01706 623305).

Red Tape

To work legally in Canada, you must obtain an Employment Authorization from a Canadian High Commission or Embassy before you leave your home country. The Canadian government offers in the neighbourhood of 13,000-15,000 temporary authorisations each year to full-time students to work temporarily in Canada. Participants in the official work exchange must be aged 18-30 years and must have proof that they will be returning to a tertiary level course of study on their return to the UK.

Interested students should check the website www.canada.org.uk/visa-info (click on 'Visiting' rather than 'Working') or obtain the general leaflet 'Student Temporary Employment in Canada' by sending a large s.a.e. with a 50p stamp and marked 'SGWHP' in the top left-hand corner to the Canadian High Commission (Immigration Section, 38 Grosvenor St, London W1K 4AA); the premium line Immigration Info number is 09068-616644 (60p per minute) which goes on interminably and does nothing more than read out the written leaflets. Note that anyone with a job fixed up in Québec must comply with separate and additional Québec immigration procedures. Processing of all work authorisations normally takes between four and six weeks.

Students who already have a written job offer from a Canadian employer may be eligible for 'Programme A'. They can apply directly to the High Commission in London for an Employment Authorization that will be valid for a maximum of 12 months and is not transferable to any other job. The other and more flexible possibility is to obtain an unspecified Employment Authorization from BUNAC already mentioned.

Certain special categories of work may be eligible for authorisation, such as nannies who are in great demand but must be qualified. There is also a category of work permits for voluntary work which takes about a month to process if you have found a placement through a recognised charitable or religious organisation. The authorisation processing fee of C$150 is not charged for the Student General Working Holiday Program nor for volunteers working for a Canadian charity.

All participants of approved student schemes benefit from orientations and back-up from the Canadian Federation of Students' SWAP (Student Work Abroad Program) offices in Toronto and Vancouver. They even organise occasional pub outings and excursions for participants, as well as advising on nitty-gritty issues like tax.

To illustrate the stringency of immigration regulations, even work-for-keep arrangements are difficult to find, as described by the Jericho Beach Youth Hostel in Vancouver (1515 Discovery St, Vancouver, BC V6R 4K5; 604-224-3208):

Unfortunately, due to Canadian employment regulations, we are unable to have foreign nationals participate in our work exchange programme at the hostel (two hours work in exchange for a free overnight). We do have an employment board at the hostel where we post notices from local companies and individuals offering employment. In addition, the front desk staff are a valuable resource for finding employment in the city.

However students with a work authorisation should be able to stay long term at a hostel in exchange for some work. For example Global Village Backpackers in Toronto, Vancouver and Banff have in the past willingly hired gap year students with permission to work; their website has a section about working visas (www.globalbackpackers.com/work.html).

One useful exception is to stay for less than three months on a visitor visa on a work for keep basis on an organic farm (see WWOOF below) or as a family helper. Au Pair Canada, 15 Goodacre Close, Red Deer, Alberta, Canada T4P 3A3 (☎/fax 403-343-1418; aupaircanada@shaw.ca) places holiday au pairs from many countries including Britain with families in Western Canada. The au pair receives free room and board, pocket money of $75 a week and, in some cases, a chance to accompany the family on holiday.

THE JOB HUNT

Those students without a pre-arranged job might encounter some difficulty finding work since the job hunt is tougher in Canada than most places. On average BUNACers take six or seven days to find a job in Canada. Even Canadian students find it hard to get summer jobs and there will be stiff competition for most kinds of seasonal work. It will be necessary to look presentable, eager to please, positive and cheerful, even if the responses are negative or the employers unhelpful.

Jobs for sales staff are advertised wherever you go in Canada. **Tanufa Kotecha** joined BUNAC's Work Canada programme and quickly learned that Canadian selling techniques are just as aggressive as American ones:

I landed a job within a week in Toronto working in a French Canadian clothing store. In my store as soon as a customer walked in, they had to be greeted by a 'sales associate' within 15 seconds! The North American way of selling is pushy and upfront, but it does get results. One must have confidence to sell.

Almost all shop jobs of this kind pay the minimum wage. In Ontario the student minimum wage is $6.40 an hour.

Skiing

The past two years have seen a remarkable increase in the number of programmes specially tailored to avid or just aspiring skiers and snowboarders taking a year out who want to improve their skiing (beginners are accepted) or train as instructors.

> **Peter Colledge joined Ski le Gap for the winter season in 2002:**
> *As I embark on my first year of university at Bath I cannot help reminiscing on my gap year and all the incredible things that I have done. Skiing is my passion and I spent over 6 months of my gap year skiing in France, Canada and Australia. Canada was the best skiing that I experienced in the year and I was on a programme called Ski Le Gap.*
> *The atmosphere of the course seemed evident as soon as 200 nervous yet extremely excited teenagers stepped off the plane, all determined to have lots of fun. On the hill, the instruction can only be described as awesome. Ski le Gap is proud of the reputation of its instructors and their unparalleled experience (many of whom have represented their country). The range of qualifications on offer was amazing. I gained several including CSIA level 3 which is an internationally recognised certification. (One other person on the course gained this level, and we were the first and only people to have ever gained level 1, 2 and 3 in just one season's skiing.) I also obtained level 1 Freeski, level 1 CSCF, a race coach qualification, and CADS, a certification allowing me to teach disabled skiers. We were also given the freedom and flexibility to achieve our individual goals. The course offered us the chance to become well qualified instructors and also to meet some fantastic people, not only on the course, but the local people as well. I can't*

> *imagine 200 British 18 year old visiting somewhere else and experiencing the same reception and respect that we were given. As for Canada as a whole, I can't stop commending it to everyone I speak to.*

Ski Le Gap (see 'Directory of Sports Courses') in Québec runs one- and three-month programmes during the ski season in the resort of Mont Tremblant. The course combines ski/snowboard instruction with French conversation lessons plus other activities such as igloo-building, dogsledding and extreme snowshoeing. The programme is geared to British students and prices are in sterling: £6,000 (2004) which includes London-Montréal airfares. Similarly *Ski-Exp-Air* (see 'Directory of Courses') offers an intensive training programme aimed at British skiers at four resorts near Québec City including Mont Ste. Anne.

Peak Leaders gap year programme in Canada takes place in the Rockies. The website of Peak Laders UK Ltd (www.peakleaders.co.uk) gives full details of the nine-week programme of ski/snowboard instructor/leader training (see 'Directory of Sports Courses'). The all-in price is £5,650.

Finally two other companies operate in British Columbia: the *International Academy* (also with a listing in the 'Directory of Courses') at Whistler and Lake Louise in the Rockies (£6,650 for a 12-week course in the latter) and *Nonstopski* whose programme runs in Fernie, BC. This is obviously a booming field, since the established gap year organisation mentioned above, Gap Challenge, has introduced a six-week Ski/Snowboard instructor programme departing in January. Experienced snowboarders who want to qualify as an instructor in Canada should check the entry for the Canadian Association of Snowboard Instructors (www.casi-acms.com) in the Directory of Courses.

A more flexible arrangement can be made through Seasons on Snow (Unit 1a, Franchise St, Kidderminster DY11 6RE; 08700 111360; info@seasonsonsnow.com/ wwwseasonsonsnow.com). This new company specialises in renting out affordable accommodation to young skiers and snowboarders for the whole season, some of whom take lessons, others work and others just ski. Through this company you can book a bed in a multi-bedded chalet in Whistler starting at £100 a week if you stay for the whole season. Packages cost £3,000 for six months including accommodation and return flights; food and lift pass (about £530 for the season) are extra.

To offset this expense, it is possible to pick up work in Whistler/Blackcomb and the other main resorts like Banff/Lake Louise, provided you have a work permit from BUNAC. Ski resorts throughout Canada create a great number of seasonal employment vacancies which can't be filled by Canadian students since they're all studying. The contact address for the Whistler/Blackcomb Resort is 4545 Blackcomb Way, Whistler, B.C. V0N 1B4 (604-938-7366; kmuller@intrawest.com). Their website (www.whistler-blackcomb.ca/company/ employment) gives dates of the annual recruiting fair and allows you to apply on-line.

A few jobs are available with UK ski tour operators though most are looking for staff who are at least 20, like the *Specialist Holidays Group* (see 'Directory of Paid Seasonal Jobs'), Hand Made Holidays Ltd (First Floor, Carpenters Buildings, Carpenters Lane, Cirencester, Glos GL7 1EE; www.handmade-holidays.co.uk), Inghams Travel Overseas Reps Dept, 10-18 Putney Hill, London SW15 6AX; 020-8780 4400; www.inghams.co.uk) and Venture Abroad (Rayburn House, Parcel Terrace, Derby DE1 1LY; www.ventureabroad.co.uk) which hires reps to guide youth groups in Canada.

James Gillespie spent the winter and summer of his gap year working in Whistler. After taking the beautiful train ride from Vancouver, it soon became clear that getting a place to stay would be a major problem. But soon he had a job as a ticket validator which came with a free ski pass and subsidised accommodation:

It was an excellent job and, although sometimes mundane, it was often livened up by violent and abusive skiers trying to get on the lift for free. Going there was the best thing I've ever done and I hope to be living there permanently eventually. I came home with a diary full of experiences, a face full of smiles, a bag full of dirty washing and pockets full of… well nothing actually. I was in debt, but it was worth it.

VOLUNTARY WORK

Some interesting practical community projects are organised by *Frontiers Foundation* (2615 Danforth Avenue, Suite 203, Toronto, Ontario M4C 1L6; 416-690-3930 or 1-800-668-4130; www.frontiersfoundation.org) in low income communities in Canada, which tend to be native communities in isolated northern areas. Some of the projects (known as Operation Beaver) consist of helping the local people to build low-cost well-heated houses or community centres. Others take place on wilderness camps for native children. Project locations have such picturesque names as Dog Creek, Rat Portage and Goose Bay. Whatever the project, Frontiers Foundation will pay all food, accommodation, travel and insurance expenses within Canada. A modest living allowance will be paid if you stay beyond the minimum period of three months (four months for the North West Territories). In addition to the C$25 application fee, the only expense will be the airfare, the volunteer visa and a medical certificate of fitness. Send three IRCs for an information pack and application form or download them from their website.

The work itself does not occupy all of your time and energies. According to **Sarah King**, there was time left over to participate in some quintessentially Canadian backwoods activities:

One of the great benefits about being a guest worker was that our activities became a focal point for the community. We played volleyball, helped break in wild horses, watched bears, made wild berry pies and rose-hip jelly, went camping, hunting, fishing and swimming, baked porcupine packed in clay, ate a delicacy of sweet and sour beaver tail, and all took up jogging around a local basketball park.

If you are interested in gaining some practical experience on organic farms or if you just want to meet Canadians, you might consider volunteering for *WWOOF-Canada* (World Wide Opportunities on Organic Farms). For a membership fee of C$35 (cash), John Vanden Heuvel (4429 Carlson Road, Nelson, BC V1L 6X3; 250-354-4417; wwoofcan@shaw.ca; www.wwoofusa.com/canada) will send a list of more than 450 farms across Canada to prospective volunteers, along with a description of the farms. All volunteers must have valid tourist visas. Obbe Verwer used his farm visits as a springboard to further travels in western Canada:

After enjoying my visits to a couple of farms listed by WWOOF, I went on by myself to Vancouver Island. I set off to hike through the rainforest along the Clayoquot Valley Witness Trail. When I came to the trailhead, I met the trail boss who was working with a group of volunteers to build boardwalks at both ends of the trails. This was to enable more people to walk part of the trail which is important because this valley has to be saved from clearcut logging. I decided to join them. Actually you are supposed to go through the organising committee to become a volunteer worker but I just pitched my tent and joined on the spot. All the wood to build the boardwalk had to be carried into the trail, steps, stringers, nails and tools. We worked till 4pm, but it was not strict at all. Sometimes it was pretty hard, but it was fun. The forest impressed me more and more. The big trees, the berries, the mushrooms and the silence in the mist. It was just amazing. It was very satisfying to be helping to save this forest.

The *Western Canada Wilderness Committee* can be visited at 341 Water St, Vancouver, BC V6B 2K7; 604-683-8220; www.wildernesscommittee.org). Volunteers should bear in mind that while building trails in the rainforests of the Pacific coast one is bound to get wet. The WCWC also needs people to work in roadside kiosks, selling T-shirts, etc. for fund-raising.

Not many international workcamps take place in Canada. One of the few organisations active in the field is in Québec, and the camps they arrange (in co-operation with UNA Exchange) are bilingual French-English. The co-ordinating organisation is *Chantiers Jeunesse,* 4545 avenue Pierre-de-Coubertin, CP 1000 Succursale M, Montréal, Québec H1V 3R2 (514-252-3015; www.cj.qc.ca).

COURSES

Although culturally hard to distinguish from the USA in some respects, Canada's French language and culture guarantee its distinctiveness. Few gap year students think of Canada when considering places to improve their French, but the French-speaking province of Québec has lots of language schools (mostly for English-speaking North Americans). For example the *Point3 Language Centre* in Montréal (see entry) and College Platon (4521 Park Ave, Montréal, Québec H2V 4E4; 514-281-1016; www.platocollege.com) offer short intensive courses with homestays at reasonable prices, e.g. 25 hours of tuition a week for four weeks costs C$675 for four weeks. The Surrey-based language agency Vis-à-Vis can place students of French in Canada as well as in France and Belgium. Bear in mind that the Québecois accent is very different from Parisian French and incorporates many more loan words from English.

The *English-Speaking Union* offers scholarships to young people to spend six or 12 months in a private Canadian high school during their gap year. The scholarship covers free board and tuition; all other expenses must be met by the exchange participant. (See entry in 'Directory of Specialist Gap Year Programmes').

For many gap students, the primary attraction of Canada is its great outdoors. Pleasant and interesting as Canada's cities are, the forests, mountains, and lakes are what give the nation its special appeal. It is possible to improve a specialist skill while exploring the wilderness, for example with *Chilcotin Holidays* in British Columbia (see Directory of Miscellaneous Courses) who offer 7- or 13-day summer training courses in guiding in the wilderness by horseback. Students who take the course have a chance of finding paid work in the field before returning to university in the autumn, providing they have a BUNAC work authorisation.

TRAVEL

For accommodation in North America (mainly Canada), get hold of the list of hostels from Backpackers Hostels Canada (Longhouse Village, RR 13, Thunder Bay, Ontario P7B 5E4, Canada; www.backpackers.ca). Contact details for hostels across Canada are available on the website.

The network of 60 student travel offices on or near Canadian university or college campuses is Travel CUTS (www.travelcuts.com). They also administer an outgoing work abroad programme for Canadian students, known as SWAP (www.swap.ca).

Israel

Israel is not a happy country. The escalating conflict between the Israelis and Palestinians often seems beyond resolution. Predictably, as the Peace Process has unravelled, Israel has lost much of its appeal for student travellers, and the number of young people choosing to head for what has been a favourite travellers' destination is drastically down. At present few if any opportunities exist in the Palestinian-governed Territories and many projects such as archaeological digs have been curtailed or cancelled because of the current situation in Israel.

But behind all the shocking violence and retaliation in the headlines, thousands of individuals and groups do not consider the situation hopeless and are working patiently towards peace and reconciliation. Spending time in Israel will enable people from outside the region to gain more insight into one of the world's most bedevilling trouble spots. Personal security is bound to be a consideration but the statistics should be reassuring, that tourists and volunteers are rarely if ever the targets of violence. If entering the country under the auspices of for example a kibbutz placement organisation, you should seek up-to-the-minute advice about where it is considered safe to go, and of course always consult the Foreign & Commonwealth Office advice (www.fco.gov.uk/travel).

Most students associate working in Israel with staying on a kibbutz or a moshav. Although there are other working opportunities, these are by far the most common ways of having a prolonged visit in Israel, and one of which many thousands of gap year students of all nationalities have taken advantage over the past decades. The popularity of kibbutz stays is no doubt partly due to the low cost of fixing up a placement and the reasonable cost of getting to Israel, typically £300-£400 altogether. Even if most of the work assigned to volunteers is not very stimulating, most participants agree that Israel is a good country in which to meet young people of different nationalities and to see something of the Middle East.

Other opportunities available to young people in Israel include au pairing (which is easy to arrange because of high demand), archaeological digs and a range of voluntary projects involving human rights work, community and social work, etc. **Laura Bennett** accepted a place at a therapeutic riding centre which she ended up enjoying although her first choice destination had been Canada:

> I was to head off to a country I knew absolutely nothing about. In fact, I was thoroughly confused about the whole situation. Some people told me Israel was very modern; others said I was mad, that I would get blown up (fortunately my father is a journalist so I didn't really fall for that one). I'm glad that it worked out the way it did. Israel is a fascinating place and the work was definitely right up my street. In addition, I'm going to read Archaeology and Anthropology, and the Middle East was obviously brilliant for that field.

Some gap year students, especially those from Jewish backgrounds, decide to spend a year in Israel learning Hebrew. A number of kibbutzim operate ulpan courses in conjunction with the Jewish Agency for Israel; the ulpan programme is designed for young people who want to gain a working knowledge of Hebrew and an understanding of the Jewish way of life and history with a view to settling in Israel. Finally, paid casual work is readily available in resorts and other tourist-related businesses, though wages are almost universally low.

Specialised Gap Year Programme

The *Friends of Israel Educational Foundation* (PO Box 7545, London NW2 2QZ; fax 020-7794 0291; info@foi-asg.org) has long run a gap year programme called the Bridge Programme for 12 candidates a year who are sent to Israel on a structured programme which includes a kibbutz stay, community service, English teaching and other projects for six months from January. After being chosen at interview in July, participants' expenses are covered apart from spending money; £600 is recommended (see entry in 'Directory of Specialist Gap Year Placements').

> **Elizabeth Petchey is a recent participant who appreciated getting to know individuals from many backgrounds and being given the chance to confront the complexities of the Middle East situation:**
> For me membership of the Bridge 2001 group was a license to become Israeli for six months. I have spent the year since my return trying to make sense of those experiences in relation to the debates and opinions that have flooded the political scene. My reflections on Israel are profoundly influenced by encounters with

> *the people I met, like Mohammed, a Christian in Jerusalem (no mistake there), Orthodox Jews in Galilee, secular Jews in Kibbutz Yahel, a Palestinian who felt trapped in Bethlehem, an Egyptian hotel owner who wanted to know details of my Israeli connections, youths telling me of their eagerness or reluctance to serve in the army, a young Russian Christian Israeli, Arab children in Peki'in, Jews motivated by Zionism and Holocaust survivors. My understanding and appreciation of the country came to be based on contact with these individuals and they served to mould any political opinions I have developed.*
>
> On her return to Europe, she felt impatient with some of the anti-Israeli positions she heard expressed so strongly:
>
> *I found myself on the defensive because so much of the hostility seemed irrationally to attack individuals I felt I actually knew. Perhaps in my naivety I could not connect Israeli soldiers on demonstrators' placards with the eighteen year olds whom I had taught English, or the Palestinian children on television to the Arab children with whom I had put on a fashion show. In July 2002 I returned to Israel to work on a summer camp for Arab and Israeli children. I could not help but feel nervous as I travelled on a bus around Tel Aviv the day after a suicide bomb attack. Yet most of all I was overwhelmed by the sheer number of people who came up to me, the majority of whom I did not know, and expressed their gratitude for my returning to help work with the children. Some said they felt they had been cut off from the world and felt I was reaching out to them.*

The Association of Jewish Sixth Formers (AJ6, Hillel House, 1/2 Endsleigh St, London WC1H 0DS; 020-8846 2277; office@aj6.org/ www.aj6.org) runs a year-out scheme in Israel for school leavers combining study and volunteer work. Participants on the Machon (Leadership) Year Out must be supported by their sponsoring youth movement. AJ6 also has more flexible volunteering schemes like the Israel Experience on which Jewish young people arrange voluntary work that suits them for 3-12 months.

KIBBUTZIM and MOSHAVIM

Everyone has some idea of what a kibbutz is: it is a communal society in which all the means of production are owned and shared by the community as a whole. For more than two generations, this idea has appealed to young people from around the world who have flocked to the 250 kibbutzim of Israel to volunteer their services and participate in this utopian community based on equality.

But recent headlines such as 'Kibbutz Kiss of Death' and 'Israel to Privatise Kibbutzim' have alerted the outside world to something that Israelis have known for some time, that the kibbutz movement is in decline or at least changing almost out of recognition. As further evidence of the decline, only one-fifth of the number of foreign volunteers who came in the 1970s arrive in Israel now, i.e. 10,000 instead of 50,000. It is symptomatic that after 33 years of placing volunteers on kibbutzim, the London and Tel Aviv-based company Project 67 has ceased trading.

Having said all that, foreign volunteers are still welcome to join some kibbutzim for two to six months and many continue to enjoy the experience. In return for their labour, volunteers receive free room and board and about £50 a month in pocket money. Many kibbutzim make considerable efforts to welcome volunteers, for example by providing organised sightseeing tours every so often.

If the kibbutz is broadly based on a socialist model, the moshav is on a capitalist model, with members owning their own machinery and houses, though the produce is marketed co-operatively. The kind of experience the volunteer has on a moshav is very different and usually more demanding. Although the term 'volunteer' is used of moshavim, a wage is paid (normally the shekel equivalent of $350-$500/£250-£350 a month) which allows a frugal person to save enough to fund further travels (normally in Egypt) especially if an end-of-season bonus is paid.

Kibbutz and moshav placements can be fixed up either inside or outside Israel. There is no doubt that registering in advance will give you peace of mind. In Britain the main kibbutz placement organisation is Kibbutz Representatives at 1A Accommodation Road, London NW11 8ED (020-8458 9235/fax 020-8455 7930; enquiries@kibbutz.org.uk/ www.kibbutz.org.il). To register with them you must be between the ages of 18 and 50 (recently raised from 32), be able to stay for a minimum of eight weeks, attend an informal interview in London or Manchester, and provide a signed medical declaration of fitness. Processing takes from three to five weeks (summer is the busiest time). The kibbutz package (which costs from £410) guarantees placement and the B4 visa, and includes flights and transport to the kibbutz. Insurance is compulsory; premiums start at £72. You can either arrange your travel independently and present yourself at the kibbutz office in Tel Aviv, or you can book flights through KR, as an individual or as part of a group. Group participants are met at the airport. The newest programme is 'The Israel Experience' which over three months combines a political and cultural introduction to the country, language instruction (Hebrew or English) and volunteering.

A number of offices in Tel Aviv are able to place volunteers who simply show up, particularly between October and May. The official Kibbutz Program Center has an active Volunteer Department (18 Frishman St, Cnr. 90 Ben Yehuda St, Tel Aviv 61030; 03-527 8874/524 6156; fax 03-523 9966; kpc@vollentir.co.il/ www.kibbutz.org.il). The office is situated in apartment 6 on the third floor, and the opening hours are Sunday to Thursday 8am-2pm. Bear in mind that if you arrive during religious holidays such as the week of Passover in the spring, working hours may be reduced or offices closed. The buses needed to reach the office are: number 222 from the airport, 10 from the railway station and 4 from the Central Bus Station. To register you will need your passport, medical certificate, insurance policy (which must show that your insurer has an Israeli representative), an airline ticket out of Israel, two passport photos and registration fee of $60. They may also want to see proof of funds ($250). Comprehensive insurance cover is compulsory, so if your policy is not sufficient, you can buy a suitable policy at the KPC for $80 which provides cover for up to 12 months. A returnable deposit is payable to guarantee that you stay for the minimum period of eight weeks.

Several moshav placement offices and agents can be tracked down through Tel Aviv's many hostels. An independent agent is *Meira's Volunteers for Moshav/Kibbutz* at 73 Ben Yehuda St, Ground Floor, Tel Aviv 63435 (03-523 7369/524 3811; meiras@netvision.net .il).

Kibbutzim are not the version of holiday camps they once were. The average working week has increased from 36 to 48 hours in recent years, though hours may be reduced in the hot summer and extended at busy times. Most of the necessities of life are provided by the kibbutz including stationery, tea, coffee, basic toiletries and cigarettes, though perks differ and have been generally shrinking as pocket money has risen. New volunteers are often assigned the undesirable jobs though most volunteer organisers are willing to transfer a dissatisfied volunteer to a different job. **Catherine Revell** claims that if you are assertive and show willingness to work hard, you can find yourself doing more interesting work; among the jobs she did on three different kibbutzim were kitchen manager, shepherdess and a sculptor's assistant.

Meeting people is the central theme of kibbutz volunteer life according to many volunteers including **Bela Lal** who decided to take a gap year to work and travel after university and before trying to break into publishing:

The wonderful benefits of being a volunteer on a kibbutz remain with you: the knowledge that such a shared/communal lifestyle can work, the feeling of complete relaxation and inner harmony and some excellent friends with whom I will definitely stay in touch. I would recommend the kibbutz experience to anyone who is open-minded, not too proud to undertake often fairly menial work, operating on a budget and most importantly wants to live in a community of people about their own age and experience something entirely unique.

Life is very different on a moshav where workers regularly get up at 5am and put in 75 hour weeks for £250-£350 a month. Often the social life is less appealing than on a kibbutz though this varies. The high season for most moshavim is November to April, so spring is when you are most likely to receive a bonus of up to two months' wages. Information about specific kibbutzim is provided in the book *Kibbutz Volunteer* published by Vacation-Work Publications (£10.99).

OTHER OPPORTUNITIES FOR GAP TRAVELLERS

Most gap year students will start their time in Israel with a spell on a kibbutz or a moshav which is an excellent way to meet other travellers and make friends. Once their stay is over, many move on to less formal arrangements.

Tourism

When Israel's tourist industry was booming, many travelling students found casual jobs in restaurants, cafés and hostels. But much of that demand has disappeared with the tourists. The best places for finding work in tourism are Eilat, Tel Aviv, Herzliya (a wealthy resort north of Tel Aviv) and to a lesser extent Haifa and Jerusalem. There is a plethora of cheap hostels around Israel, almost all of which employ two or three young foreigners to spend a few hours a day cleaning or manning the desk in exchange for a free bed and some meals. If you prove yourself a hard worker, you may be moved to a better job or even paid some pocket money.

The Youth Hostel Association of Israel (1 Shezer St, PO Box 6001, Jerusalem 91060; 02-655 8400; www.youth-hostels.org.il) can provide a list of their 32 member hostels around the country which may be in a position to offer free accommodation, meals and pocket money in exchange for six hours of work a day. Many of the dozens of hostels along Hayarkon St in Tel Aviv and elsewhere are good sources of job information or jobs themselves such as No. 1 Hostel at 84 Ben Yehuda St (03-523 7807) and the Gordon Hostel at 17 Gordon St (03-523 8329; sleepin@inter.net.il). The manager maintains a Work List which job-seekers sign and wait their turn to be matched with a vacancy. Employers phone the hostel daily with offers of jobs in construction, cleaning, dishwashing and gardening. This system is used by other hostels including Momo's Hostel at 28 Ben Yehuda St (03-528 7471).

Eilat is an important yachting and diving centre. Vacancies are sometimes posted on the gates to the Marina or on the Marina notice board, but work as crew or kitchen staff, cleaners or au pairs is usually found by asking boat to boat. **Sarah Jane Smith** had the best time of her life in Eilat after she landed a job as a deckhand and hostess on a private charter yacht for scuba divers:

> *I was taken on cruises lasting between a week and a month to the Red Sea, Gulf of Suez, etc. to some of the best diving spots in the world. I was taught how to scuba dive and also did lots of snorkelling. I saw some of the most amazing sights of my life – the sun rising over Saudi Arabia as the moon sank into Egypt, coral reefs, sharks, dolphins, and so on.*
>
> *The social life on the marina was better than the kibbutz with hundreds of other travellers working on boats or in Eilat. Every night was a party and I hardly know how I survived it. The only bad thing is the low wages (if you get paid at all) and the hard work. But the harder you work and longer you stay, the better the wages and perks become.*

Au Pairing

Demand is high for live-in childcare and any plausible candidate should have no trouble finding a job, most of which last at least six months. The salary averages $650-$800 a month. Two of the principal agencies placing young European women are *Au Pair Intermediary* (5 Moholiver, PO Box 91, Rishon le Zion, Tel Aviv; 03-965 9937; hilma@netvision.net.il) and

Au Pair International (2 Desler St, Bnei Brak 51507; 03-619 0423).

Work Experience

The English language *Jerusalem Post* (Jerusalem Post Building, Romena, Jerusalem 91000; fax 02-377646) carries all kinds of job adverts from managerial positions to English-speaking secretaries, au pairs, etc. Friday is the best day.

The Weizmann Institute of Science (PO Box 26, Rehovat 76100; 08-957 1667; www.weizmann.ac.il) accepts research students with a minimum of one year of university study to assist with interdisciplinary scientific projects for 10-16 weeks in the summer, earning a small stipend.

VOLUNTARY WORK

Connect Youth International at the British Council (10 Spring Gardens, London SW1A 2BN; 020-7389 4030/ www.britishcouncil.org/education.connectyouth/programmes/eyp/ evs.htm) offers 150-200 volunteers aged 18-25 from the UK the opportunity to spend six weeks in Israel, working with groups of young people aged 9-15. Most teach English at summer language clubs in northern Israel. Volunteers work for five hours in the morning for at least two weeks in July/August. Food, accommodation and insurance are all provided and airfares are subsidised. The deadline for applications is mid-March. For more details contact connectyouth.enquiries@britishcouncil.org.

The Jewish/Arab village of Neve Shalom/Wahat al-Salaam (which means Oasis of Peace in Hebrew and Arabic) between Tel Aviv and Jerusalem accepts a few volunteers over the age of 16 to work in the guest house, school or gardens attached to the community's School for Peace. The minimum stay is six months. In addition to board and lodging, volunteers receive $50 a month pocket money. Details are available from the Volunteer Recruiter, 99761 Doar Na Shimshon (02-991 2222; www.nswas.com).

Several organisations can use voluntary assistance for Palestinian projects. The *Universities' Trust for Educational Exchange with Palestinians* or UNIPAL (BCM UNIPAL, London EC1N 3XX; www.unipal.org.uk) sends volunteers over the age of 20 to work on short-term summer projects with Palestinian teenagers. In theory these projects take place in the West Bank, Gaza and Lebanon; however because of concerns about security, volunteers over the past couple of summers have gone only to Lebanon. Most projects involve teaching English or work with children for which relevant qualifications or experience is preferred. Applications should be in by the end of February in time for interviews at Easter. Candidates must raise £380 to contribute to expenses including airfares.

Friends of Birzeit University has assisted the Palestinian Birzeit University near Ramallah in the occupied West Bank to recruit international volunteers for summer work camps though at present Birzeit University is unable to open and the scheme is in abeyance. In previous years volunteers built the area's first park and planted trees in the refugee camps. The current position can be checked with the Co-ordinator, Friends of Birzeit University, 1 Gough Square, London EC4A 3DE (020-7373 8414; www.fobzu.org).

In Nablus, the Zajel Youth Exchange Programme was established in 2001 to encourage interested young people from the west to spend time in Nablus and participate in short, medium or longer-term volunteer projects. Accommodation is provided free in university flats belonging to An-Najah National University. Further information is available from Zajel Programs Office in the university's Public Relations Department (9-238 1113/7; youthexchange@najah.edu/ www.najah.edu).

Christian organisations are active in Israel. Each summer *World Vision UK* (599 Avebury Boulevard, Milton Keynes, Bucks. MK9 3PG; 01908 841007; studentchallenge @worldvision.org.uk) sends teams of volunteers over the age of 19 to the Holy Land. Five weeks are spent among Palestinian people; expenses are covered by World Vision. To find out about voluntary opportunities in a Christian context, contact the Christian Information

Centre in Jerusalem (PO Box 14308, 91142 Jerusalem; 02-627 2692; cicinfo@cicts.org). It keeps a list of schools and institutes mainly for people with disabilities that take on volunteers.

Archaeology

Volunteers are needed to do the mundane work of digging and sifting on a range of archaeological digs. In the majority of cases, volunteers must pay a daily fee of $25-$35 to cover food and accommodation and sometimes twice that, plus a registration fee (typically $50-$75). Most camps take place during university holidays between May and September when temperatures soar. Volunteers must be in good physical condition and able to work long hours in hot weather. Valid health insurance is required.

Archaeology Abroad's bulletins contain a sprinkling of digs in Israel. Information on volunteering at archaeological digs in Israel is available on the website of the Israel Ministry of Foreign Affairs: www.israel-mfa.gov.il/archdigs.html. An example of an ongoing dig that accepts volunteers is the excavation of the ancient port of Yavneh Yam run by the Department of Classical Studies at Tel Aviv University (69978 Ramat-Aviv; fax 03-640 9457; yavneyam@post.tau.ac.il) where the charge is a hefty $700 for two weeks.

Jennifer McKibben, who worked on a kibbutz, in an Eilat hotel and on a dig in the Negev desert, waxed most enthusiastic about the latter experience:

Actually the work was often enjoyable but not usually before the sun had risen (it gets incredibly cold at nights in the desert). It did seem madness at times when a Land Rover would take a team of us out to an unremarkable spot in the desert marked only by a wooden peg, and we were told to start digging. I think the romance of excavations quickly fades once the blisters begin to appear and that long term camps are suitable only for the initiated or fanatic.

However despite the difficulties I really enjoyed the camp. Group relations were good – there were people of all nationalities – and there was normally a camp fire going with a couple of musicians. It was wonderful just to spend time in such a beautiful desert, to go off wandering over footprintless dunes, over great red hills to look and see no sign of civilisation. More practically, it was a cheap way to eat well for a couple of weeks, see another area and extend one's all-too-short stay in Israel.

COURSES

Many of the archaeological projects mentioned above plus others listed by *Archaeology Abroad* include lectures and seminars on the history of the period of the site being excavated and on archaeological techniques. These provide an excellent practical introduction to the field for anyone planning to study ancient history, archaeology or anthropology at university. It would also be a useful addition to the CV of those hoping to get into museum work after graduation.

As of June 2003, the Israeli Ministry of Foreign Affairs is offering scholarships to Britons and most other European nationalities. Funding of up to US$600 a month will be available for summer courses, year-long courses, ulpan and research in Jewish-related subjects, but with no restriction on the field of study. Applicants must already have a university degree and be under 35. Details from the Ministry website (www.mfa.gov.il; search for 'Scholarships').

As mentioned earlier, ulpan courses are offered alongside kibbutz stays. These normally last 5½ months and include instruction in conversational Hebrew, lectures on Israel and Judaism, seminars on contemporary events and educational tours. Ulpan students usually live in a part of the kibbutz set aside for them, sometimes in a complex with classrooms and study areas. The programme is designed mainly for Jewish students, and is open both to temporary visitors to Israel and prospective settlers. Non-Jewish students can enrol in the three-month Working Hebrew Scheme which is aimed at total beginners in the language. Places are limited and acceptance competitive. Enquiries should be addressed to Kibbutz Representatives (address above).

Many dive schools are centred on Eilat offering a range of scuba courses in the Red Sea including the basic qualification, the five-day PADI Open Water Diving course which starts from about £200 including equipment hire. The largest dive centre in Israel is the Red Sea Sports Club (Ambassador Hotel, Coral Beach, Eilat 8800; 08-637 6569/fax 08-637 0655; info@redseasports.co.il). One independent tour operator offering diving instruction in the Red Sea is Regal Dive (58 Lancaster Way, Ely, Cambs. CB6 3NW; 0870 2201 777; info@regal-diving.co.uk).

Latin America

Two or three decades ago, when everybody was flocking east, few adventurous young travellers from Britain considered South or Central America. Possibly because Britain has few colonial ties with that part of the world, it was less well known than India or Southeast Asia or Africa. With the recent decline in airfares to the Americas, the situation has changed and thousands of gap year students now head to that great Spanish-speaking continent (including Portuguese-speaking Brazil). They travel independently, go on adventure tours, join a grassroots voluntary organisation or sign up with one of the specialist gap year programmes which combine volunteering in community service or scientific research, language study and active travel.

PLACEMENT AGENCIES

The gap year placement organisation *Quest Overseas* (32 Clapham Mansions, Nightingale Lane, London SW4 9AQ; www.questoverseas.com) operates a 13-week package from January to April split into three phases: an intensive Spanish language course in Quito or Sucre followed by a month-long attachment to a voluntary project (either working with deprived urban children in Peru, conserving Ecuador's rainforest or working in animal rehabilitation in Bolivia) and finally the longest stint is an expedition in the Andes. Their website gives a good flavour of their trips as does their photo-filled brochure. The current cost excluding flights and insurance is £2,790-£3,985.

Gap year specialist *Venture Co* (The Ironyard, 64-66 The Market Place, Warwick CV34 4SD (01926 411122; www.ventureco-worldwide.com) combines Spanish language course, local aid projects and expeditions on 3 programmes lasting 4 months in Latin America. *Inca Venture:* Ecuador, Peru, Chile and Bolivia; *Patagonia Venture:* Peru, Bolivia, Chile, Argentina and Tierra del Fuego; and *Maya Venture:* Guatemala, Belize, Honduras, Mexico, Nicaragua, Costa Rica and Cuba. Programmes start with 3-week intensive Spanish course given in Quito (Ecuador), Cusco (Peru) and Antigua (Guatemala). Participants then spend 4 weeks on a local aid project before embarking on an 8 or 9 week expedition through the Andes (South America) or Central America to Cuba (Maya Venture).

Madventurer (Adamson House, 65 Westgate Road, Newcastle-upon-Tyne NE1 1SG; 0845 121 1996; team@madventurer.com) arranges summer and three-month expeditions to Peru, Bolivia and Chile (as well as Africa) combining voluntary work and adventure travel. The summer fee is from £1,870. A relative newcomer is *Outreach International* (Bartletts Farm, Hayes Road, Compton Dundon, Somerset TA11 6PF; ☎/fax: 01458 274957; www.outreachinternational.co.uk) which offers gap year programmes in Mexico (a country that is under-represented in the brochures of the main agencies) and in Ecuador. The Mexican programme includes Spanish instruction during a 3-4 month voluntary placement in orphanages, running a Feed the Children programme, organising sea turtle and whale conservation, arts and crafts project with the Huicholi Indians and English teaching in coastal primary schools. There are also projects working with dolphins and volunteering at the premier dance school in Mexico. In Ecuador compassionate volunteers are needed to help run a project for street children and to work at an orphanage. Opportunities are also available to work in the Amazon rainforest.

The main gap year organisations have links with the following countries: *GAP Activity Projects* send volunteers to Argentina, Brazil, Chile, Ecuador, Mexico, Paraguay, the Falkland Islands and (just recently added) Trinidad & Tobago; *Gap Challenge* run projects in Ecuador, Peru, Belize and Costa Rica; *Project Trust* offer possibilities in Honduras, Cuba, Bolivia, Chile, Peru, Guyana and the Dominican Republic; *i-to-i* arrange supported placements in teaching, health, building, conservation, care work, tourism, eco-tourism, museums, archeology and media in Bolivia, Honduras, Ecuador, El Salvador, Dominical Republic, Brazil, Guatemala, Peru and Costa Rica. Full training and Spanish lessons are included. Projects start at £995 (excluding flights). *Teaching Abroad* send volunteer English teachers to Bolivia, Chile, Peru and Mexico. See entries in the 'Directory of Specialist Gap Year Programmes' for dates, fees, etc. See section below on Expeditions for information on Raleigh International and other expedition organisers.

Church and mission societies are especially active in this part of the world and many take volunteers from the age of 18. One that has a programme tailored to gap year students is the *Toybox Charity* (PO Box 660, Amersham, Bucks, HP6 6EA; 01494 432591/ www.toybox.org), a Christian organisation working with street children and chronically impoverished communities in Guatemala. Its year-long Gap Year Challenge programme combines three and a half months working in Guatemala City with working in the UK to raise awareness of the bleak lives for these children. **Emma Roberts** from South London heard about Toybox through her church and decided to join the programme before going to Cambridge to read Classics. Although working with children from deeply troubled backgrounds (with drugs and prostitution rife on the streets), Emma did not find the experience depressing and has stayed in touch with the friends she made at the centre since her return.

Placements generally fall into one of two categories: community service/teaching in the cities or conservation in remote areas. *Trekforce* offers a five-month programme in Central America which combines conservation work with teaching in rural communities, as well as a language course, all of which appealed to **Kitty Hill** who is now studying medicine at Newcastle University:

I always knew I wanted to do a gap year, mainly because I knew that the nature of my course meant I would not really have the chance to do this sort of travelling again. I financed my gap year with six months of 60-hour weeks plus sponsorship. The trip cost £3,500 plus international flights (£500) and spending money (£1,000) which I did not consider unreasonable. The expedition was in three phases: the first six weeks were spent 12km into the jungle at the Cockscombe Jaguar Reserve in Belize. I slept in a hammock and blithely hacked up all spiders which came too close with my foot-long machete.

We built a cabana (sleeping hut thatched with kahuna palms) and dug two 8ft latrines inside cubicles in two separate locations on the trail up Victoria Peak. It is hoped that their presence will encourage eco-tourists to do the trail, bringing revenue to the local people and the conservation agency that runs the reserve.

The second and third phases were less closely supervised but with the safety net of support from Trekforce if needed. In three weeks at the Eco-Escuela on the shores of Lake Peten Itza in Guatemala I reached roughly Spanish GCSE standard. Not half bad, though I say so myself. Then I returned to Belize for the final stage of the Expedition. For two months I lived in a village and taught at the local primary school. Teaching was amazing. I worked mainly with small groups of younger kids, teaching reading and English and surprised myself with how much I enjoyed it, and how much I actually managed to teach the kids, who were often the slowest or the most badly behaved in the class. I really believe that my presence made a difference to how much they enjoyed school. At the same time the other Trekforce volunteer and I built a fence for the school vegetable garden to keep out the chickens and pigs and I am ridiculously proud of that fence.

I did find it quite lonely and isolating at times. It takes a great deal of self-reliance and is much harder than I imagined it would be. The good side of teaching is that you get to see a country from the inside. It sometimes annoys me that everyone is always so eager when advertising things like this and gloss over the fact that teaching and some of the projects are very hard, both physically and emotionally. But I did really enjoy it and am very glad I did it.

Non-Specialist Placement Organisations in the UK

The following accept gap year students for Latin American projects if they fulfil the requirements (which in several cases include strong Christian commitment) but they do not specialise in placing year-out students:

AFS Intercultural Programmes UK, Leeming House, Vicar Lane, Leeds LS2 7JF (0113-242 6136; info-unitedkingdom@afs.org/ www.afsuk.org). AFS is very active in South and Central America with community service programme lasting 6 months in Brazil, Costa Rica, Ecuador, Guatemala, Honduras, Mexico, Panama, Paraguay, Peru and Venezuela, for volunteers generally aged 18-29. Older applicants are also welcomed. Accommodation is arranged with host families. The cost for participating is £3,300. The Schools Programme for 15-18 year olds can be requested for a Latin American destination at a cost of £3,950. Fundraising support is offered to all participants.

Cactus Language, 4 Clarence House, 30-31 North St, Brighton BN1 1EB 0845 130 4775/ fax 01273 775868; enquiry@cactusenglish.com; www.cactusenglish.com). Spanish language courses followed by voluntary placements. Short and longterm placements in fields of healthcare, education, social work and conservation in Peru, Guatemala, Mexico, Bolivia and Ecuador. Examples include working at a hatchery for Leatherback turtles on Guatemala's Pacific Coast, helping in an orphanage for girls in Cusco, Peru and teaching English in a school in Oaxaca, Mexico.

Caledonia Languages Abroad, The Clockhouse, Bonnington Mill, 72 Newhaven Road, Edinburgh EH6 5QG (0131-621 7721/fax 0131-621 7723; info@caledonialanguages.co. uk/ www.caledonialanguages.co.uk). Educational consultancy which books individuals of any nationality onto voluntary work projects as well as language courses in Brazil, Costa Rica, Cuba, Argentina, Bolivia, Ecuador and Peru.

Challenges Worldwide, 13 Hamilton Place, Edinburgh EH3 5BA (0131-332 7372; www.challengesworldwide.com). Volunteer placements in Belize, Ecuador and several Caribbean Islands, in projects run by local governments, NGOs or community groups to address issues such as environmental/conservation challenges, human rights, rural development, poverty alleviation and social development.

EIL, 287 Worcester Road, Malvern, Worcs. WR14 1AB (0800 018 4015; www.eiluk.org) provides community service opportunities in Mexico and longer-term community service programme in Ecuador (3, 6, 9 or 11 months). The month-long project in Mexico involves re-forestation projects and food distribution to 'cardboard cities'. Ecuadorian projects are in civic projects or in a social environment (e.g. orphanage, cerebral palsy centre). Community service projects also available in Argentina, Chile and Guatemala.

Global Vision International (GVI), Nomansland, Wheathampstead, St. Albans, Herts. AL4 8EJ (01582 831300; info@gvi.co.uk/ www.gvi.co.uk). Placements from 2-20 weeks. Marine conservation expeditions in Mexico, work with street children in Guatemala, biodiversity expedition to the Amazon, turtle conservation in Panama and community/ conservation projects in Ecuador. Prices from £595 to £2,450.

ICYE: Inter-Cultural Youth Exchange, Latin American House, Kingsgate Place, London NW6 4TA (☎/fax 020-7681 0983; info@icye.co.uk/ www.icye.co.uk). International exchange organisation that sends students to spend a year abroad with a host family and undertake voluntary work placements, for example in drug rehabilitation, protection of street children and ecological projects. Placements available in Bolivia, Brazil, Costa Rica, Honduras, Colombia and Mexico.

Latin Link STEP Programme, 175 Tower Bridge Road, London SE1 2AB (020-7939 9014; step.uk@latinlink.org). Self-funded team-based building projects in Argentina, Bolivia, Brazil, Ecuador, Mexico, Cuba and Peru, for committed Christians only. Spring programme runs March to July; summer programme for 7 weeks from July.

MondoChallenge, Galliford Building, Gayton Rd, Milton Malsor, Northampton NN7 3AB (01604 858225; info@mondochallenge.org). Volunteer placement in the Monte Grande region north of Santiago close to La Serena. Teaching in several small mountain village schools.

Liga Millers thought that the mountain location in Northern Chile was beautiful:
The Elqui Valley is a perfect place with a stunning climate and I think it is a great location for MondoChallenge. I am having a fantastic time here and it is a shame that this is my last week. I will have lots of fond memories of singing in a choir, climbing in the mountains and seeing condors and chinchillas, enjoying various fiestas and barbecues, playing football and dominoes with the locals and looking at Jupiter from an observatory and jointly confirming the toxic effects of Pisco Sours.

Oasis Trust, 115 Southwark Bridge Road, London SE1 0AX (020-7450 9000; enquir ies@oasistrust.org). Short and long-term practical projects in slum areas run alongside local Christian groups and churches in Brazil and Peru. Applicants should be committed Christians.

SAMS (South American Mission Society), Unit 9, Prospect Business Park, Langston Road, Loughton, Essex IG10 3TR (☎/fax 020-8502 3504; persec@samsgb.org; www.samsgb.org). Committed Christians work as self-funding volunteers, particularly in English teaching and work with underprivileged children in Peru, Bolivia, Brazil, Paraguay, Uruguay, Argentina and Chile.

TASK Brasil (Trust for Abandoned Street Kids), PO Box 4091, London SE16 3PP (020-7394 1177; www.taskbrasil.org.uk). Volunteers over 21 work on the streets of Rio. Placements cost £1,200-£2,500.

Youth with a Mission, Highfield Oval, Harpenden, Herts AL5 4BX (01582 463216/ www.ywam.uk.com). Projects working with street children followed by discipleship training in Brazil, Bolivia and Colombia for committed Christians.

Organisations in the US

American Friends Service Committee, 1501 Cherry St, Philadelphia, Pennsylvania 19102-1479, USA (215-241-7295; mexsummer@afsc.org). A Quaker organisation which recruits Spanish-speaking volunteers aged 18-26 to work for seven weeks in the summer mostly on building or teaching projects in Mexico (programme fee $900 plus travel expenses) and Cuba ($750).

AmeriSpan, PO Box 58129, Philadelphia, PA 19102 or 117 S 17th St, Suite 1401, Philadelphia, PA 19103 (800-879-6640 or 215-751-1100; info@amerispan.com; www.amerispan.com). Language training organisation which arranges internships lasting 2 weeks to 6 months in many Spanish-speaking countries.

Amigos de las Americas, 5618 Star Lane, Houston, Texas 77057 (800-231-7796; www.amigoslink.org). Runs a training programme each summer for more than 700 volunteers from the age of 16 for six to eight weeks to work mostly in community health projects in Mexico, Costa Rica, the Dominican Republic, Brazil, Honduras, Nicaragua, Bolivia and Paraguay. The fee for participation is roughly $3,200 including travel from the US. All volunteers must have studied Spanish at school or university and undergone training.

Amizade Volunteer Vacations, 920 William Pitt Union, PA 15260 (888-973-4443; volunteer@amizade.org; www.amizade.org). Short-term community service volunteer programme in Brazil and Bolivia. Cost about $2,600. Longer term opportunities in Bolivia.

Casa Alianza, SJO 1039, PO Box 025216, Miami, FL 33102-5216 (volunteer@casa-alianza.org; www.casa-alianza.org). Volunteers work with street children in Mexico City, Guatemala City, Tegucigalpa and Managua for 6-12 months. Accommodation varies according to country e.g. $70 a month in Nicaragua but up to $200 in Honduras.

Cuban Studies Institute, Center for Latin American Studies, Tulane University, Caroline Richardson Building, New Orleans, LA 70118 (504-862-8629; cuba@tulane.edu; http://intern.tulane.edu). Internships and rural homestays in Ecuador, Mexico and Cuba. 6 weeks costs $3,600.

EcoLogic Development Fund, PO Box 383405, Cambridge MA 02238-3405 (617-441-6300; www.ecologic.org). Recruits university students and professionals to work as interns and volunteers in Central America, in the fields of conservation, community development and social justice. Relevant expertise is normally needed for minimum 3-month attachments to partner organisations.

Foundation for Sustainable Development, 59 Driftwood Court, San Rafael, CA 90490 (415-482-9366; info@fsdinternational.org; www.interconnection.org/fsd). Summer and longer term internships for anyone over 18 in the field of development in Bolivia, Costa Rica, Peru, Ecuador and Nicaragua. Except for Ecuador, volunteers must be able to converse in Spanish.

The God's Child Project, 721 Memorial Highway, PO Box 1573, Bismarck, ND 58502-1573 (www.godschild.org) provides an education for slum children in Antigua and uses short- and long-term volunteers who pay about $50 a week and live with a local family after doing a Spanish course.

ICADS, Apartado 300-2050 San Pedro Montes de Oca, San José, Costa Rica (506-225 0508; icads@netbox.com; www.icadscr.com). The well regarded programmes of the Institute for Central American Development Studies combine study of the Spanish language and development issues with structured internships in Costa Rica and Nicaragua lasting a semester ($7,900) or a summer ($3,600).

WorldTeach, Center for International Development, Harvard University, 79 John F Kennedy St, Cambridge MA 02138 (617-495-5527; www.worldteach.org). Sends fee-paying college graduates to teach English for nine months in Costa Rica, Ecuador and Mexico.

EXPEDITIONS

Raleigh International, 27 Parsons Green Lane, London SW6 4HZ (020-7371 8585; www.raleighinternational.org). Chile is the longest running expedition country for Raleigh International. Projects take place in Region XI and offer a diversity of projects which might involve kayaking among sea lions, working with scientists from the Natural History Museum and tracking endangered species. Two others are in Central America: Costa Rica and Nicaragua. Applicants attend an introduction weekend and are asked to fundraise £3,500.

Jessica Green had no difficulty describing her Raleigh expedition to Chile in glowing terms when she wrote to thank her sponsors for their support:

I have just finished the expedition and have experienced the most amazing ten weeks of my life. My first project was in marine research which involved assisting senior marine biologists from the Natural History Museums of London and Santiago in describing, mapping and classifying marine life and habitats near San Rafael Laguna. The work included collecting samples of organisms, mapping penguin and sea lion colonies and surveying the shore profile. The project was exhausting but very rewarding. In order to access our base camp for the duration of the project we travelled for 20 hours aboard the cargo vessel the 'Austral III' to the Laguna. From there we spent four days man-handling inflatable boats, outboard engines, fuel and three weeks worth of rations over a 3km swamp to reach a navigable river system flowing into the study area. The scenery was spectacular; from my tent on Devil's

Island I looked over a white sand beach, a bay and sand dunes to the San Quentin Glacier. The experience of being in complete wilderness, somewhere that very few people have been able to access, was exceptional and has really helped me appreciate home comforts like plumbing, gas cookers and fresh food.
Phase II brought me back into relative civilisation (although still no plumbing or gas). Raleigh International is working to build accommodation at an existing day centre for old people in Coyhaique. In the three weeks that I worked on the site we managed to finish the foundations and lay all the floors. It is hoped that the next expedition will complete the work. The project proved an enormous challenge and I can now understand why builders take so many tea breaks, since cement mixing and floor-laying are very hard work.
Phase III took me sea kayaking, again in the San Rafael Glacier area. Between lengthy paddles and beach campsites, we were given basic training in the sport. One most memorable experience was our paddle across the glacier face through and over pack ice and icebergs. The experience was almost spiritual, with the sun shining and the water completely flat, just the sound of the huge chunks of ice falling off the glacier face. I feel immensely privileged that I have been able to see such spectacular scenery, and to work with great people. I have learned lots about myself and others.

Coral Cay Conservation, The Tower, 13th Floor, 125 High Street, Colliers Wood, London SW19 2JG (0870 750 0668; www.coralcay.org) runs expeditions in Honduras to survey the coral reefs and establish a database for coastal zone management. More recently it has introduced both reef and rainforest projects in Mexico and Cuba. A sample six-week terrestrial project would cost £1,150. A sample 6-week marine project would cost £1,800 (£2,200 for dive trainee). Prices exclude flights and insurance.

Greenforce (11-15 Betterton Street, London WC2H 9BP; 0870 770 2646/020-7470 8888; info@greenforce.org/ www.greenforce.org) is looking for volunteers to join wildlife survey projects in the Peruvian Amazon. Projects involve studying endangered species and habitats. No previous experience is necessary as training is given in the UK and in Peru. The cost is £2,550 plus flight.

Operation Wallacea, Hope House, Old Bolingbroke, Nr Spilsby, Lincolnshire PE23 4EX (01790 763194; info@opwall.com). Volunteer students, divers and naturalists assist with surveys of marine and rainforest habitats in Northern Honduras.

Trekforce Expeditions (34 Buckingham Palace Road, London SW1W 0RE; 020-7828 2275/fax 020-7828 2276; info@trekforce.org.uk/ www.trekforce.org.uk) organise and run conservation projects in the rainforests of Belize, Central America and in the Amazon jungle of Guyana, South America. The expeditions last 8, 12 or 20 weeks and offer a week of comprehensive jungle training followed by seven weeks of conservation teamwork on a challenging project. There is also the opportunity to trek into different areas of the country. The longer programmes involve expedition work followed by a phase of learning Spanish in Guatemala or Spanish/Portuguese in Brazil for a month and then teaching in rural communities for a further two months. Each expedition's project varies and in the past has included building a research centre in a jaguar reserve, or working in support of scientific research with the Natural History Museum. Help and advice on fundraising are given at introduction days and initial training is also given in the UK prior to departure.

An interesting volunteer placement scheme is run by *Native English,* a language school run by a Briton in Cuiabá (Rua Sao Benedito 306, Bairro Lixeira, Cuiabá 78.008-100; steve@terra.com.br) whereby gap year and other students provide English conversation practice and in return are taken on trips around the region to Amazonian villages, national parks, etc. The scheme offers the option of shadowing someone in an area of interest (surgeon, anthropologist, banker, naturalist); the gap year student gives the professional the chance to speak English while at the same time being exposed to that profession. Volunteers stay 3-6 months on a tourist visa and are not paid; the fee is £150 a month.

Expeditions form the final part of the programmes in South America run by Quest Overseas, as a reward for taking Spanish classes and helping on a voluntary project. For many, like **Ronan O'Kelly** who spent the first five months of 2003 with Quest Overseas, the expedition proved a fitting end to an exhilarating gap year experience:

The Quito phase was an absolute blast (though surprisingly we actually learned some Spanish!) as were the weekends off. The Yachana Project, though challenging at times (chicken feet soup took some getting used to), was a hugely fulfilling and fantastic experience. And the final phase, the expedition, really was the culmination of all the great things of the previous months. It should be taken as a compliment that the only real criticism I could find was that we did too much. I've never been so tired in my life; but likewise, never before have I fulfilled so much.

A similar scheme is run by Venture Co.

LANGUAGE COURSES

As mentioned earlier in this book, trends show that increasing numbers of people are learning Spanish. Whereas most prospective learners think of developing their language skills in Spain, more and more are looking to the many Spanish-speaking countries of South and Central America, particularly Ecuador, Peru, Mexico and Costa Rica. A number of schools have been working very hard to bring their courses, whether in travellers' survival Spanish or in advanced Spanish, to the attention of potential clients in Europe and North America. Not only are the prices very competitive when compared to courses in Spanish cities, but you are likely to receive a warmer welcome if staying with a family.

Many cultural exchange organisations and Spanish language course providers can advise or even place their 'graduates' in voluntary positions and internships where they will have a chance to immerse themselves in the Spanish language. Both *Caledonia Languages Abroad* and *Cactus Language* mentioned above can send detailed information about their courses and voluntary programmes in South and Central America. For example Caledonia offer a combined language study and volunteering programme, e.g. three weeks Spanish tuition in Peru followed by three weeks of voluntary work on the island of Amantani working within a traditional community environment (fees are £1,120 including 6 weeks accommodation). Keri Craig's successful time in Costa Rica arranged by Caledonia makes it clear why Costa Rica is another favourite destination for people who want to learn Spanish:

Everyone at the school was friendly and so helpful, whether it was organising extra classes or booking hotels at the weekend. My teacher Gaby was wonderful and my Spanish improved no end having endless gossips with Gaby each afternoon. Considering my Spanish was very basic, I was very pleased with the way it developed so quickly. It was certainly an advantage being so immersed in the culture. The dance classes after school were my particular favourite. Frank and Victor were amazing teachers and soon had us salsa-ing like the locals. My only complaint would be the Thursday night dance class outing – European boys just can't dance like the Latin men!

Gala Spanish in Spain offers intensive language courses and optional cultural programmes in various locations in South America. *CESA* is also expanding its operations in South America. **Lucy Jackson**, one of CESA's satisfied customers who studied Spanish in Ecuador after finishing university, describes how her apprehensions about travelling so far from home were soon dispelled:

I was very tired and very nervous. I was on the other side of the world from home and didn't know a soul. My fears had been fuelled by my dad who, prior to the flight, had been posting me every report on attacks on foreigners in South America. I was entirely ignorant of the continent, let alone Ecuador and had no idea what to expect from the language course in Cuenca or the two months I had set aside to travel around Ecuador and Peru with a friend. I went to refresh my very rusty Spanish and to explore a part of the world friends told me was amazing.

The most memorable aspect of my experience has to be the openness of the Ecuadorian people. During my degree I spent a year in France and it took a good three months before the French opened up enough to go out with me. Yet in Cuenca it took no more than a week and I'm still in touch with most of them now. People always wanted to help and rarely did I feel unsafe, despite my father's dire warnings.

Lessons were intensive and concentrated on grammar, oral work and consolidating lessons. We also had homework every night, which was a novelty for a uni graduate. At the end of the course I had improved way beyond my lapsed A-level ability. The combination of teacher enthusiasm, small classes (up to five) and the range of student nationalities ensured good progress. The fact that I had to speak Spanish with my host family every day was the icing on the cake. I loved the school. I was impressed by the organisation, the standard of the teachers and the extracurricular activities, e.g. cooking classes, regional and Latin American dance classes and excursions to craft villages, national parks and jungles.

Language schools in Latin America often follow up a Spanish language course with a volunteer programme such as:

APF Languages, Ave. Colon 2277 & Ulloa, Quito, Ecuador (02-2234 268; www.apflanguages.com). Combined programme of Spanish tuition with homestays and ecological or humanitarian volunteering.

Casa Xelaju, Apartado Postal 302, Quetzaltenango, Guatemala (502-761-5954; www.casaxelaju.com). Spanish courses, internships and voluntary work in Guatamala. The city of Quetzaltenango offers many opportunities to do volunteer work in the community. In exchange for a fee of $25 Casa Xelaju will search for a suitable position.

Eco-Escuela de Espanol, Calle Centromerica, Ciudad Flores, Petén 17001, Guatemala (☎/fax 502-926-3202). Language students assist local conservation projects through Ecomaya International (Calle Centroamérica Flores, Petén, Guatemala; 502-926-3202; ecomaya@guate.net; www.ecomaya.com).

Equinoccial Spanish School, Reina Victoria 1325 y Lizardo Garcia, Quito, Ecuador (011-593-2-256 4488; www.ecuadorspanish.com/en/voluntarywork). Language school that arranges unpaid environmental or community work.

Latin American Language Network, www.latinimmersion.com. Language study and internship programmes in Argentina and Chile listed on website.

Mar de Jade, US postal address: PMB 078-344, 705 Martens Court, Laredo, TX 78041-6010 (☎/fax 322 21171; www.mardejade.com). Project located on the Pacific coast of Mexico in Chacala, Nayarit, near Puerto Vallarta. Volunteer-study programme includes 3 hours of Spanish tuition daily, 15 hours of community work per week.

Nicaragua Spanish Schools, De la Rotonda Bello Horizonte, 4 cuadras al sur, 3 cuadras abajo, 1/2 cuadra al sur, casa # L-II-4, (Apartado SL-145), Managua, Nicaragua (☎/fax: +505-244-1699 or in US 805-687-9941; http://pages.prodigy.net/nss-pmc). Group of 3 schools in Managua, Nicaragua offering Spanish and cultural immersion.

San Francisco Language Institute, Av. Amazonas N22-62 y Ramírez Dávalos Edificio Vasconez, Oficina # 202, Quito, Ecuador (02-252-1306; isflc@uio.satnet.net; www.sanfranciscospanish.com). Study Spanish and volunteer work at the Asociación Exedra-María which runs pre-school education centers in the province of Pichincha. Practical training and voluntary work placements in public hospitals, law and accounting firms, travel agencies, education or according to student's preferences.

For other Spanish language courses, check entries for the following in the 'Directory of Language Courses': *CEDIC* in Buenos Aires; *Bridge-Linguatec International* with schools in Santiago, Rio de Janeiro and Buenos Aires at which you might be able to teach English while learning Spanish; *Academia de Espanol, Academia de Espanol Superior Simon Bolivar* and *Ruta del Sol* all in Quito; the *Costa Rica Spanish Institute, La Escuela de Idiomas d'Amore* and *Intercultura Language and Cultural Centre* in Costa Rica; *La Union Language School* in Guatemala; *CIS* in San Salvador; and *Experienca Centro de Intercambio Bilingue, Institute of Modern Spanish, Instituto Allende, Instituto Chac-Mool* and *OLE* in Mexico.

PAID WORK

It will not be easy for a school leaver to find paid work or work experience opportunities in South or Central America. Although demand is ubiquitous for English teachers, from dusty towns on the Yucatan Peninsula of Mexico to Punta Arenas at the southern extremity of the continent, south of the Falkland Islands, most of the customers are business people looking for something more professional than what most gap year students can offer in the way of conversation practice. Furthermore, in a land where baseball is a passion and US television enormously popular, American (and also Canadian) job-seekers have an advantage. More detailed information about teaching in Latin America can be found in the 2003 edition of *Teaching English Abroad* (£12.95 from bookshops and Vacation Work Publications).

But there are always exceptions. **Eleanor Padfield** was determined to work abroad after finishing her A-levels in June 2000 but without going through an agency where she would be with lots of other British students. After spending the first half of her year in Salamanca, Spain, she sent e-mails all over the world to fix up something to do, preferably in Latin America. Of the many schools and language schools she contacted, one of the few to reply was the Redland School in Chile (Camino El Alba 11357, Las Condes, Santiago), an upmarket private school. Although they told her that they didn't normally accept gap year students (since so many previous gappers had left prematurely to travel), they made an exception for Eleanor when she promised to stick it out till the end of the term beginning in March and ending in August. By June she was tempted to leave early but her conscience (or her mother's exhortations) persuaded her to keep her promise, though she was availing herself of any available free time to see some of Chile.

Mónica Boza recommends Cusco Peru as a promising place to pick up casual jobs in clubs like Mama Africa, Ukukus (which has the best bartenders in town), Eco, Up Town and Keros all near the main square. Few corners of the world have escaped the fashion for Irish pubs; in Cusco, try Paddy Flaherty and Rosie O'Gradys on Santa Catalina St. Similarly in the cities of Ecuador check at internet cafés such as Jamba, the Café Sutra or Pizza Net in Quito's 'Gringotown'.

People interested in taking a post-university gap year will find it easier to fix up a teaching post than will younger people. If you have a good standard of education, are carrying all your references and diplomas and are prepared to stay for an academic year, it is possible to fix up a teaching contract. After graduation, Judith Twycross received three job offers within a week of arriving in Bolivia's second city Cochabamba. Judith timed her arrival in Cochabamba so as to be a couple of weeks before the beginning of the winter term. With the advantage of a good knowledge of Spanish, she soon found employment:

> I took with me a letter of introduction and a CV both in Spanish plus a photocopy of my degree certificate. These I photocopied and delivered by hand to the directors of schools and institutes in Cochabamba. I got a list of schools from the Yellow Pages (which you could borrow at a hotel, photocopying kiosk, tourist information office, etc.). I told everyone I met what I was trying to do and received help and advice from hotel managers, taxi drivers and people I stopped on the street to ask for directions.

Leaving England for the first time, Linda Harrison travelled on a one-way ticket straight from the picturesque Yorkshire town of Kirkbymoorside to the picturesque state of Michoacàn, and suffered severe culture shock. She and a Spanish-speaking friend had pre-arranged jobs at the *Culturlingua Language Center* (Plaza Jardinadas, Local 24 y 25, Zamora, Michoacàn). Although it provided accommodation, it offered no pre-service training:

> *The director told me that I might as well start teaching the day after I arrived. I stumbled into my first class with no experience, qualifications or books. Twelve expectant faces watched while I nervously talked about England. Twelve faces went blank when I mentioned soap operas.*

The *British Council* arranges for language assistants to work in local secondary schools and higher education institutions in a number of Latin American countries for a year. Applicants must be aged 20-30 with at least A-level Spanish and preferably a degree in modern languages. Application forms are available from October for a December deadline.

English is of course not the only thing that can be taught. The flourishing skiing industry of Chile and Argentina creates some openings for ski instructors. A Scottish firm called Peak Leaders UK Ltd (Mansfield, Strathmiglo, Fife KT14 7QE; 01337 860079; www.peakleaders.co.uk) runs snowboard and ski instructor courses in the popular resort of Bariloche in Argentine Patagonia with trips to Chile and Buenos Aires, specifically for gap year and timeout students. The nine-week course (August to October) costs £5,950.

Work experience placements in Brazil are arranged by several mediating agencies include *CCUSA (Camp Counsellors USA), AFS* and *Cultural Cube*. CCUSA offers a choice of office work, sports jobs, hotel/tourism placements or working with children mainly in Sao Paulo but also in Florianópolis and Vitória (both islands) plus Rio de Janeiro.

One of the more surprising agencies to pop up in the past year or two is *Guatenannies* with an entry in the 'Directory of Paid Work'. Nannying in Guatemala is not a concept that will have occurred to many people, but this is more a cultural and language exchange.

VOLUNTARY WORK

Short-term voluntary work projects are scattered over this vast continent, and many of the opportunities are for Spanish-speakers. If you happen to have any contacts with a charity operating in South America, there is every chance you will be invited to spend time. For example during Eleanor Padfield's campaign to fill her gap year, she heard from her aunt about a Methodist mission in southern Bolivia (in a town the *Rough Guide* labels the armpit of the universe) who told her she was welcome to come and help. She helped generally with the chores and found the experience fascinating.

The internet has made it much easier to unearth opportunities for volunteering, whether from one of the mainstream databases like eVolunteer.co.uk or WorkingAbroad.com or from indigenous organisations. For instance the excellent online guide to Ecuador EcuadorExplorer.com has listings and links of teaching and voluntary work as well as what to do. In some cases a centralised placement service makes choosing a project much easier, though you will have to pay for the service as in the case of Volunteer Bolivia (wwww.volunteerbolivia.org) located in Cochabamba. They encourage their clients to sign up for a month of Spanish tuition while staying with a local family before becoming a volunteer; a combined language course, homestay and volunteer placement programme costs $740 for one month.

The student service organisation ProPeru (PO Box 21121, Billings, MT 59104-1121; 877-733-7378; info@properu.org/ www.properu.org) offers a range of internships lasting one to six months with aid agencies throughout Peru, mainly suitable for a post-university gap. The fee of $1,900 includes Spanish tuition, placement and lodgings for the first four weeks plus local transport.

Combining a Spanish language course, homestay and voluntary placement over two to six months is a route favoured by many. Spanish language course providers and cultural exchange organisations can often arrange such a programme. Among the largest are the following:

Grassroots Voluntary Organisations

Casa de los Amigos, Ignacio Mariscal 132, 06030 D.F. Mexico City (055-5705 0521; convive@avantel.net). Quaker-run guest house and service centre in Mexico City which actively matches volunteers and interns to local voluntary organisations as part of its Convive Programme. The initial fee is $50 plus $25 per month to cover admin expenses. The Casa provides simple accommodation to people involved in volunteer projects. The Casa's information centre has listings of volunteer opportunities throughout Mexico and Central America as well as other useful things such as Spanish language courses.

Casa Guatemala office, 14th Calle 10-63, Zona 1, 01001 Guatemala (Apdo. Postal 5-75-A; 502-232-5517; casaguatemal@guate.net; www.casa-guatemala.org). Orphanage and attached backpackers' hostel which relies on travellers to carry out maintenance, cooking, building, organic gardening, teaching the children English, etc. They can use as many as 100 volunteers a year preferably for a minimum of three months. The orphanage itself is about five hours north of Guatemala City, a short boat ride from the town of Fronteras on the road to the Petén region. Volunteers must pay a non-refundable fee of $180 however long they intend to stay. UK contact: Pete Brown, 30 Church Road, Upton, Wirral CH49 6JZ; 0151-606 0729.

Genesis Volunteer Program, Malecon 1312 y Ascazubi St, Bahía, Ecuador (05-692400; www.bahiacity.com/volunteer). Foreign travellers to Ecuador are invited to teach for a couple of hours a day in one of four schools in the coastal town of Bahía de Caráquez. Free local accommodation provided near beach and chance to take subsidised Spanish classes at the Escuela de Español.

One of the most acute problems in many South American cities is the number of street children. Working with one of the many charities that are tackling this problem can be both discouraging and rewarding by turns, as recounted by a volunteer in Quito for *CENIT* (Spanish acronym for Centre for the Working Girl) with an entry in the 'Directory of Voluntary Placements':

My name is Heidi and I am 20 years old. It is almost two months since I got to know CENIT, and I am so glad I started working here! What made me interested in this job is that we get in direct contact with the children in the street. There are five different sectors where the volunteers do outreach work. I work from 9.30am to 12.30pm, which is when we do most of the outreach work in the street. I have worked mostly in three sectors: the Camal Marketplace, the Villaflora (an urban neighborhood) and the local trolley station. When we walk through the big Camal market to gather the kids (aged 2-10) to play, there are usually some shy kids and parents, while other kids run towards us and their parents are happy to see us. I feel that the work in the Camal is very rewarding because you see the benefits then and there: the kids are happy to get a break from working with their parents, and the parents are happy to have a little while free from their kids.

At one of the other sectors where we work (Villaflora), we have gotten to know kids, mostly boys, between the ages of 11 and 17. These kids are true street kids since they sleep and eat on the street. Most of the volunteers love hanging out with these kids, but it is hard as well since these kids use drugs (they sniff glue).

The hard thing about this work, I think, is that sometimes I feel really useless. Often in the mornings we can sit for sometimes half an hour without any kids wanting to play with us. It happens as well occasionally that the kids don t want to talk to us at all. What is important to always keep in mind, though, is that these kids are living hard lives with a lot of abuse and abandonment. Our job is to show them there are responsible, caring adults in this world. We have to build up trust with them. Just the fact that the kids want to play with us and even come to CENIT to eat with us is a big step. Establishing this trust is not easy – it takes loads of time and many volunteers to get that far. Most of the days I have a wonderful time playing with the kids, though, and the thought that maybe one of these kids will go back to school one day makes everything worthwhile.

Conservation

An increasing number of organisations, both indigenous and foreign-sponsored, is involved in environmental projects throughout the continent. Many placements can be pre-arranged in exchange for a fee which may be equivalent to the price of a holiday. For example the Volunteer Galapagos programme (on which volunteers teach English or sport) costs about $50 a day for the first month, a third as much thereafter. Details are available in the UK from 58 Springfield Park Road, Chelmsford, Essex CM2 6EN (0845 124 9338; www.volunteergalapagos.org). A cheaper way of spending time in those famous islands is to become an International Volunteer with the Darwin Foundation (External Relations Unit, Charles Darwin Research Station, Casilla Postal 17-01-3891, Quito, Ecuador; 011-593-552-6146/147; volunteer@darwinfoundation.org). Self-funding volunteers without relevant scientific skills pay $11 a day for food and dormitory accommodation and must stay for a minimum of six months.

Staying on the mainland will be much cheaper. If in Ecuador, investigate the Ecotrackers Network (www.ecotrackers.com) which charges $45 to register plus $2 a day while you're on a project. For ecological projects in Ecuador that need volunteer input, see the entries for *FBU* and the *Fundacion Jatun Sachu* in the 'Directory of Voluntary Placements' and *Amili* in 'the Directory of Work Experience'.

The highest concentration of projects is probably in Ecuador and also in Costa Rica where the National Parks Authority runs a voluntary programme *Asociacion de Voluntarios para el Servicio en las Areas Protegidas* (ASVO). To be eligible you must be willing to work for at least one or two months, be able to speak Spanish and provide two letters of recommendation from Costa Ricans or an organisation in your home country. The work may consist of trail maintenance and construction, greeting and informing visitors, research or generally assisting rangers. Details are available from the Director, International Volunteer Program, Servicio de Parques Nacionales, Apdo. 11384-1000, San José 10104-1000 (506-257 0922; www.asvocr.com). Food and accommodation cost about $12 a day.

BUNAC has introduced a volunteering programme in Costa Rica under the auspices of the student organisation OTEC who provide back-up during the three to six month placement. Students (including gap year students) and recent graduates can participate if they have intermediate level Spanish. The programme fee for 2003 is £425 for three months, £525 for six months plus volunteers will need funds to cover their living expenses. Many other UK agencies like i-to-i run volunteer programmes in Costa Rica.

Trawling the internet for other eco-projects in Central and South America will turn up lots of lively possibilities. For example in a remote corner of Surinam you can monitor nesting sea turtles with STINASU, the Foundation for Nature Conservation in Surinam (research@stinasu.sr; www.stinasu.sr/volunteers_stm.html). They accept volunteers from February to September and expect a minimum contribution of $100.

A project in Brazil charges volunteers a reasonable $500 for three months of donating their time to carry out rainforest conservation (Iracambi, Rosário da Limeira, 36878-000 Minas Gerais, Brazil (055-32 3721 1436; www.iracambi.com). Volunteers at the remote Picaflor Research Centre in Peru (Casilla 105, Puerto Maldonado, Madre de Dios; ☎/fax 084-572589; www.picaflor.org) can stay for $10 a day provided they spend half the day clearing trails, painting boats, etc. For animal lovers the Inti Wara Yassi wildlife reserve accepts volunteers to help care for injured animals (english@intiwarayassi.org). Many volunteer possibilities are available in national parks etc. through the EcoVolunteer Program Brazil (www.br.ecovoluntarios.org).

Foreign guides are occasionally hired by expatriate or even local tour operators. For example the Tambopata Jungle Lodge (PO Box 454, Cusco, Peru; ☎/fax 084-245695;

www.tambopatalodge.com) takes on guides for a minimum of six months who must have formal training in the natural sciences and (preferably) speak Spanish, all of which should be indicated on a CV. Information about the resident naturalist programme and research opportunities in the same area can be sought in the UK from TreeS, the Tambopata Reserve Society, c/o John Forrest, PO Box 33153, London NW3 4DR). Guides for the naturalist programme must be graduate biologists, environmental scientists or geographers over the age of 20. They receive free room and board throughout their stay.

Andrew James was there in his gap year (before they began insisting on a background in biology):

> We lived in a jungle camp consisting of wooden lodges a four-hour boat trip up the Tambopata River from Puerto Maldonado. I was one of three English guides who took visitors of all nationalities in groups of about five on dawn walks to explore the rainforest and see the amazing plant life and the occasional animal. I was there for three months and was paid $150 a month for working 20 days a month with the other ten days free to do research or live it up in Puerto Maldonado (a town straight out of the Wild West).

The organisation *Rainforest Concern* (27 Lansdowne Crescent, London W11 2NS; 020-7229 2093; info@rainforestconcern.org) supports various projects in Central and South America (as well as Asia). Students and volunteers who are prepared to work for part of the day receive subsidised accommodation and meals and can stay at a cloud forest lodge in Ecuador or turtle projects in Panama and Costa Rica. *Quest Overseas* co-operates with Rainforest Concern by sending gap year volunteers to the Santa Lucia Cloudforest Reserve and to a project in and around the River Napo, both in Ecuador.

Travel

Journey Latin America and *South America Explorers* have already been recommended in the introductory chapter on 'Travel'. The alternative San Francisco-based tour company *Green Tortoise* offers tours of Costa Rica and Central America in one of their specially adapted sleeper-buses; details from 415-956-7500 or www.greentortoise.com.

Independent travellers should exercise a reasonable amount of caution. Not long ago a gap year student from London was shot and wounded by bandits who held up a bus he was travelling on between Quito and Lima. The Foreign Office advises people not to travel on public transport late at night, though for some journeys this is unavoidable; the Quito-Lima trip takes the better part of two days and two nights. Ecuador was the scene of another accident whose outcome was more tragic when a gap year student was electrocuted by a falling cable in a freak accident.

Many gap years in Peru centre on the classic Inca Trail to Machu Picchu. This is a fairly strenuous high altitude hike which takes four days confortably (three days minimum). In order to control numbers, the authorities now insist that hikers travel together in groups of nine and camp only in designated areas. All walkers must pay a registration fee.

The Caribbean

The islands of the Caribbean are far too expensive to explore unless you do more than sip rum punch by the beach. Few agencies make placements in the Caribbean, though a few are active in Cuba.

One exception is *Challenges Worldwide* which sends volunteers to several islands including Antigua, which is where Lucy Bale spent a fantastic three months at the beginning of her gap year:

Antigua was paradise compared to the rat-race I had been running four months earlier in England, work, exams, stress... It was peaceful, hot and friendly and my decision to volunteer with Challenges Worldwide was a good one. Being placed at a refuge for victims of domestic violence was a bonus I could have only dreamed of. There was never a dull moment. My duties included teaching at The Learning Centre pre-school, where I had responsibility for the 4+ age group, preparing them for primary school and teaching the basics in Maths, Reading, Writing and Science. The 'little darlings' were noisy, boisterous and naughty, much tougher than their UK counterparts but with their wide smiles, innocent eyes and broken dialect it was hard not to be amused by these colourful characters. I was also charged with teaching teachers of the Youth Skills Training Programme, a local vocational college, a task I found daunting at the start. They were educated and eager to learn; I, on the other hand, am young, inexperienced and with no formal qualifications. What could I possibly teach them? I needn't have worried, since they were very appreciative of my time and skills. Our work in Antigua was useful and good fun. The staff looked after us with true Caribbean hospitality and we were spoilt rotten!

It was definitely not all work and no play during my three-month placement. Famed for its cricket, rum, beaches and laid-back atmosphere, Antigua certainly doesn't disappoint. A short 20-minute walk from the project is Fort James beach, a gorgeous stretch of white sand, palm trees and clear blue sea – the perfect Caribbean image. And there are plenty like it. Well, 365 according to the locals, though we failed to find them all.

If you're preparing for Antigua, pack a mossie net, bikini, sun lotion and a good sense of humour. Prepare for hard work, lots of rice and male attention ('hey white girl, sexy one' being the common greeting from male passers-by). Make the most of it, time flies by and before you know it, you'll be where I am, working in an office by day, pulling pints by night scraping money together for university. I had a fantastic three months, made loads of good friends and would jump at the chance to do it again. My only regret: missing Carnival! Well there's always next year.

A number of gap year students have managed to spend time in this exotic part of the world by working for their keep, mostly on yachts.

Research opportunities exist as well. The Bermuda Biological Station for Research Inc. (Ferry Reach, St. George's, GE01 Bermuda; www.bbsr.edu) accepts students throughout the year to help scientists carry out their research and to do various jobs around the station in exchange for room and board. Volunteer interns from around the world are chosen on the basis of their academic and technical backgrounds. Summer is the peak period (applications must be in by February); otherwise apply at least four months in advance. Applicants should make personal contact with the faculty member(s) for whom they wish to work and applications should be sent direct to those faculty members. The section 'Graduate/Undergraduate Opportunities' on the website provides a list of faculty members who are looking for volunteer interns.

Cuba's economy is suffering badly from its position in world politics, but its music and vibrant culture attract some prospective year-out students. The Project Trust is one of the few UK organisations to offer Cuba as a destination, something that **Nicholas Scott** was quick to notice when he started planning his gap year. Not only did Cuba appeal because of its interesting history in terms of international relations (the course Nicholas planned to pursue) but he had spent his infancy there. He enjoyed the chance to 'party and relax, soak up the atmosphere on a beach, live a bustling life in Havana,' but his gap year also confirmed for him that he had chosen the right course of study.

The *Cuba Solidarity Campaign* (c/o Red Rose Club, 129 Seven Sisters Road, London N7 7QG; 020-7263 6452; office@cuba-solidarity.org.uk) runs a work/study scheme (called brigades) twice a year in which volunteers undertake agricultural and construction work for three weeks either in July or December/January. No specific skills or qualifications are required but applicants must be sympathetic to the revolution and be able to demonstrate a commitment to solidarity work. The cost of the brigade is approximately £800 which includes flight, accommodation, food and basic travel insurance. For further information contact the Brigade Co-ordinator.

Greenforce (11-15 Betterton Street, Covent Garden, London WC2H 9BP; 020-7470 8888; info@greenforce.org/ www.greenforce.org) is looking for volunteers to join a coral reef survey project in the Bahamas. Projects involve studying endangered species and habitats. The aim is to establish three new marine protected zones for the Bahamas National Trust. No previous experience is necessary as diving instruction and scientific training are provided. The cost is £2,750 plus flight.

United States

Jack Kerouac's On the Road continues to influence the current generation of young adults and the lure of America is as strong as ever. The home of so many heroes and of ideas which have shaped the thinking of most people in the west, the USA attracts a wide range of people, including school leavers, who want to experience the reality for themselves. Extended travel around the United States is expensive but various schemes and travel bargains can bring that vast country within reach of gap year students and older travellers. It is possible for students to qualify for an Exchange Visitor Programme visa which permits them to enter the US and work legally.

If you end up looking for a job after arrival, you will find the task infinitely easier if you have a car and a phone, tools which are synonymous with the American way of life. It also helps to have not only a tidy but a conservative appearance.

Red Tape

Despite the wide open spaces and warm hospitality so often associated with America, their official policies are discouraging for those who want to earn money while in the US. British citizens do not need to apply for a tourist visa in advance. The visa-waiver scheme is now permanent and allows ordinary tourists from approved countries to enter the US for a maximum of 90 days. Those planning trips of more than 90 days must obtain a tourist visa in advance from the Embassy. The holder of a tourist visa may be granted a stay of up to six months at the discretion of the immigration officer at the port of entry. Individuals entering visa-free under the Visa-Waiver Programme or with a visitor visa for business or tourism are prohibited from engaging in paid or unpaid employment in the US. Check the Embassy website (www.usembassy.org.uk) for full visa information and application forms or request an outline of non-immigrant visas from the Visa Branch of the US Embassy (5 Upper Grosvenor St, London W1A 2JB). The application fee for non-immigrant visas is £67 ($100), up from £32 in 2002, and candidates in most cases must now have a face-to-face interview including for the J-1.

The visa of most interest to the readers of this book is the J-1 which is available to participants of government-authorised programmes, known as Exchange Visitor Programmes (EVPs). The J-1 visa entitles the holder to take legal paid employment. You cannot apply for the J-1 without going through a recognised Exchange Visitor Programme like the British Universities North America Club (BUNAC), CIEE or Camp America. Only they can issue the document DS2019 (formerly the IAP66) necessary for obtaining a J-1 visa.

A large number of opportunities are available on summer camps and as au pairs (both described in detail below). These programmes are allowed to exist because of their educational value and many are open only to full-time students. Some will accept those between school and university, provided they have a confirmed place at a tertiary institution, and summer camp programmes are open to non-students with specific skills.

Apart from the J-1 visa available to people on approved EVPs, other possible visa categories to consider include the Q visa which is the 'International Cultural Exchange Visa' which must be applied for by the prospective employer in the US (e.g. the Disney Corporation) and approved in advance by an office of the Immigration and Naturalization Service (INS). Another possibility is the B-1 'Voluntary Service' visa. Applications must be sponsored by a charitable or religious organisation which undertakes not to pay you but may reimburse you for incidental expenses. Applicants must do work of a traditional charitable nature.

By law, all employers must physically examine documents of prospective employees within three working days, proving that they are authorised to work. Employers who are discovered by the Immigration and Naturalization Service to be hiring illegal aliens are subject to huge fines and those caught working illegally run the risk of being deported, prohibited from travelling to the US for five years and in some cases for good.

WORK AND STUDY PROGRAMMES

BUNAC (16 Bowling Green Lane, London EC1R 0QH; 020-7251 3472) administers three basic work programmes in the US: one is the 'Work America Programme' which allows full-time university students to do any summer job they are able to find before or after arrival; the second is 'Summer Camp USA' which is open to anyone over 19 interested in working on a summer camp as a counsellor; the third is 'KAMP' (Kitchen & Maintenance Programme) which is open to students who want to work at a summer camp in a catering and maintenance capacity. All participants must join the BUNAC Club (£4), travel between June and October and purchase compulsory insurance (about £100). BUNAC runs its own loan scheme for selected programmes.

As part of the application for student-only programmes, you must submit a letter from your principal, registrar or tutor on college headed paper showing that you are a full-time student in the year of travel. Gap year students should submit evidence of an unconditional offer for the September/October after they have returned from the US. You are also required to take at least $400 in travellers cheques.

To assist Work America Programme applicants in finding work, BUNAC publishes an annual Job Directory with thousands of job listings in the US from hundreds of employers, many of whom have taken on BUNAC participants in the past. The Directory is available to all potential applicants and is free of charge. To widen your scope, you might look at job search web-sites such as www.seasonalemployment.com which lists summer jobs mainly in resorts and parks. Further contacts can be found in the annually revised book Summer Jobs in the USA distributed in Britain by Vacation Work at £14.99.

BUNAC is also one of the biggest summer camp placement organisations, sending between 3,000 and 4,000 people aged between 18 and 35 to participate in the Summer Camp USA programme. The registration fee of £62 includes camp placement, return flight and land transport to camp and pocket money of $670-$730 (depending on age) for the whole nine-week period. The fact that you do not have to raise the money for the flight is a great attraction for many. Interviews, which are compulsory for all first-time applicants, are held in university towns throughout Britain between November and May.

BUNAC's other summer camp programme is called KAMP, the Kitchen and Maintenance Programme. KAMP is open to full-time students including those at the end of their gap year who are given ancillary jobs in the kitchen, laundry or maintenance department, for which they will be advanced their air fare and in some cases paid more than the counsellors, i.e. at least $900 for the nine-week period of work.

The other major camp recruitment organisation is Camp America (37a Queen's Gate, Dept. WW, London SW7 5HR; 020-7581 7333; brochure@campamerica.co.uk/ www.campamerica.co.uk) which each summer arranges for a massive 10,000 people aged 18 or over, from around the world, to work on children's camps in the USA. The work is for nine weeks between June and August where you could be teaching activities such as tennis, swimming and arts and crafts. Camp America provides a free return flight from London to New York and guidance on applying for a J-1 visa. The camp provides free board and lodging plus pocket money. At the end of your contract, you will be given a lump sum of pocket money which will range from $460 to $910 depending on your age, experience, qualifications and whether you've been on Camp America before.

Despite some initial anxiety, **Mark Welfare** enjoyed his counselling job arranged through Camp America:

> *Although I applied in January I didn't hear that I was definitely going until three weeks before departure, when I was just about to start my A-level exams. But it all worked out and I spent a very enjoyable summer working with handicapped and problem children at a camp in the Appalachian mountains of Pennsylvania. For me the Camp America scheme was ideal. I had never been away from home and it was a very easy introduction to travelling since flight, insurance, visa and job are all arranged for you.*

One way to avoid the last-minute uncertainty is to try to attend one of Camp America's recruitment fairs in London, Manchester, Birmingham, Edinburgh or Belfast in February/ March, which is what **Colin Rothwell** did:

> *At the recruitment fair at Manchester Poly, you could actually meet the camp directors from all over the States and find out more about particular camps. If you are lucky, like me and a thousand others, you can sign a contract on the spot. Then you leave all the 'dirty work' to Camp America and wait until they call you to the airport in June sometime.*

Camp America also offers two other summer programmes: Campower for students who would like to work in the kitchen/maintenance areas at camp and the Resort America programme (www.resortamerica.co.uk) whereby people work in holiday resorts and are paid $1,100 for the minimum 12-week period.

Summer Camps

Summer camps are uniquely American in atmosphere, even if the idea has spread to Europe. An estimated 8-10 million American children are sent to 10,000 summer camps each year for a week or more to participate in outdoor activities and sports, arts and crafts and generally have a wholesome experience. The type of camp varies from plush sports camps for the very rich to more or less charitable camps for the handicapped or underprivileged. Thousands of 'counsellors' are needed each summer to be in charge of a cabinful of youngsters and to instruct or supervise some activity, from the ordinary (swimming and boating) to the esoteric (puppet-making and ham radio).

After camp finishes, counsellors have up to six weeks' free time and normally return on organised flights between late August and the end of September. Camp counselling regularly wins enthusiastic fans and is worth considering if you enjoy children and don't mind hard work. Some camps are staffed almost entirely by young people from overseas, which can be useful if you are looking for a post-camp travelling companion. Others have a reasonable proportion of American employees, in which case there is a good chance that you will be invited to visit their homes when camp finishes. In the opinion of most gap year travellers who have worked on summer camps, the amazing travel opportunities after camp justify all the hard work.

After the first year of her software engineering course at Birmingham University, Victoria Jossel spent a wonderful summer in the US with Camp America which she felt really enhanced her CV:

On June 9th, I apprehensively boarded my flight to Blue Star camp in North

Carolina. Not only did I have the privilege of bonding with the children in my cabin from whom you receive constant love, caring and attention, but I also met new people from all over the world and received amazing references for my future career. I learned how to organise, motivate and lead people as well as negotiate positive outcomes to conflicts. From a normal 19 year old girl, I became a responsible, motivated, adaptable and independent person with 14 children who were my responsibility. I had never been camping and had never wanted to go camping. Yet it was the most amazing experience: I learned to start a fire on my own, cook food for all 14 girls and organise it so the kids all got EXACTLY the same amount of Hershey's chocolate.

In addition to BUNAC and Camp America, *Camp Counselors USA (CCUSA)* places young people aged 18-30 and recruits from over 60 countries. CCUSA's programme includes return flight to the US, one night's accommodation in New York City, visas and insurance, full board and lodging during placement as well as the chance to earn $400-$600 as a first year counsellor depending on your age (as of 1st June), experience, qualifications and whether you've been a camp counsellor in the US before. Enquiries should be made as early as possible to Camp Counselors (CCUSA), Green Dragon House, 64-70 High Street, Croydon CR0 9XN (020-8688 9051; info@ccusa.co.uk). Early applicants pay a lower registration fee than later ones. The deadline for applications is April 1st.

Other Work Programmes

The other principal work and travel programmes (as distinct from career-oriented internship programmes described in the next section) are those of *CIEE* (52 Poland St, London W1F 7AB; 020-7478 2020/fax 020-7734 7322; infouk@councilexchanges.org.uk) and *Camp Counselors USA* (Green Dragon House, 64-70 High Street, Croydon CR0 9XN (020-8688 9051; www.ccusaweusa.co.uk) which are broadly comparable. CCUSA's *Work Experience USA* or WEUSA programme and CIEE's Work and Travel USA programme provide students aged 18 to 30 with the opportunity to live and work in the US during the summer. Students in their year out are eligible provided they have a confirmed place on a university level course.

The CCUSA programme works with up to 100 employers in resort and vacation centres throughout the United States to find placements for participants. The 'security' programme guarantees a job to those who are accepted and costs £735 whereas to undertake the job hunt independently costs £100 less. The total package includes a Directory of Employers, return airfare from London to New York, four months insurance, meeting on arrival and two-day orientation in New York with accommodation. Interested individuals in Scotland and the north of England should contact the CCUSA office at 27 Woodside Gardens, Musselburgh, Scotland EH21 7LJ (0131-665 5843; 101355.257@compuserve.com). Most recruitment takes place before April 1st. The company has a network of interviewers around the UK and organises various open houses and recruitment fairs.

CIEE's all-in fee for Work and Travel USA starts at £335. This includes legal sponsorship necessary for the J-1 visa, full insurance for up to five months, a Job Directory and programme handbook, orientation and 24 hour emergency support.

Exchange organisations in the US often place foreign young people in jobs or with families, however many target non-English speaking foreigners rather than British candidates. One such is Intrax which has a Work/Travel Program (but no representation in the UK) though they have recently been designated by the US Department of State as an official sponsor for the International Career Training Program (also J-1) for which British candidates would be eligible to apply. Intrax can be contacted at 226 Bush St, San Francisco, CA 94115 (415-674-5252; info@intraxinc.com).

INTERNSHIPS and WORK EXPERIENCE

Internship is the American term for traineeship, normally unpaid, providing a chance to get some experience in your career interest as part of your academic course. These are typically available to undergraduates and recent graduates rather than to school leavers.

Several organisations in the UK arrange for students and graduates to undertake internships in the US. The most important is *CIEE*, 52 Poland St, London W1F 7AB (020-7478 2020; www.ciee.org.uk) which helps more than 1,500 students, graduates and young professionals arrange career-related work placements in the US lasting from 3 to 18 months. The placement can take place at any time during studies, during a sandwich year or after graduating. Although you are responsible for finding your own placement, CIEE offers a job search service as part of the programme, which includes a searchable database of internships/work placements and unlimited job advice and CV writing feedback. Students should request an Internship USA application pack and young professionals should request a PCT USA application pack. Those who qualify get a J-1 visa allowing them to work in the USA for up to 18 months. The programme fees start at £270 for a stay of up to two months.

BUNAC operates an internship programme dubbed OPT USA (Overseas Practical Training) sponsored by International Program Services of the American YMCA. The programme is open to non-students as well as students over the age of 19 and of any nationality but must be integrated into between three and 18 months of on-the-job training (and not just work experience). Programme fees vary from £190 to £440.

CDS International has practical training assignments in the US lasting between three and 18 months for Britons, Europeans and others. The opportunities for internships are limited to young professionals, aged 21-35, apart from a new training programme which is open to university students who must be evaluated by a faculty adviser (usatp@cdsintl.org).

Cultural Cube (16 Acland Rd, Ivybridge, Devon PO21 9UR; www.culturalcube.co.uk) runs two internship programmes, one for the hospitality industry, the other for business. Hospitality internships are available for 12 months in and around Atlanta (programme fee £1,490; monthly stipend $400 on top of accommodation). The business placement in Washington DC (minimum age 21) consists of optional 1-month business training workshop plus 6 or 12 month placements (fee of £1,500 or £1,900).

Cultural Homestay International in California (address below) manages a Work and Travel Programme for full-time students aged 18-30 and two internship programmes for qualifying candidates; the short-term one (1, 2 or 3 months) is for university students and recent graduates aged 20-30 and the intensive one lasting 6-10 months is for graduates and young professionals aged 22-35 (fee $3,000+). Internship programmes are also available through *InterExchange* (161 Sixth Avenue, New York, NY 10013) and *Alliances Abroad* (702 West Ave, Austin, TX 78701; info@alliancesabroad.com) which can authorise J-1 visas and arrange internships in Denver, San Francisco and Washington DC.

The Mountbatten Internship Programme (Abbey House, 74-76 St John St, 5th Floor, London EC1M 4DZ; www.mountbatten.org) annually provides work experience in New York City for about 120 people aged 20-26 with business training. Placements last one year and provide free accommodation as well as a fortnightly wage of $443. Interns pay a participation fee of £1,745.

The administration of the UK/US Career Development Programme has passed from CIEE to the National Council for Work Experience (www.work-experience.org) in conjunction with AIPT in Maryland (info@aipt.org). This programme is for people aged 18-35 with relevant qualifications and/or at least two years of work experience in their career field. A separate section of the programme is for full-time students in Hospitality & Tourism or Equine Studies. The fee to NCWE is £65 plus a variable fee of $800-$1,800 is payable to the US organiser (which the employer sometimes pays).

Young people with at least one year's practical agricultural experience may be eligible for the International Agricultural Exchange Association (IAEA) *Agriventure* exchange or the International Exchange Program UK Ltd (IEPUK) which places equine trainees in the US. Both co-operate with Communicating for Agriculture in Fergus Falls, Minnesota (http://ca.cainc.org). Participation in IEPUK costs from $1,200 plus travel and other expenses; details are available from IEPUK, The Old Rectory, Belton-in-Rutland, Oakham, Rutland LE15 9LE (01572 717381; GY@iepuk.com).

For a brief list of approved exchanges and internship programmes in the US, send an s.a.e. to the Educational Advisory Service of the *Fulbright Commission,* 62 Doughty St, London WC1N 2JZ (020-7404 6994; www.ftclondon.co.uk). Note that they can also be helpful in advising on how to study at an American university; see their useful booklet *Beginner's Guide to Undergraduate Study in the USA* which provides a list of sample tuition fees and living costs.

The 750-page book *Internships* published by Peterson's Guides lists intern positions which are paid or unpaid, can last for the summer, for a semester or for a year. The book offers general advice (including a section called 'Foreign Applicants for US Internships') and specific listings organised according to field of interest, e.g. Advertising, Museums, Radio, Social Services, Law, etc. This annually revised book is available in the UK from Vacation-Work for £19.99 plus £3 postage. Career Education Institutes in North Carolina publish 14 internship directories in specific fields such as advertising agencies or environmental organisations; check their website on www.internships-usa.com.

After a consultation with 'Taking Off', a consultancy near Boston (see page 182), **Elisabeth Weiskittel** fixed up a short internship at the Ocean Mammal Institute (www.oceanmammalinst.com) on the island of Maui in Hawaii in the middle of her gap year. Every January, the woman in charge of the Institute takes some of her students and a few interns (often people taking a year off) to Hawaii for three weeks; the 2004 fee is $1,950:

The purpose of the Institute was to study humpbacked whales and the effects of nearby boats on their behaviour. Our data was intended to support a pending law restricting the use of speedboats and other craft in these small bays where the whales and calves were swimming. One group watched and recorded the whales' behaviour in the morning and had the afternoon off, and the other group watched in the afternoon and had the morning off. I had no problem adjusting to life in Hawaii. Most people were there to get a tan and go to bars, but even if that's not your scene it's still lots of fun in Hawaii. During our last week there was a large conference on environmental issues, which all the interns were invited to attend. Some of the speakers were well-known, and one or two spoke to our group, such as the founder of Greenpeace. When the internship ended, I flew back home to New York for a few days to do my laundry and repack, and then continued my gap year in Italy.

HOMESTAYS & COURSES

Secondary school students who want to spend up to a year living with an American family and attending high school in the US should consider the programmes offered by the following:

Academic Associates International, Academic Year in the USA, 46 High St, Ewell Village, Surrey KT17 1RW (020-8786 7711; enquiry@aaiuk.org/ www.aaiuk.org).

Aspect Foundation, 350 Sansome St, Suite 740, San Francisco, CA 94104 (415-228-8050/toll-free 1-800-879-6884/fax 415-228-8051; exchange@aspect.com/ www.aspectfoundation.org). Inbound homestay programme for 15-18½ year olds and a college programme for those aged 18-21 who have finished secondary school in their country.

Challenge Educational Services, 101 Lorna Road, Hove, East Sussex BN3 3EL (01273 220261; www.challengeuk.com). Academic year in the USA programme for students aged 15-18. A semester or full Academic Year staying with an American host family and studying at a High School thoroughly immerses students in the American culture and way of life. Prices start at £2,995 for a semester and £3,495 for a full Academic Year, including visa documentation, flights and accommodation.

Cultural Homestay International, 104 Butterfield Road, San Anselmo, CA 94960, USA (415-459-5397; chimain@msn.com/ www.chinet.org).

Educational Resource Development Trust (ERDT), 475 Washington Blvd, Suite 220, Marina del Rey, CA 90292 (301-821-9977; rriske@erdtshare.org). Short-term homestays and farm or ranch stays for ages 15-18.

EIL, 287 Worcester Rd, Malvern, Worcs. WR14 1AB (0800 018 4015; www.eiluk.org). Runs an Academic Year Programme for students aged 16-19. Programme fees depend on length of placement.

English-Speaking Union, Dartmouth House, 37 Charles Street, London W1J 5ED (020-7529 1550/fax 020-7495 6108; esu@esu.org/ www.esu.org). About 30 British gap year students are offered two or three term scholarships to a school in the USA (or Canada).

International Employment Training (IET), 45 High Street, Tunbridge Wells, Kent TN1 1XL (info@jobsamerica.co.uk; www.jobsamerica.co.uk). IET works with US companies to place international applicants in a work related field experience lasting 3-18 months. Fees from £250 to £375 depending on the length of stay in the US. Wages paid on a par with US co-workers.

WISE – Worldwide International Student Exchange, PO Box 1332, Dyersburg, TN 38025 (731-287-9948; wise@wisefoundation.com). Seasonal jobs in resorts plus homestays arranged.

World Exchange, White Birch Road, Putnam Valley, NY 10579, USA (845-526-2505; www.worldexchange.org). 2, 3 or 4 week homestays for all ages. Prices start at about $475 for a fortnight near the Great Lakes to $700+ for a month in California.

Youth Exchange Service, 4675 MacArthur Court, Suite 830, Newport Beach, CA 92660 (714-955-2030; www.yesint.com). Programme for 15-18 year olds, mostly from non-English speaking countries.

Childcare

The au pair placement programme allows thousands of young Europeans with childcare experience to work for American families for exactly one year on a J-1 visa. They apply through a small number of sponsoring organisations which must follow the guidelines which govern the programme, so there is not much difference between them. The arrangement differs from au pairing in Europe since the hours are much longer and, if the au pair comes from the UK, there is no language to learn.

The basic requirements are that you be between 18 and 26, speak English, show at least 200 hours of recent childcare experience and provide a criminal record check. The childcare experience can consist of regular babysitting, helping at a local crèche or school, etc. Anyone wanting to care for a child under two must have 200 hours of experience looking after children under two and must expect the programme interviewers to delve into the experience you claim to have. The majority of candidates are young women though men with relevant experience (e.g. sole care of children under five) may be placed. (It is still not unusual to have just a handful of blokes out of hundreds of au pairs.)

The job entails working 45 hours a week (including babysitting) with at least one and a half days off per week plus one complete weekend off a month. Successful applicants receive free return flights from one of many European cities, four-day orientation in New York which covers child safety and development, and follow-up from a community counsellor. The time lag between applying and flying is usually at least two months. The counsellor's role is to advise on any problems and organise meetings with other au pairs in your area. Applicants are required to pay a good faith deposit of $400 which is returned to them at the end of 12 months but which is forfeit if the terms of the programme are broken.

The fixed amount of pocket money for au pairs is $139.05 a week, which is a reasonable wage on top of room, board and perks. An additional $500 is paid by the host family to cover the cost of educational courses (three hours a week during term-time) which must be attended as a condition of the visa. Au pairs are at liberty to travel for a month after their contract is over but no visa extension is available beyond that.

As in all au pair-host family relationships, problems do occur and it is not unusual for au pairs to chafe against rules, curfews and expectations in housework, etc. When speaking to your family on the telephone during the application period, ask as many day-to-day questions as possible, and try to establish exactly what will be expected of you, how many nights babysitting at weekends, restrictions on social life, use of the car, how private are the living arrangements, etc. The counsellors and advisers provided by the sending organisations should be able to sort out problems and in extreme cases can find alternative families. Consider carefully the pros and cons of the city you will be going to. **Emma Purcell** was not altogether happy to be sent to Memphis Tennesee which she describes as the 'most backward and redneck city in the USA':

> I was a very naïve 18 year old applying to be an au pair for a deferred year before university. During my eight months so far, I have experienced highs and lows. I have been very lucky with my host family who have made me feel one of the family. I have travelled the USA and Mexico frequently staying in suites and being treated as royalty since my host dad is president of Holiday Inn. On the bad side, I have lost numerous friends who have not had such good luck. One was working 60 hours a week (for no extra pay) with the brattiest children, so she left. Another girl from Australia lasted six months with her neurotic family who yelled at her for not cleaning the toaster daily and for folding the socks wrong. Finally she plucked up the courage to talk to her host parents and their immediate response was to throw her out. A very strong personality is required to be an au pair for a year in the States.

About half a dozen agencies in the UK send au pairs to the US, and it is worth comparing their literature. The *Au Pair in America* programme (see Directory of Specialist Gap Year Programmes) is the largest organisation placing in excess of 4,500 young people in au pair and nanny placements throughout the country. Brochures and application forms can be requested on 020-7581 7300 or online at www.aupairinamerica.co.uk. It has representatives in Europe, South Africa, Australia, etc. and agent/interviewers throughout the UK and worldwide. The programme operates under the auspices of the American Institute for Foreign Study or AIFS (37 Queens Gate, London SW7 5HR) though some of the selection has been devolved to independent au pair agencies such as Childcare International Ltd, Trafalgar House, Grenville Place, London NW7 3SA (020-8906 3116; www.childint.co.uk). Au Pair in America also has representatives in 45 countries and agent/interviewers throughout the UK.

Other active au pair Exchange Visitor Programmes are smaller but may be able to offer a more personal service and more choice in the destination and family you work for:

Au Pair Care, 2226 Bush St, San Francisco, CA 94115; 415-434-8788/1-800-428-7246; www.aupaircare.com.

EurAupair, 105 Central Way, Suite 201, Kirkland, WA 98033 plus three other regional offices in US; www.euraupair.com. UK partner is EurAupair UK, 17 Wheatfield Drive, Shifnal, Shropshire TF11 8HL; 01952 460733/ maureen@asseuk.freeserve.co.uk.

Go Au Pair, 6965 Union Park Center, Suite 100, Midvale, UT 84047-9723; 801-255-7722/ 888-287-2471; www.goAUPAIR.com. Formerly Au Pair Program USA.

InterExchange, 161 Sixth Avenue, New York, NY 10013; 212-924-1446; www.interexchange.org.

International Excahnge Centre, 35 Ivor Place, London NW1 6EA (0207-7724 4493; www.isecworld.co.uk). £410 fee.

TRAVEL

If you intend to travel widely in the States check out air passes from any branch of STA

Travel. Bus passes have already been mentioned in the 'Travel' chapter. College notice boards and student common rooms often carry notices posted by people looking for or offering rides, particularly at weekends. A contribution to the petrol will be expected, but this is vastly preferable to hitch-hiking which is decidedly dodgy in the US.

Escorted trips aimed at young people might appeal, for example those offered by Trekamerica (www.trekamerica.com), American Adventures (01295 756200; www.americanadventures.com) or Green Tortoise (mentioned on page 57).

Drive-Aways

The term 'drive-away' applies to the widespread practice of delivering private cars within North America. Prosperous Americans and Canadians and also companies are prepared to pay several hundred dollars to delivery firms who agree to arrange delivery of private vehicles to a different city, usually because the car-owner wants his or her car available at their holiday destination but doesn't want to drive it personally. The companies find drivers (an estimated three-quarters of whom are not American), arrange insurance and arbitrate in the event of mishaps. You get free use of a car (subject to mileage and time restrictions) and pay for all gas after the first tankful and tolls on the interstates. Usually a time deadline and mileage limit are fixed, though these are often flexible and checks lax. A good time to be travelling east to west or north to south (e.g. Chicago to Phoenix) is September/October when a lot of older people head to a warmer climate. On the other hand, when there is a shortage of vehicles (e.g. leaving New York in the summer), you will be lucky to get a car on any terms.

Unfortunately most companies are looking for drivers over the age of 21, so year-out students aren't eligible. If you (or an older friend) are interested in pursuing this, look up 'Automobile Transporters and Driveaway Companies' in the *Yellow Pages* of any big city. Companies to try are:

Auto Driveaway Company – www.autodriveaway.com; 1-800-621-4155. Available cars are listed on the website (updated daily) and it is possible to sign up on-line. In some cases fuel costs are covered. Website gives numbers of branch offices from Salt Lake City to Syracuse, Wichita to Winnipeg (Canada).

National Auto Transporters Inc. – www.autotransporter.com. Website does not include information for prospective drivers.

Across America Driveaway – www.transportautos.com/driveaway.htm; 1-800-677-6686.

SEASONAL JOBS

Labour demands in summer resorts sometimes reach crisis proportions especially along the eastern seaboard. Time can productively be spent searching the internet. Dozens of sites may prove useful, though www.coolworks.com is especially recommended for seasonal (and career) jobs in the outdoors tourist industry, e.g. with jobs in ski resorts, white water rafting companies, ranches and national parks. Another useful site is www.jobmonkey.com.

The majority of catering staff are paid the minimum wage, and some are paid less. Because tipping is so generous, employers can get away with offering derisory wages, e.g. $10 for an evening shift. In fact the legal minimum hourly wage for tipped employees is less than half of the standard minimum. The standard minimum wage is $5.15 an hour, though some states have legislated a higher wage, e.g. $6.75 in California, $7.10 in Connecticut (from January 2004), Washington DC, Massachusetts, Oregon and Washington state. However workers aged under 20 may be paid the youth minimum of $4.35 for the first 90 days of their employment. These can be checked on the Department of Labor's website (www.dol.gov/esa/minwage/america.htm).

Live-in jobs are probably preferable, and are often available to British students whose terms allow them to stay beyond Labor Day, the first Monday in September, when most American students resume their studies. After working a season at a large resort in Wisconsin, **Timothy Payne** concluded:

Without doubt the best jobs in the USA are to be found in the resorts, simply because they pay a reasonable wage as well as providing free food and accommodation. Since many resorts are located in remote spots, it is possible to save most of your wages and tips, and also enjoy free use of the resort's facilities. Whatever job you end up with you should have a good time due to the large number of students working there.

Popular resorts are often a sure bet, especially if you arrive in mid-August (when American students begin to leave jobs), or in April/May (before they arrive). **Katherine Smith**, who got her J-1 visa through BUNAC, describes the range of jobs she found in Ocean City, a popular seaside resort in Maryland which absorbs a large number of Britons:

I decided to spend my summer in Ocean Beach because I knew the job scene would be favourable. I found a job as a waitress in a steak restaurant and another full-time job as a reservations clerk in a hotel by approaching employers on an informal basis and enquiring about possible job vacancies. In my case this was very fruitful and I found two relatively well-paid jobs which I enjoyed very much. Other jobs available included fairground attendant, fast food sales assistant, lifeguard, kitchen assistant, chambermaid and every other possible type of work associated with a busy ocean-side town. Ocean City was packed with foreign workers. As far as I know, none had any trouble finding work; anyone could have obtained half a dozen jobs. Obviously the employers are used to a high turnover of workers, especially if the job is boring. So it's not difficult to walk out of a job on a day's notice and into another one. It really was a great place to spend the summer. I would recommend a holiday resort to anyone wishing to work hard and have a really wild time.

Other resorts to try are Wildwood (New Jersey), Virginia Beach (Virginia), Myrtle Beach (South Carolina) and Atlantic Beach (North Carolina).

The International Recruiting Department of Walt Disney's EPCOT Center (PO Box 10090, Lake Buena Vista, Florida 32830-0090) prefer to rely on the word of mouth network rather than have their six month or one year vacancies for young people to work as 'cultural representatives' widely publicised. People aged 18-28 from Britain and ten other countries are hired to represent the culture and customs of their countries; in the case of the UK this means olde worlde pubs, Scotch eggs and Royal Doulton china. Anyone applying will probably have to wait months until there is space at one of the two annual recruiting presentations which Disney organises in Britain in March and October. Any job which involves tips is usually more lucrative than others; wages can be swelled by more than $100 in a five-hour shift. The staff facilities are attractive with pools, jacuzzis, tennis courts and subsidised rent.

Paul Binfield from Kent describes the process of being hired by Disney as 'a long and patient' one:

I initially wrote to Disney in October and started my contract in January, 15 months later. It was the most enjoyable year of my life, experiencing so many excellent things and making the best friends from all over the world. The pros far outweigh the cons, though some people did hate the work. Disney are a strict company with many rules which are vigorously enforced. The work in merchandising or the pub/restaurant is taken extremely seriously and sometimes it can be hard to manufacture a big cheesy Disney smile. There are dress codes (for example men have to be clean shaven every day), and verbal and written warnings for matters which would be considered very trivial in Britain, and indeed terminations (which is a very nasty word for being fired). If you go with the right attitude it can be great fun.

Advertisements for sales positions proliferate. You may find telesales less off-putting than door-to-door salesmanship, but it will also be less lucrative. On the other hand, some gap year students do not shy away from the hard edge of selling and tackle commission-only jobs. The Southwestern Company with its headquarters in Nashville markets educational books and software door-to-door throughout the US and has a recruitment office in the UK (Goldsmiths House, Broad Plain, Bristol BS2 0JR; 0117-930 4274) which targets gap year students. Its website (www.southwestern.com) contains glowing reports from past students whose earnings have been impressive. Their statistics possibly exclude all the students who give up in disgust after a few weeks of failure.

An offbeat suggestion has been proffered by Mark Kinder who wrote from rural Maryland:

> After spending the summer on the Camp America programme, a friend and I decided to do a parachute jump. Once you have made about ten jumps, the instructors expect you to learn how to pack parachutes, which takes about five hours to learn. Once you have learnt how to pack you get paid $5 per chute cash and with a bit of practice can pack three or four chutes an hour which is good money. I would say that 90% of parachute centres in the US pay people cash for packing the chutes but you generally have to be a skydiver to do the job. It is definitely a fun way of earning money. Skydivers are very friendly people and are thrilled to meet foreigners, so they will often offer a place to stay. If not, you can always camp at the parachute centre.

A list of the 275 parachute centres in the US can be obtained from the national association USPA, 1440 Duke St, Alexandria, VA 22314 (www.uspa.org).

Soccer Coaching

Soccer has gained huge popularity in North America over the past five or ten years especially among school children. Since British football is universally admired, demand is strong for young British coaches to work on summer coaching schemes. A number of companies recruit players to work all over the States including Hawaii:

ProExcel 10281 Frosty Court, Suite 100, Manassas, VA 20109, USA (703-330-2532; www.proexcel.com). Formerly Britannia Soccer.

Goal-Line Soccer Inc, PO Box 1642, Corvallis, OR 97339 (541-753-5833; info@goal-line.com; www.goal-line.com). Minimum age 21. Mostly in Oregon and Washington. Recruits through BUNAC for July and early August only.

Major League Soccer Camps, 47 Water St, Mystic, CT 06355, USA (http://uk.mlscamps.com). The largest and best known. Registration fee of £310 includes flights from UK.

Soccer Academy Inc, PO Box 3046, Manassas, VA 20108, USA (703-385-0150; www.soccer-acdemy.com).

Others advertise in the specialist press. BUNAC knows about these companies, since they normally process the necessary J-1 visa. It is more important to be good at working with kids than to be a great football player, though of course it is easier to command the respect of the kids if you can show them good skills and a few tricks.

Among the many things Theo West did in his gap year before going to Liverpool University, he coached soccer and describes the application process and the job itself:

The procedure involved in getting a place is time-consuming and difficult but well worth the effort. It includes an interview to see if you have the right personality and experience in coaching followed by a couple of coaching days where you are evaluated at close quarters by senior coaches (which proved a slight problem for me since my home is in Inverness and the nearest coaching day was in Newcastle). Finally you accept a contract, list preferred working locations, pay a membership (which covers flights to the US), apply for a J-1 visa through BUNAC and attend an induction.

On arrival in America we were briefed on where our first week-long assignment was *to be and given our coaching equipment. The next day we headed off in hire cars for Monroe Woodbury, a rich area in upstate New York where we were introduced to the families which were to put us up for a week. The pay as a first year coach is around $140 a week for a three hour session each day and occasional adult coaching clinics. In terms of pay it was not great but the benefits generally come from the families that house you, feed you and entertain you. The benefits of an English accent in America are still many. I spent five weeks coaching in New York, Connecticut and finally worked with under-privileged kids in New Jersey. It was an amazing and draining experience as I got to meet many great people, saw some wonderful sights and negotiated myself with some difficulty into a number of bars (the strictness of the adherence to the 21 age limit for drinking proved annoying).*

VOLUNTARY WORK

The three main workcamp organisations in the USA (see chapter 'A Year Off for North Americans') have incoming programmes as well as outgoing, though prospective volunteers should register through a workcamp organisation in their own country. For example *Volunteers for Peace* (www.vfp.org) place about 500 foreign volunteers on 40-50 workcamps in the US. *CIEE* accepts around 200 individuals from abroad over the age of 18 to participate in its international voluntary service projects. In the past, volunteers have been placed on environmental projects in Yosemite National Park, the Golden Gate National Seashore and northern Idaho's Kaniksu National Forest, assisted with urban renovation and preservation of historic landmarks in New York and New Jersey, and worked with disabled children and adults on their summer holidays.

Voluntary opportunities in the US range from the intensely urban to the decidedly rural. In the former category, you can build houses in deprived areas throughout the US with *Habitat for Humanity* (Global Village, 121 Habitat St, Americus, GA 31709) or work for the *Winant Clayton Volunteers* (109 East 50th St, New York, NY 10022). Clayton volunteers work on summer play-schemes and with HIV/Aids sufferers, the homeless and in drug and psychiatric rehabilitation centres, mainly in Manhattan. Volunteers with a British passport are recruited to work for eight weeks from mid or late June followed by two or three weeks of travel; contact WCV, Davenant Centre, 179 Whitechapel Road, London E1 1DU (020-7375 0547; wcva@dircon.co.uk).

Camphill Special Schools often need volunteers to help run their programme for children with disabilities. Volunteers willing to stay more than six months will receive a monthly stipend, health insurance and will be helped to get a work visa. Details are available from Camphill Special Schools, 1784 Fairview Road, Glenmoore, PA 19343 (fax 610-469-9758; BRvolunteer@aol.com/ www.beaverrun.org).

Working outside the big cities is an attractive prospect. For example the US Forest Service organises workcamps to maintain trails, campsites and wildlife throughout the country; volunteers should apply to the individual parks; state-by-state opportunities are posted on the internet at www.fs.fed.us/people/programs/volunteer.htm.

Similarly, Wilderness Volunteers (PO Box 22292, Flagstaff, AZ 86002-2292; 928-556-0038; info@wildernessvolunteers.org) organise one-week adventure service trips throughout the country (searchable by state on their website) which cost just less than $200. The Heritage Resource Management department of the US Forest Service operates a volunteer programme to conduct archaeological surveys, record oral histories, etc. The Volunteer Co-ordinator's office is in Modoc National Forest (800 West 12th St, Alturas, CA 96101; 916-233-5811; ggates@fs.fed.us). He sends out application forms, tries to match volunteers with appropriate vacancies and assists with obtaining a J-1 visa. Volunteers/ trainees are paid a stipend of about $100 a week in addition to free accommodation.

The General Convention of Sioux YMCAs in South Dakota offers summer camp and longer positions. Volunteers live in rural Native American communities in order to help run the local YMCA Youth Center, working with Lakota children, families and schools.

The Y provides housing, a small living stipend and cultural training. Contact the YMCA for application details: PO Box 218, Dupree, South Dakota 57623 (605-365-5232; www.siouxymca.org/staff_positions.htm).

The American Hiking Society collates volunteer opportunities from around the United States to build, maintain and restore foot trails in America's backcountry. No prior trail work experience is necessary, but volunteers should be able to hike at least five miles a day, supply their own backpacking equipment (including tent), pay a $50 registration fee and arrange transport to and from the work site. Food is provided on most projects. For a schedule of projects, go to www.AmericanHiking.org or send an s.a.e. to AHS, Volunteer Vacations, 1422 Fenwick Lane, Silver Spring, MD 20910 (301-565-6704).

The US Fish & Wildlife Service in Hawaii offers 15-20 volunteers the chance to live at one of two very remote island field stations in the northwest Hawaiian archipelago. English-speaking volunteers of all nationalities work on seabird monitoring and alien plant species control for three to six months in exchange for free flights from the US mainland and free living expenses. Programme information is available from the Refuge Manager, Kauai National Wildlife Refuge Complex, P.O. Box 1128, Kilauea, Hawaii 96754; 808-828-1413; tom_alexander@fws.gov.

The Student Conservation Association Inc. (SCA, 689 River Road, PO Box 550, Charlestown, NH 03603-0550; 603-543-1700; internships@sca-inc.org) places anyone 18 or older in conservation and environmental internships in national parks and forests nationwide. Position lengths vary from 12 weeks to 12 months and provide travel expenses, housing, training and a weekly stipend. The SCA website www.theSCA.org includes a searchable database of open positions as well as an application form.

Part IV

Appendices

Currency Conversion Chart

Embassies/Consulates in London

Address List & Index of Organisations

Currency Conversion Chart

COUNTRY	£1	US$1
Eurozone	1.44 Euro	0.88 Euro
Argentina	4.5 peso	2.8 peso
Australia	A$2.48	A$1.52
Brazil	4.7 real	2.9 real
Canada	C$2.26	C$1.38
Chile	1,145 peso	701 peso
China	13.5 renminbi	8.3 renminbi
Costa Rica	653 colon	400 colon
Czech Republic	46 koruna	28 koruna
Denmark	10.7 kroner	6.6 kroner
Ecuador	1.63 US dollar	1 US dollar
Egypt	9.9 Egyptian pound	6.0 Egyptian pound
Hong Kong	12.74 HK dollar	7.8 HK dollar
Hungary	377 forint	231 forint
India	75 rupee	46 rupee
Israel	7.1 new shekel	4.4 new shekel
Japan	192 yen	118 yen
Korea	1,924 won	1,178 won
Malta	0.61 Maltese lira	0.37 Maltese lira
Mexico	17 peso	10.4 peso
Morocco	15.6 dirham	9.6 dirham
Nepal	122 rupee	75 rupee
New Zealand	NZ$2.77	NZ$1.70
Norway	12 krone	7.3 krone
Poland	6.4 zloty	3.9 zloty
Russia	50 rouble	30 rouble
Slovakia	60 koruna	36 koruna
Sweden	13.1 krona	8 krona
Switzerland	2.23 franc	1.36 franc
Thailand	68 baht	41.6 baht
Turkey	2,279,000 lira	1,395,000 lira
USA	1.63 dollar	–

Current exchange rates are available on the internet, for example at www.oanda.com or the Universal Currency Converter at www.xe.net/ucc

Appendix II

Embassies/Consulates in London

AUSTRALIA: Australia House, The Strand, London WC2B 4LA (www.australia.org.uk/vti.html)
AUSTRIA: 18 Belgrave Mews West, London SW1X 8HU (020-7235 3731; www.austria.org.uk)
BELGIUM: 103 Eaton Square, London SW1W 9AB (020-7470 3700; 09065 508963; www.belgium-embassy.co.uk)
BRAZIL: Consular Section, 6 St. Alban's St, London SW1Y 4SG (020-7930 9055; www.brazil.org.uk)
CANADA: 38 Grosvenor St, London W1X 0AA (020-7258 6600; www.dfait-maeci.gc.ca/london)
CHILE: 12 Devonshire St, London W1G 7DS (020-7580 1023; cglonduk@congechileuk.demon.co.uk)
CHINA: Visa Section, 31 Portland Place, London W1N 3AG (020-7631 1430; www.chinese-embassy.org.uk)
COSTA RICA: Flat 1, 14 Lancaster Gate, London W2 3LH (020-7706 8844; embcrlon.demon.co.uk)
CZECH REPUBLIC: 26-30 Kensington Palace Gardens, London W8 4QY (020-7243 1115)
DENMARK: 55 Sloane St, London SW1X 9SR (020-7333 0200)
ECUADOR: Flat 3b, 3 Hans Crescent, Knightsbridge, London SW1X 0LS (020-7584 8084)
EGYPT: 2 Lowndes St, London SW1X 9ET (020-7235 9777; www.egypt-embassy.org.uk)
FINLAND: 38 Chesham Place, London SW1X 8HW (020-7838 6200; www.finemb.org)
FRANCE: 21 Cromwell Road, London SW7 2EN (020-7838 2000; www.ambafrance-uk.org)
GERMANY: 23 Belgrave Square, London SW1X 8PZ (020-7824 1300/0906-833 1166; www.german-embassy.org.uk)
GREECE: 1A Holland Park, London W11 3TP (020-7221 6467)
HUNGARY: 35b Eaton Place, London SW1X 8BY (020-7235 2664/09001-171 204; http://dspace.dial.pipex.com/huemblon)
INDIA: India House, Aldwych, London WC2B 4NA (020-7836 8484; www.hcilondon.org)
ISRAEL: Consular Section, 15a Old Court Place, London W8 4QB (020-7957 9516; info@israel-embassy.org.uk)
ITALY: 38 Eaton Place, London SW1X 8AN (020-7235 9371; www.ambitalia.org.uk)
JAPAN: 101-104 Piccadilly, London W1V 9FN (020-7465 6500; www.embjapan.org.uk)
MALTA: Malta House, 36-38 Piccadilly, London W1V 0PQ (020-7292 4800)
MEXICO: 8 Halkin St, London SW1X 7DW (020-7235 6393; www.mexicanconsulate.org.uk)
NEPAL: 12a Kensington Palace Gardens, London W8 4QU (020-7229 1594; www.nepembassy.org.uk)
NETHERLANDS: 38 Hyde Park Gate, London SW7 5DP (020-7590 3200/09001-171 217; www.netherlands-embassy.org.uk)
NEW ZEALAND: New Zealand House, Haymarket, London SW1Y 4TE (0906 9100 100; £1 a minute)
NORWAY: 25 Belgrave Square, London SW1X 8QD (020-7591 5500)
PERU: 52 Sloane St, London SW1X 9SP (020-7838 9223; http://homepages.which.net/peru-embassy-uk)
POLAND: 73 New Cavendish St, London W1N 4HQ (020-7580 0476; www.poland-embassy.org.uk)
PORTUGAL: Silver City House, 62 Brompton Road, London SW3 1BJ (020-7581 8722; www.portembassy.gla.ac.uk)
RUSSIAN FEDERATION: 5 Kensington Palace Gardens, London W8 4QS (020-7229 8027; www.russialink.org.uk)
SLOVAK REPUBLIC: 25 Kensington Palace Gardens, London W8 4QY (020-7243 0803; www.slovakembassy.co.uk)
SOUTH AFRICA: South Africa House, Trafalgar Square, London WC2N 5DP (020-7451 7299; general@southafricahouse.com)
SPAIN: 20 Draycott Place, London SW3 2RZ (020-7589 8989)
SWEDEN: 11 Montagu Place, London W1H 2AL (020-7724 2101; www.swednet.org.uk/sweden)
SWITZERLAND: 16/18 Montagu Place, London W1H 2BQ (020-7616 6000; swiss.embassy@lon.rep.admin.ch; www.swissembassy.org.uk)
THAILAND: 29/30 Queen's Gate, London SW7 5JB (020-7589 2944)
TURKEY: Rutland Lodge, Rutland Gardens, London SW7 1BW (020-7589 0949; www.turkconsulate-london.com)
USA: 5 Upper Grosvenor St, London W1A 2JB (09061 500590, £1.50 a minute)

For complete and up-to-date information see the London Diplomatic List either on the website of the Foreign & Commonwealth Office (www.fco.gov.uk) or in print in a library. For Washington embassies check www.embassy.org.

Appendix III

Address List

3D Education & Adventure, Osmington Bay, Shortlake Lane, Weymouth, Dorset DT3 6EG (01305 836226/fax 01305 834070; admin@3d-jobs.co.uk/ www.3d-jobs.co.uk).....198, 203, 204

Academic Associates International, Academic Year in the USA & Europe, 46 High Street, Ewell Village, Surrey KT17 1RW (020-8786 7711/fax 020-8786 7755; enquiry@aaiuk.org/ www.aaiuk.org).....61, 310, 426

Accenture Horizons School Sponsorship Scheme, 60 Queen Victoria St, London EC4N 4TW (0500 100189; ukgraduates@accenture.com/ www.accenture.com/ ukgraduates.....112, 117

Adventure Alternative, 31 Myrtledene Road, Belfast BT8 6GQ (☎/fax 02890 701476; office@adventurealternative.com/ www.adventurealternative.com).....62, 346

Africa and Asia Venture, 10 Market Place, Devizes, Wiltshire SN10 1HT (01380 729009/ fax 01380 720060; av@aventure.co.uk/ www.aventure.co.uk).....62, 346

African Conservation Experience, PO Box 9706, Solihull, West Midlands B91 3FF (0870 241 5816; info@ConservationAfrica.net/ www.ConservationAfrica.net).....62, 125, 353

African Eco Gap, PO Box 704, Harrismith 9880, South Africa (5862 30026; fax 5862-22955; walkabout@internext.co.za).....281, 353

AfricaTrust Networks, Africatrust Chambers, PO Box 551, Portsmouth, Hants. PO5 1ZN (02392 838098; info@africatrust.gi/ www.africatrust.gi).....64, 346, 349

AFS Intercultural Programmes UK, Leeming House, Vicar Lane, Leeds LS2 7JF (0113 242 6136/fax 0113 243 0631; info-unitedkingdom@afs.org/ www.afsuk.org).....64, 293, 317, 346, 368, 408, 415

Agriventure, International Agricultural Exchange Association (IAEA), Long Clawson, Melton Mowbray, Leicestershire LE14 4NR (01664 822335/01664 823820; post@agriventure.com/www.agriventure.com).....126, 425

AIESEC International Association for Students of Economics and Management, 29-31 Cowper St, 2nd Floor, London EC2A 4AP (www.workabroad.org.uk).....115

AmeriSpan, PO Box 58129, Philadelphia, PA 19102 or 117 S 17th St, Suite 1401, Philadelphia, PA 19103 (800-879-6640 or 215-751-1100/ fax 215-751-1986; info@amerispan.com/ www.amerispan.com).....152, 184, 232, 350, 410

Anglo-Polish Universities Association (93 Victoria Road, Leeds LS6 1DR).....324

Archaeology Abroad, 31-34 Gordon Square, London WC1H 0PY/fax 020-7383 2572; arch.abroad@ucl.ac.uk/ www.britarch.ac.uk/archabroad).....38, 143, 152, 314, 405

The Army Gap Year Commission, HQ Recruiting Group, ATRA, Bldg 165, Trenchard Lines, Upavon, Wiltshire SN9 6BE (08457 300111/ www.armyofficer.co.uk).....65, 118

Art History Abroad, 26 De Laune St, London SE17 3UU (020-7277 4514/fax 020-7740 6126; info@arthistoryabroad.com/ www.arthistoryabroad.com).....66, 259, 315, 316

ATD Fourth World, 48 Addington Square, London SE5 7LB (020-7703 3231/fax 020-7252 4276; atd@atd-uk.org/ www.atd-uk.org).....153

Atlantis Youth Exchange, Kirkegata 32, 0153 Oslo, Norway (☎/fax 22 47 71 79; post@atlantis-u.no/ www.atlantis.no).....330

Au Pair in America, 37 Queen's Gate, London SW7 5HR (020-7581 7300/fax 020-7581 7355; info@aupairamerica.co.uk/ www.aupairamerica.co.uk).....66, 67, 217, 427

Azafady, Studio 7, 1A Beethoven St, London W10 4LG (020-8960 6629/fax 020-8962 0126; mark@azafady.org/ www.madagascar.co.uk).....153, 346

Base Camp Group, Howick, Balls Cross, Petworth, West Sussex GU28 9JY (01403 820899/ fax 01403 820063; contact@basecampgroup.com/ www.basecampgroup.com).....274

BBC, Work Experience Placements – www.bbc.co.uk/workexperience.....118

Blue Dog Adventures, Amwell Farm House, Nomansland, Wheathampstead, St. Albans,

Vacation Work Publications

	Paperback	Hardback
Summer Jobs Abroad	£9.99	£15.95
Summer Jobs in Britain	£9.99	£15.95
Supplement to Summer Jobs Britain and Abroad *published in May*	£6.00	-
Work Your Way Around the World	£12.95	-
Taking a Gap Year	£11.95	-
Taking a Career Break	£11.95	-
Working in Tourism – The UK, Europe & Beyond	£11.95	-
Kibbutz Volunteer	£10.99	-
Working on Yachts and Superyachts	£10.99	-
Working on Cruise Ships	£10.99	-
Teaching English Abroad	£12.95	-
The Au Pair & Nanny's Guide to Working Abroad	£12.95	-
The Good Cook's Guide to Working Worldwide	£11.95	-
Working in Ski Resorts – Europe & North America	£11.95	-
Working with Animals – The UK, Europe & Worldwide	£11.95	-
Live & Work Abroad – A Guide for Modern Nomads	£11.95	-
Working with the Environment	£11.95	-
The Directory of Jobs & Careers Abroad	£12.95	-
The International Directory of Voluntary Work	£11.95	-
Buying a House in France	£11.95	-
Buying a House in Spain	£11.95	-
Buying a House in Italy	£11.95	-
Live & Work in Australia & New Zealand	£10.99	-
Live & Work in Belgium, The Netherlands & Luxembourg	£10.99	-
Live & Work in France	£10.99	-
Live & Work in Germany	£10.99	-
Live & Work in Italy	£10.99	-
Live & Work in Japan	£10.99	-
Live & Work in Russia & Eastern Europe	£10.99	-
Live & Work in Saudi & the Gulf	£10.99	-
Live & Work in Scandinavia	£10.99	-
Live & Work in Scotland	£10.99	-
Live &Work in Spain & Portugal	£10.99	-
Live & Work in the USA & Canada	£10.99	-
Drive USA	£10.99	-
Hand Made in Britain – The Visitors Guide	£10.99	-
Scottish Islands – The Western Isles	£12.95	-
Scottish Islands – Orkney & Shetland	£11.95	-
The Panamericana: On the Road through Mexico and Central America	£12.95	-
Travellers Survival Kit Australia & New Zealand	£11.95	-
Travellers Survival Kit Cuba	£10.99	-
Travellers Survival Kit Lebanon	£10.99	-
Travellers Survival Kit Madagascar, Mayotte & Comoros	£10.99	-
Travellers Survival Kit Mauritius, Seychelles & Réunion	£10.99	-
Travellers Survival Kit Mozambique	£10.99	-
Travellers Survival Kit Oman & The Arabian Gulf	£11.95	-
Travellers Survival Kit South America	£15.95	-
Travellers Survival Kit Sri Lanka	£10.99	-

Distributors of:

	Paperback	Hardback
Summer Jobs in the USA	£14.99	-
Internships	£19.99	-
World Volunteers	£10.99	-
Green Volunteers	£10.99	-
Archaeo-Volunteers	£10.99	-

Vacation Work Publications, 9 Park End Street, Oxford OX1 1HJ
☎ **01865-241978   Fax 01865-790885**

Visit us online for more information on our unrivalled range of titles for work, travel and gap years, readers' feedback and regular updates:

www.vacationwork.co.uk